W9-AUE-271

Fodor's

VIRGINIA AND MARYLAND

8TH EDITION

Where to Stay and Eat
for All Budgets

Must-See Sights
and Local Secrets

Ratings You Can Trust

Fodor's Travel Publications   New York, Toronto, London, Sydney, Auckland
www.fodors.com

FODOR'S VIRGINIA AND MARYLAND
Editor: John D. Rambow

Editorial Production: Bethany Cassin Beckerlegge
Editorial Contributors: Loretta Chilcoat, Robin Dougherty, Natasha Lesser, Laureen Miles, Kevin Myatt, Erica Pandapas, Norman Renouf, CiCi Williamson
Maps: David Lindroth *cartographer;* Bob Blake and Rebecca Baer, *map editors*
Design: Fabrizio La Rocca, *creative director;* Guido Caroti, *art director;* Moon Sun Kim, *cover designer;* Melanie Marin, *senior picture editor*
Cover Photo: David Muench/Corbis
Production/Manufacturing: Robert B. Shields

COPYRIGHT
Copyright © 2005 by Fodors LLC

Fodor's is a registered trademark of Random House, Inc.

All rights reserved under International and Pan-American Copyright Conventions. Published in the United States by Fodor's Travel Publications, a unit of Fodors LLC, a subsidiary of Random House, Inc., and simultaneously in Canada by Random House of Canada Limited, Toronto. Distributed by Random House, Inc., New York.

No maps, illustrations, or other portions of this book may be reproduced in any form without written permission from the publisher.

Eighth Edition

ISBN 1–4000–1438–7

ISSN 1075-0711

SPECIAL SALES
This book is available for special discounts for bulk purchases for sales promotions or premiums. Special editions, including personalized covers, excerpts of existing books, and corporate imprints, can be created in large quantities for special needs. For more information, write to Special Markets/Premium Sales, 1745 Broadway, MD 6-2, New York, New York 10019, or e-mail specialmarkets@randomhouse.com.

AN IMPORTANT TIP & AN INVITATION
Although all prices, opening times, and other details in this book are based on information supplied to us at press time, changes occur all the time in the travel world, and Fodor's cannot accept responsibility for facts that become outdated or for inadvertent errors or omissions. So **always confirm information when it matters,** especially if you're making a detour to visit a specific place. Your experiences—positive and negative—matter to us. If we have missed or misstated something, **please write to us.** We follow up on all suggestions. Contact the Virginia & Maryland editor at editors@fodors.com or c/o Fodor's at 1745 Broadway, New York, New York 10019.

PRINTED IN THE UNITED STATES OF AMERICA

10 9 8 7 6 5 4 3 2 1

CONTENTS

CloseUps

ABOUT THIS BOOK

The best source for travel advice is a like-minded friend who's just been where you're headed. But with or without that friend, you'll be in great shape to find your way around your destination once you learn to find your way around your Fodor's guide.

SELECTION	Our goal is to cover the best properties, sights, and activities in their category, as well as the most interesting communities to visit. We make a point of including local food-lovers' hot spots as well as neighborhood options, and we avoid all that's touristy unless it's really worth your time. You can go on the assumption that everything in this book is recommended wholeheartedly by our writers and editors. Flip to On the Road with Fodor's to learn more about who they are. It goes without saying that no property pays to be included.
RATINGS	Orange stars ★ denote sights and properties that our editors and writers consider the very best in the area covered by the entire book. These, the best of the best, are listed in the Fodor's Choice section in the front of the book. Black stars ★ highlight the sights and properties we deem Highly Recommended, the don't-miss sights within any region. In cities, sights pinpointed with numbered map bullets ❶ in the margins tend to be more important than those without bullets.
SPECIAL SPOTS	Pleasures & Pastimes and text on chapter-title pages focus on experiences that reveal the spirit of the destination. Also watch for Off the Beaten Path sights. Some are out of the way, some are quirky, and all are worthwhile. When the munchies hit, look for Need a Break? suggestions.
TIME IT RIGHT	Check On the Calendar up front and chapters' Timing sections for weather and crowd overviews and best days and times to visit.
SEE IT ALL	Use Fodor's exclusive Great Itineraries as a model for your trip. Either follow those that begin the book, or mix regional itineraries from several chapters. In cities, Good Walks guide you to important sights in each neighborhood; ▶ indicates the starting points of walks and itineraries in the text and on the map.
BUDGET WELL	Hotel and restaurant price categories from ¢ to $$$$ are defined in the opening pages of each chapter—expect to find a balanced selection for every budget. For attractions, we always give standard adult admission fees; reductions are usually available for children, students, and senior citizens. Look in Discounts & Deals in Smart Travel Tips for information on destination-wide ticket schemes. Want to pay with plastic? AE, D, DC, MC, V following restaurant and hotel listings indicate whether American Express, Discover, Diner's Club, MasterCard, or Visa are accepted.
BASIC INFO	Smart Travel Tips lists travel essentials for the entire area covered by the book; city- and region-specific basics end each chapter. To find

the best way to get around, see the transportation section; see individual modes of travel ("Car Travel," "Train Travel") for details.

ON THE MAPS — Maps throughout the book show you what's where and help you find your way around. Black and orange numbered bullets ❶ ❶ in the text correlate to bullets on maps.

BACKGROUND — We give background information within the chapters in the course of explaining sights as well as in CloseUp boxes.

FIND IT FAST — Within the book, chapters are arranged in a roughly counterclockwise direction starting with the areas of Virginia and Maryland that are closest to Washington, D.C. Chapters are divided into small regions, with the towns inside the regions covered in geographical order; attractive routes and interesting places between towns are flagged as En Route. Heads at the top of each page help you find what you need within a chapter.

DON'T FORGET — Restaurants are open for lunch and dinner daily unless we state otherwise; we mention dress only when there's a specific requirement and reservations only when they're essential or not accepted—it's always best to book ahead. Hotels have private baths, phone, TVs, and air-conditioning and operate on the European Plan (aka EP, meaning without meals). We always list facilities but not whether you'll be charged extra to use them, so when pricing accommodations, find out what's included.

SYMBOLS

Many Listings
- ★ Fodor's Choice
- ★ Highly recommended
- ⊠ Physical address
- ✛ Directions
- ⬧ Mailing address
- ☎ Telephone
- 🖷 Fax
- ⊕ On the Web
- ✉ E-mail
- 🎫 Admission fee
- ☉ Open/closed times
- ► Start of walk/itinerary
- Ⓜ Metro stations
- ▭ Credit cards

Outdoors
- 🏌 Golf
- ⛺ Camping

Hotels & Restaurants
- 🏨 Hotel
- 🛏 Number of rooms
- ⚒ Facilities
- 🍽 Meal plans
- ✕ Restaurant
- 🍴 Reservations
- 👔 Dress code
- ⚲ Smoking
- 🍷 BYOB
- ✕🏨 Hotel with restaurant that warrants a visit

Other
- ☺ Family-friendly
- ℹ Contact information
- ⇨ See also
- ⊠ Branch address
- ☞ Take note

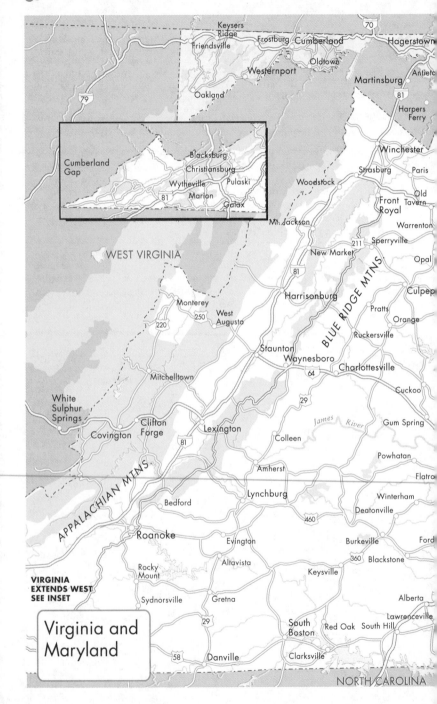

Keysers Ridge
Friendsville
Frostburg Cumberland
70
Hagerstown
Westernport
Oldtown
Martinsburg
Antiet
79
Oakland
81
Harpers Ferry
Winchester
Blacksburg
Christiansburg
Cumberland Gap
Wytheville Pulaski
81 Marion
Galax
Strasburg Paris
Woodstock
Old Tavern
Front Royal
Warrenton
Mt. Jackson
Sperryville
WEST VIRGINIA
New Market
211
Opal
81
Culpep
Monterey
Harrisonburg
BLUE RIDGE MTNS.
Pratts
Orange
250 West Augusta
220
Ruckersville
Staunton
Waynesboro
Charlottesville
64
Mitchelltown
29
Cuckoo
White Sulphur Springs
James River
Gum Spring
Clifton Forge
Lexington
Covington
81
Colleen
Powhatan
Amherst
Flatro
APPALACHIAN MTNS.
Lynchburg
Winterham
Bedford
Deatonville
460
Roanoke
Evington
Burkeville
Ford
Rocky Mount
Altavista
360 Blackstone
Keysville
VIRGINIA EXTENDS WEST SEE INSET
Sydnorsville
Gretna
Alberta
Lawrenceville
29
South Boston Red Oak South Hill
Virginia and Maryland
58
Danville
Clarksville
NORTH CAROLINA

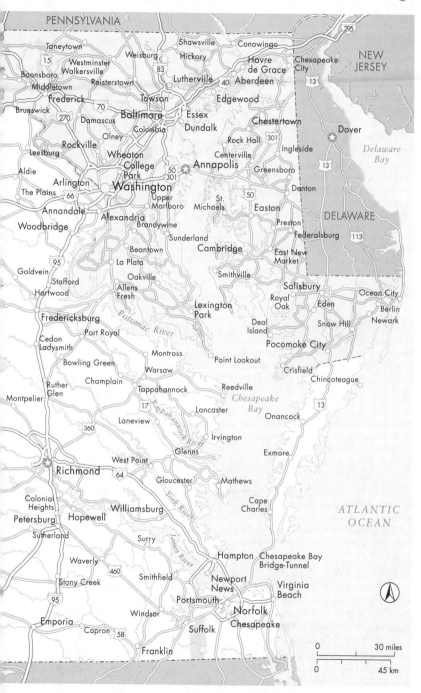

A trip takes you out of yourself. Concerns of life at home completely disappear, driven away by more immediate thoughts—about, say, what marvels will be visited the next day, or where you'll have dinner. That's where Fodor's comes in. We make sure that you know all your options, so that you don't miss something that's around the next bend just because you didn't know it was there. Because the best memories of your trip might well have nothing to do with what you came to Virginia and Maryland to see, we guide you to sights large and small all over the region. You might set out to be enveloped by Colonial Williamsburg, but back at home you find yourself unable to forget racing up Skyline Drive at dawn or chowing down on some Southern Maryland crab cakes. With Fodor's at your side, serendipitous discoveries are never far away.

Our success in showing you every corner of Virginia and Maryland is a credit to our extraordinary writers. Although there's no substitute for travel advice from a good friend who knows your style, our contributors are the next best thing—the kind of people you would poll for travel advice if you knew them.

Our updater for Northern Virginia and D.C.'s Maryland Suburbs, **Robin Dougherty**, was one of the few people who could claim to be a native of Washington, D.C. Having spent nearly 20 years in other cities, she recently returned and spent her time discovering interesting new aspects of her hometown and its environs. She also wrote a book column for the *Boston Globe* and reviewed movies for National Public Radio. We are sad to say that Robin passed away during the production of this book. She will be dearly missed.

Food and travel writer **CiCi Williamson** updated our chapter on Williamsburg and the Hampton Roads area. The author of more than 1,500 articles in newspapers and magazines and six cookbooks, her latest book is *The Best of Virginia Farms* travel guide and cookbook. She is also the host

of a PBS series based on the book. Before turning to book writing full time, she wrote a syndicated weekly food column for 22 years in 160 newspapers across the country. She has been an updater for Fodor's for 10 years.

Kevin Myatt became familiar with the towns, sites, and roads of Southwest Virginia while writing about hiking trails in the area for Roanoke.com. A copy editor at *The Roanoke Times* newspaper, he also writes a biweekly weather column that appears in the *Times* and on Roanoke.com. **Erica Pandapas** traded the Atlantic Ocean for the Blue Ridge Mountains a dozen years ago to attend Hollins College, where she also received a master's in creative writing. A New York native, she enjoys her adopted home's topography and sense of history. She has been a copy editor at *The Roanoke Times* for more than six years, while also doing volunteer writing and editing for nonprofit organizations. Fodor's updaters for the Central & Western Virginia chapter, Kevin and Erica are engaged to be married in fall 2005.

Norman Renouf, our updater for the Richmond, Fredericksburg, and the Northern Neck chapter, was born in London and educated at Charlton Secondary School, Greenwich. Always interested in travel, he started writing travel guides, articles, and newspaper contributions in the early 1990s and has covered destinations throughout Europe. Now living in Richmond, Virginia, he has also written several guides about Washington, D.C., and the mid-Atlantic region.

Natasha Lesser, a former editor at Fodor's, now lives in Baltimore with her husband and daughter. Besides writing for Fodor's, she also contributes to *The Baltimore Sun, Baltimore Style* magazine, and WYPR, the local public radio station. Two of her favorite things about Baltimore are the crab cakes at Faidley's and the architecture.

The updater for Western Maryland and the Eastern Shore, **Loretta Chilcoat** grew up among Maryland's cornfields. She also worked many hot summers in those very fields, stretching from Queenstown to Salisbury. As a former writer and editor at the Maryland Office of Tourism, she has insider knowledge of the state's most popular and hidden attractions—Maryland's mountain region is one of her favorite haunts. Now a freelance travel writer, Loretta has nine guidebooks and many articles under her belt. Although it's tough at times, she enjoys traveling with her one-year-old daughter in search of Maryland's newest hotspots.

The updater for Annapolis and Southern Maryland, Laureen Miles also edited the Maryland section in Fodor's *Road Guide* series. She provides local content for America Online's CityGuides, which cover Baltimore, Annapolis and Washington, D.C., and has spent many hours wandering the country roads of Maryland during her more than 10 years in the state.

1 Northern Virginia

Much more than a satellite of the nation's capital, northern Virginia is a repository of Colonial and Civil War history. Alexandria's Old Town holds a substantial number of historic buildings, churches, and museums; and Arlington, Fairfax, and Loudoun counties are sprinkled with historic sites and monuments such as Mount Vernon, Arlington Cemetery, and the Manassas battlefield (also known as Bull Run). Loudoun County is also Virginia's horse country, with handsome towns that include Middleburg and Leesburg. And from Great Falls Park you can view the splendid waterfalls of the Potomac.

2 D.C.'s Maryland Suburbs

Part of suburbia's sprawl, Montgomery and Prince George's counties are where you'll find the Washington Redskins, Six Flags America, the College Park Aviation Museum, and Strathmore Hall Arts Center. Naturalists appreciate the area's great green spaces, including the C&O Canal National Historical Park and Piscataway Park. Diners from Washington, D.C., and both sides of the Potomac River head to Bethesda and Silver Spring to sample cuisine from all over the world, especially Thailand and elsewhere in Asia.

3 Central & Western Virginia

Mountains rule the horizons here. The evening sun sets over the Blue Ridge for those in the cultural center of Charlottesville; nearby is Thomas Jefferson's "little mountain," Monticello. Skyline Drive and the Blue Ridge Parkway trace the spine of the Blue Ridge, creating many vistas within Shenandoah National Park and the George Washington National Forest. The Shenandoah Valley, once the home of early European settlers and later a Civil War thoroughfare, rests between the Blue Ridge and the Allegheny mountains. Farther south, inside a bowl-shaped depression encircled by bluish ridgelines, is bustling Roanoke. To the west and south of that bustling city are the New River Valley and the gorge-incised Appalachian Plateau, from whose hollows old-time mountain music still echoes.

4 Richmond, Fredericksburg & the Northern Neck

Richmond, capital of the commonwealth and former capital of the Confederacy, is not only full of historic sites but also one of the South's preeminent art cities and a major industrial center. Among its appealing restored neighborhoods is the turn-of-the-20th-century Fan District. At Petersburg, south of Richmond, the Confederacy made its last stand. In Fredericksburg, midway between Richmond and Washington, D.C., are historic 18th- and 19th-century homes, antiques shops, and Civil War battlefields. The rural peninsula of the Northern Neck extends east from Fredericksburg to the Chesapeake.

5 Williamsburg & Hampton Roads

Colonial Williamsburg, a re-created 18th-century American city complete with historic buildings, working shops, and costumed interpreters, is Virginia's most-visited attraction. Nearby are three other historical treasures: Historic Jamestowne, where the first permanent English settlers made their home; Jamestown Settlement, a re-creation of the original ships and fort; and Yorktown, site of the final major battle in the American War of Independence. Even for those with extremely limited time to spend in Virginia, these sites ought to be visited. Hampton Roads—the channel where the James, Elizabeth, and Nansemond rivers meet—is surrounded by small towns that include the historic settlements of Hampton and Portsmouth; Newport News, builder of the navy's biggest nuclear ships; the port town of Norfolk; and the busy resort town of Virginia Beach, the state's largest city.

⑥ Baltimore

Baltimore is a busy port city with newly revitalized appeal. Lively Inner Harbor, with its constellation of attractions such as the National Aquarium and the American Visionary Art Museum, is in many ways the city's heart, though Charles Street is the more established part of town. Fells Point, the center of shipbuilding in the 18th and 19th centuries, and Federal Hill are among the cobblestone neighborhoods worth exploring.

⑦ Frederick & Western Maryland

Rugged, scenic mountains dominate the landscape of western Maryland. They frame cities such as Frederick and Cumberland; they wall in pastoral valleys, state forests, and parks; they even set the stage for a popular train excursion, the Western Maryland Scenic Railroad. Once crossed by the nation's first pioneers on their westward journey, these mountains are rich with remnants of an earlier time; today you can still hike along what was once the towpath for the Chesapeake & Ohio (C&O) Canal—the region's main trade route in the mid-19th century.

⑧ Annapolis & Southern Maryland

Maryland traces its origins to the Chesapeake Bay's Western Shore, where English Colonists arrived in the 1600s. Today, Annapolis, the state capital, is rich with Colonial architecture and history. Tobacco fields, once the livelihood of early Colonists, still blanket the gentle landscape of the southern part of the state, although more sparsely than before.

⑨ The Eastern Shore

Separated from mainland Maryland by the Chesapeake Bay and bounded on the east by the Atlantic Ocean, this peninsula is a land apart. Marshy wildlife refuges, isolated islands, and rivers traversed by fishermen and sailors set the stage for a quieter way of life. (However, you'll have to share the Atlantic with quite a crowd at the thriving resort town of Ocean City.) Virginia's Eastern Shore, which extends south from Maryland and is also accessible from Virginia Beach via the Chesapeake Bay Bridge-Tunnel, is a largely undisturbed area of tiny towns and abundant wildlife, including the wild "ponies" on Assateague Island.

If you don't have time for an extended itinerary, consider the Eastern Shore or the Shenandoah Valley. They're both great choices for long weekends spent outdoors, with stops for galleries and antiques shops.

Maryland

3 days

Baltimore, the geographical and cultural center of Maryland, is a must-see for first-time visitors. Take in some of the major sights that are clustered around the colorful Inner Harbor. On Day 2, revisit Maryland's Colonial past in Annapolis, the state capital. On the third day, head farther south to view the ongoing archaeological and reconstruction work at St. Mary's City. You can stay overnight in Solomons, a longtime getaway if you love boating and the Chesapeake Bay. If you want to learn more about how the bodies of water affect people who live around here, cross the expansive Chesapeake to the Eastern Shore, stopping in such small towns as Easton and St. Michaels.

5 days

Spend your first couple of days in Baltimore before heading south to Annapolis. Historic St. Mary's City, Solomons, and other towns in St. Mary's and Calvert counties will take care of Day 4. On your last day, either cross the Chesapeake Bay to visit the Eastern Shore or head west to Frederick, a vibrant city in the foothills of the Catoctin Mountains.

Virginia

3 days

Start in the northern part of the state. Spend a day exploring the sights of Alexandria and Mount Vernon, George Washington's home; then take a nighttime drive across the river for a glimpse of the illuminated monuments of Washington, D.C. On the second day visit Manassas National Battlefield Park before heading west to the Shenandoah Valley for a spectacular drive south along Skyline Drive. Stay overnight in or outside Charlottesville, and allow at least three hours for Thomas Jefferson's plantation home, Monticello, the next morning.

5 days

Follow the three-day tour above and then proceed to Virginia's capital, Richmond, for another full day. From Richmond, it's a short jaunt south to Petersburg and Pamplin Historical Park, where General Lee's defenses were routed. The impressive museum there holds many Civil War artifacts. If you prefer, you could instead spend the fifth day in Fredericksburg's historic center.

Five days is also a fair amount of time to do justice to the historic sights surrounding Williamsburg without limiting yourself to them. Squeeze the early English settlements of Jamestown and Yorktown attractions into one full day. Allow the next two days for the museums and living history of Colonial Williamsburg. On Day 4 examine the important maritime history of the area at the Mariner's Museum in Newport News before heading across Hampton Roads to the impressive collection of the Chrysler Museum of Art in Norfolk. After these two museums, find a beach to relax at—either in Cape Charles at the tip of the Eastern Shore, or in the busy resort town of Virginia Beach.

Start your trip in Richmond and spend the day visiting its many museums and Civil War sites. On the second day, head west on I-64 to Charlottesville, where you can survey the lush, rolling countryside from Thomas Jefferson's mountaintop home, Monticello. On Day 3, take a side trip northeast up Route 20 to Orange to see Montpelier, the home of James Madison, and to tour the area's wineries. On Day 4, head west again on I-64 toward the Blue Ridge Mountains and visit Staunton; the Museum of American Frontier Culture re-creates the beginnings of agrarian life in the Shenandoah Valley. On your fifth day, take the Blue Ridge Parkway south to Lexington, home to Washington and Lee University and the Virginia Military Institute. On Day 6, stop in Roanoke for a dose of culture or head to Jefferson National Forest to commune with nature. On your final day, continue south on the scenic Blue Ridge Parkway to Abingdon for a taste of the rugged Highlands.

Virginia & Maryland
10 days

Ten days is enough time to explore the Colonial and maritime pasts of Virginia and Maryland and to visit two major cities, Baltimore and Richmond. In a concentrated area such as the triangle of Jamestown, Williamsburg, and Yorktown, five days are the minimum to see the sights and have time to unwind.

Spend your first two days exploring Baltimore's Inner Harbor sights, art museums, and historic neighborhoods. On Day 3 visit Maryland's state capital, Annapolis, and perhaps the U.S. Naval Academy there before crossing the Chesapeake to the laid-back pace of the Eastern Shore. Spend the third night in Easton and wake up well after the area's fishermen have set off. Take a day to meander through harbor towns and wildlife areas before watching the sunset from Chincoteague Island. The fifth day make your way down and off the Eastern Shore to stay overnight in the Hampton Roads area. Spend the next three days experiencing Virginia's Colonial past in Williamsburg, Jamestown, and Yorktown. After a day on the rides of Busch Gardens, buckle down with some history again in Richmond, Virginia's capital and the capital of the Confederacy.

A Civil War Tour
11 days

Civil War sites are among the most compelling reasons to visit Virginia and Maryland, and the Civil War itinerary below covers the standout attractions. When Virginia seceded from the Union in 1861, it doomed itself to become a major battleground. Thus, much of this tour is in Virginia, with a brief foray across the Mason-Dixon Line into Maryland. Richmond is the tour's hub.

Start your tour at Hampton, on the Virginia Peninsula, where the Union general George McClellan launched his drive toward Richmond. Across the channel is Fort Monroe—the Union stronghold in which the president of the Confederacy, Jefferson Davis, was imprisoned. On Day 2, drive northwest on I–64 up the peninsula to Richmond's Museum and White House of the Confederacy and the Richmond National Battlefield Park Visitor Center. Proceed 20 mi south on I–95 to Petersburg, the city that was under an extended siege by Grant's army. Visit Petersburg National Battlefield, the Siege Museum, and Pamplin Historical Park.

For Days 3 through 5, proceed north from Richmond on I–95 to Fredericksburg, which has blocks of historic Civil War–era homes. Detour to see four battlefields at Fredericksburg/Spotsylvania National Military Park. Detour an hour outside of town to see Stratfold Hall plantation, where Robert E. Lee was born. Then return to I–95 and drive northwest to Manassas National Battlefield Park, site of two important Confederate victories.

On Days 6 and 7, continue on I–95 north into Arlington and see Arlington National Cemetery and Arlington House (Lee's home for 30 years, before the Union army confiscated it and turned the grounds into the cemetery). Then head north on I–270 into Maryland. North of Frederick catch Route 34 out of Boonsboro and follow it to the Antietam National Battlefield. Return to Frederick. If you have time, visit the National Museum of Civil War Medicine, then drive southeast to Monocacy National Battlefield.

For the rest of your tour, drive back to Richmond and then southwest from the city on U.S. 360 to U.S. 460. Proceed west into Appomattox Court House, where Lee surrendered to Grant. From Appomattox you can continue west on U.S. 460 to Lynchburg's Monument Terrace, a Civil War memorial. Then take U.S. 29 north to U.S. 60 northwest into Lexington, where you can visit the Lee Chapel and Museum, where Lee is buried, and the Virginia Military Institute Museum, which has displays on Stonewall Jackson.

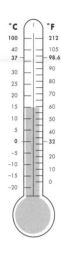

Spring brings horse racing to Baltimore, northern Virginia, and the Virginia Piedmont; the Preakness Stakes is highly festive, but many point-to-points and steeplechases are more interesting to watch and visit. Public gardens are in full bloom; garden clubs conduct tours of private properties throughout both states. In Shenandoah National Park, Skyline Drive overlooks a blooming panorama. If you happen to travel to Baltimore in early May, don't miss Sherwood Gardens, known for hundreds of thousands of tulips, azaleas, pansies, and blossoming trees.

Summer draws the largest numbers of visitors, particularly at Virginia Beach, Ocean City, and other resorts on the bay and the ocean. Baltimore's Inner Harbor can be thronged with tourists and yachtsmen. On warm days, the promenade is filled with visitors from around the world.

Autumn brings spectacular colors in the foliage of the rolling Piedmont region of Virginia and the Catoctin Mountains west of Baltimore; the temperatures become more comfortable for hiking and biking. Equestrian events resume, and in Maryland the sailboat and powerboat shows in Annapolis and the Waterfowl Festival in Easton attract thousands of people in October and November.

Winter temperatures may make it too cold to swim, yet the major resorts continue to draw vacationers with seasonal peace and quiet at much lower off-season rates. Other travelers come for romantic seclusion at a B&B. Virginia was the first Southern state to develop skiing commercially, and now both downhill and cross-country skiing are popular activities at resorts in the Shenandoah Valley and western Maryland.

Climate

The best time to visit is in spring and fall, when the temperatures are cooler. The summers in both states are very hot and humid, though the mountainous regions tend to be 10 to 15 degrees cooler. Winters are rainy and damp, though the region does occasionally get blanketed with heavy snow.

🔂 Forecasts **Weather Channel Connection** ☎ 900/932–8437, 95¢ per minute from a Touch-Tone phone ⊕ www.weather.com.

BALTIMORE, MARYLAND

Jan.	43F	6C	May	74F	23C	Sept.	79F	26C
	29	– 2		56	13		61	16
Feb.	43F	6C	June	83F	28C	Oct.	67F	19C
	29	– 2		65	18		50	10
Mar.	52F	11C	July	86F	30C	Nov.	54F	12C
	36	2		70	21		40	4
Apr.	63F	17C	Aug.	85F	29C	Dec.	45F	7C
	45	7		67	19		31	– 1

NORFOLK, VIRGINIA

Jan.	49F	9C	May	76F	24C	Sept.	81F	27C
	34	1		58	14		65	18
Feb.	50F	10C	June	83F	28C	Oct.	70F	21C
	34	1		67	19		56	13
Mar.	58F	14C	July	88F	31C	Nov.	61F	16C
	40	4		72	22		45	7
Apr.	67F	19C	Aug.	85F	29C	Dec.	52F	11C
	49	9		70	21		36	2

FESTIVALS & SEASONAL EVENTS ONGOING	
Late April–early May	Virginia Waterfront International Arts Festival (☎ 757/282–2822 ⊕ www.vafest.com) showcases performances by the Virginia Symphony, Virginia Opera, and out-of-state orchestras and artists.
Late July–early August	The two-week-long Virginia Highlands Festival (☎ 800/435–3440 or 276/676–2282 ⊕ www.vahighlandsfestival.org) in Abingdon celebrates Appalachia with juried displays and demonstrations of arts and crafts, exhibitions of animals, sales of antiques, and performances of country music.
WINTER	
December	During Illuminations (☎ 800/447–8679 ⊕ www.history.org) in Williamsburg, Virginia, 18th-century entertainment is performed on four outdoor stages. A military tattoo signals the lighting of candles in windows of the Colonial city's historic buildings.
	The Historic Alexandria Candlelight Tour (☎ 703/838–4242 ⊕ www.historicalexandria.org) is a visit to historic houses for light refreshment and performances of period music of the season.
	The Candlelight Tour of Historic Houses of Worship (☎ 301/228–2888 or 800/999–3613 ⊕ www.visitfrederick.org), in downtown Frederick, is a self-guided tour of historic churches and a synagogue, most of them within walking distance of one another. The churches are decorated for the holidays, and Christmas music and refreshments add to the festivities.
	New Year's Eve (☎ 410/752–8632 ⊕ www.bop.org) festivities in Baltimore include a concert at the Harborplace amphitheater and a midnight fireworks display over Inner Harbor. First Night Annapolis (☎ 410/268–8553 ⊕ www.firstnightannapolis.org) is a family-oriented, alcohol-free, and affordable celebration of the lively arts. Live performances are held throughout the day and evening at 40 venues.
January	Maryland's three-day Annapolis Heritage Antiques Show (☎ 410/961–5121 ⊕ www.armacostantiquesshows.com) is one of the major mid-Atlantic events of its kind.
March	Military Through the Ages (☎ 757/253–4838 ⊕ www.historyisfun.org) in Jamestown, Virginia, uses authentic weapons in a series of reenactments of battles from the Middle Ages through the 20th century.
SPRING	
April	Norfolk's Azalea Festival (☎ 757/282–2801 ⊕ www.azaleafestival.org) salutes NATO through battleship tours, a parade, an air show, concerts, a ball, and the crowning of a queen from the year's honored NATO member nation.

Historic Garden Week (☎ 804/644–7776 ⊕ www.vagardenweek. org) throughout Virginia is a time when several hundred grand private homes, otherwise closed to the public, open their doors and grounds to visitors.

The Celtic Festival and Highland Gathering of Southern Maryland (☎ 443/404–7319 ⊕ www.cssm.org), which takes place south of Annapolis in St. Leonard, includes piping and fiddling competitions, dancing, games, and the foods and crafts of the United Kingdom, Ireland, and Brittany.

May

Virginia Gold Cup (☎ 540/347–2612 ⊕ www.vagoldcup.com) steeplechase horse races, held near Middleburg in Northern Virginia, have been among the most prominent social and sporting events of the state since the 1920s.

Baltimore's Maryland Preakness Celebration (☎ 410/542–9400 ⊕ www.preakness.com) is a weeklong festival that includes parades, street parties, fund-raisers, and hot-air-balloon races. The celebration culminates in the annual running of the Preakness Stakes at Pimlico Racetrack, on the third Saturday in May.

The Chestertown Tea Party (☎ 410/778–0416 ⊕ www. chestertownteaparty.com) on Maryland's Eastern Shore commemorates patriots' 1774 act of hurling British tea into the Chester River.

Commissioning Week (☎ 410/293–2292 ⊕ www.usna.edu) at the United States Naval Academy in Annapolis, Maryland, is a time of dress parades, traditional stunts such as the Herndon Monument Climb, and a spectacular aerobatics demonstration by the navy's famous Blue Angels precision flying team.

SUMMER

June

The Fiddlers' Convention at the Carroll County Farm Museum (☎ 410/ 876–2667), an annual gathering in Westminster, Maryland, attracts some of the nation's finest bluegrass entertainers and fiddlers.

The Hampton Jazz Festival (☎ 757/838–4203 ⊕ www. hamptoncoliseum.org) in Hampton, Virginia, brings together top performers in different styles of jazz.

July

Independence Day celebrations in Baltimore culminate in a major show of fireworks over the Inner Harbor.

The Pony Swim and Auction (☎ 757/336–6161 ⊕ www. chincoteaguechamber.com) in Chincoteague, Virginia, is the annual roundup of wild ponies from Assateague Island; the foals are auctioned off to support the volunteer fire department.

August

During the first three weekends of August, "Shakespeare at the Ruins" at Barboursville Vineyards (☎ 540/832–3824 ⊕ www. barboursvillewine.com) brings outdoor performances of the Bard's classics to these beautiful vineyards, between Charlottesville and Orange in Virginia.

During the Virginia Wine Festival (☎ 410/267–6711 ⊕ www. showsinc.com) in Millwood, Virginia, you can taste vintages from roughly 50 wineries. There's also grape stomping and musical entertainment.

The Maryland State Fair (☎ 410/252–0200 ⊕ www. marylandstatefair.com), in Timonium, is 10 days of horse racing, livestock judging, live entertainment, agricultural displays, farm implements, and plenty of food.

The Maryland Renaissance Festival (☎ 410/266–7304 or 800/296–7304 ⊕ www.rennfest.com) celebrates 16th-century England with entertainment, food, and crafts shops. The grounds near Annapolis include a 5,000-seat jousting area and 10 stages. The event continues through late October.

FALL

September

Defenders' Day (☎ 410/962–4290 ⊕ www.nps.gov/fomc) celebrations at Fort McHenry in Baltimore commemorate—with music, drilling, mock bombardment, and fireworks—the battle that led to the writing of the national anthem.

Crisfield, Maryland's National Hard Crab Derby (☎ 410/968–2500 ⊕ www.crisfield.org) celebrates—what else?—the Eastern Shore's crabs with a crab race, steamed crabs, and the crowning of Miss Crustacean.

College Park Aviation Museum in Maryland hosts all sorts of airplanes at the Annual Air Fair (☎ 301/314–7777).

Baltimore's Hampden neighborhood celebrates the spirit of "Hon" with music, food, and festivities at Hampdenfest (☎ 410/235–5800 ⊕ www.hampdenfest.com).

The Virginia State Fair (☎ 804/228–3200 ⊕ www.statefair.com), in Richmond, is a classic conglomeration of carnival rides, livestock shows, displays of farm equipment, and lots of food for sale.

Ocean City, Maryland, celebrates the quest for endless summer with Sunfest Kite Festival (☎ 410/289–7855 ⊕ www.kiteloft.com), a four-day blowout with all sorts of entertainment, kite contests, and a crafts show.

The Maryland Wine Festival (☎ 410/876–2667 ⊕ ccgov.carr.org/farm-mus), at the Carroll County Farm Museum, Westminster, brings representatives from Maryland's wineries to display their products, offer tastings, and give seminars on wine making.

The Baltimore Book Festival (☎ 410/837–4636 or 800/282–6632 ⊕ www.bop.org), held in the historic Mount Vernon neighborhood, celebrates books and Baltimore's literary past.

October	

The Autumn Glory Festival (☎ 301/387–4386 ⊕ www.garrettchamber. com), held in Oakland in Maryland's westernmost county, is a celebration of the peak fall foliage that includes state banjo and fiddle championships, Oktoberfest festivities, arts, crafts, and antiques.

The October Homes Tour and Crafts Exhibit (☎ 540/882–3018 ⊕ www.waterfordva.org) in Waterford, Virginia, draws tens of thousands to this historic community.

The first Saturday of October, Bethesda restaurants sell samples of their fare at the food festival, Taste of Bethesda (☎ 301/215–6660 ⊕ www.bethesda.org).

The Chincoteague Oyster Festival (☎ 757/336–6161 ⊕ www. chincoteaguechamber.com), on Virginia's Eastern Shore, typically sells out months in advance.

Yorktown Day (☎ 757/898–2410 ⊕ www.nps.gov/colo) observances in Yorktown, Virginia, celebrate the Colonial victory in the American War of Independence (October 19, 1781) with 18th-century tactical demonstrations, patriotic exercises, and a wreath-laying ceremony.

The Virginia Film Festival (☎ 800/882–3378 ⊕ www.vafilm.com), in Charlottesville, Virginia, is becoming a major event in the motion picture industry, with screenings of important new movies and appearances by their stars.

November	

The Waterfowl Festival (☎ 410/822–4567 ⊕ www.waterfowlfestival. org) in Easton, Maryland, involves decoy exhibitions, carving demonstrations, duck-calling contests, and retriever exercises during a three-day weekend.

Waterfowl Week (☎ 757/336–6122 ⊕ www.chincoteaguechamber. com) in Chincoteague, Virginia, is when the National Wildlife Refuge opens to motor vehicles, allowing drivers to watch the Canada and snow geese on their southward migration.

PLEASURES & PASTIMES

American History These two original Colonies are full of historical attractions, from entire re-created Colonial towns to Civil War battlefields to remnants of the routes that pioneers followed on their westward treks. You can explore Colonial beginnings in Virginia's Williamsburg or Maryland's Historic St. Mary's City; amble through Richmond, Fredericksburg, Baltimore, and Frederick, where some neighborhoods appear virtually unchanged from the 18th and 19th centuries; stroll tiny Eastern Shore harbors where the waterman's way of life is now supplemented by pleasure tours on old fishing boats; or stand on the battlefields of Yorktown, Antietam, or Manassas. At Mount Vernon and Monticello you can step into the homes—and perhaps even the minds—of two of the country's most important former presidents; in Maryland, you can follow the region's former trade route by walking a portion of the historic C&O Canal, now a national park.

Biking & Hiking The three regions of Maryland and Virginia—coastal plain (or Tidewater), Piedmont, and mountains—are great for cyclists and hikers seeking an abundance of choices. National and regional trails such as the famed Appalachian Trail cross both states. In Virginia, the 500-mi section of the Trans-America Bicycle Trail extends from Breaks Interstate Park at the western fringe of the state to Yorktown on the coast; in addition, a 280-mi segment of the Maine-Richmond and Richmond-Florida coastal tracks crosses the state. In Maryland, trails, canal towpaths, and even old railroad routes are popular biking and hiking routes.

National Parks & Forests From the mountains to the seashore, many scenic and historical national parks lie within these states. In Virginia's Shenandoah Mountains lies the lovely Skyline Drive, a popular 105-mi route through Shenandoah National Park. In Maryland's smaller Catoctin Mountains sits Catoctin Mountain Park. The place is good enough for the president—Camp David, the presidential retreat, is somewhere within. Blackwater National Wildlife Refuge, southeast of Annapolis, is one of the East Coast's premier spots for viewing migratory waterfowl, bald eagles, and ospreys. The Potomac River, the waterway that divides Maryland and Virginia, is the route of the 185-mi linear park, the C&O Canal National Historical Park. It's a favorite with hikers and bicyclists.

Seafood The Chesapeake Bay, the estuary that separates mainland Maryland and Virginia from their respective Eastern Shores, provides a cornucopia of seafood. Steamed hard-shell crabs cracked with a mallet on paper-covered tables, to the accompaniment of plenty of beer, are as traditional as crab cakes seasoned with Old Bay seasoning or garlic. Cream-of-crab soup, Maryland crab soup, crab balls, crab dip, and crab imperial are just a few of the other odes to this creature. Also on the menu, in season, are bluefish, rockfish, oysters, and mussels.

Wineries Since the 1980s, Virginia has come from way behind to its spot as fifth in the nation for grape production. The state's 75 wineries, most in picturesque and historic buildings, are distributed throughout the state. Both states have wine festivals, most of which occur in the fall. Virginia alone has more than 400 annual festivals and wine-related events.

FODOR'S CHOICE

The sights, restaurants, hotels, and other travel experiences on these pages are our editors' top picks—our Fodor's Choices. They're the best of their type in the area covered by the book—not to be missed and always worth your time. In the destination chapters that follow, you can find all the details.

HISTORIC BUILDINGS & RESTORATIONS

Appomattox Court House, Virginia. In this village, now restored to its 1865 appearance, General Robert E. Lee surrendered his Confederate troops to General Ulysses S. Grant.

Colonial Williamsburg, Virginia. Once the state's capital, this restored 18th-century city is full of skilled craftspeople, orators, and actors who bring history to life (and encourage you to join in).

Monticello, Virginia. Thomas Jefferson's unique home, outside of Charlottesville, reflects the intense and multifaceted mind of this president and statesman.

Mount Vernon, Virginia. Overlooking the Potomac River, George Washington's house and farm is the most visited—and one of the most important—museums of its kind in the United States.

United States Naval Academy. Running along the Annapolis's Severn River, the Academy educates over 4,000 midshipmen annually; it's copper-clad chapel contains the remains of the Revolutionary War hero John Paul Jones.

BATTLEFIELDS & MONUMENTS

Antietam National Battlefield, Sharpsburg, Maryland. The bloodiest fight of the Civil War took place here in 1862. When it was over, more than 23,000 soldiers had either died or been wounded.

Fort McHenry, Baltimore, Maryland. This fort made of brick and earth saw battle during the War of 1812; its bombardment inspired "The Star-Spangled Banner."

Manassas National Battlefield Park, Virginia. Also known as Bull Run, this battlefield was the site of two of the most important victories for the Confederates.

Arlington National Cemetery, Virginia. The burial site of John F. Kennedy and a quarter of a million people who have served during wartime, Arlington National is a solemn site for contemplating a nation's sorrows and determination.

LODGING

$$–$$$$ **Colonial Houses, Williamsburg, Virginia.** You can step back in time (and still retain modern amenities) at these charming lodgings within Colonial Williamsburg.

$$–$$$ **The Homestead, Hot Springs, Virginia.** Eight presidents have stayed in this luxurious hotel set among the Appalachians—you can, too.

$$–$$$ **Kent Manor Inn, Stevensville, Maryland.** What was once a manor house and then a Victorian summer hotel is on 226 acres of farmland and near a creek.

BUDGET LODGING

$–$$$ **Linden Row Inn, Richmond, Virginia.** A row of 1840s Greek Revival town houses filled with antiques and reproductions makes up this charming inn.

RESTAURANTS

$$$$ **Hamptons, Baltimore, Maryland.** A view of Baltimore's Inner Harbor, elegant furnishings, and an innovative menu have earned this restaurant widespread acclaim.

$$$$ **Inn at Little Washington, Washington, Virginia.** Since 1978 chef Patrick O'Connell and his partner have been turning out New American food that wins raves from all over.

$$–$$$ **L'Auberge Provencale, White Post, Virginia.** Nationally known for its French cuisine, the bed-and-breakfast is well worth a stop for its prix-fixe dinners.

BUDGET RESTAURANTS

$ **The Homeplace, Catawba, Virginia.** In a mountain hamlet near Roanoke, the old-time country home serves mounds of fried chicken, potatoes and gravy, biscuits, and other Southern specialties. The lemonade is unlimited—and delicious.

MUSEUMS

American Visionary Art Museum, Baltimore, Maryland. The passionate creations of unconventional artists are displayed in seven galleries inside a former warehouse.

Calvert Marine Museum, Solomons, Maryland. The history of the Chesapeake Bay and the fishing, boat construction, and other industries that rely on it are explored at this southern Maryland museum.

Virginia Air and Space Center, Hampton, Virginia. Inside a nine-story waterfront building are an *Apollo 12* command capsule, a lunar lander, a dozen aircraft, and an IMAX theater. Also within is the Hampton Roads History Center.

Yorktown Victory Center, Yorktown, Virginia. This museum, next to the battlefield on which the Revolutionary War ended, helps capture what the moment meant for contemporaries.

NATURAL SIGHTS

Assateague Island National Seashore. This 37-mi-long barrier island on the border of Virginia and Maryland is a good place to find pristine beaches, wild ponies, deer, and 300 species of birds.

Natural Bridge of Virginia. Twenty miles south of Lexington, Virginia, is what Native Americans called the "Bridge of God": it's a graceful, 21-story limestone arch that now supports part of a highway.

Skyline Drive, Virginia. For more than 100 mi this highway winds up the Blue Ridge in Shenandoah National Park. It's got multiple vantage points for spectacular scenery, especially in the fall.

Sunsets at Ocean City, Maryland. Savor them outside or take a seat at any number of bay-side bars and restaurants—they're unforgettable.

SMART TRAVEL TIPS

Finding out about your destination before you leave home means you won't squander time organizing everyday minutiae once you've arrived. You'll be more streetwise when you hit the ground as well, better prepared to explore the aspects of Virginia and Maryland that drew you here in the first place. The organizations in this section can provide information to supplement this guide; contact them for up-to-the-minute details, and consult the A to Z sections that end each chapter for facts on the various topics as they relate to the region's states. Happy landings!

AIR TRAVEL

BOOKING

When you book, look for nonstop flights and remember that "direct" flights stop at least once. Try to avoid connecting flights, which require a change of plane. Two airlines may operate a connecting flight jointly, so ask whether your airline operates every segment of the trip; you may find that the carrier you prefer flies you only part of the way. To find more booking tips and to check prices and make online flight reservations, log on to www.fodors.com.

CHECK-IN & BOARDING

Always **find out your carrier's check-in policy.** Plan to arrive at the airport about two hours before your scheduled departure time for domestic flights and 2½ to 3 hours before international flights. You may need to arrive earlier if you're flying from one of the busier airports or during peak air-traffic times. To avoid delays at airport-security checkpoints, try not to wear any metal. Jewelry, belt and other buckles, steel-toe shoes, barrettes, and underwire bras are among the items that can set off detectors.

Assuming that not everyone with a ticket will show up, airlines routinely overbook planes. When everyone does, airlines ask for volunteers to give up their seats. In return, these volunteers usually get a several-hundred-dollar flight voucher, which can be used toward the purchase of another ticket, and are rebooked on the next flight out. If there are not enough volunteers, the airline must choose who will be denied boarding. The first to get bumped are passengers who checked in late and those flying on discounted tickets, so get to the gate and check in as early as possible, especially during peak periods.

Always **bring a government-issued photo ID** to the airport; even when it's not required, a passport is best.

CUTTING COSTS

The least expensive airfares to Virginia and Maryland are priced for round-trip travel and must usually be purchased in advance. Airlines generally allow you to change your return date for a fee; most low-fare tickets, however, are nonrefundable. It's smart to call a number of airlines and check the Internet; when you are quoted a good price, book it on the spot—the same fare may not be available the next day, or even the next hour. Always check different routings and look into using alternate airports. Also, price off-peak flights, which may be significantly less expensive than others. Travel agents, especially low-fare specialists (⇨ Discounts & Deals), are helpful.

Consolidators are another good source. They buy tickets for scheduled flights at reduced rates from the airlines, then sell them at prices that beat the best fare available directly from the airlines. (Many also offer reduced car-rental and hotel rates.) Sometimes you can even get your money back if you need to return the ticket. Carefully read the fine print detailing penalties for changes and cancellations, purchase the ticket with a credit card, and confirm your consolidator reservation with the airline.

Flying into BWI Airport between Baltimore and Washington, D.C. could save you on airfare; airlines, including Southwest, often have good deals to this airport. Good sales can sometimes be found to Washington Dulles International Airport and occasionally to Ronald Reagan Washington National Airport. Fares into Richmond International Airport are often more expensive.

🔢 Consolidators **AirlineConsolidator.com** ☏ 888/468-5385 ⊕ www.airlineconsolidator.com, for international tickets. **Best Fares** ☏ 800/880-1234 or

800/576-8255 ⊕ www.bestfares.com; $59.90 annual membership. **Cheap Tickets** ☏ 800/377-1000 or 800/652-4327 ⊕ www.cheaptickets.com. **Expedia** ☏ 800/397-3342 or 404/728-8787 ⊕ www.expedia.com. **Hotwire** ☏ 866/468-9473 or 920/330-9418 ⊕ www.hotwire.com. **Now Voyager Travel** ✉ 45 W. 21st St., Suite 5A, New York, NY 10010 ☏ 212/459-1616 🖷 212/243-2711 ⊕ www.nowvoyagertravel.com. **Onetravel.com** ⊕ www.onetravel.com. **Orbitz** ☏ 888/656-4546 ⊕ www.orbitz.com. **Priceline.com** ⊕ www.priceline.com. **Travelocity** ☏ 888/709-5983, 877/282-2925 in Canada, 0870/876-3876 in U.K. ⊕ www.travelocity.com.

ENJOYING THE FLIGHT

State your seat preference when purchasing your ticket, and then repeat it when you confirm and when you check in. For more legroom, you can request one of the few emergency-aisle seats at check-in, if you're capable of moving obstacles comparable in weight to an airplane exit door (usually between 35 pounds and 60 pounds)—a Federal Aviation Administration requirement of passengers in these seats. Seats behind a bulkhead also offer more legroom, but they don't have underseat storage. Don't sit in the row in front of the emergency aisle or in front of a bulkhead, where seats may not recline.

Ask the airline whether a snack or meal is served on the flight. If you have dietary concerns, request special meals when booking. These can be vegetarian, low-cholesterol, or kosher, for example. It's a good idea to pack some healthful snacks and a small (plastic) bottle of water in your carry-on bag. On long flights, try to maintain a normal routine, to help fight jet lag. At night, get some sleep. By day, eat light meals, drink water (not alcohol), and **move around the cabin** to stretch your legs. For additional jet-lag tips consult *Fodor's FYI: Travel Fit & Healthy* (available at bookstores everywhere).

FLYING TIMES

Flying time to Baltimore-Washington International Airport is nearly one hour from New York; approximately two hours from Chicago; and five hours, 40 minutes from Los Angeles. Flying time to Richmond International Airport is approximately 1½ hours from New York, two hours from Chicago, and 6½ hours from Los Angeles. A flight to D.C. is a little less than an hour from New York, about 1½ hours from Chicago, three hours from Denver and Dallas, and five hours from San Francisco. Those flying from London can expect a trip of about six hours. A trip from Sydney takes about 20 hours.

HOW TO COMPLAIN

If your baggage goes astray or your flight goes awry, complain right away. Most carriers require that you **file a claim immediately.** The Aviation Consumer Protection Division of the Department of Transportation publishes *Fly-Rights,* which discusses airlines and consumer issues and is available online. You can also find articles and information on mytravelrights.com, the Web site of the nonprofit Consumer Travel Rights Center.

▶ Airline Complaints **Aviation Consumer Protection Division** ⊠ U.S. Department of Transportation, Office of Aviation Enforcement and Proceedings, C-75, Room 4107, 400 7th St. SW, Washington, DC 20590 ☎ 202/366-2220 ⊕ airconsumer.ost.dot.gov. **Federal Aviation Administration Consumer Hotline** ⊠ For inquiries: FAA, 800 Independence Ave. SW, Washington, DC 20591 ☎ 800/322-7873 ⊕ www.faa.gov.

RECONFIRMING

Check the status of your flight before you leave for the airport. You can do this on your carrier's Web site, by linking to a flight-status checker (many Web booking services offer these), or by calling your carrier or travel agent.

AIRPORTS

Virginia has Richmond International Airport, 10 mi east of Richmond; the busy Ronald Reagan Washington National Airport, 3 mi south of downtown Washington; and Washington Dulles International Airport, 26 mi northwest of Washington. Maryland's Baltimore-Washington International (BWI) Airport is about 25 mi northeast of Washington and 10 mi south of Baltimore. Amtrak and commuter trains stop at BWI's station.

Some of the smaller regional airports have flights to Washington, D.C., Baltimore,

Richmond, and Philadelphia on USAirways; commuter planes can also sometimes be chartered. Most travelers fly to the nearest major airport and rent a car to get to the areas covered by these regional airports. Greater Cumberland Regional Airport serves western Maryland; Easton Airport, with Easton Aviation, services Maryland's middle Eastern Shore. Ocean City Municipal Airport offers private facilities close to Maryland's Atlantic seashore; Salisbury-Ocean City-Wicomico Regional Airport provides service to Maryland's lower Eastern Shore, and the Hagerstown Regional Airport has flights that go to Pittsburgh and throughout Maryland.

▶ Airport Information **Baltimore-Washington International Airport (BWI)** ⊠ Exit 2 off Baltimore-Washington Pkwy. (I-295) ☎ 410/859-7100 ⊕ www.bwiairport.com. **Richmond International Airport (RIC)** ⊠ Exit 197 off I-64 ☎ 804/226-3000. **Ronald Reagan Washington National Airport (DCA)** ⊠ Airport exit off Rte. 1 ☎ 703/417-8000 ⊕ www.mwaa.com. **Washington Dulles International Airport (IAD)** ⊠ Dulles Access Rd. off I-66 ☎ 703/572-2700 ⊕ www.mwaa.com.

▶ Commuter Airports **Easton Airport (ESN)** ⊠ 29137 Newnam Rd., Unit 1, Easton, MD ☎ 410/770-8055. **Greater Cumberland Regional Airport (CBE)** ⊠ Rte. 1, Wiley Ford, WV ☎ 304/738-0002. **Hagerstown Regional Airport (HGR)** ⊠ 18434 Showalter Rd., Hagerstown, MD ☎ 240/313-2777. **Ocean City Municipal Airport (OXB)** ⊠ 12724 Airport Rd., Berlin, MD ☎ 410/213-2471. **Salisbury-Ocean City-Wicomico Regional Airport (SBY)** ⊠ 5485 Airport Terminal Rd., Unit A, Salisbury, MD ☎ 410/548-4827.

TRANSFERS BY BUS

Reagan National, Dulles, and BWI airports are served by SuperShuttle, which will take you to a specific hotel or residence. Make reservations at the ground transportation desk. Fares vary depending on the destination. Drivers accept major credit cards in addition to cash.

▶ Bus Information **SuperShuttle** ☎ 800/258-3826.

BIKE TRAVEL

Getting around major cities and suburbs is tricky—roads are congested and, for the most part, there are no bicycle lanes. Outside the urban areas is terrain more suited for bicycling, including flat coastal plains, gentle hills, and mountains. Popular bicycling trails include the Baltimore and Annapolis Trail Park and the towpath of the C&O Canal, which runs parallel to the Potomac River on the Maryland shore, from Georgetown in Washington, D.C., to Cumberland in western Maryland.

The Maryland State Highway Administration can provide details concerning statewide bike routes. In Virginia, contact the State Bicycle Coordinator. For metropolitan Washington, D.C., the Washington Area Bicyclist Association (WABA) is a good resource.

F Maryland State Highway Administration ✉ Bicycle and Pedestrian Coordinator, Mailstop C-502, State Hwy. Administration, 707 N. Calvert St., Baltimore, MD 21203 ☎ 410/545-5656 ⊕ www.marylandroads.com. **Virginia State Department of Transportation** ✉ State Bicycle Coordinator, 1221 E. Broad St., Richmond, VA 23219 ☎ 804/371-4869 ⊕ www.virginiadot.org. **Washington Area Bicyclist Association** ✉ 733 15th St. NW, Suite 1030, Washington, D.C. 20005 ☎ 202/628-2500 ⊕ www.waba.org.

BIKES IN FLIGHT

Most airlines accommodate bikes as luggage, provided they are dismantled and boxed; check with individual airlines about packing requirements. Some airlines sell bike boxes, which are often free at bike shops, for about $20 (bike bags can be considerably more expensive). International travelers often can substitute a bike for a piece of checked luggage at no charge; otherwise, the cost is about $100. Most U.S. and Canadian airlines charge $40–$80 each way.

BOAT & FERRY TRAVEL

Water sports and activities are popular recreational pursuits in Virginia and Maryland, which share the expansive Chesapeake Bay and the Potomac River. Harbor and river cruises are offered in Baltimore, St. Michaels, Annapolis, Washington, D.C. (along the Potomac), Hampton, and Norfolk, to name a few starting points. Sailboats and other pleasure craft can be chartered for trips on the Chesa-

peake Bay or inland rivers. Popular ports include Rock Hall, Havre de Grace, and Solomons in Maryland, and Newport News and Chincoteague in Virginia.

BUSINESS HOURS

The business week runs from 9 to 5 weekdays, and in some instances, on Saturday in the metropolitan regions of Virginia and Maryland. Stores, restaurants, and other services maintain longer hours. Hours vary in small towns and resort areas, especially those dependent on seasonal visitors. In rural areas, many retail establishments close on Sunday.

Most businesses in the area close for many religious holidays and all holidays that are celebrated on a Monday. However, shopping malls and plazas, as well as restaurants, remain open.

MUSEUMS & SIGHTS

The major art and historical museums in the region are open from 10 or 11 to 5 or 6, Monday through Saturday, and noon to 5 on Sunday. Some museums are closed on Monday and/or Tuesday. Many parks and historical homes tend to have varied hours according to the season, with later closing hours in the summer. Some close during the winter months. In this book's sight reviews, open hours are denoted by a clock icon.

SHOPS

In the metropolitan areas, retail stores and shopping malls are open 10–9, Monday through Saturday, and 11–6 on Sunday. Outlet shopping centers maintain the same hours. In suburban Baltimore, Washington, and Richmond, grocery stores and superstores are open 24 hours. Retailers in small towns and in the downtown office districts close earlier and are often not open on Sunday.

BUS TRAVEL

A bus is a fairly practical way to get to a one-stop resort destination such as Ocean City or Virginia Beach, but many of Maryland's and Virginia's attractions lie outside the cities served by bus routes. Municipal buses do provide point-to-point transportation in Baltimore and Richmond and suburban Washington, D.C.

Greyhound Lines serves the following locations (among others) in Maryland: Baltimore, Cambridge, Cumberland, Easton, Frederick, Hagerstown, Salisbury, Silver Spring, and Ocean City. In Virginia it serves Abingdon, Arlington, Charlottesville, Fairfax, Fredericksburg, Hampton, Lexington, Norfolk, Richmond, Roanoke, Springfield, Staunton, Virginia Beach, and Williamsburg, as well as other towns. Peter Pan travels among Washington, D.C., Baltimore, and points north.

⚏ **Greyhound Lines** ☎ 800/231-2222 ⊕ www.greyhound.com. **Peter Pan Trailways** ☎ 800/343-9999 ⊕ www.peterpanbus.com.

CAMERAS & PHOTOGRAPHY

The *Kodak Guide to Shooting Great Travel Pictures* (available at bookstores everywhere) is loaded with tips.

⚏ Photo Help **Kodak Information Center** ☎ 800/242-2424 ⊕ www.kodak.com.

EQUIPMENT PRECAUTIONS

Don't pack film or equipment in checked luggage, where it is much more susceptible to damage. X-ray machines used to view checked luggage are extremely powerful and therefore are likely to ruin your film. Try to ask for hand inspection of film, which becomes clouded after repeated exposure to airport X-ray machines, and keep videotapes and computer disks away from metal detectors. Always keep film, tape, and computer disks out of the sun. Carry an extra supply of batteries, and be prepared to turn on your camera, camcorder, or laptop to prove to airport security personnel that the device is real.

CAR RENTAL

⚏ Major Agencies **Alamo** ☎ 800/327-9633 ⊕ www.alamo.com. **Avis** ☎ 800/331-1212, 800/879-2847 or 800/272-5871 in Canada, 0870/606-0100 in U.K., 02/9353-9000 in Australia, 09/526-2847 in New Zealand ⊕ www.avis.com. **Budget** ☎ 800/527-0700, 0870/156-5656 in U.K. ⊕ www.budget.com. **Dollar** ☎ 800/800-4000, 0800/085-4578 in U.K. ⊕ www.dollar.com. **Hertz** ☎ 800/654-3131, 800/263-0600 in Canada, 0870/844-8844 in U.K., 02/9669-2444 in Australia, 09/256-8690 in New Zealand ⊕ www.hertz.com. **National Car Rental** ☎ 800/227-7368, 0870/600-6666 in U.K. ⊕ www.nationalcar.com.

CUTTING COSTS

For a good deal, book through a travel agent who will shop around. Also, price local car-rental companies—whose prices may be lower still, although their service and maintenance may not be as good as those of major rental agencies—and research rates on the Internet. Consolidators that specialize in air travel can offer good rates on cars as well (⇨ Air Travel). Remember to ask about required deposits, cancellation penalties, and drop-off charges if you're planning to pick up the car in one city and leave it in another. If you're traveling during a holiday period, also make sure that a confirmed reservation guarantees you a car.

INSURANCE

When driving a rented car you are generally responsible for any damage to or loss of the vehicle. You also may be liable for any property damage or personal injury that you may cause while driving. Before you rent, see what coverage you already have under the terms of your personal auto-insurance policy and credit cards.

For about $9 to $25 a day, rental companies sell protection, known as a collision- or loss-damage waiver (CDW or LDW), that eliminates your liability for damage to the car; it's always optional and should never be automatically added to your bill. In Maryland the car-rental agency's insurance is primary; therefore, the company must pay for damage to third parties up to a preset legal limit, beyond which your own liability insurance kicks in. However, **make sure you have enough coverage to pay for the car.** If you do not have auto insurance or an umbrella policy that covers damage to third parties, purchasing liability insurance and a CDW or LDW is highly recommended.

REQUIREMENTS & RESTRICTIONS

In Virginia and Maryland you must be 21 to rent a car.

SURCHARGES

Before you pick up a car in one city and leave it in another, ask about drop-off charges or one-way service fees, which can be substantial. Also inquire about early-return policies; some rental agencies charge extra if you return the car before the time specified in your contract while others give you a refund for the days not used. To avoid a hefty refueling fee, fill the tank just before you turn in the car, but be aware that gas stations near the rental outlet may overcharge. It's almost never a deal to buy the tank of gas that's in the car when you rent it; the understanding is that you'll return it empty, but some fuel usually remains. Surcharges may apply if you're under 25 or if you take the car outside the area approved by the rental agency. You'll pay extra for child seats (about $8 a day), which are compulsory for children under five, and usually for additional drivers (up to $25 a day, depending on location).

CAR TRAVEL

A car is by far the most convenient means of travel throughout Maryland and Virginia, and in many areas it's the only practical way to get around. (Where it exists, public transportation is clean and comfortable, but too often it bypasses or falls short of travel high points.)

HIGHWAYS

Interstate 95 runs north–south through Maryland and Virginia, carrying traffic to and from New England and Florida and intermediate points. U.S. 50 links I–95 with Annapolis and Maryland's Eastern Shore. U.S. 97 links Baltimore with Annapolis. I–64 intersects I–95 at Richmond and runs east–west, headed east toward Williamsburg, Hampton Roads, and the bridge-tunnel to Virginia's Eastern Shore, and west toward Charlottesville and the Shenandoah Valley. At Staunton, I–64 intersects I–81, which runs north–south. Interstate 70 runs west from Baltimore's Beltway, I–695, to Hancock in western Maryland. I–68 connects Hancock to Cumberland and Garrett County. Also, U.S. 40—the National Pike—travels east and west, the entire length of Maryland. Interstate 83 journeys south from Pennsylvania to the top of I–695, the Baltimore Beltway.

ROAD MAPS

The state tourist offices of Maryland and Virginia (⇨ Visitor Information) publish official state road maps, free for the asking, that contain directories and other useful information. For the excellent, free *Maryland Scenic Byways* guide, call ☎ 877/632–9929 or look for one at a state welcome center.

RULES OF THE ROAD

The maximum speed limit is 65 mph on stretches of major highways in both states. Radar detectors are legal in Maryland, but are not permitted in Virginia, so don't forget to put it away once you cross into Virginia. Front-seat passengers in both states must wear seat belts.

In Virginia and Maryland, you may turn right at a red light after stopping if there's no oncoming traffic. When in doubt, wait for the green. Be alert for one-way streets, "no left turn" intersections, and blocks closed to car traffic.

In both states, HOV commuter lanes are restricted to a minimum of two people during rush hour. Look for the diamond on the highway and on signs telling you when the restrictions are in effect. All drivers can use HOV lanes during off-peak traffic hours.

Talking on cell phones while driving is not allowed in Washington, D.C., so don't forget to hang up when going from Maryland or Virginia into the city.

CHILDREN

Both the Maryland and Virginia state tourism Web sites list activities for children (⇨ Visitor Information, *below*).

If you're renting a car, don't forget to arrange for a car seat when you reserve. Always strap children under age six, regardless of weight, or who weigh 40 pounds or less, regardless of age, into approved child-safety seats.

For general advice about traveling with children, consult *Fodor's FYI: Travel with Your Baby* (available in bookstores everywhere).

FLYING

If your children are two or older, ask about children's airfares. As a general rule, infants under two not occupying a seat fly at greatly reduced fares or even for free.

But if you want to guarantee a seat for an infant, you have to pay full fare. Consider flying during off-peak days and times; most airlines will grant an infant a seat without a ticket if there are available seats.

Experts agree that it's a good idea to use safety seats aloft for children weighing less than 40 pounds. Airlines set their own policies: if you use a safety seat, U.S. carriers usually require that the child be ticketed, even if he or she is young enough to ride free, because the seats must be strapped into regular seats. And even if you pay the full adult fare for the seat, it may be worth it, especially on longer trips. Do **check your airline's policy about using safety seats during takeoff and landing.** Safety seats are not allowed everywhere in the plane, so get your seat assignments as early as possible.

When reserving, request children's meals or a freestanding bassinet (not available at all airlines) if you need them. But note that bulkhead seats, where you must sit to use the bassinet, may lack an overhead bin or storage space on the floor.

LODGING

Most hotels in Virginia and Maryland allow children under a certain age to stay in their parents' room at no extra charge, but others charge for them as extra adults; be sure to find out the cutoff age for children's discounts. Some resorts, B&Bs, and higher-end hotels do not allow children under a certain age; be sure to check when making a reservation.

SIGHTS & ATTRACTIONS

Places discussed in this guide that are especially appealing to children are indicated by a rubber-duckie icon (🐤) in the margin. Many historic attractions make every effort to engage children with hands-on activities and entertaining costumed reenactors.

CONSUMER PROTECTION

Whether you're shopping for gifts or purchasing travel services, **pay with a major credit card** whenever possible, so you can cancel payment or get reimbursed if there's a problem (and you can provide documentation). If you're doing business with a particular company for the first time, con-

tact your local Better Business Bureau and the attorney general's offices in your state and (for U.S. businesses) the company's home state as well. Have any complaints been filed? Finally, if you're buying a package or tour, always consider travel insurance that includes default coverage (⇨ Insurance).

BBBs Council of Better Business Bureaus ✉ 4200 Wilson Blvd., Suite 800, Arlington, VA 22203 ☎ 703/276-0100 🖷 703/525-8277 ⊕ www. bbb.org.

CUSTOMS & DUTIES

IN AUSTRALIA

Australian residents who are 18 or older may bring home A$400 worth of souvenirs and gifts (including jewelry), 250 cigarettes or 250 grams of cigars or other tobacco products, and 1,125 ml of alcohol (including wine, beer, and spirits). Residents under 18 may bring back A$200 worth of goods. Members of the same family traveling together may pool their allowances. Prohibited items include meat products. Seeds, plants, and fruits need to be declared upon arrival.

Australian Customs Service 🏢 Regional Director, Box 8, Sydney, NSW 2001 ☎ 02/9213-2000 or 1300/363263, 02/9364-7222 or 1800/020-504 quarantine-inquiry line 🖷 02/9213-4043 ⊕ www. customs.gov.au.

IN CANADA

Canadian residents who have been out of Canada for at least seven days may bring in C$750 worth of goods duty-free. If you've been away fewer than seven days but more than 48 hours, the duty-free allowance drops to C$200. If your trip lasts 24 to 48 hours, the allowance is C$50. You may not pool allowances with family members. Goods claimed under the C$750 exemption may follow you by mail; those claimed under the lesser exemptions must accompany you. Alcohol and tobacco products may be included in the seven-day and 48-hour exemptions but not in the 24-hour exemption. If you meet the age requirements of the province or territory through which you reenter Canada, you may bring in, duty-free, 1.5 liters of wine *or* 1.14 liters (40 imperial ounces) of liquor *or* 24 12-ounce cans or bottles of beer or ale. Also, if you meet the local age requirement for tobacco products, you may bring in, duty-free, 200 cigarettes and 50 cigars. Check ahead of time with the Canada Customs and Revenue Agency or the Department of Agriculture for policies regarding meat products, seeds, plants, and fruits.

You may send an unlimited number of gifts (only one gift per recipient, however) worth up to C$60 each duty-free to Canada. Label the package UNSOLICITED GIFT—VALUE UNDER $60. Alcohol and to-bacco are excluded.

🖪 **Canada Customs and Revenue Agency** ✉ 2265 St. Laurent Blvd., Ottawa, Ontario K1G 4K3 ☎ 800/461-9999 in Canada, 204/983-3500, 506/636-5064 ⊕ www.ccra.gc.ca.

IN NEW ZEALAND

All homeward-bound residents may bring back NZ$700 worth of souvenirs and gifts; passengers may not pool their allowances, and children can claim only the concession on goods intended for their own use. For those 17 or older, the duty-free allowance also includes 4.5 liters of wine or beer; one 1,125-ml bottle of spirits; and either 200 cigarettes, 250 grams of tobacco, 50 cigars, *or* a combination of the three up to 250 grams. Meat products, seeds, plants, and fruits must be declared upon arrival to the Agricultural Services Department.

🖪 **New Zealand Customs** ✉ Head office: The Customhouse, 17-21 Whitmore St., Box 2218, Wellington ☎ 09/300-5399 or 0800/428-786 ⊕ www.customs.govt.nz.

IN THE U.K.

From countries outside the European Union, including the United States, you may bring home, duty-free, 200 cigarettes, 50 cigars, 100 cigarillos, or 250 grams of tobacco; 1 liter of spirits or 2 liters of for-tified or sparkling wine or liqueurs; 2 liters of still table wine; 60 ml of perfume; 250 ml of toilet water; plus £145 worth of other goods, including gifts and souvenirs. Prohibited items include meat and dairy products, seeds, plants, and fruits.

🖪 **HM Customs and Excise** ✉ Portcullis House, 21 Cowbridge Rd. E, Cardiff CF11 9SS ☎ 0845/010-9000 or 0208/929-0152 advice service, 0208/929-6731 or 0208/910-3602 complaints ⊕ www.hmce.gov.uk.

DISABILITIES & ACCESSIBILITY

Destination Maryland, a guidebook published by the Maryland Office of Tourism, labels individual historic sites, attractions, hotels, and restaurants that are accessible to the disabled. The Virginia Tourism Corporation publishes the free *Virginia Travel Guide for Persons with Disabilities,* which provides information on parking, accessibility, and other needs of disabled travelers at attractions, parks, lodgings, campgrounds, and outdoor recreation and shopping centers.

🖪 Local Resources **Maryland Office of Tourism** ☎ 410/767-3400 or 800/634-7386 ⊕ www.visitmaryland.org. **Virginia Tourism Corporation** ☎ 804/371-0327 or 800/847-4882 ⊕ www.virginia.org.

LODGING

Despite the Americans with Disabilities Act, the definition of accessibility seems to differ from hotel to hotel. Some properties may be accessible by ADA standards for people with mobility problems but not for people with hearing or vision impairments, for example.

If you have mobility problems, ask for the lowest floor on which accessible services are offered. If you have a hearing impairment, check whether the hotel has devices to alert you visually to the ring of the telephone, a knock at the door, and a fire/emergency alarm. Some hotels provide these devices without charge. Discuss your needs with hotel personnel if this equipment isn't available, so that a staff member can personally alert you in the event of an emergency.

If you're bringing a guide dog, get authorization ahead of time and write down the name of the person with whom you spoke.

RESERVATIONS

When discussing accessibility with an operator or reservations agent, ask hard questions. Are there any stairs, inside *or* out? Are there grab bars next to the toilet *and* in the shower/tub? How wide is the doorway to the room? To the bathroom?

For the most extensive facilities meeting the latest legal specifications, opt for newer accommodations. If you reserve through a toll-free number, consider also calling the hotel's local number to confirm the information from the central reservations office. Get confirmation in writing when you can.

SIGHTS & ATTRACTIONS

Most major sites in Maryland and Virginia are accessible to the disabled. *Destination Maryland,* a guidebook published by the Maryland Office of Tourism, labels specific historic sites and attractions that are accessible. The Virginia Tourism Corporation's free *Virginia Travel Guide for Persons with Disabilities* has information on parking, accessibility, and other needs of disabled travelers at attractions, parks, and shopping centers.

TRANSPORTATION

Amtrak offers a 15% discount to the physically challenged. Wheelchair, arm, and Red Cap assistance are available at Amtrak train stations. Accessibility varies by station, so call ahead. MARC and VRE trains and stations are wheelchair accessible; call 24 hours ahead to arrange for assistance with other needs (⇨ Train Travel, *below*). The Metro and buses in suburban Washington, D.C., and the Metro, light rail, and buses in Baltimore are wheelchair accessible. Stops are generally announced. Braille can be found on all buses; braille versions of the schedule are available by calling Amtrak, the MTA, or the VRE.

🚹 Complaints **Aviation Consumer Protection Division** (⇨ Air Travel) for airline-related problems. **Departmental Office of Civil Rights** ⊠ For general inquiries, U.S. Department of Transportation, S-30, 400 7th St. SW, Room 10215, Washington, DC 20590 ☎ 202/366-4648 🖷 202/366-9371 ⊕ www.dot.gov/ost/docr/index.htm. **Disability Rights Section** ⊠ NYAV, U.S. Department of Justice, Civil Rights Division, 950 Pennsylvania Ave. NW, Washington, DC 20530 🖷 ADA information line 202/514-0301, 800/514-0301, 202/514-0383 TTY, 800/514-0383 TTY ⊕ www.ada.gov. **U.S. Department of Transportation Hotline** ☎ For disability-related air-travel problems, 800/778-4838 or 800/455-9880 TTY.

TRAVEL AGENCIES

In the United States, the Americans with Disabilities Act requires that travel firms serve the needs of all travelers. Some agencies specialize in working with people with disabilities.

🚹 Travelers with Mobility Problems **Access Adventures/B. Roberts Travel** ⊠ 206 Chestnut Ridge Rd., Scottsville, NY 14624 ☎ 585/889-9096 ⊕ www.brobertstravel.com ✎ dltravel@prodigy.net, run by a former physical-rehabilitation counselor. **Accessible Vans of America** ⊠ 9 Spielman Rd., Fairfield, NJ 07004 ☎ 877/282-8267 or 888/282-8267, 973/808-9709 reservations 🖷 973/808-9713 ⊕ www.accessiblevans.com. **Flying Wheels Travel** ⊠ 143 W. Bridge St., Box 382, Owatonna, MN 55060 ☎ 507/451-5005 🖷 507/451-1685 ⊕ www.flyingwheelstravel.com.

DISCOUNTS & DEALS

State and local tourism offices often offer discount packages; call or check out their Web sites for more information. The *Maryland Destination* guide, available from the Maryland Office of Tourism, comes with a Passport Card that gives you discounts at a selection of hotels, restaurants, attractions, and stores throughout the state. The Virginia Tourism Corporation sells various travel packages.

Be a smart shopper and compare all your options before making decisions. A plane ticket bought with a promotional coupon from travel clubs, coupon books, and direct-mail offers or purchased on the Internet may not be cheaper than the least expensive fare from a discount ticket agency. And always keep in mind that what you get is just as important as what you save.

DISCOUNT RESERVATIONS

To save money, look into discount reservations services with Web sites and toll-free numbers, which use their buying power to get a better price on hotels, airline tickets (⇨ Air Travel), even car rentals. When booking a room, always **call the hotel's local toll-free number** (if one is available) rather than the central reservations number—you'll often get a better price. Always ask about special packages or corporate rates.

Airline Tickets Air 4 Less ☎ 800/AIR4LESS, low-fare specialist.

Hotel Rooms Accommodations Express ☎ 800/444-7666 or 800/277-1064 ⊕ www.acex. net. **Hotels.com** ☎ 800/246-8357 ⊕ www.hotels. com. **Quikbook** ☎ 800/789-9887 ⊕ www. quikbook.com. **Turbotrip.com** ☎ 800/473-7829 ⊕ www.turbotrip.com.

PACKAGE DEALS
Don't confuse packages and guided tours. When you buy a package, you travel on your own, just as though you had planned the trip yourself. Fly/drive packages, which combine airfare and car rental, are often a good deal. In cities, ask the local visitor's bureau about hotel and local transportation packages that include tickets to major museum exhibits or other special events.

EATING & DRINKING
The restaurants listed are the cream of the crop in each price category. Properties indicated by an ╳☒ are lodging establishments whose restaurant warrants a special trip.

CATEGORY	COST*
$$$$	over $30
$$$	$22–$30
$$	$14–$22
$	$7–$14
¢	under $7

*Per person for a main course at dinner

MEALTIMES
Unless otherwise noted, the restaurants listed in this guide are open daily for lunch and dinner.

RESERVATIONS & DRESS
Reservations are always a good idea; we mention them only when they're essential or not accepted. Book as far ahead as you can, and reconfirm as soon as you arrive. (Large parties should always call ahead to check the reservations policy.) We mention dress only when men are required to wear a jacket or a jacket and tie.

SPECIALTIES
The treasure of the Chesapeake Bay is the blue crab. In Maryland and Virginia, the locals like crabs steamed in the shells, seasoned by the bushel, and dumped on brown-paper-covered tables in spartan crab houses. Diners use wooden mallets to crack the shells, and nimble fingers to reach the meat. Crab cakes, crab imperial (enriched crabmeat stuffed back into shells), crab soup, and a host of other such dishes can be found throughout the region. Rockfish (striped bass) is another seafood delicacy, harvested in summer and fall.

In Virginia, country ham, biscuits, collard greens, and fried chicken—Southern staples—are popular Sunday meals. Grits (often served for breakfast) and pecan and sweet-potato pies are other popular Southern foods.

WINE, BEER & SPIRITS
In Maryland, restaurants and bars can serve wine, beer, and spirits seven days a week. Alcohol is sold in liquor stores every day except Sunday. In some parts of the state you can find restaurants or bars that are also package stores where you can buy alcohol on Sunday.

In Virginia the state-run ABC liquor stores are generally open Monday–Saturday, though in some places stores are also open on Sunday afternoon. At restaurants and bars, wine, beer, and spirits are generally sold seven days a week.

HOLIDAYS
Major national holidays are New Year's Day (Jan. 1); Martin Luther King Day (3rd Mon. in Jan.); Presidents' Day (3rd Mon. in Feb.); Memorial Day (last Mon. in May); Independence Day (July 4); Labor Day (1st Mon. in Sept.); Columbus Day (2nd Mon. in Oct.); Thanksgiving Day (4th Thurs. in Nov.); Christmas Eve and Christmas Day (Dec. 24 and 25); and New Year's Eve (Dec. 31).

INSURANCE
The most useful travel-insurance plan is a comprehensive policy that includes coverage for trip cancellation and interruption, default, trip delay, and medical expenses (with a waiver for preexisting conditions).

Without insurance you'll lose all or most of your money if you cancel your trip, regardless of the reason. Default insurance covers you if your tour operator, airline, or cruise line goes out of business—the chances of which have been increasing. Trip-delay covers expenses that arise because of bad weather or mechanical delays. Study the fine print when comparing policies.

U.K. residents can buy a travel-insurance policy valid for most vacations taken during the year in which it's purchased (but check preexisting-condition coverage).

Always **buy travel policies directly from the insurance company**; if you buy them from a cruise line, airline, or tour operator that goes out of business you probably won't be covered for the agency or operator's default, a major risk. Before making any purchase, review your existing health and home-owner's policies to find what they cover away from home.

▼ Travel Insurers In the U.S.: **Access America** ✉ 2805 N. Parham Rd., Richmond, VA 23294 ☎ 800/284-8300 🖷 804/673-1491 or 800/346-9265 ⊕ www.accessamerica.com. **Travel Guard International** ✉ 1145 Clark St., Stevens Point, WI 54481 ☎ 715/345-0505 or 800/826-1300 🖷 800/955-8785 ⊕ www.travelguard.com.

FOR INTERNATIONAL TRAVELERS

For information on customs restrictions, *see* Customs & Duties.

CAR RENTAL

When picking up a rental car, non-U.S. residents need a reservation voucher for any prepaid reservations that were made in the traveler's home country, a passport, a driver's license, and a travel policy that covers each driver.

CAR TRAVEL

Gasoline stations are plentiful. Most stay open late (24 hours along large highways and in big cities), except in rural areas, where Sunday hours are limited and where you may drive long stretches without a refueling opportunity. Highways are well paved. Interstates—limited-access, multilane highways whose numbers are prefixed by "I-"—are the fastest routes. Interstates with three-digit numbers encircle urban areas, which may have other limited-access expressways, freeways, and parkways as well. Tolls may be levied on limited-access highways. So-called U.S. highways and state highways are not necessarily limited-access but may have several lanes.

Along larger highways, roadside stops with restrooms, fast-food restaurants, and sundries stores are well spaced. State police and tow trucks patrol major highways and lend assistance. If your car breaks down on an interstate, pull onto the shoulder and wait for help, or have your passengers wait while you walk to an emergency phone (available in most states). If you carry a cell phone, dial *55, noting your location on the small green roadside mileage markers.

Driving in the United States is on the right. Be sure to obey speed limits posted along roads and highways. Watch for lower limits in small towns and on back roads. On weekdays between 6 and 10 AM and again between 4 and 7 PM expect heavy traffic. To encourage carpooling, some freeways have special lanes for so-called high-occupancy vehicles (HOV)—cars carrying more than one passenger.

Bookstores, gas stations, convenience stores, and rest stops sell maps (about $3) and multiregion road atlases (about $10).

CONSULATES & EMBASSIES

▼ Australia **Australian Embassy** ✉ 1601 Mass. Ave. NW, Washington,, DC 20036 ☎ 202/797-3000 ⊕ www.austemb.org.

▼ Canada **Canadian Embassy** ✉ 501 Pennsylvania Ave. NW, Washington, DC 20001 ☎ 202/682-1740 ⊕ www.canadianembassy.org.

▼ New Zealand **New Zealand Embassy** ✉ 37 Observatory Circle, NW, Washington, DC 20008 ☎ 202/328-4800 ⊕ www.nzemb.org.

▼ United Kingdom **U.K. Embassy** ✉ 3100 Massachusetts Ave., Washington, DC 20008 ☎ 202/588-7800 ⊕ www.britainusa.com.

CURRENCY

The dollar is the basic unit of U.S. currency. It has 100 cents. Coins are the copper penny (1¢); the silvery nickel (5¢), dime (10¢), quarter (25¢), and half-dollar (50¢); and the golden $1 coin, replacing a now-rare silver dollar. Bills are denominated $1, $5, $10, $20, $50, and $100, all mostly green and identical in size; designs and background tints vary. In addition, you may come across a $2 bill, but the chances are slim. The exchange rate at this writing is US$0.53 per British pound,

US$0.77 per Euro, US$0.84 per Canadian dollar, US$0.76 per Australian dollar, and US$0.69 per New Zealand dollar.

ELECTRICITY
The U.S. standard is AC, 110 volts/60 cycles. Plugs have two flat pins set parallel to each other.

EMERGENCIES
For police, fire, or ambulance, **dial 911** (0 in rural areas).

INSURANCE
Britons and Australians need extra medical coverage when traveling overseas.

🖅 Insurance Information In the U.K.: **Association of British Insurers** ✉ 51 Gresham St., London EC2V 7HQ ☎ 020/7600-3333 🖷 020/7696-8999 ⊕ www.abi.org.uk. In Australia: **Insurance Council of Australia** ✉ Insurance Enquiries and Complaints, Level 12, Box 561, Collins St. W, Melbourne, VIC 8007 ☎ 1300/780808 or 03/9629-4109 🖷 03/9621-2060 ⊕ www.iecltd.com.au. In Canada: **RBC Insurance** ✉ 6880 Financial Dr., Mississauga, Ontario L5N 7Y5 ☎ 800/668-4342 or 905/816-2400 🖷 905/813-4704 ⊕ www.rbcinsurance.com. In New Zealand: **Insurance Council of New Zealand** ✉ Level 7, 111-115 Customhouse Quay, Box 474, Wellington ☎ 04/472-5230 🖷 04/473-3011 ⊕ www.icnz.org.nz.

MAIL & SHIPPING
You can buy stamps and aerograms and send letters and parcels in post offices. Stamp-dispensing machines can occasionally be found in airports, bus and train stations, office buildings, drugstores, and the like. You can also deposit mail in the stout, dark blue, steel bins at strategic locations everywhere and in the mail chutes of large buildings; pickup schedules are posted. You can deposit packages at public collection boxes as long as the parcels are affixed with proper postage and weigh less than one pound. Packages weighing one or more pounds must be taken to a post office or handed to a postal carrier.

For mail sent within the United States, you need a 37¢ stamp for first-class letters weighing up to 1 ounce (23¢ for each additional ounce) and 23¢ for postcards. You pay 80¢ for 1-ounce airmail letters and 70¢ for airmail postcards to most other countries; to Canada and Mexico, you need a 60¢ stamp for a 1-ounce letter and 50¢ for a postcard. An aerogram—a single sheet of lightweight blue paper that folds into its own envelope, stamped for overseas airmail—costs 70¢.

To receive mail on the road, have it sent c/o General Delivery at your destination's main post office (use the correct five-digit ZIP code). You must pick up mail in person within 30 days and show a driver's license or passport.

PASSPORTS & VISAS
When traveling internationally, carry your passport even if you don't need one (it's always the best form of ID) and **make two photocopies of the data page** (one for someone at home and another for you, carried separately from your passport). If you lose your passport, promptly call the nearest embassy or consulate and the local police.

Visitor visas aren't necessary for Canadian or European Union citizens, or for citizens of Australia who are staying fewer than 90 days.

🖅 Australian Citizens **Passports Australia** ☎ 131-232 ⊕ www.passports.gov.au. **United States Consulate General** ✉ MLC Centre, Level 59, 19-29 Martin Pl., Sydney, NSW 2000 ☎ 02/9373-9200, 1902/941-641 fee-based visa-inquiry line ⊕ usembassy-australia.state.gov/sydney.

🖅 Canadian Citizens **Passport Office** ✉ To mail in applications: 200 Promenade du Portage, Hull, Québec J8X 4B7 ☎ 819/994-3500 or 800/567-6868, 866/255-7655 TTY ⊕ www.ppt.gc.ca.

🖅 New Zealand Citizens **New Zealand Passports Office** ✉ For applications and information, Level 3, Boulcott House, 47 Boulcott St., Wellington ☎ 0800/22-5050 or 04/474-8100 ⊕ www.passports.govt.nz. **Embassy of the United States** ✉ 29 Fitzherbert Terr., Thorndon, Wellington ☎ 04/462-6000 ⊕ usembassy.org.nz. **U.S. Consulate General** ✉ Citibank Bldg., 3rd fl., 23 Customs St. E, Auckland ☎ 09/303-2724 ⊕ usembassy.org.nz.

🖅 U.K. Citizens **U.K. Passport Service** ☎ 0870/521-0410 ⊕ www.passport.gov.uk. **American Consulate General** ✉ Danesfort House, 223 Stranmillis Rd., Belfast, Northern Ireland BT9 5GR ☎ 028/9032-8239 🖷 028/9024-8482 ⊕ usembassy.org.uk. **American Embassy** ✉ For visa and immigration information or to submit a visa application via mail (enclose an SASE), Consular Information Unit, 24

Grosvenor Sq., London W1 1AE ☎ 09055/444–546 for visa information (per-minute charges), 0207/499–9000 main switchboard ⊕ usembassy.org.uk.

TELEPHONES

All U.S. telephone numbers consist of a three-digit area code and a seven-digit local number. Within many local calling areas, you dial only the seven-digit number. Within some area codes, you must dial "1" first for calls outside the local area. To call between area-code regions, dial "1" then all 10 digits; the same goes for calls to numbers prefixed by "800," "888," "866," and "877"—all toll free. For calls to numbers preceded by "900" you must pay—usually dearly.

For international calls, dial "011" followed by the country code and the local number. For help, dial "0" and ask for an overseas operator. The country code is 61 for Australia, 64 for New Zealand, 44 for the United Kingdom. Calling Canada is the same as calling within the United States. Most local phone books list country codes and U.S. area codes. The country code for the United States is 1.

For operator assistance, dial "0." To obtain someone's phone number, call directory assistance at 555–1212 or occasionally 411 (free at many public phones). To have the person you're calling foot the bill, phone collect; dial "0" instead of "1" before the 10-digit number.

At pay phones, instructions often are posted. Usually you insert coins in a slot (usually 25¢–50¢ for local calls) and wait for a steady tone before dialing. When you call long-distance, the operator tells you how much to insert; prepaid phone cards, widely available in various denominations, are easier. Call the number on the back, punch in the card's personal identification number when prompted, then dial your number.

LODGING

The lodgings we list are the cream of the crop in each price category. We always list the facilities that are available, but we don't specify whether they cost extra; when pricing accommodations, always ask what's included and what costs extra.

Properties are assigned price categories based on the range between their least and most expensive standard double rooms at high season (excluding holidays). Properties marked ✕▨ are lodging establishments whose restaurants warrant a special trip.

Assume that hotels operate on the European Plan (EP, with no meals) unless we specify that they use either the Continental Plan (CP, with a Continental breakfast), Breakfast Plan (BP, with a full breakfast), or the Modified American Plan (MAP, with breakfast and dinner) or are all-inclusive (including all meals and most activities).

CATEGORY	COST*
$$$$	over $250
$$$	$175–$250
$$	$130–$175
$	under $130

*All prices are for a standard double room, excluding state tax.

APARTMENT & HOUSE RENTALS

If you want a home base that's roomy enough for a family and comes with cooking facilities, consider a furnished rental. These can save you money, especially if you're traveling with a group. Home-exchange directories sometimes list rentals as well as exchanges.

At shoreline resorts, as well as Deep Creek Lake in western Maryland, real estate agents generally handle apartment, condo, and town house rentals. Developers and individual owners make arrangements in the mountain resorts of Virginia.

🏠 **International Agents Hideaways International** ✉ 767 Islington St., Portsmouth, NH 03801 ☎ 603/430–4433 or 800/843–4433 🖷 603/430–4444 ⊕ www.hideaways.com, annual membership $145.

🏠 **Local Agents Atkinson Realty** ☎ 757/428–4441 arranges rentals in Virginia Beach. Contact **Bud Church Coldwell Banker** ☎ 800/851–7326 for Ocean City. **Coldwell Banker** ☎ 301/387–6187 or **Railey Mountain Lake Vacations** ☎ 800/846–7368 covers Deep Creek Lake in Maryland.

🏠 **Rental Listings Property Rentals International** ✉ 1008 Mansfield Crossing Rd., Richmond, VA 23236 ☎ 804/378–6054 🖷 804/379–2073. **Hideaways International** ✉ 767 Islington St., Portsmouth, NH 03801 ☎ 603/430–4433 or 800/843–4433 🖷 603/430–4444 is a club for travelers who arrange rentals among themselves; membership $99.

BED & BREAKFASTS

Houses in this region make it a natural area for bed-and-breakfast accommodations. The majority of B&Bs in Virginia and Maryland are Victorian structures with fewer than 10 rental units; a full or a Continental breakfast is typically included in the lodging rate, and rooms rarely have their own TV. Most rooms, however, have private bathrooms.

Information & Reservation Services Bed & Breakfast Accommodations Ltd. of Washington, DC ⌂ Box 12011, Washington, DC 20005 ☎ 202/328-3510 🖷 431/582-9669 handles lodgings in Baltimore, Washington, Washington area suburbs. **Bed & Breakfast Association of Maryland** ☎ 301/432-5079. **Maryland Office of Tourism** ⌂ 217 E. Redwood St., Baltimore, MD 21202 ☎ 410/767-3400 or 800/634-7386 ⊕ www.visitmaryland.com. **Virginia Tourism Corporation** ⌂ 901 E. Byrd St., Richmond, VA 23219 ☎ 804/786-2051 or 800/847-4882 ⊕ www.virginia.org.

CAMPING

Camping is popular in the Shenandoah and Blue Ridge mountains in Virginia, and at state forests and parks in western Maryland. Be aware that black bears abound in these regions. Assateague Island State Park in Maryland and the Assateague Island National Seashore (in Maryland and Virginia) are both popular campgrounds, largely because of the pristine beaches and ocean swimming, and the opportunity to camp near wild ponies. State-maintained sites include primitive and full-service sites (with showers, bathrooms, and hookups). Private campgrounds offer more amenities.

Go Camping America ⊕ www.gocampingamerica.com. **Maryland Department of Natural Resources** ⌂ 580 Taylor Ave., Box 1869, Annapolis MD 21401 ☎ 410/260-8100 ⊕ www.dnr.state.md.us. **Virginia Department of Conservation and Recreation** ⌂ 203 Governor St., Suite 213, Richmond, VA 23219 ☎ 804/786-1712 ⊕ www.dcr.state.va.us.

HOME EXCHANGES

If you would like to exchange your home for someone else's, join a home-exchange organization, which will send you its up-

dated listings of available exchanges for a year and will include your own listing in at least one of them. It's up to you to make specific arrangements.

Exchange Clubs HomeLink International ⌂ Box 47747, Tampa, FL 33647 ☎ 813/975-9825 or 800/638-3841 🖷 813/910-8144 ⊕ www.homelink.org; $110 yearly for a listing, online access, and catalog; $70 without catalog. **Intervac U.S.** ⌂ 30 Corte San Fernando, Tiburon, CA 94920 ☎ 800/756-4663 🖷 415/435-7440 ⊕ www.intervacus.com; $125 yearly for a listing, online access, and a catalog; $65 without catalog.

HOSTELS

No matter what your age, you can save on lodging costs by staying at hostels.With few exceptions, hostels in Virginia and Maryland are near popular outdoor spots or resort communities. In Maryland, the Harpers Ferry Lodge is near the Appalachian Trail in Knoxville, across the Potomac River from Harpers Ferry. Virginia's Bears Den Lodge is near the Appalachian Trail in Bluemont, the Blue Ridge Mountains is near the Blue Ridge Parkway in Galax, and Angie's Guest Cottage Hostel is in Virginia Beach.

In some 4,500 locations in more than 70 countries around the world, Hostelling International (HI), the umbrella group for a number of national youth-hostel associations, offers single-sex, dorm-style beds and, at many hostels, rooms for couples and family accommodations. Membership in any HI national hostel association, open to travelers of all ages, allows you to stay in HI-affiliated hostels at member rates; one-year membership is about $28 for adults (C$35 for a two-year minimum membership in Canada, £14 in the U.K., A$52 in Australia, and NZ$40 in New Zealand); hostels charge about $10–$30 per night. Members have priority if the hostel is full; they're also eligible for discounts around the world, even on rail and bus travel in some countries.

Hostels HI-Angie's Guest Cottage Hostel ⌂ 302 24th St., Virginia Beach, VA 23451 ☎ 757/428-4690 ⊕ www.angiescottage.com. **HI-Bears Den Lodge** ⌂ Virginia Hwy. 601, 18393 Blueridge Mountain Rd., Bluemont, VA 20135 ☎ 540/554-8708 🖷 540/554-8708. **HI-Blue Ridge Mountains**

Blue Ridge Pkwy. at milepost 214½, east side, Galax, VA 24333 ☎ 276/236-4962. **HI-Harpers Ferry Lodge** ✉ 19123 Sandy Hook Rd., Knoxville, MD 21758 ☎ 310/834-7652 ⊟ 301/834-7652 ⊕ www.harpersferryhostel.org.

🚩 Organizations **Hostelling International–USA** ✉ 8401 Colesville Rd., Suite 600, Silver Spring, MD 20910 ☎ 301/495-1240 ⊟ 301/495-6697 ⊕ www. hiusa.org. **Hostelling International–Canada** ✉ 205 Catherine St., Suite 400, Ottawa, Ontario K2P 1C3 ☎ 613/237-7884 or 800/663-5777 ⊟ 613/237-7868 ⊕ www.hihostels.ca. **YHA England and Wales** ✉ Trevelyan House, Dimple Rd., Matlock, Derbyshire DE4 3YH, U.K. ☎ 0870/870-8808, 0870/770-8868, 0162/959-2600 ⊟ 0870/770-6127 ⊕ www.yha.org.uk. **YHA Australia** ✉ 422 Kent St., Sydney, NSW 2001 ☎ 02/9261-1111 ⊟ 02/9261-1969 ⊕ www.yha.com.au. **YHA New Zealand** ✉ Level 1, Moorhouse City, 166 Moorhouse Ave., Box 436, Christchurch ☎ 03/379-9970 or 0800/278-299 ⊟ 03/365-4476 ⊕ www.yha.org.nz.

HOTELS

The large hotels of Baltimore, Richmond, Norfolk, and the Virginia suburbs of Washington, D.C., are in competitive markets for business travelers: standards and prices are high. The beach and mountain resorts in the region are among the oldest, largest, and most expensive in the country. Accommodations at beach resorts in Maryland and Virginia can be difficult to find during summer holiday weekends—be sure to make reservations. Off season, rates often go down in both metropolitan areas and resorts.

All hotels listed have a private bath unless otherwise noted.

🚩 Toll-Free Numbers **Best Western** ☎ 800/528-1234 ⊕ www.bestwestern.com. **Choice** ☎ 800/424-6423 ⊕ www.choicehotels.com. **Comfort Inn** ☎ 800/424-6423 ⊕ www.choicehotels.com. **Days Inn** ☎ 800/325-2525 ⊕ www.daysinn.com. **Doubletree Hotels** ☎ 800/222-8733 ⊕ www.doubletree.com. **Embassy Suites** ☎ 800/362-2779 ⊕ www.embassysuites.com. **Fairfield Inn** ☎ 800/228-2800 ⊕ www.marriott.com. **Hilton** ☎ 800/445-8667 ⊕ www.hilton.com. **Holiday Inn** ☎ 800/465-4329 ⊕ www.ichotelsgroup.com. **Howard Johnson** ☎ 800/446-4656 ⊕ www.hojo.com. **Hyatt Hotels & Resorts** ☎ 800/233-1234 ⊕ www.hyatt.com. **La Quinta** ☎ 800/531-5900 ⊕ www.lq.com. **Marriott** ☎ 800/228-9290 ⊕ www.marriott.com.

Quality Inn ☎ 800/424-6423 ⊕ www.choicehotels.com. **Radisson** ☎ 800/333-3333 ⊕ www.radisson.com. **Ramada** ☎ 800/228-2828, 800/854-7854 international reservations ⊕ www.ramada.com or www.ramadahotels.com. **Sheraton** ☎ 800/325-3535 ⊕ www.starwood.com/sheraton. **Sleep Inn** ☎ 800/424-6423 ⊕ www.choicehotels.com. **Westin Hotels & Resorts** ☎ 800/228-3000 ⊕ www.starwood.com/westin.

MEDIA

NEWSPAPERS & MAGAZINES

Chesapeake Bay and *Chesapeake Life* are monthly magazines with features about natural and human history and boating. The publication is available on newsstands in Maryland, Virginia, Pennsylvania, and Washington, D.C.

Maryland's largest newspaper, the *Baltimore Sun,* predominantly covers metropolitan Baltimore and the Eastern Shore, and lists arts and entertainment events in its *Live* section on Thursday. Maryland and Virginia's Washington suburbs look to the *Washington Post* for news. The *Post* packages weekend events and entertainment in its Friday *Weekend* insert.

The free *City Paper* comes out in both Washington, D.C. and Baltimore and has listings for events and activities in the region. Magazines with information about things to do in the region include *The Washingtonian, Baltimore,* and *Style,* also in Baltimore.

RADIO

National Public Radio affiliates in Maryland include **WEAA** (88.9 FM), and **WYPR** (88.1) in Baltimore; **WESM** (91.3) in Princess Anne, and **WSCL** (89.5), Salisbury, both on the Eastern Shore. **WAMU** (88.5) in Washington, D.C. is accessible in many parts of Maryland and Virginia.

In Virginia, public radio stations include **WETA** (90.9) in Arlington; **WMRY** (103.5), **WVTU** (89.3), and **WVTW** (88.5) all in Charlottesville; **WMRA** (90.7) in Harrisonburg; **WMRL** (89.9) in Lexington; **WVTR** (91.9) in Marion; **WHRO** (90.3), **WHRV** (89.5), and **WNSB** (91.1) in Norfolk; **WCVE** (88.9) in Richmond, and **WVTF** (89.1) in Roanoke.

MONEY MATTERS

Generally, lodging, restaurants, and attractions are most expensive in Baltimore, Richmond, suburban Washington, and resort areas, especially Ocean City and Virginia Beach. Gas prices tend to be higher in the rural and mountainous regions. Lodging and restaurant costs are considerably less expensive in the western Maryland mountains and rural Virginia.

Coupons for hotel discounts and services in Virginia can be printed at www.travelcoupons.com.

Prices throughout this guide are given for adults. Substantially reduced fees are almost always available for children, students, and senior citizens. For information on taxes, *see* Taxes.

ATMS

ATMs are common throughout metropolitan Baltimore, Washington, Richmond, and the suburbs. Although ATMs are not as prevalent in western Maryland and rural Virginia, travelers should have no trouble finding them at banks and grocery stores. Banks generally have 24-hour machines.

CREDIT CARDS

Throughout this guide, the following abbreviations are used: **AE**, American Express; **D**, Discover; **DC**, Diners Club; **MC**, MasterCard; and **V**, Visa.

 Reporting Lost Cards American Express ☎ 800/992-3404. **Diners Club** ☎ 800/234-6377. **Discover** ☎ 800/347-2683. **MasterCard** ☎ 800/622-7747. **Visa** ☎ 800/847-2911.

NATIONAL PARKS

Look into discount passes to save money on park entrance fees. For $50, the National Parks Pass admits you (and any passengers in your private vehicle) to all national parks, monuments, and recreation areas, as well as other sites run by the National Park Service, for a year. (In parks that charge per person, the pass admits you, your spouse and children, and your parents, when you arrive together.) Camping and parking are extra. The $15 Golden Eagle Pass, a hologram you affix to your National Parks Pass, functions as an upgrade, granting entry to all sites run

by the NPS, the U.S. Fish and Wildlife Service, the U.S. Forest Service, and the Bureau of Land Management. The upgrade, which expires with the parks pass, is sold by most national-park, Fish-and-Wildlife, and BLM fee stations. A major percentage of the proceeds from pass sales funds National Parks projects.

Both the Golden Age Passport ($10), for U.S. citizens or permanent residents who are 62 and older, and the Golden Access Passport (free), for persons with disabilities, entitle holders (and any passengers in their private vehicles) to lifetime free entry to all national parks, plus 50% off fees for the use of many park facilities and services. (The discount doesn't always apply to companions.) To obtain them, you must show proof of age and of U.S. citizenship or permanent residency—such as a U.S. passport, driver's license, or birth certificate—and, if requesting Golden Access, proof of disability. The Golden Age and Golden Access passes are available only at NPS-run sites that charge an entrance fee. The National Parks Pass is also available by mail and via the Internet.

 National Park Foundation ✉ 11 Dupont Circle NW, 6th fl., Washington, DC 20036 ☎ 202/238-4200 ⊕ www.nationalparks.org. **National Park Service** ✉ National Park Service/Department of Interior, 1849 C St. NW, Washington, DC 20240 ☎ 202/208-6843 ⊕ www.nps.gov. **National Parks Conservation Association** ✉ 1300 19th St. NW, Suite 300, Washington, DC 20036 ☎ 202/223-6722 ⊕ www.npca.org.

 Passes by Mail & Online National Park Foundation ⊕ www.nationalparks.org. **National Parks Pass** National Park Foundation ⌂ Box 34108, Washington, DC 20043 ☎ 888/467-2757 ⊕ www.nationalparks.org; include a check or money order payable to the National Park Service, plus $3.95 for shipping and handling (allow 8 to 13 business days from date of receipt for pass delivery), or call for passes.

PACKING

If you're visiting the mountains and the caverns of Virginia, prepare for colder-than-average temperatures. Hiking along the Appalachian Trail, even in spring and fall, frequently requires a coat. A sweater is in order for a visit to Luray Caverns or

Shenandoah Caverns in all seasons of the year.

Where dress is concerned, Baltimore and Richmond are relatively conservative. In the more expensive restaurants, men are expected to wear a jacket and tie.

At the bay and ocean resorts, "formal" means long trousers and a collared shirt for men, and shoes for everybody. A tie might never get tied during a stay in these areas.

In your carry-on luggage, pack an extra pair of eyeglasses or contact lenses and enough of any medication you take to last a few days longer than the entire trip. You may also ask your doctor to write a spare prescription using the drug's generic name, as brand names may vary from country to country. In luggage to be checked, **never pack prescription drugs, valuables, or undeveloped film.** And don't forget to carry with you the addresses of offices that handle refunds of lost traveler's checks. Check *Fodor's How to Pack* (available at online retailers and bookstores everywhere) for more tips.

To avoid customs and security delays, carry medications in their original packaging. Don't pack any sharp objects in your carry-on luggage, including knives of any size or material, scissors, nail clippers, and corkscrews, or anything else that might arouse suspicion.

To avoid having your checked luggage chosen for hand inspection, don't cram bags full. The U.S. Transportation Security Administration suggests packing shoes on top and placing personal items you don't want touched in clear plastic bags.

CHECKING LUGGAGE

You're allowed to carry aboard one bag and one personal article, such as a purse or a laptop computer. Make sure what you carry on fits under your seat or in the overhead bin. Get to the gate early, so you can board as soon as possible, before the overhead bins fill up.

Baggage allowances vary by carrier, destination, and ticket class. On international flights, you're usually allowed to check two bags weighing up to 70 pounds (32 kilograms) each, although a few airlines

allow checked bags of up to 88 pounds (40 kilograms) in first class. Some international carriers don't allow more than 66 pounds (30 kilograms) per bag in business class and 44 pounds (20 kilograms) in economy. On domestic flights, the limit is usually 50 to 70 pounds (23 to 32 kilograms) per bag. In general, carry-on bags shouldn't exceed 40 pounds (18 kilograms). Most airlines won't accept bags that weigh more than 100 pounds (45 kilograms) on domestic or international flights. Expect to pay a fee for baggage that exceeds weight limits. Check baggage restrictions with your carrier before you pack.

Airline liability for baggage is limited to $2,500 per person on flights within the United States. On international flights it amounts to $9.07 per pound or $20 per kilogram for checked baggage (roughly $640 per 70-pound bag), with a maximum of $634.90 per piece, and $400 per passenger for unchecked baggage. You can buy additional coverage at check-in for about $10 per $1,000 of coverage, but it often excludes a rather extensive list of items, shown on your airline ticket.

Before departure, itemize your bags' contents and their worth, and label the bags with your name, address, and phone number. (If you use your home address, cover it so potential thieves can't see it readily.) Include a label inside each bag and **pack a copy of your itinerary.** At check-in, make sure each bag is correctly tagged with the destination airport's three-letter code. Because some checked bags will be opened for hand inspection, the U.S. Transportation Security Administration recommends that you leave luggage unlocked or use the plastic locks offered at check-in. TSA screeners place an inspection notice inside searched bags, which are resealed with a special lock.

If your bag has been searched and contents are missing or damaged, file a claim with the TSA Consumer Response Center as soon as possible. If your bags arrive damaged or fail to arrive at all, file a written report with the airline before leaving the airport.

F Complaints **U.S. Transportation Security Administration Contact Center** ☎ 866/289-9673 ⊕ www.tsa.gov.

SENIOR-CITIZEN TRAVEL

To qualify for age-related discounts, mention your senior-citizen status up front when booking hotel reservations (not when checking out) and before you're seated in restaurants (not when paying the bill). Be sure to have identification on hand. When renting a car, ask about promotional car-rental discounts, which can be cheaper than senior-citizen rates.

F Educational Programs **Elderhostel** ⊠ 11 Ave. de Lafayette, Boston, MA 02111-1746 ☎ 877/426-8056, 978/323-4141 international callers, 877/426-2167 TTY ⊟ 877/426-2166 ⊕ www.elderhostel.org.

SPORTS & OUTDOORS

From the mountains to the sea, Virginia and Maryland provide plenty of opportunities for outdoor activities and sports. The state tourism offices are a good source of information about activities in state, as are Maryland's Department of Natural Resources and Virginia's Department of Conservation and Recreation. Also see the Outdoor Activities and Sports sections in specific chapters of this guide.

F Maryland Department of Natural Resources ⊠ 580 Taylor Ave., Annapolis, MD 21401 ☎ 877/620-8367 or 410/260-8367 ⊕ www.dnr.state.md.us/outdoors. **Maryland Office of Tourism** ⊠ 217 E. Redwood St., Baltimore, MD 21202 ☎ 800/543-1036 ⊕ www.visitmaryland.org. **Virginia Department of Conservation and Recreation** ⊠ 203 Governor St., Suite 213, Richmond, VA 23219 ☎ 804/786-1712 ⊕ www.dcr.state.va.us. **Virginia Tourism Corporation** ⊠ 901 E. Byrd St., Richmond, VA 23219 ☎ 804/786-2051 or 800/847-4882 ⊕ www.virginia.org.

CANOEING & KAYAKING

Canoeing and kayaking are popular paddle sports in Maryland and Virginia. Many outfitters organize kayaking excursions on the Chesapeake Bay and its tributaries, including the Rappahannock and James rivers in Virginia, and the Patapsco and St. Mary's rivers in Maryland. The water is equally placid on Maryland's Eastern Shore and stretches of the Potomac River. White-water enthusiasts will find challenge along the Shenandoah River in Virginia and the Youghiogheny and Savage rivers in western Maryland. A rugged stretch of the Potomac River near Washington, D.C., is one of the best places in the region for white-water kayaking.

FISHING

Virginia does not require a license for saltwater fishing in the ocean, in the bay, or in rivers up to the freshwater line. A license is required for freshwater fishing in rivers, lakes, and impoundments; a license valid for one year costs $30 for nonresidents and $6 for five consecutive days.

Maryland fishing licenses are valid for one year. For nonresidents, a saltwater license is $14; freshwater licenses vary in price depending on your state of residence. You can download a license form off the Department of Natural Resources' Web site. Fishing licenses can also be obtained at many sporting-goods stores; these licenses, valid for three to five days, cost $6 or more, depending on the type of license and on the state in which you live.

F Virginia Department of Game and Inland Fisheries ⊕ Box 1104, Richmond 23230 ☎ 804/367-1000 ⊕ www.dgif.state.va.us. **Maryland Department of Natural Resources** ⊠ 580 Taylor Ave., Box 1869, Annapolis 21401 ☎ 410/260-8100 ⊕ www.dnr.state.md.us.

HIKING

Mountainous regions in Western Maryland and in Virginia's Shenandoah, Roanoke, and New River valleys make for good hiking. National and regional trails such as the famed Appalachian Trail cross both states. In Maryland, trails, canal towpaths, and even old railroad routes are popular for hiking.

SAILING

Finding places to sail is as easy as looking at a map of the states and finding big coastal cities—Baltimore, Annapolis, Newport News, and Hampton. Charter companies abound in the coastal communities, including Solomons, St. Michaels, and Ocean City in Maryland, and Virginia's Norfolk and Virginia Beach. Sailing regattas can be seen on the Chesapeake Bay throughout the summer. Because demand is heavy from mid-May through October, it's a good idea to reserve boats as soon as you know your plans.

Annapolis Sailing School ✉ 601 6th St., Box 3334, Annapolis, MD 21403 ☎ 800/638-9192. *Guide to Cruising Chesapeake Bay* ($29.95 plus $3 postage) is published by **Chesapeake Bay Magazine** ✉ 1819 Bay Ridge Ave., Suite 103, Annapolis, MD 21403 ☎ 410/263-2662.

SKIING

In the Shenandoah Valley, the Homestead Resort in Hot Springs started the southern ski industry in the 1950s and has since been joined by Wintergreen near Waynesboro, Massanutten near Harrisonburg, and other Virginia resorts. The Department of Conservation and Recreation has more information on skiing facilities and seasons.

In far western Maryland, Wisp Ski Area rises nearly 3,100 feet above sea level and overlooks Deep Creek Lake. It has 23 slopes and 14 mi of trails, from novice to expert. It's easily accessible for weekenders from Baltimore and Washington. There are additional cross-country ski trails in the region.

TAXES

Sales tax in Maryland is 5% and in Virginia it's 4.5%. The hotel tax in Maryland is 5% (an additional 7.5% city tax is added in Baltimore); in Virginia it's 9.75%.

TIME

Maryland and Virginia are in the eastern time zone. Daylight saving time is in effect from early April through late October; eastern standard time, the rest of the year. Clocks are set ahead one hour when daylight saving time begins, and back one hour when it ends. The area is 3 hours ahead of Los Angeles, 1 hour ahead of Chicago, 5 hours behind London, and 14 hours behind Sydney.

TIPPING

Tipping is expected in restaurants and bars. Waiters receive 15%-20% of the total bill, depending on the level of service; for groups of six or more, a 15%-20% gratuity may be tacked onto the bill (if gratuity is covered, additional tips aren't necessary). Bartenders get $1-$2 or more, depending on the number of drinks and the number of people in the party. Taxi drivers are generally tipped 10%-15% of the total price of the ride; more if they have been particularly helpful. Doormen carrying bags to the registration desk and porters carrying bags between the lobby and the room are usually tipped $1 per bag, as are Red Caps at the airport or the train station. Chambermaids are generally tipped $1 to $3 a night for inexpensive-to-average hotels and up to $5 a night per guest for high-end properties. Barbers, hairdressers, and masseuses are usually tipped 10%-20% of the total cost of the service, depending on the place and the amount of time spent.

TOURS & PACKAGES

Because everything is prearranged on a prepackaged tour or independent vacation, you spend less time planning—and often get it all at a good price.

BOOKING WITH AN AGENT

Travel agents are excellent resources. But it's a good idea to collect brochures from several agencies, as some agents' suggestions may be influenced by relationships with tour and package firms that reward them for volume sales. If you have a special interest, find an agent with expertise in that area. The American Society of Travel Agents (ASTA) has a database of specialists worldwide; you can log on to the group's Web site to find one near you.

Make sure your travel agent knows the accommodations and other services of the place being recommended. Ask about the hotel's location, room size, beds, and whether it has a pool, room service, or programs for children, if you care about these. Has your agent been there in person or sent others whom you can contact?

Do some homework on your own, too: local tourism boards can provide information about lesser-known and small-niche operators, some of which may sell only direct.

BUYER BEWARE

Each year consumers are stranded or lose their money when tour operators—even large ones with excellent reputations—go out of business. So check out the operator. Ask several travel agents about its reputation, and try to **book with a company that has a consumer-protection program.** (Look for information in the company's brochure.) In the United States, members of the United States Tour Operators Association are required to set aside funds ($1 million) to help eligible customers cover payments and travel arrangements in the event that the company defaults. It's also a good idea to choose a company that participates in the American Society of Travel Agents' Tour Operator Program; ASTA will act as mediator in any disputes between you and your tour operator.

Remember that the more your package or tour includes, the better you can predict the ultimate cost of your vacation. Make sure you know exactly what is covered, and beware of hidden costs. Are taxes, tips, and transfers included? Entertainment and excursions? These can add up.

🔀 Tour-Operator Recommendations **American Society of Travel Agents** (⇨ Travel Agencies). **National Tour Association** (NTA) ✉ 546 E. Main St., Lexington, KY 40508 ☎ 859/226-4444 or 800/682-8886 🖷 859/226-4404 ⊕ www.ntaonline.com. **United States Tour Operators Association** (USTOA) ✉ 275 Madison Ave., Suite 2014, New York, NY 10016 ☎ 212/599-6599 🖷 212/599-6744 ⊕ www.ustoa.com.

TRAIN TRAVEL

Amtrak trains run out of Baltimore, Maryland, north toward Boston and south toward Washington, D.C., along the busy "northeast corridor." A rail station at Baltimore-Washington International Airport serves both Baltimore (about 15 mi to the north) and Washington, D.C. (about 30 mi to the south). Some trains running between New York and Chicago stop at Charlottesville, Virginia, and at two locations in western Virginia. Trains run between Newport News, Virginia, and New York City, stopping in northern Virginia, Richmond, and Williamsburg in between. Stops in Richmond and northern Virginia are also made on runs between New York City and Florida.

The Maryland State Railroad Administration, or MARC, operates commuter trains (on weekdays only) between Baltimore's Penn Station and D.C.'s Union Station. It also operates trains from Baltimore's downtown Camden Station and from Union Station in Washington, D.C. There's free bus transportation between the Baltimore-Washington International Airport Rail Station and the airport passenger terminal.

Virginia Railway Express, or VRE, provides workday commuter service between Union Station in Washington and Fredericksburg and Manassas, with additional stops near hotels in Crystal City, Alexandria, and elsewhere.

🚆 Train Information **Amtrak** ☎ 800/872-7245 ⊕ www.northeast.amtrak.com. **Maryland State Railroad Administration** (MARC) ☎ 800/325-7245 ⊕ www.mtamaryland.com. **Virginia Railway Express** (VRE) ☎ 800/743-3873 ⊕ www.vre.org.

TRANSPORTATION AROUND VIRGINIA & MARYLAND

The best way to see these two states is by car. Interstates cross the region, allowing easy access to the mountains and beaches. The highways in and around metropolitan regions are best avoided during morning and afternoon rush hours.

Amtrak and regional trains run between some points in both states, as does Greyhound Bus Lines. But neither the train nor the bus will get you everywhere in both states. Flights between areas are very limited and not the best way to get around.

Mass transit systems exist in both the Washington suburbs and Baltimore. These can be taken to many attractions and neighborhoods, but not to all.

TRAVEL AGENCIES

A good travel agent puts your needs first. Look for an agency that has been in business at least five years, emphasizes customer service, and has someone on staff who specializes in your destination. In addition, **make sure the agency belongs to a professional trade organization.** The American Society of Travel Agents (ASTA) has more than 10,000 members in some 140 countries, enforces a strict code of ethics, and will step in to mediate agent-client disputes involving ASTA members.

ASTA also maintains a directory of agents on its Web site; ASTA's TravelSense.org, a trip planning and travel advice site, can also help to locate a travel agent who caters to your needs. (If a travel agency is also acting as your tour operator, *see* Buyer Beware *in* Tours & Packages.)

🖪 Local Agent Referrals **American Society of Travel Agents** (ASTA) ⊠ 1101 King St., Suite 200, Alexandria, VA 22314 ☎ 703/739-2782, 800/965-2782 24-hr hotline 🖶 703/684-8319 ⊕ www.astanet.com. **Association of British Travel Agents** ⊠ 68-71 Newman St., London W1T 3AH ☎ 020/7637-2444 🖶 020/7637-0713 ⊕ www.abta.com. **Association of Canadian Travel Agencies** ⊠ 130 Albert St., Suite 1705, Ottawa, Ontario K1P 5G4 ☎ 613/237-3657 🖶 613/237-7052 ⊕ www.acta.ca. **Australian Federation of Travel Agents** ⊠ Level 3, 309 Pitt St., Sydney, NSW 2000 ☎ 02/9264-3299 or 1300/363-416 🖶 02/9264-1085 ⊕ www.afta.com.au. **Travel Agents' Association of New Zealand** ⊠ Level 5, Tourism and Travel House, 79 Boulcott St., Box 1888, Wellington 6001 ☎ 04/499-0104 🖶 04/499-0786 ⊕ www.taanz.org.nz.

VISITOR INFORMATION

Learn more about foreign destinations by checking government-issued travel advisories and country information. For a broader picture, consider information from more than one country.

For city and local tourism offices, *see* Visitor Information *in* the A to Z sections at the end of each chapter.

🖪 State Tourism Offices **Maryland Office of Tourism Development** ⊠ 217 E. Redwood St., 9th fl., Baltimore, MD 21202 ☎ 410/767-3400 or 800/634-7386 🖶 410/333-6643 ⊕ www.visitmaryland.org. **Virginia Tourism Corporation** ⊠ 901 E. Byrd St., Richmond, VA 23219 ☎ 804/786-2051 or 800/847-4882 🖶 804/786-1919 ⊕ www.virginia.org.

🖪 National Park Service The **National Park Service** ⊠ National Capital Region, 1100 Ohio Dr. SW, Washington, DC 20242 ☎ 202/619-7222 🖶 202/619-7062 ⊕ www.nps.gov/parks.html.

🖪 Government Advisories **Consular Affairs Bureau of Canada** ☎ 800/267-6788 or 613/944-6788 ⊕ www.voyage.gc.ca. **U.K. Foreign and Commonwealth Office** ⊠ Travel Advice Unit, Consular Division, Old Admiralty Bldg., London SW1A 2PA ☎ 0870/606-0290 or 020/7008-1500 ⊕ www.fco.gov.uk/travel. **Australian Department of Foreign Affairs and Trade** ☎ 300/139-281 travel advice, 02/6261-1299 Consular Travel Advice Faxback Service ⊕ www.dfat.gov.au. **New Zealand Ministry of Foreign Affairs and Trade** ☎ 04/439-8000 ⊕ www.mft.govt.nz.

WEB SITES

Check out the World Wide Web when planning your trip. There you can find everything from weather forecasts to virtual tours of famous cities. Be sure to visit Fodors.com (⊕ www.fodors.com), a complete travel-planning site. You can research prices and book plane tickets, hotel rooms, rental cars, vacation packages, and more. In addition, you can post your pressing questions in the Travel Talk section. Other planning tools include a currency converter and weather reports, and there are loads of links to travel resources.

For information about travel to Maryland check out www.visitmaryland.com and for Virginia go to www.virginia.org. For Civil War buffs, www.civilwartraveler.com has information on battlefields and war-related sites and events. Wine enthusiasts can learn the basics of Maryland wines (including winery locations) at www.marylandwine.com.

NORTHERN VIRGINIA

1

2 <

Updated by
Robin
Dougherty

CLOSE TO D.C. IN MORE WAYS THAN ONE, Northern Virginia extends westward from the Potomac River to the Blue Ridge Mountains. Although its name echoes that of Confederate General Robert E. Lee's Army of Northern Virginia, today the prosperous area's business and residential life takes its cue from the national capital, to the north. Alexandria and Arlington counties were Virginia's contribution to the District of Columbia when it was created under George Washington, and their history together is complicated and tightly bound. These locales, southeast of the Potomac, were in Fairfax County before the District was formed. After many years without any federal construction, the Virginia portion of the District was returned to the state and became Alexandria and Arlington. Looking at a map of the District, what seems to be the missing left-hand quadrant of the diamond-shape city is made up of the Northern Virginia puzzle piece.

Buildings in the Old Town portion of Alexandria are reminiscent of the Federal period (1790–1820); more than 2,000 of the area's 18th- and 19th-century buildings are listed collectively on the National Register of Historic Places. Nearby areas have grown significantly and have modern housing, government, and office buildings. Tysons Corner in Fairfax County serves more than 400 corporations employing 70,000 people. Northern Virginia contains some of America's most precious acreage, including Mount Vernon and Arlington National Cemetery. Manassas (Bull Run), 26 mi from Washington, was the site of two of the most significant battles of the Civil War. Although the town is still predominately rural, suburban sprawl has taken hold, and Bull Run is the center of modern battles between the forces of development and those of preservationism. In Loudoun County many residents still cling to the illusion of romanticism through such 18th-century diversions as fox hunting and steeplechasing.

Exploring Northern Virginia

Northern Virginia is generally defined as the area close to and south and west of the Potomac River, including Arlington and Alexandria, Fairfax County, Loudoun County, and Prince William County, to the south.

About the Restaurants & Hotels

You can find a high caliber of restaurants throughout Northern Virginia, many with well-known chefs and most getting review attention from the *Washington Post*. The best restaurants here aren't all the kind likely to be found in rural inns or former Colonial outposts, however. Bragging rights to some of the D.C. area's best Asian restaurants go to Arlington, where Wilson Boulevard is lined with popular Vietnamese establishments, many of which are the proverbial holes in the wall.

In addition to a wide selection of familiar hotel chains, there are many opportunities to experience 18th-century architecture along with modern amenities. Alexandria & Arlington Bed and Breakfast Network can arrange accommodations in historic homes and other furnished guesthouses in Arlington, Alexandria, and throughout Northern Virginia.
🛈 Reservations Services **Alexandria & Arlington Bed and Breakfast Network** ✉ 512 S. 25th St., Arlington 22202 ☎ 703/549-3415 or 888/549-3415 🖷 703/549-3411 ⊕ www.aabbn.com.

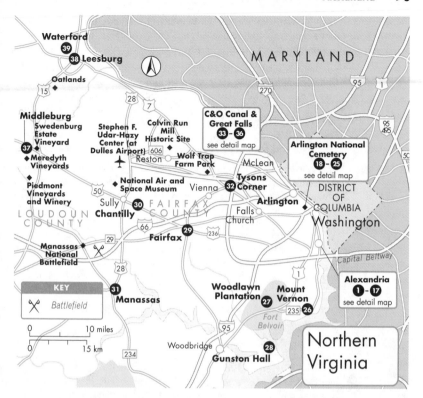

WHAT IT COSTS				
	$$$$	**$$$**	**$$**	**$**	**¢**
RESTAURANTS	over $30	$22–$30	$14–$22	$7–$14	Under $7
HOTELS	over $250	$175–$250	$130–$175	$80–$130	Under $80

Restaurant prices are per person for a main course at dinner. Hotel prices are for a standard double room, excluding state and county taxes (11% in Virginia; 10% in Maryland).

ALEXANDRIA

A lively mix of historic homes and taverns and state-of-the-art restaurants and shops, Alexandria seems to exist in two or three centuries at once. Founded in 1749 by Scottish merchants eager to capitalize on the booming tobacco trade, Alexandria first emerged as one of the most important ports in Colonial America. The city dwarfed Georgetown—Washington's oldest neighborhood—in the days before the Revolution, and, through the Civil War, had one of the country's largest slave markets. Alexandria is linked to many significant events and personages of the Colonial, Revolutionary, and Civil War periods. Members of the Lee family of Revolutionary and Civil War fame lived here, and George Washington had a town house and attended church here, though he lived a few miles south in Mount Vernon.

For many African-Americans fleeing slavery, part of their journey on the Underground Railroad included a stop in Alexandria. In fact this was true of one of the largest and most celebrated slave escapes, in which 77 individuals, many of whom labored in homes in Alexandria, took refuge on the *Pearl,* a ship bound for New Jersey, which left from Washington's 7th Street Wharf in April 1848. Unfortunately the ship was captured in Maryland and most of its passengers returned to Bruin's Slave Jail.

This vibrant past remains alive in the historic district of **Old Town Alexandria**—an area of cobbled streets, restored 18th- and 19th-century homes, churches, and taverns close to the water. The main arteries of this district are Washington Street (the G. W. Parkway as it passes through town) and King Street. Most points of interest are on the east (Potomac) side of Washington Street. Visit them on foot if you're prepared to walk 20 blocks or so; parking is usually scarce, especially close to the river, and the parking police seem to catch every violation. Parking garages within walking distance of Ramsay House provide some relief. On Saturday, parking costs $2 until 6 PM and $3 afterward.

Numbers in the text correspond to numbers in the margin and on the Old Town Alexandria map.

a good
walk

Start your walk through Old Town at the Alexandria Convention & Visitors Association, in **Ramsay House** ❶ ►, the oldest house in Alexandria. Across the street, near the corner of Fairfax and King streets, is the **Stabler-Leadbeater Apothecary** ❷, the country's second-oldest pharmacy. It was the equivalent of a corner drugstore to Alexandrians, including George Washington and the Lee family. Two blocks south on Fairfax Street, just beyond Duke Street, stands the **Old Presbyterian Meetinghouse** ❸, where Scottish patriots met during the Revolutionary War. Walk back up Fairfax Street one block and turn right on Prince Street to Gentry Row, the block between Fairfax and Lee streets. The striking edifice at the corner of Prince and Lee streets is the **Athenaeum** ❹. Many of the city's sea captains built their homes on the block of Prince Street between Lee and Union, which became known as **Captain's Row** ❺. Walk a block north on Union to King Street, where there are many shops and restaurants. One of Alexandria's most popular attractions is the **Torpedo Factory Art Center** ❻, a collection of art studios and galleries in a former World War II munitions plant (on Union at the foot of King Street). Also here is the Alexandria Archaeology Museum, with exhibits of artifacts found during excavations in Alexandria. Take Cameron Street away from the river. **Carlyle House** ❼, built in 1753, is at the corner of Cameron and North Fairfax streets.

One block west along Cameron, at Royal Street, is **Gadsby's Tavern Museum** ❽, where Washington attended parties. Continue west on Cameron Street for two blocks, turn right on St. Asaph Street, and walk up to Oronoco Street. Two historic Lee homes are on the short stretch of Oronoco between North Washington and St. Asaph streets. On the near side of Oronoco is the **Lee-Fendall House** ⑨; the **boyhood home of Robert E. Lee** ⑩ is across Oronoco on the St. Asaph Street corner.

The vast majority of African-Americans in Alexandria in 1790 were slaves, but there were nevertheless a few dozen free African-Americans living in Alexandria in 1790. This population grew to become a significant factor in Alexandria's successful development. The **Alexandria Black History Museum** ⑪, two blocks north and two blocks west of Lee's boyhood home, tells the history of blacks in Alexandria and Virginia. Head back to North Washington Street and go south to the corner of Queen Street. The **Lloyd House** ⑫, a fine example of Georgian architecture, is owned by the City of Alexandria. At the corner of Cameron and North Washington streets, one block south, stands the Georgian country-style **Christ Church** ⑬. Walk south two blocks to the **Lyceum** ⑭ at the corner of South Washington and Prince streets; it now houses two art galleries and a museum focusing on local history. The Confederate Statue is in the middle of South Washington and Prince streets, and two blocks to the west on South Alfred Street is the **Friendship Fire House** ⑮, restored and outfitted like a typical 19th-century firehouse. It's a long walk (or a quick ride on Bus 2 or 5 west on King Street) but worth the trouble to visit the **George Washington Masonic National Memorial** ⑯ on Callahan Drive at the King Street Metro station 1 mi west of the center of the city. In good weather, the open ninth-floor observation deck allows for good views. If you walk, take Duke Street for a glimpse of the Federal-style building that once housed the nefarious **Bruin's Slave Jail** ⑰.

TIMING   The Alexandria tour should take about four hours, not counting a trip to the George Washington Masonic National Memorial. A visit to the memorial adds about another hour and a half if you walk there and take the guided tour. If you're traveling by Metro, plan to finish your visit at the memorial and then get on the Metro at the King Street station.

Sights to See

Alexandria Archaeology Program. This city-operated research facility is devoted to urban archaeology and conservation. Artifacts displayed from excavations under way in Alexandria include such things as plates, cups, pipes, and coins from an early tavern, and Civil War soldiers' equipment. If digging interests you, call to sign up for the well-attended public dig days (Saturday in June and September, 1:30–3). Reservations are required. ⊠ *Torpedo Factory Art Center, 105 N. Union St., Old Town* ☎ *703/838–4399* ☐ *Museum admission free; public digs $5* ☉ *Tues.–Fri. 10–3, Sat. 10–5, Sun. 1–5.*

⑪ **Alexandria Black History Museum.** This museum, devoted to the history of African-Americans in Alexandria and Virginia from 1749 to the present, is at the site of the Robert H. Robinson Library, a building constructed in the wake of a landmark 1939 sit-in protesting the segregation of Alexandria libraries. The federal census of 1790 recorded 52 free African-Americans living in the city, and the port town was one of the largest slave exportation points in the South, with at least two bustling slave markets. ⊠ *902 Wythe St., Old Town* ☎ *703/838–4356* ⊕ *oha. ci.alexandria.va.us/bhrc* ☐ *Free* ☉ *Tues.–Sat. 10–4.*

Old Town Alexandria, Virginia

KEY

M Metro station

▶ Start of walk

④ Athenaeum. One of the most noteworthy structures in Alexandria, this striking, reddish-brown Greek Revival edifice at the corner of Prince and Lee streets stands out from its many redbrick Federal neighbors. Built in 1851 as a bank (Robert E. Lee had an account here), and then a talcum powder factory and a Union Army hospital, the Athenaeum now houses the gallery of the Northern Virginia Fine Arts Association and Alexandria Ballet. This block of Prince Street between Fairfax and Lee streets is known as **Gentry Row**, after the 18th- and 19th-century inhabitants of its imposing three-story houses. ☒ *201 Prince St., Old Town* ☎ *703/548–0035* ☞ *Free* ☉ *Wed.–Fri. 11–3, Sat. 11–3, Sun. 1–4.*

⑩ Boyhood Home of Robert E. Lee. The childhood home in Alexandria of the commander in chief of the Confederate forces is a fine example of a 19th-century Federal town house. The house was sold in 2000 to private owners who have made it their home. It's no longer open to visitors, but some of the home's furnishings are displayed at the Lyceum. ☒ *607 Oronoco St., Old Town.*

★ **⑰ Bruin's Slave Jail.** On this site, Joseph Bruin ran much of Alexandria's substantial slave trade, imprisoning in this Federal-style house African-Americans due to be sold. Harriett Beecher Stowe modeled her account of the slave trade in *Uncle Tom's Cabin* on this establishment. The building, now used as private offices, is closed to the public. ⊠ *1707 Duke St., Old Town.*

❺ Captain's Row. Many of Alexandria's sea captains once lived on this block. The cobblestones in the street were allegedly laid by Hessian mercenaries who had fought for the British during the Revolution and were held in Alexandria as prisoners of war. ⊠ *Prince St. between Lee and Union Sts., Old Town.*

❼ Carlyle House. Alexandria forefather and Scottish merchant John Carlyle built a grand house here, completed in 1753 and modeled on a country manor house in the old country. Fans of the French and Indian War era can tour the dwelling, which served as General Braddock's headquarters. The house retains its original 18th-century woodwork and is furnished with Chippendale furniture and Chinese porcelain. An architectural exhibit on the second floor explains how the house was built; outside there's an attractive garden of Colonial-era plants. ⊠ *121 N. Fairfax St., Old Town* ☎ *703/549–2997* ⊕ *www.carlylehouse.org* ▢ *$4* ⊙ *Tues.–Sat. 10–4:30, Sun. noon–4:30, guided tour every ½ hour.*

★ ⓭ Christ Church. Both Washington and Robert E. Lee were pewholders in this Episcopal church, which remains in nearly original condition. (Washington paid £36 and 10 shillings—a lot of money in those days—for Pew 60.) Built in 1773, this fine example of an English Georgian country-style church has a fine Palladian window, an interior balcony, and an English wrought-brass-and-crystal chandelier. Docents give tours during visiting hours. ⊠ *118 N. Washington St., Old Town* ☎ *703/549–1450* ⊕ *www. historicchristchurch.org* ▢ *Free* ⊙ *Mon.–Sat. 9–4, Sun. 2–4.*

Confederate Statue. In 1861, when Alexandria was occupied by Union forces, the 800 soldiers of the city's garrison marched out of town to join the Confederate Army. In the middle of Washington and Prince streets stands a statue marking the point where they assembled. In 1885 Confederate veterans proposed a memorial to honor their fallen comrades. This statue, based on John A. Elder's painting *Appomattox*, is of a lone soldier glumly surveying the battlefields after General Robert E. Lee's surrender. The names of 100 Alexandria Confederate dead are carved on the base. ⊠ *Washington and Prince Sts., Old Town.*

⟲ ⓯ Friendship Fire House. Alexandria's showcase firehouse dates from 1855 and has the appearance and implements of a typical 19th-century firehouse. According to local lore, George Washington helped found the volunteer fire company in 1774. Among early fire engines on display are a hand pumper built in Baltimore in 1851 and an Amoskeag steam pumper built in Manchester, New Hampshire, in 1860. ⊠ *107 S. Alfred St., Old Town* ☎ *703/838–3891* ⊕ *oha.ci.alexandria.va.us* ▢ *Free* ⊙ *Fri. and Sat. 10–4, Sun. 1–4.*

★ ⟲ ❽ Gadsby's Tavern Museum. This museum is in the old City Tavern and Hotel, a center of political and social life in the late 1700s. George Washington went to birthday celebrations in the ballroom here. Other noted patrons included Thomas Jefferson, John Adams, and the Marquis de Lafayette. The taproom, dining room, assembly room, ballroom, and communal bedrooms have been convincingly restored to how they probably appeared in the 1780s. The tours on Friday evenings are led by a costumed guide, who uses a lantern. ⊠ *134 N. Royal St., Old Town* ☎ *703/838–4242* ⊕ *www.gadsbystavern.org* ⌑ *$4, lantern tour $5* ⊙ *Nov.–Mar., Tues.–Sat. 11–4, Sun. 1–4, last tour at 3:15; Apr.–Oct., Tues.–Sat. 10–5, Sun. and Mon. 1–5, last tour at 4:45; tours 15 min before and after the hour. Lantern tour Mar.–Nov., Fri. 7–9:30.*

★ ⑯ **George Washington Masonic National Memorial.** Because Alexandria, like Washington, D.C., has no really tall buildings, the spire of this memorial dominates the surroundings and is visible for miles. The building fronts King Street, one of Alexandria's major east–west arteries; from the ninth-floor observation deck (reached by elevator) you get a spectacular view of Alexandria, with Washington, D.C., in the distance. The building contains furnishings from the first Masonic lodge in Alexandria. George Washington became a member of it in 1752 and held the high rank of Worshipful Master at the same time he served as president. If you don't wish to walk, the site can also be reached by DASH bus west on King Street. ⊠ *101 Callahan Dr., Old Town* ☎ *703/683–2007* ⊕ *www.gwmemorial.org* ⌑ *Free* ⊙ *Daily 9:30–5; 50-min guided tour of building and deck daily at 9:30, 10:30, 11:30, 1, 2, 3, and 4.*

➒ **Lee-Fendall House.** The short block of Alexandria's Oronoco Street between Washington and St. Asaph streets is the site of two Lee-owned houses. One is this house from 1785, the home of several illustrious members of the Lee family, and the other is the boyhood home of Robert E. Lee. The Lee-Fendall House's interior, done in several different styles, contains some family furniture. The labor leader John L. Lewis lived here from 1937 to 1969. ⊠ *614 Oronoco St., Old Town* ⌑ *$4* ⊙ *Feb.–mid-Dec., Tues.–Sat. 10–4, Sun. 1–4; sometimes closed weekends.*

⑫ **Lloyd House.** A fine example of Georgian architecture, Lloyd House was built in 1797 and is owned by the City of Alexandria. The interior is no longer open to the public, so it can be admired only from outside. ⊠ *220 N. Washington St., Old Town.*

⑭ **Lyceum.** Built in 1839 and one of Alexandria's best examples of Greek Revival design, the Lyceum is also its official history museum. Over the years, the building has served as the Alexandria Library, a Civil War hospital, a residence, and offices. Restored in the 1970s for the Bicentennial, its impressive collection includes examples of 18th-century silver, tools, stoneware, and Civil War photographs taken by Mathew Brady. ⊠ *201 S. Washington St., Old Town* ☎ *703/838–4994* ⊕ *www.alexandriahistory.org* ⌑ *Free* ⊙ *Mon.–Sat. 10–5, Sun. 1–5.*

➌ **Old Presbyterian Meetinghouse.** Except for a six-decade hiatus after the Civil War, the redbrick Old Presbyterian Meetinghouse has been an active house of worship since 1774, when Scottish pioneers established the church; a Presbyterian congregation still meets at 8:30 and 11 on Sunday morning. As its name suggests, however, the building has been more than a church—it was a gathering place vital to Scottish patriots during the Revolution. Eulogies for George Washington were delivered here on December 29, 1799. The Tomb of the Unknown Soldier of the American Revolution lies in a corner of the churchyard, where many prominent Alexandrians—including Dr. James Craik, physician to Washington, Lafayette, and John Carlyle—are interred. Still home to a very active congregation, the Presbyterian Meetinghouse is the site of sacred and secular "Concerts with a Cause" every month or so. ✉ *321 S. Fairfax St., Old Town* ☎ *703/549–6670* ⊕ *www.opmh.org* 🎟 *Free* ⊙ *Sanctuary weekdays 9–3; key available at church office at 316 S. Royal St.*

▶ ❶ **Ramsay House.** The best place to start a tour of Alexandria's Old Town is at the **Alexandria Convention & Visitors Association** in Ramsay House, the home of the town's first postmaster and lord mayor, William Ramsay. The structure is believed to be the oldest house in Alexandria. Travel counselors here provide brochures and maps for self-guided walking tours and can also give you a 24-hour permit for free parking at any two-hour metered spot. Daily guided walking tours are at 10:30 AM Monday through Saturday and 2 PM Sunday; tickets are $10. ✉ *221 King St., Old Town* ☎ *703/838–4200 or 800/388–9119, 703/838–6494 TDD* ⊕ *www.funside.com* ⊙ *Daily 9–5.*

★ ☾ ❷ **Stabler-Leadbeater Apothecary.** Once patronized by George Washington and the Lee family, the Stabler-Leadbeater Apothecary is the second-oldest apothecary in the country (the reputed oldest is in Bethlehem, PA). Some believe that it was here, on October 17, 1859, that Lt. Col. Robert E. Lee received orders to lead Marines sent from the Washington Barracks to help suppress John Brown's insurrection at Harpers Ferry (then part of Virginia). The shop now houses a small museum of 18th- and 19th-century apothecary memorabilia, including one of the finest collections of apothecary bottles in the country (some 800 bottles in all). Tours designed especially for children are available. ✉ *105–107 S. Fairfax St., Old Town* ☎ *703/836–3713* ⊕ *www.apothecarymuseum.org* 🎟 *$2.50* ⊙ *Mon.–Sat. 10–4, Sun. 1–5.*

★ ☾ ❻ **Torpedo Factory Art Center.** Torpedoes were manufactured here by the U.S. Navy during both world wars. Now the building, housing the studios and workshops of about 160 artists and artisans, has become one of Alexandria's most popular attractions. You can view the workshops of printmakers, jewelry makers, sculptors, painters, and potters, and most of the art and crafts are for sale at reasonable prices. The Torpedo Factory complex also houses the Alexandria Archaeology Program, which displays such artifacts as plates, cups, pipes, and coins from an early tavern, and Civil War soldiers' equipment. ✉ *105 N. Union St., Old Town* ☎ *703/838–4565* ⊕ *www.torpedofactory.org* 🎟 *Free* ⊙ *Daily 10–5.*

| need a break? | The **Firehook Bakery and Coffee House** (✉ 105 S. Union St., Old Town ☎ 703/519–8021 ⊕ www.firehook.com), a half block from the Torpedo Factory, serves excellent pastries, sandwiches, salads, soups, breads, and coffee. It's open weekdays 7–7 and on weekends 7–6. |

Where to Eat

★ **$$$$** ✕ **Elysium at the Morrison House.** There's no sign on the street, but Elysium is worth seeking out. The restaurant offers a "chef of your own" format, which allows diners to personally design their own menu with the executive chef. The head chef visits each table, giving diners a list of the options in the kitchen, which include fresh specimens of regional ingredients. The diner and the chef then discuss preferences and dislikes. For example, if you tell the chef that you love variations of tuna and handmade pasta, your entrée might be grilled tuna loin with tuna tartare and a side of risotto. The seven-course fixed-price meal ($74), the only option, is $112 with an optional wine pairing. ⊠ *Morrison House, 116 S. Alfred St., Alexandria* ☎ *703/838–8000* ⊕ *www.morrisonhouse. com* ⌂ *Reservations essential* ☰ *AE, DC, MC, V* ☾ *No dinner Sun., Mon., and Tues.*

$$–$$$$ ✕ **La Bergerie.** Changes in ownership and in the kitchen haven't diminished the *provençale* and Basque cooking at this elegant Old Town restaurant. Look for dishes like goat cheese and sun-dried tomato tart, escargot with garlic butter, calf's liver with sautéed onions, sea scallops with morels, quail with truffles, and sweetbreads. Don't forget to order dessert soufflés—the Grand Marnier one is exceptional—or the apple tart in advance. ⊠ *218 N. Lee St., Alexandria* ☎ *703/683–1007* ⌂ *Reservations essential* ⋔ *Jacket and tie* ☰ *AE, D, DC, MC, V* ☾ *No lunch Sun.*

★ **$$–$$$** ✕ **Gadsby's Tavern.** In the heart of the historic district, this circa-1792 tavern provides a taste of the interior decoration, cuisine, and entertainment of Colonial days. There's a strolling balladeer making the rounds on Tuesday and Wednesday nights. The tavern was a favorite of George Washington, who is commemorated on the menu ("George Washington's Favorite Duck" is half a duck roasted with peach-apricot dressing and served with Madeira sauce). Other period offerings are Gentlemen's Pye (made with veal), Sally Lunn bread, and a rich English trifle. ⊠ *138 N. Royal St., Alexandria* ☎ *703/548–1288* ⊕ *www. gadsbys.com* ☰ *D, DC, MC, V.*

$$–$$$ ✕ **Majestic Café.** A 1930s-era landmark that had been closed since 1978, the Majestic Café reopened in 2002. The art deco facade remains; inside, the café brings a modern sensibility to its 1930s origins. The cooking style moves between trendy American dishes and traditional Southern fare. Some of the best plates are the sides, such as hush puppies with *remoulade* (a mayo-based sauce that includes shallots, garlic, tarragon, and chives), fluffy spoonbread, and stewed tomatoes. Starters like a gratin of oysters and ham and main courses like balsamic-glaze salmon also satisfy. The restaurant is about eight blocks from the Metro. ⊠ *911 King St., Alexandria* ☎ *703/837–9117* ☰ *AE, D, DC, MC, V* ☾ *Closed Mon.* Ⓜ *King St.*

★ **$$–$$$** ✕ **Stella's.** Across Diagonal Road from the King Street Metro station, Stella's is set back in a pleasant courtyard. The old-fashioned wine bar, which has several domestic and European beers on tap, is just the place to relax and wait for the end of rush hour. The "New Virginia" cuisine served here takes fresh Virginia produce, meats, and seafood and uses them in nonlocal dishes, such as paella. ⊠ *1725 Duke St., Alexandria* ☎ *703/519–1946* ☰ *AE, D, DC, MC, V.*

$–$$ ✕ **Hard Times Café.** Piped-in country-and-western music and framed photographs of Depression-era Oklahoma set the tone at this casual, crowded hangout. Three kinds of chili—Texas (spicy), Cincinnati (sweeter), and vegetarian—are available. Texas chili is typically served over spaghetti—a "chili-mac"; Cincinnati comes with cheese, onions, beans, or all three. A tuna sandwich, chicken salad, and chicken wings are alternatives to the more combustive cuisine. About 30 domestic and Mexican beers are available. ⊠ *1404 King St., Alexandria* ☎ *703/837–0050* ⌕ *Reservations not accepted* ☰ *AE, MC, V* ⊙ *No lunch Sun.*

★ $–$$ ✕ **King Street Blues.** Not a place for power-lunching, this informal, relaxed café just off King Street is popular for its hearty, quirky Southern menu. Whimsical neon and papier-mâché constructions are a good foil for the waiters hustling around in T-shirts and shorts. Diners come for the baked pecan-crusted catfish, po' boy sandwiches, gumbo, glazed pork chops, BBQ, and other New Orleans specialties. Wash your choice down with the excellent house beer. ⊠ *112 N. St. Asaph St., Alexandria* ☎ *703/836–8800* ☰ *AE, D, DC, MC, V.*

★ $–$$ ✕ **Taverna Cretekou.** Whitewashed stucco walls and colorful macramé tapestries bring a bit of the Mediterranean to the center of Old Town. On the menu are lamb baked in a pastry shell and swordfish kebab. All the wines served are Greek, and in the warm months you can dine in the canopied garden. A buffet brunch is served on Sunday. ⊠ *818 King St., Alexandria* ☎ *703/548–8688* ☰ *AE, MC, V* ⊙ *Closed Mon.*

Where to Stay

$$–$$$ ☷ **Embassy Suites Old Town Alexandria.** This modern all-suites hotel is next to Alexandria's landmark George Washington Masonic Temple. A free shuttle is available to transport you to the scenic Alexandria riverfront, which has shops and restaurants. The cooked-to-order breakfast is complimentary, as is the cocktail reception every evening. There's also a playroom for children. ⊠ *1900 Diagonal Rd., Alexandria, VA 22314* ☎ *703/684–5900 or 800/362–2779* ⎙ *703/684–1403* ⊕ *www.embassysuites.com* ⇆ *268 suites* ⌕ *Restaurant, in-room data ports, kitchenettes, refrigerators, cable TV, indoor pool, gym, hot tub, recreation room, laundry facilities, laundry service, business services, meeting rooms, parking (fee)* ☰ *AE, D, DC, MC, V* ⌾⬤ *BP* Ⓜ *King St.*

★ $$–$$$ ☷ **Holiday Inn Select Old Town.** The distinctive mahogany-paneled lobby of this chain hotel suggests a club room, and the guest rooms follow this motif, with hunting-and-horse prints on the walls. Service is extraordinary here: staff will bring exercise bicycles to rooms on request and lend free bicycles for use in the area. Some rooms on the fifth and sixth floors have views of the roofs of 18th- and 19th-century buildings and the river beyond—but only after the trees have shed their leaves. There's also a free shuttle to the King Street Metro. ⊠ *480 King St., Alexandria 22314* ☎ *703/549–6080 or 800/368–5047* ⎙ *703/684–6508* ⊕ *www.hiselect.com* ⇆ *227 rooms* ⌕ *Restaurant, in-room data ports, indoor pool, hair salon, sauna, bicycles, lobby lounge* ☰ *AE, D, DC, MC, V.*

★ $$–$$$ ☷ **Morrison House.** The architecture, parquet floors, crystal chandeliers, decorative fireplaces, and furnishings here are so faithful to the Federal period (1790–1820) that it's often mistaken for a renovation rather than what it is: a structure built from scratch in 1985. The hotel blends Early American charm with modern conveniences. Some rooms have fireplaces, and all have four-poster beds. The highly regarded restaurant Elysium serves American contemporary cuisine. Morrison House is in the heart of Old Town Alexandria, seven blocks from the train and Metro stations. ✉ *116 S. Alfred St., Alexandria 22314* ☎ *703/838–8000 or 800/ 367–0800* 🖷 *703/684–6283* ⊕ *www.morrisonhouse.com* ⌑ *42 rooms, 3 suites* ♿ *2 restaurants, room service, in-room data ports, cable TV, in-room VCRs, bar, piano bar, business services, parking (fee)* ⊟ *AE, DC, MC, V* Ⓜ *King St.*

★ ¢ 🏨 **Travelers Motel.** Built in 1954, the Travelers Motel is not a glossy chain motel but a friendly, reasonable place run by the original manager. It's in a convenient location near the Wilson Bridge and Capital Beltway (I–495/I–95), and shuttle service is provided to the Huntington Metro station during the day. ✉ *5916 Richmond Hwy., Beltway Exit 1A, Alexandria 22303* ☎ *703/329–1310 or 800/368–7378* 🖷 *703/960– 9211* ⌑ *29 rooms, 1 suite* ♿ *Cable TV, pool, free parking* ⊟ *AE, DC, MC, V.*

Nightlife & the Arts

Bars & Pubs

There's something different in just about every section of the multi-level, multiroom **Fishmarket,** from a piano-bar crooner to a ragtime piano shouter and a guitar strummer. The operative word here is *boisterous.* Seafood is the specialty, and if you really like beer, order the largest size; it comes in a glass big enough to put your face in. ✉ *105 King St., Old Town, Alexandria* ☎ *703/836–5676* ⊕ *www. fishmarketoldtown.com* Ⓜ *King St.*

Murphy's Irish Pub (✉ 713 King St., Old Town, Alexandria ☎ 703/548– 1717) has authentic Irish entertainment most nights, two groups on weekends (one downstairs, one upstairs), and a blazing fire when winter comes.

Jazz

At **Basin Street Lounge** (✉ 219 King St., Alexandria, Old Town ☎ 703/ 549–1141 Ⓜ King Street), jazz combos perform Tuesday through Saturday and at brunch on Sunday. This attractive Victorian-style bar is above the 219 Restaurant. Musicians from local military bands often stop by to sit in.

★ The **Birchmere** is one of the best places outside of the Blue Ridge Mountains to hear acoustic folk and bluegrass. It also gets more than its share of headliners, including frequent visitors Mary Chapin Carpenter, Lyle Lovett, and Dave Matthews. ✉ *3701 Mt. Vernon Ave., Alexandria, VA* ☎ *703/549–7500* ⊕ *www.birchmere.com.*

Sports & the Outdoors

Hiking

Huntley Meadows Park (✉ 3701 Lockheed Blvd., Alexandria ☎ 703/768– 2525 🖾 Free ⊙ Park daily dawn–dusk; visitor center closed Tues.; call for hours other days), a 1,460-acre refuge, is made for birders. You can spot more than 200 species—from ospreys to owls, egrets, and ibis. Much of the park is wetlands, home to a variety of aquatic species. A board-walk circles through a marsh, enabling you to spot beaver lodges, and 4 mi of trails wind through the park, making it likely that you'll see deer, muskrats, and river otters as well.

The **Mount Vernon Trail** is a favorite with Washington runners and bikers. The northern section begins near the pedestrian causeway leading to Theodore Roosevelt Island (directly across the river from the Kennedy Center) and goes past Ronald Reagan Washington National Airport and on to the Alexandria waterfront. This stretch is approximately 9½ mi one way. South of National Airport, the trail runs down to the Washington Sailing Marina. The southern section of the trail (approximately 9 mi) takes you along the banks of the Potomac from Alexandria all the way to Mount Vernon. It passes Jones Point (under the Wilson Bridge), the southern apex of the original District of Columbia, just before entering protected wetlands for about 2 mi beginning at Hunting Creek.

Boating

★ The **Washington Sailing Marina** (⊠ 1 Marina Dr., Alexandria ☎ 703/548–9027 ⊕ www.washingtonsailingmarina.com), operated by the National Park Service, rents sailboats from around mid-May to September, or until the water gets too cold. Sunfish are $10 per hour, Island 17's are $17 per hour, and the larger Flying Scots are $19 per hour. There's a one-hour minimum rental for all boats; reservations are required.

Belle Haven Marina (⊠ George Washington Pkwy., Alexandria ☎ 703/768–0018), south of Reagan National Airport and Old Town Alexandria, rents three types of sailboats: Sunfish are $30 for two hours during the week and $35 for two hours on the weekend; Hobie Cat–style sailboats and Flying Scots are $46 for two hours during the week and $54 for two hours during the weekend. There are also canoes and kayaks. Rentals are available from April to October.

Shopping

Old Town Alexandria is dense with antiques shops—many of them quite expensive—that are particularly strong in the Federal and Victorian periods. The Alexandria Convention and Visitors Association has maps and lists of the dozens of stores.

The **Antique Guild** (⊠ 113 N. Fairfax St., Old Town ☎ 703/836–1048 or 800/518–7322 ⊕ www.theantiqueguild.net) is where silver flatware and estate jewelry goes when it's ready for a new home.

Sumpter Priddy III, Inc. (⊠ 323 S. Washington St., Old Town ☎ 703/299–9688 ⊕ www.sumpterpriddy.com) specializes in American furniture from the early 19th century and folk art in different media.

★ Dating to 1753, the **Saturday Morning Market at Market Square** (⊠ City Hall ☎ 703/370–8723) may be the country's oldest operating farmers' market. Vendors sell baked goods, fresh produce, plants, flowers, and high-quality crafts. Come early; the market opens at 5 AM, and by 10 AM everything has been packed up.

ARLINGTON

The Virginia suburb of Arlington County was once part of the District of Columbia. Now connected to Washington by four bridges, Arlington remains a virtual part of the capital.

Carved out of the Old Dominion when Washington was created, Arlington was returned to Virginia along with the rest of the land west of the Potomac in 1845 and until 1920 was the county of Alexandria. In the 18th century members of the Custis family, including Martha Washington's first husband, had extensive land holdings in the area. Arlington was also the home of Robert E. Lee. Since the end of World War I, the county has changed from a farming community into an urban conglomeration of large corporations, Defense Department buildings, and large-scale retailing.

Numbers in the text correspond to numbers in the margin and on the Arlington National Cemetery map.

a good walk

Begin at the visitor center of **Arlington National Cemetery** 18 ⌐. Detailed maps of the cemetery and directions to specific graves are available here. Walk out the main door to Memorial Avenue and turn left. Immediately ahead, at the end of Memorial Avenue, is the Women in Military Service for America memorial. Leaving the memorial, turn left and proceed through the gate along Schley Drive and keep walking to the crosswalk. Turn left up Custis Walk to the first cross street. A left turn here (Sheridan Drive) takes you to the **Kennedy graves** 19, where President John Kennedy, two of his children, and his wife, Jacqueline Bouvier Kennedy Onassis, are buried. To one side is the grave of President Kennedy's brother Robert Kennedy.

From the Kennedy graves, return to Custis Walk and continue uphill to the top of the walk to **Arlington House** 20. Long before it was a cemetery, this land was part of the 1,100-acre estate of George Washington Parke Custis, whose daughter married Robert E. Lee. The couple lived in this fine Greek Revival house. Leaving the house, continue along the path in front of the house, around the south flower garden to Crook Walk; turn left and continue past row upon row of simple white headstones, following the signs to the **Tomb of the Unknowns** 21. Here the remains of unknown servicemen from Korea, Vietnam, and both world wars are buried. The changing of the honor guard occurs night and day, though more frequently during daylight. Below the Tomb of the Unknowns is **Section 7A** 22, where many distinguished veterans are buried. To reach the main gate or grave sites at the northern end of the cemetery, or to make your way into the Rosslyn section of Arlington, walk downhill on Roosevelt Drive to Eisenhower Drive, and turn left past the Women's Memorial and the Memorial Gate to Custis Walk. Turn right on Custis Walk to a pedestrian gate. On your way you pass **Section 27** 23. About 1,500 United States Colored Troops of the Civil War are buried here, as are 3,800 former slaves who lived in Freedmen's Village during and shortly after the Civil War.

Leaving the cemetery through the pedestrian gate, cross Marshall Drive carefully and walk to the 49-bell **Netherlands Carillon** 24, where, even if your visit doesn't coincide with a performance, you can enjoy a good vista of Washington. To the north is the **United States Marine Corps War Memorial** 25, better known as the Iwo Jima Memorial, which commemorates the Marines who held up the flag in the decisive World War II battle on the island of the same name.

TIMING   Visiting the sites at Arlington National Cemetery could take a half day or longer, depending on your stamina and interest.

Sights to See

20 **Arlington House.** It was in Arlington that the two most famous names in Virginia history—Washington and Lee—became intertwined. George Washington Parke Custis, raised by Martha and George Washington, his grandmother and step-grandfather, built Arlington House (also known as the Custis-Lee Mansion) between 1802 and 1817 on his 1,100-acre estate overlooking the Potomac. After Custis's death, the property went to his daughter, Mary Anna Randolph Custis. In 1831 Mary married Robert E. Lee, a graduate of West Point. For the next 30 years they lived at Arlington House.

In 1861 Lee was offered command of the Union forces. He declined, insisting that he could never take up arms against his native Virginia. The Lees left Arlington House that spring, never to return. Federal troops crossed the Potomac not long after that, fortified the estate's ridges, and turned the home into the Army of the Potomac's headquarters. Arlington House and the estate were confiscated in May 1864 and sold to the federal government when the Lees failed to pay $92.07 in property taxes in person. (Survivors of General Lee were eventually compensated for the land.) Union forces built three fortifications on the land, and 200 nearby acres were set aside as a national cemetery. Sixty-five soldiers were buried there on June 15, 1864, and by the end of the Civil War more than 16,000 headstones dotted Arlington plantation's hills. Soldiers from the Revolutionary War and the War of 1812 were reinterred at Arlington as their bodies were discovered in other resting places.

The building's heavy Doric columns and severe pediment make Arlington House one of the area's best examples of Greek Revival architecture. The plantation home was designed by George Hadfield, a young English architect who, for a while, supervised construction of the Capitol. The view of Washington from the front of the house is superb. In 1955 Arlington House was designated a memorial to Robert E. Lee. It looks much as it did in the 19th century, and a quick tour takes you past objects once owned by the Custises and the Lees.

In front of Arlington House, next to a flag that flies at half staff whenever there's a funeral in the cemetery, is the flat-top **grave of Pierre-Charles L'Enfant,** designer of Washington, D.C. ⊠ *Between Lee and Sherman Drs.* ☎ *703/235–1530 or 703/557–0613* ☺ *Free* ☉ *Daily 9:30–4:30.*

▶ 18 **Arlington National Cemetery.** More than 250,000 American war dead, Fodor'sChoice   as well as many notable Americans (among them Presidents William ★   Howard Taft and John F. Kennedy, General John Pershing, and Admiral Robert E. Peary), are interred in these 612 acres across the Potomac River from Washington, established as the nation's cemetery in 1864.

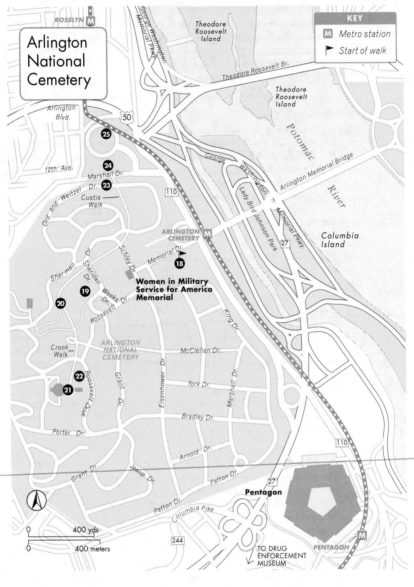

ROSSLYN Ⓜ

Arlington National Cemetery

Theodore Roosevelt Island

George Washington Memorial Pkwy

Theodore Roosevelt Br.

Arlington Blvd.

50

Theodore Roosevelt Island

Potomac

25

12th Ave.

Marshall Dr.

24

Ord and Weitzel Dr.

23

110

Custis Walk

Arlington Memorial Bridge

George Washington Pkwy

Lady Bird Johnson Park

Memorial Pkwy

River

ARLINGTON CEMETERY Ⓜ

27

Columbia Island

Sherman Dr.

Sheridan Dr.

Schley Dr.

Memorial Dr. ▶

18

19

Weeks Dr.

Women in Military Service for America Memorial

20

Roosevelt Dr.

King Dr.

Crook Walk

ARLINGTON NATIONAL CEMETERY

McClellan Dr.

Grant Dr.

Eisenhower Dr.

Marshall Dr.

22

21

Roosevelt Drive

York Dr.

Bradley Dr.

Porter Dr.

110

Grant Dr.

Jesup Dr.

Arnold Dr.

Patton Dr.

27

Pentagon

Patton Dr.

Columbia Pike

0   400 yds

0   400 meters

244

TO DRUG ENFORCEMENT MUSEUM

PENTAGON Ⓜ

While you're at Arlington there's a good chance you might hear the clear, doleful sound of a bugle playing taps, or the sharp reports of a gun salute. Approximately 20 funerals are held daily (it's projected that the cemetery will be filled in 2020). Although not the largest cemetery in the country, Arlington is certainly the best known, a place where you can trace America's history through the aftermath of its battles.

To get here, you can take the Metro, travel on a Tourmobile bus, or walk across Arlington Memorial Bridge (southwest of the Lincoln Memorial). If you're driving, there's a large paid parking lot at the skylighted visitor center on Memorial Drive. Stop at the center for a free brochure with a detailed map of the cemetery. If you're looking for a specific grave, the staff can consult microfilm records and give you directions to it. You should know the deceased's full name and, if possible, his or her branch of service and year of death.

Tourmobile tour buses leave from just outside the visitor center April through September, daily 8:30–6:30, and October through March, daily 8:30–4:30. You can buy tickets here for the 40-minute tour of the cemetery, which includes stops at the Kennedy grave sites, the Tomb of the Unknowns, and Arlington House. Touring the cemetery on foot means a fair bit of hiking, but it can give you a closer look at some of the thousands of graves spread over these rolling Virginia hills. If you decide to walk, head west from the visitor center on Roosevelt Drive and then turn right on Weeks Drive. ⊠ *West end of Memorial Bridge* ☎ *703/607–8052 to locate a grave* ⊕ *www.arlingtoncemetery.com* ▨ *Cemetery free, parking $3.75 for 1st 3 hours. Tourmobile $5.25* ☉ *Apr.–Sept., daily 8–7; Oct.–Mar., daily 8–5.*

> off the
> beaten
> path

DRUG ENFORCEMENT ADMINISTRATION MUSEUM – Across the street from the Fashion Centre at Pentagon City—a destination in itself for shoppers—is the DEA Museum, within the U.S. Drug Enforcement Administration's headquarters. It explores the impact of drugs on American society, starting with quaint 19th-century ads for opium-laced patent medicines and cocaine tooth drops (opiates, cannabis, and cocaine were unregulated then). But documentation of these addictive substances' medical dangers, as well as the corrosive political effect of the opium trade, which China detested, is hard-hitting. A similar contrast is found between the period feel of artifacts from a 1970s head shop and displays on the realities of present-day drug trafficking. ⊠ *700 Army Navy Dr., at Hayes St.* ☎ *202/307–3463* ⊕ *www.deamuseum.org* ▨ *Free* ☉ *Tues.–Fri. 10–4* Ⓜ *Pentagon City.*

★ ⓳ **Kennedy graves.** An important part of any visit to Arlington National Cemetery is a visit to the graves of John F. Kennedy and other members of his family. JFK is buried under an eternal flame near two of his children, who died in infancy, and his wife, Jacqueline Bouvier Kennedy Onassis. The graves are a short walk west of the visitor center. Across from them is a low wall engraved with quotations from Kennedy's inaugural address. The public has been able to visit JFK's grave since 1967; it's now the most-visited grave site in the country. Nearby, marked by a simple white cross, is the grave of his brother Robert Kennedy. ⊠ *Sheridan and Weeks Drs.*

24 **Netherlands Carillon.** A visit to Arlington National Cemetery gives you the chance for a lovely and unusual musical experience, thanks to a 49-bell carillon presented to the United States by the Dutch people in 1960 in gratitude for aid received during World War II. Guest carillon players perform on Saturday afternoon May through September and on July 4. Times vary; call for details. For one of the best views of Washington, look to the east across the Potomac. From this vantage point, the Lincoln Memorial, the Washington Monument, and the Capitol appear in a side-by-side formation. ⊠ *Meade and Marshall Drs.* ☎ *703/289–2500.*

Pentagon. This office building, the headquarters of the United States Department of Defense, is the largest in the world. The Capitol could fit into any one of its five wedge-shape sections. Approximately 23,000 military and civilian workers arrive daily. Astonishingly, this mammoth office building, completed in 1943, took less than two years to construct.

The structure was reconstructed following the September 2001 crash of hijacked American Airlines Flight 77 into the northwest side of the building. The damaged area was removed in just over a month, and rebuilding proceeded rapidly (in keeping with the speed of the original construction). Renovations on all areas damaged by the terrorist attack were completed by spring 2003.

Tours of the building are given on a very limited basis to educational groups by advance reservation; tours for the general public have been suspended indefinitely. ⊠ *I–395 at Columbia Pike and Rte. 27* ☎ *703/695–1776* ⊕ *www.defenselink.mil/pubs/pentagon.*

22 **Section 7A.** Many distinguished veterans are buried in this area of Arlington National Cemetery near the **Tomb of the Unknowns,** including boxing champ Joe Louis, ABC newsman Frank Reynolds, actor Lee Marvin, and World War II fighter pilot Colonel "Pappy" Boyington. ⊠ *Crook Walk near Roosevelt Dr.*

23 **Section 27.** More than 3,800 former slaves are buried in this part of Arlington National Cemetery. They're all former residents of Freedman's Village, which operated at the Custis-Lee estate for more than 30 years beginning in 1863 to provide housing, education, and employment training for ex-slaves who had traveled to the capital. In the cemetery, the headstones are marked with their names and the word "Civilian" or "Citizen." Buried at Grave 19 in the first row of Section 27 is William Christman, a Union private who died of peritonitis in Washington on May 13, 1864. He was the first soldier interred at Arlington National Cemetery during the Civil War. ⊠ *Ord and Weitzel Dr. near Custis Walk.*

off the
beaten
path

THEODORE ROOSEVELT ISLAND – The island wilderness preserve in the Potomac River has 2½ mi of nature trails through marshland, swampland, and upland forest. It's an 88-acre tribute to the conservation-minded 26th president. Cattails, arrowarum, pickerelweed, willow, ash, maple, and oak all grow on the island, which is also a habitat for frogs, raccoons, birds, lizards, and the

occasional red or gray fox. The 17-foot bronze statue of Roosevelt, reachable after a long walk toward the center of the woods, was done by Paul Manship. A pedestrian bridge connects the island to a parking lot on the Virginia shore, which is accessible by car from the northbound lanes of the George Washington Memorial Parkway.
✣ *From downtown D.C., take Constitution Ave. west across Theodore Roosevelt Bridge to George Washington Memorial Pkwy. north; follow signs or walk or bike across Bridge beginning at Kennedy Center* ☎ *703/289–2500 for park information* 🎫 *Free* ☉ *Island daily dawn–dusk* Ⓜ *Rosslyn.*

㉑ **Tomb of the Unknowns.** Many countries established a memorial to their war dead after World War I. In the United States, the first burial at the Tomb of the Unknowns took place at Arlington National Cemetery on November 11, 1921, when the Unknown Soldier from the "Great War" was interred under the large white-marble sarcophagus. Unknown servicemen killed in World War II and Korea were buried in 1958. The unknown serviceman killed in Vietnam was laid to rest on the plaza on Memorial Day 1984 but was disinterred and identified in 1998. Officials then decided to leave the Vietnam War unknown crypt vacant. Soldiers from the Army's U.S. Third Infantry ("The Old Guard") keep watch over the tomb 24 hours a day, regardless of weather conditions. Each sentinel marches exactly 21 steps, then faces the tomb for 21 seconds, symbolizing the 21-gun salute, America's highest military honor. The guard is changed with a precise ceremony during the day—every half hour from April through September and every hour the rest of the year. At night the guard is changed every hour.

The Memorial Amphitheater west of the tomb is the scene of special ceremonies on Veterans Day, Memorial Day, and Easter. Decorations awarded to the unknowns by foreign governments and U.S. and foreign organizations are displayed in an indoor trophy room. Across from the amphitheater are memorials to the astronauts killed in the *Challenger* shuttle explosion and to the servicemen killed in 1980 while trying to rescue American hostages in Iran. Rising beyond that is the mainmast of the USS *Maine,* the American ship that was sunk in Havana Harbor in 1898, killing 299 men and sparking the Spanish-American War. ✉ *End of Crook Walk.*

㉕ **United States Marine Corps War Memorial.** Better known simply as "the Iwo Jima," this memorial, despite its familiarity, has lost none of its power to stir the emotions. Honoring marines who have given their lives since the Corps was formed in 1775, the statue, sculpted by Felix W. de Weldon, is based on Joe Rosenthal's Pulitzer Prize–winning photograph of five Marines and a Navy corpsman raising a flag atop Mt. Suribachi on the Japanese island of Iwo Jima on February 19, 1945. By executive order, a real flag flies 24 hours a day from the 78-foot-high memorial. On Tuesday evening at 7 from late May to late August there's a Marine Corps sunset parade on the grounds of the memorial. On parade nights a free shuttle bus runs from the Arlington Cemetery visitors' parking lot.

North of the memorial is the Arlington neighborhood of Rosslyn. Like parts of downtown Washington and Crystal City farther to the south, Rosslyn is almost empty at night, once the thousands of people who work there have gone home. Its tall buildings provide a bit of a skyline, but this has been controversial: some say the two silvery, 31-story wing-shape towers, formerly the Gannett Buildings, are too close to the flight path followed by jets landing at Ronald Reagan National Airport.

Women in Military Service for America Memorial. What is now this memorial next to the visitor center was once the Hemicycle, a huge carved retaining wall faced with granite at the entrance to Arlington National Cemetery. Built in 1932, the wall was restored, with stairways added leading to a rooftop terrace. Inside are 16 exhibit alcoves showing the contributions that women have made to the military—from the Revolutionary War to the present—as well as the history of the memorial itself. A 196-seat theater shows films and is used for lectures and conferences. A computer database has pictures, military histories, and stories of thousands of women veterans. A fountain and reflecting pool front the classical-style Hemicycle and entry gates.

Where to Eat

$$–$$$ ✕ **Carlyle Grand Café.** Whether you eat at the bustling bar or at the dining room upstairs, you can find an imaginative, generous interpretation of modern American cooking. Start with the blue crab fritter or the housemade potato chips drizzled with blue cheese, then move on to entrées such as pecan-crusted trout, veal meat loaf, and roast pork tenderloin with a citrus glaze. The warm flourless chocolate-macadamia nut waffle with vanilla ice cream and hot fudge sauce is by now a classic. You can even buy a loaf of the bread at the restaurant's own bakery, the Best Buns Bread Company, next door. ⊠ 4000 S. 28th St., Arlington ☎ 703/931–0777 ▤ AE, D, DC, MC, V.

★ $–$$$ ✕ **Aegean Taverna.** The Aegean Taverna serves authentic Greek food indoors and outside in good weather. Good menu choices are pastitsio (baked ziti pasta with ground beef and cheese topped with béchamel sauce), moussaka, and spanakopita. Greek musicians perform Friday and Saturday nights from 7:30 to 11:30. Parking is free and easy in a large adjoining lot. ⊠ 2950 Clarendon Blvd., Arlington ☎ 703/841–9494 ▤ AE, D, DC, MC, V Ⓜ Clarendon.

★ $–$$ ✕ **Nam Viet.** Arlington's Little Saigon area has several Vietnamese restaurants, and this one is currently a favorite of knowledgeable diners. The sweet-and-spicy salmon soup has many fans, as do the cha gio (spring rolls), the soft-shell crab, and the green-papaya salad (with squid or beef jerky). Dine outside in good weather. ⊠ 1127 Hudson St., Arlington ☎ 703/522–7119 ▤ AE, D, DC, MC, V.

★ $ ✕ **Café Dalat.** In the heart of Arlington's "Little Saigon," you can find low-price Vietnamese fare in far-from-fancy but clean and pleasant Café Dalat, where service is extremely speedy. The sugarcane shrimp is excellent, and da ram gung is a sinus-clearing dish of simmered chicken and ginger. All the appetizers are winners, especially the crispy spring rolls and the tangy Vietnamese shrimp salad in lemon vinaigrette. ⊠ 3143 Wilson Blvd., Arlington ☎ 703/276–0935 ▤ MC, V Ⓜ Clarendon.

$ ✕ **Little Viet Garden.** The patrons here swear by the spring rolls, beef-broth-and-glass-noodle soups, beef tips and potato stir-fried with onion in a smoky sauce, and crispy crepes stuffed with chicken, shrimp, bean sprouts, and green onion. In warm months reserve a table on the outdoor terrace bordered by a flower box–lined white fence. ✉ *3012 Wilson Blvd., Arlington* ☎ *703/522–9686* 🚌 *AE, D, DC, MC, V* Ⓜ *Clarendon.*

Where to Stay

$$$ 🏨 **Hilton Arlington and Towers.** Traveling to Arlington Cemetery, Washington, and Alexandria sights is easy from this hotel, just above the Metro stop. Rooms make use of neutral colors and contemporary light-wood furniture, and all the suites have hot tubs. Entry to a nearby fitness club is available for a fee. The hotel has direct access via a skywalk to an adjacent shopping mall. ✉ *950 N. Stafford St., Arlington 22203* ☎ *703/528–6000 or 800/445–8667* 🖷 *703/812–5127* ⤳ *204 rooms, 5 suites* ⌂ *Restaurant, in-room data ports, cable TV, bar, laundry service, business services, meeting rooms, parking (fee)* 🚌 *AE, D, DC, MC, V* Ⓜ *Ballston.*

$$$ 🏨 **Key Bridge Marriott.** A short walk across the Key Bridge from Georgetown, this family-friendly Marriott is three blocks from a Metro stop, also allowing for easy access to sights in Northern Virginia. The hotel provides a shuttle to the station. Rooms on the Potomac side offer excellent Washington views, as does the rooftop restaurant. A 2004 renovation produced rooms freshly appointed with comfortable Colonial reproduction furniture and bedding, an updated fitness center, and expanded business amenities. ✉ *1401 Lee Hwy., Arlington 22209* ☎ *703/524–6400 or 800/228–9290* 🖷 *703/524–8964* ⤳ *588 rooms, 20 suites* ⌂ *2 restaurants, room service, in-room data ports, microwaves, cable TV, indoor pool, exercise equipment, health club, hair salon, hot tub, 2 bars, lobby lounge, laundry facilities, laundry service, business services, meeting rooms, parking (fee)* 🚌 *AE, D, DC, MC, V* Ⓜ *Rosslyn.*

$$$ 🏨 **Marriott Crystal Gateway.** This elegant, modern Marriott caters to the business traveler and those who want to be pampered. Its two towers rise 17 stories above the highway; inside is mahogany, marble, and lots of greenery. Rooms have traditional styling, with stripes and floral fabrics. ✉ *1700 Jefferson Davis Hwy., Arlington 22202* ☎ *703/920–3230 or 800/228–9290* 🖷 *703/271–5212* ⊕ *www.marriott.com* ⤳ *563 rooms, 131 suites* ⌂ *3 restaurants, 2 pools (1 indoor), gym, sauna, spa, lobby lounge, nightclub* 🚌 *AE, DC, MC, V.*

$$–$$$ 🏨 **Holiday Inn Arlington at Ballston.** You can get to the major sights of Northern Virginia quickly from this hotel, two blocks from a Metro station. Sightseers can take advantage of the hotel's proximity to Arlington National Cemetery, and the Iwo Jima, as well as monuments and museums in D.C. ✉ *4610 N. Fairfax Dr., Arlington 22203* ☎ *703/243–9800* 🖷 *703/527–2677* ⤳ *219 rooms, 2 suites* ⌂ *Restaurant, room service, in-room data ports, cable TV with video games, pool, gym, bar, laundry facilities, business services, parking (fee)* 🚌 *AE, D, DC, MC, V* Ⓜ *Ballston.*

$$ 🏨 **Best Western Pentagon.** In the shadow of the world's largest office building, this hotel has free shuttle service to three nearby Metro stops and

the Arlington attractions around them. Three two-story buildings have outside entrances and conventional motel rooms. Many of its guest rooms have good views. ⊠ *2480 S. Glebe Rd., Arlington 22206* ☎ *703/979–4400 or 800/937–8376* ☒ *703/685–0051* ⊕ *www.bestwestern.com* ↩ *206 rooms* ⚭ *Restaurant, in-room data ports, in-room safes, refrigerators, cable TV, pool, gym, bar, laundry service, business services, airport shuttle, free parking* ☰ *AE, D, DC, MC, V.*

\$\$ 🖭 **Day's Inn Arlington.** Easy to find, on U.S. Route 50 across from Fort Myer, this Day's Inn isn't frilly, but is reasonable and accommodating. You could walk to a Metro station, but a shuttle is provided during the busiest daytime hours. Coffee is complimentary. ⊠ *2201 Arlington Blvd., Arlington 22201* ☎ *703/525–0300 or 800/329–7466* ☒ *703/525–5671* ⊕ *www.daysinncrystal.com* ↩ *128 rooms* ⚭ *Restaurant, pool, bar, recreation room, meeting rooms, no-smoking rooms* ☰ *AE, D, DC, MC, V.*

\$ 🖭 **Quality Inn Iwo Jima.** Two blocks from the Marine Corps War Memorial and half a mile from the Rosslyn Metro, this budget hotel offers easy access to the many attractions at Arlington Cemetery, the restaurant district in Clarendon, and nearby Theodore Roosevelt Island. The older original section of the hotel has outside entrances and larger rooms with double-sink bathrooms. The newer high-rise section has business-class rooms with work tables, data ports, and 25-inch TVs. ⊠ *1501 Arlington Blvd., Rte. 50, Arlington, VA 22209* ☎ *703/524–5000 or 800/424–1501* ☒ *703/522–5484* ⊕ *www.qualityinniwojima.com* ↩ *141 rooms* ⚭ *Restaurant, room service, in-room data ports, microwaves, cable TV, indoor pool, exercise equipment, gym, hair salon, bar, laundry facilities, laundry service, business services, free parking, some pets allowed (fee)* ☰ *AE, D, DC, MC, V* Ⓜ *Rosslyn.*

Nightlife & the Arts

MUSIC **Galaxy Hut.** This small club and microbrewery hosts local and out-of-
★ town indie and alternative bands—a good place to see them before they get famous. There's no cover for live music on Saturday, Sunday, and Monday nights. ⊠ *2711 Wilson Blvd., Arlington* ☎ *703/525–8646* ⊕ *www.galaxyhut.com* Ⓜ *Clarendon.*

★ **Iota.** The bands at Iota play alt-country or stripped-down rock to unpretentious, attentive crowds who come mainly because they're fans of good music. Expect to fight your way to the bar—it gets crowded quickly. There's a cover almost every night. ⊠ *2832 Wilson Blvd., Arlington* ☎ *703/522–8340* ⊕ *www.iotaclubandcafe.com* Ⓜ *Clarendon.*

THEATER **Signature Theatre.** The host of the renowned 2002 Sondheim revival is
★ known for its snappy musical productions, presenting world and area premieres, Broadway revivals, and provocative contemporary works in its 136-seat black-box theater, a former bumper-plating facility. ⊠ *3806 S. 4 Mile Run Dr., Arlington* ☎ *703/820–9771* ⊕ *www.sig-online.org.*

★ **Washington Shakespeare Company** Often confused with the Shakespeare Theatre in D.C., this highly reputable company stages the works of Shakespeare, the Greeks, and other important playwrights up through modern times. ⊠ *601 S. Clark St., Arlington* ☎ *703/418–4808* ⊕ *www.washingtonshakespeare.org* Ⓜ *Crystal City.*

Shopping

Fashion Centre at Pentagon City. With Macy's at one end and Nordstrom at the other, this four-story mall includes such shops as Liz Claiborne, the Coach Store, Swatch, Baby Gap, L'Occitaine, Sephora, Crate & Barrel, Williams-Sonoma, Bang & Olufsen, a six-screen cinema, and a Discovery Channel store, as well as hair and nail salons, day spas, and jewelry repair. The skylit Food Court sells international specialties both familiar and exotic. Four full-service restaurants provide an additional selection for hungry shoppers. ⊠ *1100 S. Hayes St., Arlington* ☎ *703/415–2400* ⊕ *www.fashioncentrepentagon.com* Ⓜ *Pentagon City.*

At the **Crystal City Shops** (☎ 703/922–4636 ⊕ www.thecrystalcityshops.com) the 130 street-level and underground stores and restaurants are connected to the Crystal City Metro stop.

MT. VERNON, WOODLAWN & GUNSTON HALL

Long before Washington was planned, the shores of the Potomac had been divided into plantations by wealthy traders and gentlemen farmers. Most traces of the Colonial era were obliterated as the capital grew in the 19th century, but several splendid examples of plantation architecture remain on the Virginia side of the Potomac, 15 mi or so south of D.C. In one day you can easily visit three such mansions: Mount Vernon, the home of George Washington and one of the most popular sites in the area; Woodlawn, the estate of Washington's step-granddaughter; and Gunston Hall, the home of George Mason, author of the document on which the Bill of Rights was based. (Expect the longest wait times at Mount Vernon, particularly in spring and summer.) Set on hillsides overlooking the river, these estates offer magnificent vistas and bring back to vivid life the more palatable aspects of the 18th-century. Farther south is Woodbridge, which has a more modern attraction: the Potomac Mills outlet mall.

Numbers in the margin correspond to points of interest on the Mount Vernon, Woodlawn, and Gunston Hall map.

Mount Vernon

☾ ㉖ *16 mi southeast of Washington, D.C., 8 mi south of Alexandria, VA.*

Fodor'sChoice
★

Mount Vernon and the surrounding lands had been in the Washington family for nearly 90 years by the time George inherited it all in 1761. Before taking over command of the Continental Army, Washington was a yeoman farmer managing the 8,000-acre plantation, of which more than 3,000 acres were under cultivation. He also oversaw the transformation of the main house from an ordinary farm dwelling into what was, for the time, a grand mansion. The inheritance of his widowed bride, Martha, is largely what made that transformation possible.

The red-roof main house is elegant though understated, with a yellow pine exterior that's been painted and coated with layers of sand to resemble white-stone blocks. The first-floor rooms are quite ornate, es-

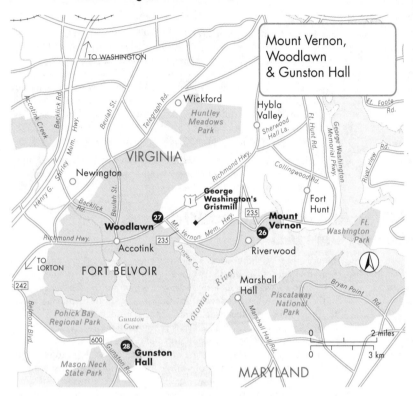

Mount Vernon,
Woodlawn
& Gunston Hall

pecially the formal large dining room, with a molded ceiling decorated with agricultural motifs. The bright colors of the walls, which match the original paint, may surprise those who associate the period with pastels. Throughout the house are smaller symbols of the owner's eminence, such as a key to the main portal of the Bastille—presented to Washington by the Marquis de Lafayette—and Washington's presidential chair. As you tour the mansion, guides are stationed throughout the house to describe the furnishings and answer questions.

The real treasure of Mount Vernon is the view from around back: beneath a 90-foot portico, the home's dramatic riverside porch overlooks an expanse of lawn that slopes down to the Potomac. In springtime the view of the river (a mile wide where it passes the plantation) is framed by dogwood blossoms. Protocol requires United States Navy and Coast Guard ships to salute when passing the house during daylight hours. Although not required, foreign naval vessels often salute, too.

You can stroll around the estate's 500 acres and three gardens, visiting the workshops, kitchen, carriage house, greenhouse, slave quarters, and—down the hill toward the boat landing—the tomb of George and Martha Washington. There's also a pioneer farmer site: a 4-acre hands-on exhibit with a reconstruction of George Washington's 16-side treading barn as its centerpiece. Among the souvenirs sold at the plantation are stripling boxwoods that began life as clippings from bushes planted in 1798, the year before Washington died. A tour of house and grounds takes about two hours. A limited number of wheelchairs is available at the main gate. Private, evening candlelight tours of the mansion with staff dressed in 18th-century costumes can be arranged.

After many years of research, George Washington's Gristmill opened in 2002 on the site of his original mill and distillery. During the guided tours, led by historic interpreters, you meet an 18th-century miller and watch the water-powered wheel grind grain into flour just as it did 200 years ago. The mill is 3 mi from Mount Vernon on Route 235 between Mount Vernon and U.S. Rte. 1. Tickets can be purchased either at the gristmill itself or at Mount Vernon's Main Gate. ⊠ *Southern end of George Washington Pkwy., Mount Vernon* ☎ *703/780–2000, 703/799–8606 evening tours* 🖷 *703/799–8609* ⊕ *www.mountvernon.org* 🖃 *$11, $4 gristmill, $13 combination ticket* ☉ *Mar., Sept., and Oct., daily 9–5; Apr.–Aug., daily 8–5; Nov.–Feb., daily 9–4.*

Woodlawn

🕐 ㉗ *3 mi west of Mount Vernon, 15 mi south of Washington, D.C.*

Woodlawn was once part of the Mount Vernon estate. From here you can still see traces of the bowling green that fronted Washington's home. The house was built for Washington's step-granddaughter, Nelly Custis, who married his favorite nephew, Lawrence Lewis. (Lewis had come to Mount Vernon from Fredericksburg to help Uncle George manage his five farms.)

The Lewises home, completed in 1805, was designed by William Thornton, a physician and amateur architect from the West Indies who drew up the original plans for the U.S. Capitol. Like Mount Vernon, the Woodlawn house is constructed wholly of native materials, including the clay for its bricks and the yellow pine used throughout its interior. Built on a site selected by George Washington, the house has commanding views of the surrounding countryside and the Potomac River beyond.

In the tradition of Southern riverfront mansions, Woodlawn has a central hallway that provides a cool refuge in summer. At one corner of the passage is a bust of George Washington set on a pedestal so the crown of the head is at 6 feet, 2 inches—Washington's actual height. The music room has a ceiling that's approximately 2 feet higher than any other in the house, built that way to improve the acoustics for the harp and harpsichord recitals that the Lewises and their children enjoyed.

Woodlawn was once a plantation where more than 100 people, most of them slaves, lived and worked. As plantation owners, the Lewises lived in luxury. Docents talk about how the family entertained and how the slaves grew produce and prepared these lavish meals as well as their own. As intimates of the Washingtons' household, the Lewises displayed a collection of objects in honor of their illustrious benefactor. Many Washington family items are on display today.

After Woodlawn passed out of the Lewis family's hands, it was owned by a Quaker community, which established a meetinghouse and Virginia's first integrated school. Subsequent owners included the playwright Paul Kester and Senator and Mrs. Oscar Underwood of Alabama. The property was acquired by the National Trust for Historic Preservation in 1957, which had been operating it as a museum since 1951. Every March, Woodlawn hosts an international needlework exhibit with more than 700 items on display.

Also on the grounds of Woodlawn is the **Pope-Leighey House.** One of Frank Lloyd Wright's "Usonian" homes, the structure was built in 1940 as part of the architect's mission to create affordable housing. It was moved here from Falls Church, Virginia, in 1964, to save it from destruction during the building of Route 66. It features many of Wright's trademark elements, including the use of local materials. ⊠ *9000 Richmond Hwy., Mount Vernon* ☎ *703/780–4000* ⊕ *www.woodlawn1805. org or www.pope-leighey1940.org* ☜ *$7.50 for either Woodlawn or Pope-Leighey House, $13 combination ticket* ☉ *Mar.–Dec., daily 10–5; limited guided tours in Mar. due to annual needlework show; tours leave every ½ hour; last tour at 4:30.*

Gunston Hall

🕐 **28** *12 mi south of Woodlawn, 25 mi south of Washington, D.C.*

Gunston Hall Plantation, down the Potomac from Mount Vernon, was the home of another important George. Gentleman farmer George Mason was a colonel of the Fairfax militia and author of the Virginia Declaration of Rights, the model for the U.S. Bill of Rights, which called for freedom of the press, tolerance of religion, and other fundamental democratic principles. Mason was a framer of the Constitution but refused to sign the final document because it didn't stop the importation of slaves, adequately restrain the powers of the federal government, or include a bill of rights. Mason's objections spurred the movement for the inclusion of the Bill of Rights into the Constitution.

Mason's home was built circa 1755. The Georgian-style mansion has some of the finest hand-carved ornamented interiors in the country. It's the handiwork of the 18th century's foremost architect, William Buckland, who also designed the Hammond-Harwood and Chase-Lloyd houses in Annapolis. Gunston Hall is built of native brick, black walnut, and yellow pine. The style of the time demanded absolute symmetry in all structures, which explains the false door set into one side of the center hallway and the "robber" window on a second-floor storage room. The house's interior, with carved woodwork in styles from Chinese to Gothic, has been meticulously restored, with paints made from the original formulas and carefully carved replacements for the intricate mahogany medallions in the moldings. Restored outbuildings include a kitchen, dairy, laundry, and smokehouse, and a schoolhouse has also been reconstructed.

The formal gardens, under excavation by a team of archaeologists, are famous for their boxwoods—some, now 12 feet high, are thought to have been planted during George Mason's time, making them among the oldest in the country. The Potomac is visible past the expansive deer park. Also on the grounds is an active farmyard with livestock and crop varieties that resemble those of Mason's era. Special programs, such as history lectures and hearth cooking demonstrations, are available throughout the year. A tour of Gunston Hall takes at least 45 minutes; tours begin at the visitor center, which includes a museum and gift shop. ⊠ *10709 Gunston Rd., Mason Neck* ☎ *703/550–9220* ⊕ *www.gunstonhall.org* ✉ *$8* ⊙ *Daily 9:30–5; 1st tour at 10, last tour at 4:30.*

Shopping
Nine miles from Gunston Hall, **Potomac Mills** (⊠ 2700 Potomac Mills Circle, Woodbridge ☎ 703/490–5948) bills itself as Virginia's most popular attraction. There are some 220 discount and outlet stores here, including Nordstrom Rack, T. J. Maxx, Saks Off Fifth, and Linens 'n Things. Swedish furniture giant IKEA is also nearby.

FAIRFAX COUNTY

In 1694 King Charles II of England gave the land that would become Fairfax County to seven English noblemen. It became a county in 1741 and was named after Thomas, sixth Lord of Fairfax. Widespread tobacco farming, the dominant industry in the 18th century, eventually depleted the land and helped steer the county toward a more industrial base. Today Fairfax County has one of the highest per capita incomes in the country. Wolf Trap, the only national park dedicated to the performing arts, is here, and throughout the year it draws concertgoers from miles around.

Fairfax

 10 mi west of Arlington.

Fairfax is completely independent of the county of the same name that surrounds it. It's a convenient place to stay while visiting the county's sights, as well as the rest of Northern Virginia.

The National Rifle Association's **National Firearms Museum** has exhibits on the role guns have played in the history of America. The permanent collection includes muzzle-loading flintlocks used in the Revolutionary War, high-tech pistols used by Olympic shooting teams, and weapons that once belonged to American presidents, including Teddy Roosevelt's .32-caliber Browning pistol and a Winchester rifle used by Dwight Eisenhower. ⊠ *National Rifle Association, 11250 Waples Mill Rd.* ☎ *703/267–1600* ⊕ *www.nrahq.org/museum* ✉ *Free* ⊙ *Daily 10–4.*

One of the oldest government buildings in the United States, the red-brick **Fairfax County Courthouse** (⊠ 4000 Chain Bridge Rd. ☎ 703/246–3410 or 703/385–8414, 703/246–3227 sheriff's office ⊕ www.co.fairfax.va.us/courts ✉ Free ⊙ By appointment) opened its doors in 1800, replacing two earlier courts. Like many buildings in Northern Virginia, it changed hands several times during the Civil War, and cannons still grace its grounds. Today, intrepid visitors can arrange to see the wills of George and Martha Washington, held in the office of the court clerk, by calling the Sheriff's Office. (Some restored pages are also on display at Mount Vernon.) The old Fairfax Jail, not open to the public, stands around the corner from the Courthouse, at 10475 Main Street, as does the William Gunnell House, the site of a renowned exploit by Confederate Ranger John Mosby, known as the "Gray Ghost" for his stealth. Free maps of this history-rich area are available from the City of Fairfax Museum and Visitor Center, at 10209 Main St.

Where to Stay

★ $$$ 🏨 **Bailiwick Inn.** Redbrick and green shutters distinguish this small luxury hotel in an 1812 building opposite the historic Fairfax County Courthouse. Expect to be pampered: there are nearly twice as many staff members as rooms. Named for prominent Virginians, guest rooms have antique and reproduction furniture, period detail, and luxurious, modern bathrooms. Four rooms have fireplaces; two have whirlpool baths. The restaurant is open Wednesday through Sunday for dinner, and lunch is served Friday. Room rates include a four-course breakfast and afternoon tea daily. Tea is open to the public on Thursday and Sunday. ⊠ *4023 Chain Bridge Rd., Fairfax, 22030* ☎ *703/691–2266* 🖨 *703/ 934–2112* ⊕ *www.bailiwickinn.com* ➥ *13 rooms, 1 suite* ♿ *Restaurant, minibars, bar* ▤ *AE, MC, V* ⦿❘ *BP.*

$ 🏨 **Best Western Fairfax.** This chain hotel has the largest outdoor pool in Northern Virginia. Landlubbers may prefer to know that the hotel is a mile from downtown Fairfax and its attractions. Rooms are unpretentious but adequate, and the restaurant only serves breakfast. ⊠ *3535 Chain Bridge Rd., Fairfax, 22030* ☎ *703/591–5500* 🖨 *703/ 591–7483* ➥ *127 rooms* ♿ *Restaurant, minibars, free parking, in-room data port, outdoor pool, fitness room* ▤ *AE, D, DC, MC, V.*

Nightlife & the Arts

Center for the Arts. This state-of-the-art performance complex on the suburban Virginia campus of George Mason University satisfies music, ballet, and drama patrons with regular performances in its 1,900-seat concert hall, the 500-seat proscenium Harris Theater, and the intimate 150-seat black-box Theater of the First Amendment. The 9,500-seat Patriot Center, site of pop acts and sporting events, is also on campus. ⊠ *Rte. 123 and Braddock Rd., Fairfax* ☎ *703/993–8888 or 202/397–7328* ⊕ *www.gmu.edu/cfa.*

Sports & the Outdoors

To squeeze in a round of golf on the way to or from Dulles Airport, try **Penderbrook Golf Club** (⊠ 3700 Golf Trail La., Fairfax ☎ 703/385–3700 ⊕ www.penderbrookgolf.com), a short but imaginative 5,927-yard, par-71 course. The 5, 11, 12, and 15 holes are exceptional. The greens fees for 18 holes are $55 Monday through Thursday, and $69 Friday through Sunday. Penderbrook is off West Ox Road and Route 50.

Chantilly

③⓪ *8 mi northwest of Fairfax.*

The main attraction for those who come to Chantilly is a Federal-period home called **Sully.** The house has changed hands many times since it was built in 1794 by Richard Bland Lee, Northern Virginia's first representative to congress. Citizen action in the 20th century saved it from destruction during construction of nearby Dulles Airport. In the 1970s the house and its outbuilding were restored to their original appearance, with a representative kitchen and flower gardens. A 45-minute tour is offered every hour on the hour, and tours of the slave quarters are available during good weather. Educational programs, craft demonstrations, and living history events are held here throughout the year. ⊠ *Rte. 28, 3601 Sully Rd.* ☎ *703/437–1794* ⊕ *www.co.fairfax.va.us/parks/sully* ⊠ *$5* ⊙ *Daily 11–4.*

Opened in 2003 to commemorate the 100th anniversary of the Wright brothers' flight, the **National Air and Space Museum Steven F. Udvar-Hazy Center** is on the grounds of Washington Dulles International Airport. The gargantuan facility displays more than 200 aircraft, 135 spacecraft, rockets, satellites, and experimental flying machines, including a Concorde, the Space Shuttle *Enterprise,* the *Enola Gay,* and the fabled Lockheed SR-71 Blackbird, which in 1990 flew from Los Angeles to Washington, DC in slightly more than an hour. An IMAX theater at this facility also shows films about flight and, in the case of *Shackleton's Antarctic Adventure,* exploration. ⊠ *14390 Air and Space Museum Pkwy., Chantilly* ☎ *202/357–2700* ⊕ *www.nasm.si.edu/udvarhazy* ⊠ *Free; round-trip shuttle from Mall, $7; IMAX, $7.50; parking, $12* ⊙ *Daily 10:30–5.*

Manassas

㉛ *16 mi southwest of Fairfax.*

⏾ The Confederacy won two important victories—in July 1861 and August 1862—at **Manassas National Battlefield Park,** or Bull Run. General Fodor'sChoice Thomas Jonathan Jackson earned his nickname Stonewall here, when ★ he and his brigade "stood like a stone wall." When the second battle ended, the Confederacy was at the zenith of its power. Originally farmland, the battlefield bore witness to the deaths of nearly 30,000 troops. The Stone House, used as a hospital during the war, still stands. President Taft led a peaceful reunion of thousands of veterans here in 1911—50 years after the first battle. The "Peace Jubilee" continues to be celebrated in Manassas every summer. A self-guided walking or driving tour of the park begins at the visitor center, whose exhibits and audiovisual presentations greatly enhance a visit. Bull Run is a 26-mi drive from Washington; from Arlington and Fairfax take I–66 west (use I–495 to get to I–66 from Alexandria) to Exit 47B (Sudley Road/Route 234 North). (Don't be fooled by the earlier Manassas exit for Route 28.) The visitor center is ½ mi north on the right. ⊠ *6511 Sudley Rd.* ☎ *703/361–1339* ⊕ *www.nps.gov/mana* ⊠ *$3* ⊙ *Park daily dawn–dusk, visitor center daily 8:30–5.*

Where to Stay

$$$ ▦ **Shiloh.** Inside a reproduction of a 19th-century house, this B&B may be named for a Civil War battle in Tennessee, but it's still just a short drive from Manassas National Battlefield Park. The grounds include a walnut grove and hiking trails. A lake full of bass, bluegill, and catfish

awaits fishing aficionados. ✉ *13520 Carriage Ford Rd., Nokesville, 20181*
☎ *703/594–2664 or 888/447–7210* ⇥ *2 suites* ⌂ *Kitchenettes, refrigerators, parking* ▭ *MC, V* ⦿⊙ *BP.*

Tysons Corner

❸❷ *11 mi northwest of Alexandria.*

A highly developed commercial area of office buildings, hotels, restaurants, and two major shopping centers, Tysons Corner is a fashionable
address in the Washington, D.C., area. Beware of the grating traffic jam
on every road, side street, and parking lot, particularly at rush hour. Routes
123 and 7, Gallows Road, and International Drive are the worst; I–495,
the Beltway, is less affected.

Where to Eat

★ **$$$$** ✗ **Maestro.** Hotel dining has suffered from a bad rap for a long time, but
this dining room in the Ritz-Carlton is one of the brightest stars in D.C.'s
metro area. Inside the state-of-the-art open kitchen, Chef Fabio Traboc-
chi emphasizes both traditional Italian cooking and what he calls *l'evo-
lutione,* his creative takes on the classics. The menu changes often, but
you might find potato ravioli in black-truffle sauce, pan-fried scallops
wrapped in focaccia, oxtail tortellini, sea bass with fennel confit, and grappa
risotto. Desserts run to sweets like bonbons filled with rose, lavender, and
peach ice cream; peppermint chocolate soufflé; or a chocolate *delice*
(chocolate custard wrapped in a chocolate turban). Three courses (any
combination) are $74; four courses, $86; and a seven-course tasting menu
is $114. Brunch is served on Sunday. ✉ *Ritz-Carlton, Tysons Corner, 1700
Tysons Blvd., Tysons Corner, VA* ☎ *703/821–1515 or 703/917–5498*
⌂ *Reservations essential* ▭ *AE, D, DC, MC, V* ⊙ *Closed Mon.*

★ **$$$–$$$$** ✗ **Capital Grille.** A small group of urban restaurants are tucked in a pocket
of high-end stores in the suburbs of Tysons Corner. Among them is the
Capital Grille, which has fine dry-aged beef cuts and traditional sides.
The Grille has more than just meat and potatoes (though there are fine
dry-aged porterhouse cuts and delicious cream-based potatoes). Don't
miss the pan-fried calamari with hot cherry peppers, for instance.
✉ *1861 International Dr., McLean* ☎ *703/448–3900* ▭ *AE, D, DC,
MC, V* ⊙ *No lunch weekends.*

$–$$$$ ✗ **Clyde's of Tysons Corner.** A branch of a popular Georgetown pub, Clyde's
has four art deco dining rooms. The Palm Terrace has high ceilings and
lots of greenery; another room is a formal dining room. The lengthy,
eclectic menu always includes fresh fish dishes, such as trout Parmesan.
The wine list is equally long. Quality is high, and service attentive.
✉ *8332 Leesburg Pike, Tysons Corner* ☎ *703/734–1900* ▭ *AE, D, DC,
MC, V.*

Where to Stay

★ **$$$** 🏨 **Hilton McLean/Tysons Corner.** This comfortable hotel provides easy
access to Manassas Battlefield and the shopping at Tysons Corner.
Rooms are decorated in bright contemporary fabrics and linens and are
full of light. The Cafe restaurant serves sumptuously prepared American cuisine, including crab cakes, Caesar salad, and cheesecake. The staff
has a reputation for friendliness. A free shuttle bus services delivers you

to the nearby shopping malls. ⊠ *7920 Jones Branch Dr., McLean, 22102* ☎ *703/847–5000* 🖷 *703/761–5100* ⊕ *www.mclean.hilton.com* 🛏 *458 rooms, 18 suites* ⚐ *Restaurant, minibars, indoor pool, health club, spa, bar* ▤ *AE, D, DC, MC, V* ꭥ *EP.*

$$$ 🏨 **Ritz-Carlton, Tysons Corner.** Rooms here are large, with antique furniture, 19th-century lithographs, and trademark elegance. Booking a room in the concierge level gives you access to an exclusive club with sweeping views of the Virginia countryside. On the third floor, the Eden Spa has everything from a juice bar to a pool with lap lanes. The lobby lounge's dark-panel walls and safari animal bronzes make it feel like a 19th-century club room. The bar's innovative menu includes pizzettes with goat cheese and smoked duck. The contemporary cuisine served in the Maestro restaurant is considered among the best in the D.C. area. A steak house with a traditional menu is also on the premises. ⊠ *1700 Tysons Blvd., McLean 22102* ☎ *703/506–4300* 🖷 *703/506–4305* ⊕ *www. ritzcarlton.com* 🛏 *366 rooms, 33 suites* ⚐ *Restaurant, minibars, indoor pool, health club, spa, bar, business services, meeting rooms* ▤ *AE, D, MC, V.*

Shopping

Tysons Corner Center. Anchored by Bloomingdale's and Nordstrom, Tysons Corner Center houses 250 other retailers. No matter when you go, be prepared to fight some of the area's heaviest traffic. A renovation of the mall, to be completed in 2005, will add a 16-screen theater, 5 new restaurants, and more than two dozen new shops. ⊠ *1961 Chain Bridge Rd., McLean* ☎ *703/893–9400* ⊕ *www.shoptysons.com.*

The **Galleria at Tysons II.** Across a busy highway from Tysons Corner Center, the Galleria has 125 generally upscale retailers, including Saks Fifth Avenue, Versace, Neiman Marcus, and F. A. O. Schwarz. ⊠ *2001 International Dr., McLean* ☎ *703/827–7730.*

Wolf Trap Farm Park for the Performing Arts

13 mi west of Alexandria.

★ A major venue in the greater D.C. area, **Wolf Trap Farm Park for the Performing Arts** is the only national park devoted to the performing arts. In warmer months popular and classical music, opera, dance, and comedy performances are given in a partially covered pavilion, the Filene Center, and in the Barns of Wolf Trap—two 18th-century barns transported from upstate New York—the rest of the year. Many food concessions are available; picnicking is permitted on the lawn, but not in the fixed seating under the pavilion.

Children's programs are emphasized at the outdoor Theater in the Woods, including mime, puppetry, animal shows, music, drama, and storytelling. (No food or drink other than water is allowed in the theater.) A major event in September is the International Children's Festival. At any event, allow extra time for parking, and expect a traffic jam after the performance. The 100-odd acres of hills, meadows, and forests here are closed to general use from two hours before to one hour after performances. Parking is free, and on performance nights, Metrorail operates a $3.50 round-trip shuttle bus between the West Falls Church Metro station and the Filene Center. The fare is exact change only, and the bus leaves 20 minutes after the show, or no later than 11 PM, whether the show is over or not. ⊠ *1551 Trap Rd., Vienna* ☎ *703/255–1900, 703/938–2404 Barns at Wolf Trap* ⊕ *www.wolf-trap.org* ⊙ *Daily 7 AM–dusk* Ⓜ *West Falls Church, then bus to Filene Center only.*

☾ **Colvin Run Mill Historic Site,** about 3 mi southeast of Wolf Trap, dates from the first decade of the 19th century, although the country store was added in the early 20th. In addition to the restored grist mill, there's a small museum inside the miller's home. It offers hourly tours, educational programs, special events, and outdoor concerts. You can picnic on the grounds, feed the ducks, and learn about America's technological roots. The Colvin Run Mill General Store originally served the local community and today offers penny candy, freshly ground cornmeal and wheat flour, popcorn, and various old-fashioned goods. The mill itself usually operates the first and third Sunday afternoons from March to November. ⊠ *Rte. 7 and 10017 Colvin Run Rd., Great Falls* ☎ *703/759–2771* ⊕ *www.co.fairfax.va.us/parks/crm* ⊠ *$5* ⊙ *Mar.–Dec., Wed.–Mon. 11–5; Jan. and Feb., Wed.–Mon. 11–4.*

C&O Canal National Historic Park & Great Falls Park

20 mi northwest of Alexandria.

The Potomac River was and still is a highway for transporting goods. In the 18th and early 19th centuries, the river was the main transport route between vital Maryland ports and the seaports of the Chesapeake Bay. Though it served as an important link with the country's western territories, the Potomac had a major drawback for a commercial waterway: rapids and waterfalls along its 190 mi made navigation of the entire distance by boat impossible.

To make the flow of goods from east to west more efficient, engineers proposed that a canal with elevator locks be built parallel to the river. George Washington founded a company to build the canal, and in 1802 (after his death) the firm opened the Patowmack Canal on the Virginia side of the river.

In 1828 Washington's canal was replaced by the Chesapeake & Ohio Canal, which stretched downtown Washington to Cumberland, Maryland. Barges moved through the C&O's 75 locks, and by the mid-19th century the canal carried a million tons of goods a year. However, by the time it had opened, newer technology was starting to make canals obsolete. The Baltimore & Ohio Railroad, which had opened the same day as the C&O, finally put the canal out of business in 1924. After Palisades residents defeated a 1950s proposal to build a highway over it, the canal was reborn as the lovely Chesapeake & Ohio Canal National Historical Park in 1971.

Numbers in the margin correspond to points of interest on the C&O Canal and Great Falls Park map.

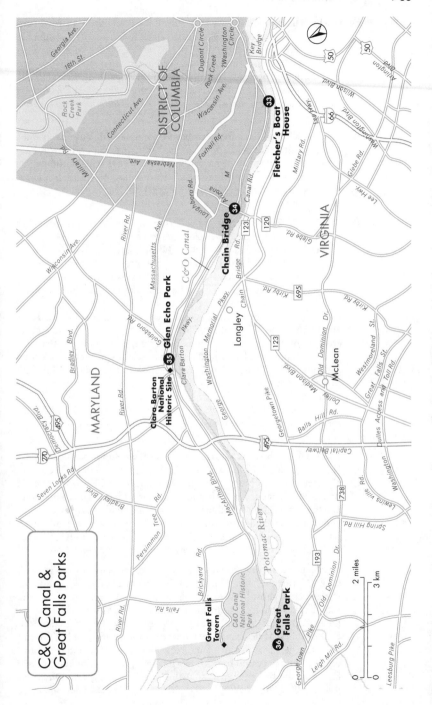

C&O Canal &
Great Falls Parks

DISTRICT OF COLUMBIA

MARYLAND

VIRGINIA

33 Fletcher's Boat House

34 Chain Bridge

35 Glen Echo Park

Clara Barton National Historic Site

36 Great Falls Park

Great Falls Tavern

C&O Canal National Historic Park

Potomac River

Langley

McLean

㉝ Fletcher's Boat House, on the D.C. side of the Potomac, rents rowboats, canoes, and bicycles and sells tackle, snack foods, and D.C. fishing licenses. Here you can catch shad, perch, catfish, striped bass, and other freshwater species. Canoeing is allowed in the canal and, weather permitting, in the Potomac. There's a large picnic area along the riverbank. ✉ *4940 Canal Rd., at Reservoir Rd., Georgetown* ☎ *202/244–0461* ◷ *Late Mar.–May, daily 7:30–7; June–Aug., daily 9–7; Sept.–Nov., daily 9–6.*

㉞ The **Chain Bridge** links the District of Columbia with Virginia. Named for the chains that held up the original structure, the bridge was built to enable cattlemen to bring Virginia herds to the slaughterhouses on the Maryland side of the Potomac. The Virginia side of the river in the area around Chain Bridge is known for its good fishing and narrow, treacherous channel.

☾ **㉟ Glen Echo Park** preserves the site of Washington's oldest amusement park (1911–68) and a stone tower from the town's earlier days. The village of Glen Echo was founded in 1891 by Edwin and Edward Baltzley, brothers who made their fortune through the invention of the egg beater. The brothers were enthusiastic supporters of the Chautauqua movement, a group begun in 1874 in New York as a way to promote liberal education among the working and middle classes. The brothers sold land and houses to further their dream, but the Glen Echo Chautauqua lasted only one season. The National Park Service administers this 10-acre property and offers year-round dances Friday through Sunday in the 1933 Spanish Ballroom, classes in the arts, two children's theaters, two art galleries with ongoing exhibits, artist demonstrations, and a Children's Museum with environmental education workshops. You can also take a ride on a 1921 Dentzel carousel May through September. ✉ *7300 MacArthur Blvd. NW, Glen Echo* ☎ *301/492–6229, 301/320–2330 events hotline* ⊕ *www.nps.gov/glec* ⌸ *Park free, carousel ride 50¢, cost varies for dances.*

Beside Glen Echo Park's parking lot is the **Clara Barton National Historic Site,** a monument to the woman who began the American Red Cross. The structure was built for her by the founders of Glen Echo, and she first used it to store Red Cross supplies; later it became both her home and the organization's headquarters. Today the building is furnished with period artifacts and many of her possessions. Access is by a 30- to 45-minute guided tour only. ✉ *5801 Oxford Rd., Glen Echo* ☎ *301/492–6245* ⊕ *www.nps.gov/clba* ⌸ *Free* ◷ *Tours on the hour 10–4.*

Maryland's **Great Falls Tavern,** headquarters for the Palisades area of C&O Canal National Historic Park, has displays of canal history and photographs that show how high the river can rise. A platform on Olmsted Island, accessible from near the tavern, gives you a spectacular view of the falls. On the canal walls are grooves worn by decades of friction from boat towlines. Mule-drawn canal boat rides ($8), about one hour roundtrip, start here between April and November from Wednesday to Monday. The tavern ceased food service long ago, so if you're hungry, head for the snack bar a few paces north. ✉ *11710 MacArthur Blvd., Potomac 20854* ☎ *301/299–3613 or 301/767–3714* ⌸ *$5 per vehicle, $3* *per person without vehicle; good for 3 days at both Great Falls Park and C&O Canal National Historic Park* ☉ *Nov.–Mar., daily 9–4:30; Apr.–Oct., daily 9–5.*

㊱ Upriver about 8 mi from the Chain Bridge, the C&O Canal National Historic Park—on the Washington, D.C., and Maryland side of the Potomac River—faces its sister national park **Great Falls Park**—on the Virginia side. Here the steep, jagged falls of the Potomac roar into the narrow Mather Gorge, the rocky narrows that make the Potomac churn.

The 800-acre park is a favorite for outings; here you can follow trails past the old Patowmack Canal and among the boulders and forests lining the edge of the falls. Horseback riding is permitted—maps are available at the visitor center—but you can't rent horses in the park. Swimming, wading, overnight camping, and alcoholic beverages are not allowed, but you can fish (a Virginia, Maryland, or D.C. license is required for anglers 16 and older), climb rocks (climbers must register at the visitor center beforehand), or—if you're an experienced boater with your own equipment— go white-water kayaking (*below* the falls only). As is true all along this stretch of the river, the currents are deadly. Despite frequent signs and warnings, there are those who occasionally dare the water and drown.

A tour of the visitor center and museum takes 30 minutes. Staff members conduct special tours and walks year-round. Maryland's Great Falls Tavern, discussed in Chapter 2, serves as a museum and has displays of canal history and a platform from which to view the falls. You can get to C&O Canal National Historical Park from Alexandria or Arlington by taking Chain Bridge to MacArthur Boulevard, then driving northwest, or by taking Exit 41 off the Beltway and following the signs to Carderock. ⊠ *Rte. 193/Old Georgetown Pike; Exit 13 off Rte. 495, the Capitol Beltway to Rte. 738, follow signs* ☏ *703/285–2966* ⊕ *www. nps.gov/gwmp/grfa* ⊠ *$4 per vehicle, good for 7 days; $3 for entry on foot, horse, motorcycle, or bicycle, good for 3 days* ☉ *Year-round, daily 7–dusk. Visitor center Apr.–Oct., daily 10–5; Nov.–Mar., daily 10–4.*

Where to Eat

★ **$$$$** ✕ **L'Auberge Chez François.** Set in the Virginia countryside, this sprawling restaurant serves the German-influence cuisine of Alsace. The decor is romantic and kitschy—a fireplace dominates the main dining room, German knickknacks line the walls, and red-jacket waiters courteously guide you through the meal. *Choucroute* (sausage, duck, smoked pork, and foie gras served atop sauerkraut), red snapper in a pastry crust for two, and medallions of beef and veal are a few of the generously portioned, outstanding entrées. You are asked in advance whether you'd like a soufflé. Say yes, unless it's the Alsatian plum tart that's calling you instead. ⊠ *332 Springvale Rd., Great Falls* ☏ *703/759–3800* ⏚ *Reservations essential* ⏛ *Jacket required* ⊟ *AE, D, DC, MC, V* ☉ *Closed Mon. No lunch.*

LOUDOUN COUNTY

Loudoun County, capital of Virginia's horse country and a half hour away from D.C., abounds with historic villages and towns, antiques shops,

CloseUp

WINE MAKING IN VIRGINIA

I N 1609 ENGLISH SETTLERS in Jamestown, Virginia, produced the first wine—however humble—in America. In the centuries that have followed, it has been either sink or swim for the state's wine industry—mostly sink. But after numerous tries, Virginia can claim some 70-odd wineries.

In 1611 the Virginia Company, which was eager to establish wine making in the Colonies, sent over French winegrowers along with slips and seeds of European vine stocks. For the next two centuries, French viticulturists attempted but failed to transplant European rootstock to the New World. In 1769 the Virginia Assembly appointed the Frenchman Andrew Estave as wine maker and viticulturist. Although he couldn't get the European stock to take either, he did realize that the problem lay with Virginia's harsher climate of cold winters and hot, humid summers. Estave believed that growers should therefore use native American grapes, which were more likely to flourish.

Thomas Jefferson was anxious to promote grape growing, both to encourage wine drinking for itself and to create a cash-crop alternative to tobacco. Although he appreciated European wines, Jefferson believed that successful wine making in America would depend on native varietals. By 1800 he and other Virginians had begun developing hybrids of American and European varieties, resulting in grapes that combined American hardiness with European finesse and complexity. The most popular are still grown today.

A strong wine-making industry developed in Virginia between 1800 and the Civil War. The war's fierce battles destroyed many vineyards. As recently as 1950, only 15 acres of grapes were being grown. In the 1960s the Virginia grape industry began a revival that has made it the sixth-largest wine-producing state. Although the revival began with American hybrids, it has shifted to French hybrids, with the cultivation of vinifera varietals appealing to more sophisticated palates.

Today Virginia's wines are winning national and international acclaim. The state produces more than 300,000 cases of wine yearly from 2,100 acres of wine grapes. The most popular variety grown, chardonnay, comes as a medium- to full-bodied dry white wine. It may be fruity, with a hint of apples or citrus. Other whites include Riesling, gewürztraminer, sauvignon blanc, seyval blanc, and vidal blanc. Virginia's reds include cabernet sauvignon, merlot, pinot noir, and chambourcin. Virginia's wineries are spread around the state in six viticultural areas. The wine industry begun by Jefferson is in the Monticello region in central Virginia. Other areas are the Shenandoah, Northern Neck George Washington Birthplace, North Fork of Roanoke, Rocky Knob, and Virginia's Eastern Shore. Each area has been designated for its unique wine-growing conditions.

The 400 wine festivals and events that take place each year attract half a million visitors. A 16-page booklet, "Virginia Wineries Festival & Tour Guide," is free at visitor information centers in the state. The guide also lists each of the state's wineries; many offer tours and tastings. You can request a copy by contacting the **Virginia Wine Marketing Program** (✆ Virginia Department of Agriculture and Consumer Services, Division of Marketing, Box 1163, Richmond 23218 ☎ 800/828–4637 ⊕ www.virginiawines.org).

—CiCi Williamson

wineries, farms, and heritage sites; the countryside is littered with stables, barns, and stacked-stone fences. The Potomac River borders the county on the north. In the major towns in Loudoun, such as Leesburg, Middleburg, and Waterford, residents emulate such traditional rural Virginia pursuits as fox hunts, steeplechases, and high-profile entertaining.

Numbers in the margin correspond to points of interest on the Northern Virginia map.

Middleburg

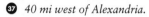

❸❼ *40 mi west of Alexandria.*

The area around here was surveyed by George Washington in 1763, when it was known as Chinn's Crossroads. It was considered strategic because of its location midway on the Winchester–Alexandria route (roughly what is now U.S. 50). Many of Middleburg's homes include horse farms, and the town is known for its steeplechases and fox hunts in spring and fall. Attractive boutiques and stores line U.S. 50 (the main street), and polo matches are played on Sunday June through Labor Day.

The vineyards in the Middleburg area often have tastings and tours. Three miles south of Middleburg, **Piedmont Vineyards and Winery** has 25 acres of vines, as well as an early 18th-century manor house. Piedmont specializes in white wines such as chardonnay and semillon, but also makes some reds. ✉ *Rte. 626* ☎ *540/687–5528* ⊕ *www.piedmontwines.com* ⊙ *Tours Apr.–Dec., daily 11–5; Jan.–Mar., Wed.–Sun. 11–5; tasting room Mon.–Sat. 10–5, Sun. 11–5.*

One mile east of Middleburg is the **Swedenburg Estate Vineyard.** The winery's modern building sits on a working farm, which raises Angus beef cattle. The Bull Run mountains form a backdrop for the vineyards. Swedenburg vineyard grows chardonnay, cabernet sauvignon, pinot noir, and Riesling. ✉ *Valley View Farm, Rte. 50/23959 Winery La.* ☎ *540/687–5219* ⊕ *www.swedenburgwines.com* ⊙ *Daily 10–4.*

Two miles east of town is the **Chrysalis Vineyard,** dedicated to producing both Old- and New-World varieties of wine and hoping to revive interest in the fabled Norton, a grape native to Virginia. ✉ *23876 Champe Ford Rd.* ☎ *540/687–8222 or 800/235–8804* ⊕ *www.chrysaliswine.com* ⊙ *Daily 11–5.*

Where to Stay

$$$$ ▦ **Goodstone Inn.** A farm cottage, a Dutch cottage, a carriage house, and a two-story 19th-century stone house are among the charming places to stay here. Take a suite decorated in rich, warm antiques and reproductions or rent an entire house on this estate in the shadow of the Blue Ridge Mountains, near walking and riding trails. A working farm provides produce and eggs for the inn's kitchen. ✉ *36205 Snake Hill Rd., 20117* ☎ *540/687–4645 or 877/219–4663* ⊕ *www.goodstone.com* ➫ *14 suites, 4 cottages* ♿ *In-room hot tubs, kitchens, 18-hole golf course, mountain bikes* ▤ *AE, MC, V* ⊙▮ *BP.*

$$–$$$ ▦ **Middleburg Country Inn.** This three-story structure, built in 1820 and enlarged in 1858, was the rectory of St. John's Parish Episcopal Church until 1907. Its medium-size rooms are furnished with antiques and period reproductions and have working fireplaces. A full country breakfast is served, and, when weather permits, you can eat your meal alfresco. ⊠ *209 E. Washington St., Box 2065, 22117* ☎ *540/687–6082 or 800/ 262–6082* 🖷 *540/687–5603* ⊕ *www.midcountryinn.com* ⟿ *5 rooms, 3 suites* ⟁ *Hot tub* 🖃 *AE, D, MC, V* ◎ *BP.*

en route Five miles south of Leesburg on Route 15, **Oatlands** is a former 5,000-acre plantation built by a great-grandson of Robert "King" Carter, one of the wealthiest pre-Revolution planters in Virginia. The Greek Revival manor house was built in 1803; a stately portico and half-octagonal stair wings were added in 1827. The house, a National Trust Historic Site, has been meticulously restored, and the manicured fields that remain host public and private equestrian events from spring to fall. Among these is the Loudoun Hunt Point-to-Point in April, a race that brings out the entire community for tailgates and picnics on blankets. The terraced walls here border a restored English garden of 4½ acres. ⊠ *20850 Oatlands Plantation La., (Rte. 15)* ☎ *703/777–3174* ⊕ *www.oatlands.org* 🖃 *$8; additional fee for special events* ◷ *Apr.–Dec., Mon.–Sat. 10–5, Sun. 1–5.*

Leesburg

38 *36 mi northwest of Alexandria.*

A staging area during George Washington's push to the Ohio Valley during the French and Indian War (1754–60), Leesburg is one of the oldest towns in northern Virginia. Its numerous fine Georgian and Federal buildings now house offices, shops, restaurants, and homes. In an early sign of changing allegiances, "George Town" changed its name to Leesburg in 1758 to honor Virginia's illustrious Lee family. When the British burned Washington during the War of 1812, James and Dolley Madison fled to Leesburg with many government records, including official copies of the Declaration of Independence and the U.S. Constitution.

The history of the Loudoun County area is detailed in the **Loudoun Museum and Gift Shop,** which displays art and artifacts of daily life from the time preceding the town's existence on through the present. ⊠ *16 W. Loudoun St. SW* ☎ *703/777–7427* ⊕ *www.visitloudoun.com* 🖃 *$3* ◷ *Mon.–Sat. 10–5, Sun. 1–5.*

Within the 1,200 acres that make up **Morven Park** is the Westmoreland Davis Equestrian Institute (a private riding school) and two museums: Morven Park Carriage Museum and the Museum of Hounds and Hunting. The mansion, the work of three architects in 1781, is a Greek Revival building that bears a striking resemblance to the White House (completed in 1800), so much so that it's been used as a stand-in for it in films. Two governors have lived here. The price of admission includes entrance to the two museums and to 16 rooms in the Morven Park mansion. ⊠ *Rte. 7, 1 mi north of Leesburg* ☎ *703/777–2414* ⊕ *www.*

morvenpark.org ⬜ *$6* ⊙ *Apr.–Oct., Tues.–Fri. noon–5, Sat. 10–5, Sun. 1–5; Nov., weekends noon–5; Christmas tours 1st 3 wks of Dec., Tues.–Sun. noon–5.*

Where to Stay & Eat

$$–$$$$ ✕ **Lightfoot Restaurant.** Housed in a Romanesque-Revival building (1888), this restaurant was the Peoples National Bank for more than half a century. Restored to its original grandeur, the restaurant was named in honor of Francis Lightfoot Lee, a signer of the Declaration of Independence. The wine "cellar" is actually the bank's vault. The seasonal American cuisine, based on local ingredients, includes Blue Ridge spinach salad, a variation on oysters Rockefeller, lamb T-bones marinated in garlic, and many kinds of seafood. ✉ *11 N. King St.* ☎ *703/771–2233* ⊕ *www. lightfootrestaurant.com* ▭ *AE, D, DC, MC, V.*

★ $$$$ ✕🖼 **Lansdowne Conference Resort.** With 205 acres of hills and tall trees bordered by the Potomac River, Lansdowne specializes in outdoor activities and has miles of hiking and jogging trails. Polished wood furniture, carpets, handsome wall decorations, and marble-accented bathrooms help make the property elegant. Tall windows in the Lansdowne Grille ($$$–$$$$) look out on Sugarloaf Mountain. The Riverside Hearth, a café overlooking a Robert Trent Jones Jr. 18-hole golf course, serves American cuisine breakfast through dinner. Its Sunday brunch buffet is renowned. ✉ *44050 Woodridge Pkwy., off Rte. 7, 22075* ☎ *703/729–8400 or 800/541–4801* 🖷 *703/729–4096* ⊕ *www.landsowneresort. com* ⬅ *291 rooms, 14 suites* ⚫ *Restaurant, 2 cafés, 18-hole golf course, tennis court, 2 pools (1 indoor), gym, billiards, racquetball, volleyball, bar* ▭ *AE, D, DC, MC, V.*

Waterford

㊴ *5 mi northwest of Leesburg, 45 mi northwest of Alexandria.*

The historic community of Waterford was founded by a Quaker miller and for many decades has been synonymous with fine crafts; its annual Homes Tour and Crafts Exhibit, held the first weekend of October, includes visits to 18th-century buildings. Waterford and more than 1,400 acres around it were declared a National Historic Landmark in 1970 in recognition of its authenticity as an almost original, ordinary 18th-century village.

NORTHERN VIRGINIA A TO Z

To research prices, get advice from other travelers, and book travel arrangements, visit www.fodors.com.

ADDRESSES

Founded as a Colonial port city, Alexandria was first settled along the Potomac River. It is this oldest area that's now called Old Town. Although the city sprawls west across I–395, this area mostly contains modern homes and shopping areas, so it's not host to any sites listed in this chapter. Although the city limits end at the I–495 "Beltway," many of the housing developments south of the Beltway still have an Alexandria postal address. If you take the G. W. Parkway toward Mount Vernon, you'll cross this area, called Alexandria South.

AIRPORT

Three major airports serve northern Virginia and Washington, D.C. The busy and often crowded Ronald Reagan Washington National Airport, 10 mi south of downtown Washington in Virginia, has scheduled daily flights by all major U.S. carriers. Washington Dulles International Airport, 26 mi northwest of Washington, is a modern facility served by the major U.S. airlines and many international carriers. Baltimore-Washington International Airport is 26 mi northeast of the capital.

🛪 Airport Information **Ronald Reagan Washington National Airport** (DCA) ☎ 703/417-8000 ⊕ www.metwashairports.com/National. **Washington Dulles International Airport** (IAD) ☎ 703/572-2700 ⊕ www.metwashairports.com/Dulles. **Baltimore-Washington International Airport** (BWI) ☎ 410/859-7100 ⊕ www.bwiairport.com.

TRANSFERS Alexandria is only a few miles from Ronald Reagan Washington National Airport. It's possible to transfer there via Metro, taxi, or public buses. Taking a taxi to Washington Dulles ($55) or Baltimore ($90) airports is extremely expensive. Baltimore is more than an hour away, but from Union Station in Washington, D.C., MARC commuter trains and many Amtrak trains stop near the airport, where a free shuttle bus transfers you to the terminal. The cheapest way to reach Washington Dulles airport is via a shuttle bus—either from Alexandria or from the Vienna Metro stop.

🛪 **SuperShuttle** ☎ 800/258-3826 ⊕ www.supershuttle.com. **United Airport Transportation Service** ☎ 703/801-4884. **Washington Flyer** ☎ 703/685-1400 ⊕ www.washfly.com.

BIKE TRAVEL

A great place to rent a bike is at the idyllic Washington Sailing Marina, which is right on the Mount Vernon Bike Trail. A 12-mi ride south will take you right up to the front doors of Mount Vernon, and a 6-mi ride north across the Memorial Bridge will put you at the foot of the Washington Monument. All-terrain bikes rent for $6 per hour or $22 per day; cruisers cost $4 per hour or $16.50 per day. The marina is open 9–5 daily.

Fletcher's Boat House rents bicycles on the D.C. side of the Potomac. The C&O Canal paths connect to the Virginia bike paths. The boat house is open late March–May, daily 7:30–7; June–August, daily 9–7; September–November, daily 9–6. It's closed December–early March and during severe weather.

🛪 Bike Rentals **Fletcher's Boat House** ⊠ 4740 Canal Rd., at Reservoir Rd., Washington, DC ☎ 202/244-0461. **Washington Sailing Marina** ⊠ 1 Marina Dr., George Washington Memorial Pkwy., Alexandria, VA ☎ 703/548-9027 ⊕ www.guestservices.com/wsm.

CAR TRAVEL

I–95 runs north–south along the eastern side of the region. I–395 begins in D.C. and joins I–95 as it crosses I–495, the Capital Beltway, which circles the District of Columbia through Virginia and Maryland, providing a circular—albeit very clogged—bypass around Washington for north- or southbound drivers. Avoid it during morning and evening rush hours. The main interchange where I–395, I–95, and I–495 converge is undergoing a major alteration, and although traffic is not being detoured, the volume of vehicles traveling through this area can cause backups, especially during rush hour.

I–66 runs east–west between Washington, D.C., and I–81 near Front Royal, which takes you south through the Shenandoah or north to West Virginia. Note that HOV restrictions prohibit single-person vehicles on I–66 inside the Beltway eastbound during morning rush hour and westbound during evening rush hour.

Once you have reached Northern Virginia, it's convenient to use the area's excellent, clean, and safe Washington Metropolitan Area Transit Authority (WMATA) system (buses and subway) or local jurisdictions' bus systems, or travel by biking or walking. In the farther-out suburbs, a car is necessary.

PARKING At the Alexandria Convention and Visitors Association, you can obtain a free 24-hour parking permit for the two-hour metered zones (you must furnish your license plate number). Giving parking tickets is one of the things Capital-area police forces do best, so if you park at meters throughout Northern Virginia and D.C., watch the time religiously and keep the meter fed lest you acquire an expensive bill stuck under your wiper blade. Also read parking signs carefully. There are many variations, and they are often quite confusing. Parking in the curb lane on major arteries during rush hour may result in your car being towed.

TRAFFIC Visitors and residents alike can be baffled by the Capital Area's tangle of highway interchanges, the sometimes confusing signage, the ongoing road repairs/improvements, and some of the nation's worst traffic. Morning and evening rush hours (6:30–9:30 and 4–7) exacerbate the situation, so avoid driving toward downtown Washington or Tysons Corner at these times. It would be prudent to select lodging north of the I–95/I–495 interchange if you plan to spend most of your time in downtown Washington or within the Beltway. The roads around Tysons Corner move very slowly during rush hours, particularly at quitting time.

DISABILITIES & ACCESSIBILITY
With the eyes of the federal government watching from across the Potomac, you can expect Northern Virginia to be almost 100% accessible, the exception being the second or third floors of historic buildings. All streets have curb cuts and many public buildings have ramps.

DISCOUNTS & DEALS
Alexandria's Key Pass provides for 15% off regular ticket prices to the historic estates of Virginia. The pass, valid April–December, includes admission to Mount Vernon, Gunston Hall, and Woodlawn plantations. It costs $20 for adults, $11 for children 6–17, and is free for children under five. The passes can be purchased from the Alexandria Convention and Visitors Association either in person or over the phone.

The Alexandria Very Important Patriot (VIP) Pass saves 20% on admission to a guided walking tour of Old Town, a boat cruise on the Potomac, and four of Old Town Alexandria's most popular attractions. The attractions are Gadsby's Tavern Museum, Carlyle House, Lee-Fendall House Museum and Garden, and the Stabler-Leadbeater Apothecary Museum. The passes, valid May–September, cost $26 for adults and $14 for children 11–17. These passes are also available from the Alexandria Convention and Visitors Association.

In addition, the Convention and Visitors Association offers different discounts and combined-ticket deals throughout the year, including passes for combination trolley tours and riverboat cruises. Call in advance to see what discounts are available for the time of your visit.

🛈 **Alexandria Convention and Visitors Association** ✉ Ramsay House, 221 King St., Alexandria 22314 ☎ 703/838-5005, 866/300-6044 toll-free ⊕ www.funside.com.

EMERGENCIES

🛈 **Emergency** ☎ 911. **Fire** ☎ 703/838-4660. **Police** ☎ 703/838-4444.

🛈 **Hospitals Alexandria Hospital** ✉ 4320 Seminary Rd., Alexandria ☎ 703/504-3000 ⊕ www.inova.com. **Inova Fair Oaks Hospital** ✉ 3600 Joseph Siewick Dr., Fairfax ☎ 703/391-3600 ⊕ www.inova.com. **Inova Fairfax Hospital and Inova Fairfax Hospital for Children** ✉ 3300 Gallows Rd., Falls Church ☎ 703/698-1110 or 703/204-6777 ⊕ www.inova.com. **Inova Mount Vernon Hospital** ✉ 2501 Parker's La., Alexandria ☎ 703/664-7000 ⊕ www.inova.com. **Virginia Hospital Center–Arlington** ✉ 1701 N. George Mason Dr., Arlington ☎ 703/558-5000 ⊕ www.virginiahospitalcenter.com.

🛈 **24-Hour Pharmacies CVS** ✉ 5101 Duke St., Alexandria ☎ 703/823-7411, 703/823-7430 pharmacy ⊕ www.cvs.com. **Rite Aid** ✉ 6711 Richmond Hwy., Alexandria ☎ 703/768-7233 ⊕ www.riteaid.com.

MAIL & SHIPPING

Alexandria's main post office is open weekdays 8–6:30 and Saturday 9–4.

Gone are the days that free coffee came with the use of the computer to check your e-mail; however, many Starbucks locations offer wireless access for a fee to those who bring their own laptops. T-Mobile subscribers log on for free. As in the rest of the universe, there are multiple locations in Northern Virginia.

🛈 Post Office **Alexandria Main Post Office** ✉ 1100 Wythe St. ☎ 703/684-7168 ⊕ www.usps.gov.

SUBWAY

Washington's Metro provides subway service in the District and in the Maryland and Virginia suburbs. The Orange, Blue, and Yellow lines are most useful for exploring Northern Virginia. You are allowed to travel with a bike on the Metro, but only in the last car of the train and between 10 and 2 on weekdays (you can do so any time on weekends). Most stations have racks.

FARES & SCHEDULES The base price is $1.10; the actual fare you pay depends on the time of day and the distance traveled. Buy your ticket with coins and bills at Farecard machines. Be sure to hang on to that flimsy ticket; you need it to exit. A $5 day pass is available at Metro Sales Outlets and at many hotels, banks, and Safeway and Giant grocery stores. For routes and schedules, contact Metro.

🛈 **Metro** ☎ 202/637-7000 ⊕ www.wmata.com.

TAXIS
🚖 Taxi Companies **Alexandria Diamond Cab** ☎ 703/549-6200. **Alexandria Yellow Cab** ☎ 703/549-2500. **Fairfax White Top Cab** ☎ 703/644-4500.

TOURS
The Alexandria Convention and Visitors Association runs walking tours that leave from its office 10:30 AM Monday through Saturday and 2 PM Sunday; tickets are $10. Alexandria Colonial Tours leads guided walking tours of historic Alexandria by reservation. Ghost-and-graveyard tours (reservations not required) are conducted Friday, Saturday, and Sunday nights.
🚶 Walking Tours **Alexandria Colonial Tours** ☎ 703/548-0100.

TRAIN TRAVEL
Amtrak has scheduled stops in Alexandria. Virginia Rail Express provides workday commuter service between Union Station in Washington and Fredericksburg and Manassas, with additional stops near hotels in Crystal City, Alexandria, and elsewhere.
🚆 Train Lines **Amtrak** ☎ 800/872-7245 Metroliner Service, 800/523-8720 Union Station, 202/484-7540 ⊕ www.amtrak.com. **Virginia Rail Express** (VRE) ☎ 800/743-3873 ⊕ www.vre.com.
🚆 Train Stations **Alexandria** ✉ 110 Callahan Dr.

VISITOR INFORMATION
Most visitor centers are open 9–5 daily.
🛈 Tourist Information **Alexandria Convention and Visitors Association** ✉ Ramsay House, 221 King St., Alexandria 22314 ☎ 703/838-4200 or 800/388-9119 ⊕ www.funside.com. **Arlington County Visitor Center** ✉1301 S. Joyce St., Arlington 22202 ☎703/228-5720 or 800/677-6267 ⊕ www.stayarlington.com. **Fairfax County Visitors Center** ✉ 8180A Silverbrook Rd., Lorton 22079 ☎ 800/732-4732 ⊕ www.visitfairfax.org. **Loudoun Tourism Council** ✉ 222 Cactocin Circle SE, Suite 100, Leesburg 20175 ☎ 703/771-2617 or 800/752-6118 ⊕ visitloudon.org. **Manassas Visitor Center** ✉ 9431 West St., Manassas ☎ 703/361-6599 ⊕ www.visitpwc.com. **Prince William Visitor Center** ✉ 200 Mill St., Occoquan ☎ 703/491-4045 ⊕ www.visitpwc.com. **Waterford Foundation** ✉ Main and 2nd Sts. ☎ 540/882-3018 ⊕ www.waterfordva.org.

D.C.'S MARYLAND SUBURBS

2

ORDER UP SOME AMERICAN CLASSICS
at the Tastee Diner ⇨*p.48*

LOOK FOR THE BRASS RING
riding Glen Echo Park's carousel ⇨*p.52*

BRING BACK FINE TREASURES
lining Kensington's Antiques Row ⇨*p.55*

HEAD OFF TO PLAY THE PONIES
at Laurel Park ⇨*p.61*

TRACE THE ROUTE OF AN ASSASSIN
at the Surratt House Museum ⇨*p.64*

Updated by
Robin
Dougherty

SUBURBAN MARYLAND IS D.C.'S BACKYARD. In 1791 Montgomery and Prince George's counties ceded 90 square mi to the new United States government to create the nation's capital, then called simply Washington. Montgomery County is to the west and north of the capital's sharply drawn boundaries, and Prince George's County is to the east. Because of their proximity to D.C., the counties are the most densely populated in Maryland, and many residents consider themselves Washingtonians. After all, what happens on Capitol Hill often has an immediate effect on residents: many people work for the federal government or are politically active.

Aside from locals commuting daily to the capital, Washington also comes to the suburbs themselves. Federal agencies that maintain offices in the area include the National Institutes of Health, the Internal Revenue Service, and the National Aeronautic Space Administration. Even the Washington Redskins play in Prince George's County.

One of the most affluent counties in the country, Montgomery County is known for Bethesda's bounty of restaurants and a breathtaking view of the powerful Potomac River and Great Falls. Prince George's County also holds the University of Maryland's College Park campus; historic houses, such as the Surratt House Museum; and great green spaces that include Fort Washington Park, the Colonial Farm, and the Merkle Wildlife Sanctuary.

Exploring Suburban Maryland

An automobile is a must to travel throughout the counties, but avoid the Capital Beltway (Interstate 495) during morning and afternoon rush hours. At those times the congestion is second only to Los Angeles. Most attractions, restaurants, and shops in Montgomery County are clustered "down-county" in areas closest to D.C. In Prince George's County, places to explore are sprinkled throughout the area.

About the Restaurants & Hotels

Bethesda residents take eating out seriously, and the range of cuisines and depth of innovation available here show it. Many Washington restaurants have opened Bethesda branches, and alfresco dining is available during good weather at most places. Bethesda's largest concentration of restaurants (about 75) are within the Woodmont Triangle, whose boundaries are formed by Old Georgetown Road, Woodmont Avenue, and Rugby Road. Bright blue signs identify parking; on weekends you can park for free in public garages.

For information about a Bethesda dining guide, Taste of Bethesda, and other special events, contact the **Bethesda Urban Partnership** (☎ 301/215–6660 ⊕ www.bethesda.org).

Even with six hotels within a mile of downtown Bethesda, it's best to book your room in advance. Occupancy rates are high, and you're likely to pay only a little less than you would in Washington. Tourists coming to see Washington's cherry blossoms make spring the busiest season. December and January tend to be the slowest and least expensive months, except around a presidential inauguration.

WHAT IT COSTS					
	$$$$	$$$	$$	$	¢
RESTAURANTS	over $30	$22–$30	$14–$22	$7–$14	under $7
HOTELS	over $250	$175–$250	$130–$175	$80–$130	Under $80

Restaurant prices are per person for a main course at dinner. Hotel prices are for a standard double room, excluding state and local taxes (11% in Virginia; 10% in Maryland).

MONTGOMERY COUNTY

Numbers in the margin correspond to points of interest on the Montgomery County map.

Montgomery County, named after Revolutionary War hero General Richard Montgomery, became (in 1776) the first Maryland county to drop the custom of naming jurisdictions after royalty. In between housing developments, strip malls, and office parks, the northern portion of the county retains traces of the area's agrarian beginnings.

Bethesda

❶ *2 mi north of Washington, D.C.*

Bethesda was named in 1871 after the Bethesda Meeting House, which was built by the Presbyterians. The name alludes to a biblical pool that had great healing power. Today people seek healing in Bethesda at the National Institutes of Health and meet here to enjoy the burgeoning restaurant scene. Bethesda has changed from a small community into an urban destination, but in certain ways time has stood still east of Bethesda in Chevy Chase, a tony town of country clubs, stately houses, and huge trees.

National Institutes of Health (NIH). One of the world's foremost biomedical research centers, with a sprawling 300-acre campus, the NIH offers tours for the public, including an orientation tour at the NIH Visitor Information Center and one at the National Library of Medicine. Although best known for its books and journals—there are more than 5 million—the National Library of Medicine also houses historical medical references dating from the 11th century. A library tour includes a look at historical documents, the library's databases, and their "visible human," which provides a view of everything from how the kneecap works to how physicians use surgical simulators. The guides have some useful advice on how to start medical research (to do any research, you must arrive at least an hour and a half before closing time). ⊠ *Visitor Information Center, 9000 Rockville Pike, Bldg. 10* ☎ *301/496–1776* ⊠ *National Library of Medicine, 8600 Rockville Pike, Bldg. 38A* ☎ *301/496–6308* ⊕ *www.nih. gov* ☜ *Free* ⊙ *Call for tour times, library hours, and information on forms of ID to bring, plus other security measures* Ⓜ *Medical Center.*

More than 750 varieties of azaleas bloom at **McCrillis Gardens and Gallery** from late March through July, and usually peak around May 1.

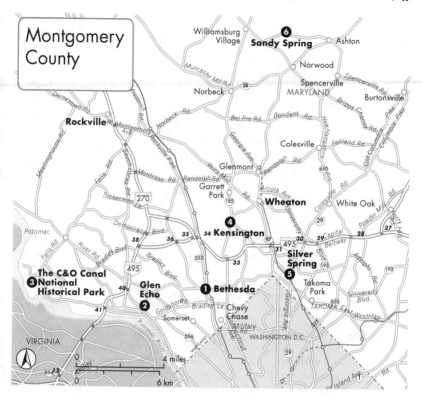

Choice ornamental trees and shrubs, including a remarkable collection of rhododendrons, bloom during the warm months. A small art gallery hosts monthly exhibitions by local artists. ✉ *6910 Greentree Rd.* ☎ *301/962–1455* ⊕ *www.mc-mncppc.org/parks/brookside/mccrilli. shtm* ✆ *Free* ⊗ *Gardens daily 10–sunset; gallery Feb.–Nov., Tues.–Sun. noon–4.*

Montgomery County Farm Woman's Cooperative Market. This market is one of the remaining vestiges of Montgomery County's agricultural society. In the midst of the Great Depression, women gathered goods from their gardens to sell in Bethesda to residents of the District of Columbia and its growing suburbs. Today the tradition continues. Baked goods, fresh fruits and vegetables, crafts, and flea-market goods are still sold in and around this low, white building in the midst of office high-rises. (A view of the market in the 1930s is depicted in a mural on the wall of the Bethesda Post Office at 7400 Wisconsin Avenue.) ✉ *7155 Wisconsin Ave.* ☎ *301/652–2291* ⊕ *montgomerycountymd. com/events/montgomery_market.htm* ⊗ *Wed. and Sat. 7–3, outdoor flea market Wed. and weekends 7–5* Ⓜ *Bethesda.*

A self-guided nature trail winds through a verdant 40-acre estate and around the **Audubon Naturalist Society.** You're never far from the trill of birdsong here, since the society has turned the grounds into something of a nature preserve, forbidding the use of pesticides and leaving some areas in a natural state. The estate is known as Woodend, as is the mansion, which was designed in the 1920s by Jefferson Memorial architect John Russell Pope. The society leads wildlife identification walks, environmental education programs, and—September through June—a weekly Saturday bird walk at its headquarters. Birders interested in new local sightings may want to call for the Audubon Society's Voice of the Naturalist tape recording. The bookstore stocks titles on conservation, ecology, and birding, as well as bird feeders, birdhouses, and nature-related gifts such as jewelry and toys. ⊠ *8940 Jones Mill Rd., Chevy Chase* ☎ *301/652–9188, 301/652–1088 for naturalist tape* ⊕ *www. audubonnaturalist.org* ⊠ *Free* ☉ *Grounds daily sunrise–sunset, bookstore weekdays 10–5, Sat. 9–5, Sun. noon–5.*

Where to Eat

★ **$$–$$$** ✕ **Cafe Bethesda.** The modern American cuisine at this intimate restaurant is conservative yet creative, and the service is attentive. Most tables are next to flower-laden window boxes. Specialties include dishes that play up local produce, game, and seafood, such as fresh rack of lamb crusted in basil and served with ratatouille, and sautéed Atlantic salmon with caramelized shallots and spinach strudel. Make reservations for Friday and Saturday nights. ⊠ *5027 Wilson La.* ☎ *301/657–3383* ⊟ *AE, D, MC, V* ☉ *Closed Mon. No lunch.*

★ **$–$$$** ✕ **Thyme Square.** The predominantly vegetarian menu at this hip-and-healthy joint is accompanied by an organic wine list. Although the menu changes seasonally, Brazilian shellfish stew—shrimp, mussels, and fish in a spicy tomato and coconut broth—remains a constant favorite. Organic steak and grilled chicken are also on the menu. ⊠ *4735 Bethesda Ave.* ☎ *301/657–9077* ⊟ *AE, D, MC, V.*

$$ ✕ **Bacchus.** The lamb dishes and appetizers ("mezze") are excellent at this Lebanese restaurant, which is much bigger—and some say better—than its location in Washington, D.C. Outdoor seating is available and both vegetarians and meat eaters will find good options on the creative menu. ⊠ *7945 Norfolk Ave.* ☎ *301/657–1722* ⊟ *AE, D, MC, V.*

$–$$ ✕ **Tara Thai.** Blue walls and paintings of sea life reflect the owner's childhood home in Huahin, Thailand: so does the extensive menu at this branch of a chain, whose many seafood dishes include fresh flounder and rockfish. Pictures of chili peppers on the menu mark the spiciness of each entrée. Favorites include the mild and traditional pad thai, and the spicy Goong Phuket, grilled black tiger shrimp topped with crabmeat and chicken sauce. ⊠ *4828 Bethesda Ave.* ☎ *301/657–0488* ⊠ *12071 Rockville Pike, Rockville* ☎ *301/231–9899* ⊟ *AE, D, DC, MC, V.*

¢–$ ✕ **Tastee Diner.** The Tastees are part of the culinary past in the Washington area, with a handful still left in Silver Spring, Laurel, and at the flagship location in Bethesda. These 24-hour diners are sentimental favorites among many area residents, who value them for their wonderful hand-formed hamburgers. Students and others on low budgets (or little sleep) ignore the dust and relish the coffee, which flows endlessly. Breakfast is served around the clock. ⊠ *7731 Woodmont Ave.* ☎ *301/ 652–3970* ⊜ *Reservations not accepted* ⊟ *MC, V.*

★ ¢ ✕ **California Tortilla.** Friendly, quick service (as well as the red chili-pepper lights hanging from the ceiling) help make this counter-service restaurant a local favorite. The blackened chicken Caesar burrito outsells other items three to one. Add spice to your meal with a dash or two from 75 hot sauces lined up on the wall, and grab a seat inside or out. On Monday nights, spin the Burrito Wheel for discounts and freebies. The Bethesda branch gave birth to a location in Potomac. ⊠ *4862 Cordell Ave.* ☎ *301/654–8226* ⊠ *7727 Tuckerman La., Potomac* ☎ *301/765–3600* ▤ *MC, V.*

Where to Stay

★ $$$$ 🏨 **Embassy Suites.** Shopping and sightseeing couldn't be more convenient at this all-suite hotel, which is adjacent to the upscale Chevy Chase Pavilion and an elevator ride up from the Friendship Heights Metro Station. Each suite includes a bedroom and separate living room with a sleeper sofa, kitchen space, and a table suitable for dining and working. The fitness center has more than 20 exercise stations and a personal trainer available at no charge. Complimentary breakfast and evening cocktails are offered daily in the sun-filled atrium. A dozen restaurants are within walking distance. ⊠ *4300 Military Rd., Washington, DC 20015* ☎ *202/362–9300 or 800/362–2779* ☎ *202/686–3405* ⊕ *www.embassysuites.com* ↝ *198 suites* ♿ *Room service, microwaves, indoor pool, health club, laundry service, parking (fee), no-smoking rooms* ▤ *AE, D, DC, MC, V* ⦿| *BP.*

$$$$ 🏨 **Hyatt Regency Bethesda.** Part of a busy nexus of restaurants, world-class shops, and movie theaters, this hotel is a convenient refuge for weary travelers. For those with energy to spare, an adjacent plaza has a small ice rink, open in winter. The room rates drop considerably on the weekend. ⊠ *1 Bethesda Metro Center, on 7400 block of Wisconsin Ave., 20814* ☎ *301/657–1234 or 800/233–1234* ☎ *301/657–6453* ⊕ *www.hyatt. com* ↝ *390 rooms, 5 suites* ♿ *Restaurant, café, room service, in-room data ports, cable TV, indoor pool, gym, health club, bar, lobby lounge, laundry service, business services, convention center, meeting rooms, parking (fee)* ▤ *AE, D, DC, MC, V.*

$–$$$ 🏨 **Holiday Inn Washington-Chevy Chase.** A short walk from the Friendship Heights Metro on the D.C. border, this comfortable hotel is inside one of the area's most upscale shopping districts. The Avenue Deli and Julian's restaurant are in the hotel, the nearby Chevy Chase Pavilion and Mazza Gallerie malls have expanded family dining options, and a wealth of good dining choices are one Metro stop away in Bethesda or a 10-minute drive down Wisconsin Avenue into Georgetown. A large outdoor swimming pool is set near the hotel's beautiful rose garden terrace. ⊠ *5520 Wisconsin Ave., Chevy Chase 20815* ☎ *301/656–1500 or 800/465–4329* ☎ *301/656–5045* ⊕ *www.sixcontinentshotels.com* ↝ *214 rooms, 10 suites* ♿ *Restaurant, snack bar, room service, in-room data ports, cable TV, pool, gym, hair salon, bar, laundry facilities, business services, meeting rooms, parking (fee), some pets allowed* ▤ *AE, D, DC, MC, V* ⦿| *CP.*

$–$$ 🏨 **American Inn of Bethesda.** At the north end of downtown Bethesda, the American Inn breaks no new fashion frontiers for motel decor, but the rooms are clean, generally bright, and affordable. The hotel houses

Guapo's restaurant, serving moderately priced Tex-Mex fare. Many other restaurants and nightclubs are within walking distance; the Bethesda Metro is a 10-minute walk away. Use of the business center—including access to the Internet and e-mail service—is free. The hotel also provides a free shuttle to the National Institutes of Health and the Naval Hospital. ⊠ *8130 Wisconsin Ave., 20814* ☎ *301/656–9300 or 800/323–7081* 🖷 *301/656–2907* ⊕ *www.american-inn.com* ⇆ *75 rooms, 1 suite* ⚑ *Restaurant, refrigerators, cable TV, pool, bar, laundry facilities, laundry service, business services, free parking, no-smoking floors* ➡ *AE, D, DC, MC, V* ⦿| *CP.*

Nightlife & the Arts

On weekends from Memorial Day through Labor Day, you can dance to the beat of live bands at free concerts held at the intersection of Wisconsin Avenue, Old Georgetown Road, and East West Highway.

NIGHTLIFE Arcade games provide the most action at **Dave & Buster's** (⊠ White Flint Mall, 11301 Rockville Pike ☎ 301/230–5151 ⊕ www. daveandbusters.com), but this 60,000-square-foot entertainment complex also includes billiard tables, shuffleboards, interactive video games and simulators, a casual restaurant, and two bars. Every other Saturday at 8 PM, a murder mystery dinner adds to the usual choices. Patrons under 21 must leave by 10 PM.

Enormously popular with well-dressed singles over 30, the **Yacht Club** (⊠ 8111 Woodmont Ave. ☎ 301/654–2396) is the brainchild of irrepressible entrepreneur and matchmaker Tommy Curtis, who measures his success by the number of engagements and marriages spawned here (at last count it was 157). Jacket and tie or turtleneck required except on Wednesday and summer evenings, when the attire is casual. The club is closed Sunday–Tuesday.

THE ARTS Opened in 2002, the 347-seat **Round House Theatre** (⊠ 7501 Wisconsin
★ Ave. ☎ 240/644–1100 ⊕ www.round-house.org) primarily produces local premieres of quirky, contemporary, off-Broadway plays as well as some Broadway fare. The season usually also includes at least one world premiere, a traditional favorite, and a holiday musical.

Strathmore Hall Arts Center. Local and national artists exhibit in the galleries and jazz, chamber, folk, and popular musicians perform year-round at this mansion built around 1900. Whimsical pieces, part of the permanent collection, are on display in the sculpture garden. A free series that includes poetry, music, art talks, and demonstrations takes place on Wednesday evening and Thursday morning (call ahead for hours). The 2,000-seat Music Hall, home to the Baltimore Symphony Orchestra in Montgomery County, opened in 2005. On Tuesday and Thursday in summer, concertgoers spread out on the expansive lawn to listen to free concerts—everything from classical to Cajun and Brit pop. Strathmore's Tea is served in a well-lit wood-panel salon, Tuesday and Wednesday at 1. ⊠ *10701 Rockville Pike* ☎ *301/530–0540* ⊕ *www. strathmore.org* ✉ *Free, Backyard Theater $6, tea $17, reservations essential* ☉ *Mon., Tues., Thurs., and Fri. 10–4, Wed. 10–9, Sat. 10–3* Ⓜ *Grosvenor/Strathmore.*

Sports & the Outdoors

The paved **Capital Crescent Trail** runs along the old Georgetown Branch, a B&O Railroad line completed in 1910 that saw its last train in 1985. Bicyclists, walkers, rollerbladers, and strollers take the 7½ mi route from near Key Bridge in Washington's Georgetown to Bethesda and Woodmont avenues in central Bethesda. The trail picks up again at a well-lit tunnel near the Thyme Square Restaurant (4735 Bethesda Avenue) and continues into Silver Spring. From Bethesda to the outskirts of Silver Spring, the 3½ mi trail is gravel. The Georgetown Branch Trail, as this section is officially named, connects with the Rock Creek Trail, which goes to Rockville in the north and Memorial Bridge past the Washington Monument in the south. When the weather's good, all sections of the trails tend to be crowded on weekends. For more information, contact the Coalition for the Capital Crescent Trail (☎ 202/234–4874 ⊕ www.cctrail.org).

★ ☾   One of the best playgrounds in the Washington area, **Cabin John Regional Park** (✉ 7400 Tuckerman La. ☎ 301/299–4160) has plastic slides, bouncing wooden bridges, swings, and mazes to delight both toddlers and preteens. On the park grounds, there's also an ice rink, indoor and outdoor tennis courts, a nature center, hiking trails, trains that operate seasonally, and a 700-seat Shirley Povich Baseball Field. Free military concerts join the chorus of cicadas every summer.

Shopping

Bethesda isn't known for bargains, although one of its best-known malls contains a Filene's Basement. In general, though, shoppers who love discounts should head north on Wisconsin Avenue to Rockville Pike (Route 355). Four of the area's seven regional malls are in Bethesda and the Chevy Chase section of Washington, D.C. Downtown Bethesda has no fewer than 13 bookstores, including a huge Barnes & Noble.

CLOTHING   **Lemon Twist.** Inside this boutique are classic women's wear and children's clothes, gifts, and more from designers such as Lilly, C. J. Lang, Susan Bristol, and CanvasBack. But most of all Lemon Twist has been known for its customer service since 1977. ✉ *8534 Connecticut Ave., Chevy Chase* ☎ *301/986–0271.*

Wear It Well. From funky jackets and slacks to tailored business suits, this local shop specializes in items that wear well and travel well. ✉ *4816 Bethesda Ave., Bethesda* ☎ *301/652–3713.*

DEPARTMENT   Most national department stores can be found at shopping malls through-
STORES   out the county.

Filene's Basement. The Boston-based upscale fashion discounter attracts bargain hunters looking for steep discounts on Calvin Klein, Hugo Boss, and other men's and women's labels. Off-price shoes, children's clothing, household goods, perfume, and accessories are sold as well. ✉ *5300 Wisconsin Ave. NW, Washington, DC* ☎ *202/966–0208* Ⓜ *Friendship Heights.*

Saks Fifth Avenue. Despite its New York origin and name, Saks is a Washington institution. It has a wide selection of European and American couture clothes; other attractions are the shoe, jewelry, fur, and lingerie departments. ⊠ *5555 Wisconsin Ave., Chevy Chase* ☎ *301/657–9000* Ⓜ *Friendship Heights.*

MALLS **Chevy Chase Pavilion.** Across from Mazza Gallerie is the newer, similarly upmarket Chevy Chase Pavilion. Its exclusive women's clothing stores include Koffi Agosu and the Steilmann European Selection (which carries KS separates). Other retail shops of note here are Pottery Barn and Anne Taylor Loft. ⊠ *5335 Wisconsin Ave. NW, Washington, DC* ☎ *202/686–5335* ⊕ *www.ccpavilion.com* Ⓜ *Friendship Heights.*

Mazza Gallerie. This four-level mall is anchored by the ritzy Neiman Marcus department store and the discounter Filene's Basement. Other draws include Williams-Sonoma's kitchenware and a seven-screen movie theater. ⊠ *5300 Wisconsin Ave. NW, Washington, DC* ☎ *202/966–6114* Ⓜ *Friendship Heights.*

Montgomery Mall. Stores in the county's largest mall include Crate & Barrel, Sears, Hecht's, and Nordstrom. Just off I–270 and I–495, it's not close to any metro stops. ⊠ *7101 Democracy Blvd.* ☎ *301/469–6000* ⊕ *www.westfield.com/montgomery.*

White Flint Mall. Bloomingdale's, Lord & Taylor, and Borders Books & Music pull in the serious shoppers. The other 125 stores and amenities include Coach, Sharper Image, Eddie Bauer, a movie theater, and Dave & Buster's. Children enjoy the KidZone, an indoor play area with balls and ramps where children can learn about gravity and similar concepts, or just indulge in free play. ⊠ *11301 Rockville Pike, North Bethesda* ☎ *301/231–7467* ⊕ *www.shopwhiteflint.com* Ⓜ *White Flint.*

Glen Echo

❷ *4 mi west of downtown Bethesda, 2½ mi from the Capital Beltway.*

Glen Echo, now a charming village of Victorian houses, was founded in 1891 by Edwin and Edward Baltzley, inventors of the eggbeater. The brothers fell under the spell of the Chautauqua movement, an organization that promoted liberal and practical education. To further their dream, the brothers sold land and houses, but the Glen Echo Chautauqua lasted only one season.

★ ☕ The Baltzley brothers' compound, **Glen Echo Park** was once noted for its whimsical architecture, including a stone tower, from the Chautauqua period. The area was later the site of an amusement park, and you can still see the skeletons of the once thriving rides. Only the splendid 1921 Dentzel **carousel** still runs (May–September, Wednesday and Thursday 10–2, weekends 10–6), and the musical accompaniment is from a rare Wurlitzer military band organ. The National Park Service administers the 10-acre property, which is the site of folk festivals as well as a puppet company and a children's theater that operate nights and Sunday afternoons in the 1933 Spanish Ballroom. Visitors can also partake of art classes and two art galleries with ongoing exhibits and demonstrations. For scheduling information, check the Weekend section in Friday's *Washington Post.* ⊠ *7300 MacArthur Blvd.* ☎ *301/492–*

6229 ⊕ *www.glenechopark.org* 🎫 *Carousel rides 50¢, puppet shows $5, plays $6, cost of dances vary* ⊙ *Daily.*

The **Clara Barton National Historic Site** is a monument to the founder of the American Red Cross. Known as the "angel of the battlefield" for nursing wounded soldiers during the Civil War, Barton used the striking Victorian structure at first to store Red Cross supplies (it was built for her by the town's founders, and it later became both her home and the organization's headquarters). Today the building is furnished with many of her possessions and period artifacts. Access is by guided tours, which last approximately 35 minutes. ⊠ *5801 Oxford Rd., next to Glen Echo Park parking lot, Glen Echo* ☎ *301/492–6245* ⊕ *www.nps.gov/ clba* 🎫 *Free* ⊙ *Daily 10–5; tours on the hour 10–4.*

Where to Eat

★ $–$$$ ╳ **Irish Inn at Glen Echo.** This turn-of-the-20th-century inn used to be a biker bar in the 1960s. Now it's a cozy, popular destination with both a pub and a restaurant, each serving excellent Irish comfort food. If you're feeling more adventurous than upscale corned beef and cabbage or shepherd's pie, try the salt-crusted salmon or braised lamb shank with roasted root vegetables. The pub, which has an attractive selection of Irish whiskey and a relatively affordable menu, stays open until 2 AM. Just don't expect to hear "Danny Boy." ⊠ *6119 Tulane Ave.* ☎ *301/ 229–2280* ▭ *AE, D, DC, MC, V.*

Potomac

8 mi north of Glen Echo, 7 mi northwest of Bethesda.

The popular translation of the Native American name "Patawomeck" is "they are coming by water." One of the best places to view the mighty Potomac River is by hiking along the towpath of the C&O canal and climbing the rocks at Great Falls, which Maryland and Virginia share a view of on opposite banks. Potomac is also known for its elegant estates and houses.

❸ **The C&O Canal National Historical Park** extends along the Potomac River 184.5 mi from Washington, D.C., to Cumberland, Maryland. Three miles south of the town of Potomac, the **Great Falls Tavern,** a museum and visitor center, serves as the park's local anchor. Barge trips and a vista on the powerful Great Falls are the draws here. A ½ mi, wheelchair-accessible walkway to the platform on Olmsted Island provides a spectacular view of the churning waters. During mule-drawn canal boat rides ($8) to Georgetown and back, costumed guides can teach you a thing or two about life along the canal in the 1800s. (Trips were canceled in 2004 because of damage to the boat, but they should be running again in 2005.) On the canal lock walls are grooves worn by decades of friction from boat towlines. Swimming and wading are prohibited, but you can fish (a Maryland license is required for anglers 16 and older), climb rocks, or go white-water kayaking below the falls (experienced boaters only). All along this stretch of the river, the currents are deadly. Despite frequent signs and warnings, people occasionally dare the water and drown. Bring your own picnic if you plan to lunch here, or head for the snack bar (open March–November) a few paces north of the tavern. ✉ *11710 MacArthur Blvd.* ☎ *301/299–3613* ⊕ *www.nps.gov/choh* 🎫 *$5 per vehicle, $3 per person without vehicle, good for 3 days on MD and VA sides of park* ☉ *Park, daily sunrise–sunset; tavern and museum, daily 9–4:45; barge trips Apr.–Oct., call for hours.*

Where to Stay & Eat

★ **$$$–$$$$** ✕ **Old Angler's Inn.** The inn, where Civil War soldiers from the North and South found respite and Teddy Roosevelt stopped after hunting and fishing, was restored in 1957 and became a fine restaurant, with a reputation that continues to this day. Diners like the cozy fireplace; menu favorites include crispy-skin Scottish salmon and cocoa-dusted venison with a black truffle sauce. ✉ *10801 MacArthur Blvd.* ☎ *301/299–9097* ⊕ *www.oldanglersinn.com* 🝔 *AE, D, MC, V* ☉ *Closed Mon.*

★ **$$–$$$** ✕ **Normandie Farm.** The French provincial cuisine here is served in romantic, rustic surroundings reminiscent of a country French farm. Many locals head to Normandie Farm to celebrate special occasions. On a menu that has remained constant for many years, the most popular dishes are beef Wellington, poached salmon, and lamb chops accompanied by fabulous popovers. Daily specials may include a grilled veal rib chop, broiled twin lobster tails, or soft-shell crabs. ✉ *10710 Falls Rd.* ☎ *301/983–8838* 🝔 *AE, DC, MC, V* ☉ *Closed Mon.*

Kensington

❹ *4 mi northeast of Bethesda.*

Established in 1890, Kensington is one of Montgomery County's earliest villages. Many elaborate Victorian houses are in both Kensington and its neighbor Garrett Park, which even has a few "Chevy houses": built in 1930, these smallish houses came with a mortgage that financed a Chevrolet in the driveway and an RCA radio inside. Walk around the Historic District, starting on Armory Avenue, to see the entire spectrum of domestic architecture here.

The **Temple of the Church of Jesus Christ of Latter-day Saints** is impossible to miss from the Beltway near Silver Spring. One of its white towers is topped with a golden statue of the Mormon angel Moroni. It's closed to non-Mormons, but a visitor center provides a lovely view of the mammoth white-marble temple and runs a film about the temple and what takes place inside. Tulips, dogwoods, and azaleas bloom in the 57-acre grounds each spring. In December locals of all faiths enjoy the Festival of Lights—400,000 of them—and a live Nativity scene. ✉ *9900 Stoney-brook Dr.* ☎ *301/587–0144* ☉ *Grounds and visitor center daily 10–9.*

Where to Eat

¢ ✕ **Café Monet.** Yellow walls and impressionist paintings lend charm to this little counter-service restaurant, a favorite of local ladies of all ages who linger over espresso, scones, and muffins. You can order a sandwich named after your favorite Impressionist artist. Outdoor seating is available. ✉ *10417 Armory Ave.* ☎ *301/946–9404* 🝔 *AE, D, MC, V* ☉ *No dinner.*

Shopping

★ At Kensington's **Antique Row** (⊠ Howard Ave. ☎ 301/949–5333), east of bustling Connecticut Avenue, more than 75 antiques dealers in 42 shops sell jewelry, china, silver, and furniture in buildings as old as some of the items. On the west side of Connecticut Avenue, Howard Avenue alternates auto body repair shops with 100,000 square feet of antiques warehouses that specialize in furniture from Belgium, England, Italy, France, and the United States. For a full listing of the **Antique Dealers of West Howard Avenue,** visit www.westhowardantiques.com. **Banning** + Low (⊠ 3700 Howard Ave. ☎ 301/933–0700) sells vintage posters and campaign memorabilia. The **Prevention of Blindness Antiques Shop** (⊠ 3716 Howard Ave. ☎ 301/942–4707) sells furniture, linens, and vintage clothing. At **Antiques-Uniques** (⊠ 3762 Howard Ave. ☎ 301/942–3324) you can find porcelain dolls, Tiffany lamps, and china.

Silver Spring

❺ *5 mi southeast of Kensington via Rte. 97.*

With a population of some 220,000, the greater Silver Spring area is one of the Washington area's largest bedroom communities and is currently undergoing something of a rebirth, with businesses and entertainment venues staking their claims in the original downtown area. Silver Spring was named when Francis Preston Blair, editor of the *Washington Globe* and a friend of President Andrew Jackson, was riding his horse through the countryside, looking for a pastoral retreat from Washington. His horse threw him, and as he looked for his mount, he noticed a spring in which sand and mica shone like silver. In 1842 he built a second home in "Silver Spring." (Blair House, his Washington home across from the White House, is the nation's official guest quarters.)

The main distinction between Silver Spring and Wheaton, a more suburban locale 4 mi to the north, is largely a line on a map. The latter is the home to the popular National Capitol Trolley Museum.

National Museum of Health and Medicine. Open since the 1860s, this medical museum illustrates medicine's fight against injury and disease. Included are displays on the Lincoln and Garfield assassinations and one of the world's largest collections of microscopes. Because some exhibits are fairly graphic (the wax surgical models and the preserved organs come to mind), the museum may not be suitable for young children or the squeamish. Adult visitors must present a photo ID to enter. ⊠ *Walter Reed Army Medical Center, 6825 16th St. NW, Adams-Morgan* ☎ *202/782–2200* ⊕ *www.nmhn.washingtondc.museum* 🎟 *Free* ☉ *Open daily 10–5:30; tours 2nd and 4th Sat. at 1:00.*

★ **American Film Institute Silver Theatre & Cultural Center.** This three-screen, state-of-the-art center for film is a restoration of architect John Eberson's art deco Silver Theatre, built in 1938. The AFI hosts film retrospectives, festivals, on-stage appearances, and tributes to stars that have included Jeanne Moreau and Russell Crowe. ⊠ *8633 Colesville Rd., Silver Spring, MD* ☎ *301/495–6700* ⊕ *www.afi.com/silver* Ⓜ *Silver Spring.*

Permanent and changing exhibits at the **George Meany Memorial Archives** document work life and United States labor history. The archives preserve the historical record of the American Federation of Labor and Congress of Industrial Organizations (AFL-CIO); Meany was their first president. ⊠ *10000 New Hampshire Ave.* ☎ *301/431–5451* ⊕ *www.georgemeany.org/archives* 🔳 *Free* ⊙ *Weekdays 9–4:30.*

A selection of the capital's historic trolleys have been rescued and restored at the **National Capital Trolley Museum,** along with streetcars from Europe, Canada, and elsewhere in America. The museum is run by volunteers whose childhood fascination with trains never left them at the station. For a nominal fare you can go on a 2-mi ride through the countryside. ⊠ *Bonifant Rd. between Layhill Rd. and New Hampshire Ave., Wheaton* ☎ *301/384–6088* ⊕ *www.dctrolley.org* 🔳 *Museum free; trolley ride $3* ⊙ *Jan.–mid-Mar. and mid-May–Nov., weekends and Memorial Day, July 4, and Labor Day noon–5; mid-Mar.–mid-May, Thurs. and Fri. 10–2, weekends noon–5; mid-June–mid-Aug., Thurs. and Fri. 11–3. Last train leaves station ½ hour before closing time.*

At the rolling 50-acre **Brookside Gardens,** formal seasonal displays of bulbs, annuals, perennials, and a sprawling azalea garden flourish. Inside, the blossoming continues in two conservatories housing seasonal displays and exotic tropicals throughout the year. The visitor center has an auditorium, classrooms for adults and children, a 3,000-volume horticulture library, a gift shop, and an information booth. ⊠ *1800 Glenallan Ave., Wheaton* ☎ *301/962–1400* ⊕ *www.brooksidegardens.org* 🔳 *Free, class fees $7–$35* ⊙ *Daily; conservatories 10–5, visitor center 9–5, gift shop Mon.–Sat. 10–4 and Sun. noon–4, horticulture library 10–3.*

Where to Stay & Eat

$$$–$$$$ ✕ **Mrs. K's Toll House.** In one of the last tollhouses in Montgomery County, Mrs. K's has welcomed diners since 1930 and continues to please both diners in search of comfort food and those with adventurous palates. Designed to resemble a country inn, the restaurant is a cozy place to dine with an appealing and sophisticated menu. Antique furniture, "Historic Old Blue" Staffordshire plates, and Nicholas Lutz glass are on display. Complete American fare lunches and dinners are served— nothing is à la carte. Both the menu and the decorations change seasonally. A live jazz band plays on Thursday night. ⊠ *9201 Colesville Rd.* ☎ *301/589–3500* ▤ *AE, D, DC, MC, V.*

★ $–$$$$ ✕ **The Original Crisfield Seafood Restaurant.** With not much more elegance than a neighborhood barbershop, the prices here might seem absurd. But you get your money's worth: no-nonsense seafood and an eyeful of Old Maryland arrested in time. Crab cakes don't get any more authentic than these, presented with just enough structural imperfection to guarantee they're made by hand; the clam chowder—creamy, chunky, and served with a bottomless bowl of oyster crackers—is rendered with similar, down-home care. The fancier (and pricier) location in Lee Plaza has an art deco style and also serves chicken and steak. It's under separate management. ⊠ *8012 Georgia Ave.* ☎ *301/589–1306* ⊠ *Lee Plaza, 8606 Colesville Rd.* ☎ *301/588–1572* ▤ *AE, MC, V* ⊙ *Original closed Mon. No lunch weekends at Lee Plaza.*

$–$$ 🏨 **Holiday Inn.** Four blocks from the Silver Spring Metro, this chain hotel doesn't offer many of luxuries, but is a dependable, pleasant place to stay. Some rooms have refrigerators, double sinks, couches, or recliners. A shuttle bus runs within a 4-mi radius on weekdays. ✉ *8777 Georgia Ave., 20910* ☎ *301/589–0800* 🖷 *301/587–4791* 🛏 *221 rooms, 10 suites* 🍴 *Restaurant, room service, indoor pool, gym, bar, free parking* ▭ *AE, D, DC, MC, V.*

$–$$ 🏨 **Ramada Inn.** This unpretentious hotel is close to Silver Spring's growing entertainment and dining hub on Colesville Road, as well as to the Silver Spring Metro. Rooms are comfortable, if unremarkable. There isn't any room service, but many local restaurants will deliver. ✉ *7990 Georgia Ave., 20910* ☎ *301/565–3444* 🖷 *301/588–2207* ⊕ *www.ramada.com* 🛏 *125 rooms* 🍴 *In-room data ports, laundry facilities, free parking* ▭ *AE, D, MC, V* ⏝ *CP.*

Sandy Spring

❻ *10 mi northwest of Rockville, 10 mi north of Wheaton.*

Best known for the refuge that the Society of Friends gave slaves here as part of the Underground Railroad, Sandy Spring is still the home of an active Quaker community. To design your own tour of this town buy a map at Sandy Spring Museum. Of the town's dozens of buildings, five homes were associated with the Underground Railroad. Unfortunately, only one of the homes, Woodlawn (16501 Norwood Road), is open for visitors and it's only to see the grounds.

Sandy Spring Museum houses a hodgepodge of items that includes Native American arrowheads and such early-20th-century memorabilia as a buggy and town-store items. A carriage museum and blacksmith shop opened on the grounds in 2002. ✉ *17901 Bentley Rd.* ☎ *301/774–0022* ⊕ *www.sandyspringmuseum.org* 🎫 *$3* ⊙ *Mon., Wed., and Thurs. 9–4, weekends noon–4.*

PRINCE GEORGE'S COUNTY

Named in 1695 for Denmark and Norway's prince (the husband of the heir to the throne of England, Princess Anne), the county was once famous for its tobacco auctions, which are still held in its southern end. Tobacco created a wealthy leisure class who enjoyed cricket; fox hunting; and horse racing, a sport still popular in the area. Much of the county today, where nearly 60% of the population is African-American, remains affluent.

Nature lovers should try to make a visit to the National Wildlife Visitor Center and the Merkle Wildlife Sanctuary. Flight fans can check out the world's oldest airport in College Park. For those who prefer 60-second thrills, Six Flags is full of roller coasters, water slides, and kiddie rides. Sports fans may not be able to see the Redskins, but they can get a fix at a Maryland Terrapins game, or at a Bowie Baysox minor-league baseball game. Historic sites, including the Surratt House Museum, are scattered throughout the county.

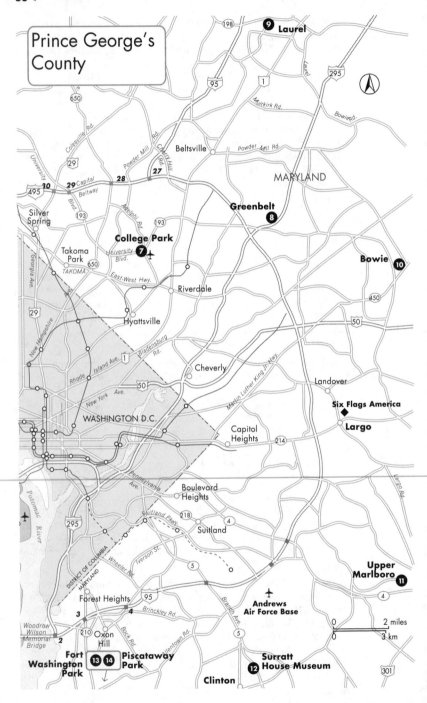

Prince George's County

9 **Laurel**

198

95 1

295

650

Mᴀʀʏʟᴀɴᴅ

Colesville Rd.

University

29

Muirkirk Rd.

Bowie Rd.

Powder Mill Rd.

Beltsville

Cherry Hill Rd.

Powder Mill Rd.

495 **30**

29 Capital Beltway

28

27

193

Silver Spring

193

Adelphi Rd.

Greenbelt
8

College Park
7

University Blvd.

Bowie **10**

Takoma Park

650

TAKOMA

East-West Hwy.

450

New Hampshire

29

Riverdale

50

Hyattsville

Georgia Ave.

1

Rhode Island Ave.

Bladensburg Rd.

Cheverly

Martin Luther King Jr. Hwy.

Landover

New York Ave.

50

WASHINGTON D.C.

♦ **Six Flags America**

Capitol Heights

Largo

214

Pennsylvania Ave.

Potomac River

Boulevard Heights

Suitland Pkwy.

218

4

295

✈

Suitland

5

Largo Rd.

Iverson St.

Upper Marlboro **11**

Wheeler Rd.

District of Columbia

Maryland

5

4

Forest Heights

95

Brinckley Rd.

Branch Ave.

✈ **Andrews Air Force Base**

3

4

0   2 miles

Woodrow Wilson Memorial Bridge

210

Rock Rd.

Allentown Rd.

5

0   3 km

2

Oxon Hill

Fort Washington Park

13 **14** **Piscataway Park**

Surratt House Museum
12

301

Clinton

To tour the county, start in College Park and work your way up to Laurel. Then head south to the heart of the county before visiting sites along the Patuxent and Potomac rivers.

College Park

❼ *6 mi east of Silver Spring via I–495, 9 mi north Washington, D.C.*

As its name implies, College Park is primarily a university town on gently rolling terrain. One of the largest campuses in the country, **University of Maryland at College Park** has an enrollment of 34,000. The College Park campus began as an agricultural college in 1856, and became part of the University of Maryland in 1920. The university's athletic teams participate in the highly competitive Atlantic Coast Conference and draw large crowds to Byrd Stadium and the 17,100-seat Comcast Center. Graduates and Marylanders from all over the state cheer on the Maryland Terrapins. The men's basketball team is almost always in contention for national championships. In Turner Hall, visitor center staff provide information about the university and maps for getting around the sprawling campus of 1,580 acres and 270 buildings. At the dairy, ice cream made from campus cows' milk is available by the cone or carton. ✉ *Turner Hall, U.S. Rte. 1 and Rossborough La.* ☎ *301/314–7777* ⊕ *www.umd.edu* ☉ *Turner Hall weekdays 8–5, Sat. 9–3. Dairy Oct.–Apr., weekdays 8–5; May–Sept., weekdays 8–5, Sat. noon–3.*

The Wright Brothers once trained military officers to fly at College Park Airport, the world's oldest continuously operating airport, which ★ ☼ is now affiliated with the Smithsonian Institution. The **College Park Aviation Museum** is a tribute to the Wright Brothers and early aviation memorabilia. Children can spin propellers and dress up like aviators. A "Speaking of Flight" lecture series is held in spring and fall. At the Peter Pan program, preschoolers make airplanes and hear stories on the second and fourth Thursday from 10:30 to noon. ✉ *College Park Airport, 1985 Corporal Frank Scott Dr.* ☎ *301/864–6029, 301/861–4765 TDD* 💺 *$4* ☉ *Daily 10–5.*

Where to Stay & Eat

★ ¢–$$ ✕ **Ledo's.** Students, alumni, and locals have made Ledo's pizza popular throughout the state. There are dozens of Ledo's franchises in Maryland, but many insist that the best pizza—with smoked provolone so gooey you need a knife and fork—comes from the original restaurant, which opened in 1955 and is still family run. Adelphi is just outside of College Park city limits. ✉ *2420 University Blvd., Adelphi* ☎ *301/422–8622* ▤ *MC, V.*

¢–$$ ✕ **R. J. Bentley's.** Most walls are covered with license plates and gas pump memorabilia, and jerseys from the university's past star athletes hang on the "wall of fame." Students and alumni head to this hangout for beer, chili, wings, and sandwiches; the bar packs in fans after home games. ✉ *7323 Baltimore Ave.* ☎ *301/277–8898* ▤ *AE, MC, V.*

$$ ▦ **The Inn and Conference Center/University of Maryland and University College.** Renovated in 2004, the center is a certified "green" building, with an air-conditioning system that is chloroflurocarbon free. Those staying here can use the campus recreation center and indoor pool for

free. Predictably, parents start booking rooms months before gradua-
tion, held in late May or early June. The hotel is less than 10 minutes
from both the College Park and Prince George's Plaza Metro stops.
✉ *3501 University Blvd. E, at Adelphi Rd., 20783* ☎ *301/985–7300
or 800/727–8622* 🖷 *301/985–7850* ⊕ *www.umuc.edu/icc* 🛏 *127
rooms, 15 suites* ♨ *2 restaurants, in-room data ports, cable TV, indoor
pool, gym, bar, business services, parking (fee)* 🖃 *AE, D, MC, V.*

Greenbelt

❽ *4 mi northeast of College Park.*

Planned as part of a New Deal program during the Great Depression,
Greenbelt was one of three communities built for low- and middle-in-
come families (the others are outside of Milwaukee and in Ohio). These
"greenbelt" communities, constructed and planned by the U.S. Department of Agriculture, were also meant to serve as models of good
suburban development. The town is now a National Historic Landmark.
Walk down Crescent Road to the Greenbelt Museum (15 Crescent
Road) for a glimpse at some representative houses, including one International Style house (10b Crescent Road) filled with artifacts from
the 1930s such as Feistaware and children's toys.

Backyard fly zappers, orange juice from concentrate, and seedless grapes
are just three examples of some of the everyday innovations that were
developed at the Agricultural Research Service's (ARS) **Beltsville Agricultural Research Center.** Even penicillin was discovered here, developed
during World War II. Today the emphasis is on charting environmental
stress, such as the depletion of the ozone, but you can also catch up on
the latest in food technology. After a brief orientation at the visitor center, inside a log lodge built in 1937 by the Civilian Conservation Corps,
you tour the farm by van or bus. Tours, which can be tailored to interests such as nutrition and genetic engineering, take at least two hours.
Because of their length and technical nature, tours are not recommended
for children below middle-school age (Field Day, held the first Saturday of June, includes hay rides, farm equipment, and lab displays and
is good for all ages). Although the researchers work to develop heartier,
safer, and sometimes tastier foods, there are no free samples and no cafe-
terias on-site. Reservations are essential; call two weeks in advance.
✉ *Bldg. 302, 10300 Baltimore Ave., 3 mi northeast of Greenbelt,
Beltsville* ☎ *301/504–9403* ⊕ *www.ars.usda.gov* 🎟 *Free* ⊙ *Weekdays
8:30–4.*

Where to Stay

$–$$$ 🏨 **Greenbelt Marriott.** This full-service hotel is a 10-minute walk from
the Greenbelt Metro and a 15-minute drive to College Park. Shuttle ser-
vice to the Metro runs every half hour from 7 AM to 9 PM. The hotel
works with four tour companies to arrange sightseeing excursions to
both Baltimore and Washington. ✉ *6400 Ivy La., 20770* ☎ *301/441–
3700 or 800/228–9290* 🖷 *301/441–3995* 🛏 *283 rooms, 4 suites*
♨ *Restaurant, room service, in-room data ports, 2 pools (1 indoor), health
club, bar, travel services, free parking* 🖃 *AE, D, DC, MC, V.*

Laurel

⑨ *7 mi north of Greenbelt.*

Three other Maryland counties claim a section of this town: Anne Arundel, Howard, Montgomery, but most of the suburb is in Prince George's.

Set on 75 acres of parkland, **Montpelier Mansion** is a masterpiece of Georgian architecture. The mansion was built and owned by the Snowdens, who earned their wealth through tobacco and an iron foundry. George Washington and Abigail Adams were among the mansion's early visitors. Interesting features include a 35- by 16-foot reproduction of a hand-painted floor cloth and an offset central hall staircase. Also on the property is a summerhouse where ladies took their tea, boxwood gardens, an herb-and-flower garden with plants grown in the 1800s, and a cultural arts center with three galleries and artists' studios. After the one-hour tour you can stroll the property's primarily gravel paths and visit the Little Teapot gift shop, which sells loose tea and imported packaged foods. A full English tea is served at the mansion about once a month: call the Little Teapot for details. ⊠ *Rte. 197 and Muirkirk Rd.* ☎ *301/953–1376, 301/953–1993 arts center, 301/498–8486 Little Teapot* ⊡ *$3* ☉ *Dec.–Feb., Sun. tours at 1 and 2; Mar.–Nov., Sun.–Thurs. noon–3, tours on the hour. Art center daily 10–5.*

★ One of the Department of the Interior's largest science and environmental education centers, the **Patuxent National Wildlife Visitor Center** showcases interactive exhibits on global environmental issues, migratory bird routes, wildlife habitats, and endangered species. A viewing station overlooks a lake area that beavers, bald eagles, and Canada geese use as a habitat. Weather permitting, you can take a 30-minute tram tour through meadows, forests, and wetlands and take your own tour on the trails. The paved Loop Trail runs ⅓ mi; another 4 mi of trails, covered with wood chips and other natural materials, crisscrosses the property. The center is between Laurel and Bowie. ⊠ *10901 Scarlet Tanager Loop, off Powder Mill Rd.* ☎ *301/497–5760* ⊕ *www.patuxent.fws.gov* ⊡ *Free, tram ride $3* ☉ *Daily 10–5:30; tram mid-Mar.–late June and early Sept.–mid-Nov., weekends 11:30–3:30; late June–late Aug., daily 11:30, 12:30, 1:30, and 2:30.*

Sports & the Outdoors

HIKING   The mission of **Patuxent Research Refuge** is to conserve and protect wildlife through research and to educate the public. The north tract of the refuge is available for fishing. Educational programs are also available here. To enter you must check in and receive an access pass. A Maryland nontidal fishing license is also required. Hunting is allowed from September through January. ⊠ *230 Bald Eagle Dr.* ☎ *410/674–3304, 410/674–4625 TDD* ⊡ *Free* ☉ *Nov.–Feb., daily 8–4:30; Mar., daily 8–6; Apr.–Aug., daily 8–8; Sept. and Oct., daily 8–6:30.*

HORSE RACING   Maryland has a long-standing love for the ponies. You can watch and wager on thoroughbreds at **Laurel Park** (⊠ Rte. 198 and Race Track Rd. ☎ 301/725–0400) during a season that runs January through March, mid-June through August, and mid-October through December. Race days are usually Wednesday through Sunday, but there are races simulcast seven days a week.

Bowie

⑩ *13 mi southeast of Laurel, 15 mi east of College Park.*

It grew up around a railroad junction in 1870, but today Bowie has more than 53,000 residents and is the home of Bowie State University, a historically black college within the University of Maryland system.

Built in the mid-1700s as a country retreat for provincial Maryland governor Samuel Ogle, the Georgian-style **Belair Mansion** was subsequently owned in the early 1900s by William Woodward, one of the first people to bring thoroughbred horses to the United States from England. The house displays British and Early American paintings, silver, and furniture. In 1914 Woodward added on to the home and built **Belair Stable**, which began the legacy of the Belair Stud, the line responsible for Omaha and his sire Gallant Fox, each of whom won the Triple Crown in the mid 1900s. One-hour tours of the mansion and stable emphasize the contributions of the families and their horses to racing history. ⊠ *12207 Tulip Grove Dr.* ☎ *301/809–3089* 🖾 *Free* ☉ *Wed.–Sun. noon–4.*

Sports & the Outdoors

FedEx Stadium (⊠ 1600 FedEx Way, Landover ☎ 301/276–6000 ⊕ www.redskins.com) is where the Washington Redskins play, but all the tickets are owned by season pass holders. Football fans who don't have megabucks to buy a ticket (they're often sold through the classifieds or through online auction sites) may be able to get tickets for other events. The Rolling Stones, George Strait, and other superstars have all performed at this 86,000-seat stadium.

★ ☺ **Bowie Baysox** (⊠ 4101 N.E. Crain Hwy. ☎ 301/805–6000 ⊕ www.baysox.com), the AA affiliate of the Baltimore Orioles, play at the 10,500-seat Prince George's Stadium. Children have major-league fun off the field at a carousel, child-oriented concession stands, and a playground. Fireworks light up the sky at every home game held on Saturday evening between April and Labor Day, as well as those on Thursday night in July and August. Tickets cost $8.

Largo

9 mi south of Bowie.

☺ Maryland's only amusement park, **Six Flags America** combines a theme park with Paradise Island, a water park. On the "dry" side, high-speed revelers ride any of eight old-fashioned wood coasters or modern steel coasters. "Batwing" puts riders headfirst, face and belly down, with nothing between them and the ground but air and a safety strap. Children under 48 inches can coast on a minimodel, "drive" an 18-wheeler, and earn their wings flying minijets. On the "wet" side, children of all ages beat the heat whizzing down water slides and swimming in pools. A barrel over Crocodile Cal's (named for Cal Ripkin, legendary star of the Baltimore Orioles) Outback Beach House dumps 1,000 gallons of water on unsuspecting passersby every few minutes. When your body has been through enough, sit back for the stage and musical entertainments. ✉ *13710 Central Ave., Largo* ☎ *301/249–1500* ⊕ *www.sixflags. com/America* ✍ *$37, kids under 48" $26, kids 3 and under free; parking $9* ⊙ *Mid-Apr.–Memorial Day, weekends 10:30–6; Memorial Day–Labor Day, daily 10:30–9; Fright Fest, Oct., Fri. 5–10, weekends noon–10.*

Where to Stay & Eat

$–$$ ✕ **Jasper's.** People come here to be seen as well as to eat. The Largo location is one of four throughout the state. On the American menu, she-crab soup, the stuffed fish of the day, and the grilled-chicken Caesar salad are at the top of the favorites; all desserts are made in-house. Jazz and rhythm and blues can be heard every night. ✉ *9640 Lottsford Ct., near US Airways Arena, Largo* ☎ *301/883–2199* ▭ *AE, D, DC, MC, V.*

$$ ▦ **New Carrollton Landover Courtyard by Marriott.** This business-district hotel caters to a corporate crowd, but it's also a convenient roosting spot for visitors to Six Flags and other sights. Free shuttle service runs to the D.C. Metro and to Amtrak's New Carrollton station, about three minutes away. Prices drop below $100 on weekends. ✉ *8330 Corporate Dr., Landover 20785* ☎ *301/577–3373* ▤ *301/577–1780* ⇆ *136 rooms, 14 suites* ⟳ *Restaurants, room service, gym, bar, in-room data ports, pool, free parking* ▭ *AE, D, DC, MC, V.*

Upper Marlboro

⓫ *14 mi south of Bowie, 11 mi east of Suitland.*

The county seat of Prince George's County was once famous for its tobacco auctions. Although tobacco is still bought and sold here, business today mostly revolves around the local government.

⟲ **Merkle Wildlife Sanctuary** is named after the conservationist Edgar A. Merkle, who began a breeding and habitat improvement program to bring Canada geese to Maryland's Patuxent River. Thousands of geese return here each September and remain through late February or early March; another 80–100 stay year-round. You can check out the geese and other fauna by hiking the nature trails or from observation decks at the visitor center, which has a discovery room where children can make crafts and observe turtles and snakes. On Sunday, from 10 to 3, the sanctuary sponsors a driving tour of the marshlands, woodlands, farm ponds, and creeks. To reach the sanctuary take Route 301 south to Route 382 and turn left on St. Thomas Church Road. ✉ *11704 Fenno Rd.* ☎ *301/888–1377* ✍ *$2 per vehicle* ⊙ *Daily dawn–dusk; weekends 10–5, hours subject to change.*

Clinton

10 mi southwest of Upper Marlboro.

The origin of the name Clinton is unclear—the town used to be called Surrattsville for Mary Surratt's husband, the postmaster John Surratt.

★ 12 The **Surratt House Museum,** once a house and tavern, is where John Wilkes Booth sought refuge after assassinating President Abraham Lincoln. For her role in the conspiracy, Mary Surratt became the first woman to be executed by the federal government. She was said to have told one of her tenants to get the "shooting irons ready" for Booth after he shot Lincoln at Ford's Theater in Washington, D.C. You can trace Booth's escape route on an electronic map at the visitor center. Costumed docents give tours of the house, talk about 19th-century life in Prince George's County, and discuss the Civil War, but they won't get into debates about Surratt's innocence or guilt. The Surratt Society, reachable through the museum, sponsors a 12-hour John Wilkes Booth escape route tour in April and September that covers the 12 days Booth spent on the run in Maryland, Virginia, and Washington, D.C. ✉ *9118 Brandywine Rd.* ☎ *301/868–1121* 🌐 *www.surratt.org* 🎟 *$3* 🕒 *Thurs. and Fri. 11–3, weekends noon–4; tours every ½ hour.*

Oxon Cove Park preserves 19th-century farm life on a site where the Piscataway Native Americans once lived. Children can feed chickens, milk cows, and take a hayride. There's also a fine view of Washington over the Potomac River. Throughout the year, the National Park Service offers programs such as sheep shearing in May, cider making in September, and "Talking Turkey"—when kids can learn about domestic and wild turkeys and get to feed them—in November. ✉ *6411 Oxon Hill Rd., 5 mi northwest of Clinton* ☎ *301/839–1176* 🌐 *www.nps.gov/nace/oxhi* 🎟 *Free* 🕒 *Daily 8–4:30.*

Fort Washington Park

13 *5 mi southwest of Clinton, 7 mi south of Oxon Hill.*

George Washington chose this site on a narrow portion of the Potomac River for the first fort to protect the nation's capital. It was destroyed during the War of 1812, only five years after its completion; the current fort was completed in 1824. Half-hour tours of the fort are given on weekend afternoons and upon request on weekdays. One Sunday per month, costumed volunteers re-create military life in the mid-1800s by firing the cannons. If you cross the drawbridge over the moat, you can see the 7-foot-thick stone and masonry walls, gun positions, and other defenses. Although the fort is impressive, most people visit the park for no other reason than to picnic along the river. ✉ *13551 Fort Washington Rd.* ☎ *301/763–4600* 🎟 *$5 per vehicle, early Apr.–late Sept.; free weekdays early Oct.–early Apr., $5 on weekends* 🕒 *Early Apr.–late Sept., daily 9–5; early Oct.–early Apr., daily 9–4:30.*

Accokeek

10 mi south of Fort Washington.

By fighting off developers in the 1950s, the Accokeek Foundation helped keep the view from Mount Vernon as George Washington would have seen. Today, the once-rural area is being developed into a suburban community. Locals call Piscataway Park, tucked away at the end of the road by the river, a hidden treasure.

On 4,000 acres of land bought to protect the view from Mount Vernon across the river, **Piscataway Park** attracts history buffs, horticulturists, naturalists, hikers, and families. At **National Colonial Farm,** you can walk through a middle-class 18th-century farm dwelling and tobacco barn, and reproductions of a smokehouse and out-kitchen used by farmers not quite as prosperous as the Washingtons on the other side of the Potomac. Guides point out the farmhouse's most valuable materials: the glass in the windows and its nails. Whenever a house burned down in the 18th century, the owners would rummage through the remains for the nails. Old-time animal breeds and heirloom crop varieties are both raised here. Also on hand is an herb garden as well as bluebirds, great blue herons, and bald eagles. If you want to compare and contrast National Colonial Farm with Mount Vernon, board the *Potomac,* a dory boat that runs every weekend between mid-June and mid-September. ⊠ *3400 Bryan Point Rd., 5 mi south of Fort Washington Park* ☎ *301/283–2113 Accokeek Foundation, 301/283–0112 National Park Service* ⊠ *$2, families $5; $7 ferry rides; $16 ferry ride includes admission to Mount Vernon* ☉ *Park, daily dawn–dusk; National Colonial Farm mid-Mar.–mid-Dec., Tues.–Sun. 10–4, tours weekends at 11, 1, and 3; ferry rides mid-June–mid-Sept., weekends at 10, noon, 2, and 4; ferry tickets must be picked up 15 min before boarding. Reservations recommended.*

SUBURBAN MARYLAND A TO Z

To research prices, get advice from other travelers, and book travel arrangements, visit www.fodors.com.

AIRPORTS

Three major airports serve both suburban Maryland and the Washington, D.C., area. Baltimore-Washington International (BWI) Airport, 10 mi south of Baltimore off I–95 and Route 295, is closer to Montgomery and Prince George's counties than Ronald Reagan National Airport or Washington Dulles International Airport.

🚹 Airport Information **Baltimore-Washington International (BWI) Airport** ☎ 410/859-7111.

BIKE TRAVEL

The Capital Crescent Trail and the canal towpath are both very popular for biking excursions. You can rent bikes at Big Wheel Bikes. Ten miles away along the towpath and 5 mi away via Falls and River roads from the Great Falls Tavern is Swain's Lock, another rental option.

🚹 Bike Rentals **Big Wheel Bikes** ⊠ 6917 Arlington Rd., Bethesda ☎ 301/652-0192. **Swain's Lock** ⊠ 10700 Swain's Lock Rd., Potomac ☎ 301/299-9006.

CAR TRAVEL

The primary transportation link throughout suburban Maryland is the Capital Beltway (I–495), which runs east–west. Interstate 95 runs north–south. Interstate 270, which intersects with I–495 in Montgomery County, reaches destinations north of Rockville in Montgomery County. Roads that run through the region and into downtown Washington include Wisconsin, Connecticut, Georgia, New Hampshire, and Pennsylvania avenues; Routes 1 and 50 (the latter turns into New York Avenue upon entering the District); Baltimore Washington Parkway; and I–295.

DISABILITIES & ACCESSIBILITY

The Metro rail system is generally accessible, but stations have only one elevator each.

🚹**Washington Metropolitan Area Transit Authority** ☎202/962–1212 elevator information.

SPORTS & THE OUTDOORS

A favorite among hikers, the C&O Canal National Historical Park is also great for cycling, fishing, and white-water kayaking.

Although snaring a seat for a Redskins game at FedEx Stadium is tough, the University of Maryland's Terrapins give sports fans a look at the future of professional sports.

🚹 **C&O Canal National Historical Park** ✉ 11710 MacArthur Blvd., Potomac ☎ 301/299–3613. **Terrapins** ✉ Byrd Stadium, University of Maryland ☎ 301/314–7070 or 800/462–8377 ⊕ www.umterps.com.

SUBWAY TRAVEL

Montgomery County is served by Metro subway system's Red Line, the system's busiest. Prince George's County is served by the Blue, Orange, and Green lines. Traveling from one country on the subway involves going through downtown Washington and transferring trains.

🚹 **Metrorail** ☎ 202/637–7000 ⊕ www.wmata.com.

TRAIN TRAVEL

Amtrak has scheduled stops in New Carrollton and at BWI Airport as part of its East Coast service. The MARC commuter train has two lines that go through Montgomery and Prince George's counties, and it also goes into Washington's Union Station.

🚹 Train Stations **New Carrollton** ✉ 4300 Garden City Dr. ☎ 202/906–3764.

🚹 Train Lines **Amtrak** ☎ 800/872–7245 ⊕ www.amtrak.com. **MARC** ☎ 800/325–7245 ⊕ www.mtamaryland.com.

VISITOR INFORMATION

🚹 Tourist Information **Bethesda Urban Partnership** ✉ 7906 Woodmont Ave., Bethesda 20814 ☎ 301/215–6660 🖶 301/215–6664 ⊕ www.bethesda.org. **Montgomery County Conference & Visitors Bureau** ✉ 11820 Parklawn Dr., Suite 380, Rockville 20852 ☎ 301/428–9702 or 800/925–0880 🖶 301/428–9705 ⊕ www.cvbmontco.com. **Prince George's County Conference & Visitors Bureau** ✉ 9200 Basil Ct., Suite 101, Largo 20774 ☎ 301/925–8300 or 888/925–8300 🖶 301/925–2053 ⊕ www.goprincegeorgescounty.com.

CENTRAL &
WESTERN VIRGINIA

3

MAKE YOUR OWN SUMMER RETREAT
to Jefferson's Poplar Forest house ⇨ *p.82*

GET SOME UNDERGROUND KNOWLEDGE
in the caverns near New Market ⇨ *p.85 and 89*

FIND SOUTH FRANCE IN VIRGINIA
at the L'Auberge Provencale inn ⇨ *p.88*

CHOW ON HOMEY FRIED CHICKEN
(with all the sides) at The Homeplace ⇨ *p.101*

FIND COUNTRY MUSIC'S ROOTS
at the Carter Fold ⇨ *p.108*

Revised by
Kevin Myatt
and Erica
Pandapas

THE NATURAL BEAUTY OF THE SHENANDOAH VALLEY, together with Skyline Drive and the Blue Ridge Parkway, provide a picturesque entry into a region rich in history and culture. About 150 mi long, the Shenandoah Valley lies between two ranges of the Appalachians—the Alleghenies to the west and the Blue Ridge to the east—in northwestern Virginia, parallel to the western edge of the state and extending to Harpers Ferry in West Virginia. East of the valley, Shenandoah National Park's nearly 200,000 acres stretch more than 80 mi along the crest of the Blue Ridge. From the roads and trails, you might see wild turkeys, white-tailed deer, and sometimes even a black bear.

Charlottesville, 71 mi northwest of Richmond, is the core of what Virginians call Mr. Jefferson's country. Although the influence of the third president of the United States echoes throughout the commonwealth, Jefferson's legacy is especially strong in Albemarle and Orange counties. Here are buildings and sites associated with him and the giants among his contemporaries. Since 1819, when Jefferson founded the University of Virginia in Charlottesville, the area has been a center of culture. More recently the countryside has been discovered by celebrities, including the actress Sissy Spacek and best-selling author John Grisham, and a growing community of writers, artists, and musicians.

The Shenandoah Valley and the Blue Ridge meet Southwest Virginia at Roanoke, a city that owes its existence to the railroads. Today, it's a commercial and medical center for the area and within easy reach of natural attractions. To the west of Roanoke is the New River Valley (named, ironically, for one of the world's oldest rivers), a region that takes pride in its inhabitants' vigorous outdoor lifestyle, its rapid growth, and Virginia Tech, the state's largest university. The Blue Ridge continues south from Roanoke to Mt. Rogers, Virginia's highest peak at 5,729 feet, then on into North Carolina. Abingdon, the oldest town west of the Blue Ridge, contains a historic district that spans twenty blocks with well-preserved 18th- and 19th-century buildings as well as the Barter Theatre, the state theater of Virginia. Covering Virginia's southwestern tip, the Appalachian Plateau is heavily wooded and incised with gorges. One of these gorges is the legendary Cumberland Gap, which leads into Kentucky and Tennessee.

Exploring Central & Western Virginia

Charlottesville, just east of the Blue Ridge, centers around Thomas Jefferson's architectural genius—Monticello and the University of Virginia. To the south, the restored Civil War–era village of Appomattox Court House is a peek back in time. Along the western rim of Virginia in the Shenandoah Valley is Winchester, which changed hands no fewer than 72 times during the Civil War. Farther south is Lexington, known for its ties to Confederate generals Robert E. Lee and Stonewall Jackson. In Roanoke, Virginia's largest city west of Richmond, Market Square is a cultural anchor for Southwest Virginia. In this area you can hike and camp in the George Washington and Jefferson national forests, float the New River, and photograph wild ponies near the state's highest mountain. Newbern and Tazewell offer remnants of life in the pioneer days, and Abingdon draws crowds to the annual Virginia Highlands Festival.

About the Restaurants & Hotels

Both locally owned and major chain motels and hotels are plentiful along the interstate highways (I–81, I–64, I–77, I–66), with a particularly heavy concentration in the Charlottesville and Roanoke areas.

Like any college city, there are a large number of apartments in Charlottesville, but most of them are occupied from fall through spring. Consulting local want ads in the *Charlottesville Daily Progress*) and contacting major national real estate and corporate housing companies such as Century 21, Aimco, and Wynne Residential are the best ways to find rental accommodations in the area.

Accommodations in private homes and converted inns are available through Blue Ridge Bed & Breakfast Reservation Service.

🔢 Reservation Services **Blue Ridge Bed & Breakfast Reservation Service** ✉ 2458 Castleman Rd., Berryville 22611 ☎ 540/955-1246 or 800/296-1246 🖷 540/955-4240 🌐 www.blueridgebb.com. **Guesthouses** 🖅 Box 5737, Charlottesville 22905 🖷 434/979-7264 🌐 www.va-guesthouses.com.

WHAT IT COSTS				
$$$$	**$$$**	**$$**	**$**	**¢**
RESTAURANTS over $30	$22–$30	$14–$22	$7–$14	Under $7
HOTELS over $250	$175–$250	$130–$175	$80–$130	Under $80

Restaurant prices are per person for a main course at dinner. Hotel prices are for a standard double room, excluding state and county taxes (11% in Virginia; 10% in Maryland).

CHARLOTTESVILLE & THE BLUE RIDGE

Surrounded by a lush countryside, Charlottesville is the most prominent city in the foothills of the Blue Ridge Mountains. Thomas Jefferson's hilltop home and the University of Virginia, the enterprise of his last years, draw appreciators of architecture. Twenty-five miles northeast, Orange County is where you find the estate of Jefferson's friend and compatriot James Madison. The tiny town of Washington, 30 mi beyond Orange, bears the stamp of another president: George Washington surveyed and plotted out this slice of wilderness in 1749. Lynchburg, to Charlottesville's south, is near the site of Jefferson's retreat home, the octagonal Poplar Forest. On the Blue Ridge itself is popular Shenandoah National Park, the park's spectacular but often-crowded Skyline Drive, and Wintergreen Resort, a haven for outdoor sports.

Numbers in the margin correspond to points of interest on the Charlottesville, the Blue Ridge, the Shenandoah Valley, and the Southwest Virginia map.

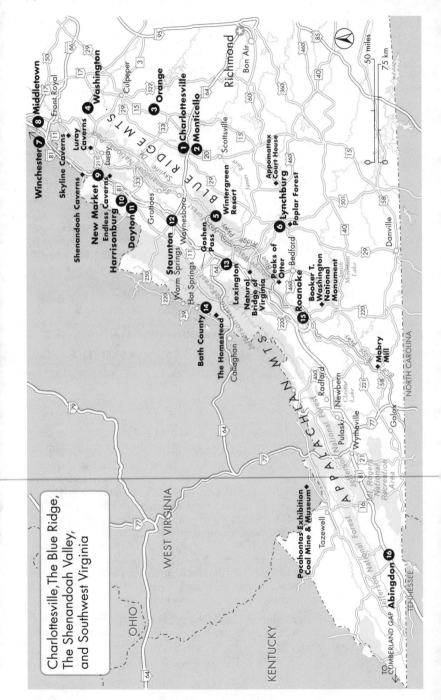

Charlottesville, The Blue Ridge,
The Shenandoah Valley,
and Southwest Virginia

Charlottesville

❶ *71 mi northwest of Richmond via I–64.*

Charlottesville, in the heart of verdant wine country, is the epitome of Virginia's Piedmont—the large, gently hilly countryside in the center of the state. The downtown pedestrian mall, a brick-paved street of restored buildings that stretches along six blocks of Main Street, is frequented by humans and canines. Outdoor restaurants and cafés, concerts, and impromptu theatrical events keep things lively. Just 2 mi southeast of Charlottesville is Monticello, the distinguished home that Thomas Jefferson designed.

Monticello Visitors Center presents a wide assortment of personal memorabilia and artifacts recovered during recent archaeological excavations at Monticello. The free, 35-minute film delves into Jefferson's political career. ⊠ *Rte. 20 S from Charlottesville, I–64 Monticello, Exit 121* ☎ *434/ 977–1783* ☉ *Mar.–Oct., daily 9–5:30; Nov.–Feb., daily 9–5.*

❷ **Monticello,** the most famous of Jefferson's homes, was constructed from
Fodor'sChoice 1769 to 1809. Every detail in the house makes a statement. The stair-
★ cases are narrow and hidden because he considered them unsightly and a waste of space, and contrary to plantation tradition, his outbuildings are in the back and not on the east side (the direction from which his guests would arrive). Throughout the house are Jefferson's inventions, including a seven-day clock and a two-pen contraption that allowed him to make a copy of his correspondence as he wrote it—without having to show it to a copyist. On-site are re-created gardens, the plantation street where his slaves lived, and a gift shop. Arrive early to avoid a long wait for a tour of the house. ⊠ *Rte. 53* ☎ *434/984–9800* ⊕ *www. monticello.org* 🎟 *$14* ☉ *Mar.–Oct., daily 8–5; Nov.–Feb., daily 9–4:30.*

Two miles from Monticello, the modest **Ash Lawn–Highland** is marked by the personality of the president who lived in it. But the building is no longer the simple farmhouse built in 1799 for James Monroe; a later owner added on a more prominent two-story section. The small rooms inside are crowded with gifts from notable people and with souvenirs from Monroe's time as envoy to France. Ash Lawn–Highland today is a 535-acre farm where peacocks and sheep roam. The outdoor Ash Lawn Opera Festival, during which one of the country's top-ranked summer opera companies performs, draws music aficionados July through August. ⊠ *1000 James Monroe Pkwy., Rte. 795 southwest of Monticello* ☎ *434/293–9539* ⊕ *www.ashlawnhighland.org* 🎟 *$9* ☉ *Apr.–Oct., daily 9–6; Nov.–Mar., daily 11–5.*

Its proximity to Monticello and Ash Lawn–Highland has made **Michie Tavern** on Route 53 a popular attraction. Most of the complex was built 17 mi away at Earlysville, in 1784, and moved here piece by piece in 1927. Costumed hostesses lead your party into a series of rooms, where historically based skits are performed and recorded historical narrations are played. The restaurant's "Colonial" lunch is fried chicken. The old gristmill has been converted into a gift shop. ⊠ *683 Thomas Jefferson Pkwy., Rte. 53* ☎ *434/977–1234* 🎟 *$8* ☉ *Daily 9–5.*

THOMAS JEFFERSON

ONE OF THE NATION'S foremost statesmen, Jefferson is best known for his first contribution to the country: drafting the Declaration of Independence in 1776. The sum of the 33-year political career that followed is better remembered than its milestones, which do bear repeating. His first office of weight was that of governor of his beloved Virginia, beginning in 1779. In 1790 he served as secretary of state under his friend George Washington (and resigned in 1793). A Republican presidential candidate in 1796, he lost by just three electoral votes to Federalist John Adams, and as rules then dictated, Jefferson became vice president. By the 1800 race, tensions between the Federalist and Republican parties were high and debilitating to a nation still finding its way. Jefferson won the nation's third presidency at this critical juncture and served two terms, after which he retired for good to Monticello.

The breadth of Jefferson's skills is bewildering to our highly specialized age. This Enlightenment man had many talents: statesman, farmer and zealous gardener, writer, scientist, musician, and philosopher. One admiring contemporary described Jefferson as a man who could "calculate an eclipse, survey an estate, tie an artery, plan an edifice, try a cause, break a horse, dance a minuet, and play a violin." As a lover of great wine, Jefferson introduced European vinifera grapes to Virginia but failed as a vintner. Today his native state's wineries are helping fulfill his vision. He has even been hailed as the father of the American gastronomic revolution, importing from France olive oil, Parmesan cheese, raisins, and pistachios. The Garden Book, which he kept for upward of half a century, contains a wealth of minutiae, from planting times to the preferred method of grafting peach trees. He kept a separate accounting book that recorded every item of cash expenditure.

It's often noted that this architect of democracy was also a slave owner (he owned about 200 slaves at any given time, and freed only seven after his death). One of the most enduring mysteries surrounding Jefferson has been whether he had a liaison with Sally Hemings, one of his slaves. DNA tests from 1998 showed that a member of the Jefferson family—many believe Thomas Jefferson himself—fathered her youngest son, Eston. Jefferson went through an inquiry into his conduct during his last year as governor of Virginia, and once he was president, Federalists accused him of improper relations with a white woman and also with Hemings. A Richmond journalist was the first to publicly allege the relationship in 1802. In 1816 Jefferson confided in a letter, "As to Federal slanders, I never wished them to be answered, but the tenor of my life, half a century of which has been on a theater at which the public have been spectators and the competent judges of its merit."

Virginians love Jefferson because he loved Virginia. Monticello, his experiment in architecture that had him making changes until the day before he died, attracts 500,000 people every year. The University of Virginia, which Jefferson called "the hobby of my old age," is now one of the nation's elite public universities. Charlottesville honors its most famous resident in a number of ways. On April 13—Jefferson's birthday—the Thomas Jefferson Center for the Protection of Free Expression presents the Muzzle Award to those guilty of trying to quash free speech. On the anniversary of his death, Independence Day, Monticello is the site of a naturalization ceremony for new Americans.

★ At the west end of Charlottesville, the **University of Virginia,** one of the nation's most notable public universities, was founded and designed by a 76-year-old Thomas Jefferson, who called himself its "father" in his own epitaph. A poll of experts at the time of the U.S. bicentennial designated this complex "the proudest achievement of American architecture in the past 200 years." Only the most outstanding students qualify for the coveted rooms that flank the Lawn, a green, terraced expanse that flows down from the Rotunda, a half-scale replica of the Pantheon in Rome. Behind the Pavilions, where senior faculty live, serpentine walls surround small, flowering gardens. Edgar Allan Poe's room—where he spent one year as a student until debts forced him to leave—is preserved on the West Range at No. 13. Tours begin indoors in the Rotunda, whose entrance is on the Lawn side, lower level. Thirty-minute to one-hour historic tours are daily at 10, 11, 2, 3, and 4. The **Bayly Art Museum** (⊠ 155 Rugby Rd. ☎ 434/924–3592 ⚏ Free ☉ Tues.–Sun. 1–5), one block north of the Rotunda, exhibits art from around the world from ancient times to the present day. ⊠ *University* ☎ *434/924–3239* ⊕ *www. virginia.edu* ⚏ *Free* ☉ *Rotunda open daily 9–4:45. University closed during winter break Dec.–Jan. and spring exams the 1st 3 wks of May.*

Housed in a converted 1916 school building, **McGuffey Art Center** contains the 2nd Street Gallery and the studios of painters, printmakers, metalworkers, and sculptors, all of which are open to the public. Dance performances are occasionally put on here. ⊠ *201 2nd St. NW, Downtown* ☎ *434/295–7973* ⊕ *www.mcguffeyartcenter.com* ⚏ *Free* ☉ *Tues.–Sat. 10–6, Sun. 1–5.*

☺ At the **Virginia Discovery Museum** children can step inside a giant kaleidoscope, explore a reconstructed log cabin, or watch bees in action in a real hive. The hands-on exhibits are meant to interest children in science, the arts, history, and the humanities. Exhibits in the Back Gallery change every few months. ⊠ *524 E. Main St., Downtown* ☎ *434/977–1025* ⊕ *www.vadm.org* ⚏ *$4* ☉ *Tues.–Sat. 10–5, Sun. 1–5.*

Where to Stay & Eat

$$$–$$$$ ✕ **OXO.** Just off the Downtown Mall, this chic restaurant has created a gastronomic fervor among Charlottesvillians since it opened in 1999. Chef-owner John Haywood puts a modern twist on classic French cuisine and changes the menu every few weeks. Notable entrées include oven-roasted beef tenderloin with truffles, mashed potatoes, and sautéed spinach, and pan-seared snapper wrapped in potato crêpes. The extensive wine list is mostly Californian. ⊠ *215 W. Water St., Downtown* ☎ *434/977–8111* ⊟ *AE, D, MC, V* ☉ *No lunch Sun. and Mon.*

$$–$$$ ✕ **Duner's.** This former motel diner 5 mi west of Charlottesville fills up early. The fanciful menu, which changes daily, emphasizes fresh, seasonal fare in its seafood and pasta dishes. Appetizers may include lamb and green peppercorn pâté with grilled bread. For an entrée, try morel-mushroom risotto cakes or shrimp in lemongrass and coconut milk over linguine. The red-tile floor and decorative copper pots on the walls keep things bright and warm. ⊠ *Rte. 250 W, Ivy* ☎ *434/293–8352* ⚍ *Reservations not accepted* ⊟ *MC, V* ☉ *No lunch.*

★ **$$–$$$**   ✕**Eastern Standard.** Chef Janet Jospe's fusion cuisine incorporates the cooking of many cultures, especially Asia and the Pacific Rim. Specialties in the formal dining room upstairs include pan-seared duck breast in a barbecue glaze and loin of lamb with mint pesto. Curries and stir-fry Asian dishes are also available. Escafé, a popular bistro downstairs with a big bar and hip furnishings, serves pastas and light fare. ⊠ *Downtown Mall, 102 Old Preston Ave., Downtown* ☎ *434/295–8668* ⊕ *www.easternstandard.com* ⊟*AE, D, DC, MC, V* ☙*Closed Sun.–Tues. No lunch.*

$$–$$$ ✕**Hamilton's at First and Main.** A local favorite, this Downtown Mall eatery has a warm terra-cotta interior and an eclectic cuisine. Try the pan-roasted halibut on Cuban black bean cake with a citrus salsa, or, if you're a pasta lover, the farfalle tossed with shrimp, country ham, sweet peppers, shiitake, and asparagus. In warmer weather, the outdoor patio doubles as a great perch to people-watch. ⊠ *101 W. Main St., Downtown* ☎ *434/ 295–6649* ⊟ *AE, D, DC, MC, V* ☙ *Closed Sun.*

★ **$–$$$**   ✕**C&O Restaurant.** A boarded-up storefront hung with an illuminated Pepsi sign conceals one of the best restaurants in town. The formal dining room upstairs, the lively bistro downstairs, and the cozy mezzanine in between share a French-influenced menu that has Pacific Rim and American Southwest touches. For a starter try the veal sweetbreads simmered in cream; the entrées include steak *chinois* (flank steak panfried with soy sauce and fresh ginger cream). The wine list is 300 strong. ⊠*515 E. Water St., Downtown* ☎ *434/971–7044* ⊕ *www.candorestaurant. com* ⊟ *AE, MC, V.*

$–$$$ ✕**Continental Divide.** A neon sign in the window of this locals' favorite says "Get in here"—you might miss the small storefront restaurant otherwise. The food is Southwestern cuisine, with quesadillas, burritos, spicy pork tacos, and enchiladas. The margaritas are potent. Cactus plants decorate the front window, and the booths have funky lights. It can get crowded and convivial, but customers like it that way. ⊠ *811 W. Main St., Downtown* ☎ *434/984–0143* ◿ *Reservations not accepted* ⊟ *D, DC, MC, V* ☙ *No lunch.*

$–$$ ✕**Hardware Store.** Deli sandwiches, burgers, crêpes, salads, seafood, and ice cream from the soda fountain are what's on sale today in this former Victorian hardware store. Your condiments will be delivered in a toolbox, and make sure to help yourself at the pickle bar. Some of the wood paneling and brick walls have been here since 1890. ⊠ *316 E. Main St., Downtown* ☎ *434/977–1518 or 800/426–6001* ⊟ *AE, DC, MC, V* ☙ *Closed Sun.*

★ **¢–$**   ✕**Crozet Pizza.** With up to 35 toppings to choose from, including seasonal items such as snow peas and asparagus spears, this out-of-the-way restaurant 12 mi west of Charlottesville is renowned for having some of Virginia's best pizza. On the weekend, takeout must be ordered hours in advance. Diners in the red clapboard restaurant find things rustic, with portraits of the owners' forebears and one wall covered with business cards from around the world. ⊠ *Rte. 240, Crozet* ☎ *434/823–2132* ⊟ *No credit cards.*

$$$–$$$$ ✕▥ **Boar's Head Inn.** Set on 55 acres in west Charlottesville, this local landmark resembles an English country inn, with flower gardens, ponds, and a gristmill from 1834. The rooms have king-size four-poster beds and Italian Anichini linens; many have balconies. Some suites have fireplaces. There are lots of activities to do here—even hot-air ballooning, through a nearby outfitter. The Old Mill Room restaurant ($$$–$$$$) serves new American cuisine and includes venison and seafood; the grilled filet mignon is a savory favorite. The $16 luncheon buffet includes an exceptional selections of salads, soups, meats, and desserts. ⊠ *U.S. 250 W, Ednam Forest, Box 5307, 22905* ☎ *434/296–2181 or 800/476–1988* 🖷 *434/972–6019* ⊕ *www.boarsheadinn.com* ↩ *171 rooms, 11 suites ♨ 3 restaurants, cable TV with movies and video games, 18-hole golf course, 20 tennis courts, 4 pools, health club, spa, fishing, racquetball, squash, shop, Internet, meeting rooms* ▭ *AE, D, DC, MC, V.*

★ $$ ✕▥ **Silver Thatch Inn.** Four-poster beds and period antiques are just part of what give charm to this 1780 white-clapboard Colonial farmhouse, 8 mi north of town. The friendly hosts help their guests arrange outdoor activities at nearby locations. The popular restaurant ($$–$$$) serves contemporary cuisine and has a very fine wine cellar. The grilled beef tenderloin here is renowned. ⊠ *3001 Hollymead Dr., 22911* ☎ *434/978–4686 or 800/261–0720* 🖷 *434/973–6156* ⊕ *www.silverthatch.com* ↩ *7 rooms ♨ Restaurant, pool; no room phones, no room TVs, no kids under 14, no smoking* ▭ *AE, DC, MC, V* ¶⦿¶ *BP.*

★ $$$$ ▥ **Keswick Hall at Monticello.** This 1912 Tuscan villa on 600 lush acres 5 mi east of Charlottesville is a luxurious, cosmopolitan retreat. Guest rooms and common areas are decorated in Laura Ashley fabrics and wallpapers, and each room is furnished with English and American antiques. Some have whirlpool baths and balconies. The 18-hole golf course, designed by Arnold Palmer, spreads across the rear of the estate. There's no check-in desk here; you are welcomed inside as if you are entering someone's home. The facilities of the private Keswick Club are open to those staying overnight. ⊠ *701 Club Dr., Keswick 22947* ☎ *434/979–3440 or 800/274–5391* 🖷 *434/977–4171* ⊕ *www.keswick.com* ↩ *44 rooms, 4 suites ♨ 2 restaurants, dining room, cable TV with movies, 18-hole golf course, 5 tennis courts, 2 pools (1 indoor), health club, spa, fishing, bicycles, croquet, meeting rooms, some pets allowed (fee)* ▭ *AE, D, DC, MC, V.*

$$–$$$ ▥ **200 South Street Inn.** Two houses, one of them a former brothel, have been combined and restored to create this old-fashioned inn in the historic district, one block from the Downtown Mall. Furnishings throughout are English and Belgian antiques. Several rooms come with a canopy bed, sitting room, fireplace, and whirlpool. ⊠ *200 South St., Downtown, 22902* ☎ *434/979–0200 or 800/964–7008* 🖷 *434/979–4403* ⊕ *www.southstreetinn.com* ↩ *16 rooms, 3 suites ♨ Cable TV, Internet; no smoking* ▭ *AE, DC, MC, V* ¶⦿¶ *CP.*

$–$$$ ▥ **High Meadows Vineyard Inn.** Two styles of architecture are joined by a hall in this bed-and-breakfast (and working vineyard). Listed on the National Register of Historic Places, the inn is 15 mi south of Monticello. Rooms have curtains and bed hangings with a handcrafted look. Dinner is served in the dining room by reservation Wednesday through Sunday. Hors d'oeuvres and samples of Virginia wines are available on the weekend. ⊠ *55 High Meadows La., Scottsville 24590* ☎ *434/286–2218 or 800/232–1832* 🖷 *434/286–2124* ⊕ *www.highmeadows.com* ↩ *10 rooms, 2 cottages ♨ Dining room; no room TVs* ▭ *AE, D, MC, V* ¶⦿¶ *BP.*

$–$$ ⊡ **Omni Charlottesville.** This attractive member of the luxury chain looms over one end of the Downtown Mall. The triangular rooms at the point of the wedge-shape building get light from two sides. Cherry-color furnishings and sage fabrics decorate the guest quarters, and potted plants soften the bright seven-story atrium lobby. ⊠ *235 W. Main St., Downtown, 22902* ☏ *434/971–5500 or 800/843–6664* 🖷 *434/979–4456* ⊕ *www.omnihotels.com* ⇥ *204 rooms, 7 suites* ⚲ *Restaurant, cable TV with movies and video games, 2 pools (1 indoor), gym, hot tub, sauna, bar, Internet* ⊟ *AE, D, DC, MC, V.*

$–$$ ⊡ **Best Western Cavalier Inn.** This facility's best feature is its location, directly across the street from the grounds of the University of Virginia and one block from the sports arena. Rates include a deluxe continental breakfast. ⊠ *105 Emmet St., University, 22903* ☏ *434/296–8111* 🖷 *434/290–3523* ⊕ *www.bestwestern.com* ⇥ *118 rooms* ⚲ *Restaurant, cable TV, pool, lounge, Internet, meeting rooms, airport shuttle, some pets allowed* ⊟ *AE, D, DC, MC, V* ⦶ *CP.*

¢   ⊡ **English Inn.** A model treatment of the B&B theme on a large but comfortable scale, the English Inn has a three-story atrium lobby with cascading plants. The suites have a sitting room, wet bar, king-size bed, and reproduction antiques; other rooms have modern furnishings. ⊠ *2000 Morton Dr., 22901* ☏ *434/971–9900 or 800/786–5400* 🖷 *434/977–8008* ⊕ *www.wytestone.com* ⇥ *67 rooms, 21 suites* ⚲ *Cable TV, indoor pool, gym, sauna* ⊟ *AE, D, DC, MC, V* ⦶ *BP.*

Nightlife & the Arts

For listings of cultural events, music, and movies, and a guide to restaurants, pick up a free copy of the *C-Ville Weekly* (www.c-ville.com) an arts and entertainment newspaper available in restaurants and hotels throughout the city. If you're near the University of Virginia campus, grab a free copy of the student newspaper, the *Cavalier Daily* (www.cavalierdaily.com), for the latest on college sports and events.

BARS & CLUBS   **Miller's** (⊠ 109 W. Main St., Downtown Mall, Downtown ☏ 434/971–8511), a large and comfortable bar, hosts blues, folk, and jazz musicians. Rock musician Dave Matthews used to tend bar here. **Tokyo Rose** (⊠ 2171 Ivy Rd., University ☏ 434/295–7673) is a sushi bar that doubles as a performance space for up-and-coming independent rock bands.

COFFEEHOUSES   **Prism Coffeehouse** (⊠ 214 Rugby Rd., University ☏ 434/977–7476 ⊕ www.theprism.org) has been a venue for folk music since a group of university students opened it in 1966. National acoustic acts have included an Appalachian string band as well as bluegrass and Irish-music performers. No smoking or alcohol is allowed. It's closed July and August.

FESTIVALS   In March, **Virginia Festival of the Book** (☏ 434/924–6890 ⊕ www.vabook.org) draws authors that have included Garrison Keillor and Michael Ondaatje. Thousands attend the festival, which is open to the public and promotes literacy while celebrating the book.

Every autumn, Charlottesville hosts the **Virginia Film Festival** (☏ 800/882–3378 ⊕ www.vafilm.com), with screenings of important new movies, panel discussions, and appearances by stars of the cinema. The movies are shown at four sites around the university and downtown.

Sports & the Outdoors

CANOEING & **James River Runners Inc.** (✉ 10082 Hatton Ferry Rd., Scottsville ☎ 434/
KAYAKING 286–2338 ⊕ www.jamesriver.com), about 35 minutes south of Charlottesville, offers canoe, kayak, tubing, and rafting trips down the James.

SPECTATOR The **University of Virginia** is part of the Atlantic Coast Conference. From
SPORTS November through February, the Cavaliers' perennially strong men's and
women's basketball teams play against other NCAA Division I-A teams
in University Hall. Fall brings football to Scott Stadium. For ticket
prices, call the University of Virginia Athletic Ticket Office (☎ 804/924–
8821 or 800/542–8821). Check the *Cavalier Daily* for game times.

Shopping

Charlottesville ranks as one of the top 10 book markets nationally (and
claims the top spot for the most avid-reading households). The city's
independent bookstores, especially those that specialize in used and antiquarian books, are great for a visit. Legal-thriller master John Grisham
kicks off book tours at **New Dominion Bookshop** (✉ 404 E. Main St. Downtown ☎ 434/295–2552). Whether it's a rare first edition you are seeking or just some unique bargains, try **Blue Whale Books** (✉ 115 W. Main
St., Downtown ☎ 434/296–4646). Run by an antiquarian book dealer,
the shop has thousands of books in all categories and price ranges, from
one dollar to several hundred. **Daedalus Bookshop** (✉ 123 4th St. NE,
Downtown ☎ 434/293–7595) has three floors of books crammed into
every nook and cranny.

Heartwood Books (✉ 5 Elliewood Ave., University ☎ 434/295–7083),
close to the university campus, stocks scholarly works, including a good
collection of theology and philosophy.

The **Downtown Mall** (✉ Main St., Downtown) is a six-block brick pedestrian mall with specialty stores, cinemas, art galleries, restaurants, and
coffeehouses in restored 19th- and early 20th-century buildings.

Orange

❸ *25 mi northeast of Charlottesville via Rte. 20, 60 mi northwest of
Richmond.*

Orange is a fertile agricultural area bearing reminders of the Civil War.
Among the many estates dotting the countryside is the home of our nation's fourth president.

The **James Madison Museum** presents a comprehensive exhibition on the
Founding Father most responsible for the Constitution (Madison became president in 1809). The collection includes some of the china and
glassware recovered from the White House before the British torched
it during the War of 1812. The fourth president's tiny Campeachy chair,
an 18th-century piece made for him by his friend Thomas Jefferson,
shows how short he was. ✉ *129 Caroline St.* ☎ *540/672–1776* 💲 *$4*
🕘 *Mar.–Nov., weekdays 9–5, Sat. 10–5, Sun. 1–5; Dec.–Feb., weekdays 9–5.*

St. Thomas's Episcopal Church (1833), the one surviving example of Jeffersonian church architecture, is a replica of Charlottesville's demolished

CloseUp

VIRGINIA WINERIES

J AMESTOWN'S COLONIAL *settlers are believed to have made the first wine in Virginia, but only in the past 25 years has the Commonwealth's wine industry truly come into its own. The number of wineries here has grown from fewer than 10 in the 1970s to more than 70 today. As you ride through the state, keep an eye out for grape-cluster signs on the highway, which identify nearby wineries. For information on winery tours and events, contact the* **Virginia Wine Marketing Program** *(☎ 800/828–463 ⊕ www. virginiawines.org) and the* **Monticello Wine Trail** *(⊕ www.monticellowinetrail.org).*

The state's Piedmont, Shenandoah Valley, and Blue Ridge regions are a particularly abundant area for wineries. They include the following:

Abingdon Vineyard & Winery. *In Washington County along the South Holston River, this farm is near to the Virginia Creeper Trail and Appalachian Trail and 7 mi from the cultural attractions of Abingdon.* ✉ 20530 Alvarado Rd., Abingdon ☎ 276/623–1255 ⊕ www. abingdonwinery.com 🎫 Tours and tastings free ⊗ Tastings and tours mid-Mar.–mid-Dec., Wed.–Sun., noon–6.

Barboursville Vineyards. *This vineyard between Charlottesville and Orange was the first one in the state to grow only vinifera (Old-World) grapes. The grapes were planted in 1976 on the former plantation of James Barbour, governor from 1812 to 1814. His house, designed by Thomas Jefferson, was gutted by fire in 1884; the ruins remain. During the last weekend of July and first three weekends of August, "Shakespeare at the Ruins" employs the site for outdoor performances.* ✉ 17655 Winery Rd. (near intersection of Rtes. 20 and 23), Barboursville ☎ 540/832–3824 ⊕ www. barboursvillewine.com 🎫 Tours free;

tastings $3 ⊗ Tastings Mon.–Sat. 10–5, Sun. 11–5.

Château Morrisette Winery. *With the Rock Castle Gorge nearby, this winery has spectacular surroundings. Tastings allow you to sample the dozen different wines produced here. A natural amphitheater on the property is the site of the annual Black Dog Jazz Festival.* ✉ Winery Rd., off Rte. 726, west of Blue Ridge Pkwy. at milepost 171.5, Meadows of Dan ☎ 540/593–2865 ⊕ www.chateaumorrisette.com 🎫 Tour and tasting $2 ⊗ Mon.–Thurs. 10–5, Fri.–Sat. 10–8, Sun. 11–5.

Jefferson Vineyards. *In 1773 Thomas Jefferson gave the land that became the Jefferson Vineyards to Italian wine maker Filippo Mazzei. Jefferson wanted him to establish a European-style vineyard; Mazzei is said to have found the soil and climate of Virginia better than Italy's. The modern-day operation has consistently produced widely appreciated wines.* ✉ 1353 Thomas Jefferson Pkwy., Charlottesville ☎ 434/977–3042, 800/ 272–3042 ⊕ www.jeffersonvineyards. com 🎫 Free ⊗ daily 11–5.

Valhalla Vineyards. *Established in 1995, Valhalla makes use of an underground barrel cave for aging. The mountaintop location allows for sweeping views of the Roanoke Valley.* ✉ 6500 Mt. Chestnut Rd., Roanoke ☎ 540/725–9463 ⊕ www.valhallawines.com 🎫 Tastings $2–$6 ⊗ Apr.–Dec., Fri. 4–7, Sat. noon–5, Sun. 1–5.

Wintergreen Winery. *Close to the Wintergreen Resort and the Rockfish River, this winery has a gift shop on the premises that's open daily.* ✉ 462 Winery Lane, Nellysford ☎ 434/361–2519 ⊕ www. wintergreenwinery.com 🎫 Tours and tastings free ⊗ Apr.–Oct., daily 10–6, Nov.–Mar., daily 10–5.

Christ Church, which Jefferson designed. It's here that Robert E. Lee worshipped during the winter of 1863–64. The church's biggest decorative asset is its Tiffany window. ☒ *119 Caroline St.* ☎ *540/672–3761* ☒ *Donation* ⊙ *Tours by appointment.*

During the Civil War, a handsome Greek revival hotel, now the **Exchange Hotel Civil War Museum,** was transformed into a Confederate receiving hospital for wounded and dying soldiers. In addition to weapons, uniforms, and the personal effects of Union and Confederate soldiers, the museum displays the often crude medical equipment used for amputations, tooth extractions, and bloodletting. One room re-creates a hospital ward; an estimated 70,000 soldiers were treated here between 1862 and 1865. ☒ *400 S. Main St., Gordonsville* ☎ *540/832-2944* ☒ *$4* ⊙ *Apr., May, and Sept.–Dec., Tues.–Sat. 10–4; June–Aug., Tues.–Sat. 10–4, Sun. 1–4.*

Just outside of Orange is **Montpelier,** the former residence of James Madison (1751–1836), the fourth president of the United States. A massive renovation is under way to remove parts of the mansion added by its 20th-century owners, the duPont family. It's fascinating to watch the mansion being restored to its early-19th-century Madisonian state; a house tour allows access to many areas being revamped, a project slated to last until 2008 at least. Some of the Madisons' possessions, as well as a tribute to the "Father of the Constitution," have been set up in an Education Center on the grounds. The walking tour includes a stop at the cemetery where James and his wife, Dolley, are buried. Exotic conifers planted by the duPonts dot the meadowlike grounds, and a walking path wanders amid an old-growth forest. The annual Montpelier Hunt Races, which are a steeplechase, have been held since 1934. When they run, on the first Saturday in November, the house tour is canceled. Admission to the races is $15. ☒ *Rte. 20, 4 mi southwest of Orange* ☎ *540/672-2728* ⊕ *www.montpelier.org* ☒ *$11* ⊙ *Apr.–Nov., daily 9:30–5; Dec.–Mar., daily 9:30–4:30.*

Where to Stay & Eat

★ **$$$$** ✕🍽 **Willow Grove Inn.** This carefully preserved 1778 Virginia plantation house, an example of Jeffersonian classical revival architecture, served as an encampment during the Revolutionary War and lay under siege during the Civil War. On 37 acres a mile north of Orange, the inn has furnishings from the 18th and 19th centuries. Rooms in the weaver's cottage and two-room schoolhouse have fireplaces and private verandas. A baby grand piano accompanies the candlelight dining in the formal dining room ($$$$), where prix-fixe dinners are served. The menu's regional Southern dishes may include smoked Rappahannock trout cakes, toasted peanut- and pecan-crusted rack of lamb, or grilled quail with corn pudding. Clark's Tavern ($–$$) is more casual, with items such as panfried catfish and crayfish étouffée. ☒ *14079 Plantation Way, 22960* ☎ *540/672–5982 or 800/949–1778* 🖷 *540/672-3674* ⊕ *www.willowgroveinn. com* ☞ *5 rooms, 6 cottages* ♿ *Restaurant, bar, pub, Internet, some pets allowed; no room TVs* ⊟ *AE, D, DC, MC, V* 🍽 *MAP.*

$$ 🍽 **Mayhurst Inn.** An architectural rarity in the South, this Italianate Victorian mansion was built in 1859 by a grandnephew of James Madison, and generals Stonewall Jackson and Robert E. Lee were early guests. Now Mayhurst is a cozy and comfortable B&B surrounded by 37 acres of woods with hiking trails. Its rooms have floor-to-ceiling windows, marble fireplaces, and antique furnishings. Some have whirlpool baths. The inn is on U.S. 15 in Orange. ⊠ *12460 Mayhurst La., 22960* ☎ *540/672–5597 or 888/672–5597* 🖷 *540/672–7447* ⊕ *www. mayhurstinn.com* ⮬ *8 rooms, 2 suites* ⚲ *Fishing, hiking; no TV in some rooms, no smoking* ⊟ *AE, MC, V* ⦿ *BP.*

Washington

❹ *63 mi north of Charlottesville.*

Known as Little Washington to differentiate it from its big sister, this tiny town packs in antiques shops, galleries, custom jewelry shops, and two theaters in roughly five blocks—perfect for an afternoon stroll.

Where to Stay & Eat

$$$$
Fodor'sChoice
★

✕⊞ The Inn at Little Washington. What began as a small-town eatery in 1978 has grown into a legend. The rich interior of the three-story white-frame inn is the work of Joyce Conway-Evans, who has designed theatrical sets and rooms in English royal houses. Plush canopy beds, marble bathrooms, and fresh flowers make the rooms sumptuous. Chef Patrick O'Connell's much-loved New American food is served in a slate-floor dining room with William Morris wallpaper. The seven-course dinner costs $158 per person on Saturday, $128 on Friday and Sunday, and $118 on weekdays, not including wine and drinks. ⊠ *Middle and Main Sts., 22747* ☎ *540/675–3800* 🖷 *540/675–3100* ⊕ *www. theinnatlittlewashington.com* ⮬ *11 rooms, 3 suites* ⚲ *Restaurant, in-room safes, bicycles* ⊟ *MC, V* ☺ *Hotel and restaurant closed Tues. except in May and Oct.* ⦿ *CP.*

$$–$$$

✕⊞ Bleu Rock Inn. This former farmhouse is set on 80 bucolic acres against a backdrop of the Blue Ridge Mountains, with a fishing pond, rolling pastures, and 7½ acres of vineyards spread across the foreground. An equestrian center on-site boards horses (you may bring your own) and trains them for riders; there's also a polo ring and steeplechase course. The guest rooms, simply furnished with light woods and lace curtains, are pleasing; the four upstairs have private balconies. Reservations are taken no later than three months in advance for the hotel, but the French country–style food ($$–$$$) is the real star here. The dishes include roasted salmon with a tapenade crust and niçoise polenta with a red wine sauce. The restaurant is closed Monday and Tuesday. ⊠ *12567 Lee Hwy., 22747* ☎ *540/987–3190* 🖷 *540/987–3193* ⊕ *www. bleurockinn.com* ⮬ *5 rooms* ⚲ *Restaurant, fishing, hiking, horseback riding, pub, some pets allowed; no room phones, no room TVs* ⊟ *AE, D, DC, MC, V* ⦿ *BP.*

Shopping

Along Main Street, you can step into the **Odyssey Collection Inc.** (⊠ 261 Main St. ☎ 540/675–1691 ⊕ www.odysseycollection.com) for pre-Columbian artifacts or handblown glass. Look for Oriental carpets at **Rare Finds** (⊠ 371 Main St. ☎ 540/675–1400).

Wintergreen Resort

❺ *25 mi southwest of Charlottesville, via I–64, U.S. 250 and Rte. 151 (Exit 107), 13 mi south of southern entrance of Shenandoah National Park, via Blue Ridge Pkwy.*

With 6,700 acres of forest, six restaurants, and three golf courses, Wintergreen is more like a community in itself than just a resort. Skiing and snowboarding are the central attractions, with 20 downhill slopes and five chairlifts. Wintergreen's snowmaking crew has been featured on the Weather Channel for its ability to keep the slopes white even when Old Man Winter isn't cooperative. On milder winter weekends you can even ski and golf on the same day for the price of a lift ticket. In summer the stunning Blue Ridge location means that hiking, mountain biking, horseback riding, golf, tennis, and swimming can all be done in the cool that comes with a high elevation. One of the golf courses, at nearly 4,000 feet, is the highest in Virginia.

off the
beaten
path

CRABTREE FALLS – A series of cascades falls a distance of 1,200 feet. Taken together, Virginia claims these cascades as the highest waterfall east of the Rockies, though no single waterfall within the series would qualify as such. Whatever the superlatives or qualifications, the falls are a wondrous sight. A trail winds up a steep mountainside all the way to the top, but the first overlook is an easy stroll just 700 feet from the lower parking lot. The best time to see the waterfalls is winter through spring, when the water is high. ⊠ *Rte. 56, 6 mi east of Blue Ridge Pkwy., or 19 mi from Wintergreen by following Rte. 151 south and then Rte. 56 west at Roseland.*

Where to Stay & Eat

$–$$$ ▥ **Wintergreen Resort.** Accommodations at the resort include everything from studio apartments to seven-bedroom houses. Most rooms have fireplaces and full kitchens; the housing units' wood exteriors blend into the surrounding forest. ⊠ *Rte. 664, Wintergreen 22958* ☎ *434/325–2200 or 800/266–2444* ₰ *434/325–8003* ⊕ *www.wintergreenresort.com* ⥂ *305 units* ௮ *6 restaurants, 9-hole golf course, 2 18-hole golf courses, 24 tennis courts, 2 pools (1 indoor), lake, gym, spa, boating, bicycles, hiking, horseback riding, downhill skiing, bar, convention center* ▤ *AE, D, MC, V.*

Sports & the Outdoors

GOLF At 3,850 feet, Wintergreen's **Devil's Knob course** (☎ 434/325–8250 ⊕ www.wintergreenresort.com) is Virginia's highest course. An 18-hole, par-70 course comes with 50-mi views from its fairways. **Stoney Creek**, a 27-hole, par-72 course, lies in the valley below.

Lynchburg

❻ *66 mi southeast of Charlottesville via Rte. 29, 110 mi west of Richmond.*

Although the city's founder, John Lynch, was a Quaker pacifist, its most prominent landmark is Monument Terrace, a war memorial: at the foot and head of the 139 limestone and granite steps that ascend to the Old City Courthouse are statues honoring a World War I dough-boy and a Confederate soldier. If you're hesitant to make the climb, at least catch the dramatic view from the bottom of Court House Hill, at Main and 9th streets. Self-guided walking tours designed by the Lynchburg Visitors Information Center cover the historic Riverfront and Diamond Hill sections.

At the **Anne Spencer House** you can step into "Edankraal," the studio of this late poet of the Harlem Renaissance. Hers is the only work of a Virginian to appear in the *Norton Anthology of Modern American and English Poetry*. A librarian at one of Lynchburg's segregated black schools, Spencer (1882–1975) penned most of her work in this back-garden sanctuary, which has been left completely intact with her writing desk, bookcases, mementos, and walls tacked with photos and news clippings. ✉ *1313 Pierce St.* ☎ *434/847–1459* 🎫 *$5* ☉ *Tours by appointment.*

At the **Legacy Museum of African-American History,** the rotating exhibits focus on such themes as health and medicine, education, business, the civil rights struggle, and the contributions African-Americans have made to society, the arts, and politics. ✉ *403 Monroe St.* ☎ *434/845–3455* 🎫 *$2* ☉ *Thurs.–Sat. noon–4, Sun. 2–4, and by appointment.*

The **Pest House Medical Museum** is on the grounds of the **Confederate Cemetery,** where a garden of 60 rosebushes has varieties dating from 1565 to 1900. The museum provides a brief but informative look into medical practices and instruments at the time of the Civil War and later. The 1840s frame building was the office of Dr. John Jay Terrell. ✉ *4th and Taylor Sts.* ☎ *434/847–1465* 🎫 *Free* ☉ *Daily dawn–dusk.*

The mansion on Daniel's Hill, **Point of Honor,** was built in 1815 on the site of a duel. Once part of a 900-acre estate, this redbrick house surrounded by lawns retains a commanding view of the James River. The facade is elegantly symmetrical, with two octagonal bays joined by a balustrade on each of the building's two stories. The interiors have been restored and furnished with pieces authentic to the early 19th-century Federal period, including wallpaper whose pattern is in the permanent collection of New York's Metropolitan Museum of Art. ✉ *112 Cabell St.* ☎ *434/847–1459* ⊕ *www.pointofhonor.org* 🎫 *$6* ☉ *Daily 10–4.*

★ Less than 5 mi southwest of Lynchburg, **Thomas Jefferson's Poplar Forest** is an impressive piece of octagonal architecture, now surrounded by only a few remaining poplars. Conceived and built by Jefferson as his "occasional retreat" (he sometimes stayed here between 1806 and 1813), this Palladian hermitage exemplifies the architect's sublime sense of order that is so evident at Monticello. Erected on a slope, the house has a front that's one story high, with a two-story rear elevation. The octagon's center is a square, skylit dining room flanked by two smaller octagons. As the ongoing restoration continues, additions made by later owners of the estate are being undone and the property is gradually being returned to Jefferson's original design. Every July 4, there's a free celebration that includes a reading of the Declaration of Independence and living-history exhibits. ✉ *Rte. 661, Forest* ☎ *434/525–1806* ⊕ *www.poplarforest.org* 🎫 *$8* ☉ *Apr.–Nov., Wed.–Mon. 10–4.*

off the beaten path

Fodor's Choice
★

APPOMATTOX COURT HOUSE – Twenty-five miles east of Lynchburg, the village of Appomattox Court House has been restored to its appearance of April 9, 1865. It was on that day that the Confederate General Lee surrendered the Army of Northern Virginia to General Grant. There are 27 structures in the national historical park; most can be entered. A highlight is the reconstructed McLean House, in whose parlor the articles of surrender were signed. The self-guided tour is well planned and introduced by exhibits and slide shows in the reconstructed courthouse. Interpreters cast as soldiers and villagers answer questions in the summer. ☒ *3 mi north of Appomattox, on State Rte. 24* ☎ *434/352–8987* ☷ *June–Aug., $4; Sept.–May, $3* ☉ *Daily 8:30–5.*

RED HILL–PATRICK HENRY NATIONAL MEMORIAL – In the town of Brookneal is the final home of Revolutionary War patriot Patrick Henry, whose "Give me liberty or give me death" speech inspired a generation. The 1770s house has been reconstructed on its original site and contains numerous furnishings owned by the Henry family. Other buildings, including a coachman's cabin and stable, stand near a formal boxwood garden. Henry's grave is on the property. ☒ *35 mi southeast of Lynchburg, off Rte. 619, Brookneal* ☎ *434/376–2044* ☷ *$6* ☉ *Apr.–Oct., daily 9–5; Nov.–Mar., daily 9–4.*

Where to Eat

$–$$ ✕ **Meriwether's Market Restaurant.** Here you can find American dishes generally made with local and regional ingredients, from game to seafood. For an entrée, try the spicy shrimp and grits, or a specialty pizza. A lighter "intermezzo" menu is available to carry you through the lull between lunch and dinner (2:30–5:30). ☒ *4925 Boonsboro Rd.* ☎ *434/ 384–3311* ⊕ *www.meriwethers.com* ☷ *AE, D, MC, V* ☉ *Closed Sun.*

Sports & the Outdoors

BIKING Lynchburg's fine municipal "greenway" system of trails is open to both bicyclists and hikers. The **Blackwater Creek Natural Area** (☎ City of Lynchburg Parks and Recreation Dept. 434/847–1640) has more than 12 mi of trails, most of them level and asphalt, which wind through a pleasant tree-shaded natural area within the city limits. One trail goes through a 500-foot tunnel. The **Percival's Island Trail,** only three blocks from one edge of the natural area and in the shadow of the downtown skyline, extends for more than a mile along a narrow strip of land in the middle of the James River.

To rent a bike, contact **Blackwater Creek Bike Rental** (☒ 1611 Concord Tpke. ☎ 434/845–0293), which is open weekdays 1 to 5 and weekends from 9 to sunset.

Shenandoah National Park

Southern entrance 18 mi west of Charlottesville via I–81; northern entrance at Front Royal.

This "Daughter of the Stars," which is the translation for the Native American word *Shenandoah,* extends more than 80 mi south along the

Blue Ridge Mountains, with several gaps in the range forming passes between the Shenandoah Valley on the west and the Piedmont on the east. Within the park's boundaries are some 60 peaks and more than 500 mi of hiking trails.

Hardwood and pine forests cover the slopes, where mountain meadows full of wildflowers open up to gorgeous panoramas that can be viewed from numerous turnoffs. Hikers and campers find beautiful terrain just yards from the highway, trout fishers may wade into more than 25 streams in seven counties, and riders can rent horses for wilderness trail rides. Those who want to know more about the area's flora and fauna may want to take a guided hike, which naturalists lead daily throughout the summer. The seasonal activities of the park are outlined in the *Shenandoah Overlook,* a free newspaper you can pick up on entering the park. The park parallels I–81; the northern limit at Front Royal is close to I–66, and the southern end at Waynesboro is close to I–64. ☞ *Park Superintendent, Box 348, Rte. 4, Luray 22835* ☎ *540/999–3500* ⊕ *www.nps.gov/shen* ☞ *Park and Skyline Dr. $10 car; $5 motorcycle, bicycle, or pedestrian; tickets are valid 7 days.*

Fodor'sChoice
★
Most people see Shenandoah National Park from **Skyline Drive,** a spectacular route that winds 105 mi south from Front Royal to Waynesboro over the mountains of the park. Beauty has its price: holiday and weekend crowds in spring through fall can slow traffic to much less than the 35 mph speed limit. Winter brings many closed facilities and occasionally ice and snow that can close parts of the drive. Nevertheless, for easily accessible wilderness and exciting views, few routes can compete with this one. Just come during the fine weather—and bring a sweater, because temperatures can be brisk.

Where to Stay

$$–$$$ 🏨 **Jordan Hollow Farm.** The oldest of the four buildings here is a 1790 farmhouse, now a restaurant serving American regional cuisine. The youngest structure, built of hand-hewn logs almost 200 years later, contains four of the inn's most luxurious rooms, which include a fireplace, whirlpool, and TV. The 150-acre horse farm is near the tiny town of Stanley, 6 mi from Luray and 15 mi from Shenandoah National Park. From here you can gaze out over pastures full of horses and playful llamas toward a backdrop of the Blue Ridge Mountains. The only "pets" allowed are horses, which can be boarded here. Nearby trails are good for both hiking and mountain biking. ⊠ *326 Hawksbill Park Rd., Stanley 22851* ☎ *540/778–2285 or 888/418–7000* 🖨 *540/778–1759* ⊕ *www.jordanhollow.com* ☞ *8 rooms, 7 suites* ♨ *Restaurant, cable TV, bicycles, hiking, bar, meeting rooms; no smoking* ☰ *AE, D, DC, MC, V* ⊙❘*BP.*

$ 🏨 **Skyland Lodge.** At the highest point on Skyline Drive (3,680 feet), with views across the Shenandoah Valley, this facility has lodging that ranges from rustic cabins and motel-style rooms to suites. There's no air-conditioning, but days above 80°F are rare at these heights. ⊠ *Milepost 41.7 on Skyline Dr., 22835* ☎ *540/999–2211 or 800/999–4714* 🖨 *540/999–2231* ☞ *177 rooms* ♨ *Restaurant, bar, Internet, meeting rooms; no a/c, no room phones, no TV in some rooms* ☰ *AE, D, DC, MC, V* ⊙ *Closed Dec.–mid-Mar.*

🏕 **Shenandoah National Park.** Shenandoah has more than 600 campsites in four campgrounds, plus a fifth primitive campground (Dundo) for large educational groups. The Big Meadows Campground, at the approximate midpoint of the park, accepts reservations; other campsites are available on a first-come, first-served basis. ☐ *Shenandoah National Park, Box 727, Luray 22835* ☎ *540/999–3231, 800/365–2267 for Big Meadows reservations* 🖷 *540/999–3601* ⊕ *www.nps.gov/shen* 🛏 *53 tent-only sites; 164 RV or tent sites, 7 sites for educational groups* 🛁 *Laundry facilities, flush toilets, dump station, drinking water, showers* 🍴 *Tent or RV sites $16–$19 per night, group sites $30* ☐ *AE, D, MC, V* ☉ *Spring through Nov.*

en route

Two miles west of the northern entrance to Skyline Drive, **Skyline Caverns** is known for the anthodites, or spiked nodes, growing from its ceilings at an estimated rate of 1 inch every 7,000 years, and for its chambers, which have descriptive names such as the Capital Dome, Rainbow Trail, Fairytale Lake, and Cathedral Hall. ☐ *U.S. 340 S, Front Royal* ☎ *540/635–4545 or 800/296–4545* ⊕ *www.skylinecaverns.com* 🎫 *$12* ☉ *Mid-Mar.–mid-June, weekdays 9–5, weekends 9–6; mid-June–Labor Day, daily 9–6; Labor Day–mid-Nov., weekdays 9–5, weekends 9–6; mid-Nov.–mid-Mar., daily 9–4.*

Luray Caverns, 9 mi west of Skyline Drive on U.S. 211, are the largest caverns in the state. For millions of years water has seeped through the limestone and clay to create rock and mineral formations. The world's only "stalacpipe organ" is composed of stalactites (calcite formations hanging from the ceilings of the caverns) that have been tuned to concert pitch and are tapped by rubber-tip plungers. The organ is played electronically for every tour and may be played manually on special occasions. A one-hour tour begins every 20 minutes. ☐ *U.S. 211, Luray* ☎ *540/743–6551* ⊕ *www.luraycaverns.com* 🎫 *$18* ☉ *Mid-Mar.–Mid-June, daily 9–6; Mid-June–Labor Day, daily 9–7; Labor Day–Nov., daily 9–6, Nov.–Mid-Mar.*

Sports & the Outdoors

CANOEING **Front Royal Canoe** (☐ U.S. 340, near Front Royal ☎ 540/635–5440 or 800/270–8808 ⊕ www.frontroyalcanoe.com) offers a $16 tube trip as well as canoe, kayak, and raft trips of one hour up to three days for $35–$120. The company also rents boats and sells fishing accessories. At **Downriver Canoe** (☐ Rte. 613, near Front Royal ☎ 540/635–5526 ⊕ www.downriver.com), day and overnight trips start at $39 per canoe (or $28 per kayak, $14 per tube, and $65 per raft). **Shenandoah River Outfitters** (☐ Rte. 684, 6502 S. Page Valley Rd., Luray 22835 ☎ 540/743–4159 ⊕ www.shenandoahriver.com) rents canoes and kayaks for $20 to $50.

FISHING To take advantage of the trout that abound in the 50 streams of Shenandoah National Park, you need a Virginia fishing license; a five-day license costs $5 ($12 for a year) and it's available in season (early April to mid-October) at concession stands along Skyline Drive.

GOLF **Caverns Country Club Resort** (⊠ Rte. 211, Luray ☎ 540/743–7111) has an 18-hole course near Luray Caverns, with the Blue Ridge Mountains and the Shenandoah River nearby. Greens fees are $30 Monday–Thursday and $38 Friday–Sunday and holidays.

HIKING The **Appalachian Trail** zigzags across Skyline Drive through the park, offering easy access by car, variable hike lengths from a few feet to many miles, and connections with the more than 500 mi of the park's own trail network. Volunteers assist the National Park Service in upkeep of the AT, which generally has a smooth surface and gentle grade through the park. Three-sided shelters provide places for long-distance hikers to sleep overnight—or for day hikers to dodge a rain shower. If you're here in May or June, expect to see "thru-hikers" with heavy backpacks trudging on their 2,000-mi journey from Georgia to Maine. But you don't have to hike 2,000 mi, or even 2,000 feet, to experience the joyous sights of the wilderness—glorious foliage, rock formations, vistas, and perhaps a deer or even a bear.

HORSEBACK **Trail rides** leave from the park's Skyland Stables several times daily from
RIDING April through October, and on weekends in November. The route follows White Oak Canyon trail, which passes several waterfalls; you can choose a one-hour ride or a 2½-hour ride. You must book 24 hours in advance. ⊠ *Skyland Lodge, milepost 41.7, near Luray* ☎ *540/999–2210* ☉ *Apr.–Oct., daily 8–5; Nov., weekends 8–5.*

SHENANDOAH VALLEY

The fertile hills of the Shenandoah Valley reminded Colonial settlers from Germany, Ireland, and Britain of the homelands they left behind. They brought an agrarian lifestyle and Protestant beliefs that eventually spread across much of the Midwest. Today, the valley is full of historic, cultural, and geological places of interest, including Civil War sites; Woodrow Wilson's birthplace, and a reproduction of Shakespeare's Globe Theatre, both at Staunton; many beautifully adorned caverns; and the famous hot mineral springs in the aptly named Bath County.

Winchester

❼ *129 mi north of Charlottesville, 136 mi northwest of Richmond.*

Winchester's small size belies its historical importance. Established in 1752, it served as a headquarters for Col. George Washington during the French and Indian War when it began two years later. During the Civil War, it was an important crossroads near the front line. It changed hands 72 times during the war, and was Gen. Stonewall Jackson's headquarters for nearly two years.

Things are more peaceful today; the biggest attraction is the Shenandoah Apple Blossom Festival in May. Specialty boutiques, regional art galleries, and antiques stores are located throughout the town's 45-block historic district, especially on the six-block pedestrian mall. Winchester's biggest claim to 20th-century fame is as the birthplace of country music legend Patsy Cline; thousands visit her gravesite each year at the

Shenandoah Memorial Park cemetery, where a bell tower memorializes her.

The **Museum of the Shenandoah Valley** brings together fine and decorative art collections and multimedia presentations that reflect the region's cultural history. The museum complex includes the Glen Burnie Historic House and Gardens, a 1736 Georgian country estate surrounded by 25 acres of formal gardens that was home of Winchester's founder, Colonel James Wood, who called it his "glen of streams." The collections include a gallery with 18th and 19th century furniture, fine arts and decorative objects gathered by the last family member to live in the house, Julian Wood Glass Jr., who died in 1992. Another gallery assembles shadow box rooms and miniatures. ⊠ *901 Amherst St.* ☎ *540/662–1473, 888/556–5799* ⊕ *www.shenandoahmuseum.org* ⊡ *$12 for museum, house, and gardens; $8 for museum or house and gardens, $6 for gardens only* ☉ *Museum Tues.–Sun., daily 10–4, house and gardens Mar.–Nov., daily 10–4.*

Stonewall Jackson's Headquarters Museum is a restored 1854 home. Jackson used this as his base of operations during the Valley Campaign in 1861–62. Among the artifacts on display are his prayer book and camp table. The reproduction wallpaper was a gift from the actress Mary Tyler Moore; it was her great-grandfather Lt. Col. Lewis T. Moore who lent Jackson the use of the house. A $7.50 block ticket purchased at the museum also includes entry to two nearby historical attractions: **George Washington's Office Museum,** a preserved log cabin where Washington briefly lived during the French and Indian War, and **Abram's Delight Museum,** the oldest residence in Winchester. The stone house was owned by Isaac Hollingsworth, a prominent Quaker. ⊠ *415 N. Braddock St.* ☎ *540/667–3242* ⊕ *www.winchesterhistory.org* ⊡ *$3.50* ☉ *Apr.–Oct., Mon.–Sat. 10–4, Sun. noon–4; Nov.–Mar., Fri. and Sat. 10–4, Sun. noon–4.*

off the
beaten
path

STATE ARBORETUM OF VIRGINIA – This arboretum, 9 mi east of Winchester, has the most extensive boxwood collection in North America. Hands-on workshops and tours are available throughout the spring, summer, and fall. You can stroll through the perennial and herb gardens and have a look at more than 8,000 trees. The arboretum is a wonderful place to bird-watch or to have a picnic. ⊠ *Rte. 50 E* ☎ *540/837–1758* ☉ *Daily dawn–dusk* ⊡ *Free.*

Where to Stay & Eat

$–$$$$ ✕ **Violino Ristorante Italiano.** Homemade pasta—about 20 different kinds—fills the menu in this cheery, yellow-stucco restaurant in the city's Old Town. Owners Franco and Marcella Stocco and their son Riccardo (the men are chefs; Marcella manages the dining room) serve up their native northern Italian cuisine, including lobster *pansotti* (lobster-filled ravioli in a sauce of white wine and lemon sauce). A strolling violinist entertains diners on the weekends. The outdoor patio, enclosed by potted plants, is a quiet spot in the midst of street bustle. ⊠ *181 N. Loudoun St.* ☎ *540/667–8006* ⊕ *www.nvim.com/violino* ⊟ *AE, D, DC, MC, V* ☉ *Closed Sun.*

$$–$$$　✕🛏 **L'Auberge Provençale.** Chef-owner Alain Borel and his wife, Celeste,
Fodor's Choice　of Avignon, France, bring the warm elegance of the south of France to
★　this 1750s country inn, originally a sheep farm owned by Lord Fairfax.
Rooms are eclectically decorated with French art and fabrics, and Victorian wicker and antiques; some have fireplaces. Breakfast includes fresh
homemade croissants and apple crêpes with maple syrup. The acclaimed
prix-fixe restaurant serves authentic Provençale cuisine ($82 per person;
reservations essential on weekends), dinner only, and is closed Monday
and Tuesday. ✉ *Rte. 340, White Post 22663* 🕿 *540/837–1375 or 800/
638–1702* 🖷 *540/837–2004* ⊕ *www.laubergeprovencale.com* 🛏 *10
rooms, 4 suites* ⚒ *Restaurant, pool; no room phones, no room TVs, no
kids under 10, no smoking* ▭ *AE, D, MC, V* ☉ *Closed Jan.* ⑩ *BP.*

Middletown

❽　*6 mi south of Winchester.*

Middletown has one of the area's loveliest historic homes. **Belle Grove,** an
elegant farmhouse and 100-acre working farm, is a monument to the rural
and the refined, two qualities that exist in harmony in the architecture
here and throughout the region. Constructed in 1797 out of limestone quar-
ried on the property, the building reflects the influence of Thomas Jefferson, said to have been a consultant. Originally built for Maj. Isaac Hite
and his wife, Nelly (President James Madison's sister), this was the headquarters of the Union general Philip Sheridan during the Battle of Cedar
Creek (1864), a crucial defeat for the Confederacy. Part of the battle was
fought on the farm, and an annual reenactment is held in October with
as many as 2,000 participants. Call for the Christmas candlelight tour schedule. ✉*Rte. 11* 🕿*540/869–2028* ⊕*www.bellegrove.org* 🎟*$7* ☉*Apr.–Oct.,
Mon.–Sat. 10–3:15, Sun. 1–4:15; Nov., Sat. 10–4, Sun. noon–5.*

Where to Stay

$　🛏 **Wayside Inn.** This inn has been welcoming travelers since 1797, when
it was a popular stagecoach stop. The 18th century is preserved through
the extensive collection of antiques and fine art, which serve to make
each room distinct. Some rooms have small bathrooms and lack a view,
but all are pleasingly decorated. Rates include a continental breakfast
on weekdays. The dining room serves regional cuisine, such as spoon
bread, peanut soup, and country ham. ✉ *7783 Main St., 22645* 🕿 *540/
869–1797* 🖷 *540/869–6038* ⊕ *www.alongthewayside.com* 🛏 *20
rooms, 2 suites* ⚒ *Restaurant, cable TV, bar, Internet, meeting rooms;
no smoking* ▭ *AE, D, DC, MC, V.*

┌─────────┐
│ **en route** │　The **Strasburg Antique Emporium** (✉ 150 N. Massanutten St.,
└─────────┘　Strasburg 🕿 540/465–3711 ☉ Fri. and Sat. 10–7, Sun.–Thurs.
10–5), 5 mi south of Middletown, covers 1.4 acres. It's in the quirky
and historic downtown of Strasburg, which was settled by Germans.
Inside the emporium, more than 100 dealers and artisans sell
everything from furniture to jewelry to vintage clothing.

Adjacent to the Strasburg Antique Emporium, the **Museum of
American Presidents** (✉ 130 N. Massanutten St., Strasburg 🕿 540/

465–8175 ⌑ $5 for president's museum; $9 for both museums
🕒 Fri.–Mon. 10–5, or by appointment) displays memorabilia of each
American president from George Washington to George W. Bush.
The prized possession is a desk where James Madison wrote some of
his most important papers. Upstairs, the **Jeane Dixon Museum**
includes the possessions, furnishings, books, and papers from the last
apartment of the famous psychic.

Shopping
Route 11 Potato Chips (✉ 2325 1st St. ☎ 540/869–0104 or 800/294–
7783 ⊕ www.rt11.com) makes chips: lightly salted, flavored with dill
or barbecue, and the extremely hot "death rain," spiced with habanero
and chipotle powder. On Friday (10–6) and Saturday (9–5), the factory
is open to the public, who can watch its potato chips take shape.

New Market

🄉 *35 mi southwest of Middletown via I–81.*

At New Market the Confederates had a victory at the late date of 1864.
Inside the Hall of Valor, in the 260-acre **New Market Battlefield Historical Park,** a stained-glass window mosaic commemorates the battle, in
which 257 Virginia Military Institute cadets, some as young as 15, were
mobilized to improve the odds against superior Union numbers; 10 were
killed. This circular building contains a chronology of the war, and a
short film deals with Stonewall Jackson's legendary campaign in the
Shenandoah Valley. A farmhouse that figured in the fighting still stands
on the premises. The battle is reenacted at the park each May. ✉ *I–81,
Exit 264* ☎ *540/740–3101* ⌑ *$8* 🕒 *Daily 9–5.*

> **off the
> beaten
> path**

SHENANDOAH CAVERNS – The spectacular calcite formations found
here, including a series resembling strips of bacon, were formed by
water dripping through long, narrow cracks in the limestone. The
colored lighting effects help differentiate the sparkling calcite crystals.
The caverns are accessible to those in wheelchairs. Also on the
grounds is **American Celebration on Parade,** an exhibit of floats
from parades across America throughout the last 50 years. ✉ *261
Caverns Rd., I–81, Exit 269* ☎ *540/477–3115* ⊕ *www.
shenandoahcaverns.com* ⌑ *$13 for caverns only; $8 for float
exhibit only; $17.50 for both* 🕒 *Mid-June–Labor Day, daily 9–6;
Labor Day–Oct., 9–5; Nov.–mid-Apr., daily 9–4; mid-Apr.–mid-
June, daily 9–5.*

ENDLESS CAVERNS – These caverns were discovered in 1879 by two
boys and a dog chasing a rabbit. Opened to the public in 1920, the
seemingly endless configurations of the caverns have baffled
numerous explorers. The tour is enhanced by lighting effects,
especially at "Snow Drift," where a sudden illumination emphasizes
the white powdery appearance of the "drift" in a room tinted brown
and yellow. ✉ *3 mi south of New Market on Rte. 11, Exit 264 or
257 off I–81* ☎ *540/896–2283* ⊕ *www.endlesscaverns.com* ⌑ *$14*

⊙ *Mid-Mar.–mid-June and Labor Day–early Nov., daily 9–5; mid-June–Labor Day, daily 9–6; mid-Nov.–mid-Mar., daily 9–4.*

Sports & the Outdoors

FISHING **Murray's Fly Shop** (⊠ 121 Main St., Edinburg ☎ 540/984–4212 ⊕ www.murraysflyshop.com), 15 mi north of New Market, is the place for advice on fishing the Shenandoah River or local trout streams. The store sells more than 30,000 flies and has hundreds of rods and reels available. A stream report, updated weekly, is available on the store's Web site.

SKIING **Bryce Resort** (⊠ Rte. 263, 11 mi west of I–81, Exit 273, Basye ☎ 540/856–2121 ⊕ www.bryceresort.com) has eight slopes and three lifts. The resort, on the eastern edge of the Allegheny Mountains, is open year-round. Golf, mountain biking, hiking, tennis, and swimming are also available.

Nightlife & the Arts

The **Shenandoah Valley Music Festival** brings classical, jazz, and folk music to the Allegheny Mountains on weekends from May to September. The events are held at the Orkney Springs Hotel, an early-19th-century spa that's now an Episcopal retreat. Arts and crafts displays and an ice-cream social precede each concert. Concertgoers can sit on the lawn for $14 or in one of two pavilions for around $21; call ahead to reserve tickets. A bus to the festival from Woodstock (Exit 283 on I–81) costs $5. ⊠ *Rte. 263, 2 mi south of Bryce Resort* ☎ *540/459–3396* ⊕ *www.musicfest.org.*

Harrisonburg

⓾ *18 mi southwest of New Market via Exit 251 from I–81.*

Harrisonburg is a workaday market town surrounded by rich farmlands. Settled in 1739, it's a stronghold of Mennonites, who wear plain clothes and drive horse-drawn buggies. The city is also a center of higher education, with James Madison University and Eastern Mennonite College in town and Bridgewater College nearby.

At the **Virginia Quilt Museum,** you can see examples of quilts made throughout the mid-Atlantic region and learn about the international heritage of quilting. ⊠ *301 S. Main St., Harrisonburg* ☎ *540/433–3818* ⊡ *$4* ⊙ *Mon. and Thurs.–Sat. 10–4, Sun. 1–4.*

Where to Stay & Eat

★ **$–$$** ✕🏠 **Joshua Wilton House.** A row of trees guards the privacy of this circa 1888 B&B, decorated in the Victorian style and set on a large yard at the edge of the "Old Town" district. The sunroom and back patio are built for relaxation. Ask for Room 4; it has a lace-draped canopy bed and a turret sitting area with a view of the Blue Ridge Mountains looming over Main Street. Room 2 has a fireplace. The restaurant's menu changes daily, its components supplied by many small, local organic farmers. As an appetizer, try the smoked salmon on apple potato cake with dill crème fraîche; for a main dish, try the grilled stuffed pork tenderloin. ⊠ *412 S. Main St., 22801* ☎ *540/434–4464* 🖷 *540/432–9525*

⊕ *www.joshuawilton.com* ⌖ *5 rooms* ⌂ *Restaurant, Internet; no room TVs, no kids under 8, no smoking* ▱ *AE, MC, V* ⭘| *BP.*

Sports & the Outdoors

Massanutten Resort (✉ Off Rte. 33, 10 mi east of Harrisonburg on Rte. 644 ☎ 540/289–9441), open year-round, has many programs geared to children. Fifteen ski slopes, a snow-tubing park, a skateboarding park, indoor and outdoor pools, pond fishing, hiking, and mountain bikes for rent are among the offerings. There's also an 18-hole golf course.

Shopping

The dozens of **antiques shops** in the Harrisonburg area are generally on or near Route 11. Contact the Harrisonburg-Rockingham Convention and Visitors Bureau for a list, or just keep an eye open while driving through communities such as Bridgewater, Dayton, Elkton, Mount Crawford, Mount Sydney, Verona, and Weyer's Cave.

> **off the beaten path**
>
> **NATURAL CHIMNEYS REGIONAL PARK –** In Mount Solon, 23 mi south of Harrisonburg, these seven freestanding limestone pylons stand from 65 to 120 feet tall and are slender like the pillars of an Egyptian temple ruin. The 500-million-year-old formations were created by some form of natural action, though their exact origins are unknown. Facilities include connecting nature trails and a swimming pool. Every June and August a jousting tournament is held at the site. ✉ *I–81, Exit 240 W, Mount Solon 22843* ☎ *540/350–2510* ⌸ *$4 per person; $8 maximum fee per car* ⊙ *Daily 9–dusk.*

Dayton

❶ *2 mi west of Harrisonburg via Rte. 33 off I–81.*

Dayton is best known for its large Mennonite population, whose black horse-drawn buggies share the road with latter-day SUVs. At the **Harrisonburg–Rockingham Historical Society,** multimedia folk art reflects the largely German and Scotch-Irish culture of the valley. One Civil War exhibit includes an electric map that traces Stonewall Jackson's famous 1862 Valley Campaign. ✉ *382 High St.* ☎ *540/879–2616 or 540/879–2681* ⊕ *www.heritagecenter.com* ⌸ *$5* ⊙ *Mon.–Sat. 10–4.*

Also known as the Daniel Harrison House, **Fort Harrison** (from circa 1749) is of fortified stone and decorated in prosperous frontier style. Costumed interpreters discuss how the furnishings—beds with ropes as slats and hand-quilted comforters—were made. Artifacts on display come from recent excavations undertaken adjacent to the house. ✉*Rte. 42* ☎*540/879–2280* ⌸*Free; donation encouraged* ⊙*Mid-May–Oct., weekends 1–5.*

Shopping

The **Dayton Farmers Market** (✉ Rte. 42, south of Dayton ☎ 540/879–9885), an 18,000-square-foot area, has homemade baked goods and fresh fruits and vegetables as well as butter churns and ceramic speckleware, made by the Mennonites who live in the area. It's one place to mingle with the craftspeople, as well as with students from James Madison University in nearby Harrisonburg. It's open Thursday–Sunday.

Staunton

12 *27 mi south of Dayton via I–81, 11 mi west of southern end of Skyline Dr. at Waynesboro off I–64.*

Staunton (pronounced *stan*-ton) was once the seat of government of the vast Augusta County, which formed in 1738 and encompassed present-day West Virginia, Kentucky, Ohio, Illinois, Indiana, and the Pittsburgh area. After the state's General Assembly fled here from the British in 1781, Staunton was briefly the state's capital. Woodrow Wilson (1856–1924), the nation's 27th president and the eighth president from Virginia, is a native son.

The **Woodrow Wilson Presidential Library** has period antiques, items from Wilson's political career, and some original pieces from when this museum was the residence of Wilson's father, a Presbyterian minister. Wilson's presidential limousine, a 1919 Pierce-Arrow sedan, is on display in the garage. The site is being expanded to become a full presidential library, with space for scholarly research. The tentative completion date is 2008. ⊠ *24 N. Coalter St.* ☎ *540/885–0897 or 888/496–6376* ⊕ *www.woodrowwilson.org* ⊡ *$8* ☉ *Mon.–Sat. 9–5, Sun. noon–5.*

★ ☪ The **Frontier Culture Museum,** an outdoor living museum, re-creates agrarian life in America. The four illustrative farmsteads, American, Scotch-Irish, German, and English, were painstakingly moved from their original site and reassembled on the museum grounds. The livestock and plants here resemble the historic breeds and varieties as closely as possible. Special programs and activities, held throughout the year, include soap and broom making, cornhusking bees, and supper and barn dances. ⊠ *1250 Richmond Rd., off I–81, Exit 222 to Rte. 250 W* ☎ *540/332–7850* ⊕ *www.frontier.va.gov* ⊡ *$10* ☉ *Dec.–mid-Mar., daily 10–4; mid-Mar.–Nov., daily 9–5.*

The **Statler Brothers Museum,** on the edge of downtown Staunton, about 2 mi from I–81, has awards and other memorabilia collected by the country-music singing group. The building that houses the museum is a former school that members Harold and Don Reid attended. Tours are given once each weekday at 2; the gift shop is open 10:30–3:30 each weekday. ⊠ *501 Thornrose Ave.* ☎ *540/885–7297* ⊕ *www.statlerbrothers. com* ⊡ *Free.*

> **need a break?**
>
> **Wright's Dairy Rite** (⊠ 346 Greenville Ave. ☎ 540/886–0435 ⊕ www.m-c-b.com/wrights), an old hangout of the Statler Brothers, still offers curbside service; orders are brought to your car. Try the homemade onion rings or a milk shake, available in nine different flavors. You can even order that 1950s staple, a malted.

Seven miles east of Staunton, the **P. Buckley Moss Museum** is a full-scale gallery of paintings and drawings by one of the Valley's most recognized artists. Moss, who moved to Waynesboro in 1964, was inspired by the quiet dignity and simplicity of the "plain people"—those in the Mennonite communities of the Shenandoah Valley—and has made these neighbors her subject matter. Her studio, a converted barn about 2 mi from the museum, opens a few times a year to the public. ✉ *2150 Rosser Ave., I–64, Exit 94, Waynesboro* ☎ *540/949–6473* ⊕ *www.p-buckley-moss. com* 🔁 *Free* ⊗ *Mon.–Sat. 10–6, Sun. 12:30–5:30.*

off the beaten path

GRAND CAVERNS – Discovered in 1804 and opened to the public just two years later, Augusta County's Grand Caverns, 23 mi from Staunton, is America's oldest show cave. Thomas Jefferson paid an early visit, and Civil War troops from both sides were among those who descended into the subterranean wonderland. One highlight: an underground room that's one of the largest of its kind in the East. ✉ *I–81, Exit 235* ☎ *540/249–5705* ⊕ *www.grandcaverns.com* 🔁 *$15* ⊗ *Apr.–Oct., daily 9–5; Mar., weekends 9–5.*

Where to Stay & Eat

★ ¢–$$ ✕ **Mrs. Rowe's Restaurant.** A homey restaurant with plenty of booths, Rowe's has been operated by the same family since 1947 and enjoys a rock-solid reputation for inexpensive and delicious Southern meals. The fried chicken—skillet-cooked to order—is a standout. A local breakfast favorite is oven-hot biscuits topped with gravy (your choice of sausage, tenderloin, or creamy chipped beef). For dessert, try the mince pie in the fall or the rhubarb cobbler in summer. ✉ *I–81, Exit 222* ☎ *540/ 886–1833* ⊕ *www.mrsrowes.com* ☐ *D, MC, V.*

$–$$$ ✕🔲 **Belle Grae Inn.** The sitting room and music room of this restored 1870 Victorian house have been converted into formal dining rooms, with brass wall sconces, Oriental rugs, and candles at the tables. The menu ($$$$), which changes weekly, has continental cuisine with a regional flair. Accommodations are furnished with antique rocking chairs and canopied or brass beds; a complimentary snifter of brandy awaits in each one. ✉ *515 W. Frederick St., 24401* ☎ *540/886–5151 or 888/ 541–5151* 🖷 *540/886–6641* ⊕ *www.bellegrae.com* 🔁 *8 rooms, 7 suites, 2 cottages* ⌕ *Restaurant, some microwaves, Internet; no smoking* ☐ *AE, D, MC, V* ⦿ *MAP.*

$–$$$ 🔲 **Frederick House.** Six restored town houses dating from 1810 make up this inn in the center of the historic district. All rooms are decorated with antiques, and some have fireplaces and private decks. A pub and a restaurant are adjacent. ✉ *28 N. New St., 24401* ☎ *540/885–4220 or 800/334–5575* 🖷 *540/885–5180* ⊕ *www.frederickhouse.com* 🔁 *11 rooms, 12 suites* ⌕ *Cable TV, meeting rooms; no smoking* ☐ *AE, D, DC, MC, V* ⦿ *BP.*

$–$$ 🔲 **Sampson Eagon Inn.** Across the street from the Woodrow Wilson Presidential Library in the Gospel Hill section of town, this restored Greek revival (circa 1840) has a lot of period charm. In the spacious guest rooms are antique canopy beds, cozy sitting areas, and modern amenities. Don't miss the Kahlúa Belgian waffles for breakfast. ✉ *238 E. Beverley St., 24401* ☎ *540/886–8200 or 800/597–9722* ⊕ *www.eagoninn. com* 🔁 *5 rooms, one with shower only* ⌕ *Cable TV with movies; no kids under 12, no smoking* ☐ *AE, MC, V* ⦿ *BP.*

Nightlife & the Arts

THEATER Experience Shakespeare's plays the way the Elizabethans did at **Blackfri-**
★ **ars Playhouse** (✉ 10 S. Market St. ☎ 540/885–5588 ⊕ www.

shenandoahshakespeare.com), a near-duplicate of the Globe Theatre that has rapidly gained worldwide acclaim for its attention to detail. Like those in 17th-century London, most seating consists of benches (modern seat backs and cushions are available), and some stools are right on stage.

Shopping

At **Sheridan Sunspots Studios & Designs** (⊠ 202 S. Lewis St. ☎ 540/885–8557), near downtown, you can see artisans at work, blowing glass and melding copper. Their exquisite items for the house and garden are available for purchase. In spring the studio hosts the Virginia Hot Glass Festival, which brings together hot-glass artists from across the region. **Virginia Made Shop** (⊠ I–81, Exit 222 ☎ 540/886–7180) specializes in Virginia-made products, from pottery and wind chimes to peanuts and wine. At **Virginia Metalcrafters** (⊠ 1010 E. Main St., I–64, Exit 94, Waynesboro ☎ 540/949–9400 or 800/368–1002) you can find a broad line of gifts and decorative accessories that are hand-cast in brass, iron, bronze, and pewter. All are made using the same techniques employed since the company was founded in 1890.

Lexington

⑬ *30 mi south of Staunton via I–81.*

Two deeply traditional Virginia colleges sit side by side in this town, each with a memorial to a soldier who was also a man of peace.

Washington and Lee University, the ninth-oldest college in the United States, was founded in 1749 as Augusta Academy and later renamed Washington College in gratitude for a donation from George Washington. After Robert E. Lee's term as its president (1865–70), it received its current name. Today, with 2,000 students, the university occupies a campus of white-column, redbrick buildings around a central colonnade. Twentieth-century alumni include the late Supreme Court Justice Lewis Powell, newsman Roger Mudd, and novelist Tom Wolfe. The campus's **Lee Chapel and Museum** contains many relics of the Lee family. Edward Valentine's statue of the recumbent general, behind the altar, is especially moving: the pose is natural and the expression gentle, a striking contrast to most other monumental art. Here you can sense the affection and reverence that Lee inspired. ⊠ *Jefferson St., Rte. 11* ☎ *540/463–8768* ⊕ *www2.wlu.edu* ⊠ *Free* ☺ *Chapel open Apr.–Oct., Mon.–Sat. 9–5, Sun. 1–5; Nov.–Mar., Mon.–Sat. 9–4, Sun. 1–4; campus tours Apr.–Oct., weekdays 10–4, Sat. 9:45–noon; Jan.–Mar., weekdays 10 and noon, Sat. 11.*

Adjacent to Washington and Lee University are the imposing Gothic buildings of the **Virginia Military Institute** (VMI), founded in 1839 and the nation's oldest state-supported military college. With an enrollment of about 1,300 cadets, the institute has admitted women since 1997. The **Virginia Military Institute Museum,** in the George C. Marshall Museum until renovations to Jackson Memorial Hall are completed in 2007, displays 15,000 artifacts, including Stonewall Jackson's stuffed and mounted horse, Little Sorrel, and the general's coat, pierced by the bullet that killed him at Chancellorsville. ⊠ *Letcher Ave.* ☎ *540/464–7232* ⊕ *www.vmi. edu* ⊠ *$3* ☺ *Daily 9–5.*

The **George C. Marshall Museum** preserves the memory of the World War II army chief of staff. Exhibits trace his brilliant career, which began when he was aide-de-camp to John "Black Jack" Pershing in World War I and culminated when, as secretary of state, he devised the Marshall Plan, a strategy for reviving postwar Western Europe. Marshall's Nobel Peace Prize is on display; so is the Oscar won by his aide Frank McCarthy, who produced the Academy Award–winning Best Picture of 1970, *Patton*. An electronically narrated map tells the story of World War II. *VMI campus* ⊠ *Letcher Ave.* ☎ *540/463–7103* 🖃 *$3* ☉ *Daily 9–5.*

Confederate general Jackson's private life is on display at the **Stonewall Jackson House,** where he is revealed as a dedicated Presbyterian who was devoted to physical fitness, careful with money, musically inclined, and fond of gardening. The general lived here only two years, while teaching physics and military tactics to the cadets, before leaving for his command in the Civil War. This is the only house he ever owned; it's furnished now with period pieces and some of his belongings. ⊠ *8 E. Washington St.* ☎ *540/463–2552* ⊕ *www.stonewalljackson.org* 🖃 *$6* ☉ *Mon.–Sat. 9–5, Sun. 1–5.*

The inventor of the first mechanical wheat reaper is honored at the **Cyrus McCormick Museum,** which sits about a mile off I–81. Follow the signs to Walnut Grove farm; now a livestock research center, this mill farmstead is where McCormick did his work. In addition to the museum and family home, you can tour a blacksmith shop and gristmill. All are registered as national historic landmarks. ⊠ *State Rte. 606, 5 mi north of Lexington* ☎ *540/377–2255* 🖃 *Free* ☉ *Daily 8:30–5.*

off the beaten path

Fodor'sChoice
★

NATURAL BRIDGE OF VIRGINIA – About 20 mi south of Lexington, this impressive limestone arch (which supports Route 11) has been gradually carved out by Cedar Creek, which rushes through 215 feet below. The Monacan Native American tribe called it the Bridge of God. Surveying the structure for Lord Halifax, George Washington carved his own initials in the stone; Thomas Jefferson bought it (and more than 150 surrounding acres) from George III. The after-dark sound-and-light show may be overkill, but viewing and walking under the bridge itself and along the wooded pathway beyond are worth the price of admission. On the property are dizzying caverns that descend 34 stories, a wax museum, a toy museum, and an 18th-century village constructed by the Monacan Indian Nation. ⊠ *I–81 S, Exit 180, I–81 N, Exit 175* ☎ *540/291–2121 or 800/533–1410* ⊕ *www.naturalbridgeva.com* 🖃 *Bridge $10, all attractions $22.50* ☉ *Mar.–Nov., daily 8 AM–dark.*

Where to Stay & Eat

$–$$$ ✕ **Wilson-Walker House.** This stately 1820 Greek revival house is ideal for eating elegant regional cuisine. Seafood dishes are a specialty—try the pan-seared, potato-encrusted trout. The restaurant is not as expensive as you might expect, and is particularly affordable during the $5 chef's-special luncheon. ⊠ *30 N. Main St.* ☎ *540/463–3020* ☰ *AE, MC, V* ☉ *Closed Sun. and Mon.*

$–$$ ✕ **The Palms.** Once a Victorian ice-cream parlor, this full-service restaurant in an 1890 building has indoor and outdoor dining. Wood booths line the walls of the plant-filled room: the pressed-metal ceiling is original. Specialties on the American menu include broccoli-cheese soup, charbroiled meats, and teriyaki chicken. ⊠ *101 W. Nelson St.* ☎ *540/463–7911* ⚑ *Reservations not accepted* ▤ *AE, D, MC, V.*

$$–$$$ ✕▦ **Maple Hall.** For a taste of Southern history, spend a night at this country inn of 1850. Once a plantation house, it's set on 56 acres 6 mi north of Lexington. All rooms have period antiques and modern amenities; most have gas log fireplaces as well. Dinner is served in three ground-floor rooms and on a glassed-in patio; the main dining room ($$–$$$) has a large decorative fireplace. Among notable entrées on the seasonal menu are beef fillet with green peppercorn sauce; veal sautéed with mushrooms in hollandaise sauce; and chicken Chesapeake, a chicken breast stuffed with spinach and crabmeat. ⊠ *Rte. 11, 24450* ☎ *540/463–6693 or 877/283–9680* ⊟ *540/463–7262* ⊕ *www.lexingtonhistoricinns.com/maplehall.htm* ⇖ *17 rooms, 4 suites* ⚲ *Restaurant, tennis court, pool, fishing, hiking, meeting rooms* ▤ *D, MC, V* ⌾ *BP.*

¢–$ ▦ **Natural Bridge Hotel.** Within walking distance of the spectacular rock arch of the same name (there's also a shuttle bus), the Colonial-style brick hotel has a beautiful location as well as numerous recreational facilities. Long porches with rocking chairs allow leisurely appreciation of the Blue Ridge Mountains. Rooms are done in a Colonial Virginia style. ⊠ *Rte. 11, Box 57, Natural Bridge 24578* ☎ *540/291–2121 or 800/533–1410* ⊟ *540/291–1896* ⊕ *www.naturalbridgeva.com* ⇖ *180 rooms* ⚲ *Restaurant, snack bar, some microwaves, cable TV with movies and video games, miniature golf, 2 tennis courts, pool, hiking, bar, meeting rooms* ▤ *AE, D, DC, MC, V.*

Nightlife & the Arts

The **Theater at Lime Kiln** (⊠ Lime Kiln Rd. ☎ 540/463–7088 ⊕ www.theateratlimekiln.com) stages musicals, concerts, and performances as varied as Russian clowns and Vietnamese puppeteers. The Kiln's solid rock walls create a dramatic backdrop. Original musicals are staged Tuesday through Saturday, and contemporary music concerts are given on Sunday throughout the summer. In winter, productions continue in a downtown theater on Main Street. To get here from I–81, follow U.S. 60 west 0.4 mi past the Washington and Lee University pedestrian bridge, turn left on Borden Road, and follow it 0.2 mi.

en route The drive to Bath County on the 35-mi stretch of Route 39 north and west from Lexington provides a scenic trip through 3-mi **Goshen Pass,** a dramatic gorge that follows the boulder-strewn Maury River through the Allegheny Mountains. Before the coming of railroads, it was the principal stagecoach route into Lexington. In May, the scene becomes lush with rhododendrons and other flowering plants; in October, the colors of the rainbow paint the maples and oaks that fill the gorge. A day-use park enables picnickers to bask in this forest preserve, where the river allows for fishing, swimming, and tubing.

Sports & the Outdoors

The **Virginia Horse Center** (⊠ 487 Maury River Rd. ☎ 540/463–2194) on Route 39 stages competitions—show jumping, hunter trials, multi-breed shows—several days a week. An indoor arena permits year-round operation. Most events are free.

Bath County

⑭ *20 mi northwest of Lexington via Rte. 39.*

As residents are proud to point out, there are no traffic lights in all of Bath County and only 10 year-round inhabitants per square mile. In fact, there often seem to be almost as many visitors as inhabitants here, particularly around the historic Homestead resort in Hot Springs. The healing thermal springs were what originally brought visitors to town in the 1700s. Although they're less fashionable today, the sulfurous waters still flow at Warm Springs, Hot Springs, and Bolar Springs, their temperatures ranging from 77°F to 104°F. Try "taking the cure" at the Jefferson Pools in Warm Springs, where the rustic men's and ladies' bathhouses (built in 1761 and 1836, respectively) are largely unchanged.

Where to Stay & Eat

★ **$$–$$$** ✕ **Waterwheel Restaurant.** Part of a complex of five historic buildings, this restaurant is in a gristmill that dates from 1700. A walk-in wine cellar, set among the gears of the original waterwheel, has 100 wine selections; diners may step in and choose for themselves. The dining area is decorated with Currier & Ives and Audubon prints. Some menu favorites are fresh smoked trout and chicken Fantasio (breast of chicken stuffed with wild rice, sausage, apple, and pecans). Desserts include such Old Virginny recipes as a deep-dish apple pie baked with bourbon. On Sunday look for the hearty but affordable brunch. ⊠ *Grist Mill Sq., Warm Springs* ☎ *540/839–2231* ▭ *D, MC, V* ☉ *Closed Tues. Nov.–May.*

$$–$$$ 🏨 **Homestead.** Host to a prestigious clientele since 1766, the Homestead
FodorsChoice has evolved from a country spa to a 15,000-acre resort and conference
★ facility. From the glorious columns of the entry hall to the stunning views of the Appalachian Mountains, magnificence surrounds those here from the first moment to the last. Rooms in the sprawling redbrick building, built in 1891, have Georgian-style furnishings; some have fireplaces. As for what to do, there's 4 mi of streams stocked with rainbow trout, 100 mi of riding trails, skeet and trap shooting, and nine ski slopes (snow-boarding allowed). The Homestead was the site of the South's first downhill skiing in 1959, and one of the golf courses, laid out in 1892, includes the oldest tee in continuous use in the United States. An orchestra plays nightly in the formal dining room (dinner is included in the room rate), where continental cuisine and regional specialties take their place in its six-course extravaganzas. ⊠ *Rte. 220, Hot Springs 24445* ☎ *540/ 839–1766 or 800/838–1766* 🖷 *540/839–7670* ⊕ *www.thehomestead. com* ⇌ *429 rooms, 77 suites* ♿ *6 restaurants, cable TV with movies and video games, 3 18-hole golf courses, 8 tennis courts, 2 pools (1 indoor), spa, bicycles, bowling, horseback riding, downhill skiing, ice-skating, cinema, video game room, Internet, meeting rooms, airport shuttle* ▭ *AE, D, DC, MC, V* ✝◎❙ *MAP.*

★ **$–$$** 🏠 **Inn at Gristmill Square.** Occupying five restored buildings at the same site as the Waterwheel Restaurant, the rooms of this state historical landmark inn are in a Colonial Virginia style. Four units are in the original miller's house; others occupy the former blacksmith's shop, hardware store, gristmill, and cottage. Some of the rooms have fireplaces and patios. ✉ *Rte. 645, Box 359, Warm Springs 24484* ☎ *540/839–2231* 🖷 *540/839–5770* ⊕ *www.gristmillsquare.com* ⇨ *12 rooms, 5 suites, 1 apartment* ⟆ *Restaurant, cable TV, 3 tennis courts, pool, sauna, bar, meeting rooms* ▭ *D, MC, V* ⌦ *BP.*

$–$$ 🏠 **Milton Hall.** This 1874 Gothic brick house, built as an elegant country retreat by English nobility, is on 44 acres. It's close to the George Washington National Forest and its abundant outdoor activities. The spacious rooms have Victorian furnishings and large beds. Box lunches can be ordered in advance. ✉ *207 Thorny La., I–64, Exit 10, at Callaghan, Covington 24426* ☎ *540/965–0196 or 877/764–5866* ⊕ *www.milton-hall.com* ⇨ *6 rooms, 1 suite* ⟆ *Cable TV with movies, hiking; no smoking* ▭ *D, MC, V* ⌦ *BP.*

¢ 🏠 **Roseloe Motel.** The modest and clean lodgings in this motel from the '50s are all homey and conventionally decorated. The Roseloe is halfway between Warm Springs and Hot Springs, where the fresh mountain air is bracing. ✉ *Rte. 1, Box 590, Hot Springs 24445* ☎ *540/839–5373* ⇨ *14 rooms* ⟆ *Some kitchenettes, refrigerators, cable TV* ▭ *AE, D, MC, V.*

Nightlife & the Arts

Garth Newel Music Center (✉ Rte. 220, Warm Springs ☎ 540/839–5018 or 877/558–1689 ⊕ www.garthnewel.org) has weekend chamber-music performances in summer; you can make reservations and plan to picnic on the grounds.

Sports & the Outdoors

GOLF The **Homestead** has three excellent 18-hole golf courses. The par-70, 6,679-yard Cascades course, the site of USGA and Senior PGA events, has gently sloped fairways amid rugged terrain. The par-72, 6,752-yard Lower Cascades course, designed by Robert Trent Jones, has more wide-open fairways with many bunkers and breaks. The par-72, 6,211-yard Old Course is most famous for its first tee, established in 1892. It's the oldest tee still in continuous use in the United States.

HIKING & The Warm Springs Ranger District of the **George Washington and Jef-**
MOUNTAIN **ferson National Forests** (☎ 540/839–2521) has information on hundreds
BIKING of miles of local trails. At **Douthat State Park** (✉ Exit 27, 7 mi north of I–64 near Clifton Forge ☎ 540/862–8100), there are more than 40 mi of well-signed, smoothly groomed, and sometimes steep trails for hiking and biking. The trails pass by waterfalls and majestic overlooks.

SNOW SPORTS **Homestead** has nine slopes for snowboarding or cross-country, downhill, or night skiing. Snowmobiling tours take you around the 15,000-acre property, or you could take to the trails in snowshoes day or night (with the help of headlamps and guides). Ice skating and snowtubing add options for staying outdoors in the cold.

SOUTHWEST VIRGINIA

Southwest Virginia is a rugged region of alternating mountain ridges and deep valleys. Modern urban life is juxtaposed with spectacular scenery in the Roanoke and New River valleys. Other areas retain the quiet charm of yesteryear: they have many pleasant meadows, old country churches, and towns with just one stop sign. The gorge-incised Appalachian Plateau in far southwest Virginia is abundant in coal. Interstate 81 and Interstate 77 form a kind of "X" across the region, and the Blue Ridge Parkway roughly defines Southwest Virginia's eastern edge.

Roanoke

🕕 *49 mi south of Lexington (via I–81).*

The bowl-shape Roanoke Valley, although considered the geological southern end of the Shenandoah Valley, has historic and cultural ties that link it more closely to rugged Southwest Virginia than to the genteel Shenandoah. Roanoke, population 95,000, is Virginia's largest city west of Richmond and in many ways the area's capital. The metropolitan area of 230,000 has enough city flavor to provide a degree of culture and elegance, but its location between the Blue Ridge Parkway and Appalachian Trail means that the wilds aren't too far away either; mountains dominate its horizons in all directions. Salem, next door to Roanoke, is its smaller and older neighbor in the valley. Fiercely independent, Salemites hate to have their town called a suburb.

Even in daylight, the Roanoke skyline is dominated by a star. The 100-foot-tall **Mill Mountain Star,** which was the world's largest man-made star when constructed in 1949, stands in a city park 1,000 feet above the Roanoke Valley. From either of the park's two overlooks, Roanoke, the "Star City of the South," looks like a scale model of a city. From the overlooks you can also see wave after wave of Appalachian ridgelines. ⊠ *Mill Mountain Park, follow Walnut St. south 2 mi from downtown Roanoke; or take Parkway Spur Rd. 3 mi north from Blue Ridge Pkwy. at milepost 120.3.*

🕲 Sharing the mountaintop with the star is the **Mill Mountain Zoo,** one of only two nationally accredited zoos in Virginia. Asian animals are center stage here, including a rare Siberian tiger, snow leopards, and red pandas. ⊠ *Mill Mountain Park, follow Walnut St. south 2 mi from downtown Roanoke; or take Parkway Spur Rd. 3 mi north from Blue Ridge Pkwy. at milepost 120.3* ☎ *540/343–3241* ⊕ *www.mmzoo.org* 🎟 *$6.75* 🕗 *Daily 10–5; gate closes at 4:30.*

Market Square is the heart of Roanoke, with Virginia's oldest continuous farmer's market, a multiethnic food court inside the restored City Market Building, and several restaurants, shops, and bars. A restored warehouse called **Center in the Square** (⊠ 1 Market Sq. SE ☎ 540/342–5700 ⊕ www.centerinthesquare.org) contains the Mill Mountain Theatre and three regional museums covering science, history, and art. A combined $11 ticket grants access to the science museum, which has many interactive exhibits, as well as the MegaDome theater and Hopkins Planetarium.

☺ Near Market Square, the **Virginia Museum of Transportation** has the largest collection of diesel and steam locomotives in the country—not surprising, considering Roanoke got its start as a railroad town and was once the headquarters of the Norfolk & Western railroad. The dozens of original train cars and engines, many built here in town, include a massive Nickel Plate locomotive—just one of the many holdings that constitute an unabashed display of civic pride. The sprawling model train and miniature circus setups please young and old alike. ⊠ *303 Norfolk Ave.* ☎ *540/342–5670* ⊕ *www.vmt.org* 🖃 *$7.40* ☉ *Weekdays 11–4, Sat. 10–5, Sun. 1–5.*

★ You can relive the final days of steam trains at the **O. Winston Link Museum,** inside a renovated passenger train station. Link spent several years in the late 1950s and early 1960s photographing Norfolk & Western's last steam engines in the railroads of Southwest Virginia. The hundreds of stunning black and white photographs on display do much more than evoke nostalgia—they also capture day-to-day life: a horse-drawn carriage awaiting an oncoming train, a locomotive rocketing past lovers watching a drive-in movie. ⊠ *101 Shenandoah Ave.* ☎ *540/ 982–5465* ⊕ *www.linkmuseum.org* 🖃 *$5* ☉ *Mon.–Sat. 10–5, Sun. noon–5.*

Dixie Caverns is unusual in that, rather than descending into the cave, you first must walk upstairs into the heart of a mountain. The spacious Cathedral Room, formations dubbed Turkey Wing and Wedding Bell, and an earthquake fault line are among the sights. There's also a mineral and fossil shop attached to the caverns. ⊠ *5753 W. Main St., take I–81 to Exit 132, which links up with Rte. 11/460, Salem* ☎ *540/380– 2085* 🖃 *$7.50* ☉ *May–Sept. daily 9:30–6; Oct.–Apr. daily 9:30–5.*

off the
beaten
path

NATIONAL D-DAY MEMORIAL – When Allied forces landed at Normandy on June 6, 1944, in what would be the decisive military move of World War II, the small town of Bedford lost nearly an entire generation of its young men. The town of 3,200 lost 19 on D-Day, and four more in days to come. Because its losses on D-Day were proportionally heavier than any other U.S. community, Bedford was chosen as the site of this memorial. Its focal point is a huge granite arch and flag plaza on a hill overlooking the town. There are also granite statues of soldiers in combat and a reflecting pool that periodically shoots up spurts of water, as if struck by bullets. ⊠ *U.S. 460, 27 mi east of Roanoke, Bedford* ☎ *800/351–3329* ⊕ *www. dday.org* 🖃 *$10* ☉ *Daily 10–5.*

BOOKER T. WASHINGTON NATIONAL MONUMENT – This restored tobacco farm 25 mi southeast of Roanoke and 21 mi south of Bedford is a National Monument. Washington (1856–1915), born into slavery on this farm, was a remarkable educator and author who went on to advise Presidents McKinley, Roosevelt, and Taft and to take tea with Queen Victoria. More important, he started Tuskegee

Institute in Alabama and inspired generations of African-Americans. Covering 224 acres, the farm's restored buildings; tools; crops; animals; and, in summer, interpreters in period costume all help show what life during slavery was like. ☒ *Rte. 122, 21 mi south of Bedford* ☎ *540/721–2094* ⊕ *www.nps.gov/bowa* ☒ *Free* ☉ *Daily 9–5.*

need a break?

At the **Homestead Creamery** (☒ Rte. 122, just east of intersection with Rte. 116, Burnt Chimney ☎ 540/721–5808), you can sample farm-fresh milk. No plastic or paper cartons here—it's stored and sold in glass bottles, the way milkmen used to bring it. Gulping the chocolate milk is like drinking a chocolate cake. Unusual milk flavors such as mocha and orange cream are often available.

Where to Stay & Eat

★ **$-$$$** ✕ **Carlos Brazilian International Cuisine.** High on a hill with a spectacular view, this lively restaurant has French, Italian, Spanish, and Brazilian dishes. Try the *porco reacheado* (pork tenderloin stuffed with spinach and feta cheese) or the *moqueca mineira* (shrimp, clams, and whitefish in a Brazilian sauce). Brazilian radio often accompanies the meal. ☒ *4167 Electric Rd.* ☎ *540/345–7661* ☰ *AE, MC, V* ☉ *Closed Sun.*

$$-$$$ ✕ **The Library.** This quiet, elegant restaurant in the Piccadilly Square shopping center is decorated with shelves of books. Its frequently changing menu specializes in seafood dishes. Expect dishes such as sautéed Dover sole with almonds, fillet of beef with béarnaise sauce, and lobster tail. ☒ *3117 Franklin Rd. SW* ☎ *540/985–0811* ⌕ *Reservations essential* ☰ *AE, DC, MC, V* ☉ *Closed Sun.–Mon. No lunch.*

$ ✕ **Mac 'N' Bob's.** The enormous growth in seating since 1980, from 10 to 250, testifies to the popularity of this establishment in downtown Salem. Sports memorabilia lines the walls of the attractive redbrick building near Roanoke College, and sporting events are likely to be on the TVs near the bar. The menu runs from hamburgers to steak to seafood to pizza. If you have a big appetite, try a fully loaded calzone, which flops off the sides of your plate like a flounder. ☒ *316 E. Main St., Salem* ☎ *540/389–5999* ☰ *AE, D, MC, V.*

$ ✕ **The Homeplace.** Bring a big appetite with you on the drive up and over

FodorsChoice ★ Catawba Mountain to get to the Homeplace. Famished Appalachian Trail hikers in grimy shorts and suave diners in their Sunday best eat side by side in this farm home in a tiny country hamlet—come as you are. Old-fashioned cooking is dished up grandma style, with all-you-can-eat fried chicken, mashed potatoes and gravy, green beans, pinto beans, baked apples, hot biscuits, and an extra meat selection of your choice is served to each table for $11 a person (throw in another dollar for yet another meat selection). No alcohol is served, but the lemonade is delicious. ☒ *7 mi west of Salem on Rte. 311 N, Exit 141 off I–81, Catawba* ☎ *540/ 384–7252* ⌕ *Reservations not accepted* ☰ *MC, V* ☉ *No lunch Thurs.–Sat., no dinner Sun.*

$-$$$ ✕⌂ **Hotel Roanoke and Conference Center.** This elegant Tudor revival building, listed on the National Register of Historic Places, was built in 1882 by the Norfolk & Western Railroad. The richly paneled lobby has Florentine marble floors and ceiling frescos. The formal restaurant serves regional Southern cuisine ($$–$$$); perennial favorites include peanut soup and steak Diane, prepared table-side. The Market Square Bridge, a glassed-in walkway, goes from the hotel to downtown attractions. ⊠ *110 Shenandoah Ave., 24016* ☎ *540/985–5900* 🖷 *540/345–2890* ⊕ *www. hotelroanoke.com* ➥ *313 rooms, 19 suites* ⚹ *2 restaurants, cable TV with movies and video games, pool, gym, bar, Internet, convention center, meeting rooms, airport shuttle* ⊟ *AE, D, DC, MC, V.*

$$–$$$ 🏨 **Bernard's Landing.** A resort set on Smith Mountain Lake 45 minutes southeast of Roanoke, Bernard's rents one- to three-bedroom condominiums with water views and two- to five-bedroom town houses (all waterfront) for periods of up to two weeks. Because the units are separately owned, the way they are furnished varies widely, but all units have full kitchen facilities and private decks. Conferences are scheduled here year-round, and summer vacationers come for the many sports available. ⊠ *775 Ashmeade Rd., Moneta 24121* ☎ *540/721–8870 or 800/ 572–2048* 🖷 *540/721–8383* ⊕ *www.bernardslanding.com* ➥ *60 units* ⚹ *Restaurant, kitchens, microwaves, cable TV, 6 tennis courts, 2 pools, gym, sauna, boating, fishing, racquetball, playground, Internet, meeting rooms* ⊟ *AE, D, MC, V.*

Nightlife & the Arts

BARS & CLUBS   Roanoke's nightlife centers on the Market Square area of downtown, which is often bustling and lively on weekend nights. Near the Square, **Corned Beef and Co.** (⊠ 107 Jefferson St. ☎ 540/342–3354) has live jazz and funk music on Friday and Saturday nights. For something a bit out of the ordinary, try **Kara O'Caen's Irish Pub** (⊠ 303 S. Jefferson St. ☎ 540/344–5509), where live Irish folk music plays many nights.

Outdoor Activities & Sports

GOLF   **Hanging Rock Golf Course** (⊠ 1500 Red La., I–81, Exit 140, Salem ☎ 540/389–7275 ⊕ www.hangingrockgolf.com) has regularly received accolades as a top golf course in the state and region.

HIKING   The **Appalachian Trail** is north and west of Roanoke, crossing the valley at Troutville, 5 mi to the north. Two of the most photographed formations on the entire 2,000-mi route from Georgia to Maine, McAfee Knob and Dragon's Tooth, are accessible from trailheads on the Virginia 311 highway, west of the valley. The **Star Trail** (trailhead on Riverland Road, 2 mi southeast of downtown Roanoke) winds through a forest oasis amid the metropolitan area as it works its way up 1½ mi to the Mill Mountain Star. Other trails can be found along the Blue Ridge Parkway to the east and south and in the George Washington and Jefferson national forests to the north and west. For more information contact the national forests' **Supervisor's Office** (⊠ 5162 Valleypointe Pkwy., Roanoke ☎ 540/ 265–5100 or 888/265–0019).

HORSE SHOW   The **Roanoke Valley Horse Show** (⊠ Salem Civic Center ☎ 540/375–3004 ⊕ www.roanokevalleyhorseshow.com), in June, is one of the top all-breed shows, attracting more than 1,000 entries each year.

SPECTATOR   Each April and October, **Martinsville Speedway** (⊠ U.S. 220, Ridgeway
SPORTS   ☎ 276/638–7332 or 276/627–1900 ⊕ www.martinsvillespeedway.com)

fills its 86,000 seats with those who want to see NASCAR's top drivers in the Winston Cup series races held here, 50 mi south of Roanoke.

Shopping

Head to Market Square for offbeat stores, including **The Binaba Shop** (⌂ 120 Campbell Ave. SE ☎ 540/376–7064), which sells African artifacts, clothing, and jewelry. **Wertz's Country Store** (⌂ 215 Market St. SE ☎ 540/342–5133), beside the downtown farmer's market, sells country hams, homemade jams and jellies, sorghum molasses, and many sorts of nuts. For a furry companion that nevertheless doesn't bite or growl, visit **Blue Ridge Bears & Gifts** (⌂ 3109 Brambleton Ave. SW ☎ 540/989–4995 ⊕ www.nvo.com/blueridgebears), where the bears range in size from an inch to 3 foot tall.

Blue Ridge Parkway

5 mi east of Roanoke.

The Blue Ridge Parkway takes up where Skyline Drive leaves off at Waynesboro, weaving south for 471 mi to Great Smoky Mountains National Park in North Carolina. The parkway goes up to higher elevations than the drive, up to 4,200 feet at Apple Orchard Mountain, and even higher in North Carolina. Roanoke is the largest city along its entire route; with the exception of Asheville, N.C., the rest of the parkway bypasses populated areas, as was the intention of its New Deal–era designers. In Virginia, the parkway is especially scenic between Waynesboro and Roanoke, winding through the George Washington National Forest, visiting numerous ridge-top overlooks that provide views of crumpled-looking mountains and patchwork valleys. South of Roanoke, the route becomes more gently rolling as the Blue Ridge becomes more like a plateau on its way to North Carolina. Call the National Park Service's office in Vinton (☎ 540/857–2490) for information on Virginia's section of the Blue Ridge Parkway.

Peaks of Otter Recreation Area, 25 mi northeast of Roanoke, offers a close-up view of cone-shape Sharp Top Mountain, which no less an authority than Thomas Jefferson once called America's tallest peak. At 3,875 feet it's not even the tallest in the park—nearby Flat Top is 4,004 feet. You can hike to both peaks (the Sharp Top trail is often crowded on weekends) and to little brother Harkening Hill, as well as to Fallingwater Cascades, a thrilling multitier waterfall. For those not up to the climb, a bus heads most of the way up Sharp Top hourly throughout the day. The peaks rise about the shores of Abbott Lake, a bucolic picnic spot. A pleasant lakeside lodge and campground along the placid lake below are an ideal base for local trekking. ⌂ *Blue Ridge Pkwy., mile marker 86* ☎ *540/586–4357* ⊕ *www.peaksofotter.com* ▣ *Free.*

☼ **Explore Park,** a 1,100-acre recreational park near Roanoke, depicts life in Virginia from three distinct periods between 1671 and 1850. Costumed interpreters represent early Native American life, the Colonial frontier experience, and the life of a 19th-century settlement, with schoolhouse and blacksmith's shop. The park has 6 mi of hiking trails along the Roanoke River gorge as well as good opportunities for mountain biking, fishing, canoeing, and kayaking. Inside the park is the **Blue Ridge Parkway Visitors Center,** open 9–5 daily year-round. ⊠ *1½ mi north of milepost 115 on the Blue Ridge Pkwy.* ☎ *540/427–1800 or 800/842–9163* ⊕ *www.explorepark.org* ⌺ *$8* ⊙ *May–Oct., Wed.–Sat. 10–5, Sun. noon–5.*

Mabry Mill, north of Meadows of Dan and the Blue Ridge Parkway's junction with U.S. 58 at milepost 176, 55 mi south of Roanoke, is one of the parkway's most popular stops for photographers. The restored water-powered, weather-worn gristmill grinds cornmeal and buckwheat flour, which are for sale. There are regular demonstrations of blacksmithing and other trades. A short hiking trail rings the property. ⊠ *Blue Ridge Pkwy., milepost 176* ☎ *276/952–2947* ⌺ *Free* ⊙ *May–Oct., daily 8–6.*

Where to Stay & Eat

$–$$$ 🏨 **Doe Run Lodge.** This resort at Groundhog Mountain, a rustic lodge on the crest of the Blue Ridge, has grand views of the Piedmont. Golfing, skiing, and hunting are all nearby. Each unit has a fireplace and kitchen, and floor-to-ceiling windows allow for full appreciation of the view. ⊠ *Milepost 189, Box 280, Fancy Gap 24328* ☎ *276/398–2212 or 800/325–6189* 🖶 *276/398–2833* ⊕ *www.doerunlodge.com* 🛏 *39 chalets, 3 villas, 2 cabins* ⚃ *Restaurant, some microwaves, 3 tennis courts, pool, sauna, fishing, basketball, hiking, volleyball, meeting rooms, some pets allowed (fee); no a/c in some rooms* ☰ *AE, MC, V.*

¢–$ 🏨 **Peaks of Otter Lodge.** This unpretentious, peaceful lodge is so popular that reservations are accepted beginning October 1 for the following year. Every room looks out on Abbott Lake from a private terrace or balcony, and their interiors have a folksy quality. The restaurant's big draw is the Friday night seafood buffet for $21.95. ⊠ *Milepost 86, Rte. 664, Box 489, Bedford 24523* ☎ *540/586–1081 or 800/542–5927* 🖶 *540/586–4420* ⊕ *www.peaksofotter.com* 🛏 *63 rooms* ⚃ *Restaurant, fishing, hiking, bar, pub, meeting rooms; no room phones, no room TVs, no a/c* ☰ *MC, V.*

New River Valley

41 mi southwest of Roanoke via I–81.

Despite its name, derived from being "new" to explorers when it was first discovered, the New River is actually one of the oldest rivers in the world: legend says only the Nile is older. The only river that flows from south to north completely through the Appalachian Mountains, it may have been there before the mountains came, some 300 million years ago. In Virginia the New River cuts a bluff-graced valley for 60 mi from Galax near the North Carolina line to Pearisburg, just over the West Virginia line. With an economy centered on research at Virginia Tech and manufacturing, the once-small towns of Blacksburg, Christiansburg, Radford, and Pulaski at the heart of the valley now sprawl together until it's hard to tell where one ends and the other begins. Visitors will find cozy downtown areas in each and many opportunities for outdoor recreation just outside the towns' limits.

With 26,000 students, **Virginia Tech** is Virginia's largest university. A small college just a few decades ago, Tech is now known for top-notch research programs and its Hokies football team, regularly ranked in the top 10. The focal point of the sprawling campus is the Drillfield, a vast green space surrounded by hefty neo-Gothic buildings built of what is known locally as "Hokie Stone" masonry. The **Virginia Museum of Natural History** (⊠ 428 N. Main St. ☎ 540/231–3001) presents rotating exhibits on local and national wildlife; a separate geology museum in Deering Hall displays gems and minerals. ⊠ *Blacksburg* ☎ *540/231–6000* ⊕ *www.vt.edu.*

Almost a century before Virginia Tech's founding in 1872, the **Historic Smithfield** plantation was built on what was then the frontier wilds. Aristocratic colonist and Revolutionary War patriot William Preston moved his family to the estate in 1774, a year before the war began. Among his descendants were three Virginia governors and four U.S. senators. Today, costumed interpreters, authentic period furniture, and Native American artifacts reveal how different life in the New River Valley was more than two centuries ago. ⊠ *100 Smithfield Plantation Rd., Blacksburg* ☎ *540/231–3947* ⊕ *www.civic.bev.net/smithfield* ⊠ *$5* ⊙ *Apr.–Dec., Thurs.–Sun. 1–5.*

What is now the **Wilderness Road Regional Museum** was once lodgings for settlers making their way west on a Native American route that went from Pennsylvania through the Cumberland Gap. The man who founded the town of Newbern built this house in the same year, and the structure has since served as a private home, a tavern, a post office, and a store. Today the house contains antique dolls, swords and rifles, an old loom, and other artifacts of everyday life. A self-tour map of Newbern, the only Virginia town entirely within a National Register of Historic Places district, is available at the museum. ⊠ *I–81, Exit 98, Newbern* ☎ *540/674–4835* ⊕ *www.rootsweb.com/~vanrhs/wrrm* ⊠ *$2* ⊙ *Mon.–Sat. 10:30–4:30, Sun. 1:30–4:30.*

Each October, the **Radford Highlanders Festival** brings Scotland to the New River Valley through bagpipes, games, parades, dancing, crafts, and sheep dog demonstrations. Men in traditional kilts challenge each other's machismo in the caber toss and hammer throw. Clan gatherings and genealogists on-site help visitors trace their Scottish roots. ⊠ *I–81, Exit 109, Radford* ☎ *540/831–5021 or 540/831–5324* ⊕ *www.radford. edu/festival* ⊠ *Free.*

off the beaten path

AUDIE MURPHY MONUMENT – On May 28, 1971, America's most decorated World War II veteran, who later became an actor, died when his plane struck Brush Mountain amid thick fog. A peaceful half-mile ridge-top walk leads to a simple monument, built by the Christiansburg Veterans of Foreign Wars, that marks the site of the crash and summarizes Audie Murphy's life. An overlook below the monument has a fine view of the Craig Creek Valley. Although the path to the monument is relatively smooth, the road to the top of Brush Mountain is winding, steep, and rocky; the monument is also accessible via a steep 4-mi Appalachian Trail climb. ⊠ *Forest*

Service Rd. 188.1, from Blacksburg, follow Mount Tabor Rd. [Rte. 624] 12 mi east, turn left onto Rte. 650 at the sign, follow it 5 mi as it becomes a forest service road to the dead end on top of Brush Mountain.

Where to Stay & Eat

$ ✕ **Boudreaux's Restaurant.** What started as a project in business marketing for a pair of Virginia Tech students is now an established part of Blacksburg's downtown. The canopied rooftop is a particularly relaxing area to enjoy jambalaya or Cajun catfish, all the while watching playful sparrows pick up the crumbs. Live bands often perform in the evenings. ✉ *205 N. Main St., Blacksburg* ☎ *540/961–2330* ⊕ *www.boudreauxs. com* ▭ *AE, D, MC, V.*

$ ✕ **The Cellar.** A gathering place and watering hole near the Virginia Tech campus, this storefront restaurant serves eclectic, inexpensive dishes. Try the Greek spaghetti with sautéed feta, garlic, and olives, or the "Mac Daddy": a single large meatball in marinara sauce and Parmesan. In the basement tavern you can choose from a particularly large list of beers; local bands often play there into the wee hours. ✉ *302 N. Main St., Blacksburg* ☎ *540/953–0651* ⊕ *www.the-cellar.com* ▭ *MC, V.*

$$–$$$$ ▥ **Mountain Lake.** Centered around the highest natural lake east of the Mississippi, this resort has more than 20 different types of accommodations, including spartan cottages and plush suites in a majestic sandstone hotel from 1930 (the resort itself predates the Civil War). Atop 4,000-foot Salt Pond Mountain, Mountain Lake resort has an overwhelming number of outdoor activities available: you can hike, mountain bike, ride horses, swim, and boat within the 2,500-acre Mountain Lake Wilderness, which surrounds the hotel and is operated by a nonprofit organization. The adjacent Jefferson National Forest offers even more recreation, including a segment of the Appalachian Trail. ✉ *115 Hotel Circle, 7 mi north of U.S. 460 on Rte. 700, Pembroke, 24136* ☎ *540/626–7121* ⊕ *www.mountainlakehotel.com* ➥ *28 cottages, 16 lodge rooms, 43 hotel rooms* ♿ *Dining room, some microwaves, some refrigerators, pool, hot tub, bicycles, archery, hiking, video game room, shop, Internet, meeting rooms; no a/c, no room TVs* ▭ *AE, D, MC, V* ◖*MAP* ⊘ *Closed Dec.-Apr.*

$$–$$$ ▥ **Holiday Inn University.** This hotel is particularly distinguished for its location, across the street from Virginia Tech, with a golf course, movie theater, numerous restaurants and shopping areas, and even a beach volleyball court nearby. The rooms are modern and comfortable, with two phone lines in each one. ✉ *900 Prices Fork Rd., Blacksburg 24060* ☎ *540/ 552-7001* 🖶 *540/552-0827* ⊕ *www.bnt.com/4Points* ➥ *147 rooms, 1 suite* ♿ *Restaurant, dining room, cable TV with movies and video games, tennis court, 2 pools (1 indoor), lounge, recreation room, Internet, meeting rooms, airport shuttle* ▭ *AE, D, DC, MC, V.*

$ ▥ **Best Western Radford Inn.** Service and amenities (such as a bathroom phone) distinguish this facility from the other highway motels it resembles in the same area. The Colonial-decorated rooms have views of the Blue Ridge Mountains that are not utterly spoiled by the surrounding parking lot. ✉ *1501 Tyler Ave., Rte. 177, Radford 24141* ☎ *540/639–3000* 🖷 *540/633–0251* ⊕ *www.bestwestern.com* ⤴ *104 rooms* ♨ *Restaurant, microwaves, cable TV, indoor pool, gym, sauna, bar, Internet, meeting rooms, some pets allowed* ▭ *AE, D, DC, MC, V.*

Sports & the Outdoors

BIKING The 52-mi **New River Trail**, Virginia's narrowest state park, runs from Pulaski to Galax following what was once a railroad bed. It parallels the river for 39 of those miles, passing through two tunnels. The trail is also open to hikers and horseback riders. **Mountain Lake** (✉ 115 Hotel Circle, 7 mi north of U.S. 460 on Rte. 700, Pembroke ☎ 540/626–7121 ⊕ www.mountainlakehotel.com) has more than 20 mi of mountain bike trails, with bicycles available at the hotel. The Jefferson National Forest's **Pandapas Pond Recreation Area,** on the edge of Blacksburg, is a popular place for mountain biking.

CANOEING & The **New River** is open to canoeing, kayaking, and fishing. For more in-
FISHING formation, or to rent or buy boats or fishing gear, contact any of the following local outfitters: **Back Country Ski & Sport** (✉ 3710 S. Main St., Blacksburg ☎ 540/552–6400 ⊕ www.bcski.com). **New River Adventures** (✉ 1007 N. 4th St., Wytheville ☎ 276/228–8311 or 276/699–1034 ⊕ www.newriveradventures.com). **Tangent Outfitters** (☎ 540/731–5202 ⊕ www.newrivertrail.com).

HIKING The 4-mi loop at **Cascades Recreation Area** (✉ Jefferson National Forest, off U.S. 460, 4 mi north of Pembroke on Rte. 623) passes a rushing stream and a 60-foot waterfall. This hike is popular locally and becomes crowded on weekends when the weather's good. The **Appalachian Trail** crosses the New River Valley, visiting overlook sites such as Angel's Rest and Wind Rock. For more information on area hikes in the Jefferson National Forest, contact the **Blacksburg Ranger Station** (✉ 110 Southpark Dr., Blacksburg ☎ 540/552–4641).

SPECTATOR **Virginia Tech** competes in the Atlantic Coast Conference in several var-
SPORTS sity NCAA Division I sports, including football, baseball, and basketball. Its football team, commonly ranked in the top 10, plays in 65,000-seat **Lane Stadium** (☎ 540/231–6731 tickets).

Abingdon

16 *135 mi southwest of Roanoke (via I–81).*

Abingdon, near the Tennessee border, is a cultural crossroads in the wilderness: the town of nearly 7,000 draws tens of thousands of people each year because of a fine theater company and exuberant local celebrations. By far the most popular event here is the **Virginia Highlands Festival** during the first two weeks of August: 200,000 people come to hear live music performances ranging from bluegrass to opera, to visit the exhibitions of mountain crafts, and to browse among the wares of more than 100 antiques dealers. This is followed by the **Burley Tobacco Festival,** held in September, during which country-music stars perform and prize farm animals are proudly displayed.

CloseUp

MOUNTAIN MUSIC

SOUTHWEST VIRGINIA'S HILLS *and valleys have long reverberated with the sounds of fiddles, banjoes, mandolins, and acoustic guitars. Scotch-Irish settlers brought these sounds with them, and for the generations before radio and television, front-porch gatherings and community dances entertained local families isolated, geographically and culturally, from the rest of civilization.*

Whether called bluegrass, roots, or old-time country, the notes first plucked in the rugged hollers of Appalachia now echo much farther. It's in the Virginia-Tennessee border town of Bristol that some people mark the start of the commercial country-music industry. In 1927 a makeshift recording studio was set up downtown by the talent scout Ralph Peer. Peer advertised for musicians to play and have their songs recorded. From these sessions came such seminal acts as the Carter Family and Jimmie Rodgers. "Hillbilly music" had come out of the hollers, eventually sparking a multibillion-dollar industry.

Those rich sounds cultivated by generations are still played in Southwest Virginia. Two centers are Galax and Floyd, though many other towns, large and small, have festivals or events. Here are a few other local places for the finest in old-time country and bluegrass music:

Carter Fold *(⊠ U.S. 58/421, 19 mi west of Bristol, Hiltons,* ☎ *276/386–6054 or 276/386–9480* ⊕ *www.carterfamilyfold. org* ✉ *$5 for shows, $18 for festival). At this 1,000-seat auditorium, live music is performed on Saturday night; a two-day festival is held each August. A museum in an adjacent old store building nearby displays memorabilia from the Carter family; descendants often perform in the shows.*

Old Fiddlers Convention *(⊠ Galax* ☎ *276/236–8541* ⊕ *www. oldfiddlersconvention.com* ✉ *$5 Mon.–Thurs., $8 Fri., $10 Sat. or $30 for the week). Hundreds of musicians and thousands of fans gather the second week of August for performances, contests, camaraderie, and informal jam sessions that last until early morning.*

Rex Theatre *(⊠ 113 E. Grayson St., Galax* ☎ *276/238–8130 or 276/236–0668* ⊕ *www.rextheatregalax.org* ✉ *Free). Bluegrass, country, and gospel music is broadcast from here each Friday night on WBRF, FM–98.1.*

Blue Ridge Music Center *(⊠ Blue Ridge Pkwy. milepost 213, near N.C. line* ⊕ *www.blueridgemusiccenter.net). This center launched an ambitious concert series at its outdoor amphitheater in summer 2002 that included the likes of Ricky Skaggs and Doc Watson.*

Floyd Country Store *(⊠ Floyd* ☎ *540/745–4563* ⊕ *www.floydcountrystore.com* ✉ *$3). What were once just sessions have evolved into a Friday Night Jamboree attended by local folks and visitors from far off. In summer, music often breaks out all around the store as well. "Granny Rules" are in effect—"no smokin', no cussin', and no drinkin'." But clogging on the dance floor is fine.*

Ralph Stanley Museum and Traditional Mountain Music Center *(⊠ Clintwood* ☎ *276/926–5591* ⊕ *www. ralphstanleymuseum.com). Housed in a 100-year-old, four-story house, the Ralph Stanley Museum opened in 2004 in order to preserve traditional mountain music. Focusing on the life and career of local legend Ralph Stanley, the exhibits allow visitors to hear the music of Stanley and other artists. In time the site will host performances.*

Regional artists exhibit their folk art and crafts at the **William King Regional Arts Center,** which also has an outdoor sculpture garden. ☒ *415 Academy Dr.* ☎ *276/628–5005* ☞ *Free* ☉ *Tues. 10–9, Wed.–Fri. 10–5, weekends 1–5.*

Where to Stay & Eat

$$–$$$ ✕ **The Starving Artist Cafe.** This eatery, which doubles as an art gallery, has many seafood and pasta dishes. The Friday and Saturday menu includes Cajun-style prime rib. ☒ *134 Wall St. NW* ☎ *276/628–8445* ▭ *AE, MC, V* ☉ *Closed Sun. No dinner on Mon.*

$$–$$$ ✕ **The Tavern.** Inside a building from 1779 is a very cozy restaurant. The three dining rooms and cocktail lounge all have fireplaces, stone walls, and brick floors. In warm weather you can dine outdoors on a balcony overlooking historic Court House Hill or on a brick patio surrounded by trees and flowers. The menu includes rack of lamb and fresh seasonal seafood such as stuffed trout. ☒ *222 E. Main St.* ☎ *276/628–1118* ▭ *AE, D, MC, V.*

★ $$–$$$$ ✕▦ **Camberley's Martha Washington Inn.** Constructed as a private house in 1832, turned into a college dormitory in 1860, and then used as a field hospital during the Civil War, the Martha Washington finally became an inn in 1935. Across from the Barter Theater, the inn has rooms furnished with Victorian antiques; some have fireplaces. The restaurant's contemporary American cuisine ($$$) includes roasted rainbow trout with crayfish, loin of lamb with hominy cheese grits, and—for dessert—Martha's marbled strawberry shortcake. There is complimentary afternoon tea on Friday and Saturday on the porch of the inn. ☒ *150 W. Main St., 24210* ☎ *276/628–3161 or 800/555–8000* ☏ *276/628–8885* ⊕ *www.marthawashingtoninn.com* ☞ *50 rooms, 11 suites* ♿ *Restaurant, bar, meeting rooms* ▭ *AE, D, DC, MC, V.*

¢ ▦ **Alpine Motel.** The spacious, modern rooms of this clean motel have striking views of Virginia's highest mountain peaks: Mt. Rogers and Whitetop. The motel is set far back from the road and is therefore popular with families, as well as traveling salespeople. The Barter Theatre is nearby. ☒ *882 E. Main St., 24210* ☎ *276/628–3178* ☏ *276/628–3179* ☞ *19 rooms* ♿ *Cable TV, Internet* ▭ *AE, D, MC, V.*

Nightlife & the Arts

From April through the Christmas season, audiences flock to the prestigious **Barter Theatre** (☒ *133 W. Main St.* ☎ *276/628–3991* ⊕ *www. bartertheatre.com*), America's longest-running professional repertory theater. Founded during the Depression by local actor Robert Porterfield, the theater got its name in the obvious way: early patrons who could not afford the 40¢ tickets could pay in produce. Kevin Spacey, Ned Beatty, and Gregory Peck are among the many stars who began their careers at the Barter, which today presents the classics of Shakespeare as well as works by contemporary playwrights such as David Mamet. Although times have changed since Noël Coward was given a Virginia ham for his contributions, the official policy still permits you to barter for your seat. But don't just show up at the box office with a bag of arugula—all trades must be approved by advance notice. Plays change every four weeks.

The Outdoors

HIKING At the end of Abingdon's Main Street is the beginning of the 34-mi **Virginia Creeper Trail**, a former railbed of the Virginia-Carolina Railroad. You can hike it, bike it, or take to it on horseback. The trail has sharp curves, steep grades, and 100 trestles and bridges. It joins the Appalachian Trail at Damascus, a town known for its friendly attitude and the many businesses targeted toward hikers and cyclists. In May the town celebrates Trail Days, a festival celebrating hikers. ⊠ *Trailhead at end of Main St.* ☎ *540/676–2282 or 800/435–3440.*

Wild ponies on open grasslands studded with rocky knobs give the area around **Mt. Rogers** an appearance distinct from any other in Virginia. At 5,729 feet, Mt. Rogers is Virginia's highest point, but you don't need to hike all the way to its summit to experience the grandeur of Western-like terrain—a short walk of about a mile from **Grayson Highlands State Park** (⊠ U.S. 58, 20 mi east of Damascus ☎ 276/579–7092 🖲 $2) into the adjacent **Mount Rogers Recreation Area** is all that's required. Through the 5,000-acre state park and 120,000-acre recreation area run an extensive network of riding and hiking trails; the Appalachian Trail passes through on its way to North Carolina and Tennessee, just south. Hunting and fishing are permitted in season; permits are available in most sporting goods stores. ⊠ *Mount Rogers National Recreation Area, 3714 Hwy. 16, Marion 24354* ☎ *276/783–5196* 🖲 *Free.*

Appalachian Plateau

About 60 mi west of Abingdon via Alternate U.S. Rte. 58.

Gorges and "hollers" cut deeply into this elevated land in the far southwestern tip of Virginia. **Breaks Interstate Park** and **Cumberland Gap National Historic Park** both on the Virginia-Kentucky line, preserve two of the better known of these valleys. Like neighboring Kentucky and West Virginia, coal has long been the driving force here; the area has suffered as coal mining jobs have dwindled amid mechanization and environmental concerns. Nevertheless, the plateau is inviting and inspiring country, evoking some sense of how Virginia was in the time of the pioneers. George Washington Vanderbilt loved mountain-encircled Burke's Garden near Tazewell so much that he wanted to build a huge country mansion there; he was rebuffed by suspicious locals and instead chose Asheville, N.C., for Biltmore, his estate. And the mountains around the town of Big Stone Gap inspired the 1908 novel and later movie *The Trail of the Lonesome Pine*, by John Fox Jr.

Next to the Lonesome Pine theater is the 1880s **June Tolliver House.** Rooms are furnished from the period, and local arts and crafts, including coal carvings and quilts, are for sale. ⊠ *Climpon Ave., Big Stone Gap* ☎ *276/523–4707* 🖲 *Free* ☉ *Mid-May–mid-Dec., Tues.–Sat. 10–5, Sun. 2–6.*

In a Victorian mansion built during the coal boom of 1888–93, the **Southwest Virginia Historical Museum** holds a mine-manager's home furnishings and other exhibits. ⊠ *10 W. 1st St., Rte. 58 Alternate* ☎ *276/523–1322* 🖲 *$3* ☉ *Memorial Day–Labor Day, Mon.–Thurs. 10–4, Fri.*

9–4, Sat. 10–5, Sun. 1–5; Labor Day–Dec. and Mar.–Memorial Day, Tues.–Thurs. 10–4, Fri. 9–4, Sat. 10–5, Sun. 1–5.

On 110 acres that were once part of a hunting ground for the Shawnee and Cherokee nations, **Crab Orchard Museum and Pioneer Park** presents visitors with relics of many different historical periods. An archaeological dig at the site yielded many Native American tools and pieces of furniture. The history that followed the arrival of the Europeans is also illustrated through artifacts, as are the social changes caused by farming and regional mining. Among the diverse exhibits are an early European map showing the Pacific Ocean in West Virginia, the remains of a woolly mammoth, and an instrument used to bleed patients. Farm buildings and crafts shops nearby are fully accessible to people with disabilities. To get to Tazewell, take Exit 45 off I–81 at Marion, then go north 30 mi on Route 16. ⊠ *Rtes. 19/460, Tazewell* ☎ *276/988–6755* ⊕ *www. craborchardmuseum.com* ⊠ *$7* ⊙ *Mon.–Sat. 9–5.*

Visitors can get their best glimpse of the coal mining life at **Pocahontas Exhibition Coal Mine and Museum.** Inside this former mine is a 13-foot-tall coal seam that helps you understand how mammoth an operation it once was. Opened in 1882, the mine produced more than 44 million tons of coal during its 73-year existence; its famous "Pocahontas No. 3" coal was the fuel of choice for the U.S. Navy. Guides explain the story of mining and how hand-loading succumbed to mechanization. The town of Pocahontas, once with a population of 5,000 as it bustled with coal miners who came from Hungary, Wales, Russia, Poland, and Italy, now has a population of fewer than 500. From Tazewell, take U.S. 460 northeast to Rte. 102. ⊠ *Rte. 644, off Rte. 102, Pocahontas* ☎ *276/ 945–2134* ⊠ *$6* ⊙ *Apr.–Oct., Mon.–Sat. 10–5, Sun. noon–6.*

CENTRAL & WESTERN VIRGINIA A TO Z

To research prices, get advice from other travelers, and book travel arrangements, visit www.fodors.com.

AIRPORTS

The region's three largest airports are small and relatively hassle-free, so, except during peak holiday periods, travelers need allow no more time than for the typical security clearances. Regional carriers using small jets and turboprops are the norm, though larger jets sometimes serve Roanoke. The regional carriers primarily offer access to Washington, Charlotte, and Atlanta, but flights to and from Chicago, Pittsburgh, Cincinnati, New York, and Detroit are also available. Many travelers to western Virginia prefer to fly into international airports in Washington, Richmond, or Greensboro, N.C., then commute by rental car; all three major city airports are within two hours' drive of western Virginia destinations. Tri-City Regional Airport is just across the state line in Blountville, Tenn., for easy access to the Abingdon area.

⌨ Airport Information **Charlottesville-Albemarle Airport** ⊠ 8 mi north of Charlottesville at intersection of Rtes. 606/649 off Rte. 29 ☎ 434/973-8342 ⊕ www.gocho.com. **Lynchburg Regional Airport** ⊠ Rte. 29 S ☎ 434/455-6090. **Roanoke Regional Airport** ⊠ Off

I-581 ☎ 540/362-1999 ⊕ www.roanokeairport.com. **Tri-Cities Regional Airport** ✉ Blountville, TN ☎ 423/325-6000 ⊕ www.triflight.com.

TRANSFERS Van on the Go shuttles guests from the Charlottesville airport to hotels, downtown, and area tourist attractions. Reservations are required. Several taxi services also serve the airport (*see* Taxis).

🔗 **Van on the Go** ✉ Charlottesville-Albermarle Airport ☎ 434/975-8267 or 877/973-7667.

🔗 CAR RENTALS

Airports in Charlottesville, Roanoke, and Lynchburg are served by national car rental firms. Travelers in Charlottesville might want to consider Autorent, a smaller company that serves several central and eastern Virginia cities. The company meets passengers at the airport, bus station, and train station, and has four-wheel-drive vehicles, convertibles, and large vans among its fleet of rentals.

🔗 **Local Agencies Autorent** ✉ 1744 Rio Hill Shopping Center, Rte. 29 N ☎ 434/973-1144 or 877/467-3681 ⊕ www.gorent.com.

CAR TRAVEL

The many pleasant highways and routes that snake through western Virginia's rolling countryside make driving a particularly good way to travel. The region's interstates (I–64, I–81, and I–77) are remarkably scenic, but the same mountainous terrain that contributes to their beauty can also make them treacherous. Dense valley fog banks, mountain-shrouding clouds, and gusty ridge-top winds are concerns at any time of the year, and winter brings ice and snow conditions that can change dramatically in a few miles when the elevation changes.

Charlottesville is where U.S. 29 (north–south) meets I–64. Lynchburg is the meeting point of U.S. 460 between Richmond and Roanoke and Route 29 south from Charlottesville. U.S. 460 meets I–81 at Roanoke.

Interstate 81 and Route 11 run north–south the length of the Shenandoah Valley and continue south into Tennessee. Interstate 66 west from Washington, D.C., which is 90 mi to the east, passes through Front Royal to meet I–81 and Route 11 at the northern end of the valley. Interstate 64 connects the same highways with Charlottesville, 30 mi to the east. Route 39 into Bath County connects with I–81 just north of Lexington. Interstate 77 cuts off the southwest tip of the state, running north–south and crossing I–81 at Wytheville. Interstate 77 crosses two major ridges and passes through two mountain tunnels in Virginia.

TRAFFIC Travelers will rarely find bumper-to-bumper traffic jams in Charlottesville or any other city in the region. The major exception: autumn Saturdays when the University of Virginia has a home football game. Virginia Tech games can similarly snarl traffic in the Roanoke–New River Valley area, including on I–81.

EMERGENCIES

Charlottesville is served by six locations of CVS. Pharmacies inside Kroger and Wal-Mart are also open 24 hours a day.

🔗 **Doctors & Dentists Martha Jefferson Hospital, Physician Referral Services** ☎ 434/982-8450.

☑ Emergency Services Albemarle County Office of Emergency Services ☏ 434/971–1263. **Ambulance, Fire, Police** ☏ 911.

☑ Hospitals Charlottesville: Martha Jefferson Hospital ✉ 459 Locust Ave. ☏ 434/982–7000. **University of Virginia Medical Center** ✉ Lee St. ☏ 434/982–3865. Roanoke:**Carilion Roanoke Memorial Hospital** ✉ Belleview Ave. and Jefferson St. ☏ 540/981–7000. **Lewis-Gale Medical Center** ✉ 1900 Electric Rd., Salem ☏ 540/776–4000.

SPORTS & THE OUTDOORS

There are plentiful golf courses in the hills that dominate the region. Downhill skiing is available, typically from December to March, with start and end dates highly dependent on the whims of a variable climate, at four locations: Wintergreen, Bryce, Massanutten, and Homestead resorts.

With two sprawling national forests and a number of streams and rivers flowing out of the mountains, hunting and fishing are among the most popular outdoor sports in western Virginia.

☑ Golf Virginia State Golf Association ✉ 600 Founders Bridge Blvd., Midlothian 23113 ☏ 804/378–2300 ⊕ www.vsga.org.

☑ Hunting & Fishing Virginia Department of Game and Inland Fisheries ✉ 4010 W. Broad St., Richmond 23230 ☏ 804/367–1000 ⊕ www.dgif.virginia.gov.

TOURS

For $16, the Lexington Carriage Company will take visitors around town in a horse-drawn carriage for 45–50 minutes, from April through October. Tours begin and end at the Lexington Visitor Center. A self-guided walking-tour brochure of the town is available from the Lexington Visitor Center. The Historic Staunton Foundation offers free one-hour walking tours Saturday morning at 10, Memorial Day through October, departing from the Woodrow Wilson Birthplace at 24 North Coalter Street. A brochure for a self-guided tour is available from the Staunton/Augusta Travel Information Center.

☑ Horse-Drawn Tours Lexington Carriage Company ☏ 540/463–5647.

☑ Walking Tours Historic Staunton Foundation ✉ 1205 Augusta. St. ☏ 540/885–7676. **Lexington Visitor Center** ✉ 106 E. Washington St. ☏ 540/463–3777.

TRAIN TRAVEL

Amtrak has service three days a week to Charlottesville and Staunton, en route from New York and Chicago. The same train stops at Clifton Forge for the Homestead resort in Bath County. A complimentary shuttle bus on Sunday, Wednesday, and Friday connects Roanoke (Campbell Court and Roanoke Airport Sheraton) and Clifton Forge Rail Station. Amtrak's *Crescent* runs between New York City and New Orleans and stops daily in Lynchburg and Charlottesville.

☑ Train Stations Clifton Forge ✉ 400 Ridgeway St. **Kemper Street Station** ✉ 825 Kemper St. , Lynchburg ☏ 434/847–8247. **Staunton** ✉ 1 Middlebrook Ave. **Union Station** ✉ 810 W. Main St., Charlottesville ☏ 434/296–4559.

☑ Train Lines Amtrak ☏ 800/872–7245 ⊕ www.amtrak.com.

VISITOR INFORMATION

☑ Tourist Information Abingdon Convention & Visitors Bureau ✉ 335 Cummings St., Abingdon 24210 ☏ 276/676–2282 ⊕ www.abingdon.com/tourism. **Charlottesville/**

Albemarle Convention and Visitors Bureau ✉ Rte. 20 S, Box 178, Charlottesville 22902 ☎ 434/293-6789 or 877/386-1102 ⊕ www.charlottesvilletourism.org. **Lynchburg Regional Convention and Visitors Bureau** ✉ 216 12th St., Lynchburg 24504 ☎ 434/847-1811 or 800/732-5821. **Roanoke Valley Convention and Visitors Bureau** ✉ 101 Shenandoah Ave. NE, Roanoke 24011 ☎ 540/342-6025 or 800/635-5535 ⊕ www.visitroanokeva.com. **Shenandoah Valley Travel Association** ✉ I-81, Exit 264 ⊕ Box 1040, New Market 22844 ☎ 540/740-3132 or 800/847-4878 ⊕ www.shenandoah.org.

RICHMOND, FREDERICKSBURG & THE NORTHERN NECK

4

GET A TASTE OF TUDOR ENGLAND
exploring Richmond's Agecroft Hall ⇨*p.126*

ORDER A ROUND OF SANGRIA
from the Europa tapas bar ⇨*p.128*

MAKE LIKE SCARLETT O'HARA
Walking down the Jefferson
Hotel's grand staircase ⇨*p.130*

PAY YOUR RESPECTS
at Petersburg National Battlefield ⇨*p.133*

LINGER IN LUXURY
at the Tides Inn, between two rivers ⇨*p.151*

Updated by
Norman
Renouf

A HOST OF PATRIOTS AND PRESIDENTS have lived and worked in the heart of the Old Dominion, an area that takes in Richmond, Fredericksburg, Petersburg, and the Northern Neck. The birthplaces, boyhood homes, or graves of notable figures such as George Washington, James Monroe, John Tyler, and Robert E. Lee can be found here, and the area has many associations with other leaders, including Patrick Henry and Thomas Jefferson. Serving as Virginia's capital since 1880, Richmond is also the former capital of the Confederacy. Besides numerous Revolutionary War and Civil War sites, the city also contains the Fan District, full of 19th-century homes and the Virginia state capitol, designed by Thomas Jefferson.

A half hour south of Richmond, Petersburg is a delightful antebellum city with many historic attractions. Besieged by the Union Army in 1864, the townspeople bravely did their best to protect the Confederacy. Less than an hour north of Richmond sits the appealing city of Fredericksburg, a history buff's dream, with hundreds of impressive 18th- and 19th-century homes. The nearby Fredericksburg/Spotsylvania National Military Park presents the story of the area's role in the Civil War.

East of Fredericksburg, away from the blood-soaked and fought-over grounds, peace and quiet reign in a 90-mi-long peninsula Virginians call "The Northern Neck." This outdoorsman's escape was the birthplace of three presidents, including the Father of Our Country. Here, wide rivers and the briny Chesapeake Bay entice water lovers and sports anglers. Gazing across the peaceful property where Washington was born, it's easy to see why he longed to choose a life at Mount Vernon instead of serving two terms as our first president.

Exploring the Area

Richmond, 100 mi south of Washington, D.C., on the James River, is the state's historic capital. It's easy to get here on I–95. Midway between Washington and Richmond (50 mi from each) on I–95, Fredericksburg is a lovely place to relax and retrace 18th- and 19th-century history in homes and museums and on nearby battlefields. About 20 mi east of Fredericksburg, the Northern Neck begins. There's no public transportation to this rural area, but a car lets you wander at will among its many historic sites and water views. Petersburg, with its Civil War history, is a mere half hour south of Richmond.

About the Restaurants & Hotels

Keep in the mind that hotel rooms can be very hard to come by during Richmond's NASCAR Nextel Cup races, held over two weekends in May and September. If you have your heart set on a bed-and-breakfasts, look to Petersburg, Fredericksburg and the Northern Neck: there aren't many in Richmond.

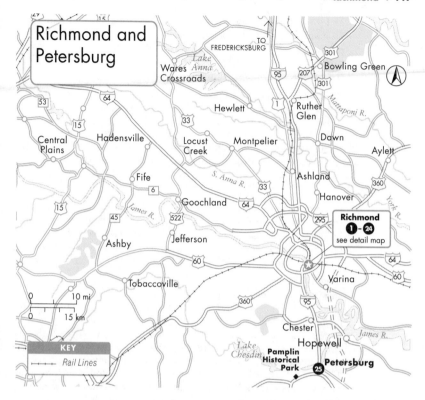

Richmond and Petersburg

TO FREDERICKSBURG

Wares Crossroads
Lake Anna
Bowling Green
Hewlett
Ruther Glen
Mattaponi R.
Central Plains
Hadensville
Locust Creek
Montpelier
Dawn
Aylett
Fife
S. Anna R.
Ashland
Hanover
Goochland
James R.
Jefferson
Ashby
Richmond
1 - **24**
see detail map
York R.
Tobaccoville
Varina
Chester
Lake Chesdin
Pamplin Historical Park
Hopewell
James R.
Petersburg
25

0 ——— 10 mi
0 ——— 15 km

KEY
┼┼┼ *Rail Lines*

WHAT IT COSTS				
$$$$	**$$$**	**$$**	**$**	**¢**
RESTAURANTS over $30	$22–$30	$14–$22	$7–$14	under $7
HOTELS over $250	$175–$250	$130–$175	$80–$130	under $80

Restaurant prices are per person for a main course at dinner. Hotel prices are for a standard double room, excluding state tax.

RICHMOND

Centered on the fall line of the James River, about 75 mi upriver from the Chesapeake Bay, Richmond completes the transition from Tidewater Virginia into the Piedmont, the central section of rolling plains that reaches toward the mountain barrier in the west. Not only is Richmond the capital of the Commonwealth, but it was also the capital of the Confederacy. As a result, the city is studded with historic sites.

At the start of the Civil War, Richmond was the most industrialized city in the South, and it remains an important city for national industries. After years of urban decay, Richmond transformed itself into a lively and sophisticated modern town, adding high technology to traditional economic bases that include shipping and banking. It's one of the South's preeminent art cities, flourishing with avant-garde painting and sculpture in addition to artifacts and magnificent traditional works, such as the Fabergé eggs in the Virginia Museum of Fine Arts.

Richmond is also a great place for genealogy and history researchers. The following libraries or archives are interesting stops for the casual browser as well as for those in search of ancestors: the Library of Virginia, Virginia Historical Society Museum of Virginia History, Beth Ahabah Museum and Archives, American Historical Foundation Museum, and Black History Museum & Cultural Center of Virginia.

Downtown

Richmond's historic attractions lie north of the James River, which bisects the city with a sweeping curve. The heart of old Richmond is the Court End district downtown. This area, close to the capitol, contains seven National Historic Landmarks, three museums, and 11 additional buildings on the National Register of Historic Places—all within eight blocks.

Running west from the Court End district is Main Street, lined with banks; stores are concentrated along Grace Street, to the north. Cary Street, an east–west thoroughfare, becomes, between 12th and 15th streets, the cobblestone center of Shockoe Slip. This area (once the city's largest commercial trading district) and Shockoe Bottom (on land formerly a Native American trading post) are unique restored areas filled with trendy shops, restaurants, and nightlife. Shockoe Bottom landmarks include the 17th Street Farmers' Market, operating since 1775, and Main Street Station, an elaborate Victorian structure capped by red tiles that was Richmond's first train station. To the east above the James River is Church Hill, which on the south side of Broad Street has become a fashionable neighborhood of restored 18th- and 19th-century homes and churches.

Drive west beyond the historic downtown to see a fascinating group of close-in, charming, and distinctive neighborhoods. Not far from the capitol is Jackson Ward, called the "Home of Black Capitalism," a cultural and entrepreneurial center after the Civil War.

Numbers in the text correspond to numbers in the margin and on the Richmond map.

a good tour

Because the historic sites in Richmond are fairly spread out, it's best to do a series of walks, either driving or taking public transportation between groups of attractions. The city's many one-way streets may make for a circuitous route to some sights.

A good place to start is at the east side of downtown on Church Hill but a word of caution is needed here. Although the south side of Broad Street has seen considerable gentrification, the northern side is still one of the city's poorest neighborhoods and should be avoided. At the **Chimborazo Medical Museum** ❶ ⌐, one of the National Park Service's five Richmond-area visitor centers, you can pick up information about Richmond and the Civil War battlefields nearby.

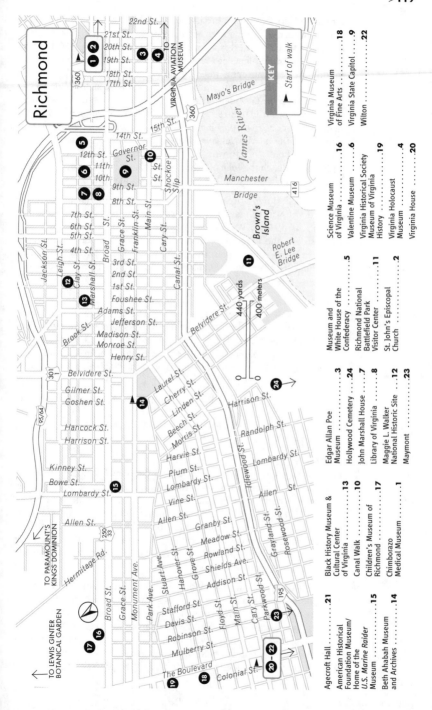

Richmond

KEY

▲ *Start of walk*

Virginia Museum
of Fine Arts **18**
Virginia State Capitol **9**
Wilton **22**

Science Museum
of Virginia **16**
Valentine Museum **6**
Virginia Historical Society
Museum of Virginia
History **19**
Virginia Holocaust
Museum **4**
Virginia House **20**

Museum and
White House of the
Confederacy **5**
Richmond National
Battlefield Park
Visitor Center **11**
St. John's Episcopal
Church **2**

Edgar Allan Poe
Museum **3**
Hollywood Cemetery ...**24**
John Marshall House ...**7**
Library of Virginia **8**
Maggie L. Walker
National Historic Site ..**12**
Maymont **23**

Black History Museum &
Cultural Center
of Virginia **13**
Canal Walk **10**
Children's Museum of
Richmond **17**
Chimborazo
Medical Museum **1**

Agecroft Hall **21**
American Historical
Foundation Museum/
Home of the
U.S. Marine Raider
Museum **15**
Beth Ahabah Museum
and Archives **14**

Drive nine blocks west on Broad Street (each intersection is a four-way stop) and turn left down 25th Street to park and visit **St. John's Episcopal Church** ❷. Continue down 25th Street and take a right on Main Street to reach the **Edgar Allan Poe Museum** ❸. One block to the south is Richmond's newest museum, the **Virginia Holocaust Museum** ❹. Parking downtown can be difficult, but you can park free near the **Museum and White House of the Confederacy** ❺. To get here drive west on Broad Street and turn right on 11th Street, then right on Clay Street. Parking is free in the adjacent hospital parking garage with ticket validation at this museum or at the nearby **Valentine Museum** ❻, which deals with city history. From here you can walk south on 10th Street and then right on Marshall to reach the **John Marshall House** ❼. Across the street is the **Library of Virginia** ❽, which has free underground parking.

A short walk down 9th Street will bring you to the **Virginia State Capitol** ❾. If you want to take in a view rather than moving on to another museum, stroll **Canal Walk** ❿, beginning south of the capitol at 12th and Main streets and following the locks on the James River. The Shockoe Slip area of upscale shops starts at Cary and 12th. The **Richmond National Battlefield Park Visitor Center** ⓫ is close to the river near 5th and Tredegar streets.

You could also stretch your legs walking the 12 blocks to the next site, but it's probably best to retrieve the car. Drive west on Broad Street, turn right on 2nd Street, and drive four blocks north to visit the **Maggie L. Walker National Historic Site** ⓬, in Jackson Ward, honoring the achievements of a pioneering black entrepreneur. Next go west on Leigh Street and turn left on Saint James Place to the **Black History Museum & Cultural Center of Virginia** ⓭, on Clay Street.

TIMING To visit all these sites would take an entire day. Allow at least an hour for each site or museum—two hours for the Museum and White House of the Confederacy. If you plan to do research at the Library of Virginia, allow a half day here.

Sights to See

❶ **Black History Museum & Cultural Center of Virginia.** The goal of this museum in the Jackson Ward is to gather visual, oral, and written records and artifacts that commemorate the lives and accomplishments of blacks in Virginia. On display are 5,000 documents, fine art objects, traditional African artifacts, textiles from ethnic groups throughout Africa, and artwork by artists Sam Gilllam, John Biggers, and P. H. Polk. ✉ *00 Clay St., at Foushee St.* ☎ *804/780–9093* ⊕ *www.blackhistorymuseum.org* 🎟 *$5* ⊙ *Tues.–Sat. 10–5, Sun. 1–5.*

❿ **Canal Walk.** The 1¼-mi Canal Walk meanders through downtown Richmond along the Haxall Canal, the James River, and the Kanawha Canal, and can be enjoyed on foot or in boats. Along the way, look for history exhibits such as the Flood Wall Gallery, bronze medallions, and other exhibits placed on Brown's Island and Canal Walk by the Richmond Historical Riverfront Foundation. Many sights intersect with Canal Walk, including the Richmond National Battlefield Park Civil War Visitor Center and those places at which 5th, 7th, Virginia, 14th, 15th, and 17th streets meet the water.

The James River–Kanawha Canal was proposed by George Washington to bring ships around the falls of the James River. Brown's Island hosts festivals and concerts in warmer months. **Richmond Canal Cruises** (✉ 139 Virginia St. ☎ 804/649–2800) operates a 35-minute ride on the canal in a 38-seat open boat. Tours, which cost $5, depart from the Turning Basin near 14th and Virginia streets. Tours run from April through Thanksgiving; call for times. If you're in a car, try to find the site before parking. Lack of prominent signage makes it challenging to find, and parking lots are a few blocks away. ⊕ *www.richmondriverfront. com/canalwalk.shtml.*

❶ Chimborazo Medical Museum. This was once the Civil War's largest and best-equipped hospital. Chimborazo opened in 1861 and treated more than 76,000 Confederate soldiers between 1862 and 1865. It could house more than 3,000 patients in its 100 wards. This site—once more than 40 acres—now houses a National Park Service visitor center and a small medical museum that tells the story of the patients, hospital, and physicians through uniforms, documents and other artifacts. ✉ *3215 Broad St.* ☎ *804/226–1981* ⊕ *www.nps.gov/rich* ☞ *Free* ☉ *Daily 9–5.*

❸ Edgar Allan Poe Museum. Richmond's oldest residence, the Old Stone House in the Church Hill Historic District just east of downtown, now holds a museum honoring the famous writer. Poe grew up in Richmond, and although he never lived in this early- to mid-18th-century structure, his disciples have made it a shrine with some of the writer's possessions on display. The Raven Room has illustrations inspired by his most famous poem. ✉ *1914 E. Main St.* ☎ *804/648–5523 or 888/213–2703* ⊕ *www. poemuseum.org* ☞ *$6* ☉ *Tues.–Sat. 10–5, Sun. 11–5. Guided tours on the hr; last tour departs at 4.*

❼ John Marshall House. John Marshall was chief justice of the U.S. Supreme Court for 34 years—longer than any other. He built his red-brick Federal-style house with neoclassical motifs in 1790. Appointed to the court by President John Adams, Marshall also served as secretary of state and ambassador to France. The house, fully restored and furnished, has wood paneling and wainscoting, narrow arched passageways, and a mix of period pieces and heirlooms. The house has been a beautifully maintained museum since 1913. ✉ *9th and Marshall Sts.* ☎ *804/648–7998* ⊕ *www.apva.org/apva/marshall.html* ☞ *$6* ☉ *Tues.–Sat. 10–5, Sun. noon–5.*

❽ Library of Virginia. As the official state archive, this library preserves and provides access to more than 96 million manuscript items documenting four centuries of Virginia history. The library also houses and makes available to researchers more than 1½ million books, bound periodicals, microfilm reels, newspapers, and state and federal documents. Its collections include 240,000 photographs, prints, engravings, posters, and paintings. The building has free underground parking. ✉ *800 E. Broad St.* ☎ *804/692–3500* ⊕ *www.lva.lib.va.us* ☞ *Free* ☉ *Mon.–Sat. 9–5.*

⑫ **Maggie L. Walker National Historic Site.** From 1904 to 1934, this restored 28-room brick building was the home of a pioneering African-American businesswoman and educator whose endeavors included banking, insurance, and a newspaper. You can take a 45-minute tour of the house and see a movie about her accomplishments. ⊠ *Visitor center, 600 N. 2nd St.* ☎ *804/771–2017* ⊕ *www.nps/gov/malw* ⊠ *Free* ☉ *Mon.–Sat. 9–5.*

★ ⑤ **Museum and White House of the Confederacy.** These two buildings provide a look at a crucial period in the nation's history. The museum (a good place to start) has elaborate permanent exhibitions on the Civil War era. The "world's largest collection of Confederate memorabilia" includes such artifacts as the sword Robert E. Lee wore to the surrender at Appomattox. Next door, the "White House" has in fact always been painted gray. Made of brick in 1818, the building was stuccoed to give the appearance of large stone blocks. Preservationists have painstakingly re-created the interior as it was during the Civil War, when Jefferson Davis lived in the house. During the 45-minute guided tour, you see the entry hall's period 9-foot-tall French rococo mirrors and its floor cloth, painted to resemble ceramic tiles. You can park free in the adjacent hospital parking garage; the museum will validate tickets. ⊠ *1201 E. Clay St.* ☎ *804/649–1861* ⊕ *www.moc.org* ⊠ *Combination ticket $10; museum only, $7; White House only, $7* ☉ *Mon.–Sat. 10–5, Sun. noon–5.*

off the beaten path

PARAMOUNT'S KINGS DOMINION – This entertainment complex in Doswell, 20 mi north of Richmond, is great for children, but parents will need to bring lots of money and patience; lines often begin forming an hour before the park opens. The more than 100 rides include a roller coaster that's launched on compressed air and the "Xtreme SkyFlyer," a variation on the bungee-jumping theme. ⊠ *I–95, Doswell Exit 98* ☎ *804/876–5000* ⊕ *www.kingsdominion.com* ⊠ *$32, parking $5* ☉ *May and Sept., weekends; hrs vary, call ahead; June–Aug., daily 10 AM–10:30 PM.*

⑪ **Richmond National Battlefield Park Visitor Center.** Inside what was once the Tredegar Iron Works, this is the best place to get maps and other materials on the Civil War battlefields and attractions in the Richmond area. A self-guided tour and optional tape tour for purchase covers the two major military threats to Richmond—the Peninsula Campaign of 1862 and the Overland Campaign of 1864—as well as the impact on Richmond's home front. Three floors of exhibits in the main building include unique artifacts on loan from other Civil War history institutions. Other original buildings on-site are a carpentry shop, gun foundry, office, and company store.

Built in 1837 the ironworks, along with smaller area iron foundries, made Richmond the center of iron manufacturing in the southern United States. When the Civil War began in 1861, the ironworks geared up to make the artillery, ammunition, and other matériel that sustained the Confederate war machine. Its rolling mills provided the armor plating for warships, including the ironclad CSS *Virginia.* The works—saved from burning in 1865—went on to play an important role in rebuilding the devastated South; it also produced munitions in both world wars. A café is adjacent to the visitor center. If you're lucky, you may still find free on-street parking; a pay lot at the visitor center costs $4. ⊠ *5th and Tredegar Sts.* ☎ *804/771–2145* ☒ *Free* ☉ *Daily 9–5.*

❷ St. John's Episcopal Church. For security reasons, the rebellious Second Virginia Convention met in Richmond instead of at Williamsburg; it was in this 1741 church on March 23, 1775, that Patrick Henry delivered the speech in which he declared, "Give me liberty or give me death!" His argument persuaded the Second Virginia Convention to arm a Virginia militia. The speech is reenacted May–September on Sunday at 2 PM. The cemetery includes the graves of Edgar Allan Poe's mother, Elizabeth Arnold Poe, and many famous early Virginians, notably George Wythe, a signer of the Declaration of Independence. The chapel gift shop, in the old Victorian Gothic house on the grounds, has Colonial crafts and other items for sale. Guided tours are led on the half hour. ⊠ *2401 E. Broad St., at 24th St.* ☎ *804/648–5015* ⊕ *www.historicstjohnschurch. org* ☒ *$3* ☉ *Mon.–Sat. 10–4, Sun. 1–4.*

❻ Valentine Museum. This museum impressively documents the life and history of Richmond with exhibits that cover topics from architecture to race relations. **Wickham House** (1812), a part of the Valentine, is more rightly a mansion; it was designed by architect Alexander Parris, the creator of Boston's Faneuil Hall. John Wickham was Richmond's wealthiest citizen of the time, and Daniel Webster and Zachary Taylor were frequent guests. The house interiors are stunning, but not everything at the museum is opulent: the slave quarters, also meticulously restored, provide a chilling contrast to the mansion's splendor. ⊠ *1015 E. Clay St.* ☎ *804/649–0711* ⊕ *www.valentinemuseum.org* ☒ *$5* ☉ *Tues.–Sat. 10–5, Sun. noon–5; guided Wickham House tours Tues.–Sat 11–4 and Sun 1–4.*

off the beaten path

VIRGINIA AVIATION MUSEUM – The legendary SR-71 Blackbird spy plane, once able to travel faster than three times the speed of sound and at an elevation of more than 85,000 feet (near the edge of the earth's atmosphere) sits proudly outside this museum. The U.S. Air Force's 32 Blackbirds were used on reconnaissance missions from 1964 to 1990. The museum also has Captain Dick Merrill's 1930s open cockpit mail plane; airworthy replicas of the Wright brothers' 1900, 1901, and 1902 gliders; a replica 1903 Flyer; and a World War I SPAD VII in mint condition. Virginia's Aviation Hall of Fame is also housed at this branch of the Science Museum of Virginia. To get here, take Exit 197 off I–64E and follow signs to the museum. ⊠ *Richmond International Airport, 5701 Huntsman Rd.* ☎ *804/236–3622* ⊕ *www.vam.smv.org* ☒ *$6* ☉ *Mon.–Sat. 9:30–5, Sun. noon–5.*

❹ Virginia Holocaust Museum. The city's newest, and most poignant, museum is housed in the former Climax Warehouse, which stored tobacco in Richmond's Shockoe Bottom. In keeping with the museum's aim to teach "tolerance through education," the museum details the experiences of Holocaust survivors from across Virginia, who have recorded their stories and shared their memories. One permanent exhibit, the Ipson Saga, follows the life of a family who went from pre-war Lithuania to the Kovno ghetto concentration camp, as well as their escape and eventual resettlement in Virginia. After an introductory film in which six Richmond-based survivors tell their stories, visitors receive a book for a self-guided tour. The museum's auditorium, the Chore Shell, is a replica of the beautiful 18th-century interior of the only surviving synagogue in Lithuania. Because of the nature of the exhibits, the museum is not recommended for young children. ⊠ *2000 E. Cary St.* ☎ *804/257–5400* ⊕ *www.va-holocaust.com* ⊠ *Donations accepted* ⊙ *Weekdays 9–5, weekends 11–5.*

★ ❾ **Virginia State Capitol.** Thomas Jefferson designed this grand edifice in 1785, modeling it on a Roman temple—the Maison Carrée—in Nîmes, France. Due to extensive renovations the interior of the Capitol is off limits until January 2007, and even the beautiful gardens are now being dug up so that a new Visitors center can be constructed there. ⊠ *Capitol Sq.* ☎ *804/698–1788.*

The Fan District

To the west of downtown, Monument Avenue, 140 feet wide and divided by a verdant median, is lined with statues of Civil War heroes, as well as a newer one commemorating Arthur Ashe, and the stately homes of some of the first families of Virginia. A block south, a series of streets fanning out southwesterly from Park Avenue near Virginia Commonwealth University creates the Fan District, a treasury of restored turn-of-the-20th-century town houses that has become a popular neighborhood. Adjacent to it is Carytown, a restored area of shops and eateries along Cary Street.

a good tour

Follow Broad Street west, and turn left on Laurel Street to reach the **Beth Ahabah Museum and Archives** ⑭. For the **American Historical Foundation Museum/Home of the U.S. Marine Raider Museum** ⑮, continue west on Broad, turn left on Lombardy Street, and drive one block before turning left into the museum. Plan to spend a couple of hours at the **Science Museum of Virginia** ⑯, about five blocks farther west on Broad Street. Next door is the **Children's Museum of Richmond** ⑰. There's lots of free parking here. After your visit take the Boulevard south to the **Virginia Museum of Fine Arts** ⑱. In the same block is the **Virginia Historical Society Museum of Virginia History** ⑲. Trendy Cary Street is four blocks farther south.

TIMING Even if you select only two or three museums to visit, allow four–five hours for this tour.

Sights to See

⑮ **American Historical Foundation Museum/Home of the U.S. Marine Raider Museum.** Housing the largest collection of military knives and bayonets in the United States, this museum has other exhibits that chronicle the deeds of the World War II Marine Raiders, a group started by Colonel Evan Carlson to raid Pacific Islands such as Makin. There's also a pictorial history of the monuments of Monument Avenue. ⊠ *1142 W. Grace St.* ☎ *804/353–1812* ⊕ *www.ahfrichmond.com* ⊠ *Free* ⊙ *Weekdays 11–3.*

⓮ **Beth Ahabah Museum and Archives.** This repository contains articles and documents related to the Richmond and southern Jewish experience, including the records of two congregations. ⊠ *1109 W. Franklin St.* ☎ *804/353–2668* ⊕ *www.bethahabah.org* ⊠ *Free, $3 donation suggested* ☉ *Sun.–Thurs. 10–3.*

🖑 ⓱ **Children's Museum of Richmond.** A welcoming, hands-on place for children and families, the museum is a place to climb, explore, experiment, and play until every surface area is smudged with fingerprints. Bright, colorful, and crowded, the museum's different sections keep an eye out for a child's best interests. How It Works lets children experiment with tools, materials, and their own endless energy. The Feeling Good Neighborhood has a functioning apple orchard as well as a monster-size digestive system. Our Great Outdoors houses the museum's most popular attraction, The Cave, where children explore a 40-foot replica of a Virginia limestone cave and are introduced to earth science, oceanography, and rock collecting. In the Art Studio, the paint gets on someone else's walls for a change. Specific exhibits include Children's Bank, Health and Safety, TV Studio, SuperMarket, Computer Station, Art Studio, StagePlay, and In My Own Backyard (for toddlers). ⊠ *2626 W. Broad St.* ☎ *804/474–2667* ⊕ *www.c-mor.org* ⊠ *$7* ☉ *Tues.–Sat. 9:30–5, Sun. noon–5.*

off the beaten path

LEWIS GINTER BOTANICAL GARDEN – Founded in 1984 the Lewis Ginter Botanical Garden features year-round beauty, dining, and shopping. On the 80-acre property northwest of downtown, 40 acres are landscaped in nine main areas. These areas include one of the largest and most diverse perennial gardens on the East Coast, a formal Victorian garden, a study garden with an extensive collection of daffodils and daylilies, a wetland garden teeming with wildlife, and an Asian and conifer garden. In 2005 a new Children's Garden with a botanical maze, international village, and a handicap-accessible Tree House will open. The highlight of the Garden, literally, is the Conservatory, which has a 63-foot dome, a central palm house, and a wing full of tropical plants. ⊠ *1800 Lakeside Ave.* ☎ *804/262–9887* ⊕ *www.lewisginter.org* ⊠ *$9* ☉ *Daily 9–5.*

★ 🖑 ⓰ **Science Museum of Virginia.** Aerospace, astronomy, electricity, physical sciences, computers, crystals, telecommunications, and the Foucault pendulum are among the subjects covered in exhibits here, many of which strongly appeal to children. The biggest spectacle is the Ethyl IMAX Dome and Planetarium, which draws the audience into the movie or astronomy show. The museum is in a former train station with a massive dome. ⊠ *2500 W. Broad St.* ☎ *804/367–1080* ⊕ *www.smv.org* ⊠ *Museum $8.50; IMAX $8.50; IMAX and planetarium $16* ☉ *Mon.–Sat. 9:30–5, Sun. 11:30–5.*

⓳ **Virginia Historical Society Museum of Virginia History.** With 7 million manuscripts and 200,000 books, the library here is a key stop for researchers and genealogists. The visitor-friendly museum mounts regularly changing exhibits and has permanent exhibitions that include an 800-piece collection of Confederate weapons and equipment and "The

Story of Virginia, an American Experience," which covers 16,000 years of history and has galleries on topics such as Becoming Confederates and Becoming Equal Virginians. ⊠ *428 N. Blvd., at Kensington Ave.* ☎ *804/358–4901* ⊕ *www.vahistorical.org* ☎ *$5* ⊘ *Mon.–Sat. 10–5, Sun., galleries only, 1–5. Research library closed Sun.*

★ ⑱ **Virginia Museum of Fine Arts.** The panorama of world art here, spanning the ages from ancient times to the present, features such important works as the Mellon collections of British Sporting Art and French impressionist and postimpressionist art—including nine original wax sculptures and seven bronzes by Edgar Degas; works by Goya, Renoir, and Monet; Classical and Egyptian art; Roman marble statues, and one of the world's leading collections of Indian, Nepalese, and Tibetan art. The museum's most beloved pieces are its five Fabergé eggs. Through 2008 the museum is undergoing a major expansion that will double existing gallery space, create a sculpture garden, and enlarge parking. During this time some galleries and collections will be off view: call ahead for specific information. ⊠ *200 N. Blvd.* ☎ *804/340–1400* ⊕ *www.vmfa. state.va.us* ☎ *Free, $5 suggested donation* ⊘ *Wed.–Sun. 11–5.*

Richmond's Estates

Not far from downtown are mansions and country estates, two with buildings transported from England. Presidents and Confederate leaders are buried in Hollywood Cemetery.

a good drive

Virginia House, Agecroft Hall, and Wilton are on the west side of Richmond, about 10 minutes from the Museum of Fine Arts. Take Boulevard south to Grove Avenue and turn right. Turn left on Malvern Avenue (which turns into Canterbury, then Sulgrave Road) to visit **Virginia House ⑳** and **Agecroft Hall ㉑**. To see **Wilton ㉒**, follow Berkshire Street to Route 147 and turn left. Turn left again at Wilton Road; the historic house is at the end of the road. If you want to visit **Maymont ㉓**, drive back out on Wilton Road and turn right on Route 147. After reaching Carytown, turn right on Pump House Road to visit Maymont's petting zoo or continue straight and turn right on Meadow Street to see the mansion. **Hollywood Cemetery ㉔** will be on the left side of Meadow Street.

TIMING To visit each mansion, allow anywhere from 30 to 60 minutes for its guided tour. Additionally Virginia House and Maymont have extensive gardens to wander. Most of these country estates are closed Monday.

Sights to See

㉑ **Agecroft Hall.** Built in Lancashire, England, in the 15th century during the reign of King Henry VIII, Agecroft Hall was transported here in 1926. It's the finest Tudor manor house in the United States. Set amid gardens planted with specimens typical of 1580–1640, the house contains an extensive assortment of Tudor and early Stuart art and furniture (1485–1660) as well as collector's items from England and elsewhere in Europe. ⊠ *4305 Sulgrave Rd.* ☎ *804/353–4241* ⊕ *www.agecrofthall.com* ☎ *$7* ⊘ *Tues.–Sat. 10–4, Sun. 12:30–5.*

㉔ **Hollywood Cemetery.** Many noted Virginians are buried here, including presidents John Tyler and James Monroe; Confederate president Jefferson

Davis; generals Fitzhugh Lee, J. E. B. Stuart, and George E. Pickett; the statesman John Randolph; and Matthew Fontaine Maury, a naval scientist. ⊠ *Cherry and Albemarle Sts.* ☎ *804/648–8501* 🗩 *Free* ⊙ *Mon.–Sat. 7–5, Sun. 8–5.*

㉓ Maymont. On this 100-acre Victorian estate is the lavish Maymont House museum, a carriage collection, and elaborate Italian and Japanese gardens. A true family attraction, Maymont's complex includes the new Nature & Visitor Center, native wildlife exhibits, and a children's farm. A café is open for lunch. Tram tours and carriage rides are available. ⊠ *2201 Shields Lake Dr.* ☎ *804/358–7166* ⊕ *www.maymont.org* 🗩 *Free, donation suggested* ⊙ *Grounds daily 10–7; mansion, nature center, and barn Tues.–Sun. noon–5.*

⑳ Virginia House. Alexander and Virginia Weddell had this 12th-century English monastery shipped across the Atlantic and up the James River in the 1920s. After three years of reconstruction and the planting of lush year-round gardens, the couple realized their dream of a re-created European estate. Alexander Weddell spent a lifetime in the diplomatic service in Mexico, Argentina, and Spain, and the house contains an extensive collection of Spanish and Latin American antiques. The estate (named after Mrs. Weddell, and not the state) passed to the Virginia Historical Society when the Weddells died in a New Year's Day train accident in 1948. ⊠ *4301 Sulgrave Rd.* ☎ *804/353–4251* 🗩 *$5* ⊙ *Fri. and Sat. 10–4, Sun. 12:30–5; last tour begins 1 hr before closing.*

㉒ Wilton. William Randolph III built this elegant Georgian house in 1753 on the only James River plantation in Richmond. Once 14 mi downriver, the home was moved brick by brick to its current site when industry encroached upon its former location. Wilton is the only house in Virginia with complete floor-to-ceiling panels in every room, and the pastel-painted panels and sunlit alcoves are a large part of its beauty. The home's 1815 period furnishings include the family's original desk bookcase and an original map of Virginia drawn by Thomas Jefferson's father. The Garden Club of Virginia landscaped the terraced lawns that overlook the James River. ⊠ *215 S. Wilton Rd., off Cary St.* ☎ *804/ 282–5936* ⊕ *www.wiltonhousemuseum.org* 🗩 *$5* ⊙ *Mar.–Jan., Tues.–Fri. 1–4:30, Sat. 10–4:30, Feb. by appointment only.*

Where to Eat

$$$$ ✕ **Mortons.** When speaking of steak houses Morton's always comes to the top of the list, and this is the place for a true beef connoisseur. In a formal dining room with mahogany panels, leather booths, and engraved glass partitions, you can dine on the finest quality aged grain-fed beef shipped directly from Chicago, with fresh fish and other seafood also on the menu. The separate bar also includes fine cigars for sale. ⊠ *111 Virginia St.* ☎ *804/648–1662* ☰ *AE, D, DC, MC, V.*

$$$$ ✕ **Old Original Bookbinder's.** Opened in 1865, the original branch of this restaurant has been a Philadelphia institution and has played host to the likes of astronauts, princesses, movie stars, and many other celebrities. Now the tradition continues in a beautifully renovated old tobacco warehouse near the James River. Surrounded by exposed brick walls, a live lobster tank, and an open kitchen, you can enjoy meat and seafood dishes such as a grilled double-cut pork chop, Bookbinder's Steak, and crusted Mahimahi. ⊠ 2306 E. Cary St. ☎ 804/643–6900 ⊟ AE, MC, V ⊗ No lunch.

$$$–$$$$ ✕ **Lemaire.** Named after Etienne Lemaire, Maitre d'Hotel to Thomas Jefferson from 1794 until the end of his presidency, this is the grandest restaurant in Richmond. Jefferson's tastes included adding light sauces and fresh herbs to dishes prepared with the region's more than abundant supply of ingredients. Today the menu follows that theme with updated regional Southern cuisine that includes dashes of European classical and American contemporary influences. Typical dishes might include rack of venison, or crispy-skinned Chesapeake Bay rockfish. ⊠ Jefferson Hotel, 101 W. Franklin St. ☎ 804/788–8000 ⊕ www.jeffersonhotel.com ⊟ AE, D, DC, MC, V.

$$$ ✕ **Amici Ristorante.** A perennial Richmond favorite since opening in 1991, the restaurant serves Northern Italian dishes such as housemade ravioli filled with spinach and ricotta cheese, grilled buffalo rib eye with a port and black truffle sauce, and shrimp, scallops, clams and fresh fish in a light tomato broth. In the cozy first floor, the walls around the booths are adorned with flowered tapestries and oil paintings of Italy. The second floor is more formal, with white walls trimmed with stenciled grapes and vines. There's also a small outdoor terrace. ⊠ 3343 W. Cary St. ☎ 804/353–4700 ⊟ AE, MC, V.

$$$ ✕ **The Dining Room.** This restaurant's rich mahogany paneling and impressionistic paintings create a feeling of warmth. The American cuisine here includes such dishes as a beef tenderloin served with oyster tempura, grilled asparagus, and béarnaise sauce. In addition to a tempting three-course prix-fixe menu, available at all times, there's a perennially popular champagne brunch on Sunday. ⊠ Berkeley Hotel, 1200 E. Cary St. ☎ 804/343–7300 or 888/343–7301 ⊕ www.berkeleyhotel.com ⊟ AE, D, DC, MC, V.

★ **$$–$$$** ✕ **Europa.** At this Mediterranean café and tapas bar, there are plenty of enticing main dishes, but many diners opt for making a meal from the extensive list of tapas priced in the single digits, including Spanish meats and cheeses, lamb meatballs, codfish fritters, and stewed squid. Housed in a former warehouse in Shockoe Bottom a few blocks from the capitol, the lively restaurant has a quarry-tile floor and original brick walls. Paella fanciers can choose from three versions: "La Valencia" (the traditional meats, fish, and shellfish); "La Marinera" (fish and shellfish); or "La Barcelonesa" (chicken, chorizo, and lamb). You can wash it all down with sangria made in-house. ⊠ 1409 E. Cary St. ☎ 804/643–0911 ⊕ www.europarichmond.com ⊟ AE, MC, V ⊗ Closed Sun.; no lunch Sat.

$$–$$$ ✕ **The Hard Shell.** This fun and unpretentious restaurant has many fresh and local seafood dishes, and those with other tastes can choose from such options as filet mignon and prime rib and even vegetarians are well cared for. Raw Bar enthusiasts will be enticed, too, with choice being the only problem. The Sunday Brunch is especially attractive, as are the specialty drinks, especially the martinis. ⊠ 1411 E. Cary St. ☎ 804/643–2333 ⊕ www.thehardshell.com ⊟ AE, D, DC, MC, V ⊗ No lunch weekends.

$$-$$$ ✕ **The Iron Horse.** Twenty feet from this restaurant are the busiest train tracks on the East Coast, and the passing trains are certainly a novelty when dining here. The lunch menu includes tapas, pizzas, and sandwiches, and there are two major options for dinner. The more casual dinner menu, served in the Calvert Room and the lounge, includes sandwiches and other entrées and sandwiches named after local celebrities. The à la carte menu, served in the Calvert room only, changes seasonally and has more creative dishes, such as braised lamb shanks and roasted monkfish. ⊠ *100 S. Railroad Ave., Ashland* ☎ *804/752–6410* ▭ *AE, D, DC, MC, V* ⊘ *No lunch weekends; no dinner Mon.*

$$-$$$ ✕ **Julep's.** In the River District, and in the city's oldest commercial building (1817), Julep's has a spiral staircase joining the upper and lower dining areas. The specialty here is new Southern cuisine, with seasonal lunch and dinner menus that include tempting dishes such as roasted game hen stuffed with a risotto of country ham, green peas, and mushrooms. The wine list is one to linger over. And try not to leave without sampling one of the restaurant's namesakes. ⊠ *1719–21 E. Franklin St.* ☎ *804/377–3968* ⊕ *www.juleps.net* ▭ *AE, MC, V* ⊘ *Closed Sun. No lunch Sat. No dinner Mon.*

$$-$$$ ✕ **Limani Fish Grill.** This is a serious seafood experience—it's one of the best seafood restaurants in the city—in an interesting minimalist dining room. Selecting only the freshest line-caught fish, Limani seasons them with sea salt, bastes them with oregano-infused olive oil, and then grills them over an open fire using oak and fruitwoods. Most dishes are priced by the half-pound. ⊠ *W. Cary St.* ☎ *804/353–5323* ▭ *AE, MC, V* ⊘ *Closed Sun. No lunch.*

$-$$ ✕ **Legend Brewing Company.** Central Virginia's oldest and largest microbrewery is not a legend in name only; its finely brewed unpasteurized beers are legendary in the region. You can take home one-liter "growlers" of your favorite tipple. The menu of sophisticated pub food, which may include jambalaya, a bratwurst platter, and crab quesadillas, can be taken in the large dining room or, whenever the weather allows, on the large terrace: the views are over the James River to downtown Richmond on the northern bank. ⊠ *321 W. 7th St.* ☎ *804/232–3446* ⊕ *www.legendbrewery.com* ▭ *AE, D, DC, MC, V.*

¢-$ ✕ **3rd Street Diner.** Built on the site of a famous Confederate hospital, this friendly American diner has been serving great food, including breakfast dishes, sandwiches, and entrées like baked spaghetti and roast pork with stuffing, since 1926. The mix of booths and tables downstairs, and tables upstairs, are surrounded by large prints of the era. The diner's open 24 hours a day. ⊠ *3rd and Main St.* ☎ *804/788–4750* ▭ *MC, V.*

¢-$$ ✕ **Strawberry Street Cafe.** An unlimited salad bar ($5) in a claw-foot bathtub is this Fan District café's trademark. Homemade soups, unique sandwiches, and broiled crab cakes are among the offerings. Brunch is available on Sunday, and there's a Strawberry Street Market next door. ⊠ *421 Strawberry St.* ☎ *804/353–6860* ⊕ *www.strawberrystreetcafe.com* ▭ *AE, MC, V.*

¢-$ ✕ **Penny Lane Pub & Restaurant.** A Richmond institution since 1976, the name and the presence of the Liver Bird (the symbol of Liverpool) here is a clue that tells you that this is a little piece of that British city in Virginia. The host Terry O'Neill is a genuine scouser (Liverpudlian native). The menu is full of typical English favorites like cottage pie and fish-and-chips. The selection of beers on tap here is the best in central Virginia. Premiership soccer lovers will feel at home here, and there's also darts and pool available. ⊠ *421 E. Franklin St.* ☎ *804/780–1682* ⊕ *www.pennylanepub.com* ▤ *AE, D, MC* ☉ *Closed Sun. No lunch Sat.*

Where to Stay

Of the nearly 150 hotels and motels in the Richmond area, these are among the most noteworthy.

★ $$$–$$$$ 🏨 **Jefferson Hotel.** The inspiration for this majestic hotel was Major Lewis Ginter, who wanted it to be one of the finest hotels in the country when it was opened in 1895. Reopened in 1907 after a fire, it hosted the famous and the rich until closing in 1980. Rebuilt again, it opened in 1986. In this National Historic Landmark, there's a magnificent sweeping staircase with 36 steps that's reminiscent of the one in *Gone With the Wind*, embellished faux-marble columns, a 70-foot high ceiling with a stained glass skylight, rich tapestries, and replicas of traditional Victorian furniture. The rooms are done in a total of 57 different styles. ⊠ *101 W. Franklin St., at Adams St., 23220* ☎ *804/788–8000 or 800/424–8014* 🖷 *804/225–0334* ⊕ *www.jeffersonhotel.com* ⇆ *228 rooms, 36 suites* ♖ *2 restaurants, room service, indoor pool, health club, bar* ▤ *AE, D, DC, MC, V.*

$$–$$$ 🏨 **Richmond Marriott.** The lobby of this luxury hotel near the 6th Street Marketplace has crystal chandeliers and marble flooring. Rooms are furnished in a contemporary style; a tanning salon keeps the beauty-conscious crowd content. ⊠ *500 E. Broad St., 23219* ☎ *804/643–3400 or 800/228–9290* 🖷 *804/788–1230* ⊕ *www.marriotthotels.com/ricdt* ⇆ *400 rooms* ♖ *2 restaurants, in-room data ports, indoor pool, health club, hot tub, lobby lounge, concierge* ▤ *AE, D, DC, MC, V.*

$–$$$ 🏨 **Linden Row Inn.** Edgar Allan Poe played in the garden that became
Fodor'sChoice the beautiful brick courtyards within this row of 1840s Greek Revival
★ town houses. The main building is furnished in antiques and period reproductions; the carriage-house garden quarters are decorated in Old English style and have homemade quilts. Mornings begin with a free newspaper and deluxe continental breakfast; afternoons end with a wine-and-cheese reception in the beautiful parlor. Also complimentary are transportation to nearby historic attractions and passes to the YMCA's health club. The inn's dining room, open for breakfast, lunch, and dinner, is in the former stables. ⊠ *101 N. 1st St., at Franklin St., 23219* ☎ *804/783–7000 or 800/348–7424* 🖷 *804/648–7504* ⊕ *www.lindenrowinn.com* ⇆ *60 rooms, 10 suites* ♖ *Restaurant, in-room data ports, dry cleaning, laundry service, no-smoking rooms* ▤ *AE, D, DC, MC, V* ⦿ *CP.*

★ $$ 🏨 **Commonwealth Park Suites Hotel.** When it was the Rueger back in 1846, this hotel was a bootlegging saloon with rooms for its clientele. After a fire during the Civil War, it fell into disrepair for 50 years. After being rebuilt in 1912 and after several renovations, it now has 59 luxurious rooms and suites. Because the Commonwealth is across from the Capitol, some senators and representatives make this their home when the state legislature is in session. ✉ *901 Bank St., 23219* ☎ *804/343–7300 or 888/343–7301* 🖷 *804/343–1025* 🛏 *10 rooms, 49 suites* ⚐ *Minibars, in-room broadband, dry cleaning, laundry service, meeting rooms, no-smoking rooms* 🖃 *AE, D, DC, MC, V.*

★ **$–$$** 🏨 **Berkeley Hotel.** Although built in the style of the century-old warehouses and buildings that surround it, this boutique hotel dates from 1988. Those seeking extra space and luxury should opt for the Governor's Suite, which has a luxurious king bed, a private terrace, and a living room with panoramic views over the historic Shockoe Slip area. Norman guest rooms have four-poster beds and traditional furnishings. Guests staying here get free entry to the Capital Club health and fitness facilities. ✉ *1200 E. Cary St., 23219* ☎ *804/780–1300 or 888/780–4422* 🖷 *804/343–1885* ⊕ *www.berkeleyhotel.com* 🛏 *54 rooms, 1 suite* ⚐ *Restaurant, some in-room broadband, gym, lobby lounge, dry cleaning, laundry service, concierge, meeting rooms, no-smoking rooms, parking (fee)* 🖃 *AE, D, DC, MC, V.*

$ 🏨 **Henry Clay Inn.** Named after the local orator and statesman who was a three-time candidate for President in the early 1800s, this inn re-creates the Georgian Revival splendor of two inns that used to be nearby. Opened in 1992 the Henry Clay is furnished with reproductions of antiques as well as period pieces. The suites all have refrigerators, microwaves, and Jacuzzis. The Kings Dominion theme park is just to the north, and the Virginia Commons Center mall is to the south, between Ashland and Richmond. ✉ *114 N. Railroad Ave., Ashland 23005* ☎ *804/798–3100 or 800/343–4565* 🖷 *804/752–7555* ⊕ *www. henryclayinn.com* 🛏 *11 rooms, 3 suites* ⚐ *Restaurant, some in-room hot tubs, some microwaves, some refrigerators, cable TV, free parking; no smoking* 🖃 *AE, D, DC, MC, V.*

¢–$ 🏨 **Comfort Inn Executive Center.** On the northwest side of Richmond, this three-building redbrick motel is near the University of Richmond and convenient to I–95 and I–64. From the street it looks attractive, but it also appears deceptively small; you see only the first of three buildings. The others stretch away from the street in a sort of private cul-de-sac. A deluxe continental breakfast is included. Thirty rooms have whirlpool bathtubs. ✉ *7201 W. Broad St., 23294* ☎ *804/672–1108* 🖷 *804/755–1625* ⊕ *www.comfortinn.com* 🛏 *123 rooms* ⚐ *Pool, gym, lobby lounge, laundry facilities* 🖃 *AE, D, DC, MC, V* ⏹ *CP.*

¢ 🏨 **Days Inn.** This high-rise motel on the northwest side of Richmond is off West Broad Street, near several office buildings. A deluxe continental breakfast and in-room movies are free. Rooms are reached via secure interior corridors. "WorkZone" rooms with king-size beds are equipped for the business traveler. ✉ *2100 Dickens Rd., 23230* ☎ *804/ 282–3300 or 800/329–7466* 🖷 *804/288–2145* ⊕ *www.daysinn.com* 🛏 *180 rooms* ⚐ *Pool, shop* 🖃 *AE, D, DC, MC, V* ⏹ *CP.*

¢ 🏨 **Econo Lodge Richmond.** This basic hotel with exterior corridors is near I–64 and five full-service restaurants. ✉ *7300 W. Broad St., Exit 183C off I–64, 6 mi from downtown, 23294* ☎ *804/672–8621 or 800/228–2800* 🖷 *804/755–7155* ⊕ *www.fairfieldinn.com* 🛏 *124 rooms, 1 suite* ⚐ *In-room data ports, cable TV, pool, no-smoking rooms* 🖃 *AE, D, DC, MC, V* ⏹ *CP.*

Nightlife & the Arts

The **Richmond Coliseum** (✉ 601 E. Leigh St. ☎ 804/780–4956 ⊕ www. richmondcoliseum.net) has been a Richmond institution since the early 1970s. With 11,330 permanent seats, and nearly 2,000 more for concerts, it hosts top entertainers and artists, the Ringling Brothers circus, Richmond Riverdogs hockey team, wrestling, and other large events.

Bars
Tonic (✉ 14 N. 18th St. ☎ 804/648–4300) is Richmond's newest martini bar and cocktail lounge. Among the delights is the "Strawberries and Champagne" cocktail. Tonic also serves a dinner menu of Mediterranean dishes; entrées are under $15.

Dance
The **Richmond Ballet** (✉ 407 E. Canal St. ☎ 804/344–0906 ⊕ www. richmondballet.com), the city's professional classical ballet company, usually performs at the Carpenter Center and at the Theatre Virginia in the Virginia Museum of Fine Arts.

Music
The **Richmond Symphony** (☎ 804/788–1212 ⊕ www.richmondsymphony. com), founded in 1957, often utilizes internationally known soloists at performances in the Carpenter Center. The Richmond Symphony All-Star Pops hosts popular guest artists.

Theater
Barksdale Theatre (✉ 1601 Willow Lawn Dr. ☎ 804/282–2620 ⊕ www. barksdalerichmond.org), the area's oldest not-for-profit theater, began in 1953. Performances ranging from classics to innovative new works are staged Thursday through Saturday evening and on Sunday afternoon.

Carpenter Center (✉ 600 E. Grace St. ☎ 804/225–9000 ⊕ www. carpentercenter.org), a restored 1928 motion picture palace, is now a performing-arts center that mounts opera, traveling shows, symphonic music, and ballet.

Landmark Theatre (✉ 6 N. Laurel St. ☎ 804/646–4213) was built in an extremely elaborate style with towering minarets and desert murals: when it was built by the Shriners in 1926, it was called "the Mosque." Just to the west of downtown, the Landmark is known for its excellent acoustics and has the largest permanent proscenium stage on the East Coast. Many of America's most famous entertainers have performed here, and it continues to be used for the road versions of Broadway shows, symphony performances, ballet, children's theater, concerts, and fashion shows.

Sports & the Outdoors

Baseball
The Richmond Braves, a Triple-A farm team for Atlanta, play at the **Diamond** (✉ 3001 N. Blvd. ☎ 804/359–4444 ⊕ www.rbraves.com).

Car Racing

Richmond International Raceway (✉ Laburnum Ave. exit, off I–64 ☎ 804/
345–7223 or 866/455–7223 ⊕ www.rir.com) holds two NASCAR
Nextel Cup Series races, held on Saturday nights in May and September, as well as other races. Tickets for the series cost $50–$110 and are
extremely hard to come by, but tickets for all other events are readily
available. Children under 12 are admitted free.

Golf

In Richmond aficionados tee off most of the year. The area has 24 golf
courses open to the public—the **Virginia State Golf Association** (⊕ www.
vsga.org) has a good handle on them all; its Web site even allows you
to book tee times online.

Rafting

Richmond is the only city within the U.S. that has rafting within its city
limits. **Richmond Raft** (☎ 804/222–7238 or 800/222–7238 ⊕ www.
richmondraft.com) conducts white-water rafting trips through the city
on the James River (Class III and IV rapids), as well as float trips from
March through November.

Shopping

Sixth Street Marketplace has specialty shops, chain stores, and eating
places. **Shockoe Slip** (✉ E. Cary St. between 12th and 15th Sts.), a neighborhood of tobacco warehouses during the 18th and 19th centuries, has
some boutiques. The open-air **Farmers' Market** (✉ 17th and Main Sts.),
beside the old Main Street Station, is surrounded by art galleries, boutiques, and antiques shops, many in converted warehouses and factories.

PETERSBURG

❷ Historic **Petersburg,** 20 mi south of Richmond on I–95, lies along the
Appomattox River. During the Civil War, the city was under siege by
Union forces from June 1864 to April 1865—the so-called last stand of
the Confederacy. A major railroad hub, the city was a crucial link in
the supply chain for Lee's army, and its surrender brought about the evacuation of Richmond and the surrender at Appomattox.

The 🏛 **Petersburg Visitors Center** sells the Fort Henry Pass, which allows
admission to the Siege Museum, Centre Hill Mansion, and Blandford
Church for $11. The center also has information about Lee's Retreat
Trail, a 26-stop driving tour around the area. Free parking is plentiful
near the center. ✉ *McIlwaine House, 425 Cockade Alley* ☎ *804/733–
2400 or 800/368–3595* ⊕ *www.petersburg-va.org.*

To walk **Petersburg National Battlefield** is to be where more than 60,000
Union and Confederate soldiers died during the siege of the city. A pronounced depression in the ground is the eroded remnant of the Crater,
the result of a 4-ton gunpowder explosion set off by Union forces in one
failed attack. The 1,500-acre park is laced with several miles of earth-
works and includes two forts. In the visitor center, maps and models
convey background information vital to the self-guided driving tour, dur-

ing which you park at specified spots on the tour road and proceed on foot to nearby points of interest. ⊠ *Rte. 36, 2½ mi east of downtown* ☎ *804/732–3531* ⊕ *www.pps.gov/pete* ⊠ *$4 car, $2 cyclist or pedestrian* ⊙ *Park mid-June–Labor Day, daily 8:30–dusk; Labor Day–mid-June, daily 8–5. Visitor center daily 8:30–5:30.*

★ The **Siege Museum,** inside a former commodities market from 1839, tells the story of how the city's lavish life style gave way to a bitter struggle for survival during the Civil War: a single chicken could cost as much as $50. A 16-minute movie narrated by Petersburg-born actor Joseph Cotten dramatizes the upheaval. ⊠ *Exchange Bldg., 15 W. Bank St.* ☎ *804/733–2404* ⊠ *$5* ⊙ *Daily 10–5.*

Centre Hill Mansion. This, the third home of the Bolling family, was originally built in 1823. Having been remodeled twice since then, it illustrates changing architectural styles; it was and is the grandest home in Petersburg. Inside are ornate woodwork, plaster motifs and period furnishings, and an 1840s service tunnel in the basement that once connected the work area of the house to the street below. ⊠ *1 Centre Hill Circle* ☎ *804/733–2401* ⊠ *$5* ⊙ *Daily 10–5.*

A parish church from the 18th century, **Old Blandford Church** is a memorial to the Southern soldiers who died during the Civil War. Some 30,000 Confederate soldiers are buried in the churchyard, which is surrounded by ornamental ironwork. The church's 15 spectacular stained-glass windows by Louis Comfort Tiffany are memorials donated by the Confederate states. The Memorial Day tradition is said to have begun in this cemetery in June 1866. ⊠ *319 S. Crater Rd., 2 mi south of town* ☎ *804/733–2396* ⊠ *$5* ⊙ *Daily 10–5.*

★ On April 2, 1865, in what is now **Pamplin Historical Park,** Union troops successfully attacked General Robert E. Lee's formerly impenetrable defense line, forcing Lee to abandon Petersburg. Today you are greeted by the 300-foot-long facade of the Battlefield Center, a concrete representation of the Confederate battle lines. Besides the center, which focuses on the April 2 battle, there's a 2-mi battle trail with 2,100 feet of 8-foot-high earthen fortifications, reconstructed soldier huts, and original picket posts. Also on the grounds is Tudor Hall, an 1812 plantation home that served as the 1864 headquarters for Confederate general Samuel McGowan. Costumed interpreters bring the era to life, and reconstructed outbuildings have exhibits and displays. The **National Museum of the Civil War Soldier** on the grounds has interactive displays and nearly 1,000 artifacts. You can select an audio guide that includes the actual letters and diaries of a soldier. The park also has a café and a large store. Allow at least two hours to visit the park and museum. ⊠ *6125 Boydton Plank Rd., off U.S. 1, I–85 S. to Exit 63A* ☎ *804/861–2408 or 877/726–7546* ⊕ *www.pamplinpark.org* ⊠ *$13.50* ⊙ *Mid-Aug.–mid-June, daily 9–5; mid-June–mid-Aug 9–6.*

Where to Eat & Stay

$$–$$$ ✕ **Alexander's Fine Food.** White tablecloths flare from beneath glass tops at the tables of this Greek-American restaurant, which also has a

bar. A souvlaki platter, leg of lamb, and Athenian-style chicken are specialties. ⊠ *101 W. Bank St.* ☎ *804/733–7134* ▤ *No credit cards* ☉ *Closed Sun. No dinner Mon. and Tues.*

$–$$ ✕ **Leonardo's Deli & Cafe.** Rag-painted cherry walls contrast with white wooden booths at this casual deli and café, which serves meals from breakfast through dinner. The tin ceiling and ceiling fans point to the building's age, and the *Mona Lisa* copy on the wall alludes to the café's namesake. ⊠ *7 Bollingbrook St.* ☎ *804/863–4830* ▤ *AE, MC, V.*

$ ▣ **Ragland Mansion.** This stunningly attractive Italianate villa dates from the 1850s; it was the residence of General "Black Jack" Pershing during World War I. Inside are large formal rooms with crown moldings, French windows, 14-foot ceilings, mosaic parquet floors, European and American artworks. The rooms and suite are furnished with antique furniture, claw-foot tubs, brass and iron beds, and paintings and engravings. It's a short walk from downtown and the Historic District. ⊠ *205 S. Sycamore St., 23803* ☎ *804/861–1932 or 800/861–8898* ▤ *804/861–5943* ⊲ *7 rooms, 1 suite* ⚷ *Internet, free parking* ▤ *AE, MC, V.*

¢–$ ▣ **Hampton Inn.** Near the front door of this chain hotel, large greenhouse windows frame a bright breakfast room for the extensive Continental breakfast. Each room has a hair dryer, iron, ironing board, and coffeemaker. The inn is between two interstates (Exit 9B off I–295 and Exit 52 off I–95), 4 mi from downtown Petersburg and near the Petersburg National Battlefield. Several restaurants are nearby. A shuttle runs to the Fort Lee army base in the morning and returns in the afternoon. ⊠ *5103 Plaza Dr., Hopewell 23860* ☎ *804/452–1000 or 800/426–7866* ▤ *804/541–8584* ⊕ *www.hamptoninn.com* ⊲ *72 rooms, 2 suites* ⚷ *Refrigerators, in-room broadband, in-room VCRs, pool, gym, sauna, dry cleaning, laundry facilities, meeting rooms, no-smoking rooms* ▤ *AE, D, DC, MC, V* ⦿ *CP.*

¢ ▣ **Best Western Steven Kent.** This pristine two-story motel has a home-style family restaurant, an Olympic-size swimming pool, and nearly 20 acres of recreational facilities. Local calls and newspapers are free, and rooms have a coffeemaker, hair dryer, iron, and ironing board. ⊠ *12205 S. Crater Rd., 23805* ☎ *804/733–0600 or 800/284–9393* ⊕ *www.bestwestern.com* ▤ *804/862–4549* ⊲ *133 rooms* ⚷ *Restaurant, microwaves, in-room broadband, putting green, 2 tennis courts, pool, basketball, horseshoes, bar, lounge, playground, laundry facilities, business services, meeting rooms* ▤ *AE, D, DC, MC, V* ⦿ *CP.*

FREDERICKSBURG

Halfway between Richmond and Washington near the falls of the Rappahannock River, Fredericksburg is a popular destination for history buffs. The town's 40-block National Historic District contains more than 350 original 18th- and 19th-century buildings, including the house George Washington bought for his mother; the Rising Sun Tavern; and Kenmore, the magnificent 1752 plantation owned by George Washington's sister. The town is a favorite with antiques collectors, who cruise the dealers' shops along Caroline Street on land once used by Native American tribes as fishing and hunting ground.

Although its site was visited by explorer Captain John Smith as early as 1608, Fredericksburg wasn't founded until 1728. It was named after England's crown prince at the time, Frederick Louis, the eldest son of King George II. The streets still bear names of his family members: George, Caroline, Sophia, Princess Anne, William, and Amelia. Established as a frontier port to serve nearby tobacco farmers and iron miners, Fredericksburg was at one point the 10th largest port in the colonies.

George Washington knew Fredericksburg well, having grown up just across the Rappahannock on Ferry Farm, his residence from age 6 to 19. The myths about chopping down a cherry tree and throwing a coin (actually a rock) across the Rappahannock (later confused with the Potomac) refer to this period of his life. In later years Washington often visited his mother here on Charles Street.

Fredericksburg prospered in the decades after independence, benefiting from its location midway along the route between Washington and Richmond—an important intersection of railroad lines and waterways. When the Civil War broke out, it became the linchpin of the Confederate defense of Richmond and therefore the target of Union assaults. In December 1862, Union forces attacked the town in what was to be the first of four major battles fought in and around Fredericksburg. In the battle of Sunken Road, Confederate defenders sheltered by a stone wall at the base of Marye's Heights mowed down thousands of Union soldiers who charged across the fields.

At Chancellorsville in April 1863, General Robert E. Lee led 60,000 troops to a brilliant victory over a much larger Union force of 134,000, and this resulted in Lee's invasion of Pennsylvania. The following year, Grant's troops battled Lee's Confederates through the Wilderness, a region of dense thickets and overgrowth south of the Rapidan River, then fought them again at Spotsylvania. Although neither side was victorious, Grant continued heading his troops toward the Confederate capital of Richmond.

By the war's end, fighting in Fredericksburg and at the nearby Chancellorsville, Wilderness, and Spotsylvania Court House battlefields resulted in more than 100,000 dead or wounded. Fredericksburg's cemeteries hold the remains of 17,000 soldiers from both sides. Miraculously, despite heavy bombardment and house-to-house fighting, much of the city remained intact.

Today the city is being overrun for a different reason. The charming, historic town appeals to commuters fleeing the Washington, D.C., area for kinder, less expensive environs. The railroad lines that were so crucial to transporting Civil War supplies now bring workers to and from the nation's capital an hour away, and the sacred Civil War battlegrounds share the area with legions of shopping centers.

Numbers in the text correspond to numbers in the margin and on the Fredericksburg map.

Downtown Fredericksburg

Fredericksburg, a modern commercial town, includes a 40-block National Historic District with more than 350 original 18th- and 19th-century buildings. No play-acting here—residents live in the historic homes and work in the stores, many of which sell antiques.

a good tour

Begin at the **Fredericksburg Visitor Center ❶** to get maps or directions, or to join a tour. Walk northwest on Caroline Street to the **Hugh Mercer Apothecary Shop ❷**, passing numerous antiques shops and boutiques along the way. Continue another three blocks to the **Rising Sun Tavern ❸**, built by George Washington's brother. Walk back to Lewis Street, turn right, and walk two blocks to the **Mary Washington House ❹**. Continue on Lewis Street and turn right on Washington Avenue to the entrance of **Kenmore ❺**, where George's sister lived. To see the **Mary Washington Grave and Monument ❻**, turn right on Washington Avenue and walk two blocks. On the southern end of Washington Avenue is the **Confederate Cemetery ❼**. From the cemetery take William Street back toward the center of town. At Charles Street turn right to reach the **James Monroe Museum and Memorial Library ❽**. Return to the corner of Charles and William and walk one block to Princess Anne Street to visit the **Fredericksburg Area Museum and Cultural Center ❾**. To return to the visitor center, walk two more blocks along Princess Anne, turn left on Hanover, and right on Caroline Street. To return to the visitor center, turn left on Hanover and right on Caroline Street. To get to the **Mary Washington College Galleries ❿**, it's best to drive unless you want to walk almost a mile from where you are now. Drive five blocks northwest on Caroline Street and turn left on Amelia. Follow Amelia and turn left on Washington Avenue. One block later, turn right onto William Street. At College Avenue, turn right and drive ½ mi to the gallery on your right. Parking (on College Avenue and two reserved spots in the staff lot at the corner of College and Thornton Street) may be tight on weekdays when the college is in session. The galleries have a fine collection of Asian art, as well as works by modern masters.

TIMING A walking tour through the town proper takes three to four hours; battlefield tours will take at least that long. (The Park Service's cassettes last about 2½ hours for an automobile tour.) A self-guided tour of the University of Mary Washington Galleries takes about 30 minutes. Spring and fall are the best times to tour Fredericksburg on foot, but because Virginia weather is temperate intermittently in winter, you may find some suitable walking days then. Summers—especially August—can be hot, humid, and not very pleasant for a long walk.

Sights to See

❼ **Confederate Cemetery.** This cemetery contains the remains of more than 2,000 soldiers (most of them unknown) as well as the graves of generals Dabney Maury, Seth Barton, Carter Stevenson, Daniel Ruggles, Henry Sibley, and Abner Perrin. ✉ *1100 Washington Ave., near Amelia St., Historic District* ☉ *Daily dawn–dusk.*

❾ **Fredericksburg Area Museum and Cultural Center.** In an 1816 building once used as a market and town hall, this museum's six permanent exhibits

Fredericksburg,
Virginia

KEY

Ⓜ *Metro station*

► *Start of walk*

tell the story of the area from prehistoric times through the Revolutionary and Civil wars to the present. The Civil War exhibits emphasize the civilian experience, although attention is also paid to the soldier. Military items on display include a Henry rifle, a sword with "CSA" carved into the basket, and a Confederate officer's coat. Most weapons and accessories were found on local battlefields. Other displays include dinosaur footprints from a nearby quarry, Native American artifacts, and an 18th-century plantation account book with an inventory of slaves. The first and third floors have changing exhibits. ⊠ *907 Princess Anne St., Historic District* ☎ *540/371–3037* ⊕ *www.famcc.org* ☞ *$5* ⊙ *Mar.–Nov., Mon.–Sat. 10–5, Sun. 1–5; Dec.–Feb., Mon.–Sat. 10–4, Sun. 1–4.*

► ❶ **Fredericksburg Visitor Center.** Beyond the usual booklets, pamphlets, and maps, this visitor center has passes that enable you to park for a whole day in what are usually two-hour zones as well as money-saving passes to city attractions ($24 for entry to nine sights; $16 for four sights). Before beginning your tour, you may want to see the center's 10-minute orientation slide show. The center building itself was constructed in 1824 as a residence and confectionery; during the Civil War it was used as a prison. Before leaving, don't forget to get a pass for free parking anywhere in the Old Town. It's valid for the entire day. ⊠ *706 Caroline*

St., Historic District ☎ *540/373–1776 or 800/678–4748* ⊕ *www. fredericksburgvirginia.net* ⊙ *Daily 9–5; hrs extended in summer.*

<table>
<tr><td>

need a
break?

</td><td>

Have an old-fashioned malt in **Goolrick's Pharmacy** (✉ 901 Caroline St., Historic District ☎ 540/373–9878), a 1940s drugstore. In addition to malts and egg creams (made of seltzer and milk, but not egg or cream), Goolrick's serves light meals weekdays 8:30–7 and Saturday 8:30–6. **Virginia Deli** (✉ 101 William St., Historic District ☎ 540/371–2233 ⊙ Weekdays 8–4, Sat. 8–6) serves breakfast, specialty sandwiches, and Virginia favorites. For freshly made soups, sandwiches, and desserts, drop by **Olde Towne Wine and Cheese Deli** (✉ 707 Caroline St., Historic District ☎ 540/373–7877), across the street from the visitor center.

</td></tr>
</table>

🐚 ❷ **Hugh Mercer Apothecary Shop.** Offering a close-up view of 18th- and 19th-century medical instruments and procedures, the apothecary was established in 1761 by Dr. Mercer, a Scotsman who served as a brigadier general of the Continental Army (he was killed at the Battle of Princeton). Dr. Mercer may have been more careful than other colonial physicians, but his methods might still make you cringe. A costumed hostess explicitly describes amputations and cataract operations before the discovery of anesthetics. You can also hear about therapeutic bleeding, see the gruesome devices used in colonial dentistry, and watch a demonstration of leeching. ✉ *1020 Caroline St., at Amelia St., Historic District* ☎ *540/ 373–3362* 💲 *$5* ⊙ *Mar.–Nov., Mon.–Sat. 9–5, Sun. 11–5; Dec.–Feb., Mon.–Sat. 10–4, Sun. noon–4.*

❽ **James Monroe Museum and Memorial Library.** This tiny one-story building—on the site where Monroe, who became the fifth president of the United States, practiced law from 1787 to 1789—contains many of Monroe's possessions, collected and preserved by his family until the present day. They include a mahogany dispatch box used during the negotiation of the Louisiana Purchase and the desk on which the Monroe Doctrine was signed. ✉ *908 Charles St., Historic District* ☎ *540/654–1043* 💲 *$5* ⊙ *Mar.–Nov., Mon.–Sat. 9–5, Sun. 1–5; Dec.–Feb., Mon.–Sat. 10–4, Sun. 1–4.*

★ ❺ **Kenmore.** Named Kenmore by a later owner, this house was built in 1775 on a 1,300-acre plantation owned by Colonel Fielding Lewis, a patriot, merchant, and brother-in-law of George Washington. Lewis sacrificed his fortune to operate a gun factory and otherwise supply General Washington's forces during the Revolutionary War. As a result, his debts forced his widow to sell the home following his death. The outstanding plaster moldings in the ceilings are even more ornate than those at Mount Vernon. It's believed that the artisan responsible for the ceilings worked frequently in both homes, though his name is unknown, possibly because he was an indentured servant. Most of the lavish furnishings are in storage while the mansion undergoes a major restoration slated to be finished by 2006. Guided 45-minute architectural tours of the home are conducted by docents; the subterranean Crowningshield museum on the grounds displays Kenmore's collection of fine Virginia-made furniture and family portraits as well as changing exhibits on Fred-

ericksburg life. ⊠ *1201 Washington Ave., Historic District* ☎ *540/
373–3381* ⊕ *www.kenmore.org* 🎫 *$6* ☉ *Jan. and Feb., Sat. 11–5;
Mar.–late May, daily 11–5; Memorial Day weekend through Labor
Day weekend, daily 10–5; early Sept.–Dec., daily 11–5.*

⑩ Mary Washington College Galleries. On campus are two art galleries. The
Ridderhof Martin Gallery hosts exhibitions of art from various cultures
and historical periods. The du Pont Gallery, in Melchers Hall, displays
paintings, drawing, sculpture, photography, ceramics, and textiles by
art faculty, students, and contemporary artists. Free gallery-visitor
parking is available in the lot at the corner of College Avenue at Thornton Street. ⊠ *1301 College Ave., Historic District* ☎ *540/654–2120*
🎫 *Free* ☉ *When college is in session, Mon., Wed., and Fri. 10–4,
weekends 1–4.*

⑥ Mary Washington Grave and Monument. A 40-foot granite obelisk, dedicated by President Grover Cleveland in 1894, marks the final resting
place of George's mother. It was laid at "Meditation Rock," a place on
her daughter's property where Mrs. Washington liked to read.

④ Mary Washington House. George purchased a three-room cottage for his
mother in 1772 for £225, renovated it, and more than doubled its size
with additions. She spent the last 17 years of her life here, tending the
garden where her original boxwoods still flourish today, and where many
a bride and groom now exchange their vows. The home has been a museum since 1930. Inside, displays include Mrs. Washington's "best
dressing glass," a silver-over-tin mirror in a Chippendale frame; her teapot;
Washington family dinnerware; and period furniture. The kitchen and
its spit are original. Tours begin on the back porch with a history of the
house. From there you can see the brick sidewalk leading to Kenmore,
the home of Mrs. Washington's only daughter. ⊠ *1200 Charles St., Historic District* ☎ *540/373–1569* 🎫 *$5* ☉ *Mar.–Nov., Mon.–Sat. 9–5,
Sun. 11–5; Dec.–Feb., Mon.–Sat. 10–4, Sun. noon–4.*

③ Rising Sun Tavern. In 1760 George Washington's brother Charles built
as his home what later became the Rising Sun Tavern, a watering hole
for such patriots as the Lee brothers (the only siblings to sign the Declaration of Independence); Patrick Henry, the five-term governor of
Virginia who said, "Give me liberty or give me death"; and future presidents Washington and Jefferson. A "wench" in period costume leads
a tour without stepping out of character. From her you hear how travelers slept and what they ate and drank at this busy institution. ⊠ *1304
Caroline St., Historic District* ☎ *540/371–1494* 🎫 *$5* ☉ *Mar.–Nov.,
Mon.–Sat. 9–5, Sun. 11–5; Dec.–Feb., Mon.–Sat. 10–4, Sun. noon–4.*

off the beaten path	**BLUE & GRAY BREWING COMPANY –** To tour a home-grown brewery and have a free tasting, drive 2½ mi southeast of the visitor center, where the beers include Fred Red Ale, Falmouth American Pale Ale, and Blue & Gray Classic Lager. ⊠ *Bowman Center Industrial Park, 3321 Dill Smith Dr.* ☎ *540/538–2379* ⊕ *www. blueandgraybrewingco.com* ☉ *Wed. 3–6, Fri. 5–8, Sat. 10–1.*

Around Fredericksburg

Surrounding the town of Fredericksburg are historic sites and beautiful vistas where, in 1862, Union forces once stood. Today you see only the lively Rappahannock and beautiful homes on a lovely drive across the river.

a good drive

From downtown Fredericksburg drive east on William Street (Route 3) across the Rappahannock River 1 mi to **George Washington's Ferry Farm** ⓫ ▶, on the right. Living here from age 6 to 19, Washington received his formal education and taught himself surveying. Here you can see exhibits and ongoing archaeological excavations. Return on Route 3 toward Fredericksburg and turn right at the signs to **Chatham Manor** ⓬, just east of the river. This Georgian mansion has views of the Rappahannock River and Fredericksburg. From Chatham Manor take River Road (Route 607) about a mile along the river, crossing U.S. 1 (Jefferson Davis Highway) to Route 1001 and **Belmont** ⓭, a spacious Georgian house furnished with many antiques and works of art. Return to Route 1 via Route 1001 and turn right (south) and cross the river. Turn left on Princess Anne Street and go 1½ mi to the train station. This takes you past many old homes, churches, the main business district, and the museum. Turn right on Lafayette Boulevard; the **Fredericksburg/Spotsylvania National Military Park** ⓮ and **National Cemetery** ⓯ are ½ mi ahead on the right. Exhibits, films, and ranger-led tours describe Fredericksburg's role in the Civil War.

TIMING   Allow 5 minutes to drive to Ferry Farm and 10 minutes each to drive to Belmont and Chatham Manor. A tour of Belmont takes about an hour, as does Chatham Manor if you tour the museum and gardens. The battlefields of Wilderness, Chancellorsville, and Spotsylvania Court House are each within 15 mi of Fredericksburg. It can take one to several hours to tour each one, depending on your level of interest. At the Fredericksburg Battlefield Visitor Center, allow an hour or two—there's a 22-minute video, a small museum, and frequent walking tours.

Sights to See

⓭ **Belmont.** The last owner of this 1790s Georgian-style house was American artist Gari Melchers, who chaired the Smithsonian Commission to establish the National Gallery of Art in Washington; his wife, Corinne, deeded the 27-acre estate and its collections to Virginia. Belmont is now a public museum and a Virginia National Historic Landmark administered by Mary Washington College. You can take a one-hour tour of the spacious house, which is furnished with a rich collection of their antiques. Galleries in the stone studio, built by the Melchers in 1924, house the largest repository of his work. An orientation movie is shown in the reception area, which was once the carriage house. ⊠ *224 Washington St., Falmouth, VA* ☎ *540/654–1015* ⊕ *www.mwc.edu/belmont* ☞ *$7* ☉ *Mar.–Nov., Mon.–Sat. 10–5, Sun. 1–5; Dec.–Feb., Mon.–Sat. 10–4, Sun. 1–4.*

⓬ **Chatham Manor.** A fine example of Georgian architecture, Chatham Manor was built between 1768 and 1771 by William Fitzhugh, a plantation owner, on a site overlooking the Rappahannock River and the town of Fredericksburg. Fitzhugh frequently hosted luminaries such as George Washington. During the Civil War, Union forces commandeered the house and converted it into a headquarters and hospital. President Abraham Lincoln conferred with his generals here; Clara Barton (founder of the American Red Cross) and poet Walt Whitman tended the wounded. After the war, the house and gardens were restored by private owners and eventually donated to the National Park Service. The home itself is now a museum. Five of the 10 rooms in the 12,000-square-foot mansion are open to the public and house exhibits spanning several centuries. ⊠ *120 Chatham La., Falmouth, VA* ☎ *540/373–4461* ⊕ *www.nps.gov* 🎫 *Free* ☉ *Daily 9–5.*

★ ⓮ **Fredericksburg/Spotsylvania National Military Park.** The 9,000-acre park actually includes four battlefields and three historic buildings. At the Fredericksburg and Chancellorsville visitor centers you can learn about the area's role in the Civil War by watching a 22-minute video for $2, and by viewing displays of soldiers' art and battlefield relics. In season, park rangers lead walking tours. The centers offer tape-recorded tour cassettes ($4.95 rental, $7.50 purchase) and maps that show how to reach hiking trails at the Wilderness, Chancellorsville (where General Stonewall Jackson was mistakenly shot by his own troops), and Spotsylvania Court House battlefields (all within 15 mi of Fredericksburg).

Just outside the Fredericksburg battlefield park visitor center is Sunken Road, where from December 11 to 13, 1862, General Robert E. Lee led his troops to a bloody but resounding victory over Union forces attacking across the Rappahannock (there were 18,000 casualties on both sides). Much of the stone wall that protected Lee's sharpshooters is now a re-creation, but 100 yards from the visitor center, part of the original wall overlooks the statue *The Angel of Marye's Heights,* by Felix de Weldon (sculptor of the famous *Marine Corps War Memorial* statue in Arlington). This memorial honors Sergeant Richard Kirkland, a South Carolinian who risked his life to bring water to wounded foes; he later died at the Battle of Chickamauga. ⊠ *Fredericksburg Battlefield Visitor Center, 1013 Lafayette Blvd., and Sunken Rd., Historic District* ☎ *540/ 373–6122* ⊠ *Chancellorsville Battlefield Visitor Center, Rte. 3 W, Plank Rd., Chancellorsville* ☎ *540/786–2880* ⊕ *www.nps.gov/frsp* 🎫 *Free* ☉ *Visitor centers daily 9–5; driving and walking tours daily dawn–dusk.*

☙ ▶ ⓫ **George Washington's Ferry Farm.** If it hadn't been for the outcries of historians and citizens, a Wal-Mart would have been built on this site, the boyhood home of our first president. The land was saved by the Historic Kenmore Foundation, and the discount store found a location farther out on the same road. Ferry Farm, which once consisted of 600 acres, is across the Rappahannock River from downtown Fredericksburg and was the site of a ferry crossing. Living here from ages 6 to 19, Washington received his formal education and taught himself surveying while *not* chopping a cherry tree or throwing a coin across the Rappahannock— legends concocted by Parson Weems. The mainly archaeological site also has an exhibit on "George Washington: Boy Before Legend." The ongoing excavations include a summer program for children and adults,

"Digging for Young George." Colonial games are held daily June through August. Ferry Farm became a major artillery base and river-crossing site for Union forces during the Battle of Fredericksburg. ⊠ *Rte. 3 E, 268 Kings Hwy., at Ferry Rd., Fredericksburg, VA 22405* ☎ *540/370–0732* ⊕ *www.kenmore.org* ☒ *$3* ⊙ *Jan. and Feb., Sat. 10–5; Mar.–May, daily 10–5; Memorial Day Weekend through Labor Day weekend daily 10–5, after Labor Day–Dec., daily 10–4.*

⑮ National Cemetery. The National Cemetery is the final resting place of 15,000 Union dead, most of whom have not been identified. ⊠ *Lafayette Blvd. and Sunken Rd., Historic District* ☎ *540/373–6122* ⊙ *Daily dawn–dusk.*

Where to Eat

$$–$$$$ ✕ **Augustine's at Fredericksburg Square.** Named after Augustine Washington, George's father, who owned most of the property along Caroline Street, this is the place to go in Fredericksburg for a formal dinner. In this very formal environment, the well spaced tables are set in the traditional European style, including the use of gold charger plates. The creative and attractively presented dishes here, prepared in a New American style, might include saffron-braised angler Fish and ricotta gnocchi. The wine list is not only extensive in its selections but also creatively presented. ⊠ *525 Caroline St.* ☎ *540/310–0063* ⊕ *www.augustinesrest. com* ⊟ *AE, D, DC, MC, V* ⊙ *Closed Sun. and Mon. No lunch.*

$$–$$$ ✕ **Bistro 309.** In an 1833 storefront that served as a general store, buttermilk-color walls display local art. Copper chandeliers and original heart-of-pine floors lend a warm glow; when the weather's fine, tables are brought out onto the sidewalk for alfresco dining. In addition to an extensive wine list and daily blackboard specials, entrées include the signature dish, chili-rubbed quail; trout stuffed with crab meat; brined pork chops; and free-range chicken. ⊠ *309 William St.* ☎ *540/371–9999* ⊕ *www.bistro309.com* ⊟ *AE, D, MC, V* ⊙ *Lunch and dinner Tues.–Sat.; Sun. brunch* ⊙ *Closed Mon.*

$$–$$$ ✕ **Claiborne's.** On the walls of this swank eatery in the 1910-era Fredericksburg train station are historic train photographs. The restaurant, decorated in dark green and navy with mahogany-and-brass bars, specializes in low-country Southern dishes, including crawfish, grits, and collard greens. Accompanying the steaks, chops, and seafood are ample vegetable side dishes served family style. On Sunday there's a lunch buffet. ⊠ *200 Lafayette Blvd., Historic District* ☎ *540/371–7080* ⊕ *www. claibornesrestaurant.com* ⊟ *AE, DC, MC, V.*

$$–$$$ ✕ **Ristorante Renato.** This family-owned restaurant, decorated with lace curtains, red carpeting, and walls covered with paintings, specializes in Italian cuisine, including veal, chicken, pasta, and seafood. Standouts include veal Florentine, fettuccine Alfredo, eggplant parmigiana, steamed mussels, and Italian desserts such as cannoli, spumoni, and tiramisu. ⊠ *422 William St., Historic District* ☎ *540/371–8228* ⊟ *AE, MC, V* ⊙ *No lunch weekends.*

$$–$$$ ✕ **The Riverview.** There's a view of the Rappahannock River and Chatham Manor from both the dining room, which has a cozy fireplace, and the brick patio—a lovely place to eat alfresco in summer. The Riverview describes its offerings as "The Best of Beef, Bay, and Bottle," and its specialties are prime rib and fresh seafood. The restaurant has been a favorite with locals since it open in the 1980s. ⊠ *1101 Sophia St., Historic District* ☎ *540/373–6500* ▤ *AE, D, DC, MC, V.*

$–$$$ ✕ **Merriman's Restaurant & Bar.** Inside an old brick storefront, Merriman's dining room is painted a bright yellow. On the eclectic menu are Mediterranean dishes such as linguine Mykonos, Greek salad, and Middle Eastern hummus, which jostle against classic Virginia meats and seafood. Desserts are made fresh daily. ⊠ *715 Caroline St., Historic District* ☎ *540/371–7723* ⊕ *www.merrimansrestaurant.com* ▤ *AE, D, DC, MC, V.*

$$ ✕ **Six-twenty-three American Bistro and Tapas.** A 1769 house once known as "The Chimneys" is now a decidedly modern place to eat. Main dishes include pasta, quail, rainbow trout, chicken adobo, flank steak, duck, and stuffed pork loin. If you are in the mood for something less imposing, look to the tapas menu, where there are almost 20 dishes $8 and under that include risottos, clams, mussels, and vegetarian dishes. From 5 to 7 PM Wednesday to Friday there's a 25% discount on tapas. Brunch is served Sunday, and you can eat on the patio when the weather permits. Across from the visitor center, the restaurant shares the premises with a wine shop. ⊠ *623 Caroline St., Historic District* ☎ *540/361–2640* ▤ *AE, D, DC, MC, V* ⊙ *Closed Mon. and Tues. No lunch Wed.–Sat.*

$–$$ ✕ **La Petite Auberge.** Housed in a pre–Civil War brick general store, this white-tablecloth restaurant actually has three dining rooms decorated like a French garden, with numerous paintings by local artists for sale. The interesting menu changes with the seasons and the chef uses local produce and seafood. Specialties like house-cut beef, French onion soup, and seafood are all served with a continental accent. A fixed-price ($14) three-course dinner is served from 5:30 to 7 Monday through Thursday. ⊠ *311 William St., Historic District* ☎ *540/371–2727* ▤ *AE, D, MC, V* ⊙ *Closed Sun.*

$–$$ ✕ **Smythe's Cottage & Tavern.** Entering this cozy dining room in a blacksmith's house built in the early 1800s is like taking a step back in time. The lunch and dinner menus are classic Virginia: seafood pie, quail, stuffed flounder, peanut soup, and Smithfield ham biscuits. ⊠ *303 Fauquier St., Historic District* ☎ *540/373–1645* ▤ *MC, V* ⊙ *Closed Tues.*

¢–$$ ✕ **Sammy T's.** Vegetarian dishes, healthy foods, and homemade soups and breads share the menu with hamburgers and dinner platters at this unpretentious place. The bar is stocked with nearly 50 brands of beer. There's a separate no-smoking section around the corner, but a tin ceiling, high wooden booths, and wooden ceiling fans make the main dining room much chummier and more homey. ⊠ *801 Caroline St., Historic District* ☎ *540/371–2008* ⊕ *www.sammyts.com* ▤ *AE, D, MC, V.*

Where to Stay

$–$$$ ▥ **Richard Johnston Inn.** This elegant B&B was constructed in the late 1700s and served as the home of Richard Johnston, mayor of Fredericksburg from March 1809 to March 1810. Guest rooms are decorated with period antiques and reproductions. The aroma of freshly baked breads and muffins entices you to breakfast in the large Federal-style dining room, where the table's set with fine china, silver, and linens. The inn is just across from the visitor center and two blocks from the train station. Ample private parking is behind the inn. ⊠ *711 Caroline St., Historic District 22401* ☎ *540/899–7606 or 877/557–0770* ⊕ *www. the richardjohnstoninn.com* ➷ *7 rooms, 2 suites* ♦ *Cable TV, in-room VCRs, Wi-Fi, free parking; no smoking* ⊟ *AE, MC, V* ⦿ *CP.*

$–$$ ▦ **Kenmore Inn.** This 18th-century historic home is easily recognizable by its magnificent and inviting front porch. There are two types of rooms. The deluxe ones, in the original part of the house, have working fireplaces and canopy beds; the slightly smaller standard rooms have colonial furnishings. The English pub, which serves lighter dishes and imported draft beer, is open Tuesday to Sunday evenings. ⊠ *1200 Princess Anne St., Historic District, 22401* ☎ *540/371–7622* ☐ *540/ 371–5480* ⊕ *www.kenmoreinn.com* ➷ *9 rooms* ♦ *Restaurant, some cable TV, pub; no TV in some rooms* ⊟ *AE, D, DC, MC, V* ⦿ *CP.*

$ ▦ **WyteStone Suites.** Near a small outlet mall, several restaurants, and the Spotsylvania County Tourism Office, this modern hotel is 2 mi from the historic area. Each suite has king or double beds with quilted bedspreads and a sofa bed in the living room. Rooms are entered from inside walkways around the six-story atrium. ⊠ *4615 Southpoint Pkwy., take Exit 126 off I–95, bear right onto U.S. 1 South, turn left onto Southpoint Pkwy. to hotel on right, 22407* ☎ *540/891–1112 or 800/794–5005* ☐ *540/ 891–5465* ➷ *85 suites* ♦ *In-room data ports, microwaves, refrigerators, cable TV, indoor pool, laundry facilities* ⊟ *AE, D, DC, MC, V* ⦿ *BP.*

$ ▦ **Wingate Inn.** Built in 2001, this four-story hotel has large rooms equipped for the business traveler. Guest rooms are decorated in a soothing cream and moss. Coffeemakers are standard in every room. The large lobby hosts the expanded continental breakfast and evening dessert and beverage pantry. There's a complimentary local shuttle. The Wingate is set back from U.S. Route 17 (Exit 133 off I–95, north toward Warrenton). Turn left at the first signal light west of I–95. ⊠ *20 Sanford Dr., 22406* ☎ *540/368–8000 or 800/228–1000* ☐ *540/368–9252* ⊕ *www.mywingate.com* ➷ *83 rooms, 10 suites* ♦ *In-room data ports, microwaves, refrigerators, indoor pool, health club, spa, meeting rooms, free parking* ⊟ *AE, MC, V* ⦿ *CP.*

¢–$ ▦ **Fredericksburg Colonial Inn.** This 1920s motel with moss green siding and forest green awnings has a beautifully decorated central staircase in the lobby. Rooms are furnished with antiques and appointments from the Civil War period, and the lobby has an old-time upright piano. Breakfast includes beverages, cereal, and coffeecake. ⊠ *1707 Princess Anne St., Historic District, 22401* ☎ *540/371–5666* ☐ *540/371–5884* ⊕ *www.fci1.com* ➷ *30 rooms* ♦ *Refrigerators, free parking; no smoking* ⊟ *AE, MC, V* ⦿ *BP.*

¢–$ ▦ **Hampton Inn.** This may be a typical chain motel, but it's neat and clean, and the continental breakfast is extensive. Because it's on a main artery in a busy retail area, ask for a room facing the interior courtyard. Local phone calls from your room are free, as is the HBO. Several restaurants are a block or two away. ⊠ *2310 William St., Exit 130-A off I–95, Fredericksburg West, 22401* ☎ *540/371–0330* ☐ *540/371–1753* ⊕ *www. hamptoninn.com* ➷ *166 rooms* ♦ *In-room data ports, cable TV, pool,* *laundry facilities, meeting rooms, free parking* ⊟ *AE, D, DC, MC, V* ¶Ol *CP.*

THE NORTHERN NECK

Between Fredericksburg and the Chesapeake Bay is the "Northern Neck," an area attractive to nature lovers, anglers, and boaters. This 90-mi-long peninsula has a 1,200 mi total shoreline and is bathed on three sides by the Potomac and Rappahannock rivers, and the mighty Chesapeake Bay. Settled more than 300 years ago, the Northern Neck is the birthplace of presidents George Washington, James Monroe, and James Madison as well as General Robert E. Lee and Washington's mother, Mary Ball.

The Northern Neck peninsula is as unspoiled today as when Captain John Smith first visited in 1608. Even at the peninsula's start, the area is forested and tranquil. You can find charming B&Bs; fresh-off-the-boat seafood; dozens of marinas; excursion boats to islands in the Chesapeake Bay; historic homes and museums; and places to commune with nature.

The sites below are listed in geographical order beginning at the intersection of Routes 3 and 301. Though it's unusual that three presidents' birthplaces are in such proximity, that of James Madison and James Monroe are just markers off the highway, whereas Washington's is a national monument. A marker on Highway 301 in Port Conway, King George County, memorializes the onetime plantation where James Madison was born in 1751; an outline of the house and a marker in neighboring Westmoreland County identifies the birthplace of James Monroe, born in 1758, on Highway 205 between Oak Grove and Colonial Beach.

Numbers in the text correspond to numbers in the margin and on the Northern Neck map.

George Washington Birthplace National Monument

❶ *32 mi east of Fredericksburg on Rte. 3.*

After you pass the town of Oak Grove on Route 3, all signs point to the national park on the Potomac River. At Pope's Creek, **George Washington Birthplace National Monument** is a 550-acre park mirroring the peaceful rural life our first president preferred. The house in which Mary Ball Washington gave birth to George in 1732 burned in 1779, but native clay was used to make bricks for a representative 18th-century plantation home. Costumed interpreters lead tours through the house, which has items dating from the time of Washington's childhood. The grounds include a kitchen, garden, cemetery with 32 Washington family graves, and the Colonial Living Farm, worked by methods employed in Colonial days. Picnic facilities are available year-round. ⊠ *Rte. 3* ☎ *804/ 224–1732* ⊕ *www.nps.gov/gewa* ☞ *$3* ⊗ *Daily 9–5.*

Where to Stay

¢–$ ▦ **Westmoreland State Park.** This 1,300-acre, full-service park is one of Virginia's most beautiful campgrounds, with hiking trails winding

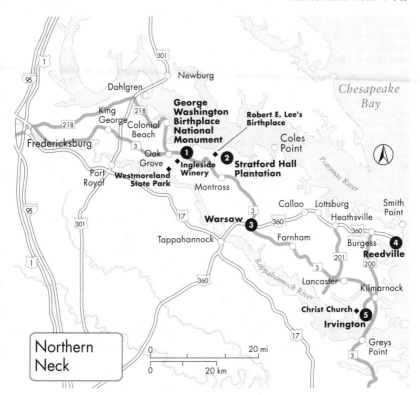

Northern
Neck

George
Washington
Birthplace
National
Monument

Robert E. Lee's
Birthplace

Ingleside
Winery

Stratford Hall
Plantation

Westmoreland
State Park

Christ Church

Irvington

through marshlands, woods, meadows and along the Potomac River.
There are also places to fish, rent boats or kayaks, or simply picnic. The
comfortable, climate-controlled cabins have complete kitchens with
microwave oven and toaster, dishes, silverware, and cooking utensils (bring
your own dishwashing supplies). Living rooms have a sofa, dining table,
and working fireplace. The basic furnishings include linens for four beds.
From Memorial Weekend to Labor Day Weekend there is a one-week
minimum; at all other times the minimum is two nights. Westmoreland
also has 118 campsites available. ⊠ *1650 State Park Rd., Rte. 1, Box
600, Montross 22520-9717* ☎ *804/493–8821 or 800/933–7275* 🖷 *804/
493–8329* ⊕ *www.dcr.state.va.us/parks/westmore.htm* ⚘ *Grocery, picnic area, kitchens, pool, boating, fishing, hiking, laundry facilities; no
room phones, no room TVs* ⟳ *27 cabins* ⊟ *AE, MC, V.*

⚠ **Westmoreland State Park campsites.** In addition to sites for RVs and
tents, Westmoreland also has six camping cabins that provide a shelter
but few other amenities. ⊠ *1650 State Park Rd., Rte. 1, Box 600,
Montross 22520-9717* ☎ *804/493–8821 or 800/933–7275* 🖷 *804/
493–8329* ⊕ *www.dcr.state.va.us/parks/westmore.htm* ⚑ *Partial
hookups $21, no hookups and tent sites $16* ⚘ *Grills, laundry facilities, flush toilets, partial hookups (electric and water), drinking water,
showers, fire grates, picnic tables, electricity, general store* ⟳ *42 par-*

tial hookups, 74 without hookups, 129 tent sites, 6 cabins ▭ *AE, MC, V* ☻ *Open Mar.–Nov.*

Stratford Hall Plantation

❷ *8 mi east of George Washington Birthplace National Monument via Rte. 3.*

Robert E. Lee, who became the commander of the Confederate Army, was born in the Great House of **Stratford Hall Plantation,** one of the country's finest examples of Colonial architecture. Eight chimneys in two squares top the H-shape brick home, built in the 1730s by one of Lee's grandfathers, Colonial governor Thomas Lee. The house contains Robert E. Lee's crib, original family pieces, and period furnishings. The working Colonial plantation covers 1,600 acres and has gardens, a kitchen, smokehouse, laundry, orangery, springhouses, coach house, stables, slave quarters, and a gristmill that grinds from 11 to 2 on the first whole weekend of each month from April through September. The Plantation Dining Room, a log cabin restaurant, serves meals and sandwiches daily from 11:30 to 3. There's also a Plantation Picnic Buffet ($16) available on weekends in summer. Its outdoor screened deck overlooks the woodlands. ✉*Rte. 3, Stratford* ☎ *804/493–8038 or 804/493–8371* ⊕ *www.stratfordhall. org* ▤ *$10* ☻ *Visitor center 9:30–5, house tours 10–4.*

Where to Stay

$ ⌂ **Stratford Hall.** Of the two guesthouses on the plantation property, Cheek, the larger one, has 15 rooms, which come with either two twin beds or a king-size bed. Astor, named after Lady Astor and made from a log cabin, is directly across from the Plantation Dining Room. Both guesthouses have a fully equipped kitchen, a living room with fireplace, and decks. ✉ *485 Great House Rd., 22558* ☎ *804/493–8038 or 804/493–8371* 🖷 *804/493–0333* ⊕ *www.stratfordhall.org* ⤳ *20 rooms* ♨ *Restaurant, parking* ▭ *MC, V* ⑩ *CP.*

⚠ **Cole's Point Plantation.** This 110-acre wooded campground on the Potomac River has a 575-foot fishing pier, a boat ramp, and a 120-slip full-service marina. The facility has four log cabins that can sleep 4–13 people. Reservations are essential. ✉ *Rte. 612, north of Rte. 202, Rte. 728, Box 77, Coles Point 22442* ☎ *804/472–3955* 🖷 *804/472–4488* ⊕ *www.colespoint.com* ♨ *Pool, flush toilets, full hookups, partial hookups (electric and water), swimming (river)* ⤳ *74 full hookups or tent sites, 35 partial hookups or tent sites, 1 tent-only site, 4 cabins* ▤*Cabins $50, full hookups $26, partial hookups $21, tent sites $19* ▭ *AE, MC, V* ☻ *Open May–Oct.*

Warsaw

❸ *15 mi southeast of Stratford Hall via Rte. 3.*

The county seat of Richmond County, Warsaw is a pleasant town of 7,000 that's shaded by large oak trees. Near the U.S. 360 bridge over the Rappahannock, it's therefore closer to the city of Tappahannock (on the other side) than to its fellow towns on the Northern Neck.

A cruise 20 mi up the river to Ingleside Plantation—a Virginia winery—leaves from Tappahannock. **Rappahannock River Cruises** enlists its ship *Capt. Thomas* to take passengers on the narrated day cruise. A buffet lunch is served at the winery ($11), snacks are served on board, or you can bring your own. To reach the dock, take Highway 17 south from Tappahannock to Hoskins Creek. The cruise departs daily at 10, returning at 4:30. ⊠ *Hoskins Creek* ☎ *804/453-2628* ⊕ *www.tangiercruise. com* 🖃 *$22* ☉ *May–Oct., daily at 10.*

Ingleside Plantation Vineyards is one of Virginia's oldest and largest wineries. It produces one of the few sparkling wines from Virginia. There are also white wines (viognier, sauvignon blanc, pinot gris, and chardonnay) and reds (sangiovese, cabernet franc, and sauvignon) as well as specially produced labels. The vineyards cover about 50 acres of gently rolling countryside whose climate and sandy loam soil, is similar to that of Bordeaux, France. The winery has a tasting bar; a gift shop with grape-related gifts; a large outdoor patio with umbrella tables and a fountain; and a large indoor room for group tastings and buffet lunch. The winery is about 40 minutes east of Fredericksburg and only a few miles from the Washington Birthplace National Monument. ⊠ *5872 Leedstown Rd., from Rte. 3, turn south on Rte. 638 at winery's signpost, Oak Grove* ☎ *804/224-8687* ⊕ *www.ipwine.com* ☉ *Mon.–Sat. 10–5, Sun. noon–5.*

Camping

¢–$ 🏕 **Heritage Park Resort & Belle Mount Vineyards.** On Menokin Bay, this campground has panoramic views overlooking the Rappahannock River and scenic wildlife settings. The rustic, wooden, two-bedroom cottages are heated and air-conditioned so they can be rented year-round. Each has a living room with navy plaid chairs and sofa, a dining room, and a fully equipped kitchen. With its banquet facilities for 300, the resort is a good place for picnics, receptions, and family reunions. There are also 78 campsites, some of which have full hookups or partial hookups. Tours and tastings at the winery on the premises are available Wednesday through Sunday from mid-Mar.–mid-Dec. ⊠ *2570 Newland Rd., Rte. 674, 2½ mi west of U.S. 360, Warsaw 22572* ☎ *804/333-4038* 🖷 *804/333-4039* ⊕ *www.heritagepark.com* 🛏 *5 cottages, 78 campsites (20 with water and electric and 25 with water, electric, and sewer)* ♿ *Kitchens, tennis court, pool, boating; no smoking* ▤ *AE, D, MC, V.*

Reedville

❹ *31 mi from Warsaw via U.S. 360, 46 mi from Stratford Hall via Rtes. 202 and 360.*

This small town at the eastern tip of the Northern Neck was the home of wealthy fishermen and businessmen who made their fortunes from the menhaden fish abundant in the nearby Chesapeake Bay and Potomac waters.

The educational and activity-oriented **Reedville Fishermen's Museum** is housed in a restored fisherman's home and a larger building. Permanent and rotating exhibits document the area's fishing industry, and there are two fishing boats here, including a skipjack and a buy boat. ⊠ *Main St.*

☎ 804/453–6529 ⊕ *www.rfmuseum.org* ⊠ *$3* ☉ *Early-Mar–late Apr., weekends 10:30–4:30; May–Oct., daily 10:30–4:30; early Nov.–mid-Jan., Fri.–Mon. 10:30–4:30; mid-Jan.–early Mar. by appointment for groups.*

Popular cruises to Smith and Tangier islands in the Chesapeake Bay leave from Reedville. The 150-passenger ship *Captain Evans* of **Smith Island and Chesapeake Bay Cruises** sails from the KOA Kampground at Smith Point on Route 802, departing at 10 AM and returning at 3:45 PM daily. The 13½-mi trip takes 1½ hours and passes a 5,000-acre waterfowl and wildlife refuge. Now a part of Maryland, Smith Island—a Methodist colony settled by British Colonists from Cornwall in the early 1700s—can also be reached from Crisfield, on Maryland's Eastern Shore. Lunch is available at several restaurants on the island. Reservations are required. ⊠ *382 Campground Rd., behind KOA Kampground* ☎ 804/453–3430 ⊕ *www.eaglesnest.net/smithislandcruise* ⊠ *$25* ☉ *May–mid-Oct.*

Tangier is a Virginia island in the Chesapeake Bay named by Captain John Smith. This largely unspoiled fishing village with quaint, narrow streets also happens to be the soft crab capital of the nation. There's a small airport here for private planes and it also can be reached by the ship *Chesapeake Breeze* of **Tangier Island & Chesapeake Cruises** (ships also leave from Onacock, Virginia, and Crisfield, Maryland, on the Eastern Shore). The ship departs at 10 AM and returns at 3:30 PM daily, cruising 1½ hours each way. The island has several restaurants serving lunch. From the intersection of Highways 360 and 646, drive 1½ mi; then turn left on Highway 656 (Buzzard's Point Road), which leads to the dock. Reservations are required. ⊠ *468 Buzzard's Point Rd.* ☎ 804/453–2628 ⊕ *www.tangiercruise.com* ⊠ *$22* ☉ *May–Oct., daily.*

Where to Stay

$$ ▥ **Fleeton Fields.** Set amid beautifully manicured lawns and gardens, this lovely Colonial-style inn also overlooks a tidal pond in which you may be lucky enough to see ospreys, Great Blue Herons, and eagles. Inside the inn, you're greeted by fresh flowers and soothing music before being escorted to one of the three beautifully furnished suites. Cool evenings are warmed by inviting fireplaces, and each morning's breakfast is served using china, crystal, and silver. ⊠ *2783 Fleeton Rd., 22539* ☎ *804/453–5014 or 800/497–8215* ⊕ *www.fleetonfields.com* ⮡ *3 suites* ☍ *Cable TV, minibars* ▤ *AE, D, DC, MC, V* ⧓ *BP.*

$ ▥ **The Gables.** A four-story redbrick Victorian mansion built in 1909, the Gables was built by Captain Albert Fisher, one of the founders of the local fishing industry. The house has been lovingly restored and has period antiques throughout. There are two guest rooms in the main house and four more in the adjacent carriage house. The Gables has its own deepwater dock on Cockrell's Creek with easy access to the Chesapeake Bay. ⊠ *Main St., 22539* ☎ *804/453–5209* ⮡ *6 rooms* ☍ *Dock; no kids under 13* ▤ *MC, V* ⧓ *BP.*

(en route) After leaving Reedville on Route 360, turn left on Route 200 and drive 13 mi to Kilmarnock. Turn right on Route 3 and drive to the little town of Lancaster, home of the **Mary Ball Washington Museum and Library.** This four-building complex honors George

Washington's mother, who was born in Lancaster County. Lancaster House, built about 1798, contains Washington family memorabilia and historic items related to the county and the Northern Neck. The Steuart-Blakemore Building houses a genealogical library, and the Old Jail is a lending library and archives. ⊠ *8346 Mary Ball Rd., Lancaster* ☎ *804/462–7280* ⊕ *www.mbwm.org* ☞ *$2 museum house and grounds; $5 to work at library* ☉ *Tues.–Fri. 10–4; library Wed.–Sun. 10–4.*

Irvington

❺ *5 mi from Kimarnock.*

Although much older than the resort, the lovely town of Irvington has been associated with the Tides Inn for more than 50 years.

The **Historic Christ Church** was completed in 1735, when George Washington was three years old. The Georgian-style structure, on the National Register of Historic Places, was built by Robert "King" Carter and contains a rare "triple decker" pulpit made of native walnut. Bricks for the church were fired in a great kiln near the churchyard. A 12-minute video is screened in the museum. ⊠ *420 Christ Church Rd., from Irvington drive 1½ mi north on Rte. 200* ☎ *804/438–6855* ⊕ *www.christchurch1735.org* ☞ *Free* ☉ *Church daily; museum Apr.–Nov., Mon.–Sat. 10–4, Sun. 2–5; Dec.–Mar., weekdays 8:30–4:30.*

Where to Stay & Eat

$$–$$$ ✕ **Trick Dog Cafe.** This neat little wooden restaurant is one of the best on the Northern Neck. The interestingly innovative dishes here may include such dishes as tandoori chicken with cumin-spiced red potatoes, Indian-spiced eggplant, chickpeas, caramelized onions, and cucumber raita (a yogurt salad). The Sunday Brunch is particularly popular. ⊠ *4537 Irvington Rd.* ☎ *804/438–1055* ⊕ *www.trickdogcafe.com* ▤ *AE, MC, V* ☉ *Closed Mon. No lunch Tues.–Sat. No dinner Sun. Mon.–Sun. for lunch Tue.–Sat.*

¢ ✕ **White Stone Wine & Cheese.** This shop sells Mediterranean-style sandwiches, soups, and baked goods as well as wine and cheese. There are tables available to eat your picnic. ⊠ *101 William St.* ☎ *540/371–2233* ▤ *MC, V* ☉ *Closes at 5 daily.*

★ $$$–$$$$ 🏨 **The Tides Inn.** Surrounded by manicured grounds overlooking Carters Creek, the Tides Inn, here since 1947, is sandwiched between the Potomac and Rappahannock rivers. Many of the rooms and suites, which are decorated in a British Colonial style, have spectacular water views. The Golden Eagle Golf course is challenging, the par-3 course less so; the ponds are well-stocked with fish; and bird-watchers should take their binoculars. There's also a sailing school that's set up for all ages and experience levels, and you can take a cruise along the Rappahannock River on a 127-foot yacht. ⊠ *480 King Carter Dr., 22480* ☎ *804/438–5000 or 800/843–3746* ☎ *804/438–5222* ⊕ *www.tidesinn.com* ☞ *84 rooms, 22 suites* ₺ *4 restaurants, in-room DVD players, in-room data ports, 18-hole golf course, 9-hole golf course, 4 tennis courts, 3 pools, gym, spa, boating, marina, fishing, bicycles, croquet, horseshoes, shuf-*

fleboard, lounge, dance club, shops, babysitting, children's programs (ages 4–12), laundry facilities, airport shuttle, some pets allowed (fee) ☰ *AE, D, DC, MC, V.*

$$ 🏠 **The Hope and Glory Inn.** This 1890 schoolhouse is now a pale-honey color Victorian B&B. The first-floor classrooms have been opened into an expansive, columned lobby with a painted checkerboard floor. The upstairs bedrooms and small cottages behind the inn are decorated in what might be called California romantic, with pastel painted floors and interesting (nonruffled) window treatments. In the garden, surrounded by a tall wooden fence, there's a completely open-air bathroom that can be booked by adventurous couples. In 2004 the inn built new cottages, called "tents," in an allusion to turn-of-the-20th-century Methodist tent communities. On wooded bluffs overlooking the headwaters of Carter's Creek, the tents each have three bedrooms and a kitchen, and there's a pool and dock for canoes and kayaks planned for 2005. ⌧ *634 King Carter Dr., 22480* ☎ *804/438–6053 or 800/497–8228* 🖷 *804/438–6053* ⊕ *www.hopeandglory.com* ⤳ *7 rooms, 4 cottages* ☰ *MC, V* ⦿ *BP.*

RICHMOND & ENVIRONS A TO Z

To research prices, get advice from other travelers, and book travel arrangements, visit www.fodors.com.

AIRPORTS
Richmond International Airport, 10 mi east of the city, Exit 197 off I–64, has scheduled flights by nine airlines.
🛫 Airport Information **Richmond International Airport** ⌧ Airport Dr. ☎ 804/226–3000 ⊕ www.flyrichmond.com.

TRANSFERS A taxi ride to downtown Richmond from the airport costs $20–$22.

BIKE TRAVEL
Multiuse trails throughout the region give mountain bikers, cyclists, hikers, and runners a variety of urban and rural settings for enjoying their sports. Richmond's Forest Hill Park, Dorey Park in Henrico County, Poor Farm Park in Hanover County, and Pocahontas State Park in Chesterfield County are some of the most popular sites for bicyclists. For more information about area bicycling, contact the Richmond Area Bicycling Association or Mountain Bike Virginia.

There are no shops that rent bicycles in Richmond.
🛫 **Mountain Bike Virginia** ⊕ www.mountainbikevirginia.com. **Richmond Area Bicycling Association** ☎ 804/266-2453 ⊕ www.raba.org.

BUS TRAVEL
Greyhound buses depart seven times a day from Washington to Fredericksburg and Richmond between 7 AM and 5 PM. A round-trip ticket is $18.50 to Fredericksburg and $37 to Richmond, but a ticket doesn't guarantee a seat, so arrive early and get in line to board. Fredericksburg buses stop at a station on Alternate Route 1, about 2 mi from the center of town; cabs and a cheap regional bus service are available there.

Greater Richmond Transit operates bus service in Richmond. Buses run daily, 5 AM–1 AM; fares are $1.50 (exact change required). Most buses are wheelchair accessible.

There is no bus service within the Northern Neck.

🚌 Bus Depots **Fredericksburg Greyhound** ✉ 1400 Jefferson Davis Hwy. ☎ 540/373–2103. **Richmond Greyhound** ✉ 2910 N. Blvd. ☎ 804/254–5910.

🚌 Bus Lines **Greater Richmond Transit** ☎ 804/358–4782 ⊕ www.ridegrtc.com. **Greyhound Lines** ☎ 800/231–2222 ⊕ www.greyhound.com.

BUS TRAVEL WITHIN FREDERICKSBURG

You can ride FRED, the city's excellent little bus, for only 25¢. Six lines— red, yellow, blue, orange, green, and purple—serve the region and stop at all historic sites as well as shopping malls and other modern areas of the city from 7:30 AM to 8:30 PM.

🚌 Bus Information **FRED** ☎ 540/372–1222 ⊕ www.efredericksburgva.gov.

CAR RENTAL

Most major car-rental companies are represented at Richmond Airport. Enterprise, also has locations in Richmond, Ashland, Fredericksburg, and Petersburg.

🚗 **Enterprise** ✉ 10056 W. Broad St., Richmond ☎ 804/346–9500 ✉ 6th and Franklin Sts., Richmond ☎ 804/648–7612 ✉ 4410A Lafayette Blvd., Fredericksburg ☎ 540/891–2200 ✉ 514-C N. Washington Hwy., Ashland ☎ 804/752–2319 ✉ 3206 S. Crater Rd., Petersburg ☎ 804/861–9305.

CAR TRAVEL

Having a car is advisable in Richmond and Fredericksburg. It's essential for touring outlying attractions, including historic homes and battlefields, and the Northern Neck.

Richmond is at the intersection of Interstates 95 and 64, which run north–south and east–west, respectively. U.S. 1/301 also runs north–south past the city. To drive to **Fredericksburg** from Washington, D.C., take I–95 south to Route 3 (Exit 130-A), turn left, and follow the signs. The drive takes about an hour one-way; add 45 minutes during rush hour.

To reach the **Northern Neck** from Fredericksburg either take Route 3 South or U.S. 17 to Route 360, crossing the Rappahannock River at the Tappahannock Bridge. Driving north from Williamsburg and Hampton roads, cross the river at Greys Point by driving north on Route 3. Access from Maryland and Washington, D.C., is over the Potomac River toll bridge on Route 301. If you cross here, you shortly come upon Virginia's Potomac Gateway Visitors Center in King George.

EMERGENCIES

Fredericksburg's Medic 1 Clinic is open weekdays 8 AM–9 PM, Saturday 9–7, and Sunday 9–3.

🚑 **Ambulance, Fire, Police** ☎ 911.

🏥 Hospitals **Medical College of Virginia Hospital** ✉ 401 N. 12th St., Richmond ☎ 804/828–9000. **Medic 1 Clinic** ✉ 3429 Jefferson Davis Hwy., Fredericksburg ☎ 540/371–1664.

🏥 24-Hour Pharmacies **CVS Pharmacy** ✉ 2738 W. Broad St., Richmond ☎ 804/359–2497.

TAXIS

Cabs are metered in Richmond; they charge $2.50 for the first mile and
$1.50 for each additional mile.

🔁 Taxi Companies **Bumbreys Independent Cab Service** ✉ 209 Lafayette Blvd., Fredericksburg ☎ 540/373–6111. **City Cab** ✉ Fredericksburg ☎ 540/372–4484. **Groome Transportation** ✉ Richmond Airport, Richmond ☎ 804/222–7222. **Metro Taxicab Service**
✉ 2405 Westwood Ave., Richmond ☎ 804/353–5000. **Yellow Cab of Fredericksburg**
✉ 2217 Princess Anne St., Fredericksburg ☎ 540/368–8120. **Yellow Cab Service Inc.**
✉ 3203 Williamsburg Rd., Richmond ☎ 804/222–7300.

TOURS

Historic Richmond Tours, a service of the Valentine Richmond History
Center, offers guided tours that cover such topics as the historic Hollywood Cemetery and the River District and Jackson Ward. You can take
either a walking tour or travel throughout the city in your own vehicle
with a "step-on guide" (one who rides with you).

Richmond Discoveries' excursions includes tours that highlight Civil
War history, horseback tours, and customized trips for large groups or
small families.

Fredericksburg Trolley Tours runs a 75-minute narrated tour of Fredericksburg's most important sights. Tours, which are conducted Friday
to Sunday from January through March, and daily from April through
October, cost $15 and leave from the visitor center.

The Living History Company of Fredericksburg can tailor walking
tours to match what you want to see. In addition, the tour coordinator
at the Fredericksburg Visitor Center can arrange a group walking tour
of the city as well as of battlefields and other historic sites to which you
can drive. Reservations are required. The Fredericksburg Department
of Tourism (in the visitor center) publishes a booklet that includes a short
history of Fredericksburg and a self-guided tour covering 29 sights.

Lee's Retreat is a 26-stop self-guided driving tour from Petersburg to
Appomattox. For a route map and other information, contact the Petersburg Visitor Center (⇨ Visitor Information).

TOURS **Fredericksburg Trolley Tours** (☎ 540/898–0737 ⊕ www.
fredericksburgtrolley.com). **Historic Richmond Tours** (☎ 804/649–
0711 ⊕ www.richmondhistorycenter.com). **Living History Company of
Fredericksburg** (☎ 540/899–1776 or 888/214–6384 ⊕ www.
historyexperiences.com). **Richmond Discoveries** (☎ 804/222–8595
⊕ www.richmonddiscoveries.com).

TRAIN TRAVEL

Amtrak trains operate between Washington's Union Station, Alexandria,
Fredericksburg, Richmond, and a number of commuter stops several times
daily. Richmond's train station is north of town. The unmanned Fredericksburg station is two blocks from the historic district.

A one-way ticket costs $22 between Fredericksburg and Washington and
$29 between Washington and Richmond. Amtrak service between New
York City and Newport News or Florida passes through Richmond daily.

The Virginia Rail Express, which uses the same tracks and station as Amtrak, provides workday commuter service between Fredericksburg and Washington's Union Station with additional stops near hotels in Crystal City, L'Enfant Plaza, and elsewhere. A round-trip ticket from Washington's Union Station to Fredericksburg costs $16.20.

There's no mass transit to the Northern Neck, but you can take the train to Fredericksburg and rent a car.

🚂 Train Stations **Fredericksburg station** ✉ Caroline St. and Lafayette Blvd. **Richmond train station** ✉ 7519 Staples Mill Rd. ☎ 804/553-2903.

🚂 Train Lines **Amtrak** ☎ 800/872-7245 ⊕ www.amtrak.com. **Virginia Rail Express** (VRE) ☎ 703/684-1001 or 800/743-3873 ⊕ www.vre.org.

VISITOR INFORMATION

Northern Neck Visitor Information is available at the Potomac Gateway Visitor Center, at the Northern Neck Tourism Council, and other sites throughout the Northern Neck. There's no tourist bureau at Reedville, but tourist brochures are available in the Reedville Fishermen's Museum.

Richmond tourist brochures are available at the National Park Service's five Richmond area visitor centers (*see* Richmond National Battlefield Park Civil War Visitor Center *and* Chimborazo Medical Museum).

🚏 Tourist Information **Fredericksburg Visitor Center** ✉ 706 Caroline St., 22401 ☎ 540/373-1776 or 800/678-4748 🖨 540/372-6587 ⊕ www.fredericksburgvirginia.com. **Hanover Visitor Center** ✉ 112 N. Railroad Ave., I-95, Exit 92B, Ashland ☎ 804/752-6766 or 800/897-1479 ⊕ www.town.ashland.va.us. **Richmond Regional Visitor Center** ✉ 401 N. 3rd St., 23210 ☎ 804/783-7450 or 888/742-4666 ⊕ www.richmond.com/visitors. **Visitor Center at Richmond International Airport** ✉ 1 Richard E. Byrd Terminal Dr., 23210 ☎ 804/236-3260 ⊕ www.richmond.com/visitors. **Petersburg Visitor Center** ✉ 425 Cockade Alley ☎ 804/733-2400 or 800/368-3595 ⊕ www.petersburg-va.org ✉ Information by mail ✉ 15 Bank St., Petersburg 23803 ☎ 804/733-2402 🖨 804/861-0883. **Potomac Gateway Visitor Center** ✉ 3540 James Madison Pkwy., King George 22485 ☎ 540/663-3205 ⊕ www.northernneck.org. **Reedville** 🗃 Box 312, Reedville 22539 ☎ 800/453-6167. **Virginia Tourism Corporation** ✉ 901 E. Byrd St., Richmond ☎ 800/932-5827 ⊕ www.richmondva.org ✉ Bell Tower at Capitol Sq., 9th and Franklin Sts., Richmond ☎ 804/648-3146 ✉ Information by mail ✉ 403 N. 3rd St., 23219.

WILLIAMSBURG & HAMPTON ROADS

5

Updated by
CiCi
Williamson

PERHAPS NO OTHER REGION IN VIRGINIA contains more variety and options than its eastern coastline. Colonial Williamsburg has evoked the days of America's forefathers since its restoration began during the 1920s. Jamestown and Yorktown also help to make the area one of the most historically significant in the United States. When it's time for pure recreation, you can head to theme parks such as Busch Gardens Williamsburg and resort areas, including Virginia Beach.

At the end of the Virginia peninsula is the enormous Hampton Roads harbor, where the James, Elizabeth, and Nansemond rivers flow together and on into Chesapeake Bay. Hampton Roads has also played a crucial role in the discovery and settlement of the nation, its struggle for independence, and the conflict that nearly dissolved the Union.

This entire area, known as the Tidewater, is technically defined as the area in which all river flow is eastward, toward the Chesapeake Bay. The cities in southeast Virginia take on different personalities depending on their proximity to the Chesapeake Bay and the rivers that empty into it. Hampton contains the world's largest naval base, and enormous shipbuilding yards are in Norfolk and Newport News. The area is also committed to recreation and tourism: there are many resort hotels, a bustling beachfront, and boardwalk attractions. Virginia Beach, which in the 1950s claimed to have the world's longest public beach, is now working hard to fight oceanfront erosion and rebuild its once showy boardwalk.

Linked to the Hampton Roads area by the unusual Chesapeake Bay Bridge-Tunnel is Virginia's "other coastline," the quiet, largely untrafficked Eastern Shore.

Exploring Williamsburg & Hampton Roads

To keep the chronology straight, visit Virginia's "historic triangle" in the order of Jamestown, Williamsburg, and then Yorktown. Although Jamestown is somewhat overshadowed by the much-larger Williamsburg, Jamestown Island was the first permanent English settlement (1607) in North America. Just a short drive along the tree-lined Colonial Parkway is Williamsburg, which subsequently grew into the political and economic center of the Virginia Colony. The 173 acres of modern-day Colonial Williamsburg contains re-created and restored structures peopled with costumed interpreters. Everything from momentous political events to blacksmithing is portrayed. Completing the "historic triangle," is Yorktown, 20 mi away, the site of the battle that ended the war for independence from England. Several 18th- and 19th-century plantations lie west of Williamsburg, along the James River. South of Yorktown are Newport News, the shipbuilding capital of Virginia, and Hampton. To see the rest of this waterfront area of Virginia, you can cross the James River at Hampton and visit Norfolk, Portsmouth, and, to the east, the Virginia Beach resort area.

About the Restaurants & Hotels

Dining rooms within walking distance of Colonial Williamsburg's restored area are often crowded, and reservations (☎ 800/447–8679) are necessary. Many nationally known chain eateries line both sides of U.S. 60 on the east side of the city.

There are more than 200 hotel properties in Williamsburg. For a complete list, contact the **Williamsburg Area Convention and Visitors Bureau** (✉ 201 Penniman Rd., Box 3585, Williamsburg 23187-3585 ☎ 757/253–0192 or 800/368–6511).

APARTMENT & Apartment and house rentals are not common in the Williamsburg area,
HOUSE RENTALS but quite the thing to do at Virginia Beach. Rentals vary greatly in size, cost, and relative amount of luxury, so research possibilities thoroughly. 🏠 Local Agents **Long and Foster Real Estate** ✉ 317 30th St., Virginia Beach ☎ 757/428–4600 or 800/941-3333. **Siebert Realty** ✉ 601 Sandbridge Rd., Virginia Beach 23456 ☎ 757/426-6200 or 877/422-2200 ⊕ www.siebert-realty.com.

BED-AND- There are many bed-and-breakfasts in the Williamsburg area, especially
BREAKFASTS near the James River Plantations off Route 10. Most are housed in historic properties with charming antiques. Rates usually include a full country breakfast.

Reservations at inns can be made through the Virginia Division of Tourism Reservation Service. Virginia Beach Reservations can make a reservation in your choice of about 75 hotels. Williamsburg Vacation Reservations, representing more than 70 hostelries, provides free lodging reservation services.
🏠 Reservation Services **Virginia Beach Reservations** ☎ 800/822-3224. **Virginia Division of Tourism Reservation Service** ☎ 800/934-9184. **Williamsburg Vacation Reservations** ☎ 800/446-9244.

WHAT IT COSTS				
	$$$$	**$$$**	**$$**	**$**	**¢**
RESTAURANTS	over $30	$22–$30	$14–$22	$7–$14	under $7
HOTELS	over $250	$175–$250	$130–$175	$80–$130	under $80

Restaurant prices are per person for a main course at dinner. Hotel prices are for a standard double room, excluding state tax.

THE HISTORIC TRIANGLE

Colonial Williamsburg, a careful restoration of the former Virginia capital, gives you the chance to walk into another century and see how earlier Americans lived. The streets may be unrealistically clean for that era, and you can find hundreds of others exploring the buildings with you, but the rich detail of the re-creation and the sheer size of the city could hold your attention for days. A ticket or pass (price is based on the number of attractions and the duration of visit) admits the holder to sites in the restored area, but it costs nothing just to walk around and absorb the atmosphere.

The 23-mi Colonial Parkway joins Williamsburg with two other significant historical sites on or near the peninsula bounded by the James and York rivers. Historic Jamestowne was the location of the first permanent English settlement in North America, and it's an excellent place to begin a visit to the area; Yorktown was the site of the final major battle in the American Revolutionary War. The sites themselves are maintained today by the National Park Service. Close by are Jamestown Settlement and the excellent Yorktown Victory Center, both run by the Jamestown-Yorktown Foundation. Like Colonial Williamsburg, these two sights re-create the buildings and activities of the 18th century, using interpreters in period dress.

Numbers in the margin correspond to points of interest on the Williamsburg and Environs map.

Jamestown

❶ *9 mi southwest of Colonial Williamsburg via Colonial Pkwy.*

Jamestown takes you to the beginnings of English settlement in this country: its two major sights are places to explore the early relationship between the English and Native Americans.

Historic Jamestowne, separated from the mainland by a narrow isthmus, was the site of the first permanent English settlement in North America (1607) and the capital of Virginia until 1699. The first settlers' bitter struggle for survival here, on the now uninhabited land, makes for a visit that stirs the imagination. Redbrick foundation walls roughly outline the settlement, and artists' conceptions of the original buildings can be seen at several locations. The only standing structure is the ruin of a church tower from the 1640s, now part of the Memorial Church built in 1907; the markers within indicate the original church's foundations. Other monuments around the site also date from the tercentenary celebration in 1907. Statues portray the founder of Jamestown, Captain John Smith, and his advocate, the Native American princess Pocahontas, who Smith credited with saving him from being beheaded.

Along with Yorktown Battlefield and the Colonial Parkway, Historic Jamestowne is part of Colonial National Historical Park, run by the National Park Service. Ranger guided tours, held daily, explore many different events in Jamestown's history. Living-history programs are presented daily in summer and on weekends in spring and autumn.

The visitor center and museum exhibits are closed until late 2006. A modest Visitor Information Station contains orientation services, exhibits, and a museum store until the new visitor center is completed near the main parking lot. On-site, archaeologists from the Association for the Preservation of Virginia Antiquities continue to dig up evidence of colonists' and Native Americans' ways of life, including the remains of the original 1607 fort.

A 5 mi nature drive that rings the island is posted with informative signs and paintings. On leaving Historic Jamestowne, you can stop at the reconstructed Glasshouse to observe a demonstration of glassblowing, an unsuccessful business venture of the early colonists. The products of today are for sale in a gift shop. ⊠ *Off Colonial Pkwy.* ☎ *757/898–2410* 💲 *$8* ⊙ *Daily 9–5; gates close at 4:30.*

Adjacent to but distinct from Historic Jamestowne, a mainland living-history museum called **Jamestown Settlement** holds a version of the early James Fort. Within it, interpreters in costume cook, forge metal, and describe what life was like living under thatch roofs and between walls of wattle and daub (stick framework covered with mud plaster). The largest structure in the complex is the church, where attendance was required twice a day. In the Powhatan Indian Village you can enter a *yehakin* (house) and see buckskin-costumed interpreters cultivate a garden and make tools. This is one museum where everything can be handled. At the pier are full-scale reproductions of the ships in which the settlers arrived: *Godspeed, Discovery,* and *Susan Constant.* The *Godspeed* retraced the original voyage in 1985, and all the vessels are seaworthy. You may climb aboard the *Susan Constant* and find out more from the sailor-interpreters. Indoor exhibits examine the lives of the Powhatans and their English-born neighbors, their interaction, and world conditions that encouraged colonization. A riverfront discovery area that opened in 2004 provides information about 17th-century water travel, commerce, and cultural exchange, reflecting Powhatan Indian, European and African traditions. Dugout canoe making takes place in this area. There's also a 15-minute docudrama called *Jamestown: The Beginning.* Thursday and Friday in April and May; October and November bring lots of school groups, so it's best to arrive after 2 PM on those days. ✉ *Rte. 31 off Colonial Pkwy.* ☎ *757/253–4838 or 888/593–4682* ⊕ *www.historyisfun. org* 🎫 *$11.75; combination ticket with Yorktown Victory Center $17* ⊙ *June 15–Aug. 15, daily 9–6; Aug. 16–June 14, daily 9–5.*

Colonial Williamsburg

51 mi southeast of Richmond via I–64.

Williamsburg was the capital of Virginia from 1699 to 1780, after Jamestown and before Richmond. Williamsburg hasn't been politically important for a long time, but now that **Colonial Williamsburg** is there to represent it in its era of glory, it's a jewel of the commonwealth. Outside the restored area is a modern city with plenty of dining and lodging options and attractions, including outlet shops and a large water park.

*Fodor's*Choice
★

All vehicular traffic is prohibited within Colonial Williamsburg to preserve the illusion. Shuttle buses run continuously to and from the visitor center.

Colonial Williamsburg sells a number of all-inclusive tickets that cost just a bit more than a $33 one-day pass. The Freedom Pass ($39), which allows you to visit for one full year, also includes admission to special events. The Liberty Pass ($69), also valid for a year includes all the benefits of the Freedom Pass as well as admission to all special events, access to a VIP visitor lounge, and special discounts.

Numbers in the margin correspond to points of interest on the Colonial Williamsburg map.

② The **Visitor Center** is the logical first stop at Colonial Williamsburg. Here you can park free; buy tickets; see a 35-minute introductory movie, *Williamsburg—the Story of a Patriot*; and pick up the *Visitors Companion*, which has a list of regular events and special programs and a map of the Historic Area. Tickets are also sold at the Lumber House in the historic area and at the Williamsburg Attraction Center. ✉ *102 Information Center Dr., off U.S. 60* ☎ *757/220–7645 or 800/447–8679* ⊕ *www.colonialwilliamsburg.com* 🎫 *Annual Passes, $39–$59 good for 1 year, admit bearer to every Colonial Williamsburg–run site. General admission, $33 for 1st day, can be upgraded to annual pass and include all museums and exhibitions. Various less-expensive tickets allow for more restricted visits* ⊙ *Daily 9–5.*

The spine of Colonial Williamsburg's restored area is the broad 1-mi-long **Duke of Gloucester Street.** On Saturday at noon, from March to October, the Junior Fife and Drum Corps marches the length of the street and performs a stirring drill. Along this artery alone, or just off it, are two dozen attractions. Walking west on Duke of Gloucester Street from the Capitol, you can find a dozen 18th-century shops—including those of the apothecary, the wig maker, the silversmith, and the milliner.

❸ The **Capitol** is the building that made this town so important. It was here that the pre-Revolutionary House of Burgesses (dominated by the ascendant gentry) challenged the royally appointed council (an almost me-

COLONIAL WILLIAMSBURG BASICS

THE RESTORATION PROJECT that gave birth to Colonial Williamsburg began in 1926, inspired by a local pastor, W. A. R. Goodwin, and financed by John D. Rockefeller Jr. The work of the archaeologists and historians of the Colonial Williamsburg Foundation continues to this day. A total of 88 original 18th-century and early-19th-century structures have been meticulously restored, and another 40 have been reconstructed on their original sites. In all, 225 period rooms have been furnished from the foundation's collection of more than 100,000 pieces of furniture, pottery, china, glass, silver, pewter, textiles, tools, and carpeting. Period authenticity also governs the landscaping of the 90 acres of gardens and public greens. The restored area covers 173 acres; surrounded by a greenbelt, it's all controlled by the foundation, which guards against development that could mar the illusion of the Colonial city.

Despite its huge scale, Colonial Williamsburg can seem almost cozy. One million people come here annually, and all year long hundreds of costumed interpreters, wearing bonnets or three-corner hats, rove and ride through the streets (you can even rent outfits for your children). Dozens of skilled craftspeople, also in costume, demonstrate and explain their trades inside their workshops. They include the shoemaker, the cooper (he makes barrels), the gunsmith, the blacksmith, the musical instrument maker, the silversmith, and the wig maker. Their wares are for sale nearby. Four taverns serve food and drink that approximate the fare of more than 220 years ago.

Colonial Williamsburg makes an effort to not just represent the lives of a privileged few, and to not gloss over disturbing aspects of the country's history. Slavery, religious freedom, family life, commerce and trade, land acquisition, and the Revolution are portrayed in living-history demonstrations. In the 1½-hour "About Town" walking tour, you can be personally escorted by such famous patriots as Thomas Jefferson or Martha Washington. Free black and enslaved men struggle with issues of identity and survival in "Among the Dipping Gourds." At the meetinghouse, you can step into the controversial world of the Reverend James Waddell, a "Licensed Dissenter." The vignettes that are staged throughout the day take place in the streets and in public buildings. These may include dramatic afternoon court trials or fascinating estate appraisals. Depending on the days you visit, you may see the House of Burgesses dissolve, its members charging out to make revolutionary plans at the Raleigh Tavern. There's even a love story at play as Mr. Drinkard and Miss Grant become involved in a terrible miscommunication before the eyes of camera-clad tourists.

Because of the size of Colonial Williamsburg and the large crowds (especially in the warmer months), the best plan may be to begin a tour early in the day; it's a good idea to spend the night before in the area. The foundation suggests allowing three or four days to do Colonial Williamsburg justice, but that will depend on your own interest in the period—and that interest often increases on arrival. Everyone should allow at least one full day to tour the city. A number of guided walks or tours are available. Museums, exhibits, and stores close at 5 PM, but the town is open 24 hours, and walks and events take place in the evenings, usually ending by 10 PM. Some sites close in winter on a rotating basis.

dieval body made up of the bigger landowners). In 1765 the House eventually arrived at the resolutions, known as Henry's Resolves (after Patrick Henry), that amounted to rebellion. An informative tour explains the development, stage by stage, of American democracy from its English parliamentary roots. In the courtroom a guide recites the harsh Georgian sentences that were meted out: for instance, theft of more than 12 shillings was a capital crime. Occasional reenactments, including witch trials, dramatize the evolution of American jurisprudence.

What stands on the site today is a reproduction of the 1705 structure that burned down in 1747. Dark-wood wainscoting, pewter chandeliers, and towering ceilings contribute to a handsome impression. That an official building would have so ornate an interior was characteristic of aristocratic 18th-century Virginia. This was in telling contrast to the plain town meeting halls of Puritan New England, where other citizens were governing themselves at the same time. ⊠ *East end of Duke of Gloucester St.*

4 **Raleigh Tavern** was the scene of pre-Revolutionary revels and rallies that were often joined by Washington, Jefferson, Patrick Henry, and other major figures. The spare but elegant blue-and-white Apollo Room is said to have been the first meeting place of Phi Beta Kappa, the scholastic honorary society founded in 1776. The French general Marquis de Lafayette was feted here in 1824. In 1859 the original structure burned, and today's building is a reconstruction based on archaeological evidence and period descriptions and sketches of the building. ⊠ *Duke of Gloucester St., west of Capitol.*

5 **Wetherburn's Tavern,** which offered refreshment, entertainment, and lodging beginning in 1743, may be the most accurately furnished building in Colonial Williamsburg, with contents that conform to a room-by-room inventory taken in 1760. Excavations at this site have yielded more than 200,000 artifacts. The outbuildings include the original dairy and a reconstructed kitchen. Vegetables are still grown in the small garden. ⊠ *Duke of Gloucester St., across from Raleigh Tavern.*

6 At **James Anderson's Blacksmith Shop,** smiths forge the nails, tools, and other iron hardware used in construction throughout the town. The shop itself was reconstructed by carpenters using 18th-century tools and techniques. ⊠ *Between Botetourt and Colonial Sts., on south side of Duke of Gloucester St.*

7 The original **Magazine** (1715), an octagonal brick warehouse, was used for storing arms and ammunition—at one time, 60,000 pounds of gunpowder and 3,000 muskets. It was used for this purpose by the British, then by the Continental army, and again by the Confederates during the Civil War. Today, 18th-century firearms are on display within the arsenal. ⊠ *West of Queen St., on south side of Duke of Gloucester St.*

8 The **Guardhouse** once served in the defense of the Magazine's lethal inventory; now it contains a replica fire engine (1750) that is seen on the town streets in the warmer months. Special interpretive programs about the military are scheduled here. ⊠ *Duke of Gloucester St. near Queen St.*

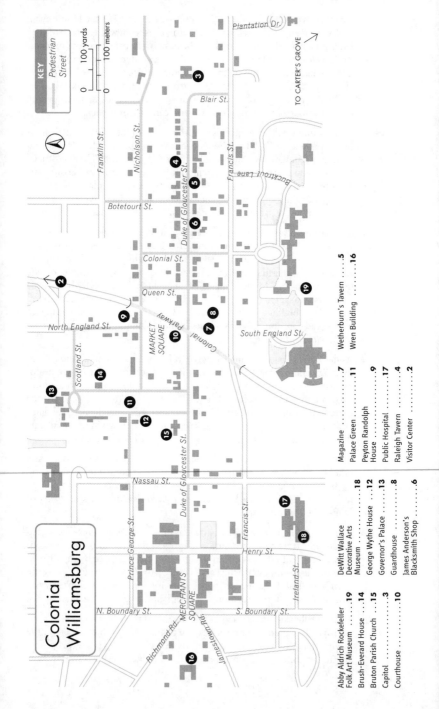

Colonial Williamsburg

KEY

Pedestrian Street

0   100 yards
0   100 meters

Plantation Dr.

TO CARTER'S GROVE

Franklin St.

Nicholson St.

Blair St.

Botetourt St.

Francis St.

Bucktrout Lane

Duke of Gloucester St.

Colonial St.

Queen St.

North England St.

Scotland St.

MARKET SQUARE

Colonial Parkway

South England St.

Nassau St.

Prince George St.

Duke of Gloucester St.

N. Boundary St.

MERCHANTS SQUARE

S. Boundary St.

Henry St.

Francis St.

Ireland St.

Richmond Rd.

Jamestown Rd.

Abby Aldrich Rockefeller
Folk Art Museum **19**
Brush-Everard House . . . **14**
Bruton Parish Church . . . **3**
Capitol **10**

DeWitt Wallace
Decorative Arts
Museum **18**
George Wythe House . . . **12**
Governor's Palace **13**
Guardhouse **8**
James Anderson's
Blacksmith Shop **6**

Magazine **7**
Palace Green **11**
Peyton Randolph
House **9**
Public Hospital **17**
Raleigh Tavern **4**
Visitor Center **2**

Wetherburn's Tavern **5**
Wren Building **16**

In **Market Square,** an open green between Queen and Palace streets along Duke of Gloucester, cattle, seafood, dairy products, fruit, and vegetables were all sold—as were slaves. Both the market and slave auctions are sometimes reenacted.

9 The **Peyton Randolph House** was the home of a prominent colonist and revolutionary who served as attorney general under the British, then as Speaker of the House of Burgesses, and later as president of the first and second Continental Congresses. The oak-panel bedroom and Randolph family silver are remarkable. ⊠ *Nicholson St. at N. England St.*

East of the Peyton Randolph House, on Nicholson Street, is the **military encampment,** where you can get a feeling for military life in the 1700s. During warm weather," Join the Continental Army," an interactive theater performance, lets you experience military life on the eve of the Revolution. Under the guidance of costumed militiamen, visitors drill and make camp in a 45-minute participatory program. If you want to join the ranks for a little while, you can volunteer at the site.

On the outskirts of the Historic Area, you can follow the pleasant fragrance of wood burning to **Robertson's Windmill,** where rural trades such as basket making, pit sawing (two men on either side of a long saw in a pit), and barrel making are demonstrated. When the weather is willing, the windmill powers the fires inside that tradespeople use for their craft. The coopers smolder metal strands that wrap around the barrels, keeping them taut. ⊠ *N. England St.*

10 The original **Courthouse** of 1770 was used by municipal and county courts until 1932. Civil and minor criminal matters and cases involving slaves were adjudicated here; other trials were conducted at the Capitol. The stocks once used to punish misdemeanors are outside the building: they can make for a perverse photo opportunity. The courthouse's exterior has been restored to its original appearance. Visitors often participate in scheduled reenactments of court sessions. ⊠ *North side of Duke of Gloucester St., west of Queen St.*

11 The handsome **Palace Green** runs north from Duke of Gloucester Street up the center of Palace Street, with the Governor's Palace at the far end and a notable historic house on either side.

12 The **George Wythe House** was the residence of Thomas Jefferson's law professor; Wythe was also a signer of the Declaration of Independence. General Washington used the house as a headquarters just before his victory at Yorktown. The large brick structure, built in the mid-18th century, is conspicuously symmetrical: each side has a chimney, and each floor has two rooms on either side of a center hallway. The garden in back is similarly divided. The outbuildings, including a smokehouse, kitchen, laundry, outhouses, and a chicken coop, are reconstructions. ⊠ *West side of Palace Green.*

13 His Majesty's Governor Alexander Spotswood built the original **Governor's Palace** in 1720, and seven British viceroys, the last of them Lord Dunmore in 1775, lived in this appropriately showy mansion. The 800 guns and swords arrayed on the walls and ceilings of several rooms herald the power of the Crown. Some of the furnishings are original, and the rest are matched to an extraordinary inventory of 16,000 items. Lavishly appointed as it is, the palace is furnished to the time just before the Revolution. During the Revolution, it housed the commonwealth's first two governors, Patrick Henry and Thomas Jefferson. The original residence burned down in 1781, and today's reconstruction stands on the original foundation.

A costumed guide greets you at the door for a tour through the building, offering commentary and answering questions. Notable among the furnishings are several pieces made in Williamsburg and owned by Lord Dunmore. Social events are described on the walk through the great formal ballroom, where you might even hear the sounds of an 18th-century harp, clavichord, or piano, or see colonists dancing to the hit tunes of the times. The supper room leads to the formal garden and the planted terraces beyond. ⊠ *Northern end of Palace Green.*

⑭ The **Brush-Everard House** was built in 1717 by John Brush, a gunsmith, and later owned by Thomas Everard, who was twice mayor of Williamsburg. The yellow wood-frame house contains remarkable, ornate carving work but is open only for special-focus tours. Temporary exhibits and vignettes on slaves' lives are held here in summer. ⊠ *Scotland St. and Palace Green.*

⑮ The lovely brick Episcopal **Bruton Parish Church** has served continuously as a house of worship since it was built in 1715. One of its 20th-century pastors, W. A. R. Goodwin, provided the impetus for Williamsburg's restoration. The church tower, topped by a beige wooden steeple, was added in 1769; during the Revolution its bell served as the local "liberty bell," rung to summon people for announcements. The white pews, tall and boxed in, are characteristic of the starkly graceful Colonial ecclesiastical architecture of the region. When sitting in a pew, listening to the history of the church, keep in mind that you could be sitting where Thomas Jefferson, Ben Franklin, or George Washington once listened to sermons. The stone baptismal font is believed to have come from an older Jamestown church. Many local eminences, including one royal governor, are interred in the graveyard. The fully operational church is open to the public; contributions are accepted. ⊠ *Duke of Gloucester St. west of Palace St.*

need a break? At the west end of Duke of Gloucester Street, for a block on both sides, **Merchants Square** has more than 40 shops and restaurants, some serving fast food. Services also include three banks and a drugstore.

⑯ The **Wren Building** is part of the College of William and Mary, founded in 1693 and the second-oldest college in the United States after Harvard University. The campus extends to the west; the Wren Building (1695) was based on the work of the celebrated London architect Sir Christopher Wren. Its redbrick outer walls are original, but fire gutted the interiors several times, and the current quarters are largely reconstructions of the 20th century. The faculty common room, with a table covered with green felt and an antique globe, suggests Oxford and Cambridge universities, the models for this New World institution. Jefferson studied and later taught law here to James Monroe and others. Tours, led by undergraduates, include the chapel where Colonial leader Peyton Randolph is buried. ⊠ *West end of Duke of Gloucester St.*

⑰ The **Public Hospital,** a reconstruction of a 1773 insane asylum, provides an informative, shocking look at the treatment of the mentally ill in the 18th and 19th centuries. It also serves as cover for a modern edifice that houses very different exhibitions; entrance to the DeWitt Wallace Decorative Arts Museum is through the hospital lobby. ⊠ *Francis St.*

⑱ The **DeWitt Wallace Decorative Arts Museum** adds another cultural dimension that goes well beyond Colonial history. Grouped by medium are English and American furniture, textiles, prints, metals, and ceramics of the 17th to the early 19th century. If you're yawning at the thought of fancy tableware, stop: presentations here tend to be creative and surprising. Prizes among the 8,000 pieces in the collection are a full-length portrait of George Washington by Charles Willson Peale and a royally commissioned case clock surmounted by the detailed figure of a Native American. You enter the museum through the Public Hospital. ⊠ *Francis St.*

⑲ The **Abby Aldrich Rockefeller Folk Art Museum** showcases American "decorative usefulware"—toys, furniture, weather vanes, coffeepots, and quilts—within typical 19th-century domestic interiors. There are also folk paintings, rustic sculptures, and needlepoint pictures. Since the 1920s, the 2,000-piece collection has grown from the original 400 pieces acquired by the wife of Colonial Williamsburg's first and principal benefactor. ⊠ *S. England St.*

The reconstructed **Carter's Grove plantation,** created after extensive archaeological investigation, examines 400 years of history, starting in 1619 with the fortified hamlet called Wolstenholme Towne. Exhibits in the **Winthrop Rockefeller Archaeology Museum** provide further insight. The 18th century is represented by slave dwellings on their original foundations, where costumed interpreters explain the crucial role African-Americans played on plantations. Dramatic plays take place here during the evening. Finally, you may tour the **mansion,** built in 1755 by Carter Burwell, whose grandfather," King" Carter, made a fortune as one of Virginia's wealthiest landowners and greatest explorers. The mansion was extensively remodeled in 1919, and further additions were made in the 1930s. The interior is notable for the original wood paneling and elaborate carvings. A one-way country road, also used for biking, leads from Carter's Grove through woods, meadows, marshes, and streams back to Williamsburg. ⊠ *U.S. 60, 6 mi east of Colonial Williamsburg* ☎ *757/229–1000* ⊠ *$18, included in any regular Williamsburg pass. Play $10* ⊙ *Mid-Mar.–Dec., Tues.–Sun. 9–5.*

off the
beaten
path

WILLIAMSBURG WINERY – Carrying on a Virginia tradition of wine making that began with early settlers, the winery offers guided tours, a well-stocked wine shop, a 17th-century tasting room, and a museum of wine-making artifacts. A casual lunch is served in the Gabriel Archer Tavern. Be sure to give the cabernets and merlots a try. ⊠ *5800 Wessex*

168 <

CloseUp

ROBERT "KING" CARTER

ROBERT "KING" CARTER *was the richest man in the English Colonies of North America and one of the wealthiest men in the world. At his death in 1732 at the age of 69, Carter held 1,000 slaves, 300,000 acres, and @10,000. The will disposing of his possessions covered 53 sheets of paper. Although he inherited limited holdings from his father and half brother, his astuteness in the tobacco business, politics and land speculation greatly increased his wealth. Carter grew tobacco; he also owned the tobacco warehouses and the ships to carry the product to Europe. Carterís self-importance and political acumen led to others giving him the somewhat sarcastic nickname of "King."*

Carter's family was a very old one—some of his ancestors had fought alongside King William at the Battle of Hastings in 1066. By the time the first permanent English settlement was founded at Jamestown in

1607, the family's old name, Cartier, had been anglicized to Carter. Around 1612, members of the Carter business cartel began looking at the potential of the emerging tobacco trade in Virginia and emigrated here.

Carter held influential political positions throughout his life: he was speaker of the Virginia House of Burgesses, treasurer of the colony, colonel and commander-in-chief of the Lancaster-Northumberland Counties militia, and acting governor of the Virginia Colony.

No other Virginian of his generation was so successful in his political career, in the marriages made by his children, and so ruthless in building his estate for the benefit of those children. His family dynasty, estimated to have over 50,000 descendants living today, includes six governors of Virginia, three signers of the Declaration of Independence, and two presidents of the United States.

Hundred, off Lake Powell Rd. and Rte. 199, Williamsburg ☎ 757/ 229–0999 ☑ $6, includes tasting of 5–7 wines and a souvenir glass ⊘ Mid-Feb.–mid-Jan., Mon.–Sat. 10:30–5:30, Sun. 11–5:30.

Where to Eat

$$–$$$$ ✕ **Le Yaca.** A mall of small boutiques is the unlikely location for this French-country restaurant. The dining room has soft pastel colors, hardwood floors, candlelight, and a central open fireplace. The menu is arranged in the French manner, with four prix-fixe menus and 10 entrées, including whole duck breast with black truffle sauce, leg of lamb with rosemary garlic sauce, and fresh scallops and shrimp with champagne sauce. Le Yaca is on U.S. 60 East, near Busch Gardens. ⊠ *Village Shops at Kingsmill, 1915 Pocahontas Trail* ☎ 757/220–3616 ▭ *AE, D, DC, MC, V* ⊘ *Closed Sun. and 1st 2 wks of Jan.*

★ $$–$$$$ ✕ **The Trellis.** With vaulted ceilings and hardwood floors, the Trellis is an airy and pleasant place. The imaginative lunch and dinner menus change with the seasons. A good wine list complements such dishes as homemade tomato bisque, wild boar, and soft-shell crabs. The seafood entrées are particularly good, and many patrons wouldn't leave without ordering the rich Death by Chocolate, the restaurant's signature dessert. ⊠ *Merchants Sq., 403 Duke of Gloucester St.* ☎ *757/229–8610* ▭ *AE, MC, V.*

$–$$$$ ✕ **Aberdeen Barn.** Saws, pitchforks, oxen yokes, and the like hang on the barn walls, but the wood tables are lacquered, and the napkins are linen. Specialties include slow-roasted prime rib of beef; baby-back Danish pork ribs barbecued with a sauce of peach preserves and Southern Comfort; and shrimp Dijon. An ample but not esoteric wine list is dominated by California vintages, but there are Virginia selections. ⊠ *1601 Richmond Rd.* ☎ *757/229–6661* ▭ *AE, D, MC, V* ⊙ *No lunch.*

★ **$–$$$$** ✕ **Regency Room.** This hotel restaurant is known for its elegance, its attentive service, and quality cuisine. Among crystal chandeliers, Asian silk-screen prints, and full silver service, you can sample chateaubriand carved tableside, as well as rack of lamb, Dover Sole, lobster bisque, and rich ice-cream desserts. It may almost seem as if you're treated like royalty. A jacket and tie are required at dinner and optional at Sunday brunch. ⊠ *Williamsburg Inn, 136 E. Francis St.* ☎ *757/229–1000* ♣ *Reservations essential* ▭ *AE, D, DC, MC, V.*

$$–$$$ ✕ **Berret's Restaurant and Raw Bar.** One of the most reliable seafood spots around, Berret's is in Merchants Square. Upscale but casual, the restaurant lights crackling fires during colder months and opens up its pleasant outdoor patio when it's warm. Entrées and appetizers employ fresh Chesapeake Bay seafood. It's usually a sure bet to try any of the nightly specials of fresh fish, which often include perfectly prepared tuna. The she-crab soup, a house favorite, blends crabmeat, cream, and crab roe with just a hint of sherry. ⊠ *199 Boundary St.* ☎ *757/253–1847* ▭ *AE, D, DC, MC, V* ⊙ *Jan.–early Feb., closed Mon.*

$$ ✕ **The Seafare of Williamsburg.** Here in one of the area's few places for "fine dining," the waiters are tuxedo-clad, the tablecloths crisp linen. The menu's offerings resemble those available on a luxury cruise ship. Rum buns begin the meal, where the highlights include enormous crab cakes and filet mignon filled with crabmeat and rich béarnaise sauce. Order one of the showy flambé desserts, which are prepared tableside. ⊠ *1632 Richmond Rd.* ☎ *757/229–0099* ▭ *AE, D, DC, MC, V.*

$–$$ ✕ **Peking.** You might not guess by its appearance, but this Chinese restaurant with a Mongolian grill is a treat. The daily buffet offers both stick-to-your-ribs Chinese and Mongolian dishes. At the grill, choose the ingredients you want in your entrée, and watch the cooks prepare it in front of you. The shopping center location is just outside the historic district. ⊠ *120 J. Waller Mill Rd.* ☎ *757/229–2288* ▭ *AE, D, MC, V.*

$–$$ ✕ **Sal's Restaurant by Victor.** Locals love this family Italian restaurant and pizzeria. Victor Minichiello and his staff cook in a wood-fired oven and serve up pasta, fish, chicken, and veal dinners as well as subs and pizzas. The restaurant delivers free to nearby hotels. ⊠ *1242 Richmond Rd.* ☎ *757/220–2641* ▭ *AE, D, MC, V.*

★ **$–$$** ✕ **The Whaling Company.** Fresh seafood is the drawing card at this large wooden building, which wouldn't look out of place in a New England fishing village. Despite its out-of-town look, the restaurant has an authenticity sometimes hard to find in touristy towns. Locals come in for the fresh scallops, fish, and other seafood. Steaks are available, but no poultry or other meats are served. The restaurant is off U.S. 60 West just after the Route 199 interchange. ✉ *494 McLaws Circle* ☎ *757/229–0275* ▭ *AE, DC, MC, V* ⊙ *No lunch.*

¢–$ ✕ **College Delly.** It's easy to forget that this is a college town, but this cheerful dive keeps up the school spirit. The white-brick eatery with forest-green canvas awnings is dark and scruffy inside. Walls are hung with fraternity and sorority pictures, graduation snapshots, and sports-team photos. Booths and tables are in the William and Mary colors of green and gold. Deli sandwiches, pasta, stromboli, and Greek dishes are all prepared with fresh ingredients and are all delicious, and there's a wide selection of beers on tap. The Delly delivers orders free to nearby hotels from 6 PM to 1 AM. ✉ *336 Richmond Rd.* ☎ *757/229–6627* ▭ *MC, V.*

¢–$ ✕ **Old Chickahominy House.** Reminiscent of old-fashioned Virginia tearooms, this Colonial-style restaurant has delectable goodies served up by sweet, grandmotherly types. For breakfast there's Virginia ham and eggs, made-from-scratch biscuits, country bacon, sausage, and grits. Lunch brings Brunswick stew, Virginia ham biscuits, fruit salad, and homemade pie. ✉ *1211 Jamestown Rd.* ☎ *757/229–4689* ▭ *MC, V* ⊙ *No dinner.*

COLONIAL TAVERNS

The four reconstructed "taverns" in Colonial Williamsburg are essentially restaurants with beer and wine available. Colonial-style food is served at lunch, dinner, and Sunday brunch. Formerly the taverns were all fairly expensive. However, in an effort to attract more business, new casual dining and reasonable prices have been instituted in several of the taverns. Although the food can be uneven (excellent one night and mediocre the next) a meal at any tavern is a good way to get into the spirit of the era.

No reservations are taken for lunch, but it's recommended that you make dinner reservations up to two or three weeks in advance. Hours also change according to season, so check by calling the reservations number (☎ 800/447–8679). Smoking is not permitted in any of the taverns. To see tavern menus, go to: www.history.org/visit/diningExperience/.

$$$–$$$$ ✕ **Christiana Campbell's Tavern.** George Washington's favorite tavern is across the street from the Capitol. The menu includes items such as oyster fritters, crab cakes, and softshell crabs. The Mrs. Campbell's Waterman's Supp'r assortment comes with crab-stuffed shrimp, oyster stew, grilled salmon, seared scallops, and seasonal seafood. Meals can also be eaten in the garden. ✉ *Waller St.* ▭ *AE, D, DC, MC, V.*

$–$$$$ ✕ **Kings Arms.** In this 18th-century-style chop house, generous cuts of prime aged beef, tender pork, and lamb are on offer. It's the best of the Historic Area's four Colonial taverns. The genteel surroundings imitate those experienced by Thomas Jefferson and Patrick Henry. Don't miss favorite such as peanut soup or Norfolk Pottage Pie, a game pie made of venison, rabbit, duck, vegetables, and bacon in a wine sauce. Weather permitting, you can eat from a separate lighter menu in a garden behind the tavern. ✉ *Duke of Gloucester St.* ▭ *AE, D, DC, MC, V.*

¢–$$ ✕ **Chownings Tavern.** A reconstructed 18th-century alehouse, Chowning's serves casual quick fare for lunch, including traditional pit-style BBQ ordered from the new walk-up service area in the tavern garden. You can eat either inside the tavern or under an garden arbor. After 5 PM, Chownings becomes a true 18th-century tavern and Gambol's (a lively nighttime program presented for 25 years) operates throughout the evening. Costumed balladeers lead family sing-alongs, and costumed servers play popular games of the day. From 8 PM until closing, Chowning's caters to a more mature audience. ⊠ *Duke of Gloucester St.* ⊟ *AE, D, DC, MC, V.*

¢–$$ ✕ **Shields Tavern.** The James Shields Tavern has returned to its roots as an 18th-century coffee house, with costumed interpreters engaging guests in "events of the day." The tavern's menu of light fare—soups, salads and sandwiches—is served throughout the day. After 3, a part of the restaurant is given over to serving coffee and other beverages. ⊠ *Duke of Gloucester St.* ⊟ *AE, D, DC, MC, V.*

Where to Stay

★ $$$$ 🏨 **Williamsburg Inn.** This grand hotel from 1937 is owned and operated by Colonial Williamsburg. Rooms are beautifully and individually furnished with reproductions and antiques in the English Regency style, and genteel service and tradition reign. Rooms come with such perks as morning coffee and afternoon tea, a daily newspaper, turndown service, and bathrobes. The Providence Wings, adjacent to the inn, are less formal; rooms are in a contemporary style with Asian accents and overlook the tennis courts, a private pond, and a wooded area. ⊠ *136 E. Francis St., Box 1776, 23187-1776* 📞 *757/229–1000 or 800/447–8679* 📠 *757/220–7096* ⊕ *www.colonialwilliamsburg.com* 🛏 *62 rooms, 14 suites* ♨ *3 restaurants, room service, in-room VCRs, 9-hole golf course, 2 18-hole golf courses, tennis court, pool, health club, spa, croquet, hiking, lawn bowling, lounge, piano, children's programs (ages 5–12), dry cleaning, laundry service, Internet, concierge, meeting rooms, no-smoking rooms* ⊟ *AE, D, DC, MC, V.*

$$–$$$$ 🏨 **Colonial Houses.** A stay here seems particularly moving at night, FodorsChoice when the town's historic area is quiet and you have Williamsburg pretty ★ much to yourself. Five of the 25 homes and three lodging taverns are 18th-century structures; the others have been rebuilt on their original foundations. Lodgings are furnished with antiques, period reproductions; modern amenities include hair dryers, irons, ironing boards, coffeemakers, a complimentary fruit basket and bottle of wine; the staff is costumed. The Colonial Houses share the facilities of the adjacent Williamsburg Inn and the Lodge. ⊠ *136 E. Francis St., Box 1776, 23187-1776* 📞 *757/229–1000 or 800/447–8679* 📠 *757/565–8444* ⊕ *www. colonialwilliamsburg.com* 🛏 *77 rooms* ♨ *Room service, dry cleaning; no smoking* ⊟ *AE, D, DC, MC, V.*

★ $$–$$$$ 🏨 **Kingsmill Resort and Spa.** This manicured 2,900-acre resort on the James River owned by Anheuser-Busch is home to the largest golf resort in Virginia: it hosts the LPGA's Michelob ULTRA Open each May. You can play year-round on three championship courses, including the newly renovated River Course. The 9-hole course is free if you stay here, and so is a shuttle bus to Busch Gardens, Water Country USA, and Colonial Williamsburg. The guest rooms, renovated in 2004, have fireplaces and are decorated with Colonial-style furniture. The inventive menu at the expensive Bray Bistro emphasizes seafood, game birds, and steak. ⊠ *1010 Kingsmill Rd., Williamsburg 23185* 📞 *757/253–1703 or 800/ 832–5665* 📠 *757/253–8246* ⊕ *www.kingsmill.com* 🛏 *235 rooms,*

175 suites ⚅ 6 restaurants, in-room data ports, cable TV, 9-hole golf course, 3 18-hole golf courses, putting green, 15 tennis courts, 2 pools (1 indoor), wading pool, health club, sauna, spa, steam room, beach, boating, marina, boat ramp, fishing, billiards, bar, babysitting, dry cleaning, laundry service, concierge, business services, meeting rooms ⊟ AE, D, DC, MC, V.

$$–$$$$ 🏨 **Williamsburg Lodge.** This classic hotel is under total renovation and will reopen in phases, with roughly half of the rooms open by the end of 2005. A new conference center opens in 2006. Every room will have a hair dryer, iron, and ironing board. ⊠ *310 S. England St., 23187-1776* ☎ *757/229–1000 or 800/447–8679* 🖷 *757/220–7799* ⊕ *www. colonialwilliamsburg.com ➳ 323 rooms ⚅ Restaurant, 9-hole golf course, 2 18-hole golf courses, 1 pool, bicycles, lobby lounge, dry cleaning, laundry facilities, laundry service, concierge, business services, meeting rooms, no-smoking rooms ⊟ AE, D, DC, MC, V.*

★ $$$ 🏨 **Liberty Rose.** Century-old beeches, oaks, and poplars surround this slate-roof, white-clapboard house on a hilltop-acre 1 mi from Colonial Williamsburg. The inn was constructed in the early 1920s; furnishings include European antiques and plenty of silk and damask. Most remarkable is that every room has windows on three sides. The large room on the first floor has a unique bathroom with a claw-foot tub, a red-marble shower, and antique mirrors. Breakfast is served on a sunporch. This two-story bed-and-breakfast does not have an elevator. ⊠ *1022 Jamestown Rd., 23185* ☎ *757/253–1260 or 800/545–1825* ⊕ *www. libertyrose.com ➳ 4 rooms ⚅ No smoking ⊟ AE, MC, V* ⊠◯ *BP.*

¢–$$$ 🏨 **Woodlands Hotel and Suites.** An official Colonial Williamsburg property with contemporary furnishings, this 300-room hotel is adjacent to the Huzzah restaurant and the visitor center complex. The lobby and breakfast area has an open fireplace. Suites come with refrigerators and microwaves, and all guest rooms have high-speed Internet. ⊠ *102 Visitor Center Dr., 23185* ☎ *757/229–1000 or 800/447–8679* 🖷 *757/ 565–8797* ⊕ *www.colonialwilliamsburg.com ➳ 204 rooms, 96 suites ⚅ Restaurant, pool, horseshoes, Ping-Pong, lobby lounge, playground ⊟ AE, D, DC, MC, V* ⊠◯ *CP.*

$$ 🏨 **The Fife and Drum Inn.** On the second floor of Merchant's Square and practically across the street from the historic district stands this family-run B&B (there's no elevator). Each room is stylishly decorated by the owner in a motif that spotlights an aspect of Williamsburg town history. Modern amenities include a hair dryer and in-room phones with voice mail. Rooms have either a shower or a combination tub/shower. Included in the rates are afternoon appetizers, homemade cookies, non-alcoholic beverages, and a full hot breakfast. ⊠ *441 Prince George St., 23185* ☎ *757/345–1776 or 888/838–1783* 🖷 *757/253–1675* ⊕ *www. fifeanddruminn.com ➳ 7 rooms, 2 suites ⚅ Cable TV, in-room VCR players, free parking ⊟ AE, D, DC, MC, V* ⊠◯ *BP.*

★ $$ 🏨 **Williamsburg Sampler Bed & Breakfast Inn.** Charming and hospitable, this redbrick inn near the historic district is modeled after a plantation-style house from the 1700s. Rooms have 18th- and 19th-century antiques, pewter pieces, four-poster beds, and pleasant views of the city. The suites are particularly inviting: each has a separate sitting room, French doors, and a porch overlooking gardens. There are no phones in the rooms, but local calls are free from the inn's foyer. ⊠ *922 Jamestown Rd., 23185* ☎ *757/253–0398 or 800/722–1169* 🖷 *757/253–2669* ⊕ *www. williamsburgsampler.com* 🛏 *4 rooms, 2 suites* ♿ *Dining room, exercise room, sauna; no smoking* ▤ *AE, D, DC, MC, V* ⍑ *BP.*

¢–$ ▦ **Howard Johnson's–Historic Area.** Not your typical chain hotel, this family-run franchise inn with washers and dryers on each floor, spacious guest rooms, and a friendly staff make this a good choice for families. Colonial furnishings, marble fireplaces, and high-back wooden chairs in the lobby lend the hotel some charm. Take time out in the pool or exercise room when you need a break from sightseeing. The Howard Johnson is 1 mi from Colonial Williamsburg. ⊠ *7135 Pocahontas Trail, U.S. Hwy. 60, 23185* ☎ *800/841–9100* 🖷 *757/220–3211* ⊕ *www. hojo.com* 🛏 *96 rooms, 4 suites* ♿ *Pool, gym, video game room, laundry facilities, concierge, business services* ▤ *AE, D, DC, MC, V* ⍑ *CP.*

¢–$ ▦ **Quality Inn Lord Paget.** Tall white columns front this modern motel. Eight rooms are accessed via stairs off the spacious lobby, which has Oriental carpets; others have parking at the front door. Some rooms have canopy beds. Refrigerators and microwaves are available for a fee. The property has a 2½-acre lake and lovely gardens. Newspapers and local phone calls are free. ⊠ *901 Capitol Landing Rd., 23185* ☎ *757/229–4444 or 800/537–2438* 🛏 *94 rooms* ♿ *Coffee shop, putting green, pool, dock, fishing, laundry service, no-smoking rooms* ▤ *AE, D, DC, MC, V* ⍑ *BP.*

$ ▦ **War Hill Inn.** This inn was designed by a Colonial Williamsburg architect to resemble a period structure: the two-story redbrick building at the center has two wood-frame wings. Inside are appropriate antiques and reproductions. The War Hill is inside a 32-acre operating cattle farm, 4 mi from the Colonial Williamsburg information center. Those in search of privacy may want one of the cottages or the first-floor suite (other rooms open onto a common hallway). ⊠ *4560 Long Hill Rd., 23188* ☎ *757/565–0248 or 800/743–0248* ⊕ *www.warhillinn.com* 🛏 *6 rooms, 2 cottages* ♿ *Cable TV* ▤ *MC, V* ⍑ *BP.*

¢–$ ▦ **Heritage Inn.** This comfortable three-story inn is decorated inside and out in Colonial style. Room furnishings include postered headboards, Colonial Williamsburg prints, and an armoire concealing a TV. Some quarters open directly onto the parking lot, but this is an unusually quiet, leafy site, and the pool is within a garden. An independent caterer serves breakfast in the restaurant. ⊠ *1324 Richmond Rd., 23185* ☎ *757/ 229–6220 or 800/782–3800* 🖷 *757/229–2774* 🛏 *54 rooms* ♿ *Pool, some pets allowed* ▤ *AE, D, DC, MC, V* ⍑ *CP.*

¢ ▦ **Governor Spottswood Motel.** This one-story redbrick motel has been extended gradually, section by section, since the 1950s. Furnishings reflect the influence of Colonial Williamsburg. In classic motel style, each room faces its parking space. There's lawn space and a sunken garden area for the swimming pool. Seven cottages sleep four to seven people, and 14 rooms have kitchens. It's a good value for the location. ⊠ *1508 Richmond Rd., 23185* ☎ *757/229–6444 or 800/368–1244* 🖷 *757/ 253–2410* ⊕ *www.govspottswood.com* 🛏 *78 rooms* ♿ *Pool, playground, laundry facilities* ▤ *AE, DC, MC, V.*

Nightlife & the Arts

Busch Gardens Williamsburg (✉ U.S. 60 ☎ 757/253–3350 ⊕ www. buschgardens.com) hosts popular song-and-dance shows (country, gospel, opera, German folk) in several theaters; in the largest, the 5,000-seat Royal Palace, pop stars often perform. **Music Theatre of Williamsburg** (✉ 3012 Richmond Rd. ☎ 757/564–0200 or 888/687–4220 ⊕ www.musictheater. com) offers family-oriented live country music and comedy. Shows run Monday through Saturday beginning at 8 PM. Well-known artists on tour play at the 10,000-seat **Phi Beta Kappa Hall** (✉ Jamestown Rd. entrance to campus ☎ 757/221–3340) at the College of William and Mary.

Sports & the Outdoors

AMUSEMENT PARKS
Busch Gardens Williamsburg, a 100-acre amusement and theme park, has more than 40 rides and six beautifully landscaped "countries" with re-creations of European and French Canadian hamlets. In addition to roller coasters, bumper cars, and water rides, the park has eight mainstage shows, a magical children's area, and a small walk-through nature preserve, where gray wolves are the highlight. Costumed actors add character to the theme areas, and two covered trains circle the park while cable-car gondolas pass overhead. ✉ *U.S. 60, 3 mi east of Williamsburg* ☎ *757/253–3350 or 800/343–7946* ⊕ *www.buschgardens.com* ✆ *$47; parking $7* ⊙ *Apr.–mid-May, Sat. 10–10, Sun. 10–7; mid-May–mid-June, Sun.–Fri. 10–7, Sat. 10–10; mid-June–July, daily 10–10; Aug., Sun.–Fri. 10–10, Sat. 10–midnight; Sept. and Oct., Fri. 10–6, weekends 10–7.*

At **Water Country USA,** the more than 30 water rides and attractions, live entertainment, shops, and restaurants have a colorful 1950s and '60s surf theme. The Meltdown is a four-person toboggan with 180-degree turns and a 76-foot drop. The Nitro Racer is a super-speed slide down a 382-foot drop into a big splash. The largest attraction is a 4,500-square-foot heated pool. ✉ *Rte. 199, 3 mi off I–64, Exit 242B* ☎ *757/253–3350 or 800/343–7946* ⊕ *www.4adventure.com* ✆ *$36* ⊙ *Mid-May, weekends 10–6; early–mid-June, daily 10–6; mid-June–mid-Aug., daily 10–8; mid–late Aug. daily 10–7; early Sept., daily 10–6; mid-Sept., weekends 10–6.*

GOLF
Colonial Williamsburg (☎ 757/220–7696 or 800/447–8679) operates three courses—the excellent 18-hole Golden Horseshoe Course; the 18-hole Golden Horseshoe Green; and the 9-hole Spottswood Course. **Kingsmill Resort** (✉ 1010 Kingsmill Rd. ☎ 757/253–3906), near Busch Gardens, has three 18-hole golf courses and a par-3, 9-hole course.

Shopping

Merchants Square, on the west end of Duke of Gloucester Street, has non-Colonial, upscale shops that include Laura Ashley, the Porcelain Collector of Williamsburg, and the J. Fenton Gallery. There's also Quilts Unlimited and the Campus Shop, which carries William and Mary gifts and clothing.

CRAFTS
Nine stores and shops in Colonial Williamsburg imitate those once run in the 1700s. Typical wares include silver tea services, jewelry, pottery, pewter and brass items, ironwork, tobacco and herbs, candles, hats, baskets, books, maps and prints, and baked goods. Two **crafts houses** sell approved reproductions of the antiques on display in the houses and

WILLIAMSBURG OUTLET SHOPPING

YOU CAN FIND many outlet malls less than 10 minutes' west of Colonial Williamsburg, in the tiny town of Lightfoot. If you're driving from Richmond to Williamsburg on I–64 take Exit 234 west to Lightfoot. When you reach U.S. 60 (Richmond Road), the outlets—both freestanding and in shopping centers—are on both sides of the road. Most outlet shops are open Monday–Saturday 10–9, Sunday 10–6. In January and February, some stores close weekdays at 6.

The **Williamsburg Pottery Factory** (✉ U.S. 60 W, Lightfoot ☎ 757/564–3326), an attraction in itself, has a parking area that's usually crammed with tour buses. Covering 200 acres, the enormous outlet store sells luggage, clothing, furniture, food and wine, china, crystal, and—its original commodity—pottery. Individual stores such as Pfaltzgraff and Banister Shoes are within the compound. At the **Candle Factory Outlet** (✉ 7521 Richmond Rd., Lightfoot ☎ 757/564–3354), you can watch candles being made.

The largest of the outlets, **Prime Outlets at Williamsburg** (✉ U.S. 60, Lightfoot ☎ 757/565–0702) has more than 85 stores. Liz Claiborne, Jones New York, Royal Doulton, L. L. Bean, Waterford-Wedgwood, Mikasa, Eddie Bauer, Tommy Hilfiger, Brooks Bros., Nike, Guess, Nautica, and Cole Haan are all here. It's also the country's only outlet for Lladro, known for its figurines.

The **Williamsburg Outlet Mall** (✉ U.S. 60 W, Lightfoot ☎ 888/746–7333) has more than 60 shops, including the Jockey Store, Linens 'n Things, Farberware, Levi's, and Bass.

Patriot Plaza (✉ 3032 Richmond Rd., Lightfoot ☎ 757/564–7570) has Lenox, Dansk, Prince Michel Wineshop, Villeroy & Boch, Polo Ralph Lauren, and other factory outlets.

---

museums. ✉ Craft House, Merchants Sq. ☎ 757/220–7747 ✉ Craft House Inn, S. England St. ☎ 757/220–7749.

Yorktown

 14 mi northeast of Colonial Williamsburg via Colonial Pkwy.

It was at Yorktown that the combined American and French forces surrounded Lord Cornwallis's British troops in 1781—this was the end to the Revolutionary War. In Yorktown today, as at Jamestown, two major attractions complement each other. Yorktown Battlefield, the historical site, is operated by the National Park Service; and Yorktown Victory Center, which has re-creations and informative exhibits, is operated by the state's Jamestown–Yorktown Foundation.

Yorktown remains a living community, although it's a small one. Route 238 leads into town, where along Main Street are preserved 18th-century buildings on a bluff overlooking the York River. Its quiet character stands out amid the theme park–like attractions of the area.

Settled in 1691, Yorktown had become a thriving tobacco port and a prosperous community of several hundred houses by the time of the Revolution. Nine buildings from that time still stand, some of them open to visitors. **Moore House,** where the terms of surrender were negotiated, and the elegant **Nelson House,** the residence of a Virginia governor (and a signer of the Declaration of Independence), are open for tours in summer and are part of the Yorktown Victory Center's entrance fee.

The **Swan Tavern,** a reconstruction of a 1722 structure, houses an antiques shop. **Grace Church,** built in 1697 and damaged in the War of 1812 and the Civil War, was rebuilt and has an active Episcopal congregation; its walls are made of native marl (a mixture of clay, sand, and limestone containing fragments of seashells). On Main Street, the **Somerwell House,** built before 1707, and the **Sessions House** (before 1699) are privately owned and closed to the public: they're the oldest houses in town. The latter was used as the Union's local headquarters during General George McClellan's Peninsula Campaign of the Civil War.

Yorktown Battlefield preserves the land where the British surrendered to American and French forces in 1781. The museum in the visitor center has on exhibit part of General George Washington's original field tent. Dioramas, illuminated maps, and a short movie about the battle make the sobering point that Washington's victory was hardly inevitable. A look around from the roof's observation deck can help you visualize the events of the campaign. Guided by an audio tour purchased from the gift shop ($3.95 for cassette, $4.95 for CD), you may explore the battlefield by car, stopping at the site of Washington's headquarters, a couple of crucial "redoubts" (breastworks dug into the ground), and the field where surrender took place. ⊠ *Rte. 238 off Colonial Pkwy.* ☎ *757/ 898–2410* ☜ *$5* ☼ *Visitor center daily 9–5.*

On the western edge of Yorktown Battlefield, the **Yorktown Victory Center** has wonderful exhibits and demonstrations that bring to life the American Revolution. Textual and graphic displays along the Road to Revolution walkway cover the principal events and personalities. The trail enters the main museum, where the story of Yorktown's critical role in the achievement of American independence is told. Life-size tableaux show 10 "witnesses," including an African-American patriot, a loyalist, a Native American leader, two Continental army soldiers, and the wife of a Virginia plantation owner. The exhibit galleries contain more than 500 period artifacts, including many recovered during underwater excavations of "Yorktown's Sunken Fleet" (British ships lost during the siege of 1781). Outdoors, in a Continental army encampment, interpreters costumed as soldiers and female auxiliaries reenact and discuss daily camp life. In another outdoor area, interpreters re-create 18th-century farm life. ⊠ *Rte. 238 off Colonial Pkwy.* ☎ *757/253–4838 or 888/593–4682* ⊕ *www.historyisfun.org* ☜ *$8.25; combination ticket for Yorktown Victory Center and Jamestown Settlement, $17* ☼ *June 15–Aug. 15, daily 9–6; Aug. 16–June 14, daily 9–5.*

FodorsChoice ★

Where to Stay & Eat

¢–$$ ✕ **Waterstreet Landing.** The fare runs to seafood, steaks, pizza, and sandwiches at this cream-color brick café across the street from the York River. There's also a bar here. ⊠ *114 Water St.* ☎ *757/887–5269* ▭ *MC, V.*

$–$$ 🏨 **Marl Inn.** Far from the crowds of Williamsburg and Jamestown, this white picket–fence inn is known for its quiet, relaxing setting and for the innkeepers' famous Crab Cake Benedict, served for breakfast. The inn is steeped in history: it's on the grounds of the last battle of the Revolution. Antique and 18th-century reproduction furnishings are inside. ✉ *220 Church St., 23690* ☎ *757/898–3859 or 800/799–6207* ⊕ *www. marlinnbandb.com* 🛏 *1 room, 3 suites* ⚹ *Cable TV, bicycles, some pets allowed* ⊟ *AE, MC, V* ❑ *BP.*

¢–$ 🏨 **Duke of York Motel.** All rooms in this classic 1960s motel face the water and are only a few steps from a public beach. The furnishings include quilted bedspreads and Queen Anne–style reproduction wood furniture. The motel also has a swimming pool and a restaurant that serves breakfast and lunch daily. ✉ *508 Water St., 23690* ☎ *757/898–3232* 🖷 *757/ 898–5922* ⊕ *www.dukeofyorkmotel.com* 🛏 *57 rooms* ⚹ *Restaurant, pool* ⊟ *AE, D, DC, MC, V.*

Charles City County

35 mi northwest of Colonial Williamsburg via Rte. 5.

Colonists founded Charles City County in 1616. Today you can get a taste of those early days by following Route 5 on its scenic route, parallel to the James River, past nine plantations—some of which are now bed-and-breakfasts.

㉑ **Evelynton Plantation,** originally part of Westover estate, is believed to have been part of the dowry of William Byrd II's eldest daughter, Evelyn. However, her father refused to allow her to wed her favorite suitor, and she never married. The plantation was purchased in 1846 by the Ruffin family, which had settled on the south shore of the James River in the 1650s. Edmund Ruffin, a celebrated agronomist prior to the Civil War, was a strident secessionist who fired the first shot at Fort Sumter. Evelynton was the scene of fierce skirmishes during the 1862 Peninsula Campaign; the manor house and outbuildings were destroyed during the war.

The present Colonial Revival–style house on a hill at the end of a cedar-and-dogwood alley was built two generations later, using 250-year-old brick, under the direction of the architect Duncan Lee. The house is furnished with 18th-century English and American antiques and has a handsomely landscaped lawn and gardens. Since it opened to the public in 1986, it has earned a reputation for artistic, abundant flower arrangements in every season. The house, gardens, and grounds are part of a 2,500-acre working plantation still operated by Ruffin descendants. Afternoon tea is held on the terrace during Historic Garden Week and the Christmas season. Flower arranging seminars are held three times a year; call for details. ✉ *Rte. 5, 6701 John Tyler Memorial Hwy., Charles City* ☎ *804/829–5075 or 800/473–5075* 🎟 *$10.50* ⊙ *Daily 9–5.*

㉒ **Westover** was built in 1735 by Colonel William Byrd II (1674–1744), an American aristocrat who spent much of his time and money in London. He was in Virginia frequently enough to serve in both the upper and lower houses of the Colonial legislature at Williamsburg and to write one of the first travel books about the region (as well as a notorious secret diary, a frank account of plantation life and Colonial politics). Byrd lived here with his beloved library of 4,000 volumes. The house, celebrated for its moldings and carvings, is open only during Garden Week in late April. The grounds are arrayed with tulip poplars at least 100 years old, and gardens of roses and other flowers are well tended. Three wrought-iron gates, imported from England by the colonel, are mounted on posts topped by figures of eagles with spread wings. Byrd's grave is here, inscribed with the eloquent, immodest, lengthy, and apt epitaph he composed for himself. ⊠ *Rte. 5, 7000 Westover Rd., Charles City* ☎ *804/829–2882* ☜ *$2* ☉ *Grounds daily 9–6, house daily in late Apr.; call for hours.*

② Virginians say that the first Thanksgiving was celebrated at **Berkeley** on December 14, 1619, not in Massachusetts in 1621. This plantation was the birthplace of Benjamin Harrison, a signer of the Declaration of Independence, and of William Henry Harrison, who was briefly president in 1841. Throughout the Civil War, the Union general George McClellan used Berkeley as headquarters; during his tenure, his subordinate general Daniel Butterfield composed the melody for taps on the premises. The brick Georgian house, built in 1726, has been carefully restored and furnished with period antiques following a period of disrepair after the Civil War. The gardens are in excellent condition, particularly the boxwood hedges. ⊠ *Rte. 5, 12602 Harrison Landing Rd., Charles City* ☎ *804/829–6018* ⊕ *www.berkeleyplantation.com* ☜ *$10.50* ☉ *Daily 9–5; last tour 4:30.*

★ ② **Shirley,** the oldest plantation in Virginia, has been occupied by a single family, the Carters, for 10 generations. Their claim to the land goes back to 1660, when it was settled by a relative, Edward Hill. Robert E. Lee's mother was born here, and the Carters seem to be related to every notable Virginia family from the Colonial and antebellum periods. The approach to the elegant 1723 Georgian manor is dramatic: the house stands at the end of a drive lined by towering Lombardy poplars. Inside, the hall staircase rises for three stories with no visible support. Family silver is on display, ancestral portraits are hung throughout, and rare books line the shelves. ⊠ *501 Shirley Plantation Rd., Charles City* ☎ *804/829–5121* ⊕ *www.shirleyplantation.com* ☜ *$10.50* ☉ *Daily 9–5; last tour 4:45.*

Where to Stay & Eat

★ $$–$$$ ✕ **Indian Fields Tavern.** Housed in a restored farmhouse, this restaurant specializes in southern dishes, especially regional specialties such as crab cakes and bread pudding. Other main dishes include Tidewater shellfish in a tomato-and-crab broth and a veal porterhouse chop. In season you can eat on the screened porch overlooking gardens. There's brunch on Sunday. ⊠ *9220 John Tyler Memorial Hwy.* ☎ *804/829–5004* ⊕ *www.indianfields.com* ⊟ AE, D, MC, V.

$$ ▥ **Edgewood Plantation.** Three stories high, the Victorian Edgewood sits behind a porch on 5 largely wooded acres, ½ mi west of Berkeley Plantation and less than an hour from Williamsburg. The house includes a graceful three-story staircase and 10 fireplaces (four in bedrooms) and is furnished with an overabundance of antiques and country crafts. Rooms have 18th- and 19th-century canopied king or queen beds and

Oriental rugs; period clothing is used as decoration. Breakfast is served in the formal dining room. Two gazebos sit in the English garden. Even if you don't stay here, you can take a tour of this 1849 Victorian wood house (daily, house $8, grounds $2). ⊠ *Rte. 5, 4800 John Tyler Memorial Hwy., Charles City 23030* ☎ *804/829–2962 or 800/296–3343* 🖷 *804/829–2962* 🛏 *8 rooms* ⚐ *Dining room, some refrigerators, pool; no room phones* ▤ *AE, MC, V* ⧉ *BP.*

★ $$ ⊡ **North Bend Plantation Bed & Breakfast.** The road to this historic home winds past trailer homes and cottages before a gravel road turns to the left between farm fields. As a working farm, it stands out from similar B&Bs. The 1819 Greek Revival home was built for Sarah Harrison, sister of President William Henry Harrison, by her husband John Minge. Inside, antebellum-era antiques, as well as Civil War maps and artifacts decorate every room. Room amenities include robes and TVs. The southern breakfast here might include buttermilk biscuits, Smithfield ham, apple butter, bacon, and grits, along with strong coffee. ⊠ *12200 Weyanoke Rd., Box 13A, Charles City 23030* ☎ *804/829–5176* 🖷 *804/ 829–6828* 🛏 *4 rooms, 1 suite* ⚐ *In-room VCR players, pool, bicycles, croquet, horseshoes; no room phones* ▤ *MC, V* ⧉ *BP.*

HAMPTON ROADS AREA

The region known today as the Hampton Roads Area is made up of not only the large natural harbor, into which five rivers flow, but of the peninsula to the north that extends southeast from Williamsburg, and the Tidewater area between the mouth of the harbor and the Atlantic Ocean. On the peninsula are the cities of Newport News and Hampton; to the south and east are Norfolk, Portsmouth, Chesapeake, and Virginia Beach. These cities have been shaped by their proximity to the Chesapeake Bay and the rivers that empty into it, either as ports and shipbuilding centers or, in the case of Virginia Beach, as a hugely popular beach town. Hampton and Norfolk are the "old" cities of this area; recent development and revival efforts have made them worthy of a second look.

During the Civil War, the Union waged its thwarted 1862 Peninsula Campaign here. General George McClellan planned to land his troops on the peninsula in March of 1862 with the help of the navy, and then press westward to the Confederate capital of Richmond. Naval forces on the York and James rivers would protect the advancing army. However, beginning with the blockade that the ironclad CSS *Virginia* (formerly the USS *Merrimack*) held on the James until May, events and Confederates conspired to lengthen and foil the campaign.

Numbers in the margin correspond to points of interest on the Hampton Roads Area map.

Newport News

㉕ *23 mi southeast of Williamsburg.*

Newport News stretches for almost 35 mi along the James River from near Williamsburg to Hampton Roads. Known mostly for its struggling

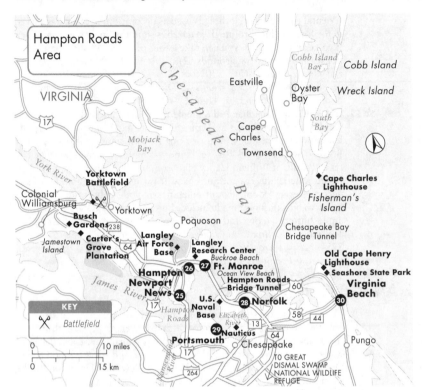

shipbuilding industry, the city is largely residential and is a suburb for both Williamsburg and the Tidewater area. Newport News has a number of Civil War battle sites and a splendid municipal park. The fabulous Mariners' Museum may be the best museum in the state. Close by, the Virginia Living Museum is a pleasant zoo experience for kids. The city's small, but busy, airport is convenient to both Williamsburg and the beach, making it a good base from which to visit both areas.

Newport News first appeared in the Virginia Company's records in 1619. It was probably named after Christopher Newport, captain of the *Susan Constant,* largest of the three ships in the company of Captain John Smith that landed at Jamestown in 1607. Newport News Shipbuilding is one of the largest privately owned shipyards in the world, and with approximately 18,000 employees, probably the second-largest employer in Virginia. It's the only shipyard in the country capable of building nuclear aircraft carriers.

Built in 1769 by Col. William Harwood Jr., the white frame **Endview Plantation** played a role in three wars. The Revolutionary War brought 3,000 militiamen to its lands; it was used as a training ground during the War of 1812; and both sides used it as a hospital during the Civil War. Guided tours take 30 minutes. ⊠ *362 Yorktown Rd., Exit 247 off*

I–64, 23603 ☎ *757/887–1862* ⊕ *www.endview.org* ✉ *$6* ☉ *Apr.–Dec., Mon. and Wed.–Sat. 10–4, Sun. 1–5.*

The Italianate redbrick **Lee Hall Mansion,** built in 1858 by affluent planter Richard Decauter Lee, was on the front lines of the Civil War 1862 Peninsula Campaign. A ladies' parlor, dining room, music room, and two bedrooms have been restored to their 1862 appearance, and so has the room by Maj. Gen. John B. Magruder's headquarters. Inside an exhibit gallery are a tablecloth from the USS *Monitor* and items recovered from the Peninsula Campaign. ⊠ *163 Yorktown Rd., Exit 247 off I–64* ☎ *757/ 888–3371* ⊕ *www.leehall.org* ✉ *$5* ☉ *Apr.–Dec., Mon. and Wed.–Sat. 10–4, Sun. 1–5.*

★ ℭ A world history of seagoing vessels and the people who sailed them occupies the outstanding **Mariners' Museum,** inside a 550-acre park. An alliance between the museum and the South Street Seaport Museum in New York City allows the two institutions to share collections, exhibitions, and educational programs. Many of the authentic scale models hand-carved by August Crabtree are so tiny that you must view them through magnifying glasses; they portray shipbuilding accomplishments from ancient Egypt to 19th-century Britain. Among the more than 50 full-size craft on display are a Native American bark canoe, a sailing yacht, a speedboat, a gondola, a Coast Guard cutter, and a Chinese sampan. In separate galleries you can often watch the progress of a boat under construction; view ornate and sometimes huge figureheads; examine the watermen's culture of the Chesapeake Bay; and learn about the history of the U.S. Navy.

Such nautical gear as trail boards, rudder heads, and paddle boxes are on display, along with a selection of the intricate whale-tusk carvings called scrimshaw. Photographs and paintings recount naval history and the story of private-sector seafaring. The museum also holds artifacts from the RMS *Titanic* and the ironclad USS *Monitor,* which served in the 1862 Peninsula Campaign and today lies off the coast of North Carolina. You can see the gigantic turret and its cannons by climbing up platforms and looking down into the tank of water that preserves the artifacts. An indoor exhibit displays the anchor, distress lantern, steering wheel, iron plates, original letters, and silverware from the CSS *Virginia.* Under construction for a planned 2007 opening is the Monitor Center, which will house materials, research, and programming related to the history of the USS *Monitor* and the CSS *Virginia.* ⊠ *100 Museum Dr., I–64, Exit 258A* ☎ *757/595–0368 or 800/581–7245* ⊕ *www. mariner.org* ✉ *$8* ☉ *Daily 10–5.*

ℭ The **Peninsula Fine Arts Center** is a community-supported arts facility with changing exhibitions of visual arts. There's a special "Hands on for Kids" program. ⊠ *101 Museum Dr., I–64, Exit 258A* ☎ *757/596–8175* ⊕ *www.pfac-va.org* ✉ *$4* ☉ *Tues.–Sat. 10–5, Sun. 1–5.*

The **Virginia War Museum** houses more than 60,000 artifacts from all over the world. The collection includes a graffiti-covered section of the Berlin Wall, a Civil War blockade runner's uniform, weapons, uniforms, wartime posters, photographs, and other memorabilia. It traces military history from 1775 to the Gulf War and includes an outdoor exhibition of seven tanks and cannons, and the history of African-Americans and women in the military. Several war memorials are on the grounds of Huntington Park. An annual "Christmas in the Field" Civil War reenactment is performed the second weekend of December. ⊠ *9285 Warwick Blvd., Rte. 60* ☎ *757/247–8523* ⊕ *www.warmuseum. org* ⊠ *$5* ☉ *Mon.–Sat. 9–5, Sun. 1–5.*

The **U.S. Army Transportation Museum,** at Fort Eustis, traces the history of army transportation by land, sea, and air, beginning with the Revolutionary War era. More than 90 vehicles, including experimental craft and numerous locomotives and trains dating to the 1800s, are on display. The museum's Korean War and World War II–era tanks can be toured inside and out. ⊠ *Besson Hall, Bldg. 300, I-64, Exit 250A* ☎ *757/878–1115* ⊠ *Free* ☉ *Tues.–Sun. 9–4:30.*

☾ At the **Virginia Living Museum,** animals indigenous to the region live in wild or simulated lakefront habitats that allow you to observe their natural behavior. A trail leads to the water's edge, where otters and blue herons can be spotted, then upland past de-scented skunks, lame bald eagles (wounded by hunters), and cute but unpettable bobcats. A 40-foot-tall outdoor aviary re-creates a wetlands habitat. Indoors, the Planetarium (children under three not admitted) offers more celestial sights; call for show times. The tacky Safari minigolf site may be fun for children, but it lessens the splendor of the environment. ⊠ *524 J. Clyde Morris Blvd.* ☎ *757/595–1900* ⊠ *Museum $9, planetarium $3, combination ticket $11* ☉ *Memorial Day–Labor Day, daily 9–6; Labor Day–Memorial Day, Mon.–Sat. 9–5, Sun. noon–5.*

Where to Stay & Eat

$–$$ ▥ **Ramada Inn and Conference Center.** This Ramada's contemporary exterior is a takeoff of the typical column porticos of nearby plantation homes. The rooms have patterned spreads and wallpaper above the chair rails. It's in a good location, making it a good alternative to the high-price summer rates of Williamsburg hotels. ⊠ *950 J. Clyde Morris Blvd., Exit 258 off I-64, 23601* ☎ *757/599–4460 or 800/841–1112* 🖷 *757/599–4336* ⊕ *www.ramada.com* ➷ *149 rooms* ♿ *Restaurant, in-room data ports, indoor pool, gym, business services, airport shuttle, no-smoking rooms* ▤ *AE, D, DC, MC, V.*

★ $ ✕ **Bill's Seafood House.** This reasonably priced seafood restaurant is a favorite with locals. The interior is simple—café curtains, tubular chairs, wood-grain Formica tables and nautical paintings. Seafood platters (broiled or fried) and other seafood dishes arrive with hush puppies and a choice of sides. For the landlubber, rib-eye steaks, chicken strips, and homemade pork barbecue are on the menu. No alcohol is served. ⊠ *10900 Warwick Blvd., U.S. Hwy. 60* ☎ *757/595–4320* ▤ *No credit cards* ☉ *No lunch Sat.–Wed. No dinner Sun.*

★ $ ▥ **Hilton Garden Inn Newport News.** New in July 2004, this light and airy motel is within walking distance of a mall, restaurants, and movie theaters. Room amenities include free high-speed Internet access, a large work desk, irons, ironing boards, and coffeemakers. ⊠ *180 Regal Way, Exit*

256B (Victory Blvd.), right at Commonwealth Dr. then right on Regal Way ☎ *757/947–1080* 🖷 *757/947–1081* ⊕ *http://hiltongardeninn. hilton.com* ⟿ *122 rooms* ⚭ *Restaurant, microwaves, refrigerators, indoor pool, gym, spa, dry cleaning, laundry services, Internet, business services, meeting rooms, no-smoking rooms* ⊟ *AE, D, DC, MC, V.*

★ $ ✕🖾 **Omni Newport News Hotel.** The burgundy, green, and gold color scheme of the lobby carries over to the guest rooms, which look out on the indoor pool below. Rooms have mahogany furnishings, granite vanities, desks, and sofas. Mitty's Ristorante and Piano Lounge ($–$$$) serves regional Italian cuisine and local seafood, with exceptional homemade pasta and veal dishes. Specialties include ziti with broccoli and shrimp Capri (shrimp paired with spinach and fresh Italian herbs). To reach the hotel, take Exit 258A off I–64 and make the first right; turn right at the hotel sign. ⊠ *1000 Omni Blvd., 23606* ☎ *757/873–6664 or 800/873–6664* 🖷 *757/873–1732* ⊕ *www.omnihotels.com* ⟿ *183 rooms, 4 suites* ⚭ *Restaurant, in-room data ports, indoor pool, gym, sauna, bar, lobby lounge, nightclub, laundry facilities, business services, meeting rooms, no-smoking rooms* ⊟ *AE, D, DC, MC, V.*

¢–$ 🖾 **Comfort Inn.** This well-maintained, three-story redbrick inn is adjacent to Patrick Henry Mall and several restaurants. Amenities include health-club privileges as well as 24-hour coffee served in the large lobby, which is decorated with Federal-style furnishings. Refrigerators and microwaves are available for a fee. ⊠ *12330 Jefferson Ave., Exit 255A off I–64 and south on Clarie La., 23602* ☎ *757/249–0200 or 800/368–2477* 🖷 *757/249–4736* ⟿ *124 rooms* ⚭ *In-room data ports, pool, laundry facilities, meeting rooms, no-smoking rooms* ⊟ *AE, D, DC, MC, V* ⵙ *CP.*

Sports & the Outdoors

FISHING & **BOATING** Around Newport News you can expect excellent catches of striper, flounder, and the occasional catfish. The **Mariners' Museum** (⊠ 100 Museum Dr. ☎ 757/591–7799 ⊕ www.mariner.org) rents boats for use on Lake Maury, which is on the museum's grounds. The lake is open for fishing in spring and summer. Encircling the lake is the 5 mi Noland Trail.

The **James River Bridge Fishing Pier** (☎ 757/247–0364) is open year-round; call for hours.

GOLF **Newport News Golf Club at Deer Run** (⊠PU–901 Clubhouse Way, Exit 250B off I–64 ☎ 757/886–7925 ⊕ www.nngolfclub.com) has two par-72, 18-hole courses within Newport News Park. Greens fees are about $32.

Kiln Creek Golf Club and Resort (⊠ 1003 Brick Kiln Blvd., Exit 255B off I–64 ☎ 757/988–3222 ⊕ www.kilncreekgolf.com) has one 27-hole championship course. Greens fees are $48–$58.

Hampton

 5 mi north of Newport News, 16 mi northwest of Norfolk.

Founded in 1610, Hampton is the oldest continuously existing English-speaking settlement in the United States. It also holds the country's first aviation research facility, NASA Langley Research Center. The center was headquarters for the first manned space program in the United States: Astronauts for the *Mercury* and *Apollo* missions trained here.

Hampton was one of Virginia's major Colonial cities. In 1718 the pirate William Teach (better known as Blackbeard) was killed by Virginia sailors in a battle off North Carolina. As a warning to other pirates, the sailors brought his head back and mounted it on a pole at the entrance to the Hampton River (now Blackbeard Point, a residential area).

The city has been partially destroyed three times: by the British during the Revolution and again during the War of 1812, then by Confederates preempting Union invaders during the Civil War. Since the mid-1990s, Hampton has been undergoing a face-lift. It hosts many summer concerts and family festivals.

The **Virginia Air and Space Center** traces the history of flight and space exploration. The nine-story, futuristic, $30 million center is the official repository of the NASA Langley Research Center. Its space artifacts include a 3-billion-year-old moon rock, the *Apollo 12* command capsule, and a lunar lander. The center also holds a dozen full-size aircraft, southeast Virginia's only IMAX theater, and hands-on exhibits that let you see yourself as an astronaut. ✉ *Downtown Waterfront, 600 Settlers Landing Rd., I–64, Exit 267* ☎ *757/727–0800* ⊕ *www.vasc.org* ▤ *Space Center $8.50, IMAX movie $7.50, Space Center and 1 IMAX movie $12* ☉ *Memorial Day–Labor Day, Mon.–Wed. 10–5, Thurs.–Sun. 10–7; Labor Day–Memorial Day, Mon.–Sat. 10–5, Sun. noon–5.*

★ ☺ Once inside the Virginia Air and Space Center, the **Hampton History Museum** has moved into its own site a few blocks away. Encompassing 10 galleries of permanent and changing exhibits, the museum depicts the area's colorful history through archaeological and audiovisual exhibitions that include partial reproductions of Colonial buildings. Full-scale reproductions of the gun turret of the USS *Monitor* and a portion of the CSS *Virginia* show how the two ironclads changed the course of naval history at the start of the 1862 Peninsula Campaign. ✉ *120 Old Hampton La.* ☎ *757/727–1610* ⊕ *www.hampton.va.us/history_museum* ▤ *$5* ☉ *Mon.–Sat. 10–5, Sun. 1–5.*

In a waterfront park near the Virginia Air and Space Center is the **Hampton Carousel.** Its prancing steeds and bright-color chariots carry riders round and round to the tunes of carnival music. Expert artisans have meticulously restored the 1920 carousel, which was a fixture at the city's former Buckroe Beach Amusement Park for 60 years. ✉ *602 Settlers Landing Rd.* ☎ *757/727–6381* ▤ *$1, 50 cents with ticket to Virginia Air and Space Center* ☉ *May–Sept., Mon.–Wed. noon–5, Thurs.–Sun. noon–7; call for fall and winter hours.*

Little of early Hampton survived the shellings and conflicts of the past, but the brick walls of **St. John's Church** (1728) have. Today a stained-glass window honors Pocahontas, the Native American princess who is said to have saved the life of Captain John Smith in 1608. The communion silver on display, made in London in 1618, is the oldest such service still used in this country. The parish, founded in the same year as the city (1610), also claims to be the oldest in continuous service in

America. You may listen to a taped interpretation or take a guided tour (by arrangement) and visit a small museum in the parish house. ⊠ *100 W. Queens Way* ☎ *757/722–2567* ⊕ *www.stjohnshampton.org* ⊠ *Free* ☉ *Weekdays 9–3, Sat. 9–noon.*

Hampton University was founded in 1868 as a freedmen's school, and ever since has had a distinguished history as an institution of higher education for African-Americans. Booker T. Washington was an early graduate. The **Hampton University Museum,** on the riverfront campus, is notable for its extensive and diverse collection of African art, which includes 2,000 pieces from 87 ethnic groups and cultures. Other valuable holdings include Harlem Renaissance paintings, Native American artwork and crafts, and art from Oceania. ⊠ *Museum, Huntington Bldg., off Tyler St.; I–64, Exit 267, to campus* ☎ *757/727–5308* ⊕ *www. hamptonu.edu* ⊠ *Free* ☉ *Weekdays 8–5, Sat. noon–4.*

Where to Stay & Eat

$$$ ✕**Captain George's.** Although you can order steaks off the à la carte menu, the main pull here is the 70-item, all-you-can-eat buffet of fried, steamed, and broiled seafood. Highlights are steamed Alaskan crab legs, steamed shrimp with Old Bay seasoning, broiled flounder, steamed mussels, and she-crab soup. Among the 15 desserts are baklava and five fruit cobblers. A mural of the Chesapeake Bay dominates the largest of four dining rooms, which has tables with tops embedded with seashells. ⊠ *2710 W. Mercury Blvd., Exit 263 south off I–64* ☎ *757/826–1435* ⊟ *AE, MC, V* ☉ *No lunch Mon.–Sat.*

$$–$$$ ✕**The Grate Steak.** Farm implements and unfinished pine walls decorate the four dining rooms, which are casual and boisterous. You may choose your own steak and then grill it yourself on a huge barbecue grill. The menu also includes fried shrimp, grilled tuna, and salad bars. Prime rib, served on the bone if you like, is slowly roasted by a professional chef. ⊠ *1934 Coliseum Dr.* ☎ *757/827–1886* ⊟ *AE, D, DC, MC, V* ☉ *No lunch.*

$$–$$$ ✕**Pier 21.** Overlooking the Hampton marina inside the Radisson Hotel Hampton is this ship-shape restaurant serving three meals daily plus Sunday brunch. The contemporary decor is carried out in forest green, brass, and natural woods. The all-you-can-eat salad, soup, and pasta bar at lunch is a good value at $5.95 ($8.95 including pasta). Sunday brunch is $14.95. Main dishes at dinner include halibut, mahi mahi, surf and turf, steaks, and pasta. ⊠ *700 Settlers Landing Rd.* ☎ *757/727–9700* ⊟ *AE, D, DC, MC, V.*

¢–$ ✕**The Grey Goose Tearoom.** You're greeted by an enticing aroma and a gift shop with tea-related items when you enter this cozy room decorated with Victorian tea-party prints in gilded frames, antique teapots, and knickknacks. Brunswick stew, creamy Hampton blue-crab soup, and biscuits are permanent fixtures on the "everything-homemade" menu, and daily specials, such as chicken and dumplings, are posted on the wall. Desserts are especially good, but avoid the canned fruit salad on iceberg lettuce. The tearoom is open for lunch daily and some weekend nights for "Dinnertainment," during which local theater players and singers perform. ⊠ *1101–A W. Queens Way* ☎ *757/723–7978* ⊟ *AE, D, DC, MC, V* ☉ *Closed Sun.*

$-$$$ 🏨 **Radisson Hotel Hampton.** The nine-story Radisson has the premier location in town, right at a marina and a block away from the Virginia Air and Space Center. Most rooms look over the harbor or the handsome plaza in front of the space center. Guest rooms have an autumn color scheme with bleached wood furniture, a desk, and an easy chair. Amenities include hair dryers, irons, ironing boards, and coffeemakers. ✉ *700 Settlers Landing Rd., 23669* ☎ *757/727–9700 or 800/333–3333* 🖷 *757/722–4557* ⊕ *www.radisson.com* ⇌ *172 rooms* ⟜ *Restaurant, café, in-room data ports, refrigerators, pool, gym, bar, dataport* ▭ *AE, D, DC, MC, V.*

$-$$ 🏨 **Courtyard by Marriott.** The smell of homemade chocolate cookies greets you Monday through Thursday at the front desk of this modern hotel, where the chef refills a bottomless basket. As the naval items on the walls suggest, this Marriott takes in the local influence. The pool is set amid landscaped grounds. The restaurant serves breakfast only. ✉ *1917 Coliseum Dr., 23666* ☎ *757/838–3300* 🖷 *757/838–6387* ⊕ *www.courtyard.com* ⇌ *146 rooms* ⟜ *Restaurant, cable TV, pool, health club, dry cleaning, laundry service* ▭ *AE, D, DC, MC, V.*

$-$$ 🏨 **Holiday Inn Hampton.** Halfway between Colonial Williamsburg and Virginia Beach, this complex of buildings stands on 13 beautifully landscaped acres. About half the rooms have a pink-and-green color scheme; others have a darker look, with cherrywood dressers and tables. Many have sofas. Some rooms overlook the indoor pool in the atrium, and others have doors that open, motel-style, onto the parking lot. ✉ *1815 W. Mercury Blvd., 23666* ☎ *757/838–0200 or 800/842–9370* 🖷 *757/838–4964* ⊕ *www.sixcontinentshotels.com* ⇌ *320 rooms* ⟜ *Restaurant, 2 pools (1 indoor), gym, sauna, bar, convention center* ▭ *AE, D, DC, MC, V.*

Sports & the Outdoors

FISHING **Venture Inn Charters** (✉ 766 Settlers Landing Rd. ☎ 757/850–8960 or 800/853–5002) organizes half- and full-day charter trips from April to December, leaving from the Hampton Downtown Public Piers. The fishing excursions turn up spot, croaker, flounder, gray trout, and striped bass.

SPECTATOR **Langley Speedway** (✉ 3165 N. Armistead Ave. ☎ 757/865–1100) has
SPORTS the NASCAR Weekly Racing Series from April through October. Its nightly races cost $12.

Ft. Monroe

❷⁷ *Inside Hampton, at the end of Mercury Blvd.*

The channel between Chesapeake Bay and Hampton Roads is the "mouth" of Hampton Roads. On the north side of this passage is Hampton's Ft. Monroe, built in stages between 1819 and 1834. The largest stone fort in the country, it's also the only one still in operation to be enclosed by a moat. Robert E. Lee and Edgar Allan Poe served here in the antebellum years, and it remained a Union stronghold in Confederate territory throughout the Civil War. After the war, Confederate president Jefferson Davis was imprisoned for a time in one of the fort's casemates (a chamber in the wall); his cell and adjacent casemates now house the Casemate Museum. Exhibits of weapons, uniforms, models, drawings, and extensive Civil War relics retell the fort's history, depict coastal artillery activities, and describe the military lifestyle through the Civil War years. ⊠ *Rte. 258, Mercury Blvd.* ☎ *757/788–3391* ⊠ *Free* ⊙ *Daily 10:30–4:30.*

Norfolk

❷ *16 mi southeast of Hampton.*

Norfolk is reached from the peninsula by the Hampton Roads Bridge-Tunnel (I–64) as well as Route 460. There's plenty to see in this old navy town, but the sites are spread out. Like many other old Southern towns, Norfolk has undergone a renaissance, one that's especially visible in the charming shops and cafés in the historic village of Ghent.

The springtime Azalea Festival is one highlight of the lovely 155-acre **Norfolk Botanical Garden** on the eastern edge of the city. Besides growing an abundance of azaleas, rhododendrons, and camellias, the garden has a fragrance garden for the blind, with identification labels in Braille. A delicately landscaped Japanese garden has trees native to that country, including unusual strains of cherry and maple. From mid-March to October, boats and trams carry you along routes to view seasonal plants and flowers, including 4,000 varieties of roses on 3½ acres. Year-round, you can stroll 12 mi of paths. Eleven marble statues of famous artists, carved in the late 19th century by Moses Ezekiel, enhance the natural beauty of the gardens. The lakeside is ideal for picnics. ⊠ *6700 Azalea Garden Rd.* ☎ *757/441–5831* ⊕ *www.norfolkbotanicalgarden.org* ⊠ *Garden $6, boat tours $3* ⊙ *Mid-Apr.–mid-Oct., daily 9–7; mid-Oct.–mid-Apr., daily 9–5.*

Occupying a 16th-century English Tudor–style house that was reproduced by a textile tycoon around 1900, the **Hermitage Foundation Museum** contains the largest privately owned collection of Asian art in the United States. Ivory and jade carvings, ancient bronzes, and a 1,400-year-old marble Buddha from China are all here. The decorative-art collections include Tiffany glass, Persian rugs, and furniture from the Middle East, India, Europe, and America. You can picnic on the grounds along the Lafayette River. ⊠ *7637 N. Shore Rd.* ☎ *757/423–2052* ⊕ *www.hermitagefoundation.org* ⊠ *$5* ⊙ *Mon.–Sat. 10–5, Sun. 1–5.*

★ By any standard the **Chrysler Museum of Art** downtown qualifies as one of America's major art museums. The permanent collection includes works by Rubens, Gainsborough, Renoir, Picasso, van Gogh, Andy Warhol, and Pollock—a list that suggests the breadth available here. Classical and pre-Columbian civilizations are also represented. The decorative-arts collection includes exquisite English porcelain and art nouveau furnishings. Every American glassmaker between 1825 and 1950 is represented in the glass collection, which has an extensive number of Tiffany pieces, as well as artifacts from ancient Rome and the Near and Far East. ⊠ *245 W. Olney Rd.* ☎ *757/664–6200* ⊕ *www.chrysler.org* ⊠ *$7; Wed. by voluntary contribution* ⊙ *May–Oct., Wed. 10–9, Thurs.–Sat. 10–5, Sun. 1–5, Tues. 10–2; Nov.–Apr., Wed. 10–9, Thurs.–Sat. 10–5, Sun. 1–5* ⊙ *Closed Mon.*

The federal redbrick **Moses Myers House,** built by its namesake in 1792, is exceptional, and not just for its elegance. In the long dining room, a wood writing desk holds a collection of fine china—and a set of silver kiddush cups (Moses Myers was Norfolk's first permanent Jewish resident). A transplanted New Yorker, Myers made his fortune in Norfolk in shipping, then served as a diplomat and a customhouse officer. His grandson married James Madison's grandniece, his great-grandson served as mayor, and the family kept the house for five generations. The furnishings, 70% of them original, include family portraits by Gilbert Stuart and Thomas Sully. ⊠ *331 Bank St.* ☎ *757/333–1085* ⊕ *www. chrysler.org/houses.asp* ⬚ *$5* ⊘ *Wed.–Sat. 10–4, Sun. 1–4.*

The **Douglas MacArthur Memorial** is the burial place of the war hero. An "army brat" with no hometown, General MacArthur (1880–1964) designated this navy town as the site for a monument to himself because it was his mother's birthplace—and perhaps because no one as well known as he had a monument nearby (MacArthur's ego was formidable). In the rotunda of the old City Hall, converted according to MacArthur's design, is the mausoleum; 11 adjoining galleries house mementos of MacArthur's career, including his signature corncob pipe and the Japanese instruments of surrender that concluded World War II. Next door the general's staff car is on display, and a 24-minute biography is shown. ⊠ *Bank St. and City Hall Ave.* ☎ *757/441–2965* ⊕ *www. macarthurmemorial.org* ⬚ *By donation* ⊘ *Mon.–Sat. 10–5, Sun. 11–5.*

St. Paul's Church, constructed in 1739, was the only building in town to survive the bombardment and conflagration of New Year's Day 1776; a cannonball fired by the British fleet remains embedded in the southeastern wall. An earlier church had been built on this site in 1641, and the churchyard contains graves dating from the 17th century. ⊠ *St. Paul's Blvd. and City Hall Ave.* ☎ *757/627–4353* ⬚ *By donation* ⊘ *Tues.–Fri. 10–4.*

The **Waterside Festival Hall** is a mixture of stores and entertainment. Waterside has become the nightlife hot spot of the area, with 11 restaurants and bars, including Jillian's and Bar Norfolk. Musical performances and temporary art exhibitions take place in the public spaces, and there are restaurants and plenty of places to snack as you shop. The **Hampton Roads Transit kiosk** (☎ 757/623–3222) is a source of visitor information and the launching point for tours of the city. ⊠ *Waterfront, 333 Waterside Dr.* ⊕ *www.watersidemarketplace.com.*

The **Norfolk Naval Station,** on the northern edge of the city, is an impressive sight, sometimes berthing as many as 100 ships of the Atlantic Fleet. The base was built on the site of the Jamestown Exposition of 1907: many of the original buildings survive and are still in use. Several large aircraft carriers, built at nearby Newport News, call Norfolk home port and can be seen from miles away, especially at the bridge-tunnel end of the base. You may see four or even more, each with a crew of up to 6,300, beside slightly smaller amphibious carriers that discharge marines in both helicopters and amphibious assault craft. The submarine piers, floating drydocks, supply center, and air station are all worth seeing. Hampton Roads Transit operates tour trolleys most of the year, departing from the naval-base tour office. A photo identification card is required for everyone entering the base. ✉ *9079 Hampton Blvd.* ☎ *757/444–7955, 757/444—1577 visitor's office* ⊕ *www.navstanorva.navy.mil/tour* 🎫 *Tour $7.50* ⊙ *Tours daily 1:30.*

A popular attraction on Norfolk's redeveloped waterfront is **Nauticus,** the National Maritime Center. With more than 70 high-tech exhibits on three "decks," the site places ancient shipbuilding exhibits next to interactive displays depicting the modern naval world. Weather satellites, underwater archaeology, and the Loch Ness Monster all come together here. Also available are some rare movies of the days when scout planes were catapulted from cruisers and battleship and then made water landings beside the ship. The battleship USS *Wisconsin,* still maintained in a state of reduced readiness to allow reactivation, has found a home here. Most of its interior is off-limits, but its enormous gun turrets and conning tower are impressive up close. The *Wisconsin,* tied up just outside the museum, and the Hampton Roads Naval Museum, within Nauticus, are both operated by the U.S. Navy and can be toured without paying Nauticus's admission price. There are additional fees for the AEGIS Theater and Virtual Adventures. ✉ *1 Waterside Dr.* ☎ *757/ 664–1000* ⊕ *www.nauticus.org and www.hrnm.navy.mil* 🎫 *$10* ⊙ *Memorial Day–Labor Day, daily 10–6; Labor Day–Memorial Day, Mon.–Sat. 10–5, Sun. noon–5* ⊙ *USS Wisconsin closed Mon.*

☺ **Virginia Zoological Park,** the largest in the state, has more than 100 species living on 55 acres—including rhinos and ostriches as well as such domesticated animals as sheep. With the assistance of docents, children can handle some of the animals. In the Africa exhibit, elephant demonstrations are scheduled regularly in summer. ✉ *3500 Granby St.* ☎ *757/ 441–2706* 🎫 *$6* ⊙ *Daily 10–5.*

Where to Eat

★ $–$$$ ✕ **La Galleria.** This restaurant has earned a reputation as one of the best in Norfolk. The interior, not done in the usual homey Southern style, may appear cold, but it's impressive. Decorations include Ionic columns and large urns imported from Italy. A pianist entertains with soft music. Among the menu choices are *vongole al forno* (baked clams sprinkled with herbs, garlic, and bread crumbs) as an appetizer, and many excellent pastas and main courses, such as veal, chicken, steaks and fish (for example, salmon sautéed in herbs, garlic, and white wine. Before dinner, you may want to check out the d'Art Center across the street, a working community for the visual arts. ✉ *120 College Pl.* ☎ *757/623–3939* 🍴 *AE, DC, MC, V.*

$–$$ ✕ **Basil's.** Fresh seafood dishes are this eatery's specialty, but the freshly made pastas stand out as well. Try the ravioli à la basil for a starter and the tuna *romanga* to get a real taste for the kitchen's strengths. Marble columns and fine wood furnishings make the place perfect for a quiet evening. ✉ *Clarion James Madison Hotel, 345 Granby St.* ☎ *757/ 622–6682* 🍴 *AE, D, DC, MC, V.*

★ $–$$ ✕ **Freemason Abbey Restaurant and Tavern.** This former church near the historic business district has 40-foot-high cathedral ceilings and large windows. You can sit upstairs, in the large choir loft, or in the main part of the church downstairs. Beside the bar just inside the entrance, you can order lighter fare. Regular appetizers include artichoke dip and bacon-wrapped scallops. There's a dinner special every weeknight, with lobster on Wednesday night. Friday is wild game night: wild boar, alligator, or another unusual special. ⊠ *209 W. Freemason St.* ☎ *757/622–3966* ▭ *AE, D, DC, MC, V.*

★ $–$$ ✕ **The Wild Monkey.** From its scrumptious $10 meat loaf to the smoked salmon with blue cheese, this Ghent restaurant wows to the last bite. Its ever-changing wine list is list, and there's even a board with recommended wine and food pairings. For a starter, try the pork and ginger dumplings; end with the pecan pie. If you go for Sunday brunch, the Cuban sandwich is fine, and the frittata is a unique take on the traditional Mexican dish of huevos rancheros. Make sure to get here early; the Monkey is tiny. ⊠ *Colley Ave.* ☎ *757/627–6462* ⚭ *Reservations not accepted* ▭ *AE, MC, V* ☉ *No dinner Sun.*

★ ¢–$$ ✕ **No Frill Bar and Grill.** This expansive café is in an antique building in the heart of Ghent. The wooden tables are beneath a tin ceiling and exposed ductwork are surrounded by walls of cream and mustard. A bar is in the center of several dining spaces. Signature items include its ribs; the Funky Chicken Sandwich, a grilled chicken breast with bacon, tomato, melted Swiss cheese, and Parmesan pepper dressing on rye; and the Spotswood Salad of baby spinach, Granny Smith apples, and blue cheese. ⊠ *806 Spotswood Ave., at Colley Ave.* ☎ *757/627–4262* ▭ *AE, D, DC, MC, V.*

★ ¢–$ ✕ **Doumar's.** After he introduced the world to its first ice-cream cone at the 1904 World's Fair in St. Louis, Abe Doumar founded this drive-in institution in 1934. It's still operated by his family. Waitresses carry to your car the specialties of the house: barbecue, limeade, and ice cream in waffle cones made according to an original recipe. ⊠ *20th St. and Monticello Ave.* ☎ *757/627–4163* ▭ *No credit cards* ☉ *Closed Sun.*

Where to Stay

$$–$$$ ▦ **Norfolk Waterside Marriott.** This 1991 addition to the redeveloped downtown area is connected to the Waterside Festival Hall shopping area by a ramp and is close to Town Point Park, site of many festivals. The handsome lobby, with wood paneling, a central staircase, silk tapestries, and Federal-style furniture, sets a high standard that continues throughout the hotel. Rooms are somewhat small, but each has most everything the business traveler could ask for—including two telephones, voice mail, and Internet access. ⊠ *235 E. Main St., 23510* ☎ *757/627–4200 or 800/ 228–9290* 🖷 *757/628–6452* ⊕ *www.marriott.com* 🛏 *396 rooms, 8 suites* ⚭ *2 restaurants, in-room data ports, indoor pool, lobby lounge* ▭ *AE, D, DC, MC, V.*

$–$$$ ▦ **Sheraton Norfolk Waterside Hotel.** Modern is the word for the way this hotel is furnished, from the bright, spacious lobby to the ample rooms and large suites. A ground-floor bar with dramatic 30-foot windows overlooks the Elizabeth—many rooms also have a beautiful view over the water. This property is convenient to the Waterside Festival Hall shopping area. ⊠ *777 Waterside Dr., 23510* ☎ *757/622–6664* 🖷 *757/625– 8271* ⊕ *www.sheraton.com* 🛏 *426 rooms, 20 suites* ⚭ *Restaurant, pool, lounge* ▭ *AE, D, DC, MC, V.*

$-$$ 🏨 **Hilton Airport.** Don't let the gray exterior scare you away; the interior of this six-story highway-side Hilton is neither drab nor harsh. The hotel has an atrium, a concierge floor, and some rooms with king-size beds. Outside there's a place for picnics. ✉ *1500 N. Military Hwy., 23502* ☎ *757/466–8000 or 800/422–7474* 🖷 *757/466–8000* ⊕ *www.hilton. com* ⌁ *249 rooms, 4 suites* ♿ *3 restaurants, coffee shop, picnic area, in-room data ports, tennis court, pool, health club, 2 bars, airport shuttle* ☰ *AE, D, DC, MC, V.*

$-$$ 🏨 **Holiday Inn Select Airport.** Surprisingly plush for a Holiday Inn property, this airport location, which opened in 2000, welcomes business travelers with an elegant lobby bar and fireplace. Rooms are outfitted with two phone lines, high-speed DSL Internet access, and voice mail. ✉ *Lake Wright Executive Center, 1570 N. Military Hwy., 23502* ☎ *757/213– 2231* 🖷 *757/213–2232* ⊕ *www.hiselect.com/norfolkva* ⌁ *147 rooms* ♿ *Restaurant, microwaves, refrigerators, indoor pool, gym, hot tub, lobby lounge, business services, laundry facilities, meeting rooms, airport shuttle* ☰ *AE, D, DC, MC, V.*

★ $ 🏨 **Clarion James Madison Hotel.** In the early 1900s, this hotel was the skyscraper of Norfolk—topping out at eight stories. The boutique hotel still maintains a domineering presence downtown. You can sip a microbrew on a leather seat in the lobby's lounge, where exquisite Tiffany chandeliers, mahogany wood pillars, and Oriental rugs recall the Jazz Age. Rooms, renovated in 2004, have varied color schemes. Most rooms have stand-up showers; about 40 have tubs. ✉ *345 Granby St., 23510* ☎ *757/622–6682 or 888/402–6682* 🖷 *757/683–5949* ⌁ *127 rooms, 54 suites* ♿ *Restaurant, cable TV with video games, in-room data ports, refrigerators, lobby lounge, dry cleaning, laundry facilities, concierge, meeting rooms, free parking* ☰ *AE, D, MC, V.*

Nightlife & the Arts

Town Point Park (✉ Waterfront), between Nauticus and Waterside Festival Hall, is the site of many free outdoor festivals and concerts, including Harborfest in spring. Fun, food, and music are here most Fridays from May through October.

DINNER CRUISE   The *Spirit of Norfolk* (✉ 333 Waterside Dr., Norfolk ☎ 757/625–1748 ⊕ www.spiritcruises.com) operates the area's only dinner-dance cruises with live music and entertainment. Lunch and brunch cruises are also available.

MUSIC   The **Virginia Opera Company** (✉ 160 E. Virginia Beach Blvd. ☎ 757/623– 1223 ⊕ www.vaopera.org) is often joined by major guest artists during its season (October through March). The elegant Harrison Opera House has good acoustics.

Sports & the Outdoors

BASEBALL   Gleaming over the Norfolk harbor area is Harbor Park, home to the **Norfolk Tides** (✉ Waterside Dr. ☎ 757/622–2222 ⊕ www.norfolktides. com). The Tides are the International League, Triple-A team for the New York Mets. Harbor Park seats 13,000 fans and has a full-service restaurant and bar. For added fun, travel to the ball game via the Elizabeth River Ferry. Ferries leave every 30 minutes on game days from the North Landing Pier in Olde Towne Portsmouth.

FISHING   Charters and pier fishing are available in season at **Harrison Boat House** (✉ 414 W. Ocean View Ave. ☎ 757/588–9968). **Willoughby Bay Marina** (✉ 1651 Bayville St. ☎ 757/588–2663) has fishing charters.

Shopping
An eclectic mix of chic shops, including antiques stores and eateries, are in **Ghent,** a turn-of-the-20th-century neighborhood that runs from the Elizabeth River to York Street, to West Olney Road and Llewellyn Avenue. Colley Avenue and 21st Street is the hub.

You can watch painters, sculptors, glassworkers, quilters, and other artists at work in their studios at the **d'Art Center** (✉ 125 College Pl. ☎ 757/625–4211 ⊕ www.d-artcenter.org); the creations are for sale in two galleries on the premises.

The center of Norfolk's downtown, the **MacArthur Center Mall** (✉ 300 Monticello Ave. ☎ 757/627–6000) has more than 100 stores, as well as anchors Nordstrom and Dillard's. The restaurants inside, including such as Johnny Rockets and Castaldi's, are good value for the food and price.

In Ghent, the upscale clothing and shoe boutiques at the **Palace Shops** (✉ 21st St. and Llewellyn Ave. ☎ 757/622–9999) are a good place to search out some finery. Antiques hunters will probably want to check out the **Ghent Market and Antique Center** (✉ 1400 Granby St. ☎ 757/625–2897) with a full city block of goods. Fine kitchen equipment and accessories can be found at the lovely **Bouillabaisse** (✉ 1611 Colley Ave., #A ☎ 757/627–7774).

Rowena's Jam and Jelly Factory (✉ 758 W. 22nd St. ☎ 757/627–8699) tempts your sweet tooth with factory tours Monday through Wednesday; make arrangements in advance. For sale in the shop are homemade jams, cooking sauces, fruit curds, and cookies.

Portsmouth

 6 mi southwest of Norfolk via I–264.

Portsmouth, across the Elizabeth River from Norfolk, has a well-maintained historic area called Olde Towne, which has handsome buildings from the 18th and 19th centuries. A five-minute pedestrian ferry makes traveling between Portsmouth and Norfolk easy.

The **Portsmouth Naval Shipyard Museum,** one block from the waterfront and close to the pedestrian ferry landing, has exhibits on naval history that include uniforms, medals, photographs, artifacts and models of 18th-century warships. You can explore the retired Coast Guard lightship *Portsmouth,* a floating lighthouse whose quarters below deck have been authentically furnished and are open to visitors. ✉ *2 High St.* ☎ *757/393–8591 shipyard museum, 757/393–8741 lightship* ⊕ *www.portsnavalmuseums.com* 🎫 *$3, includes lightship* ⊗ *Tues.–Sat. 10–5, Sun. 1–5.*

The **Portsmouth Children's Museum** has rooms where children can learn engineering and scientific principles by playing with bubbles and blocks. ✉ *221 High St.* ☎ *757/393–8393* ⊕ *www.childrens-museum.org*

🖺 *$5, includes Portsmouth Naval Shipyard Museum* ⊙ *Tues.–Sat. 10–5, Sun. 11–5.*

Where to Stay

¢–$ 🏨 **Holiday Inn Olde Towne.** With the Portsmouth waterfront just out the door, and Olde Towne's attractions so nearby, this hotel is very well situated. The undistinguished appearance of the building hides pleasant things inside: public and guest rooms vary in size, but all have a modern look. The bar and restaurant have long windows beside the Elizabeth River: it's the perfect spot for watching ships and boats and the Portsmouth and Norfolk waterfronts. High-speed Internet is being added to the guest rooms. ⊠ *8 Crawford Pkwy., 23704* ☎ *757/393–2573 or 800/465–4329* 🖷 *757/399–1248* ⊕ *www.sixcontinentshotels. com* ⇨ *210 rooms, 5 suites* ᗉ *Restaurant, in-room data ports, pool, gym, lobby lounge, laundry facilities, laundry service, Internet, meeting rooms* ▤ *AE, D, DC, MC, V.*

Nightlife & the Arts

Inside the restored 1945 **Commodore Theatre** (⊠ 421 High St. ☎ 757/393–6962), crystal chandeliers and wall murals make a handsome setting for light dinner fare and first-run movies. There are tables on the main floor, and the balcony has traditional theater seating.

off the beaten path

GREAT DISMAL SWAMP NATIONAL WILDLIFE REFUGE – The forbidding name was assigned to the area by William Byrd on one of his early-18th-century surveying expeditions. George Washington once hoped to drain it. Today the swamp is a 106,000-acre refuge that harbors bobcats, black bears, and more than 150 varieties of birds. A remarkably shallow lake—3,000 acres, 6 feet deep—is surrounded by skinny cypress trees that lend the scene a primeval quality. One hundred miles of hiking and biking trails, including a wheelchair-accessible boardwalk, make this a spectacular contrast to nearby downtown Portsmouth and Norfolk. ⊠ *Follow signs from Rte. 32, Suffolk 23434* ☎ *757/986–3705* ⊙ *Apr.–Sept., daily 6:30–8; Oct.–Mar., daily 6:30–5.*

Virginia Beach

③⓪ *18 mi east of Norfolk via I–64 to Rte. 44.*

The heart of Virginia Beach—a stretch of the Atlantic shore from Cape Henry south to Rudee Inlet—has been a popular summertime destination for years. With 6 mi of public beach, high-rises, amusements, and a busy 40-block boardwalk, Virginia's most populated city is now a place for peaceful communion with nature. The Boardwalk and Atlantic Avenue have teak benches, an oceanfront park, an old-fashioned fishing pier with shops and a restaurant with bar, and a 3 mi bike trail. Bikes (two- or four-wheel) can be rented at several shops and hotels along the beach. The farther north you go, the more beach you find in proportion to bars, T-shirt parlors, and video arcades. Most activities and events in town are oriented toward families.

Along the oceanfront, the **Old Coast Guard Station,** inside a 1903 Seat-ack Lifesaving Station, contains photographic exhibits, examples of lifesaving equipment, and a gallery that depicts German U-boat activity off the coast during World War II. ⊠ *24th St. and Atlantic Ave.* ☎ *757/422–1587* ✆ *$3* ⊙ *Tues.–Sat. 10–5, Sun. noon–5.*

Inland from the shore is the late 17th-century **Adam Thoroughgood House,** named for the prosperous plantation owner who held a land grant of 5,350 acres and died in 1640. This 45-by-22-foot brick house, probably constructed by a Thoroughgood grandson, recalls the English cottage architecture of the period, with a protruding chimney and a steeply pitched roof. The four-room early plantation home has a 17th-century garden with characteristic hedges. ⊠ *1636 Parish Rd.* ☎ *757/460–7588* ✆ *$2* ⊙ *Tues.–Sat. 10–5, Sun. noon–5.*

★ The sea is the subject at the popular **Virginia Aquarium and Marine Science Center,** a massive facility with more than 200 exhibits. This is no place for passive museum goers; many exhibits require participation. You can use computers to predict the weather and solve the pollution crisis, watch the birds in the salt marsh through telescopes on a deck, handle horseshoe crabs, take a simulated journey to the bottom of the sea in a submarine, and study fish up close in tanks that re-create underwater environments. The museum is almost 2 mi inland from Rudee Inlet at the southern end of Virginia Beach. ⊠ *717 General Booth Blvd.* ☎ *757/425–3474* ✆ *$12* ⊙ *After Labor Day–before Memorial Day, daily 9–5; Memorial Day–Labor Day, daily 9–7.*

Sandwiched between high-rise hotels is the **Atlantic Wildfowl Heritage Museum,** which holds fine waterfowl art and artifacts, including decoys (thousands of waterfowl migrate through eastern Virginia on their way north and south). The building, a small renovated cottage built in 1895 by Virginia Beach's first mayor and postmaster, Bernard Holland, is the oldest building of its kind on the oceanfront. Purchased in 1909 by a Norfolk banker and cotton broker, it's listed as the de Witt Cottage on the National Register of Historic Places. ⊠ *1113 Atlantic Ave.* ☎ *757/437–8432* ⊕ *www.awhm.org* ✆ *Free* ⊙ *Memorial Day–Sept., Mon.–Sat. 10–5, Sun. noon–5; Oct.–Memorial Day, Tues.–Sat. 10–5, Sun. noon–5.*

At the northeastern tip of Virginia Beach, on the cape where the mouth of the bay meets the ocean, the historic **Old Cape Henry Lighthouse** is near the site where the English landed on their way to Jamestown in 1607. This lighthouse, however, didn't light anyone's way until 1792. You can still climb to the top of the old lighthouse in summer; a new, working lighthouse is closed to visitors. ⊠ *U.S. 60* ☎ *757/422–9421* ✆ *$3* ⊙ *Mid-Mar.–Oct., daily 10–5; Nov. and Jan.–mid-Mar., daily 10–4.*

Botanists will have a field day at **First Landing State Park,** which is inland from the Cape Henry lighthouses and the army installation at Fort Story. Spanish moss grows no farther north than here, and blue spruce appears no farther south. The park is also a haven for red and gray foxes, raccoons, opossums, water snakes, and other denizens of swamp and dune. Boardwalks built just above the water level let you get close to flora and fauna while keeping your feet dry, and there are campgrounds, picnic areas, and guided tours. ☒ *2500 Shore Dr., U.S. 60* ☎ *757/ 412–2300* 🖃 *Apr.–Oct., weekdays $3 per car, weekends $4; Nov.–Mar., $2* ۞ *Apr.–Oct., park daily 8* AM*–dusk, visitor center weekdays 8–4, weekends 9–4; Nov.–Mar., park Sun.–Fri. 8* AM*–dusk, visitor center weekdays 8–4, Sun. 9–4.*

Where to Stay

$–$$$ ✕ **Croaker's.** A great local favorite, Croaker's isn't a restaurant that many people passing through the area know about. Far from the crowds, it's at the north end of Shore Drive. Along with melt-in-your-mouth crab cakes, Croaker's serves a mean Oysters William (oysters with white wine, butter, and shallots). Another surprise is the excellent steaks, which are cut to order. ☒ *3629 Shore Dr.* ☎ *757/363–2490* ▭ *AE, D, DC, MC, V* ۞ *No lunch.*

★ **$–$$** ✕ **Coastal Grill.** Though it's in a mall, this place has a warm, even elegant look, with a big, open bar and artful lighting. But food is the reason to come: chef-owner Jerry Bryan prepares American classics with an innovative, irresistible twist. Spinach salad is paired with sautéed chicken liver and balsamic vinaigrette; New York strip steak comes with sautéed onions and horseradish cream; and the fresh seafood dishes, including seasonal oysters on the half shell, are sublime. The moderately priced wine list comes with suggestions for wine-and-food pairings. Come early and expect a wait. ☒ *1427 Great Neck Rd.* ☎ *757/496–3348* 🖎 *Reservations not accepted* ▭ *AE, D, DC, MC, V* ۞ *No lunch.*

★ **$–$$** ✕ **Havanna's.** This upbeat bistro serves Cuban-inspired cuisine in fun, tropical surroundings. The cedar furnishings and low-hanging lights over the long tables make this local favorite look sophisticated. With dishes such as grilled flank steak *mojo* (marinated with peppers and spices), saffron-infused bouillabaisse, and *picadillo* (spicy ground beef), this tony place leaves you craving a cigar and a cocktail. If you like both, you're in luck: there's a fine line of cigars as well as an assortment of margaritas. ☒ *1423 N. Great Neck Rd.* ☎ *757/496–3333* ▭ *AE, D, MC, V.*

$–$$ ✕ **Rockafeller's.** The Down East architecture of this local favorite with double-deck porches hints at the seafood that's available. The restaurant has a bar, a raw bar, and alfresco dining in good weather (in cool weather, the large window wall still gives you a water view). Seafood, pasta, chicken, and beef share the menu with salads and sandwiches. Rockafeller's (and several others) are on Rudee Inlet. To get here, go south on Pacific Avenue and turn right on Winston-Salem immediately before the Rudee Inlet bridge. The street ends at Mediterranean Avenue. ☒ *308 Mediterranean Ave.* ☎ *757/422–5654* ▭ *AE, D, DC, MC, V.*

$ ✕ **Murphy's Irish Pub.** A relatively new place a block from the boardwalk, Murphy's has plenty of easy parking. It's a combination Irish pub, sports bar, and restaurant. The large central dining room has an open fireplace in the middle, a bar on one side, and a smaller dining room at one end. The menu includes steaks and Irish, Italian, and seafood entrées as well as snacks and sandwiches. The Sunday brunch is very reasonable, and so are the weekday dinner specials. ☒ *2914 Pacific Ave.* ☎ *757/417–7701* ▭ *AE, D, DC, MC, V.*

Where to Stay

$–$$$$ 🏨 **Best Western Oceanfront.** The small, neat lobby of this seven-story chain property opens onto the boardwalk and beach. All rooms have an ocean view and are decorated with tropical floral spreads and beach paintings. Coffeemakers and hair dryers are included in rates. ✉ *1101 Atlantic Ave., 23451* ☎ *757/422–5000 or 866/829–2326* 🖷 *757/425–2356* 🌐 *www.bestwestern.com* 🛏 *96 rooms, 14 suites* ♿ *Restaurant, in-room safes, microwaves, refrigerators, indoor-outdoor pool, gym, sauna, bar, dry cleaning, laundry facilities, meeting rooms, no-smoking rooms* 🖃 *AE, D, MC, V.*

$$–$$$ 🏨 **Cavalier Hotels.** In the quieter north end of town, this 18-acre resort complex combines the original Cavalier Hotel of 1927, a seven-story redbrick building on a hill, with an oceanfront high-rise built across the street in 1973. The clientele is about evenly divided between conventioneers and families. F. Scott and Zelda Fitzgerald stayed regularly in the older section (it has since been lavishly refurbished). If you stay on the hilltop, you can see the water—and get to it easily by shuttle van or a short walk. The newer building overlooks 600 feet of private beach. There's a fee for tennis, but the other athletic facilities are free. ✉ *Atlantic Ave. and 42nd St., 23451* ☎ *757/425–8555 or 888/746–2327* 🖷 *757/425–0629* 🌐 *www.cavalierhotel.com* 🛏 *400 rooms* ♿ *5 restaurants, in-room data ports, putting green, 4 tennis courts, 2 pools (1 indoor), wading pool, gym, beach, croquet, volleyball, babysitting, playground, no-smoking rooms* 🖃 *AE, D, DC, MC, V.*

★ **$–$$$** 🏨 **Ramada Plaza Resort Oceanfront.** With its 17-story tower, this Ramada is the tallest hotel in the city. Rooms that do not face the ocean directly have either a partial view or overlook the swimming pool. The modern lobby has a skylit atrium. Each guest room has a coffeemaker, iron, ironing board, and hair dryer. Beds have quilted spreads and striped draperies. Gus' Mariner Restaurant's varied menu includes good seafood. An adjoining small pub serves soup and sandwiches after 4 PM. ✉ *57th St. and Oceanfront, 23451* ☎ *757/428–7025 or 800/365–3032* 🖷 *757/428–2921* 🌐 *www.ramada.com* 🛏 *247 rooms* ♿ *Restaurant, in-room safes, microwaves, refrigerators, indoor-outdoor pool, gym, sauna, bar, dry cleaning, laundry service, convention center, meeting rooms, no-smoking rooms* 🖃 *AE, D, DC, MC, V.*

★ **¢–$** 🏨 **Crowne Plaza Virginia Beach.** This sparkling white, modern hotel is well situated, midway between Norfolk and the beach and 15 mi from Norfolk International Airport. The skylit lobby overlooks a glassed-in indoor pool. Rooms have a sitting area with sofa and desk; there are floral spreads and moss-color carpeting, with prints of flowers on the wall. Every room has a hair dryer, iron, ironing board, and coffeemaker. ✉ *4453 Bonney Rd., 23462* ☎ *757/473–1700 or 800/847–5202* 🖷 *757/552–0477* 🛏 *149 rooms* ♿ *Restaurant, in-room data ports, refrigerators, pool, gym, hot tub, lobby lounge, dry cleaning, laundry service, meeting rooms, no-smoking rooms* 🖃 *AE, D, DC, MC, V.*

¢–$ 🏨 **Extended Stay America.** Designed for business travelers and their long-term stays, this affordable lodging is clean, with weekly rates from $399 to $429. Decorated with white walls with burgundy patterned spreads and cherrywood furniture, rooms are austere but have an iron and ironing board, a kitchen with stove, microwave, coffeemaker, and cooking utensils. The hotel is midway between Norfolk and Virginia Beach. ⊠ *4548 Bonney Rd., 23462* ☎ *757/473–9200 or 800/398–7829* ⊕ *www.extendedstayhotels.com* ⇨ *120 rooms* ♨ *In-room data ports, laundry facilities, no-smoking rooms* ▤ *AE, D, DC, MC, V.*

Nightlife

There's free nightly entertainment from April through Labor Day weekend at the 24th Street stage or 24th Street Park on the Boardwalk. **Murphy's Grand Irish Pub and Restaurant** (⊠ 2914 Pacific Ave. ☎ 757/417–7701) has entertainment every night in summer and Tues.–Sat. during winter—there's typically an Irish musician or two. **Harpoon Larry's** (⊠ 24th and Pacific Sts. ☎ 757/422–6000) is a local watering hole with true character, not a tourist trap. Don't be surprised to see a great white shark staring back at you as you eat a juicy piece of that shark's cousin (mahimahi) stuffed with fresh Chesapeake Bay crabmeat, or enjoy raw oysters and a cold Corona. Some come just for the pool table.

Sports & the Outdoors

BOATING & CANOEING
For canoe rentals, try **Munden Point Park** (☎ 757/426–5296).

GOLF
There are four public golf courses in Virginia Beach, each with moderately priced fees. Except for Kempsville Greens, all ask that you reserve a tee time one week in advance. **Cypress Point Country Club** (⊠ 5340 Club Head Rd. ☎ 757/490–8822) has greens fees of $29 for weekdays before noon and $49 for weekends. Caddies are available. **Hell's Point** (⊠ PU–2700 Atwoodtown Rd. ☎ 757/721–3400) has power carts, which are included in the greens fees ($57 weekdays and $67 weekends). **Honey Bee Golf Club** (⊠ 2500 S. Independence Blvd. ☎ 757/471–2768) has a greens fee of weekdays $35, weekends $39. Inquire about caddies, if you want one. **Kempsville Greens Municipal Golf Course** (⊠ 4840 Princess Anne Rd. ☎ 757/474–8441) is the least expensive course (weekdays $19, weekends $21). There are no caddies; power carts cost $12 per person. There's open play on weekdays, and weekend times are taken beginning at 8 AM on Friday.

WATER SPORTS
Chick's Beach Sailing Center (☎757/460–2238) offers Hobie Cat and Windsurfer rentals and lessons. You can use **Wild River Outfitters** (☎ 757/431–8566) for guided kayak tours, dolphin tours, and more. **Lynnhaven Dive Center** (☎ 757/481–7949) leads dives and gives lessons.

WILLIAMSBURG & HAMPTON RDS. A TO Z

To research prices, get advice from other travelers, and book travel arrangements, visit www.fodors.com.

AIRPORTS

The three major airports in the region are served by many national and international carriers. Ticket prices are often much less expensive flying out and into Norfolk and Newport News than nearby Richmond. All three airports are relatively small and are easy to navigate in and around.

Newport News/Williamsburg International Airport is served primarily by US Airways. Norfolk International Airport, between Norfolk and Virginia Beach, is served by major carriers as well as several smaller ones. Richmond International Airport, 10 mi east of Richmond, off I–64 at Exit 197, is about 45 mi from Williamsburg.

🛩 Airport Information **Newport News/Williamsburg International Airport** ✉ 12525 Jefferson Ave., at I–64, Newport News 🕾 757/877–0221. **Norfolk International Airport** ✉ Norview Ave. 🕾 757/857–3351. **Richmond International Airport** ✉ Airport Dr. 🕾 804/226–3000.

BIKE TRAVEL

Biking around Colonial Williamsburg is a wonderful way to explore its 173 acres. Rental bikes are available for those staying at the Williamsburg Inn, Lodge, or Colonial Inns. Bikesmith, in Williamsburg, rents bikes to all. Bike rentals are also available from Bikebeat, about 3 mi from the restored area. The pamphlet "Biking through America's Historic Triangle" maps a 20 mi route along the bike path of the scenic Colonial Parkway, which goes past Williamsburg, Yorktown, and Jamestown. The guide is available at area bike shops.

In Virginia Beach, there are numerous locations along the boardwalk where you can rent bikes. The covered multiperson bikes are especially fun for families.

🚲 Bike Rentals **Bikebeat** ✉ 4640–9B Monticello Ave., Williamsburg 🕾 757/229–0096. **Bikesmith** ✉ 515 York St., Williamsburg 🕾 757/229–9858. **Jamestown Bicycle Rental Co.** ✉ Jamestown 🕾 757/291–2266. **Ocean Rentals Beach Service** ✉ Virginia Beach 🕾 757/481–5191. **Seashore Bike Shop** ✉ Virginia Beach 🕾 757/491–9312. **Williamsburg Lodge** ✉ 310 S. England St. 🕾 757/229–1000 ⊕ www.colonialwilliamsburg.com.

BOAT & FERRY TRAVEL

The Elizabeth River Ferry conveys pedestrians from Waterside Festival Hall, in Norfolk, to Portsmouth's Olde Towne. Taking the five-minute ferry trip is more fun than driving through the tunnel; it departs Norfolk 15 minutes before and after every hour.

🚢 Boat & Ferry Lines **Elizabeth River Ferry** 🕾 757/222–6100 💲 75¢ ⊗ Daily 7:15 AM–11:45 PM.

BUS TRAVEL

Greyhound Lines typically has half a dozen or so departures daily from Hampton, Norfolk, Virginia Beach, Suffolk, and Williamsburg.

🚌 Bus Depots **Williamsburg Transportation Center** ✉ 468 N. Boundary St., Williamsburg 🕾 757/229–1460 or 800/231–2222. **Charles Carr/Hampton Depot** ✉ 2 W. Pembrook Ave., Hampton 🕾 757/722–9861. **Greyhound Norfolk Depot** ✉ 701 Monticello Ave., Norfolk 🕾 757/625–7500. **Myles of Travel** ✉ 1017 Laskin Rd., Virginia Beach 🕾 757/422–2998. **Newbreed Travel Center** ✉ 1562 Holland Rd., Suffolk 🕾 757/934–8068. 🚌 Bus Lines **Greyhound Lines** 🕾 800/231–2222.

CAR TRAVEL

Williamsburg is west of I–64, 51 mi southeast of Richmond; the Colonial Parkway joins Williamsburg with Jamestown to the southwest and Yorktown to the east.

The I–664 road creates a circular beltway through the Hampton Roads area. I–664 connects Newport News and Norfolk, via Suffolk. I–64 runs northwest through Norfolk to intersect with I–664 in Hampton and I–95 at Richmond. U.S. 58 and what was once I–44 is now just an extension of I–264 (part of I–64).

PARKING Parking near the Colonial Williamsburg historic area can be difficult during summer months and special events. It's best, if you are touring the historic area, to park at the visitor center and ride the shuttle to the park. The parking lot behind the Merchants Square shopping area is a good bet if you're planning a short visit or going out to eat around the area.

Virginia Beach has no shortage of public parking lots and spaces. The cost for a day of parking is approximately $7.50 and includes free trolley passes for up to four people to travel up and down Atlantic Avenue. Municipal lots/decks are at 4th Street (metered only), 9th Street and Pacific Avenue, 19th Street and Pacific Avenue, 25th Street and Pacific Avenue, 31st Street and Atlantic Avenue, and Croatan and Sandbridge beaches. Metered spaces have a three-hour limit.

TRAFFIC The area is well served with expressways and interstate highways, but you have to share these routes with many local drivers. Because the ragged coastline is constantly interrupted by water, driving from one town to another usually means going through a tunnel or over a bridge, either one of which may create a traffic bottleneck. The entrance to the tunnel between Hampton and Norfolk can get very congested, especially on weekends, so listen to your car radio for updated traffic reports.

Williamsburg, despite a wealth of tourist attractions, is still a small town of sorts. You can travel from Colonial Williamsburg to Busch Gardens in 10–20 minutes, depending on traffic conditions. All attractions are well signed and it's difficult to get lost.

The Tidewater area, however, is another story. With a long list of tunnels and bridges connecting myriad waterways, it's easy to find yourself headed in the wrong direction. Highways have adequate signs, but sometimes it may be too late to merge before entering a tunnel/bridge. Traffic is highly congested during rush hour and during peak summer months, when the beach traffic can grind everything to a halt.

In congested periods, use the less-traveled I–664. The 17½ mi Chesapeake Bay Bridge-Tunnel is the only connection between the southern part of Virginia and the Eastern Shore; U.S. 13 is the main route up the spine of the Eastern Shore peninsula into Maryland.

DISABILITIES & ACCESSIBILITY
In Colonial Williamsburg, vans for people with disabilities are allowed by prior arrangement. Some structures in the park have wheelchair ramps. For more information on services for people with disabilities, call Colonial Williamsburg at 757/229–1000 Ext. 2473.

In Virginia Beach, there are access ramps for the disabled on every beach from 1st to 58th streets. There are handicap-accessible wooden walkways that extend from the boardwalk to the water at 8th, 17th,

24th, and 30th streets. There's also designated on-street parking for people with disabilities at the Rudee Loop, between 2nd and 38th streets. Designated handicap parking is also available at all off-street municipal parking lots.

🔏 Local Resources **Al's Wheelchair Transportation** ✉ Virginia Beach ☎ 757/474-1968. **Association of Retarded Citizens of The Virginia Peninsula** ✉ Williamsburg ☎ 757/826-6461. **Peninsula Center for Independent Living** ✉ Williamsburg ☎ 757/827-0275 or 757/564-1880. **TLC Transportation** ✉ Virginia Beach ☎ 757/449-4852.

EMERGENCIES
🆘 **Ambulance, Fire, Police** ☎ 911.

🆘 Doctors & Dentists **Physicians Referral Services of Williamsburg** ✉ Williamsburg ☎ 757/229-4636. **Virginia Beach Medical Referral Service** ✉ Virginia Beach ☎ 757/640-1958.

🆘 Hospitals **Riverside Regional Medical Center** ✉ 500 J. Clyde Morris Blvd. ☎ 757/594-2000, 757/594-2050 emergency room. **Sentara Bayside Hospital** ✉ 800 Independence Blvd., Virginia Beach ☎ 757/363-6137. **Sentara Norfolk General Hospital** ✉ 600 Gresham Dr. ☎ 757/668-3551. **Williamsburg Community Hospital** ✉ 301 Monticello Ave., Williamsburg ☎ 757/259-6000, 757/259-6005 emergency room.

🆘 24-Hour Pharmacies **Rite Aid** ✉ 525 W. 21st St., Norfolk ☎ 757/625-6073 ✉ 801 Frederick Blvd., Portsmouth ☎ 757/397-5981 ✉ 5795 Princess Ann Rd., Virginia Beach ☎ 757/490-0307.

MEDIA
The main local newspaper in Williamsburg and Newport News is the *Newport News Daily Press*. The *Virginia Gazette* is published in Williamsburg. The *Virginian-Pilot* is the main paper for the entire Tidewater region.

TAXIS
You don't see their cars often, but there are a few taxi companies in Williamsburg. Norfolk and Virginia Beach have quite a few more because of airport traffic and the military bases. Unless you're at Newport News/Williamsburg International Airport or Norfolk International Airport, you must phone for a cab. Rates are metered and tipping is expected.

🚖 Taxi Companies **Beach Taxi** ✉ Virginia Beach ☎ 757/486-6585. **Beach Yellow Cab** ✉ Virginia Beach ☎ 757/460-0606. **Black and White Cabs** ✉ Norfolk ☎ 757/855-4444. **Groome Transportation** ✉ Williamsburg ☎ 757/877-9477. **Yellow Cab** ✉ Norfolk ☎ 757/622-3232. **Yellow Cab** ✉ Williamsburg ☎ 757/722-1111.

TOURS
Most Williamsburg tours depart from the Greenhow Lumber House, where you can purchase tickets and make reservations.

American Rover Sailing Tours, which offers boat tours aboard a striking 135-foot topsail schooner, cruises around Hampton Roads's nautical historical landmarks and the Norfolk Naval Station. The *Carrie B*, a scaled-down reproduction of a Mississippi riverboat, cruises Hampton Roads for 2½ hours to give you a look at the naval shipyard and the site of the encounter of the USS *Monitor* and the CSS *Virginia* during the Civil War. A luxury yacht's Discovery Cruise explores Virginia Beach's Broad Bay.

Carriage and wagon rides are available daily, weather permitting. General ticket holders may purchase tickets on the day of the ride at the Lumber House.

The Hampton Circle Tour is a self-guided driving route that passes all of Hampton's attractions. Maps are available from the Visitors Bureau. The Virginia Beach Tour driving trip goes past both beach and historic points. Maps are available at the visitor center, but signs also mark the route.

Lanthorn Tours take you on an evening walking tour of trade shops where jewelry and other products are made in 18th-century style. The separate ticket required for this program may be purchased at the visitor center or from the Greenhow Lumber House.

The Norfolk Trolley has a guided tour of the historic downtown area that allows you to get on and off as you please. Tickets are available at the Hampton Roads Transit kiosk at Waterside Festival Hall. Portsmouth's Olde Towne Trolley Tour gives you the inside story of major historical events. It departs from various points in downtown on Sunday and Wednesday at 10:45.

Hour-long guided walking tours of the historic area depart from the Greenhow Lumber House daily from 9 to 5. Reservations should be made on the day of the tour at the Lumber House and can be made only by those with tickets to Colonial Williamsburg. "The Original Ghosts of Williamsburg" Candlelight Tour is based on the book of the same name by L. B. Taylor Jr. The tour is offered every evening at 8 (there's also an 8:45 tour June–August). The 1¼-hour, lantern-lit guided tour through historic Williamsburg costs $8.50. Interpreters well versed in Williamsburg and Colonial history are available to lead groups on tours of the Historic Area.

🚤 Boat Tours **American Rover Sailing Tours** ☎ 757/627-7245. *Carrie B* ☎ 757/393-4735. **Discovery Cruise** ☎ 757/422-2900.

🚗 Driving Tours **Hampton Circle Tour** ☎ 757/727-1102. The **Virginia Beach Tour** ☎ 757/473-4888 or 800/822-3224.

🚋 Trolley Tours **Norfolk Trolley** ✉ 333 Waterside Dr. ☎ 757/640-6300. **Olde Towne Trolley Tour** ✉ 6 Crawford Pkwy. ☎ 757/393-5111.

🚶 Walking Tours **Greenhow Lumber House** ✉ Duke of Gloucester St. ☎ 757/220-7645 or 800/447-8679. **Interpreters** ☎ 800/228-8878. **"The Original Ghosts of Williamsburg" Candlelight Tour** ☎ 757/253-1058.

TRAIN TRAVEL

Amtrak trains stop in Williamsburg on their way from Boston; New York; Philadelphia; Washington, D.C.; and Richmond to Newport News, with one train daily in each direction. At Newport News, a shuttle bus connects to Norfolk. Trains stop at Williamsburg on their way from New York, Washington, and Richmond to Newport News.

🚆 Train Stations **Newport News Amtrak Station** ✉ NPN, 9304 Warwick Blvd. ☎ 757/245-3589. **Williamsburg Transportation Center (WBG)** ✉ 468 N. Boundary St. ☎ 757/229-8750.

🚆 Train Lines **Amtrak** ☎ 800/872-7245.

VISITOR INFORMATION

Visitor Information Centers throughout the area generally operate daily 9–5. Call ahead to get visitor packets from Colonial Williamsburg and Virginia Beach: they both include a wealth of information and great maps. The Virginia Beach packet also includes a useful coupon booklet.

🚹 Tourist Information **Colonial National Historical Park** ⛫ Box 210, Yorktown 23690 ☎ 757/898–3400 ⊕ www.apva.org. **Colonial Williamsburg Dining and Lodging Reservations** ☎ 800/447–8679. **Colonial Williamsburg Visitor Center** ⛫ Box 1776, Williamsburg 23187-1776 ☎ 800/246–2099 ⊕ www.history.org. **Hampton Convention and Visitors Bureau** ✉ 710 Settlers Landing Rd., Hampton 23669 ☎ 757/727–1102 or 800/800–2202 ⊕ www.hampton.va.us/. **Newport News Tourism and Conference Bureau** ✉ 2400 Washington Ave., Newport News 23607 ☎ 757/928–6843 or 888/493–7386 ⊕ www.newport-news.org. **Newport News Visitor Information Center** ✉ 13560 Jefferson Ave., 1–64, Exit 250B ☎ 757/886–7777 or 888/493–7386. **Norfolk Convention and Visitors Bureau** ✉ End of 4th View St., 23503 ☎ 757/441–1852 or 800/368–3097 ⊕ www.norfolkcvb.com. **Portsmouth Convention and Visitors Bureau** ✉ 505 Crawford St., Suite 2, Portsmouth 23704 ☎ 757/393–5327 or 800/767–8782 ⊕ www.ci.portsmouth.va.us. **Virginia Beach Visitor Information Center** ✉ 2100 Parks Ave., Virginia Beach 23451 ☎ 757/437–4888 ⊕ www.vbfun.com. **Williamsburg Area Convention and Visitors Bureau** ✉ 201 Penniman Rd., Box 3585, Williamsburg 23187-3585 ☎ 757/253–0192 or 800/368–6511. **Williamsburg Attraction Center** ✉ 5715–62A U.S. 60, Prime Outlets, Williamsburg 23187 ☎ 757/253–1058.

BALTIMORE

6

STARE OUTSIDER ART IN THE FACE
at the American Visionary Art Museum ⇨ *p.216*

BASK IN BALTIMORE'S WATERY PAST
starting with the Inner Harbor's
Maritime Museum ⇨ *p.217*

SEE WHERE THE "BANNER STILL WAVES"
on your approach to Fort McHenry ⇨ *p.218*

DEVOUR A WHOLE GRILLED FISH
where seafood is supreme:
the Black Olive ⇨ *p.235*

LOAD UP ON FREE BOOKS
at the Book Thing ⇨ *p.248*

Updated by
Natasha Lesser

BALTIMORE IS A CITY OF NEIGHBORHOODS. From the cobblestone streets of historic Fells Point and Federal Hill, up the wide avenues of elegant Mount Vernon, and across the countless modest blue-collar enclaves, the city wears many different faces. On the east and west sides, seamless blocks of the city's trademark redbrick row houses, each fronted by white marble steps, radiate outward from the modern towers of downtown Baltimore. Uptown, marble mansions, grand churches, and philanthropic institutions proudly bearing their founders' names mark the city's progress: fortunes earned on the harbor flowed north to create these monuments to wealth and power.

Baltimore was established by the Colonial government in 1729, at the end of the broad Patapsco River that empties into the Chesapeake Bay. Named for George Calvert, the first Lord Baltimore and the founder of Maryland, the town grew as a port and shipbuilding center and did booming business during the War of Independence.

A quantum leap came at the turn of the 19th century: from 6,700 in 1776, the population reached 45,000 by 1810. Because it was the home port for U.S. Navy vessels and for the swift Baltimore clipper ships that often preyed on British shipping, the city was a natural target for the enemy during the War of 1812. After capturing and torching Washington, D.C., the British fleet sailed up the Patapsco River and bombarded Baltimore's Fort McHenry, but in vain. The 30- by 42-foot, 15-star, 15-stripe flag was still flying "by the dawn's early light," a spectacle that inspired "The Star-Spangled Banner."

After the War of 1812, Baltimore prospered as a slave market, and during the Civil War the population's sympathies were divided between North and South, provoking riots. Frederick Douglass escaped his childhood enslavement in the shipyards of Fells Point to become a famed orator and abolitionist. The first bloodshed of the Civil War occurred in Baltimore when the Sixth Massachusetts Regiment was stoned by an angry group of Baltimoreans. (This is a town whose regional identity has always been, and remains, ambiguous.) Soon after, President Lincoln, mistrusting the loyalty of certain city officials, had them summarily detained—an act that was no doubt strategically effective but was probably unconstitutional.

In the late 1800s, Baltimore became a manufacturing center of iron, steel, chemical fertilizer, and textiles. It also became the oyster capital of the world, packing more of those tasty mollusks in 1880 than anywhere else. After a 1904 fire destroyed 1,500 structures, Baltimore rebuilt valiantly and rode the economic roller coaster through World War I and the Great Depression. World War II brought an influx of people and industry to the city. After the war, a steady flow of residents to the newly developed suburbs drained the city of vitality as well as population; the loss of manufacturing jobs also hurt this blue-collar town, and many neighborhoods seriously declined.

Starting in the late 1950s, the city began trying to revive itself. The construction of Charles Center in 1961 was one early attempt. By the late 1960s, plans were in effect to invigorate the city's waterfront. But it wasn't until the early 1980s when Harborplace opened that the Inner Harbor became what it is today. Hotels, office buildings, and attractions such as the Maryland Science Center, the stellar National Aquarium, and Oriole Park at Camden Yards were built around Inner Harbor. Restaurants and shops proliferated in the once-downtrodden downtown area and then beyond.

Development continues to spread along the waterfront into the formerly industrial areas of Fells Point, Canton, and Locust Point, and many young professionals and businesses are moving in—to the dismay of some, who see the impending loss of the city's waterfront industries. In fact, neighborhoods all over the city are being revitalized. Other areas, like Roland Park, Guilford, Homeland, and Mt. Washington in north Baltimore, remain the tony residential neighborhoods they've always been. Yet just east and west of downtown are blocks of boarded up homes, signs of the problems that the city still faces. It is this stark contrast that Baltimore continues to address.

EXPLORING BALTIMORE

Many of Baltimore's biggest attractions are around the Inner Harbor—the National Aquarium in Baltimore, the Visionary Arts Museum, and Camden Yards. Farther uptown are the Walters Museum of Art, in Mount Vernon, and the Baltimore Museum of Art, near Johns Hopkins University, in Charles Village. The neighborhoods themselves are fun to explore. Historic Federal Hill, just south of the Inner Harbor, is home to some of the oldest houses in the city. Fells Point and Canton, farther east, are lively waterfront communities. Mount Vernon and Charles Village have wide avenues lined with grand old row houses that were once home to Baltimore's wealthiest residents. Farther north are Roland Park (Frederick Law Olmsted Jr. contributed to its planning), Guilford, Homeland, and Mt. Washington, all leafy, residential neighborhoods with cottages, large Victorian house, and redbrick Colonials.

It's easy to explore the Inner Harbor and neighborhoods such as Mount Vernon, Charles Village, and Fells Point by foot. For traveling between areas, however, a car is the most efficient means of transportation. Parking around the Inner Harbor is primarily in garages, though meters can be found along Key Highway. In other neighborhoods, you can generally find meter parking on the street.

Pratt Street runs east along the Inner Harbor; from here the major northbound arteries are Charles Street and the Jones Falls Expressway (I–83). Cross street addresses are marked "East" or "West" according to which side of Charles Street they are on; similarly, Baltimore Street marks the dividing line between north and south. Residents refer to areas of the city by direction of these major arteries: thus, South Baltimore, North Baltimore, East Baltimore, West Baltimore, Northeast Baltimore, Northwest Baltimore, etc.

A light-rail runs north–south along Howard Street, going between Camden Yards and Hunt Valley in the northern suburbs. Buses also run throughout the city. But neither is particularly quick, and they don't go

Baltimore

Chase St.

TO
BALTIMORE
ZOO

TO HAMPDEN, JOHNS
HOPKINS UNIVERSITY,
AMTRAK PENN STATION,

13 – 18
see inset

TO
BALTIMORE
STREETCAR
MUSEUM

Greenmount Ave.

TO BOLTON
HILL

Read St.

Eager St.

Cathedral St.

N. Charles St.

St. Paul Street

Calvert St.

Read St.

MOUNT
VERNON

Jones Falls Expwy.

45

Martin Luther King Jr. Blvd.

Orchard St.

St. Mary St.

Madison St.

Monument St.

11

12

10

7

6

9

8

5

Centre St.

Front St.

Hillen St.

Guilford Ave.

40

Park Ave.

Franklin St.

4

3

2

Mulberry St.

1

Charles St.

St. Paul Place

Pleasant St.

Fallsway

Gay St.

Front St.

40

Greene St.

Eutaw St.

Howard St.

Saratoga St.

Liberty St.

43

Lexington
Market

Lexington St.

Greyhound
Bus Terminal Site

CITY
CENTER

38

37

42

Paca St.

Fayette St.

Baltimore St.

WEST
BALTIMORE

45

44

1st Mariner
Arena

Lombard St.

Light St.

South St.

Custom House Ave.

Gay St.

Holocaust
Memorial

36

29
Commu
College
of Balti
Harbor
Campus

Market Pl.

49 50

Eutaw St.

Pratt St.

46

Camden St.

Convention
Center

Conway St.

47

ORIOLE PARK AT
CAMDEN
YARDS

395

Charles St.

Calvert St.

Light St.

19

25

20

Pier 1

Pier 2

27

26

28

Pier 3

Pier 4

Inner Harbor

Pier 5

Lee St.

Martin Luther King
Jr. Blvd.

W. Hamburg St.

48

TO
BWI
AIRPORT

Lee St.

Visitor
Center
i

Hughes St.

Hanover St.

Montgomery St.

Sharp St.

Howard St.

Light St.

22

FEDERAL
HILL

RASH FIELD

Key Hwy.

FEDERAL
HILL PARK

Covington St.

24

TO BALTIM
MUSEUM
OF INDUS

23

Warren St.

to every part of town. Cabs can be a good way to get around the city, but you must call first to arrange a pickup. A fun way to travel between waterfront attractions such as Fort McHenry and Fells Point is to take one of the water taxis that ply the harbor.

Mount Vernon

Baltimore's cultural center, Mount Vernon is home to the Walters Museum of Art and the Peabody Institute, one of the country's top music schools. The area was named for the nation's first significant monument to George Washington, erected at the neighborhood's center in Mount Vernon Place. In the 19th century Mount Vernon was home to some of Baltimore's wealthiest residents, including Enoch Pratt, a wealthy merchant who donated funds for the first public library; Robert Garrett, of the Baltimore & Ohio Railroad, and Henry and William Walters, who founded the art gallery that bears their name. Though some of the grand houses here remain single family residences, many have been turned into apartments or offices.

Charles Street is the neighborhood's main thoroughfare; here you can find shops, restaurants, and cafés. It takes about 25 to 30 minutes to walk up Charles from the Inner Harbor, or you could drive or take the No. 3 bus.

Numbers in the text correspond to numbers in the margin and on the Baltimore map.

a good tour

Begin by parking along Charles Street somewhere between Mulberry and Madison streets. Just south of Mulberry Street is the **Woman's Industrial Exchange** ❶ ☞, a Baltimore institution. Back up Charles, one block west on Mulberry Street is the **Basilica of the Assumption** ❷, the nation's oldest Catholic cathedral. West of the basilica is the **Enoch Pratt Free Library** ❸, the nation's first free public library. Returning to Charles Street, take note of the **First Unitarian Church** ❹, at Franklin Street, one block up. About two blocks north is the **Walters Art Museum** ❺, an impressive museum with more than 30,000 paintings, sculpture, and other artworks. The gallery marks the southern end of **Mount Vernon Place** ❻, where a series of lovely parks is dominated by the **Washington Monument** ❼. The **Peabody Institute** ❽ and the **George Peabody Library** ❾ are on the southeast side of Mount Vernon Square. Head west on Mount Vernon Place to see the **Garrett-Jacobs Mansion** ❿, designed by Stanford White. Continue west and Mount Vernon Place turns into Monument Street, where you can visit the **Maryland Historical Society** ⓫ for an intriguing look at the past. If you're up for more art, head south on Park Avenue back to Centre Street, to visit the **Contemporary Museum** ⓬.

TIMING The many sights of historic Mount Vernon merit at least an entire morning.

Sights to See

❷ **Basilica of the Assumption.** Completed in 1821, the Catholic Basilica of the Assumption is the oldest cathedral in the United States. Designed by Benjamin Latrobe, architect of the U.S. Capitol, it stands as a paragon of neoclassicism, with a grand portico fronted by six Corinthian columns that suggest an ancient Greek temple. Two towers are surmounted by cupolas. The church, including 24 original skylights in the dome, which were covered over after World War II, are being restored; the building will be closed for work until 2006, the bicentennial of the laying of the church's cornerstone. ⊠ *Mulberry St. at Cathedral St., Mount Vernon* ☎ *410/727–3564* ⊗ *Call for hours.*

⑫ Contemporary Museum. New works are created expressly for the museum by artists invited from all over the world to work in residence here. The pieces must be created in collaboration with a local community or institution and be relevant to the city in some way. What results is some very creative work, shown both on-site and off, using traditional mediums and innovative approaches. ⊠ *100 W. Centre St., Mount Vernon* ☎ *410/783–5720* ⊕ *www.contemporary.org* ⊠ *$3.50 suggested donation* ⊗ *Thurs.–Sat. noon–5.*

❸ Enoch Pratt Free Library. Donated to the city of Baltimore in 1882 by its namesake, a wealthy merchant, the Enoch Pratt Free Library was one of the country's first free-circulation public libraries; it remains one of the country's largest. The Pratt was remarkable for allowing any citizen to borrow books at a time when only the wealthy could afford to buy them. When the collection outgrew its original fortresslike rococo structure in 1933, Pratt's democratic ideals were incorporated into the new building's grand yet accessible design. Innovations such as a sidewalk-level entrance and department store–style exhibit windows set the standard for public libraries across the country. The building is still a treat to explore. A huge skylight illuminates the grand Central Hall's marble floors, gilded fixtures, mural panels depicting the history of printing and publishing, and oil portraits of the Lords Baltimore. The Children's Department, where there's a fish pond, puppet theater, and a large selection of books, is a real gem for little ones. An audio architecture tour of the museum is available at the circulation desk. ⊠ *400 Cathedral St., Mount Vernon* ☎ *410/396–5500* ⊕ *www.pratt.lib.md.us* ⊗ *June–Sept., Mon.–Wed. 11–7, Thurs. 10–5:30, Fri. and Sat. 10–5; Oct.–May, Mon.–Wed. 11–7, Thurs. 10–5:30, Fri. and Sat. 10–5; Sun. 1–5.*

off the
beaten
path

AMERICAN DIME MUSEUM – Baltimore's most eccentric museum is named for the traveling collections of man-made and natural curiosities that were popular in the 19th century (they were called "dime museums" after the typical cost of admission.) It's all a tribute to the art of the carnival sideshow, displaying a collection of colorful artifacts such as sideshow banners, props, and believe-it-or-not displays that include a "genuine" unicorn. Exhibitions explain the attractions and even let you in on the secrets of the business. Sword swallowers, contortionists, and other sideshow professionals occasionally perform. ⊠ *1808 Maryland Ave., Midtown* ☎ *410/230–0263* ⊕ *www.dimemuseum.com* ⊠ *$5* ⊗ *Wed.–Fri. noon–3, weekends noon–5.*

BALTIMORE STREETCAR MUSEUM – This often-overlooked museum lets you travel back to an era when streetcars dominated city thoroughfares. A film traces the vehicle's evolution, and there are beautifully restored streetcars to explore. Best of all, you can take unlimited rides on a working streetcar. ⊠ *1901 Falls Rd., Midtown* ☎ *410/547–0264* 🖅 *$6* ⊙ *June–Oct., weekends noon–5; Nov.–May, Sun. noon–5.*

❹ **First Unitarian Church.** Designed by Maximilian Godefroy in 1819, the church that year was the site for the sermon that definitively established Unitarianism as a denomination (the sermon was given by the church's founder, Dr. William Ellery Channing). ⊠ *At Charles and Franklin Sts., entrance at 1 W. Hamilton St. Mount Vernon* ☎ *410/685–2330* ⊙ *Weekdays 9–3.*

❾ **George Peabody Library.** The Peabody Library is a fine example of neo-Renaissance architecture. Its stunning reading room reflects the scholarly interests of the 19th century, with more than a quarter of a million books lining the shelves. Most impressive, though, are the cast-iron balconies towering above the black-and-white marble floor. A skylight, 61 feet above, brightens the library, which some have called "the most beautiful room in Baltimore." ⊠ *1 E. Mt. Vernon Pl., Mount Vernon* ☎ *410/ 659–8179* 🖅 *Free* ⊙ *Tues.–Fri. 9–5, Sat. 9–1; public viewing 10–10:15 and 3–3:15.*

☯ **Maryland Zoo in Baltimore.** The 150 acres of the Maryland Zoo in Baltimore—the third-oldest zoo in the country—are a natural stomping ground for little ones seeking out the spectacle of elephants, lions, giraffes, hippos, and penguins, among the 2,000 animals that make this their home. Don't miss the warthog exhibit, said to be the nation's only dedicated environment for the bumpy beasts. Favorite sights include a chimpanzee house and leopard lair, polar bears frolicking in an arctic pool, and a petting zoo with a re-created barnyard. If you make it all the way to the Africa exhibit and are too tired to walk back, you can hop on a tram that goes back to the entrance. Surrounding the zoo is Druid Hill Park, which was designed by Frederick Law Olmsted Jr.; the park has seen better days, but it's worth a drive through. ⊠ *Druid Hill Lake Dr., Druid Hill* ☎ *410/366–5466* ⊕ *www.baltimorezoo.org* 🖅 *$12* ⊙ *Mar.–Dec. 10–4:30.*

❿ **Garrett-Jacobs Mansion.** Originally built in 1893 by Stanford White for Robert Garrett, the president of the Baltimore & Ohio Railroad, this mansion was the largest and most expensive ever constructed in Baltimore (the neighbors objected to its size). After Garrett died in 1896, his widow, Mary, and her second husband, Dr. Henry Barton Jacobs, had John Russell Pope build an extension of equal size. ⊠ *11 W. Mt. Vernon Pl., Mount Vernon* ☎ *410/539–6914* ⊕ *www.garrett-jacobsmansion. org* 🖅 *$3* ⊙ *Tours Mon. at 3 and by appt.; reservations required.*

⓫ **Maryland Historical Society.** More than 200,000 objects serve to celebrate Maryland's history and heritage at this museum. One major attraction is the original manuscript of "The Star-Spangled Banner." The first floor is devoted to an exhibit about Marylanders' pursuit of liberty, with a focus on religious freedom, voting rights, labor, and war. Featured on the second floor are portrait paintings by the Peale family and Joshua

Johnson, America's first African-American portrait artist, as well as 18th- and 19th-century Maryland landscape paintings juxtaposed against present-day photographs of the same places. Furniture manufactured and designed in Maryland from the 18th century to the present is on the third floor. There's also a library with 7 million works that relate to the state's history. ⊠ *201 W. Monument St., Mount Vernon* ☎ *410/685–3750* ⊕ *www.mdhs.org* ⌨ *$8 museum, $6 library* ⊗ *Museum: Wed.–Sun. 10–5; library: Wed.–Sat. 10–4:30.*

★ ❻ **Mount Vernon Place.** One of the country's most beautifully designed public spaces, Mount Vernon Place came into being when John Eager Howard donated the highest point in Baltimore as a site for a memorial to George Washington. With the monument as its center, the square is composed of four parks, each a block in length, that are arranged around Mount Vernon Place (which goes east–west) and Washington Place (north–south). The sculptures in the parks deserve a close look; of special note is a bronze lion by Antoine-Louis Barye in the middle of West Mount Vernon Place. Northeast of the monument is Mount Vernon Methodist Church, built in the mid-1850s on the site of Francis Scott Key's home and place of death. Take a moment to admire the brownstones along the north side of East Mount Vernon Place. They're excellent examples of the luxurious mansions built by 19th-century residents of Baltimore's most prestigious address.

❽ **Peabody Institute.** Established in 1857 by philanthropist George Peabody, this beautiful building was the first academy of music in America. It's still one of the most preeminent music conservatories in the country. Since 1977 it has been a division of Johns Hopkins University. ⊠ *1 E. Mt. Vernon Pl., Mount Vernon* ☎ *410/659–8100* ⊕ *www.peabody.jhu.edu.*

★ ❺ **Walters Art Museum.** The Walters's prodigious collection of more than 30,000 artworks provides an organized overview of human history over 5,500 years, from the 3rd millennium BC to the early 20th century. The original museum (1909) houses the museum's major collections of Renaissance and baroque paintings as well as a sculpture court. In two other buildings are Egyptian, Greek and Roman, Byzantine, and Ethiopian art collections, among the best in the nation, along with many 19th-century paintings. There are also medieval armor and artifacts, jewelry, and decorative works; Egyptology exhibits; a wonderful gift shop; and a café. ⊠ *600 N. Charles St., Mount Vernon* ☎ *410/547–9000* ⊕ *www.thewalters.org* ⌨ *$10; free 1st Thurs. of month and Sat. 11–1* ⊗ *Wed.–Sun. 10–5.*

need a break? Donna's (⊠ 800 N. Charles St. ☎ 410/385–0180) is a Mount Vernon spot for coffee; soups, salads, and sandwiches are also served. At artsy and elegant **Sascha's 527** (⊠ 527 N. Charles St. ☎ 410/539–8880) you can choose from a selection of salads and sandwiches.

❼ **Washington Monument.** Completed on July 4, 1829, Baltimore's Washington Monument was the first monument dedicated to the nation's first president. The 160-foot white marble tower is capped with an 18-foot statue depicting Washington in 1783 as he resigned his position as the commander in chief of the Continental Army at the Annapolis statehouse. A total of 228 steps spiral up to the top of the monument, where incomparable views of the city are available from four portals. The tower was designed and built by Robert Mills, the first architect born and educated in the United States; 19 years after completing Baltimore's Washington Monument, Mills designed and erected the national Washington Monument in D.C. ⊠ *Mt. Vernon Pl., Mount Vernon* ☎ *410/396–1049* ⊑ *$1* ⊙ *Wed.–Sun. 10–4.*

❶ **Woman's Industrial Exchange.** This Baltimore institution was organized in 1882 as a way for destitute women, many of them Civil War widows, to support themselves in a ladylike fashion through sewing and other domestic handiworks. To this day you can still purchase handmade quilts, embroidered baby clothes, sock monkeys, and many other crafts. But most come for lunch in the tearoom, where old-fashioned fare such as tomato aspic, chicken salad, yeast rolls, and homemade cakes are served. It's closed on weekends. ⊠ *333 N. Charles St., Mount Vernon* ☎ *410/685–4388* ⊕ *www.womansindustrialexchange.org* ⊙ *Weekdays 10–3, gift shop open until 4.*

off the beaten path
GREAT BLACKS IN WAX MUSEUM – Though not as convincing as the likenesses at a Madame Tussaud's, the more than 100 wax figures on display here do a good job of recounting the triumphs and trials of Africans and African-Americans. The wax figures are accompanied by text and audio. Baltimoreans honored include Frederick Douglass, who as a youth lived and worked in Fells Point; singer Billie Holiday; and jazz composer Eubie Blake. To get here from Mount Vernon, take Charles north and turn left at North Avenue. ⊠ *1601 E. North Ave., East Baltimore* ☎ *410/563–3404* ⊕ *www.greatblacksinwax. org* ⊑ *$6* ⊙ *Mid-Jan.–mid-Oct., Tues.–Sat. 9–6, Sun. noon–6; mid-Oct.–mid-Jan., Tues.–Sat. 9–5, Sun. noon–5. Closed Mon. except in Feb., July, Aug., Martin Luther King Jr. Day, and most federal holidays; holiday hours 10–4.*

MARYLAND INSTITUTE COLLEGE OF ART – Better known as MICA, Maryland's premier art school was established in 1826. The school's buildings are primarily found along Mt. Royal Avenue, which borders Bolton Hill, a neighborhood of handsome 19th-century row houses. The main building, at 1300 Mount Royal, was built in 1908 in Renaissance revival style. The Mount Royal Station building at Cathedral Street was once a stop for the B&O Railroad, but since 1964 it has been home to MICA's sculpture department. Up the street is the contemporary Brown Center, which opened in 2003; some love it, some hate it, but the translucent building definitely makes a statement. ⊠ *1300 Mt. Royal Ave., Bolton Hill* ☎ *410/669–9200* ⊕ *www.mica.edu.*

Charles Village

Anchored by Johns Hopkins University and the Baltimore Museum of Art, Charles Village is home to many students and professors. Writers and artists, too, are drawn to the area's intellectual atmosphere. The row houses along Charles, St. Paul, and Calvert Streets—some of them quite large—were built in the late 1890s and early 1900s for merchants, bankers, and other professionals. These early developments were constructed on old family estates, one of which became the basis for the present-day Johns Hopkins campus. Some of the old mansions still exist and are now museums, including Johns Hopkins's Homewood House and the Evergreen House, which also belongs to the university. On the eastern and northern sides of the Johns Hopkins campus are the neighborhoods of Tuscany-Canterbury and Roland Park. Farther to the north and east are Homeland and Guilford, tony areas worth exploring for their beautiful homes and lovely, tree-lined streets.

a good tour

About 4 mi north of downtown and the Inner Harbor, on Charles Street, is the **Baltimore Museum of Art** ⑬, where an excellent art collection is housed in a John Russell Pope–designed building. The art museum is contiguous to the Homewood campus of **Johns Hopkins University** ⑭; you can enter the campus at a few spots along Charles Street. At the main entrance on Charles and 34th streets is the exquisite **Homewood House Museum** ⑮, the historic house of John Carroll Jr., which is open to the public. Next to the playing fields, on the University Parkway side of the campus, is the **Lacrosse Museum and National Hall of Fame** ⑯.

From Johns Hopkins University, drive several blocks north on Charles Street to Stratford. Turn right on Stratford and drive to where it intersects with Greenway to reach the **Sherwood Gardens** ⑰, an urban oasis where tulips and azaleas abound each spring. Backtrack one block to St. Paul Street, which then curves northwest to meet Charles Street; two blocks north of that intersection, at Charles Street and Cold Spring Lane, stands the grand **Evergreen House** ⑱, where a guided tour gives you a sense of the lives of the rich and famous at the turn of the 20th century.

TIMING   Give yourself at least half a day to visit the Baltimore Museum of Art and walk around the Johns Hopkins campus. Add an additional hour or two for each of the smaller museums.

Sights to See

★ ⑬ **Baltimore Museum of Art.** Works by Matisse, Picasso, Cézanne, Gauguin, van Gogh, and Monet are among the 90,000 paintings, sculptures, and decorative arts on exhibit at this impressive museum, near Johns Hopkins University. Particular strengths include an encyclopedic collection of postimpressionist paintings donated to the museum by the Cone sisters, Baltimore natives who were pioneer collectors of early 20th-century art. The museum also owns the world's second-largest collection of Andy Warhol works, and many pieces of 18th- and 19th-century American painting and decorative arts. The museum's neoclassical main building was designed by John Russell Pope, the architect of the National Gallery in Washington; the modern aluminum and concrete wing houses the contemporary art collection. From Gertrude's, the museum restaurant, you can look out at 20th-century sculpture displayed in two landscaped gardens. The first Thursday of each month, the museum is free and has music, lectures, children's activities, and a cash bar. ⊠ *10 Art Museum Dr., Charles Village* ☎ *410/396–7100,* ⊕ *www.artbma.*

org ⌨ *$7; free 1st Thurs. of month* ☉ *Wed.–Fri. 11–5, weekends 11–6, 1st Thurs. of month 11–8.*

⑱ Evergreen House. Built in the 1850s, this 48-room Italianate mansion was the home of the 19th-century diplomat and collector John Work Garrett, whose father was president of the Baltimore & Ohio Railroad (the Garrett family continued to live here until the 1950s). Garrett bequeathed the house, its contents (an exquisite collection of books, paintings, and porcelain), and 26 acres of grounds to Johns Hopkins University. He required that the estate remain open to "lovers of music, art, and beautiful things." A tour of the mansion is a fascinating look at the luxury that surrounded a rich American family at the turn of the 20th century. ⊠ *4545 N. Charles St., Homeland* ☎ *410/516–0341* ⌨ *$6* ☉ *Tues.–Fri. 11–4, weekends noon–4.*

⑮ Homewood House Museum. This elegant Federal-period mansion was once the home of Charles Carroll Jr., son of Charles Carroll of Carrollton, a signer of the Declaration of Independence. Deeded to Johns Hopkins University in 1902 along with 60 acres, the house served as faculty club and offices before being fully restored to its 1800 grandeur (it's one of the finest examples of the neoclassical architecture of the period). ⊠ *3400 N. Charles St., at 34th St., Charles Village* ☎ *410/516–5589* 🖶 *410/516–7859* ⌨ *$6* ☉ *Tues.–Fri. 11–4, weekends noon–4.*

⑭ Johns Hopkins University. The school was founded in 1876 with funds donated by Johns Hopkins, director of the Baltimore & Ohio Railroad. Much of the neo-Colonial architecture of the Homewood campus dates from the early 1900s, when the present-day campus was laid out. Dominating the school's main quad is Gilman Hall, which was built in 1904 and named for Hopkin's first president, Daniel Coit Gilman. Pathways lead through campus; maps throughout can help you find your way. The medical school and hospital are in East Baltimore. ⊠ *3400 N. Charles St., Charles Village* ☎ *410/516–8000* ⊕ *www.jhu.edu.*

Lovely Lane Methodist Church. Built in 1882, Lovely Lane Methodist Church is honored with the title "The Mother Church of American Methodism." Stanford White designed the Romanesque sanctuary after the basilicas of Ravenna, Italy; the stained-glass windows are excellent examples of Italian mosaic art. The buildings to the north that resemble the church are the original campus of the Women's College of Baltimore, now called Goucher College (the school moved to Towson in the 1950s). Dr. Goucher, the college's founder, was a pastor at Lovely Lane. Today, the building next to the church is occupied by the Baltimore Lab School. Tours of the church and the Methodist Historical Society are by appointment. ⊠ *2200 St. Paul St., North Charles* ☎ *410/ 889–1512* ⊕ *www.lovelylane.net* ☉ *Weekdays 9–3.*

Waverly Farmer's Market. Every Saturday morning locals gather to shop for fresh produce and baked goods at this popular farmer's market. You can get a cup of coffee and a muffin or a tasty grilled mushroom sandwich to snack on as you check out the scene. ⊠ *Parking lot at 33rd St. and Greenmount Ave., Waverly* ☎ *No phone* ⌨ *Free* ☉ *Sat. 7–noon.*

🔞 **Lacrosse Museum and National Hall of Fame.** Photos, objects, and videos tell the story of the history of lacrosse, a very popular sport in Maryland. One room is dedicated to outstanding players who have been honored by the U.S. Lacrosse association since 1957. ⊠ *113 W. University Pkwy., Tuscany-Canterbury* ☎ *410/235–6882* ⊕ *www.uslacrosse.org* ⊠ *$3* ⊙ *June–Jan., weekdays 10–3; Feb.–May, Tues.–Sat. 10–3.*

need a break? Stop into the **One World Cafe** (⊠ 100 W. University Pkwy.) for coffee, a smoothie, or some creative vegetarian fare.

🔞 **Sherwood Gardens.** A popular spring destination for Baltimore families, this 6-acre park contains more than 80,000 tulips that bloom in late April. Azaleas peak in late April and the first half of May. The gardens are usually at their best around Mother's Day. ⊠ *Stratford Rd. and Greenway, east of St. Paul St., Guilford* ☎ *410/785–0444* ⊠ *Free* ⊙ *Daily dawn–dusk.*

Inner Harbor

The revival of the Inner Harbor in the early 1980s was a success story for the city. Once an area of run-down warehouses and industrial buildings, the Inner Harbor was transformed into Baltimore's main destination. Hotels, office buildings, and attractions such as the National Aquarium, Harborplace, and the Maryland Science Center are all in the area; Camden Yards is a few blocks west. Still a working port, the harbor is a place where merchant ships unload cargo or undergo dry-dock repairs while nearby pleasure boats tie up for a visit along the promenade. Landlubbers can enjoy Baltimore's maritime scene as well: sailboat tours, water taxis, and boat rentals all let you tour the city by sea.

South of the Inner Harbor, and best accessed by car or water taxi, Fort McHenry, now preserved as a national monument, was bombarded by the British during the War of 1812. During a long night's siege by cannon and artillery the fort never fell, and the sight of the American flag flying above the fort's walls inspired Francis Scott Key to pen a poem that became the national anthem.

a good walk Begin at the northwest corner of the Inner Harbor at **Harborplace and the Gallery** ⑲, where two glass-enclosed market pavilions invite you to graze at the food stalls and boutiques. Tour the **USS Constellation** ⑳, a restored 1854 wooden naval warship docked at the heart of Harborplace. You can pick up the water taxi to **Fort McHenry** ㉑ right in front of Harborplace (look for the signs) or drive there later.

Walk down the west side of the Inner Harbor to the glass-enclosed **Visitor Center.** Continue down to the southwest corner of the harbor, to the **Maryland Science Center** ㉒, where an IMAX movie theater and hundreds of hands-on exhibits are for both children and adults. From there it's just a short walk to the best view in Baltimore at **Federal Hill Park** ㉓ and the adjacent **American Visionary Art Museum** ㉔.

Return to Harborplace and walk east along the northern edge of Inner Harbor to Pier 2: here, at the **World Trade Center** ㉕, you can enjoy the panoramic vista from 27 floors up. At Piers 3 and 4 is the **National Aquarium in Baltimore** ㉖, with thousands of colorful fish, sharks, dolphins, jellyfish, reptiles, and amphibians. Docked just to the west on Pier 3 is the **Baltimore Maritime Museum** ㉗, whose three vessels include the USS *Torsk,* the submarine credited with sinking the last two Japanese warships during World War II. On Pier 4 is the **Power Plant** ㉘, which is now home to Barnes & Noble, Hard Rock Cafe, and ESPN Zone. It's an option if you want to break for lunch, although Harborplace offers a wider selection of eateries.

Across Pratt Street is **Port Discovery—The Baltimore Children's Museum** ㉙, which the young and young-at-heart climb, crawl, slide, and swing their way through. The museum shares the plaza with Power Plant Live!, a retail and entertainment complex; head across it to find Maryland Art Place, a gallery of contemporary local artists. On the other side of President Street, at the corner of Pratt, is the dramatic, black, red, and yellow **Reginald F. Lewis Museum** ㉚, devoted to African-American history and culture.

If time allows, there are a few more small museums at the east end of the Inner Harbor. Right past Pier 6, the **Baltimore Public Works Museum** ㉛ allows you a peek at the city's underground workings, from steam pipes to sewers. A block farther east, at President and Fleet streets, the **Baltimore Civil War Museum–President Street Station** ㉜ considers Baltimore's divided sympathies during the War Between the States.

If you're ready for more, head back up President Street and east on Pratt Street to Albemarle Street and the **Star-Spangled Banner House** ㉝. The American flag that flew at Fort McHenry when Francis Scott Key wrote "The Star-Spangled Banner" was sewn here. One block north, on Lombard Street, is the **Carroll Mansion** ㉞, once home to Charles Carroll, one of the signers of the Declaration of Independence. Continue east on Lombard Street another few blocks into Historic Jonestown to reach the **Jewish Museum of Maryland** ㉟. Head back along Lombard Street and north to Baltimore Street to find **Nine Front Street** ㊱, home to Baltimore's second mayor, and the redbrick **Phoenix Shot Tower** ㊲. Cross over President and follow Baltimore Street to Holliday Street, and take a right to get to **Baltimore City Hall** ㊳.

TIMING   Allow at least a whole day for Inner Harbor attractions. Arrive early at the National Aquarium to ensure admission, which is by timed intervals; by noon, the wait is often two or three hours.

Sights to See

㉔ **American Visionary Art Museum.** The nation's primary museum and education center for self-taught or "outsider" art has won great acclaim by both museum experts and those who don't even consider themselves art aficionados. Seven galleries exhibit the unusual creations—paintings, sculptures, relief works, and pieces that defy easy classification—of untrained "visionary" artists working outside the mainstream art world. In addition to the visual stimulation of amazingly intricate or refreshingly inventive works, reading the short bios of artists will give you in-

FodorsChoice
★

sight to their often moving spiritual and expressive motivations. The museum's unusual, playful philosophy extends outside its walls, with large exhibits installed in a former whiskey warehouse and a 55-foot whirligig twirling in the museum's plaza. The Joy America Cafe has a view of the Baltimore Harbor and an exuberant menu to match its name. ⊠ *800 Key Hwy., Federal Hill* ☎ *410/244–1900* ⊕ *www.avam.org* ☜ *$11* ⊙ *Tues.–Sun. 10–6.*

38 Baltimore City Hall. Built in 1875, Baltimore City Hall consists of mansard roofs and a gilt dome over a 110-foot rotunda, all supported by ironwork. Inside you can get tours of the chambers and view exhibits on Baltimore's history. Directly across the street is **City Hall Plaza,** on what was originally the site of the Holliday Street Theatre. The theater was owned and operated by the Ford brothers; they also operated Ford's Theatre in Washington, D.C., where President Lincoln was assassinated. "The Star-Spangled Banner" was first publicly sung here. ⊠ *100 N. Holliday St., Downtown* ☎ *410/396–3100* ☜ *Free* ⊙ *Weekdays 8–4:30.*

32 Baltimore Civil War Museum-President Street Station. President Street Station offers a glimpse of the violence and divided loyalties that the war caused in Maryland, a state caught in the middle. Originally the Baltimore terminus of the Philadelphia, Wilmington, & Baltimore Railroad, the relocated station, built in 1849, contains exhibits that depict the events that led to mob violence. It began when troops from the Sixth Massachusetts Regiment bound for Washington, D.C., walked from this station to the Camden Station (near Oriole Park). In what would be the first bloodshed of the Civil War, 4 soldiers and 12 civilians were killed; 36 soldiers and a number of civilians were wounded. The riot lasted for several hours and inspired the secessionist poem "Maryland, My Maryland," today the state song. Guided tours of the route of the Sixth Massachusetts are offered at 1 PM on weekends. ⊠ *601 President St., Inner Harbor East* ☎ *410/385–5188* ☜ *$3; guided tour $5* ⊙ *Daily 10–5.*

27 Baltimore Maritime Museum. Consisting of three docked vessels and a restored lighthouse, this museum gives a good sense of Baltimore's maritime heritage as well as American naval power. On the west side of the pier, the submarine USS *Torsk,* the "Galloping Ghost of the Japanese Coast," is credited with sinking the last two Japanese warships in World War II. The lightship *Chesapeake,* built as a floating lighthouse in 1930 and now out of commission, remains fully operational. The *Taney* is a Coast Guard cutter that saw action at Pearl Harbor. Built in 1856, the Seven Foot Knoll Lighthouse marked the entrance to the Baltimore Harbor from the Chesapeake Bay for 133 years before its move to the museum. ⊠ *Pier 3, Inner Harbor* ☎ *410/396–3453* ⊕ *www.baltomaritimemuseum.org* ☜ *$7* ⊙ *June–Aug., daily 10–5:30; Sept.–Nov. and Mar.–May, Sun.–Thurs. 10–5, Fri. and Sat. 10–6; Dec.–Feb., Fri.–Sun. 10–5.*

off the beaten path   **BALTIMORE MUSEUM OF INDUSTRY** – Housed in an 1865 oyster cannery, the fascinating and kid-friendly Baltimore Museum of Industry covers the city's industrial and labor history and is worth the ½ mi walk south of the Inner Harbor along Key Highway. Here you can watch and help operate the functional re-creations of a machine shop circa 1900, a print shop, a cannery, and a garment workroom. A restored steam-driven tugboat that plied the waterfront for the first half of this century is docked outside. ⊠ *1415 Key Hwy., Federal Hill* ☎ *410/727–4808* ⊕ *www.thebmi.org* ⊠ *$6* ☺ *Mon.–Sat. 10–5, Sun. noon–5.*

③ **Baltimore Public Works Museum.** A short walk east of the Inner Harbor, this museum is an unusual collection of artifacts displayed in an unusual location: the old Eastern Avenue Sewage Pumping Station, built in 1912. Here you can examine several generations of water pipe, including wood piping nearly 200 years old. Other exhibits tell the history of such city services as trash removal. Outdoors, a life-size model reveals what lies underneath Baltimore streets. ⊠ *751 Eastern Ave., Inner Harbor* ☎ *410/396–5565* ⊠ *$2.50* ☺ *Tues.–Sun. 10–4.*

need a break?

Espresso, cannolis, and other delicious Italian pastries can be found at **Vaccaro's** (⊠ 222 Albermarle St., Little Italy ☎ 410/685–4905). **Whole Foods** (⊠ 1001 Fleet St., Inner Harbor East ☎ 410/528–1640) has tables and chairs for eating pre-made sandwiches, sushi, and salads.

③ **Carroll Mansion.** This house was once the winter home of Charles Carroll, one of the signers of the Declaration of Independence. It's now a museum dedicated to the history of the city and the neighborhood, Historic Jonestown, as told through the various occupants of the house through the years. ⊠ *800 E. Lombard St., Historic Jonestown* ☎ *410/605–2964* ⊠ *$5* ☺ *Sat. noon–4 or by appt.*

② **Federal Hill Park.** On the south side of Inner Harbor, Federal Hill Park was named in 1788 to commemorate Maryland's ratification of the U.S. Constitution. Later it was the site of Civil War fortifications, built by less-than-welcome Union troops under the command of Major General Benjamin "Spoonie" Butler. Until the early 1900s, a signal tower atop Federal Hill displayed the "house" flags of local shipping companies, notifying them of the arrival of their vessels. Some of the oldest homes in Baltimore surround the park, and its summit provides an excellent view of the Inner Harbor and the downtown skyline. The best vantage point for photographing Baltimore, the park is also a favorite spot for watching holiday fireworks. ⊠ *Battery Ave. and Key Hwy., Federal Hill.*

☺ ② **Fort McHenry.** This star-shape brick fort is forever associated with Francis Scott Key and "The Star-Spangled Banner," which Key penned while **FodorsChoice** ★ watching the British bombardment of Baltimore during the War of 1812. Key had been detained onboard a truce ship, where he had been negotiating the release of one Dr. William Beanes, when the bombardment began; Key knew too much about the attack plan to be released. Through the next day and night, as the battle raged, Key strained to be sure, through the smoke and haze, that the flag still flew above Fort McHenry—indicating that Baltimore's defenders held firm. "By the dawn's early light" of September 14, 1814, he saw the 30-foot by 42-foot "Star-Spangled Banner" still aloft and was inspired to pen the words to a poem (set to the tune of an old English drinking song). The flag that flew above Fort McHenry that day had 15 stars and 15 stripes, and was hand-sewn for the fort. A visit to the fort includes a 16-minute history film, guided tour, and frequent living history displays (including battle reenactments) on weekends. To see how the formidable fortifications might have appeared to the bombarding British, catch a water taxi from the Inner Harbor to the fort instead of driving. ⊠ *E. Fort Ave., Locust Point, from Light St., take Key Hwy. for 1½ mi and follow signs* ☎ *410/962–4290* ⊕ *www.nps.gov/fomc* ⊠ *$5* ☉ *Memorial Day–Labor Day, daily 8–8; Labor Day–Memorial Day, daily 8–5.*

⑲ Harborplace and the Gallery. Inside two glass-enclosed marketplaces are a plethora of shops and eateries: the Light Street Pavilion has two stories of food courts and restaurants and the Pratt Street Pavilion is dedicated mainly to retail stores. More than a dozen restaurants, including the Capitol City Brewing Company, Phillips, and City Lights, offer waterfront dining, and such local specialty shops as Best of Baltimore and Maryland Bay Company carry interesting souvenirs. In summer, performers entertain at an outdoor amphitheater between the two pavilions, and paddleboats are available for rent south of the Pratt Street building. A skywalk from the Pratt Street Pavilion leads to **The Gallery,** an upscale four-story shopping mall with 70 more shops, including April Cornell, J. Crew, Coach, and Godiva Chocolatiers. ⊠ *100 Pratt St., Inner Harbor* ☎ *410/332–4191* ⊕ *www.harborplace.com* ☉ *Mon.–Sat. 10–9, Sun. 11–7. Harborplace and the Gallery have extended summer hours; some restaurants open earlier for breakfast, and most close late.*

㉟ Jewish Museum of Maryland. Sandwiched between two 19th-century synagogues, the Jewish Museum of Maryland has changing exhibits of art, photography, and documents related to the Jewish experience in Maryland. The Lloyd Street Synagogue, to the left of the museum, was built in 1845 and was the first in Maryland and the third in the United States. The other, B'nai Israel, was built in 1876 in a uniquely Moorish style. Tours of both synagogues are available. ⊠ *15 Lloyd St., Historic Jonestown, follow Pratt St. east from Inner Harbor, turn left on Central Ave., left again onto Lombard St., and then right onto Lloyd St.* ☎ *410/ 732–6400* ⊕ *www.jewishmuseummd.org* ⊠ *$8* ☉ *Tues.–Thurs. and Sun. noon–4 and by appt.; tours of the synagogues Tues.–Thurs. 1 and 2:30.*

Maryland Art Place. Surrounded by bars and restaurants in the Power Plant Live! complex, this cutting-edge gallery highlights works by contemporary local and regional artists. ⊠ *8 Market Pl., Suite 100, Inner Harbor* ☎ *410/962–8565* ⊕ *www.mdartplace.org* ⊠ *Free* ☉ *Tues.–Sat. 11–5.*

★ ☺ **㉒ Maryland Science Center.** Originally known as the Maryland Academy of Sciences, this 200-year-old institution is one of the oldest scientific institutions in the United States. Now housed in a contemporary building, the three floors of exhibits on the Chesapeake Bay, Earth science, physics, the body, dinosaurs, and outer space are an invitation to engage, experiment, and explore. The center has a planetarium, a simulated archaeological dinosaur dig, an IMAX movie theater with a screen five stories high, and a playroom especially designed for young children. ⊠ *601 Light St., Inner Harbor* ☎ *410/685–5225* ⊕ *www.mdsci.org* 🎦 *$14; IMAX tickets $8* ⊙ *Tues.–Fri. 10–5, Sat. 10–6, Sun. 11–5.*

★ ☾ ㉖ **National Aquarium in Baltimore.** The most-visited attraction in Maryland has more than 10,000 fish, sharks, dolphins, and amphibians dwelling in 2 million gallons of water. They're joined by the reptiles, birds, plants, and mammals inhabiting the center's rain-forest environment, inside a glass pyramid 64 feet high. This ecosystem harbors two-toed sloths in calabash trees, parrots in the palms, iguanas on the ground, and red-bellied piranhas in a pool (a sign next to it reads DO NOT PUT HANDS IN POOL). Each day in the Marine Mammal Pavilion, seven Atlantic bottlenose dolphins are part of several entertaining presentations that highlight their agility and intelligence. The aquarium's famed shark tank and Atlantic coral reef exhibits are spectacular; you can wind through an enormous glass enclosure on a spiral ramp while hammerheads and brightly hued tropical fish glide by. Hands-on exhibits include such docile sea creatures as horseshoe crabs and starfish. ⊠ *Pier 3, Inner Harbor* ☎ *410/576–3800* ⊕ *www.aqua.org* 🎦 *$17.50* ⊙ *Mar.–June, Sept., and Oct., Sat.–Thurs. 9–5, Fri. 9–8; July and Aug., Sun.–Thurs. 9–6, Fri. and Sat. 9–8; Nov.–Feb., Sat.–Thurs. 10–5, Fri. 10–8; visitors may tour for up to 1½ hours after closing. Timed tickets may be required on weekends and holidays; purchase these early in day.*

㊱ **Nine Front Street.** This cute two-story brick town house, built in 1790, was once the home of Mayor Thorowgood Smith, the second mayor of Baltimore. The Women's Civic League, which has its home there, gives tours of the house and of city hall; call for an appointment. ⊠ *9 Front St., Historic Jonestown* ☎ *410/837–5424* ⊙ *Tues.–Thurs. 9–2:30, Fri. 9–2; call ahead.*

㊲ **Phoenix Shot Tower.** The only remaining tower of three of this type that once existed in Baltimore, this brick structure was used to make shot by pouring molten lead from the top. As the drops fell, they formed balls that turned solid in cold water at the bottom. ⊠ *801 E. Fayette St., Historic Jonestown* ☎ *410/605–2964* 🎦 *$1* ⊙ *May–Aug., Fri.–Sun. noon–4; Sept.–Apr., by appt.*

☾ ㉙ **Port Discovery—The Baltimore Children's Museum.** At this interactive museum adults are encouraged to play every bit as much as children. A favorite attraction is the three-story KidWorks, a futuristic jungle gym on which the adventurous can climb, crawl, slide, and swing their way through stairs, slides, ropes, zip-lines, and tunnels, and even cross a narrow footbridge three stories up. In Miss Perception's Mystery House, youngsters help solve a mystery surrounding the disappearance of the Baffeld family by sifting through clues; some are written or visual, and others are gleaned by touching and listening. Changing interactive exhibits allow for even more play. ⊠ *35 Market Pl., Inner Harbor* ☎ *410/727–8120* ⊕ *www.portdiscovery.com* 🎦 *$11* ⊙ *Memorial Day–Labor Day, daily 10–6; Labor Day–Memorial Day, Tues.–Sat. 10–5, Sun. noon–5.*

☕ ㉘ **The Power Plant.** What really was the city's former power plant is now a retail and dining complex that includes a Hard Rock Cafe, a Barnes & Noble, and a 35,000 square foot ESPN Zone. Next door is the **Pier 4 Building,** which houses a Chipotle Mexican Grill and the Pier 4 Kitchen and Bar. ✉ *Pier 5, 601 E. Pratt St., Inner Harbor* ☎ *No phone.*

㉚ **Reginald F. Lewis Museum.** Named for the former CEO of TLC Beatrice International, the Reginald F. Lewis Museum is dedicated to the African-American experience in Maryland. The contemporary, predominately red and black building holds exhibits on African-American history, art, and culture as told through the lives of such individuals as Frederick Douglass, Billie Holiday, and Kweisi Mfume. Facilities include an oral history recording and listening studio and an information resource center. The museum also organizes walking tours of Baltimore that cover African-American history and culture. ✉ *830 East Pratt St. Inner Harbor* ☎ *443/263–1800* ⊕ *www.africanamericanculture.org* 💲 *$8* ⊘ *Tues.–Sun., 10–5.*

㉝ **Star-Spangled Banner House.** Built in 1793, this Federal-style home was where Mary Pickersgill hand-sewed the 15-star, 15-stripe flag that survived the British bombardment of Fort McHenry in 1814 and inspired Francis Scott Key to write "The Star-Spangled Banner." The house contains Federal furniture and American art of the period, including pieces from the Pickersgill family. Outdoors, a map of the United States has been made of stones from the various states. A museum connected to the house tells the history of the War of 1812. ✉ *844 E. Pratt St., Historic Jonestown* ☎ *410/837–1793* ⊕ *www.flaghouse.org* 💲 *$6* ⊘ *Tues.–Sat. 10–4.*

⑳ **USS *Constellation*.** Launched in 1854, the USS *Constellation* was the last—and largest—all-sail ship built by the U.S. Navy. Before the Civil War, as part of the African Squadron, she saw service on antislavery patrol; during the war, she protected Union-sympathizing U.S. merchant ships from Confederate raiders. The warship eventually became a training ship for the navy before serving as the relief flagship for the Atlantic Fleet during World War II, finally arriving in Baltimore in 1955 for restoration to her original condition. You can tour the USS *Constellation* for a glimpse of life as a 19th-century navy sailor, and children can muster to become Civil War–era "powder monkeys." Recruits receive "basic training," try on replica period uniforms, participate in a gun drill, and learn a sea chantey or two before being discharged and paid off in Civil War money at the end of their "cruise." ✉ *Pratt and Light Sts., Inner Harbor* ☎ *410/539–6238* ⊕ *www.constellation.org* 💲 *$7.50* ⊘ *May–mid-Oct., daily 10–6; mid-Oct.–Apr., daily 10–4.*

Visitor Center. Stop by the sweeping, all-glass center for information on the city, brochures, tickets, and hotel and restaurant reservations. In the parking lot behind the center, the first 45 minutes are free. ✉ *401 Light St., Inner Harbor* ☎ *877/225–8466* ⊕ *www.baltimore.org* 💲 *Free* ⊘ *Mon.–Thurs. and Sun. 9–6, Fri. and Sat. 9–7:30.*

㉕ **World Trade Center.** With 32 stories, this building, designed by I. M. Pei's firm, is the world's tallest pentagonal structure. The 27th-floor observation deck ("Top of the World") allows an unobstructed view of Baltimore and beyond from 423 feet. ✉ *401 E. Pratt St., Inner Harbor* ☎ *410/837–8439* ⊕ *www.bop.org* ✉ *$5* ☉ *Memorial Day–Labor Day, weekdays and Sun. 10–6, Sat. 10–8; Apr., May, Sept., and Oct., Wed.–Sun. 10–6.*

Fells Point

A Colonial-era neighborhood once populated by shipbuilders and sailors, Fells Point (along with Canton, farther east) is one of the city's most popular waterfront communities. The neighborhood was founded in 1726 when Englishman William Fell purchased the peninsula, seeing its potential for shipbuilding and shipping. Beginning in 1763, his son Edward and his wife, Ann Bond Fell, divided and sold the land; docks, shipyards, warehouses, stores, homes, churches, and schools sprang up, and the area quickly grew into a bustling seaport. Fells Point was famed for its shipyards (the notoriously speedy clipper ships built here irritated the British so much during the War of 1812 that they tried to capture the city, a move resulting in Fort McHenry's bombardment). During the 1830s Frederick Douglass was employed at a shipyard at the end of Thames Street. Around the 1840s the shipbuilding industry started to decline, in large part because of the rise of steam ships, which were being built elsewhere.

Today people come to Fells Point to stroll the waterfront promenade, browse the small shops, and go to one of its many bars (day and night). Most restaurants, bars, and shops are on Thames (pronounced with a long "a") Street, running east–west, and Broadway, running north–south. Beyond these busy thoroughfares is a quiet National Register Historic District neighborhood of 18th-century brick homes. The neighborhood, a five-minute drive from downtown, can also be reached via an Inner Harbor water taxi.

TIMING   A few hours is probably all you need to explore the neighborhood and visit its two small museums.

a good walk

For a historic walking tour map, stop by the **Fell's Point Visitor Center** on South Ann Street. Next door is the small **Robert Long House Museum** ㊴, the city's oldest home. From there, turn right on cobblestone Thames Street, flanked on the north by blocks of small shops and restaurants and on the south by sailboats and working tugs docked along the harbor. The television show *Homicide* was filmed at the old Broadway Pier. You can find out more about the history of the area at the **Fells Point Maritime Museum** ㊵ on Thames. Continue to Broadway, where there's the pier where water taxis depart. To the north is a pedestrian promenade and the **Broadway Market** ㊶.

Sights to See

㊶ **Broadway Market.** For a drink or light snack, visit the twin pavilions, which have provided neighborhood residents with fresh produce, fish, and meat for more than 100 years. These days you can also find pizza, sandwiches, and oysters at a raw bar. ✉ *Broadway, between Fleet and Lancaster Sts., Fells Point.*

⑩ Fells Point Maritime Museum For the history of the shipbuilding industry in Fells Point and the people involved in it, head to this small museum. You can find out about the speedy Baltimore clipper schooners, which once made this area famous; the cargoes they carried; and the shipbuilders, merchants, and sailors who sought their fortunes here. ⊠ *1724 Thames St. Fells Point* ☎ *410/732–0278* ⊕ *www.mdhs.org* 💲 *$4* ☉ *Thurs.–Mon. 10–5.*

Fell's Point Visitor Center. This visitor center is also the home of the Society for the Preservation of Federal Hill and Fell's Point, which is why the center uses the apostrophe in "Fell's" (it's not commonly used). There's a gift shop here and a historic walking tour brochure for the taking. Neighborhood tours depart from here on Friday evening and Saturday morning (April–October) and focus on topics such as maritime history or slavery and Frederick Douglass's tenure in Fells Point. ⊠ *808 S. Ann St., Fells Point* ☎ *410/675–6750* ⊕ *www.preservationsociety.com* ☉ *Apr.–Oct., daily 10–5; Nov.–Mar. noon–5.*

㊴ Robert Long House Museum. The city's oldest existing residence, this small brick house was built in 1765 as both home and business office for Robert Long, a merchant and quartermaster for the Continental Navy who operated a wharf on the waterfront. Furnished with Revolutionary War–era pieces, the parlor, bedroom, and office seem as if Long himself just stepped away. A fragrant herb garden flourishes in warm months. ⊠ *812 S. Ann St., Fells Point* ☎ *410/675–6750,* ⊕ *www. preservationsociety.com* 💲 *$3* ☉ *Tours daily Apr.–Nov., 1 and 2:30.*

> **need a break?** The **Daily Grind** (⊠ 1720 Thames St., Fells Point ☎ 410/558–0399) is the neighborhood spot for coffee.

West Baltimore

A few blocks west of the Inner Harbor is the centerpiece of West Baltimore: Oriole Park at Camden Yards. South of Camden Yards is the M&T Bank Stadium, where the Baltimore Ravens football team plays. The working-class neighborhoods of West Baltimore have been home to some of the city's most colorful residents: Babe Ruth, Edgar Allan Poe, and Charles Carroll, a member of the Continental Congress. The area is also home to the medical campus of the University of Maryland. Because the sights are far apart and the streets are less safe than those in downtown Baltimore, parts of this area are best visited by car.

> **a good drive** Start this tour at Fayette and Greene streets, where the **Westminster Cemetery and Catacombs** ㊷ hold the remains of Edgar Allan Poe—perhaps Baltimore's most renowned literary figure. Just up Paca Street you can buy a fine lunch at the Lexington Market. Less than a mile away you can find the **Poe House** ㊸, where Edgar Allan Poe wrote his first horror story. To get here, follow Fayette Street west to Schroeder Street. Go two blocks, and turn right onto Saratoga Street. Go 1/4 of a block and turn right onto Amity Street. Because of the possibility of street crime in this area, take safety precautions: don't go alone, and don't go at night.

Next, venture back east along Baltimore Street, to the campus of the University of Maryland at Baltimore. Take a right on Greene Street; at the corner of Lombard Street is **Davidge Hall** ㊹, the oldest building in the United States to be used continuously for teaching medicine. Adjacent to it is the **Dr. Samuel D. Harris National Museum of Dentistry** ㊺.

Just south of Pratt Street, on Emory Street, is the **Babe Ruth Birthplace and Museum** ㊻. From here, follow the baseballs on the sidewalk, or, if you're traveling by car, head back up to Pratt Street and take a right on Eutaw to get to **Oriole Park at Camden Yards** ㊼, three blocks away. South of the Camden Yards is the **M & T Bank Stadium** ㊽, where the Baltimore Ravens play.

From Ravens stadium, head north on Martin Luther King Boulevard, then turn left onto Washington Boulevard. At the eighth traffic light, turn into Carroll Park on the right. At the top of the hill is the **Mount Clare Museum House** ㊾, which once belonged to Charles Carroll, a member of the Continental Congress. Return downtown by driving east along Pratt Street and take a right onto Poppleton Street to the **B&O Railroad Museum** ㊿, the birthplace of railroading in America.

TIMING　Several hours should be enough to cover all the sights on this tour. Reserve an extra hour around lunchtime to stroll among the food stands at Lexington Market. Sights are dispersed on the drive, and the neighborhoods are less safe than downtown Baltimore.

Sights to See

😊 ㊻ **Babe Ruth Birthplace and Museum.** This modest brick row house, three blocks from Oriole Park at Camden Yards, was the birthplace of "the Bambino." Although Ruth was born here in 1895, his family never lived here; they lived in a nearby apartment, above a tavern run by Ruth's father. The row house and the adjoining buildings make up a museum devoted to Ruth's life and to the local Orioles baseball club. Film clips, rare photos of Ruth, Yankees payroll checks, a scorebook from Ruth's first professional game, and many other artifacts can be found here. ✉216 *Emory St., West Baltimore* ☎ 410/727–1539 ⊕ *www.baberuthmuseum. com* 💲*$6* ⊙ *Apr.–Oct., daily 10–5; Nov.–Mar., daily 10–4; until 7 before Oriole home games.*

★ 😊 ㊿ **B&O Railroad Museum.** The famous Baltimore & Ohio Railroad was founded on the site that now houses this museum, which contains more than 120 full-size locomotives and a great collection of railroad memorabilia, from dining car china and artwork to lanterns and signals. The 1884 roundhouse (240 feet in diameter and 120 feet high) adjoins one of the nation's first railroad stations. From this station, the legendary race between the *Tom Thumb* (a working replica of the steam locomotive is inside) and a gray horse took place: the horse won when *Tom Thumb* lost a fan belt. Samuel Morse's first transmission of Morse code, WHAT HATH GOD WROUGHT?, in 1844, passed through wires here, en route from Washington to the B&O Pratt Street Station. Train rides are available on weekends. The Iron Horse Café serves food and drinks. ✉ *901 W. Pratt St., West Baltimore* ☎ 410/752–2490 ⊕ *www.borail. org* 💲 *$14* ⊙ *Weekdays 10–4, Sat. 10–5, Sun. noon–5.*

44 Davidge Hall. Built in 1812 for $35,000, this green-dome structure has been used for teaching medicine for nearly two centuries. Part of the downtown campus of the University of Maryland at Baltimore, Davidge Hall is a relic of the days when dissection was illegal; the acoustically perfect anatomy theater was lighted by skylights instead of windows so that passersby would not witness students working on cadavers. ⊠ *522 W. Lombard St., West Baltimore* ☎ *410/706–7454* ☜ *Free* ⊘ *Weekdays 8:30–4:30.*

45 Dr. Samuel D. Harris National Museum of Dentistry. This unusual museum, which has a set of George Washington's dentures, is on the Baltimore campus of the University of Maryland, the world's first dental school. Housed in a Renaissance Revival–style building, the museum has exhibits on the anatomy and physiology of human and animal teeth and the history of dentistry; you can also play a tune on the "Tooth Jukebox." One popular exhibit displays the dental instruments used in treating Queen Victoria in the mid-19th century. ⊠ *31 S. Greene St., West Baltimore* ☎ *410/706–0600* ☜ *$4.50* ⊘ *Wed.–Sat. 10–4, Sun. 1–4.*

48 M & T Bank Stadium. The Baltimore Ravens football team calls this state-of-the art stadium home. Games are played here from August to January. ⊠ *1101 Russell St., West Baltimore* ☎ *410/261–7283* ⊕ *www.baltimoreravens.com.*

49 Mount Clare Museum House. One of the oldest houses in Baltimore, this elegant mansion was begun in 1754. It was the home of Charles Carroll, author of the Maryland Declaration of Independence, member of the Continental Congress, and one of Maryland's major landowners. The state's first historic museum house has been carefully restored to its Georgian elegance; more than 80% of the 18th-century furniture and artifacts, including rare pieces of Chippendale and Hepplewhite silver, crystal, and Chinese export porcelain, were owned and used by the Carroll family. Washington, Lafayette, and John Adams were all guests here. The greenhouses are famous in their own right: they provided rare trees and plants for Mount Vernon. ⊠ *1500 Washington Blvd., Southwest Baltimore* ☎ *410/837–3262* ☜ *$6* ⊘ *Tues.–Sat. 10–4; tours are every hour until 3.*

★ ☾ **47 Oriole Park at Camden Yards.** Since it opened in 1992, this nostalgically designed baseball stadium has inspired other cities to emulate its neo-traditional architecture and amenities. Home of the Baltimore Orioles, Camden Yards bustles on game days. The Eutaw Street promenade, between the warehouse and the field, has a view of the stadium; look for the brass baseballs embedded in the sidewalk that mark where home runs have cleared the fence, or visit the Orioles Hall of Fame display and the monuments to retired Orioles. Daily tours take you to every nook and cranny of the ballpark, from the immense JumboTron scoreboard to the dugout to the state-of-the-art beer delivery system. ⊠ *333 W. Camden St., Downtown* ☎ *410/685–9800 general information, 410/547–6234 tour times, 410/481–7328 tickets to Orioles home games* ⊕ *www.theorioles.com* ☜ *Eutaw St. promenade free; tour $5* ⊘ *Eutaw St. promenade daily 10–3, otherwise during games and tours.*

43 Poe House. Though the "Master of the Macabre" lived in this tiny row house only three years, he wrote "MS Found in a Bottle" and his first horror story, "Berenice," in the tiny garret chamber that's now furnished in an early-19th-century style. Besides visiting this room, you can view changing exhibits and a video presentation about Poe's short, tempestuous life. Because of the possibility of crime, it's best to visit this neighborhood during daylight hours as part of a group. ⊠ *203 N. Amity St., West Baltimore* ☎ *410/396–7932* ⊕ *www.eapoe.org/balt/poehse.htm* 🎫 *$3* ☾ *Wed.–Sat. noon–3:45; call ahead.*

㊷ Westminster Cemetery and Catacombs. The city's oldest cemetery is the final resting place of Edgar Allan Poe and other famous Marylanders, including 15 generals from the American Revolution and the War of 1812. Dating from 1786, the cemetery was originally known as the Old Western Burying Grounds. In the early 1850s a city ordinance demanded that burial grounds be part of a church, so a building was constructed above the cemetery, creating catacombs beneath it. In the 1930s the schoolchildren of Baltimore collected pennies to raise the necessary funds for Poe's monument. In one of Baltimore's quirkier traditions, each year on Poe's birthday a mysterious stranger leaves three roses and a bottle of cognac on the writer's grave. ⊠ *W. Fayette and Greene Sts., Downtown* ☎ *410/706–2072* ☾ *Daily 8–dusk.*

need a break? **Lexington Market** (⊠ Lexington St. between Paca and Eutaw Sts., West Baltimore ☎ 410/685–6169) is in a bit of a dodgy area, but a trip there for Faidley's crab cakes is well worth your while.

WHERE TO EAT

Think about eating in Baltimore and you think about crabs. That's the specialty here—served both steamed and in crab cakes. Ask a resident about the best place for crabs, and you're sure to get an opinion. But just because Baltimore loves crabs, that doesn't mean that's all there is to eat. The city has Afghan, Greek, American, tapas, and more. The city's dining choices may not compare to New York, or even Washington, but it does have some real standouts.

North of Saratoga Street in Mount Vernon, Charles Street is the place for dining. Choices around the Inner Harbor often mean chains or hotel restaurants; head south to Federal Hill for more interesting options. In Little Italy, at the eastern end of the Inner Harbor, are Italian restaurants serving different regional variations (although most tread the classic Southern Italian, spaghetti-with–garlic-bread road). Fells Point has some renowned local restaurants. Charles Village, near Johns Hopkins University is, and Hampden, just west, have some good casual options. Note that places generally stop serving by 10 PM, if not earlier.

WHAT IT COSTS				
$$$$	**$$$**	**$$**	**$**	**¢**
RESTAURANTS over $30	$22–$30	$14–$22	$7–$14	under $7

Restaurant prices are per person for a main course at dinner.

Mount Vernon

★ $$$–$$$$ ✕ **The Prime Rib.** Bustling and crowded, this luxuriously dark dining room is just north of Mount Vernon Square and five minutes from the Inner Harbor. Tables are set close together under a low ceiling, keeping things intimate for the bankers and lawyers who often eat here, as well as couples on expensive dates. The Prime Rib has a traditional menu headed by a superb prime rib and an even better filet mignon; the jumbo lump crab cakes are also great. The surprisingly short wine list is predominantly Californian. ⊠ *1101 N. Calvert St., Mount Vernon* ☎ *410/539–1804* ⊕ *www.theprimerib.com* ⌒ *Reservations essential* ⋔ *Jacket required* ⊟ *AE, D, DC, MC, V.*

$$–$$$$ ✕ **Saffron.** The name reflects more than just the main ingredients of this creative Indian restaurant, where traditional flavors and techniques are fused with North African, Latin, and French influences. The space, too, is as warm and luxurious as the menu, with saffron-hue walls and flowing fabrics embracing streamlined banquettes and clean white table settings. Favorites include the chicken stuffed with pistachios and figs in a coconut sauce and lobster simmered in tomato and cilantro sauce. ⊠ *802 N. Charles St., Mount Vernon* ☎ *410/528–1616* ⌒ *Reservations recommended* ⊟ *AE, D, DC, MC, V* ⊘ *No lunch.*

$$–$$$ ✕ **The Brewer's Art.** Part brew pub, part restaurant, this spot in a redone mansion seems young but urbane, with an ambitious menu, a clever wine list, and the Belgian-style beers it brews itself: try the potent Resurrection ale. The menu of seasonal dishes uses high-quality, locally available ingredients to create European-style country fare that is both hearty and sophisticated. The classic steak frites are a best bet, as are the fresh homemade ravioli made with seasonal ingredients such as pumpkin in autumn and tomatoes and artichokes in the summer. ⊠ *1106 N. Charles St., Mount Vernon* ☎ *410/547–6925* ⊕ *www.belgianbeer.com* ⊟ *AE, D, DC, MC, V* ⊘ *Closed Mon.*

$$–$$$ ✕ **Tio Pepe.** Candles light up the whitewashed walls of these cellar dining rooms, where the menu covers all regions of Spain. The staple is *paella à la Valenciana* (chicken, sausage, shrimp, clams, and mussels with saffron rice); a less-well-known Basque preparation is red snapper with clams, mussels, asparagus, and boiled egg. Make dinner reservations well in advance; walk-in weekday lunch seating is usually available. ⊠ *10 E. Franklin St., Mount Vernon* ☎ *410/539–4675* ⌒ *Reservations essential* ⋔ *Jacket and tie* ⊟ *AE, D, DC, MC, V.*

★ $$ ✕ **Abacrombie.** Across from Meyerhoff Symphony Hall, this elegant, clubby-feeling spot on the bottom floor of a B&B is popular for preconcert meals. But it's also worth coming at other times, when it's not as busy, for the creative, seasonal menu, which might include dishes such as roasted pork tenderloin with rutabaga puree or rock fish with smoked paprika sauce. Or try the three-course, prix-fixe dinner, which comes with matching wines for each course. ⊠ *58 W. Biddle St., Mount Vernon* ☎ *410/837–3630* ⌒ *Reservations essential* ⊟ *AE, D, DC, MC, V* ⊘ *Closed Mon. and Tues. No lunch.*

★ $$ ✕ **The Brass Elephant.** The rooms of this grand antebellum house on Charles Street are filled with classical music and the chatter of diners (the Teak

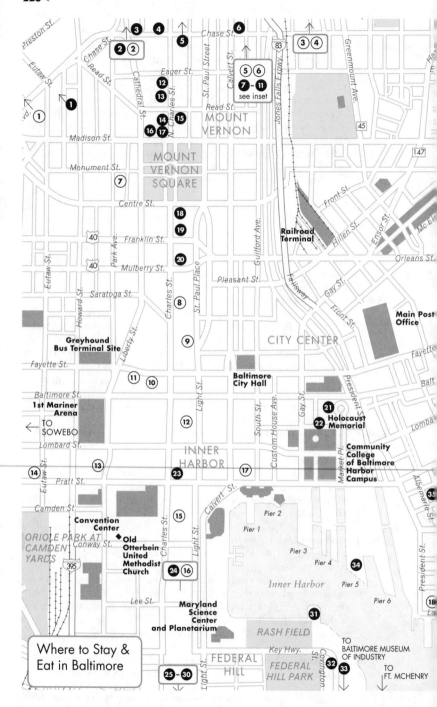

Where to Stay &
Eat in Baltimore

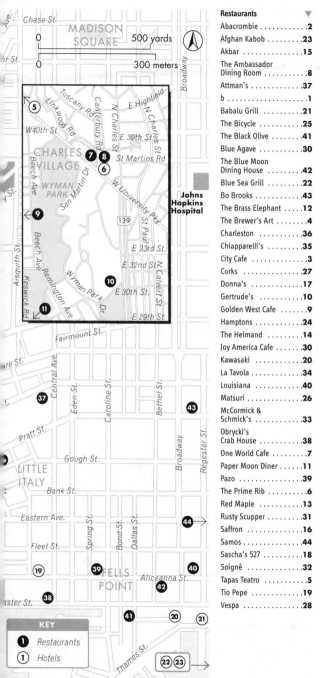

Room is the quietest, the Oak Room the noisiest). The northern Italian menu includes traditional piccatas and marinaras as well as updated versions of Italian classics, such as homemade cannelloni filled with duck confit, woodland mushrooms, and ricotta. Upstairs, the softly lit Tusk Lounge is a comfortable, classy spot to meet for drinks. ✉ *924 N. Charles St., Mount Vernon* ☎ *410/547–8480* ⊕ *www.brasselephant.com* ⊟ *AE, DC, MC, V.*

$–$$$ ✕ **Sascha's 527.** High ceilings, warm yellow walls hung with paintings, and a giant crystal chandelier add drama to this spacious, artsy spot near the Walters. Choose from an eclectic menu of "tastes"—appetizer-size plates, "grills," chicken, lamb, or fish served with a selection of unusual sauces, and other American fare with a twist. At lunch there's counter service only, with a choice of fancy sandwiches and inventive pizzas and salads. On Thursday nights live jazz accompanies dinner. ✉ *527 N. Charles St., Mount Vernon* ☎ *410/539–8880* ⊟ *AE, DC, MC, V* ☺ *Closed Sun. No lunch Sat.*

★ **$–$$** ✕ **The Helmand.** Owned by Hamid Kharzai's brother, Qayum Karzai, Helmand serves outstanding Afghan fare in a casual yet elegant space. Beautiful woven textiles and traditional dresses adorn the walls, adding color to the simple white table settings. Try one of the many outstanding lamb dishes such as *sabzy challow* (spinach sautéed with chunks of beef) or the vegetarian *aushak* (Afghan ravioli). For starters, *kaddo*, a sweet-and-pungent pumpkin dish, is unforgettable. ✉ *806 N. Charles St., Mount Vernon* ☎ *410/752–0311* ⊟ *AE, DC, MC, V* ☺ *No lunch.*

$–$$ ✕ **Tapas Teatro.** Connected to the Charles Theater, the place for art films in Baltimore, the Tapas Teatro is a popular pre- and post-movie spot. It's often a scene, especially in warm weather, when the glass front is open and tables spill onto the street. Tapas include marinated red peppers, spinach sautéed with crab, and lamb tenderloin. There's also an extensive list of wines by the glass. But be careful: it's so much fun to keep sampling that it's easy to run up a hefty bill. ✉ *1711 N. Charles St., Station North Arts District* ☎ *410/332–0110* ⊟ *AE, MC, V* ☺ *Closed Mon. No lunch.*

$–$$ ✕ **Akbar.** A few steps below street level, this small restaurant is usually crowded and always filled with pungent aromas and the sounds of Indian music. Among the vegetarian dishes, *alu gobi masala*, a potato-and-cauliflower creation, is prepared with onions, tomatoes, and spices. Tandoori chicken is marinated in yogurt, herbs, and strong spices, then barbecued in a charcoal-fired clay oven. Akbar also makes a good choice for an interesting Sunday brunch. ✉ *823 N. Charles St., Mount Vernon* ☎ *410/539–0944* ⊕ *www.akbar-restaurant.com* ⊟ *AE, D, DC, MC, V.*

$–$$ ✕ **City Cafe.** The lofty space and black-and-white tile floors give this casual spot a feeling of past grandeur. Come here for basic American fare—sandwiches, salads, pasta, big brunches—and stick to that: the more creative ambitious attempts on the menu often fall short. In summer, the frozen cappuccino is a sweet, creamy treat. ✉ *1001 Cathedral St., Mount Vernon* ☎ *410/539–4252* ⊟ *AE, D, DC, MC, V.*

$–$$ ✕ **Donna's.** Basic black-and-light wood are the backdrop for this casual American, part of a local chain (other locations are on St. Paul in Charles Village and in Cross Keys in Roland Park). For breakfast, bagels and muffins are served on weekdays and brunch is available Sunday;

sandwiches, soups, and salads are the lunchtime offerings; dinner might include balsamic-glaze salmon, herb chicken breast with artichoke hearts, or a daily pasta dish. You can also just stop in for a cup of coffee any time of the day. ⊠ *800 N. Charles St., Mount Vernon* ☎ *410/385–0180* ☰ *AE, D, MC, V.*

$–$$ ✕ **Kawasaki.** This lively dining room is good for a convivial dinner or weekday lunch. Cases on the wall hold the personal chopsticks of Kawasaki's many regulars. Menu standouts are sparkling fresh sushi and sashimi—without a doubt the best in town. Try one of the creative sushi rolls, such as the Number 5, with scallops, orange slices, and Japanese mayonnaise. ⊠ *413 N. Charles St., Mount Vernon* ☎ *410/659–7600* ☰ *AE, DC, MC, V* ☽ *Closed Sun.*

$–$$ ✕ **Red Maple.** Theatrical, stylish Red Maple doesn't have a sign out front: a small red maple tree icon on the front door is the only way it announces its presence. Inside, the striking, minimalist space is warmed by a fireplace, candlelight, and sumptuous suede banquettes. The food is equally arresting: Asian-inspired tapas, artfully conceived and beautifully presented. The 16 different small plates are inexpensive, but it's easy to run up your tab because each is so compelling. ⊠ *930 N. Charles St., Mount Vernon* ☎ *410/547–0149* ☰ *AE, DC, MC, V* ☽ *No lunch.*

Bolton Hill

$–$$ ✕ **b.** In a residential neighborhood of lovely, large row houses, this casual corner bistro serves imaginative, Mediterranean-influenced fare. The seasonal menu includes such dishes as roasted vegetable ravioli in sage butter and sesame-encrusted salmon with honey horseradish creme fraiche. Or choose from one of the chalkboard specials, such as the risotto of the day or the "butcher's special." On Sunday, b is a popular spot for brunch. ⊠ *1501 Bolton St., Bolton Hill* ☎ *410/383–8600* ☰ *AE, D, MC, V* ☽ *Closed Mon. No lunch.*

Charles Village

$$–$$$ ✕ **The Ambassador Dining Room.** A Tudor-style dining room in a 1930s apartment building is the setting for subtle, superb Indian fare. Go for the classics such as chicken *tikka masala* (grilled chicken in a sauce of red pepper, ginger, garlic, and yogurt) or *alu gobi* (spicy potatoes and cauliflower), or sample more creative options such as lamb tenderloin with fennel and chive sauce. In summer the lovely garden is a favorite spot for outdoor dining. You may want to finish your meal with a dish of cardamom ice cream. ⊠ *3811 Canterbury Rd. Tuscany-Canterbury* ☎ *410/366–1484* ☰ *AE, MC, V.*

$–$$$ ✕ **Gertrude's.** In the Baltimore Museum of Art, this casual yet classy spot cooks up creative Maryland cuisine. Crab cakes, served in many forms, are one option, as are cornmeal-encrusted catfish or one of the many daily specials. In warm weather the outdoor terrace overlooking the sculpture garden makes for very pleasant dining. On Tuesday nights, entrées are only $10. ⊠ *10 Art Museum Dr., Charles Village* ☎ *410/889–3399* ⚑ *Reservations essential.* ☰ *AE, MC, V* ☽ *Closed Mon.*

¢–$ ✕ **One World Cafe.** A favorite of Johns Hopkins students, this low-key restaurant, café, and bar is open morning until night for tasty vegetarian fare. Settle onto a couch or one of the small tables for a portobello sandwich with caramelized onions and feta cheese, tofu baked with ginger and served with steamed vegetables, or One World's version of that Baltimore specialty: a crabless crab cake. Smoothies, espresso drinks, microbrews, and mixed drinks from the full bar fill out the menu. ⊠ *100 W. University Pkwy., Tuscany-Canterbury* ☎ *410/235-5777* ⊟ *AE, DC, MC, V.*

¢–$ ✕ **Paper Moon Diner.** Everywhere you look in this funky, colorful diner are toys, as well as a mix of other objects glued to the ceilings and walls. People come at all hours (it's open 24/7) for the overstuffed omelettes, big stacks of pancakes, burgers, and other classic fare. The waiters have diner attitude—they don't always seem too interested in serving—but the place is always lively and entertaining. ⊠ *227 W. 29th St., Charles Village* ☎ *410/889–4444* ⊟ *MC, V.*

Hampden

★ ¢–$ ✕ **Golden West Cafe.** On "The Avenue," funky Hampden's main commercial street, Golden West is the go-to spot for breakfast, lunch, and dinner. The place is colorful and eclectic, and so is the menu of diner fare with a Tex-Mex and Asian twist. Try the cold Vietnamese salad with shrimp or the hefty *huevos montuleños*—fried eggs with yellow corn cakes covered in beans, feta, salsa, and a fried banana (and served at all hours). Large tables make it a good spot for groups, and the bar makes it good for pre- or post-dinner drinks. ⊠ *1105 W. 36th St., Hampden* ☎ *410/889–8891* ⊟ *AE, D, MC, V* ☉ *Closed Tues.*

Inner Harbor

$$$$ ✕ **Hamptons.** A panoramic view of the Inner Harbor competes with the

Fodor'sChoice restaurant's elegant interior: Sheraton-style tables, set with bowls of flow-

★ ers, are spaced generously in a dining room decorated to resemble an English country house. Expect carefully composed seasonal cuisine at once contemporary and classic: roasted pheasant with butternut squash and mushroom risotto in Madeira demi-glace, for instance. The Sunday champagne brunch is a major draw. For a more casual meal, try the hotel's other restaurant, Brighton's. ⊠ *Harbor Court Hotel, 550 Light St., Inner Harbor* ☎ *410/347–9944* ⊕ *www.harborcourt.com* ⌦ *Reservations essential* 🍴 *Jacket and tie* ⊟ *AE, D, MC, V* ☉ *Closed Mon.*

$$–$$$$ ✕ **Babalu Grill.** The prominent portrait of Desi Arnaz; the conga drum bar stools; the live salsa music on weekends: this place is all about fun. Many of the classic Cuban dishes on the menu come from owner Steve DeCastro's family recipes, such as savory *ropa vieja* (a stew of shredded beef) and seafood paella, brimming with shrimp, shellfish, and chorizo. The bar serves an impressive list of obscure rums and tequilas, and the wine list focuses on South American and Spanish vintages. ⊠ *32 Market Pl., Inner Harbor* ☎ *410/234–9898* ⊕ *www.serioussteaks. com/Babalu* ⊟ *AE, D, DC, MC, V.*

$$–$$$$ ✕ **Rusty Scupper.** A perennial tourist favorite, the Rusty Scupper undoubtedly has the best view along the waterfront; sunset here is magical, with the sun sinking slowly into the harbor as lights twinkle on the city's skyscrapers. The interior is decorated with light wood and win-

dows from floor to ceiling; the house specialty is seafood, particularly the jumbo lump crab cake, but the menu also includes beef, chicken, and pasta. Reservations are essential on Friday and Saturday. ⊠ *402 Key Hwy., Inner Harbor* ☎ *410/727–3678* ⊟ *AE, D, DC, MC, V.*

$$–$$$ ✕ **Blue Sea Grill.** Blue is the color, cool is the mood, and the ocean is the source for the fresh seafood served here in many forms. Start with a plate of raw oysters or a bowl of Maryland crab soup, then order from a selection of whole fishes—grilled, broiled, or pan-fried. ⊠ *614 Water St., Inner Harbor* ☎ *410/837-7300* ⊕ *www.blueseagrill.com* ⊟ *AE, D, DC, MC, V* ☉ *No lunch. Closed Sun.*

$$–$$$ ✕ **McCormick & Schmick's.** McCormick & Schmick's is a chain restaurant, but it's a very good one. From its expansive Baltimore location at the end of Pier 5, on the east side of the waterfront, there's a terrific harbor view; ask to be seated on the patio. More than two-dozen varieties of fish and seafood, available on a daily basis, are flown in from all over the world: the large menu changes daily. Choose from the more than half-dozen choices of oysters available on the half shell, or go for the signature cedar-plank wild Oregon king salmon. ⊠ *711 Eastern Ave., Inner Harbor* ☎ *410/234–1300* ⊕ *www.mccormickandschmicks.com* ⊟ *AE, D, MC, V.*

$ ✕ **Afghan Kabob.** A couple of blocks up from the Inner Harbor, this barebones spot serves simple, delicious Afghan fare. Order at the counter—start with the pumpkim appetizer, then try the lamb kebab, which comes with salad, rice, and fresh pita bread, or a vegetarian plate that might include chickpeas, lentils, and okra—and grab a table. It's a good alternative to the pricier options by the water for lunch or an early dinner (it closes at 8 PM). ⊠ *37 S. Charles St., City Center* ☎ *410/727–5511* ⊟ *AE, MC, V* ☉ *Closed Sun.*

¢–$ ✕ **Attman's.** Open since 1915, this authentic New York–style deli near the Jewish Museum is the king of Baltimore's "Corned Beef Row." Don't be put off by the long lines: the outstanding corned beef sandwiches are worth the wait, as are the pastrami, homemade chopped liver, and other oversize creations. Attman's closes at 6:30 PM daily. ⊠ *1019 Lombard St., Historic Jonestown* ☎ *410/563–2666* ⊟ *AE, DC, MC, V.*

Federal Hill

$$$ ✕ **Corks.** The creative American cuisine is as stellar as the impressive wine list at Corks. Suggested wines are paired with dishes, or you can ask the knowledgeable waitstaff for suggestions. Outstanding dishes in the seasonal menu might include the monkfish osso buco and the braised veal breast with woodland mushrooms and crispy sweetbreads. It's so cozy in the dimly lit, wood-panel dining room that you may never want to leave. ⊠ *1026 S. Charles St., Federal Hill* ☎ *410/752-3810* ⚐ *Reservations essential* ⊟ *AE, D, MC, V* ☉ *No lunch.*

$$–$$$ ✕ **The Bicycle.** Bright, energetic, and often noisy Bicycle serves intelligent, creative cuisine. Caribbean, Asian, and Southwestern flavors influence the short but engaging menu, which is supplemented by specials that make use of the fresh seafood and local seasonal produce. Tables are close in this small bistro, but proximity enhances its liveliness. ⊠ *1444 Light St., Federal Hill* ☎ *410/234–1900* ⊕ *www.bicyclebistro.*

com ⌖ *Reservations essential* ▭ *AE, D, MC, V* ☉ *Closed Sun. and Mon. No lunch.*

★ **$$–$$$** ✕ **Joy America Cafe.** On the top floor of the offbeat American Visionary Art Museum, this restaurant (and its appropriately unconventional menu) does the place justice. The food is inspired by the New World: South and Central America, Cuba, and the Caribbean all influence the kitchen. Exuberant flavors abound, such as the chili-spiced shrimp ceviche with lime and coconut milk. Sunday brunch fare includes interesting twists such as crab omelets. ⊠ *American Visionary Art Museum, 800 Key Hwy., Federal Hill* ☏ *410/244–6500* ▭ *AE, DC, MC, V* ☉ *Closed Mon.*

$$–$$$ ✕ **Soigné.** Polished but relaxed, Soigné presents an Asian- and French-influenced fusion menu in attractively spare, comfortable surroundings. The creative menu succeeds beautifully with such ambitious dishes as seared foie gras with scallops, the richness of which is leavened with caramelized mango in a sake-spiked demi-glace. ⊠ *554 E. Fort Ave., Federal Hill* ☏ *410/659–9898* ⌖ *Reservations essential* ▭ *AE, D, MC, V* ☉ *Closed Sun. No lunch.*

$–$$ ✕ **Blue Agave.** At this authentic regional Mexican and American Southwestern restaurant, every sauce and salsa is made daily to create pure, concentrated flavors—the traditional mole sauces here are delicious. Dishes such as grilled quail served with both green and spicy yellow moles, or the more familiar chicken enchiladas with mole poblano, demonstrate the kitchen's command of this rich, complex concoction. More than 80 different kinds of tequila are available, and you won't find a finer margarita anywhere. ⊠ *1032 Light St., Federal Hill* ☏ *410/576–3938* ⊕ *www.blueagaverestaurant.com* ▭ *AE, D, MC, V* ☉ *Closed Tues. and Wed. No lunch.*

$–$$ ✕ **Matsuri.** Sit down at the counter or make your way to one of the tables as this small, spare sushi place, a Federal Hill favorite. You can order by the piece, or opt for one of the bento boxes, udon soups, or tempura dishes like the signature crab and shrimp, wrapped in rice and seaweed and deep fried. ⊠ *1105 S. Charles St., Federal Hill* ☏ *410/752–8561* ▭ *AE, D, MC, V* ☉ *No lunch weekends.*

$–$$ ✕ **Vespa.** For hip, hopping Italian, this sleek restaurant is the spot. Try a thin-crusted pizza topped with spicy sausage, raisins, and roasted peppers. Equally delicious are the pasta dishes and entrées like grilled game hen with crispy polenta, all matched with wines. ⊠ *1117 S. Charles St., Federal Hill* ☏ *410/385–0355* ▭ *AE, MC, V* ☉ *Closed Sun. No lunch.*

Little Italy

$$–$$$ ✕ **Chiapparelli's.** At this neighborhood favorite, families come to celebrate milestones—baptisms, communions, graduations, and such. Pictures of the Baltimore landscape adorn the redbrick walls, and some white-cloth tables overlook one of Little Italy's main streets. The reasonably priced pasta selections rely on standards, but there's also more upscale fare such as chicken Giuseppe: breaded chicken breast with spinach, crabmeat, and provolone in a lemon wine sauce. ⊠ *237 S. High St., Little Italy* ☏ *410/837–0309* ⊕ *www.chiapparellis.com* ▭ *AE, D, DC, MC, V.*

$$ ✕ **La Tavola.** Specializing in homemade, inventive pasta dishes, La Tavola is a cut above other Little Italy spaghetti houses. Don't miss the *mafalde alla fiorentina,* wide pasta with spinach, ricotta, pine nuts, and raisins in a nutmeg-flavor cream sauce. Veal cannelloni in béchamel tomato sauce is another standout. If you're still hungry after one of La Tavola's generous plates of pasta, the fresh fish is a good bet, as is the roasted veal chop. ✉ *248 Albemarle St., Little Italy* ☎ *410/685–1859* ⊕ *www.la-tavola.com* ▤ *AE, D, DC, MC, V.*

Fells Point

★ **$$$–$$$$** ✕ **The Black Olive.** One of the best Greek restaurants in the country, the Black Olive specializes in impeccably fresh seafood. Let the waiter give you a guided tour of the catch of the day, which reclines on a bed of ice in the kitchen case. You can have your selection simply grilled, lightly dressed, and filleted for you table-side, accompanied by a glass from the wine list's thoughtful selection of oft-neglected Greek vintages. For an appetizer be sure to try the *kakavia,* a spicy Greek bouillabaisse served with irresistible bread warm from the brick oven. ✉ *814 S. Bond St., at Shakespeare St., Fells Point* ☎ *410/276–7141* ⊕ *www.theblackolive. com* ⌂ *Reservations essential* ▤ *AE, D, MC, V* ☾ *Closed Mon. No lunch.*

★ **$$$–$$$$** ✕ **Charleston.** The kitchen here may have a South Carolina low-country accent, but it's also skilled in the fundamentals of French cooking. Inside the glowingly lit dining room, such classics as she-crab soup, crisp cornmeal-crusted oysters, and spoon bread complement more elegant fare, such as squab roasted with apples. Best bets are Southern-inspired dishes such as shrimp sautéed with andouille and Cajun ham served over creamy grits. ✉ *1000 Lancaster St., Fells Point* ☎ *410/332–7373* ⊕ *www.charlestonrestaurant.com* ⌂ *Reservations essential* ▤ *AE, D, MC, V* ☾ *Closed Sun. No lunch.*

$$–$$$ ✕ **Louisiana.** Fells Point's most elegant dining room feels like a spacious, opulent antebellum parlor. The menu mixes creole and French with a touch of New American, and is accompanied by an expansive, thoughtful wine list. The lobster bisque, with a dollop of sherry added at the table by one of Louisiana's impeccable waiters, is sublime, and crawfish étouffée is a worthy follow-up course. ✉ *1708 Aliceanna St., Fells Point* ☎ *410/327–2610* ▤ *AE, DC, MC, V* ☾ *No lunch.*

$$–$$$ ✕ **Obrycki's Crab House.** For 50 years Obrycki's has served steamed crabs with its unique black pepper seasoning. Go for the crabs: beyond that, the seafood menu is standard and the food just fair. ✉ *1727 E. Pratt St., Fells Point* ☎ *410/732–6399* ⊕ *www.obryckis.com* ▤ *AE, D, DC, MC, V* ☾ *Closed mid-Dec.–early Mar.*

$–$$ ✕ **Samos.** East of Fells Point is Greektown (15 minutes by car from Inner Harbor hotels), home to Baltimore's Greek population. An informal restaurant, done in classic blue and white, it serves excellent Greek fare. Portions are generous, with lamb souvlaki leading the menu. ✉ *600 Oldham St., Greektown* ☎ *410/675–5292* ▤ *AE, D, DC, MC, V* ☾ *Closed Sun.*

$ ✕ **Blue Moon Dining House.** A cozy café with a celestial motif appropriate to its name, the Blue Moon is a favorite spot for breakfast, served until 3 PM daily. Start with one of the enormous housemade cinnamon rolls, but save room for excellent brunch fare such as crab Benedict and sky-high French toast topped with fruit compote. On Friday and Saturday the Moon reopens at 11 PM and stays open all night, attracting revelers from Fells Point's many clubs and bars. On weekend mornings there's often a line, but it's well worth the wait. ⊠ *1621 Aliceanna St., Fells Point* ☎ *410/522–3940* ⌔ *Reservations not accepted* ▭ *AE, D, MC, V.*

¢–$ ✕ **Pazo.** An expansive 19th-century warehouse is now home to this fashionable, two-level restaurant serving Mediterranean-influenced fare. Enjoy tapas in the rich, red-hued setting lit by giant wrought-iron chandeliers, or head upstairs to the mezzanine and watch the crowd below. ⊠ *1425 Aliceanna St. Fells Point* ☎ *410/534–7296* ▭ *AE, DC, MC, V* ☾ *No lunch.*

Canton

$–$$$ ✕ **Bo Brooks.** Picking steamed crabs on Bo Brooks's waterfront deck with a pitcher of cold beer at hand as sailboats and tugs ply the harbor is a quintessential Baltimore pleasure. Brooks serves its famous crustaceans year-round, along with a menu of Chesapeake seafood classics. Locals know to stick to the Maryland crab soup, jumbo lump crab cakes, and fried oysters. ⊠ *2701 Boston St., Canton* ☎ *410/558–0202* ⊕ *www. bobrooks.com* ▭ *AE, D, MC, V.*

WHERE TO STAY

All hotels listed are within a short drive or a half hour's walk of the Inner Harbor. Fells Point is less than a mile from downtown Baltimore and the Inner Harbor—a commute that's especially enjoyable by water taxi. Lodging reservations must be made well in advance in summer and for Preakness weekend, the third weekend in May. Hunt Valley, a suburb about 25 minutes' drive north of Baltimore on I-83, has several convenient budget options. In summer, prices are significantly higher than off-season.

	WHAT IT COSTS				
	$$$$	**$$$**	**$$**	**$**	**¢**
HOTELS	over $250	$175–$250	$130–$175	$80–$130	Under $80

Hotel prices are for a standard double room, excluding state (5% in Maryland) and Baltimore City tax (7.5%) for a total of 12.5% room tax.

Mount Vernon

$$$$ ▭ **Peabody Court.** Built as a luxury apartment house in 1924, this 13-story hotel faces the Washington Monument. The hotel retains its original distinguished lobby and other period touches such as marble bathrooms. Rooms have desks and two-line speakerphones with data ports; a lobby business center has a fax machine, copier, and computer station. Rooms with park views are the best choice. A courtesy shuttle will ferry you to destinations within a 2-mi radius. The hotel bistro, George's on Mount Vernon Square, serves American and Italian cuisine. ✉ *612 Cathedral St., Mount Vernon, 21201* ☎ *410/727–7101* 🖨 *410/ 789–3312* 🌐 *www.peabodycourthotel.com* 🛏 *104 rooms* ⚲ *Restaurant, in-room safes, minibars, refrigerators, cable TV, gym, library, Internet, business services, meeting rooms, parking (fee), no-smoking floors* 🍴 *AE, D, DC, MC, V* ❖ *CP.*

★ **$–$$** 🏨 **Abacrombie.** In a large, late 19th-century building, once a private house, this intimate inn has rooms furnished in Victorian style and an outstanding restaurant. It's across the street from the Meyerhoff Symphony Hall and in walking distance of MICA, the University of Baltimore, and Amtrak's Penn Station. Breakfast is served in the parlor room. The inn has no elevator. ✉ *58 W. Biddle St., Mount Vernon, 21201* ☎ *410/244–7227 or 888/922–3437* 🖨 *410/244–8415* 🌐 *www.badger-inn.com* 🛏 *12 rooms* ⚲ *Restaurant, bar, cable TV, free parking; no smoking* 🍴 *AE, D, MC, V* ❖ *CP.*

Bolton Hill

$$ 🏨 **Mr. Mole Bed & Breakfast.** This elegant town house in Bolton Hill, a lovely neighborhood of large row houses west of Mount Vernon, gets its name from a character in the children's book *The Wind in the Willows.* Each of the six guest rooms is whimsically decorated, and comes with fresh flowers and a direct-dial phone with voice mail. Typically, the Dutch-style breakfast consists of fresh fruits, Amish cheeses and meats, homemade breads, and coffee cake. Mr. Mole is within walking distance of the Myerhoff Symphony Hall, MICA, and Howard Street's Antique Row. ✉ *1601 Bolton St., Bolton Hill, 21217* ☎ *410/728–1179* 🖨 *410/ 728–3379* 🌐 *www.mrmolebb.com* 🛏 *6 rooms* ⚲ *Free parking; no room TVs, no kids under 10, no smoking* 🍴 *AE, D, DC, MC, V* ❖ *CP.*

City Center

$$–$$$ 🏨 **Hampton Inn and Suites.** The free breakfast and the logo may be the same, but this Hampton Inn tries to be more urban and chic than others in the chain. The hotel, in anearly 1900s office building that lay vacant for many years, follows the historical direction of the structure, but keeps things contemporary. Rooms, done in warm mauve and beige and dark wood, have a clubby, streamlined look. The biggest and most expensive rooms, on the top floor, are studio suites in the former executive offices. ✉ *131 E. Redwood, City Center, 21202* ☎ *410/539–7888* 🖨 *410/539– 7405* 🌐 *www.baltimorehamptoninn.com* 🛏 *116 rooms, 10 studio suites* ⚲ *Cable TV, indoor pool, gym, Internet, business center, 2 meeting rooms, parking (fee), no-smoking floors* 🍴 *AE, D, DC, MC, V.*

$$–$$$ 🏨 **Radisson Plaza Lord Baltimore.** Baltimore's historic landmark hotel, the Radisson extends its Jazz Age elegance to the guest rooms, which have been restored to their original style. Built in 1928, this 23-story hotel is distinguished by an elegantly gilded art deco lobby. Rooms on the south side have the best view, and from the top three floors you can see the harbor. The hotel is quiet and comfortable, and the location is central, three blocks from the Baltimore Convention Center or Harborplace. ✉ *20*

W. Baltimore St., City Center, 21202 ☎ 410/539–8400 🖶 410/625–1060 ⊕ www.radisson.com/lordbaltimore ➾ 419 rooms, 10 suites ⚛ 2 restaurants, cable TV, gym, sauna, bar, Internet, business services, meeting rooms, parking (fee), no-smoking floors ▭ AE, D, DC, MC, V.

★ $$–$$$ 🏨 **Tremont Park.** Built in the 1960s as an apartment house, the 13-story Tremont is now a European-style all-suites hotel that's elegant but still comfortable. The lobby and hotel restaurant, 8 East, are intimate and private—qualities attracting guests who might be easily recognized. The suites come in two sizes: both have a toaster oven and a coffeemaker (complete with freshly ground beans). The Tremont is near Mount Vernon and the Inner Harbor. The concierge will help arrange local transportation, which in most cases is free. ⊠ 8 E. Pleasant St., City Center, 21202 ☎ 410/576–1200 or 800/873–6668 🖶 410/244–1154 ⊕ www.1800-tremont.com ➾ 60 suites ⚛ Restaurant, kitchenettes, microwaves, cable TV, gym, bar, concierge, 2 meeting rooms, parking (fee) ▭ AE, D, DC, MC, V.

★ $$–$$$ 🏨 **Tremont Plaza Hotel.** This 37-story building, once an apartment building, is in the densest part of the business district. Its plain facade and minuscule brass-and-marble lobby belie the tasteful earth-tone guest rooms, which are a favorite of musicians and actors performing at local theaters. The suites come in six sizes. The best views of the city and the small park in the center of St. Paul Place are from rooms with numbers ending in 06. The restaurant, Tugs, has a nautical theme and a menu rich in seafood. ⊠ 222 St. Paul Pl., City Center, 21202 ☎ 410/727–2222 or 800/873–6668 🖶 410/685–4215 ⊕ www.1800-tremont.com ➾ 253 suites ⚛ Restaurant, kitchenettes, cable TV, pool, gym, sauna, bar, concierge, Internet, 4 meeting rooms, parking (fee) ▭ AE, D, DC, MC, V.

$$–$$$ 🏨 **Wyndham Inner Harbor.** One of Baltimore's largest, this hotel (four blocks from the harbor) divides its rooms between two towers and also houses the largest ballroom in the city, which makes it especially popular with conventioneers. Rooms, decorated in light colors, have a contemporary flair and marble-floor bathrooms. Amenities include in-room voice mail, Internet access, hair dryers, and ironing boards. The hotel restaurant is Don Shula's Steak House, where the menu is presented on an official NFL football autographed by Shula, a former coach for the Baltimore Colts. ⊠ 101 W. Fayette St., City Center, 21201 ☎ 410/752–1100 🖶 410/752–0832 ⊕ www.wyndham.com/BaltimoreInnerHarbor ➾ 707 rooms, 21 suites ⚛ 2 restaurants, refrigerators, cable TV, Internet, business services, 24 meeting rooms, pool, gym, bar, convention center, parking (fee), no-smoking rooms ▭ AE, D, DC, MC, V.

Inner Harbor

★ $$$–$$$$ 🏨 **Harbor Court.** The entrance to the most prestigious hotel in Baltimore is set back from the street by a brick courtyard that provides an immediate sense of tranquillity. A grand spiral staircase dominates the lobby, which is decorated in English country opulence. All guest rooms include such deluxe touches as twice-daily maid service, plush bathrobes, and TVs in the bathrooms; upscale suite amenities also include 6-foot marble tubs with separate shower, canopied four-poster beds, and CD players. Waterside rooms have a commanding view of the harbor, but court-yard rooms are quietest. ✉ *550 Light St., Inner Harbor, 21202* ☎ *410/234–0550 or 800/824–0076* 🖷 *410/659–5925* ⊕ *www.harborcourt.com* 🛌 *195 rooms, 23 suites* ♨ *2 restaurants, coffee shop, minibars, TV with movies and video games, tennis court, indoor pool, health club, sauna, racquetball, bar, library, concierge, Internet, business services, convention center, 10 meeting rooms, parking (fee), no-smoking floors* ▭ *AE, D, DC, MC, V.*

$$$–$$$$ 🏨 **Hyatt Regency.** This stretch of Light Street is practically a highway, but the unenclosed skyways allow ready pedestrian access to both Inner Harbor attractions and the convention center. Rooms have rich gold and black-purple prints, cherrywood furniture, and marble in the bathrooms; most rooms have views of the harbor or the city. The lobby has glass elevators and the chain's trademark atrium. The 12th floor is the club level, with complimentary breakfast, evening hors d'oeuvres, and a private concierge available. Atop the hotel, the Pisces restaurant and lounge provides stunning city views, especially at night. ✉ *300 Light St., Inner Harbor, 21202* ☎ *410/528–1234 or 800/233–1234* 🖷 *410/685–3362* ⊕ *baltimore.hyatt.com* 🛌 *486 rooms, 25 suites* ♨ *2 restaurants, 3 tennis courts, pool, gym, sauna, 2 bars, Internet, business services, parking (fee), no-smoking floors* ▭ *AE, D, DC, MC, V.*

$$$–$$$$ 🏨 **Marriott Baltimore Waterfront.** The city's tallest hotel and the only one directly on the inner harbor itself, this upscale 32-story Marriott has a neoclassical interior that uses multihue marbles, rich jewel-tone walls, and photographs of Baltimore architectural landmarks. Although it's at the eastern end of the Inner Harbor, all downtown attractions are within walking distance; there's also a water taxi stop right by the front door. Most rooms offer unobstructed views of the city and harbor; ask for one that faces west toward downtown for a splendid panorama of the waterfront and skyscrapers. ✉ *700 Aliceanna St., Inner Harbor East, 21202* ☎ *410/385–3000* 🖷 *410/895–1900* ⊕ *www.marriotthotels.com/BWIWF* 🛌 *750 rooms* ♨ *Restaurant, coffee shop, in-room safes, minibars, indoor pool, health club, lounge, Internet, business services, 15 meeting rooms, parking (fee), no-smoking floors* ▭ *AE, D, DC, MC, V.*

$$$–$$$$ 🏨 **Renaissance Harborplace Hotel.** The most conveniently located of the Inner Harbor hotels—across the street from the shopping pavilions—the Renaissance Harborplace meets the needs of tourists, business travelers, and conventioneers. Guest rooms are light and cheerful, with amenities that include coffeemakers, terry robes, hair dryers, and ironing boards. Some rooms have a view of the harbor, the downtown landscape, or the indoor courtyard. The hotel adjoins the Gallery, a four-story shopping mall. ✉ *202 E. Pratt St., Inner Harbor, 21202* ☎ *410/547–1200 or 800/468–3571* 🖷 *410/539–5780* ⊕ *www.renaissancehotels.com/BWISH* 🛌 *562 rooms, 60 suites* ♨ *Restaurant, minibars, indoor pool, gym, sauna, bar, Internet, business services, convention center, 19 meeting rooms, parking (fee), no-smoking rooms* ▭ *AE, D, DC, MC, V.*

$$$ 🏨 **Baltimore Marriott Inner Harbor.** This 10-story hotel is a block away from Oriole Park at Camden Yards, Harborplace, and the convention center. The public areas are nondescript but surprisingly tranquil, as are the pastel-hued rooms, decorated in teal, mauve, and gray. The best views are from rooms facing the Inner Harbor and the ballpark. Rooms on the 10th floor come with concierge-level privileges. ⊠ *110 S. Eutaw St., Inner Harbor, 21201* ☎ *410/962–0202 or 800/228–9290* 🖷 *410/625–7832* ⊕ *www.marriott.com* ⇨ *524 rooms, 2 suites* ⚭ *Restaurant, cable TV, indoor pool, gym, sauna, bar, concierge, Internet, business services, 20 meeting rooms, parking (fee), no-smoking rooms* ⊟ *AE, D, DC, MC, V.*

\$\$–\$\$\$ 🔲 **Days Inn Inner Harbor.** Less than three blocks from the Inner Harbor, this nine-story redbrick building provides reliable and relatively economical accommodations in the center of town. The utilitarian, pastel-hue guest rooms are sparsely furnished, but each has a small desk and phone with voice mail and Internet access. ⊠ *100 Hopkins Pl., Inner Harbor East, 21201* ☎ *410/576–1000* 🖷 *410/576–9437* ⊕ *www.daysinnerharbor. com* ⇨ *250 rooms, 8 suites* ⚭ *Restaurant, refrigerators, pool, bar, Internet, business services, 3 meeting rooms, parking (fee), no-smoking rooms* ⊟ *AE, D, DC, MC, V.*

\$–\$\$\$ 🔲 **Courtyard by Marriott Baltimore Inner Harbor.** One block from the Inner Harbor waterfront and adjacent to Little Italy, this lodging is the farthest east of the Inner Harbor hotels. With sunny rooms in soothing neutral tones, the Courtyard Inner Harbor is a comfortable and attractive alternative to more central hotels with similar amenities and higher rates. Most downtown attractions are still within walking distance, though the stadiums and convention center are more comfortably reached by car or cab. ⊠ *1000 Aliceanna St., Inner Harbor East, 21202* ☎ *443/923–4000* 🖷 *443/923–9970* ⊕ *www.marriott.com/BWIDT* ⇨ *205 rooms* ⚭ *Restaurant, cable TV, Internet, business services, 4 meeting rooms, pool, gym, business services, parking (fee), no-smoking floors* ⊟ *AE, D, DC, MC, V.*

Fells Point

\$\$\$–\$\$\$\$ 🔲 **Inn at Henderson's Wharf.** Built in the mid-1800s as a B&O Railroad tobacco warehouse, this richly decorated, warmly inviting B&B–style inn has harbor or garden views from all of its rooms. The inn is at the water's edge, on the very peninsula that gave Fells Point its name. Adjacent to the inn is a marina with slips to 150 feet; all possible amenities are available to visiting yachtsmen. ⊠ *1000 Fell St., Fells Point, 21231* ☎ *410/522–7777 or 800/522–2088* 🖷 *410/522–7087* ⊕ *www. hendersonswharf.com* ⇨ *38 rooms* ⚭ *Gym, concierge, Internet, business center, meeting rooms, free parking; no smoking* ⊟ *AE, DC, MC, V* ¶⊙¶ *CP.*

\$\$\$ 🔲 **The Admiral Fell Inn.** This inn is an upright anchor at the center of action in funky Fells Point. By joining together buildings constructed between the late 1770s and the 1920s, the owners created a structure that resembles a small, European-style hotel, with lots of character and quirks. The rooms, which vary in shape, all have four-poster canopy beds. Three suites and eight rooms have whirlpool baths. Some hallways have a few stairs, and some rooms face a quiet, interior courtyard: if steps or street noise bother you, let the reservation agent know. ⊠ *888 S. Broadway, Fells Point, 21231* ☎ *410/522–7377 or 800/292–4667* 🖷 *410/522–0707* ⊕ *www.admiralfell.com* ⇨ *80 rooms* ⚭ *Restau-*

rant, pub, cable TV, Internet, meeting rooms, free parking ⊟ *AE, DC, MC, V* ¶❍¶ *CP.*

$$–$$$ 🏠 **Celie's Waterfront Bed & Breakfast.** Proprietors Nancy and Kevin Kupec oversee every detail of this small inn in the heart of Fells Point. Guest rooms, all with private bath, are furnished in Early American style; two suites accommodate large groups. Upscale amenities include down comforters, terry robes, fireplaces, and whirlpool baths. Continental breakfast is served in the cozy dining room. The rooftop deck provides a wonderful view of Baltimore's skyline and harbor. ✉ *1714 Thames St., Fells Point, 21231* ☎ *410/522–2323 or 800/432–0184* 🖷 *410/522–2324* ⊕ *www.celieswaterfront.com* ➷ *7 rooms* ᘖ *Dining room, cable TV, Internet, parking (fee)* ⊟ *AE, D, MC, V* ¶❍¶ *CP.*

Canton

$$–$$$ 🏠 **Inn at 2920.** In the heart of one of the city's liveliest neighborhoods, this stylish B&B is dedicated to tranquil, luxurious living. Low-allergen surroundings (natural fiber carpeting, low-chemical cleaning products, purified air) and high thread–count sheets are standard amenities, and each room has a Jacuzzi bathtub, satellite television with VCR, and CD player. Full-course breakfasts generally include fresh fruit salad, omelets, and waffles or pancakes, but different dietary needs can be accommodated. ✉ *2920 Elliott St., 21224* ☎ *410/342–4450* 🖷 *410/342–6436* ⊕ *www.theinnat2920.com* ➷ *4 rooms* ᘖ *Cable TV, in-room VCRs, Internet; no room phones, no kids under age 13, no smoking* ⊟ *AE, MC, V* ¶❍¶ *BP.*

Roland Park

$–$$$ 🏠 **Inn at the Colonnade.** Directly across the street from Johns Hopkins and within walking distance of the Baltimore Museum of Art, this hotel is also 10 minutes north of downtown. Rooms are welcoming, with rich, warm furnishings, and there are extras such as a glass-dome swimming pool, whirlpools, and free transportation to center-city destinations. ✉ *4 W. University Pkwy., Tuscany-Canterbury, 21218* ☎ *410/235–5400* 🖷 *410/235–5572* ⊕ *www.doubletree.com* ➷ *106 rooms, 19 suites* ᘖ *Restaurant, cable TV, Internet, indoor pool, gym, hot tub, lobby lounge, business services, meeting rooms, parking (fee), no-smoking rooms* ⊟ *AE, D, DC, MC, V.*

$–$$ 🏠 **Radisson Hotel at Cross Keys.** This secluded hotel is in the gated Village of Cross Keys, which occupies 72 acres of wooded grounds. Ten minutes north of downtown, it's a respite from city bustle. Rooms come with high-speed Internet access along with cheerful French country style. The health conscious will appreciate the wooded walking trails, tennis courts, and state-of-the-art exercise equipment. The hotel is adjacent to an outdoor mall with high-end boutique shopping. There's complimentary shuttle service to the Inner Harbor. ✉ *5100 Falls Rd., Roland Park, 21210* ☎ *410/532–6900 or 800/756–7285* 🖷 *410/532–2403* ⊕ *www.radisson.com* ➷ *147 rooms, 7 suites* ᘖ *Restaurant, pool, gym, lounge, cable TV, Internet, business services, meeting rooms, free parking, no-smoking floors* ⊟ *AE, D, DC, MC, V.*

Northern Suburbs

$ ⛉ **Courtyard by Marriott Hunt Valley.** About 25 minutes from downtown, in an affluent suburb that's a growing corporate center, this motel is comfortable and affordable. The simple guest rooms are as standardized as Courtyard's signature white-stucco exterior; coffeemakers, ironing boards, and hair dryers are added conveniences. The neighbors are office buildings, which means that rooms are quiet at night but have uninteresting views. The nearby York and Shawan road corridors have many restaurants, and there's public transportation to downtown via the light-rail Hunt Valley stop. ✉ *221 International Circle, Hunt Valley, 21030* ☎ *410/584–7070* 🖷 *410/584–8151* ⊕ *www.marriotthotels.com/BWIHU* ➯ *144 rooms, 12 suites △ Restaurant, indoor pool, gym, hot tub, bar, Internet, business services, free parking* ▤ *AE, D, DC, MC, V.*

$ ⛉ **Hampton Inn Hunt Valley.** Guest rooms at this suburban hotel are brightly decorated with basic furnishings. The property is within walking distance to a light-rail station for transportation to downtown Baltimore; the city is an easy 25-minute drive directly down I–83. Although there's no restaurant in the hotel, a free breakfast bar is available every morning, and many restaurants are nearby. ✉ *11200 York Rd., Hunt Valley, 21031* ☎ *410/527–1500* 🖷 *410/771–0819* ⊕ *www.hamptoninn.com* ➯ *125 rooms △ Cable TV, refrigerators, gym, Internet, free parking* ▤ *AE, D, DC, MC, V* ⛁ *CP.*

NIGHTLIFE & THE ARTS

The most comprehensive and complete calendar for Baltimore events appears in the *City Paper* (www.citypaper.com), a free weekly distributed in shops and yellow street-corner machines; it's published every Wednesday. Other event listings appear in the "Maryland Live" Thursday supplement to the *Baltimore Sun* and the monthly *Baltimore* magazine.

Fells Point, just east of the Inner Harbor, has scores of bars, restaurants, and clubs attracting a rowdy, largely collegiate, crowd. If you're seeking quieter surroundings, head for the upscale comforts of downtown or Mount Vernon clubs and watering holes.

Bars & Lounges

Upstairs at **The Brewer's Art** (✉ 1106 N. Charles St., Mount Vernon ☎ 410/547–6925) is an elegant bar and lounge with armchairs, marble pillars, and chandeliers, plus a dining room with terrific food; downstairs, the dark basement bar specializes in Belgian-style beers. With its stylized art deco surroundings, the funky **Club Charles** (✉ 1724 N. Charles St., North Arts District ☎ 410/727–8815) is a favorite hangout for an artsy crowd, moviegoers coming from the Charles Theater across the street, and, reputation has it, John Waters. The patio at the waterside **DuClaw Brewery** (✉ 901 South Bond St., Fells Point ☎ 410/563–3400) is a great spot for an early-evening pint; the restaurant serves bar fare with a twist, but stick to the standards.

The well-heeled gather at the Harbor Court Hotel in the **Explorer's Lounge** (⌗ 550 Light St., Inner Harbor ☎ 410/234–0550), where there are antique elephant-tusk lamps and faux leopard-skin chairs. Enjoy a cigar and pick a single-malt scotch from the largest selection in town. A pianist performs every night, and on Friday and Saturday nights there's a jazz trio. **Red Maple** (⌗930 N. Charles St., Mount Vernon ☎410/547–0149) is a stylish spot for drinks and tapas. The **Tusk Lounge** (⌗ 924 N. Charles St., Mount Vernon ☎ 410/547–8480), above the Brass Elephant restaurant, is a cozy, classy place for drinks.

At **DSX** (⌗ 200 W. Pratt St., Inner Harbor ☎410/659–5844), sports fans banter about trivia, dispute scores, and commiserate over scandals. This is a favorite postgame hangout for Orioles and Ravens fans. **Mc-Cafferty's** (⌗ 1501 Sulgrave Ave., Mount Washington ☎ 410/664–2200), named for former Baltimore Colts coach Don McCafferty, is a haven for fans of both pigskin and beef.

The Funk Box (⌗ 8 E. Cross St., Federal Hill ☎ 410/625-2000) is Baltimore's premier spot for live music, from rock and reggae, to jazz, blues, and soul. The **Horse You Came In On** (⌗ 1626 Thames St., Fells Point ☎ 410/327–8111) is a dim, quiet neighborhood tavern during the week, and a raucous bar with live music on weekends. **Ottobar** (⌗ 2549 N. Howard St., Mount Vernon ☎ 410/662–0069) is the city's venue for live alternative music.

Club Hippo (⌗ 1 W. Eager St., Mount Vernon ☎ 410/547–0069 ⊕ www.clubhippo.com) is Baltimore's longest-reigning gay bar. **Gallagher's** (⌗940 S. Conkling St., Canton ☎410/327–3966) is the city's most popular lesbian bar. A dance club, martini bar, and pub have all helped make **Grand Central** (⌗ 1003 N. Charles St., Mount Vernon ☎ 410/752–7133) into a hip gay hotspot.

Film

The **Charles Theater** (⌗ 1711 N. Charles St., Mount Vernon ☎ 410/727–3456 ⊕ www.thecharles.com) is Baltimore's preeminent venue for first-run, foreign, and art films. **Rotunda Cinematheque** (⌗ 11 W. 40th St., Roland Park ☎ 410/235–4800) has two small theaters showing independent films. The **Senator Theatre** (⌗ 5904 York Rd., Belvedere Square ☎ 410/435–8338) is the city's grande dame, a rare surviving example of a neighborhood theater built during Hollywood's golden age.

Music

An die Musik (⌗ 409 N. Charles St., Mount Vernon ☎ 410/385–2638 ⊕ www.AndieMusikLIVE.com) is an intimate space for classical, jazz, and world music. **Meyerhoff Symphony Hall** (⌗ 1212 Cathedral St., Mount Vernon ☎ 410/783–8000 ⊕ www.baltimoresymphony.org) is the city's principal concert hall. It's the home of the Baltimore Symphony Orchestra, led by maestro Yuri Temirkanov. **Friedberg Hall** (⌗ E. Mount Vernon Pl. and Charles St., Mount Vernon ☎ 410/659–8124 ⊕ www.peabody.jhu.edu), part of the Peabody Conservatory of Music, is the scene of recitals, concerts, and opera performances by students, faculty, and distinguished guests. At the outdoor **Pier Six Concert Pavilion** (⌗ Pier 6 at Pratt St., Inner Harbor ☎ 410/752–8632 ⊕ www.bop.org) there's both pavilion and lawn seating for concerts showcasing top national musicians and groups. Concerts run from June to September.

Theater

The **Baltimore Theatre Project** (✉ 45 W. Preston St., Mount Vernon ☎ 410/752–8558 ⊕ www.theatreproject.org) is dedicated to showing original and experimental theater, music, and dance. **Center Stage** (✉ 700 N. Calvert St., Mount Vernon ☎ 410/332–0033 ⊕ www.centerstage. org) performs works by Shakespeare and Samuel Beckett as well as contemporary playwrights. The intimate **Fells Point Corner Theater** (✉ 251 S. Ann St., Fells Point ☎ 410/276–7837 ⊕ www.fpct.org), an 85-seat venue focused on acting and directing workshops, stages eight off-Broadway productions a year, along with readings and poetry slams. A beautifully restored 1914 movie palace is home to the **France-Merrick Performing Arts Center at the Hippodrome** (✉ 12 N. Eutaw, West Baltimore ☎ 410/8837–7400 ⊕ www.france-merrickpac.com), a stage for concerts, Broadway musicals, and other big productions.

Lyric Opera House (✉ 140 W. Mt. Royal Ave., Mount Vernon ☎ 410/685–5086) hosts plays and musicals in addition to opera productions. **Morris A. Mechanic Theatre** (✉ 25 Hopkins Plaza, at Baltimore and Charles Sts., City Center ☎ 410/625–4230) houses road productions of Broadway hits and serves as a testing ground for Broadway-bound productions. **Spotlighters Theater** (✉ 817 St. Paul St., Mount Vernon ☎ 410/752–1225 ⊕ www.spotlighters.org) is a true community theater, staging locally produced (and cast) works that include original productions, Shakespeare, and musicals; there's one production a month, with performances on weekends. The **Vagabond Players** (✉ 806 S. Broadway, Fells Point ☎ 410/563–9135 ⊕ www.bcpl.net/~thevag/) hosts performances of recent Broadway hits and theater favorites every weekend.

SPORTS & THE OUTDOORS

Participant Sports

Bicycling

Baltimore lacks any kind of defined network of bicycling paths; exploring the city by bike means riding on the streets, a frequently hazardous experience. Or you could head to one of the city's parks or out of town to dedicated cycling trails. Bikes can be rented from **Light Street Cycles** (✉ 1015 Light St., Federal Hill ☎ 410/685–2234); ask for a map of local trails. Just south of the city is the **Baltimore and Annapolis Trail** (☎ 410/222–6244); to get on the trail near BWI airport, follow I–695 to I–97 south, take Exit 15 onto Dorsey Road, heading west away from the airport. Look for signs for Saw Mill Creek Park, which has 13 mi of paved trails, open space, bridges, and woodlands. North of the city, the 21-mi **Northern Central Railroad Hike and Bike Trail** (☎ 410/592–2897 ⊕ www.dnr.state.md.us/publiclands/central/gunpowder.html) extends along the old Northern Central Railroad to the Maryland–Pennsylvania line. It begins at Ashland Road, just east of York Road in Hunt Valley, and heads north 20 mi to the Pennsylvania border. Parking is available at seven points along the way.

Bowling

Invented in Baltimore in 1900, duckpin bowling uses smaller balls and pins. For some fun and some real Baltimore character, head to the **Patterson Bowling Center** (✉ 2105 Eastern Ave., Fells Point ☎ 410/675–1011), the oldest duck pin bowling center in the country.

Golf

The *Baltimore Sun*'s **golf guide** (⊕ www.sunspot.net/sports/golf/bal-golfguide.special) gives a detailed and thorough overview of local courses.

Public **Forest Park** (✉ 2900 Hillsdale Rd., North Baltimore ☎ 410/448–4653), has 18 holes (par 71) and is a challenging course, with a tight, tree-lined front 9 holes and open back 9. Greens fees are $18 weekdays and $19 on weekends; reservations are accepted. Designed in 1936, **Mount Pleasant** (✉ 6001 Hillen Rd., North Baltimore ☎ 410/254–5100) was for many years the site of the Eastern Open. It has 18 holes of par-71 golf on bent grass. Greens fees are $23 on weekdays and $24 on weekends.

North of the city, **Pine Ridge** (✉ 2101 Dulaney Valley Rd., Lutherville ☎ 410/252–1408) is an attractive, well-maintained 18-hole, par-54 course with water in play; greens fees are $23 on weekdays and $24 on weekends.

Health & Fitness Clubs

A few clubs offer temporary membership to visitors. Your hotel may provide this as a courtesy, so ask the concierge. Of hotels, the **Harbor Court** has by far the best athletic facilities. At the **Downtown Athletic Club** (✉ 210 E. Centre St., Mount Vernon ☎ 410/332–0906), you can pay a daily fee of $20 to play squash and racquetball and to use the indoor pool and exercise equipment. **Gold's Gym** (✉ 601 E. Pratt St., Inner Harbor ☎ 410/576-7771) in the Power Plant charges $15 per day for use of its gym. The exercise facilities and squash courts at the **Meadow Mill Athletic Club** (✉ 3600 Clipper Mill Rd., Hampden ☎ 410/235–7000) are $11 per day.

Running

Scenic places to run around the Inner Harbor include the promenade around the water; Rash Field, on the south side, adjacent to the Science Center and Federal Hill Park; and the path at the water's edge at Fort McHenry. If you're staying in Mount Vernon, head north up Charles Street towards Charles Village and Johns Hopkins University.

Tennis

Courts can be found in the city's public parks, though if you're a serious player, you may be better off using hotel courts or tennis clubs.

Druid Hill Park (✉ Druid Hill Lake Dr., West Baltimore ☎ 410/396–6106) has 24 courts. **Patterson Park** (✉ Eastern Ave., East Baltimore ☎ 410/396–3774) has 10 courts.

Rates at private courts are roughly $40–$50. Open year-round, the **Cross Keys Tennis Club** (✉ 5100 Falls Rd., Roland Park ☎ 410/433–1800) has courts available for an hourly fee. The courts at the **Orchard Indoor**

Tennis Club (✉ 8720 Loch Raven Blvd., Towson ☎ 410/821–6206) are available to nonmembers for an hourly rate.

Spectator Sports

Baseball

The **Baltimore Orioles** (✉ Oriole Park at Camden Yards, 333 W. Camden St., West Baltimore ☎ 410/685–9800 general information, 410/481–7328 for tickets ⊕ www.theorioles.com) play in their beautiful ballpark from early April until early October. Think twice about settling on a hot dog and Budweiser for your meal: the stadium also sells lumpmeat crab cakes, former Orioles first baseman Boog Powell's barbecued pork loin and beef, and local microbrews, such as Clipper City's Ft. McHenry Lager.

Football

The **Baltimore Ravens** (✉ 1101 Russell St., West Baltimore ☎ 410/261–7283 ⊕ www.baltimoreravens.com) play in the state-of-the-art M &T stadium from August to January.

Horse Racing

On the third Saturday in May the prestigious Preakness Stakes, the second race in the Triple Crown, is run at Baltimore's **Pimlico Race Course** (✉ Hayward and Winner Aves., Northwest Baltimore ☎ 410/542–9400 ⊕ www.marylandracing.com). The course has additional Thoroughbred racing from April through June, Wednesday through Sunday, and September through mid-October, Thursday through Sunday.

Lacrosse

Lacrosse is serious business in Baltimore: outdoor high school and college lacrosse is very popular and fiercely played in spring, and there's even a professional team. The **Baltimore Bayhawks** (✉ 2219 York Rd. ☎ 866/994–2957 ⊕ www.baltimorebayhawks.com) play major league lacrosse from May through August at the Unitas Stadium at Towson University, which is about 20 minutes north of the Inner Harbor. The **Johns Hopkins University Blue Jays** (✉ Homewood Field, Charles St. and University Pkwy., Charles Village ☎ 410/516–7490 ⊕ hopkinssports. fansonly.com) are a perennial favorite. The **Loyola Greyhounds** (✉ Charles St. and Cold Spring La., North Baltimore ☎ 410/617–5014 ⊕ www. loyola.edu/athletics/mlax_sked.htm), play on their college's campus.

Soccer

The **Blast** (✉ Baltimore Arena, 201 W. Baltimore St., West Baltimore ☎ 410/732–5278 team, 410/347–2020 arena ⊕ www.baltimoreblast. com), a team in the Eastern Division of the Major Indoor Soccer League, plays from October to April.

SHOPPING

Baltimore isn't the biggest shopping town, but it does have some malls and some good stores here and there. Hampden (the "p" is silent), a neighborhood west of Johns Hopkins University, has funky shops selling everything from housewares to housedresses along its main drag,

36th Street (better known as "The Avenue"). Some interesting shops can be found along Charles Street in Mount Vernon and along Thames Street in Fells Point. Federal Hill has a few fun shops, particularly for furnishings and vintage items.

Shopping Malls

About 7 mi north of downtown, at Northern Parkway and York Road, is **Belvedere Square** (⊠ E. Belvedere Ave. at York Rd. ☎ 410/464–9773), a small, open-air mall with shops for women's and children's clothing, furniture, and gifts as well as a number of gourmet food shops (the soup at Atwater's is delicious). At the Inner Harbor, the Pratt Street and Light Street pavilions of **Harborplace and the Gallery** (☎ 410/332–4191) contain almost 200 specialty shops that sell everything from business attire to children's toys. The Gallery has J. Crew, Banana Republic, and the Gap, among others. **Owings Mills Town Center** (⊠ Owings Mills exit from I–795, 20 min northwest of the Inner Harbor, Owings Mills ☎ 410/363–1234 ⊕ www.owingsmillsmall.com) has Macy's and Hecht's department stores; specialty clothing stores; and shoe, toy, and bookstores as well as a multiplex cinema. The mall is at the northern terminus of the city's metro system. **Towson Town Center** (⊠ Dulaney Valley Rd. and Fairmount Ave., ½ mi south of I–695 at Exit 27A, Towson ☎ 410/494–8800 ⊕ www.towsontowncenter.com) has nearly 200 shops, including Hecht's, Nordstrom, the Gap, and Anthropologie. **Village of Cross Keys** (⊠ 5100 Falls Rd., North Baltimore ☎ 410/323–1000), about 6 mi north of downtown, is an eclectic collection of 30 stores, including Talbot's, Chico's, Williams-Sonoma, Ann Taylor, and some small, high-end boutiques shops for women's clothing and gifts.

Department Stores

Merchandise at **Hecht's** includes men's, women's, and children's clothing along with housewares. There are five locations around Baltimore, including ones in Owings Mills Town Center and Towson Town Center. Shop for top-name designer goods accompanied by courteous, service-oriented sales staff and live music from a grand piano at **Nordstrom** (⊠ Towson Town Center, 825 Dulaney Valley Rd., Towson ☎ 410/494–9111).

Food Markets

Baltimore's indoor food markets, all of which are at least 100 years old, are a mix of vendors selling fresh fish, meat, produce, and baked goods and a food court, with stands for street food such as crab cakes, sausages, fried chicken, and pizza. Lexington Market is the largest and most famous, and Broadway and Cross Street markets are close behind in terms of local, taste-tempting foods. City markets are generally open year round, every day but Sunday, until 6.

Broadway Market (⊠ Broadway and Fleet St., Fells Point) has many stalls with fresh fruit, prepared foods, a raw bar, and baked goods that can be eaten at counters or taken outside for picnics along the waterfront. **Cross Street Market** (⊠ Light and Cross Sts., Federal Hill) has a terrific sushi bar along with stands selling produce, sandwiches, steamed crab, and baked items. Cross Street is open late on Friday and Saturday, when the market hosts one of the city's most popular happy hour scenes, attracting crowds of youngish professionals. The city's oldest and largest public market, **Lexington Market** (⊠ Lexington St. between Paca and Eutaw Sts., Downtown ☎ 410/685–6169 ⊕ www.lexingtonmarket. com) has more than 150 vendors selling meat, produce, seafood, baked goods, delicatessen items, poultry, and food products from around the world. Don't miss the world-famous crab cakes at Faidley's Seafood; other local specialties with market stalls are Rheb's chocolates, Polock Johnny's Polish sausages, and Berger's Bakery's chocolate-iced vanilla wafer cookies.

Specialty Stores

Antiques

Many of Baltimore's antiques shops can be found on historic Antique Row, which runs along the 700 and 800 blocks of North Howard Street. Shops include cluttered kitsch boutiques as well as elegant, high-end galleries of furniture and fine art. Fells Point shops are concentrated on Eastern, Fleet, and Aliceanna streets. Hampden shops are found primarily on 36th Street.

The **Antique Warehouse at 1300** (⊠ 1300 Jackson St. and Key Hwy., Federal Hill ☎ 410/659–0663) has 35 dealers under one roof. **Avenue Antiques** (⊠ 901 W. 36th St., Hampden ☎ 410/467–0329) is a collection of multiple dealers, selling antiques from Victorian to mid-century modern. At **Gaines McHale Antiques and Home** (⊠ 836 Leadenhall St., Federal Hill ☎ 410/625–1900 ⊕ www.gainesmchale.com) the owners build new pieces with old wood, turning antique armoires, for example, into entertainment centers. There's also a large selection of unaltered, high-quality country and traditional antiques from England and France. **Second Chance** (⊠ 1645 Warner St. Southwest Baltimore ☎ 410/385–1101) salvages unique architectural pieces from old buildings being renovated or destroyed; the store is open Thursday–Saturday 9–5. **The Turnover Shop** (⊠ 3855 Roland Ave., Hampden ☎ 410/235–9585) is a consignment shop selling high-end antiques.

Books

Barnes & Noble (⊠ 601 E. Pratt St., Inner Harbor ☎ 410/385–1709,), in the Power Plant complex at the Inner Harbor, is the city's largest general-interest bookseller.

The **AIA/Baltimore Bookstore** (⊠ 11 ½ W. Chase St., Mount Vernon ☎ 410/625–2585) carries all kinds of architecture books. **Atomic Books** (⊠ 1100 W. 36th St., Hampden ☎ 410/662–4444 ⊕ www.atomicbooks. com) specializes in obscure titles and small-press publications, including independent comics and 'zines, along with videos. There's also a formidable selection of pop-culture toys such as lunch boxes, cookie jars, and stickers. **Book Thing** (⊠ 3001 Vineyard La., Waverly ☎ 410/662–5631 ⊕ www.bookthing.org) takes donations and gives away free books—as many as you like, as long as you promise not to resell them; it's open weekends 9–6. **The Children's Bookstore** (⊠ 737 Deepdene Rd.,

Roland Park ☎410/532–2000) is a cozy, well-stocked resource for current and classic children's literature. The **Kelmscott Bookshop** (⊠ 32 W. 25th St., Charles Village ☎ 410/235–6810 ⊕ www.kelmscottbookshop.com) is known for its enormous, well-preserved stock of old and rare volumes in every major category, especially art, architecture, American and English literature, and travel. **Lambda Rising** (⊠ 241 W. Chase St., Mount Vernon ☎410/234–0069) is Baltimore's gay, lesbian, and bisexual bookstore. **Mystery Loves Company** (⊠ 1730 Fleet St., Fells Point ☎ 410/276–6708 ⊕ www.mysterylovescompany.com) specializes in books and gifts for whodunit fans; the shop stocks an excellent selection of works by Baltimore native son (and inventor of the genre) Edgar Allan Poe.

Gifts

Many of the city's museums have excellent shops, which are good sources for gifts. **Best of Baltimore** (⊠ 301 S. Light St., Harbor Pl. ☎410/332–4191) carries city-related souvenirs and local specialty products. For unique, truly local mementos of Baltimore, like crab-shape twinkle lights and a kit for cleaning row-house marble steps, **Hometown Girl** (⊠ 1001 W. 36th St., Hampden ☎410/662–4438) is the place to go. It also stocks local history books and Baltimore guidebooks.

The **Tomlinson Craft Collection** (⊠ The Rotunda, 711 W. 40th St., Roland Park ☎410/338–1572) is a gallery of local artisan handiworks, from fine jewelry to ceramics and metalwork. The **Store Ltd.** (⊠ Village of Cross Keys, Roland Park ☎ 410/323–2350) has an eclectic mix of top-quality (and pricey) jewelry, women's sportswear, glassware, and other high-design gifts.

Jewelry

Amaryllis (⊠ The Gallery, 200 E. Pratt St. ☎410/576–7622) specializes in handcrafted jewelry from more than 400 artists. Designers come from all over the world for the incredibly wide selection of beads at **Beadazzled** (⊠ 501 N. Charles St., Mount Vernon ☎ 410/837–2323); there's also a selection of already made jewelry.

Children's Clothing

Raw Sugar (⊠ 524 E. Belvedere Ave., Belvedere Square ☎410/464-1240) carries clothing for the funky, fashionable six and under set as well as maternity wear and toys.

Men's Clothing

Jos. A. Bank's Clothiers (⊠ 100 E. Pratt St., Inner Harbor ☎410/547–1700) is a century-old Baltimore source for men's tailored clothing and casual wear. **Samuel Parker Clothier** (⊠ Mt. Washington Mill, Mt. Washington ☎ 410/464-6180) carries a fine selection of updated traditional clothing by the likes of Ralph Lauren and Samuelson.

Women's Clothing

Jones & Jones (⊠ Village of Cross Keys, Roland Park ☎410/532–9645) carries stylish sportswear and business attire. **Ruth Shaw** (⊠ Village of Cross Keys, Roland Park ☎410/532–7886) sells the work of European designers like Gaultier and Paul Smith as well as chic evening wear. **Something Else** (⊠ 1611 Sulgrave Ave., Mt. Washington ☎410/542–0444) is the source for sophisticated hippie wear: Flax-brand clothes, flowing skirts, big scarves, and colorful sweaters.

Ma Petite Shoe (⊠ 832 W. 36th St., Hampden ☎ 410/235-3442) sells chocolates as well as funky, fabulous shoes. **Oh! Said Rose** (⊠ 840 W. 36th St., Hampden ☎ 410/235–5170) carries fun, feminine clothing with a vintage look. **The Shine Collective** (⊠ 3554 Roland Ave., Hampden ☎ 410/366–6100) carries hip accessories and clothing made by a group of local young designers.

SIDE TRIPS FROM BALTIMORE

Not far from Baltimore, Maryland's landscape is dotted with well-preserved 18th- and 19th-century towns. Harford County's Havre de Grace, at the top of the bay, and nearby Aberdeen, with a legacy of military history, make for an ideal day trip. Historic Ellicott City, southwest of Baltimore in Howard County, is a fun place to explore, have lunch, and shop.

Havre de Grace

40 mi northeast of Baltimore (via I–95).

On the site of one of Maryland's oldest settlements is the neatly laidout town Havre de Grace, reputedly named by the Marquis de Lafayette. This "harbor of mercy," on the Chesapeake Bay at the mouth of the Susquehanna River, was shelled and torched by the British in the War of 1812, and few structures predate that period.

Havre de Grace is about a 40-minute drive from downtown Baltimore. From downtown, take I–395 to I–95; pick up I–95 north to New York and follow it to Harford County and Havre de Grace. Route 155 off Exit 89 leads to downtown Havre de Grace.

One of the few 18th-century structures in Havre de Grace, **Rodgers House** (⊠ 226 N. Washington St.) is a two-story redbrick Georgian town house topped by a dormered attic. The town's most historically significant building, it was the home of Admiral John Rodgers, who fired the first shot in the War of 1812. Like most of the other historic houses in Havre de Grace, it's closed to the public but still worth a drive past.

The **Havre de Grace Decoy Museum,** housed in a converted power plant, has 1,200 facsimiles of ducks, geese, and swans made from wood, iron, cork, papier-mâché, and plastic. Three classes—decorative, decorative floater, and working decoys—are represented. On weekends, decoy carvers demonstrate their art in the museum basement. A festival during the first full weekend in May includes carving contests and demonstrations by retrievers. ⊠ *Giles and Market Sts.* ☎ *410/939–3739* ⊕ *www.decoymuseum.com* ⊠ *$6* ☉ *Daily 11–4.*

The **Susquehanna Museum,** at the southern terminal of the defunct Susquehanna and Tidewater Canal, tells the history of the canal and the people who lived and worked there. From 1839 until 1890 the canal ran 45 mi north to Wrightsville, Pennsylvania. It was a thoroughfare for mule-drawn barges loaded with iron ore, coal, and crops. The museum, in a lock tender's cottage built in 1840, is partially furnished with modest mid-century antiques that recall its period of service. ⊠ *Erie and Conesto Sts.* ☎ *410/939–5780* 🖃 *$2* ⊙ *May–Oct., weekends 1–5; candlelight tour 2nd Sun. in Dec.*

The conical **Concord Point Lighthouse** is the oldest continuously operated lighthouse on the Chesapeake Bay. Built in 1827, it was restored in 1980. You can climb up 30 feet for views of the bay, the river, and the town. ⊠ *Concord and Lafayette Sts. at the Susquehanna River, Havre de Grace* ☎ *410/939–9040* 🖃 *Free* ⊙ *Apr.–Oct., weekends 1–5.*

Susquehanna State Park, 6 mi upriver from Havre de Grace, sits on 2,500 acres. You can fish, bird-watch, hike, bike, and camp. A covered stone pavilion by the river is a good place for picnics. ⊠ *Rte. 155* ☎ *410/836–6735* 🖃 *Free* ⊙ *Daily 9–sunset.*

The **Steppingstone Museum** is a 10-acre complex of seven restored turn-of-the-20th-century farm buildings plus a replica of a canning house. Among the 12,000-plus artifacts in the collection are a horse-drawn tractor and an early gas-powered version, manual seeders and planters, and horse-drawn plows. A blacksmith, a weaver, a wood-carver, a cooper, a dairymaid, and a decoy artist regularly demonstrate their trades in the workshops. ⊠ *Susquehanna State Park, 461 Quaker Bottom Rd.* ☎ *410/939–2299* 🖃 *$3* ⊙ *May–Sept., weekends 1–5.*

★ The **Ladew Topiary Gardens** displays the life's work of Harvey Smith Ladew. The trees and shrubs are sculpted into geometric forms and lifelike renditions of animals such as a fox and hounds, swans, and even a seahorse. The 15 different formal gardens cover 22 acres. Besides the amazing topiary displays are rose, berry, and herb gardens, and a tranquil Japanese garden with pagoda, lily ponds, and lush flowers. In summer there are special events such as concerts and polo matches. The 18th-century manor house is filled with English antiques, paintings, photographs, and fox-hunting memorabilia. A café on the grounds serves lunch and light snacks. ⊠ *3535 Jarrettsville Pike, 14 mi north of I–695, Monkton* ☎ *410/557–9466* ⊕ *www.ladewgardens.com* 🖃 *House and gardens $12, gardens only $8* ⊙ *Mid-Apr.–Oct., weekdays 10–4, weekends 10:30–5.*

Where to Stay & Eat

$$–$$$ ✕ **Crazy Swede.** A nautical theme prevails in this restaurant on a tree-lined avenue. Windows and mirrors on all sides keep the dining room well lighted whether or not the sailboat lanterns on the tables are burning. On the menu, beef, seafood, and pasta dishes are all well represented. Veal Havre de Grace, served with shrimp and lump crabmeat in a Chablis cream sauce, is a specialty. ⊠ *400 N. Union Ave., Havre de Grace* ☎ *410/939–5440* ⊕ *www.crazyswederestaurant.com* ▤ *AE, MC, V.*

$$–$$$ ✕ **MacGregor's.** Behind the redbrick facade of a bank built in 1928, Mac-Gregor's occupies two dining rooms on two levels, with glass walls on three sides looking onto the Chesapeake Bay. The interior is adorned with carved duck decoys, mounted guns, and antique prints of the town; there's also outdoor dining on a deck with a gazebo. Seafood is the specialty, and the kitchen claims to have the best crab cakes on the

bay. ⊠ *331 St. John's St., Havre de Grace* ☎ *410/939–3003* ⊕ *www.macgregorsrestaurant.com* ⊟ *AE, D, DC, MC, V.*

$–$$ 🏠 **Vandiver Inn.** This three-story wood house, built in 1886 and listed on the National Register of Historic Places, is 1½ blocks from the bay. Green with a dark green trim on the outside, the inn has a Victorian look, with antique beds and other period pieces. A porch extends the width of the house front, and the gazebo in the backyard is as old as the house itself. ⊠ *301 S. Union Ave., Havre de Grace, 21078* ☎ *410/939–5200 or 800/245–1655* ⊕ *www.vandiverinn.com* 🛏 *17 rooms* ⚭ *Cable TV, Internet, meeting rooms; no smoking* ⊟ *AE, D, MC, V* ⧖ *BP.*

$–$$ 🏠 **Spencer-Silver Mansion.** This house was built in 1886 from gray granite quarried at nearby Port Deposit—the same kind of granite was used to build the Brooklyn Bridge. Characteristic Victorian details include stained-glass windows, a wraparound porch, and a turret. The carriage house is a lovely two-story stone cottage with loft bedroom, Jacuzzi, and fireplace; it sleeps up to four but is ideal for couples seeking a romantic hideaway. All rooms are furnished with period antiques supplemented by select reproductions. ⊠ *200 S. Union Ave., 21078* ☎ *410/939–1097 or 800/780–1485* ⊕ *www.spencersilvermansion.com* 🛏 *4 rooms, 1 suite* ⚭ *Internet; no smoking* ⊟ *AE, MC, V* ⧖ *BP.*

Aberdeen

30 mi northeast of Baltimore.

A site for artillery testing since 1917, Aberdeen celebrates its heritage every year on Armed Forces Day (the third Saturday in May) with tank parades and firing demonstrations. The town is also the birthplace of Cal Ripken Jr., who made baseball history in 1995 by breaking Lou Gehrig's record for most consecutive games played.

Aberdeen loves its native son so much that they gave part of City Hall to honor the legendary Baltimore Oriole shortstop. The small but heartwarming **Ripken Museum** holds memorabilia from Cal's career with the team, both major- and minor-league, as well as items pertaining to brother Billy, who played for the O's, and father Cal Sr., who coached and managed the team. A gift shop sells autographed baseballs and other Ripken mementos. ⊠ *8 Ripken Plaza* ☎ *410/273–2525* 🏷 *$3* ⊙ *Memorial Day–Labor Day, daily 11–3; Labor Day–Apr., Fri. and Mon. 11–3, Sat. 11–4, Sun. noon–3:30; May–Memorial Day, Thurs., Fri., and Mon. 11–3, Sat. 11–4, Sun. noon–3:30.*

Cal Ripken Stadium (⊠ 873 Long Dr. ☎ 410/297–9292 ⊕ www.ripkenbaseball.com) brings Single-A baseball to town with the IronBirds, an Orioles minor-league affiliate team. Owned by Cal Ripken, the team plays short-season ball every June to September in Ripken Stadium, a 5,500-seat venue complete with skyboxes.

Ellicott City

12 mi southwest of Baltimore

Ellicott City was founded in 1772 by three Quaker brothers—John, Andrew, and Joseph Ellicott. By the 1860s, Ellicott City had become one of the most prominent milling and manufacturing towns in the east. Today the town retains its historical flavor and is a pleasant place to stroll and browse the many stores and antiques shops. The Howard County Office of Tourism (☎ 410/313–1900 or 800/288–8747) offers walking tours of the town.

Ellicott City was the B & O Railroad's first stop. The **Ellicott City B & O Railroad Station Museum,** built in 1831, is the oldest railroad terminal in America. Exhibits focus on the history of the railroad and on its role in the Civil War. ⊠ *Corner of Maryland Ave. and Main St., Ellicott City* ☎ *410/461–1944* ⊕ *www.ecbo.org* ⊠ *$5* ⊙ *Fri. and Sat. 11–4, Sun. noon–4.*

The **Oella Mill** was once just that; these days it houses antiques dealers and artisans under its very large roof. ⊠ *840 Oella Ave., Ellicott City* ☎ *410/465–8708.*

BALTIMORE A TO Z

To research prices, get advice from other travelers, and book travel arrangements, visit www.fodors.com.

ADDRESSES

Laid out in a more-or-less regular grid pattern, Baltimore is fairly easy to navigate. The navigational center of town is the intersection of Charles and Baltimore streets; all east–west demarcations use Charles Street as the starting (zero) block, and north–south distinctions originate at Baltimore Street. The major downtown north–south thoroughfares are Charles and Saint Paul (north of Baltimore Street) and Light Street (south of Baltimore). Downtown, east–west traffic depends heavily on Pratt and Lombard streets. The downtown area is bounded by Martin Luther King Boulevard on the west and by the Jones Falls Expressway (President Street) on the east.

AIRPORTS

Baltimore's major airport is Baltimore-Washington International Airport (BWI), just south of town. BWI is easily reached by car, taxi, or light-rail; for most agencies, rental cars are returned to lots off the airport premises.

🖪 Airport Information **Baltimore-Washington International Airport (BWI)** ⊠ 10 mi south of Baltimore off Rte. 295/Baltimore-Washington Pkwy. ☎ 410/859–7111 for information and paging ⊕ www.bwiairport.com.

TRANSFERS By Bus: **BWI Super Shuttle** provides van service between the airport and downtown hotels, every half hour, 4 AM–midnight. Travel time is about 30 minutes; the fare is $20 for the first person, $5 per additional passenger. Hotel vans, which operate independently of the hotels, take 30 minutes on average. Some hotels may provide complimentary limousine service.

By Limousine: **Carey Limousines** provides sedan service, which costs $80; make reservations 24 hours in advance. **Private Car/RMA Worldwide**

Chauffeured Transportation has sedans, limos, and vans; the cost to the Inner Harbor is about $40 for a sedan.

By Taxi: **Airport Taxis** stand by to meet arriving flights. The ride into town on I–295 takes 20 minutes; a trip between the airport and downtown costs about $25. Airport Taxi service is available only *from* BWI; for transportation to the airport, consult a local cab company such as **Jimmy's Cab Co.** or **Arrow Taxicab.**

By Train: **Amtrak** service between the BWI Airport rail station and Baltimore's Penn Station is available daily at irregular intervals, so call ahead. The ride takes 15 minutes and costs $13. **Maryland Area Rail Commuter** (MARC) trains travel between the BWI Airport and Penn Station in about 20 minutes, weekdays 7 AM–10 PM, at a fare of $4 one-way; trains leave once an hour. Light-rail train service also connects the airport with downtown Baltimore, Penn Station, and other destinations. The fare is $1.60 one-way, $3.20 round-trip, and $3.50 for a one-day pass; trains run about every 20 minutes. For information and schedules, contact the **Maryland Transit Administration.**

🚹 **Airport Taxis** ☎ 410/859-1100 ⊕ www.bwiairporttaxi.com. **Arrow Taxicab** ☎ 410/358-9696. **Amtrak** ☎ 800/872-7245. **BWI Airport rail station** ☎ 410/672-6167. **BWI Super Shuttle** ☎ 800/258-3826. **Carey Limousines** ☎ 410/880-0999 or 888/880-0999. **Jimmy's Cab Co.** ☎ 410/296-7200. **Maryland Area Rail Commuter (MARC)** ☎ 800/325-7245 or 410/539-5000. **Maryland Transit Administration (MTA)** ☎ 800/325-7245 or 410/539-5000 ⊕ www.mtamaryland.com. **Penn Station** ✉ Charles St. and Mt. Royal Ave., Mount Vernon ☎ 410/291-4269. **Private Car/RMA Worldwide Chauffeured Transportation** ☎ 410/519-0000 or 800/878-7743 ⊕ www.rmalimo.com.

BIKE TRAVEL

Navigating Baltimore by bicycle is an uneasy proposition. The vast majority of residents rely on four-, rather than two-wheeled, vehicles. There are practically no bike-oriented amenities such as bicycle lanes or even bike racks. However, with caution and awareness on the part of the rider, the compact center core of the city can be navigated and even enjoyed on two wheels.

🚹 **Bike Rentals** **Light Street Cycles** ✉ 1015 Light St., Federal Hill ☎ 410/685-2234.

BUS TRAVEL

Travel to Baltimore by bus is easy and convenient. Passengers can arrive at the downtown bus terminal or at the Baltimore Travel Plaza just off I–95; the plaza has long-term parking and local bus service to downtown and other destinations. Greyhound Lines has scheduled daily service to and from major cities in the United States and Canada. Peter Pan/Trailways Bus Lines offers slightly nicer travel to many destinations in the Northeast, including Washington, D.C., New York, and Boston.

🚹 **Bus Depots** **Baltimore Travel Plaza** ✉ 5625 O'Donnell St., at I-95, East Baltimore ☎ 800/231-2222. **Downtown Bus Terminal** ✉ 2110 Hanes St., at Russell St., City Center ☎ 410/752-7682.

⏹ Bus Lines **Greyhound Lines** ☎ 800/231-2222 ⊕ www.greyhound.com. **Maryland Transit Administration** (MTA) ☎ 800/325-7245 or 410/539-5000 ⊕ www.mtamaryland.com. **Peter Pan/Trailways Bus Lines** ☎ 800/237-8747 ⊕ www.peterpanbus.com.

BUS TRAVEL WITHIN BALTIMORE

Buses provide an inexpensive way to see much of Baltimore, though you may have to transfer several times. The Maryland Transit Administration has more than 70 bus routes. There's also MTA bus service between Baltimore and Annapolis.

FARES & SCHEDULES
Route and schedule information is available by contacting the Maryland Transit Administration. Bus and transit schedules are also available inside the Charles Center metro station (Charles and Baltimore streets downtown), but sometimes these run out and are not immediately replaced. Fare is $1.60 (exact change is required). All-day passes are $3.50 and can be used with light-rail or metro travel. Some routes have service 24 hours daily.

⏹ **Maryland Transit Administration** (MTA) ☎ 800/325-7245 or 410/539-5000 ⊕ www.mtamaryland.com.

CAR RENTALS

Baltimore is served by all major car-rental agencies at BWI Airport. Enterprise and Thrifty have the most numerous and convenient locations around town.

⏹ Agencies **Enterprise** ☎ 800/736-8222 ⊕ www.enterprise.com. **Thrifty** ☎ 410/859-4900 ⊕ www.thrifty.com.

CAR TRAVEL

From the northeast and south, I–95 cuts across the city's east side and the harbor; Route 295, the Baltimore–Washington Parkway, follows a similar route farther to the east and is the best route downtown from the airport. From the north, I–83, also called the Jones Falls Expressway, winds through Baltimore and ends at the Inner Harbor. I–395 serves as the primary access to downtown from I–95. From the west, I–70 merges with the Baltimore Beltway, I–695. Drivers headed downtown should use I–395.

PARKING
Parking in downtown Baltimore tends to be difficult; on weekdays, many garages fill up early with suburban commuters. When the Orioles or Ravens play a home game, parking around the Inner Harbor can be nearly impossible to find. Best bets for parking are hotel garages, which seem to often have spaces available. Attended parking lots are located around the downtown periphery and cost less than garages.

It's hard to find a metered parking spot downtown, though in other areas it's much easier. Most meters in well-traveled areas charge 25¢ per 15-minute period and have a two-hour limit; around the Inner Harbor vicinity meters are in effect 24 hours a day.

TRAFFIC
Weekday rush hour traffic can be quite heavy, particularly around the I–95 tunnels, on I–695, and on I–83. When the Orioles or Ravens play a home game, the stadium area becomes extremely congested, and it's better to avoid driving in that vicinity as well as on I–295 (the most convenient entrance/exit area for the stadiums) altogether.

CHILDREN IN BALTIMORE

BABYSITTING Baltimore lacks a babysitter referral service. Most hotels provide child-care referral services for guests; check with the concierge desk. Rates range from $8 to $20 per hour.

DISABILITIES & ACCESSIBILITY

Major attractions and points of interest in Baltimore, from the 18th-century fortifications at Fort McHenry to Ravens Stadium, are accessible to those with disabilities; many have especially helpful resources. The National Aquarium, for example, offers Assistive Listening Devices, ASL interpreters, audio and Braille tours, express entry for visitors with special needs, and reserved seating for the dolphin show. Local organizations such as LINC (Learning Independence Through Computers) are the best source for getting information on accessibility at area hotels, restaurants, and attractions; LINC's Web site has a comprehensive list of local support organizations and accessible facilities in the Baltimore area. The Maryland Transit Authority provides transporation services to people with special needs; contact the Maryland Transit Authority (MTA) Mobility Office.

Baltimore's Center Stage, Mechanic Theater, and Lyric Opera House all provide accessible performances, which include audio description, Braille, and large-print programs for events. The group Maryland Arts Access works to make arts, recreation, and cultural activities throughout the state available to all, regardless of disability.

🚩 **Local Resources LINC** ✉ 1001 Eastern Ave., East Baltimore ☎ 410/659-5462 ⊕ www. linc.org/TextOnly/mdres_text.html. **Maryland Arts Access** ✉ 1 N. Charles St., Downtown ☎ 410/347-1650 ⊕ www.mdtap.org/md_arts.html. **MTA Mobility Office** ☎ 410/727-3535 ⊕ www.mtamaryland.com.

DISCOUNTS & DEALS

The Baltimore Visitor Center offers the three-day Harbor Pass, which saves you on admission to local attractions and gives you discounts on parking, hotels, and tours.

Numerous Web sites offer discounted hotel rooms in Baltimore, but fewer sites do the same thing for dining. If you're willing to dine at off-peak hours to save up to 30% off your dinner bill, visit the Dinner Broker Web site, where you can see what restaurants participate and make free online reservations.

🚩 **Baltimore Visitor Center** ✉ 401 Light St. Inner Harbor ☎ 877/225-8466, ⊕ www. baltimore.org. **Dinner Broker** ☎ 888/432-8288 [888/432-8288 ⊕ www.dinnerbroker.com.

EMERGENCIES

To report non-life-threatening situations that are nonetheless of concern, the Baltimore City Police Department operates an alternative phone line, **311,** which connects directly to a police operator. For emergencies, call 911.

Mercy Medical Center has set up a "Dial a Downtown Doctor" hotline for physician referrals and appointments. The service is available around the clock, seven days a week. Also downtown, the University of Maryland Medical Center operates a similar service from 7 AM to 7 PM daily, and can provide access to dentists as well as medical doctors.

🔳 **Ambulance, fire, police** ☎ 911.

🔳 **Doctors & Dentists Dial a Downtown Doctor** ☎ 800/636-3729 ⊕ www.mdmercy. com. **University of Maryland Physicians Referral** ☎ 800/492-5538 ⊕ www.umm.edu. 🔳 **Hospitals GBMC** ✉ 6701 Charles St., Towson ☎ 410/849-2225. **Johns Hopkins Hospital** ✉ 600 N. Wolfe St., East Baltimore ☎ 410/955-2280. **Mercy Medical Center** ✉ 301 St. Paul Pl., City Center ☎ 410/332-9000. **Sinai Hospital** ✉ 2401 Belvedere Ave., Mt. Washington ☎ 410/601-8800. **University of Maryland University Hospital** ✉ 22 S. Greene St., West Baltimore ☎ 410/328-8667.

🔳 **24-Hour Pharmacies CVS** ✉ 4625 Falls Rd., Roland Park ☎ 410/662-1670. **Rite Aid** ✉ 250 W. Chase St., Mount Vernon ☎ 410/752-4473 ✉ Rotunda shopping center, 711 W. 40th St., Charles Village ☎ 410/467-3343.

MAIL & SHIPPING

Baltimore's main post office is convenient to downtown and open 24 hours. Federal Express and UPS have offices downtown, and operators such as Kinko's and Mail Boxes Etc. offer packing and shipping services.

Free public Internet access is available at the Enoch Pratt Free Library (just ask the librarian for a temporary library card).

🔳 **Main Post Office** ✉ 900 E. Fayette St., Inner Harbor East ☎ 410/347-4425. **FedEx** ✉ 36 S. Charles St. ☎ 800/463-3339. **Kinko's** ✉ 3003 N. Charles St., City Center ☎ 410/223-2000. **UPS Store** ✉ 211 E. Lombard St., Inner Harbor ☎ 410/659-9360. 🔳 **Internet Enoch Pratt Free Library** ✉ 400 Cathedral St., Mount Vernon ☎ 410/ 396-5500.

SIGHTSEEING TOURS

Tours of Baltimore, on foot or four wheels, run from traditional surveys of historic buildings and sites to quirkier explorations such as the Fells Point Ghost Tour.

TROLLEY TOURS The Baltimore Shuttle offers a 90-minute narrated trolley tour of the city; tours are $18 and depart daily at 11 and 2 from the Visitor Center at the Inner Harbor.

🔳 **The Baltimore Shuttle** ☎ 410/732-5098.

WALKING TOURS For a general overview of Baltimore, energetic, irrepressible Zippy Larson offers many different walking tours with historic, cultural, and architectural themes. Zippy's witty, well-researched tours start at $60 per person (which includes a restaurant meal) and take you outside the tourist bubble.

A particularly fascinating experience is local historian Wayne Schaumburg's guided tour to Greenmount Cemetery. Baltimore's largest and most prestigious burial ground is the final resting place of John Wilkes Booth, Johns Hopkins, and other native sons and daughters. Tours take place Saturday mornings in May and October and are $10 per person.

The Fells Point Ghost Tour interweaves narrative about the maritime neighborhood's colorful past with tales of its spectral inhabitants. Tours, which are suitable for children, run every Friday and Saturday evening at 7 PM from July to October, and Saturday only March to June and

November; the cost is $12 per adult; reservations are recommended. The Fells Point Visitors Center also offers a Fells Point Ghost Walk as well as tours focusing on such topics as maritime history and immigration.

For building buffs, the Baltimore Architectural Foundation sponsors walking tours of the historic and architecturally significant neighborhood of Mount Vernon; reservations are required and the cost is $10. The Mount Vernon Cultural District also organizes tours of Mount Vernon and other nearby neighborhoods.

🗐 **Baltimore Architectural Foundation** ☎ 410/962-0241 ⊕ www.baltimorearchitecture. org. **Fells Point Ghost Walk** ☎ 410/522-7400 ⊕ www.fellspointghost.com. **Fells Point Visitors Center Tours** ☎ 410/675-6750 ⊕ www.preservationsociety.com. **Greenmount Cemetery Tours** ☎ 410/256-2180 ⊕ home.earthlink.net/~wschaumburg. **Mount Vernon Cultural District** ⊠ 217 N. Charles St., Mount Vernon ☎ 410/605-0462 ⊕ www. mvcd.org. **Zippy Larson's Shoe Leather Safaris** ☎ 410/817-4141 ⊕ www.bcpl. net/~zipbooks.

WATER TOURS Most cruise and tour boats depart from docks in the Inner Harbor. The tall ship *Clipper City* offers excursions around the harbor aboard a 158-foot replica of an 1850s topsail schooner. The two-hour tours depart twice a day from May to October from the pier in front of Harborplace's Light Street Pavilion. Harbor Cruises, Ltd. and Pintail Yachts present lunch, dinner, and evening cruises around the harbor. Ride the Ducks of Baltimore provides a tour of the city by both land and water.

🗐 **Clipper City** ⊠ Inner Harbor ☎ 410/539-6277 ⊕ www.sailingship.com. **Harbor Cruises, Ltd.** ☎ 410/727-3113 or 800/695-2628 ⊕ www.harborcruises.com. **Pintail Yachts** ⊠ Pier 5, Inner Harbor ☎ 410/539-3485. **Ride the Ducks of Baltimore** ⊠ 25 Light St., Inner Harbor ☎ 410/727-3825. Subway Travel

The Baltimore metro serves those coming into the city from the suburban northwest. Stops include Charles Center and Lexington Market, both within walking distance of the Inner Harbor. The single line runs from Owings Mills to Johns Hopkins Hospital, east of downtown. There's also a light-rail that runs between points north and south in the city (⇨ Train Travel below).

FARES & Fare is $1.60; day passes are $3.50. Trains run weekdays 5 AM–mid-
SCHEDULES night, Saturday and Sunday 6 AM–midnight.

🗐 **Maryland Transit Administration (MTA)** ☎ 800/325-7245 or 410/539-5000 ⊕ www. mtamaryland.com.

TAXIS

Taxis in Baltimore are not usually flagged or hailed in the street. Instead, call to have a cab pick you up, ask your hotel concierge or doorman to summon a taxi, or go to the cab stand at Pratt and Light streets in the center of the Inner Harbor zone. Local companies include Arrow Taxicab and Jimmy's Cab Co.

🗐 Taxi Companies **Arrow Taxicab** ☎ 410/358-9696. **Jimmy's Cab Co.** ☎ 410/ 296-7200.

TRAIN TRAVEL

All Amtrak trains on the northeast corridor between Boston and Washington stop at Baltimore's Penn Station. Maryland Area Rail Commuter (MARC) trains travel between Baltimore's Penn Station and Washington, D.C., Camden Station and Washington, and BWI Airport and Penn Station. The trip to Washington, D.C. takes about 1 hour and costs $7; the trip to BWI Airport from Penn Station takes about 20 minutes and costs $4. Trains run weekdays 4:45 AM–9:30 PM (note that MARC trains do not run on weekends).

Light-rail is an easy, comfortable way to reach downtown from the northern and southern suburbs. Stops near downtown include Oriole Park at Camden Yards, Howard Street, and Centre Street near Mount Vernon. The city's cultural center can be reached by the Cathedral Street stop. Light-rail extends to Hunt Valley, BWI Airport, and Glen Burnie. The fare is $1.60 (exact change is required); day passes are $3.50.

🚆 Train Stations **Amtrak Penn Station** ⊠ Charles St. and Mt. Royal Ave., Mount Vernon ☎ 410/291-4269.

🚆 Train Lines **Amtrak** (800/872-7245). **Maryland Area Rail Commuter** (MARC) ☎ 800/325-7245 or 410/539-5000. **Maryland Transit Administration** (MTA) ☎ 800/325-7245 or 410/539-5000 ⊕ www.mtamaryland.com.

VISITOR INFORMATION

Contact the Baltimore Visitor Center for information on the city. A live operator can answer your questions weekdays 9–5:30; otherwise an automated system is in place. The Web site is also full of information about the city. The drop-in Visitor Center is open Monday through Thursday and Sunday 9–6, and Friday and Saturday 9–7:30. A parking lot is behind it; the first 45 minutes are free.

The Baltimore Office of Promotion's Web site has the most detailed information on city events such as New Year's Eve, the Waterfront Festival, the Book Festival, Hampdenfest, and the Thanksgiving Parade (the Saturday before Thanksgiving).

The Fell's Point Visitor Center has information particular to the neighborhood, including a handout that covers many buildings' histories and architecture.

For more information on Havre de Grace and Aberdeen, contact the Harford County Tourism Council or the local visitor centers. For more information on Ellicott City, contact the Howard County Tourism Council.

🚆 Tourist Information **Baltimore Convention Center** ⊠ 100 W. Pratt St., Inner Harbor ☎ 410/649-7000 ⊕ www.bccenter.org. **Baltimore Office of Promotion** ☎ 410/752-8632 ⊕ www.bop.org. **Baltimore Visitor Center** ⊠ 401 Light St., Inner Harbor ☎ 877/225-8466 ⊕ www.baltimore.org. **Fell's Point Visitor Center** ⊠ 808 S. Ann St., Fells Point ☎ 410/675-6750 ⊕ www.preservationsociety.com. **Harford County Tourism Council** ⊠ 211 W. Belair Rd., Aberdeen ☎ 410/272-2325 or 800/597-2649 ⊕ www.harfordmd.com. **Havre de Grace Visitor Center** ⊠ 450 Pennington Ave., Havre de Grace ☎ 410/939-2100. **Howard County Office of Tourism** ⊠ 8267 Main St., Ellicott City ☎ 410/313-1900 or 800/288-8747 ⊕ www.visithowardcounty.com.

WATER TAXIS

Ed Kane's Water Taxis and the Seaport Taxi are fun and convenient ways to get around the Inner Harbor. They make stops at 16 points along the waterfront, including Fells Point, the National Aquarium, museums, restaurants, and Fort McHenry. All-day tickets for both services are $6. Look for stops, marked with signs, all along the waterfront; depending on season, boats arrive every 10–15 minutes in season or you can call to be picked up at a particular location.

🚢 **Ed Kane's Water Taxis** ☎ 410/563-3901 ⊕ www.thewatertaxi.com. **Seaport Taxi** ☎ 410/675-2900 ⊕ www.natlhistoricseaport.org/taxi.html.

FREDERICK &
WESTERN
MARYLAND

7

BE GLAD FOR MODERN SCIENCE
after seeing the exhibits at the
Museum of Civil War Medicine ⇨*p.264*

MAKE A STYLISH RETREAT
to the Antrim 1844 inn ⇨*p.269*

CONTEMPLATE JOHN BROWN'S LEGACY
at Harpers Ferry Park ⇨*p.272*

PAY YOUR RESPECTS
at Antietam Battlefield ⇨*p.277*

RIDE SOME VINTAGE LOCOMOTION
on the Western Maryland Scenic RR ⇨*p.280*

Updated by
Loretta
Chilcoat

MARYLAND'S MOUNTAINSIDE used to be known to few people beyond the locals. But the secret's out now. Stretching from the Piedmont region's rolling farmland to the remote mountaintops of Garrett County and the heights of the Appalachians, the area is a land where white-tail deer, wild turkey, and even black bear roam among its miles of oaks, hickories, and maples. Seeking a temporary escape from the bustle of urban and suburban life, travelers head here to camp under light-pollution-free skies, hike along waterfall trails in lush state parks and sink into plush, goose-down beds in bed-and-breakfasts.

The past is alive (and often reenacted) here in its historic towns and Civil War battlefields. You're virtually guaranteed to hit a friendly festival celebrating anything from the intense colors of fall to the snowy peaks of Wisp Mountain.

In the early 1700s Germans and other immigrants came to farm the fertile valleys of Frederick and Washington counties, where large dairy farms still dot the pastoral landscape. The Irish and Scots arrived in the first half of the 19th century to help build railroads, the National Road, and the Chesapeake & Ohio (C&O) Canal. Western Maryland was an important transportation gateway for the nation's first pioneers. The Historical National Road, the nation's first federally funded road, paved the way for future settlers, and today travelers can still journey on the twisty road that parallels Interstate 70. The dream of the Chesapeake & Ohio (C&O) Canal revolutionizing the way goods would be transported was short lived, as the railroad came into the region at the same time. However, remnants of this nearly 185-mi-long waterway, paralleling the meandering Potomac River from Washington's Georgetown to Cumberland, remain, and today the canal's towpath is a popular hiking and biking trail. The railroad was big business in Hagerstown and Cumberland, providing jobs and a speedy link to Baltimore and Washington, D.C.

Because of its proximity to Baltimore and Washington, Frederick, the region's largest city, became a staging area for many important events in American history. Ben Franklin helped plan aspects of the French and Indian War from Braddock Heights, a mountain on Frederick's western edge. Meriwether Lewis stopped by before meeting up with William Clark on their trek westward. During the Civil War, Confederate and Union troops clashed on the streets of Frederick, on their way to the battles of South Mountain and Antietam.

A surprising number of American presidents have visited Frederick. George Washington slept and ate his way through here. Abraham Lincoln passed through after the Battle of Antietam, which was fought on the other side of the green mountains that border Frederick on the western horizon. Franklin Roosevelt showed British prime minister Winston Churchill the town before moving on to Camp David.

The region's other big towns, Hagerstown and Cumberland, were transportation hubs in earlier centuries. Though the railroad plays a much less important role in both cities today, its past is used to lure visitors. Hagerstown is known for its Roundhouse Museum, which has an extensive collection of railroad memorabilia, history books, and a miniature railroad layout. Cumberland is in the midst of turning the western terminus of the Chesapeake and Ohio Canal into a heritage and recreational area. A new visitor center has already opened at the C&O Canal National Historical Park. The city's Victorian-era train station has been restored and is the starting point of a popular excursion up the mountains. Eventually, a stretch of the canal will be restored for tours on replicas of the original canal boats.

The region's mountains, forests, and world-famous rivers are an equally important draw. Kayakers and white-water rafters rave about the rapids on the Savage River and the north-flowing Youghiogheny River, and hikers, bicyclists, and campers flock to state parks throughout the region. Deep Creek Lake, the state's largest, is frequented by boaters and anglers.

Disagreement lingers on just where western Maryland begins. For Baltimoreans, more familiar with the Eastern Shore and Ocean City, anything west of their beltway is western Maryland. Washingtonians, on the other hand, tend to lump Frederick and points west together as a distinct region. For the people who live in the hills of Allegany and Garrett counties, western Maryland begins just west of a man-made cut in a mountain called Sideling Hill. This unusual geological formation has become an attraction among motorists tooling along Interstate 68. Passing rock formations several million years old, the highway opens to sweeping views of mountain ridges, shaded blue in the fading sunset. These are the Alleghenies, Maryland's mountainside.

Exploring Frederick & Western Maryland

Frederick, Maryland's second-largest city, is surrounded by rolling farmlands and rugged mountains, where outdoor activities beckon. In Washington County, northwest of Frederick, Hagerstown is the county seat and a great base for excursions to the C&O Canal, various state parks, and the Appalachian Trail. Farther west, the rugged mountains of Allegany County are crossed by the Old National Highway: today the site of a scenic railroad excursion, this is the same route that westward pioneers traveled in covered wagons. Maryland's westernmost county, Garrett County, was once the vacation destination of railroad barons and Washington's high society; today it's a big destination for boaters, fishermen, and outdoors enthusiasts.

About the Restaurants & Hotels

WHAT IT COSTS				
$$$$	$$$	$$	$	¢
RESTAURANTS over $30	$22–$30	$14–$22	$7–$14	under $7
HOTELS over $250	$175–$250	$130–$175	$80–$130	under $80

Restaurant prices are per person for a main course at dinner. Hotel prices are for a standard double room, excluding state tax.

FREDERICK

Frederick has one of the best-preserved historic districts in Maryland, perhaps second only to Annapolis. Within the 50-block district, tree-shaded streets are lined with buildings from the 18th and 19th centuries, and brick walks connect lovely courtyards. Eclectic shops, museums, antiques stores, and fine restaurants attract crowds of weekend visitors.

Numbers in the text correspond to numbers in the margin and on the Frederick map.

a good walk

Frederick's Historic District is easily accessible by foot, though not all the worthwhile sites are within walking distance. Begin a leisurely tour at the **Frederick Visitor's Center** downtown, which is amid restaurants, boutiques, and shops. A few must-see historic sites and museums are nearby. South of the visitor center on Patrick Street, scene of a skirmish between Union and Confederate troops before the Battle of Antietam in 1862, is the **National Museum of Civil War Medicine.** A few blocks west of the museum is the **Barbara Fritchie House and Museum,** where the bold, patriotic Fritchie waved a Union flag outside her window as Confederate troops marched through town. A few blocks south of the Fritchie home on Bentz Street is the **Roger Brooke Taney House,** a museum dedicated to Supreme Court Justice Taney and his brother-in-law, Francis Scott Key.

TIMING   It will take three to four hours to cover these sights.

Sights to See

★ **Barbara Fritchie House and Museum.** After you visit this modest brick cottage, a reproduction of the original, it's easy to imagine Dame Fritchie sticking her white-capped head out of a second-floor window and waving a Union flag at Confederate troops. Poet John Greenleaf Whittier made her famous; his poem "Barbara Fritchie" appeared in the *Atlantic Monthly* a year after Confederate troops passed through Frederick. His stirring account of Fritchie defiantly waving the flag at the invading Confederates stirred patriotism and made the 95-year-old woman a heroine. Her unusual life, at least as told by Whittier, has fascinated history enthusiasts around the world. Even British prime minister Winston Churchill visited the house; on his way to Camp David with President Franklin Roosevelt, he stood outside and recited Whittier's poem: "Shoot if you must, this old gray head, but spare your country's flag. . . ." A tea set Fritchie used to serve George Washington is on display. ⊠ *154 W. Patrick St.* ☎ *301/698–0630* 🎫 *$2* ⊘ *Call for hours.*

Frederick Visitor's Center. At the center you can pick up brochures of historic sites and maps for a self-guided tour or join a guided 90-minute walking tour. Tours begin at 1:30 PM and are offered on holidays and weekends April through November. ⊠ *19 E. Church St.* ☎ *301/228–2888 or 800/999–3613* ⊕ *www.fredericktourism.org* 🎫 *Tour $7* ⊘ *Daily 9–5.*

National Museum of Civil War Medicine. The only museum devoted to the study and interpretation of Civil War medicine is also rumored to be haunted. No wonder: the museum is inside what was once a furniture

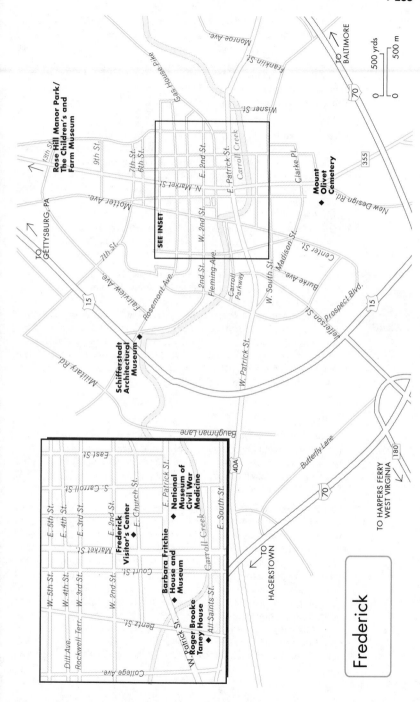

Frederick

store in 1830 and then a funeral home until 1978: the dead from the Battle of Antietam (1862) were taken here for embalming. Exhibits at the museum cover "Recruitment," "Camp Life," "Medical Evacuation," and "Veterinary Medicine." More than 3,000 artifacts are on display, including a Civil War ambulance and the only known surviving Civil War surgeon's tent. Photographs and a video help explain the state of the healing arts during this period. ⊠ *48 E. Patrick St.* ☎ *301/695–1864* ⊕ *www. civilwarmed.org* 🖃 *$6.50* ⊙ *Mon.–Sat. 10–5, Sun. 11–5.*

Roger Brooke Taney House. A two-story Federal-style house contains a museum dedicated to Taney (1777–1864) and his brother-in-law Francis Scott Key, author of the "Star-Spangled Banner." History remembers Supreme Court Justice Taney as the author of the 1857 Dred Scott Decision, which stated that blacks had no constitutional rights. Taney and Key practiced law together in Frederick; their office still stands across from City Hall. Personal belongings of both men are on display at the Taney House. Behind the home is the former slave quarters, one of the few such surviving structures in the region. ⊠ *121 S. Bentz St.* ☎ *301/663–1188* 🖃 *$2* ⊙ *Mid-Apr.–Dec., Sat. 10–4, Sun. 1–4.*

a good drive

Begin at the **Schifferstadt Architectural Museum** ☛ on the city's west side, near Baker Park. Drive back toward downtown along Rosemont Avenue. Turn right onto Rockwell Terrace and then left on Market Street and head north to the **Rose Hill Manor Park/The Children's and Farm Museum,** the home of Maryland's first governor. Finally, retrace the drive south via Court Street. Turn left on South Street and then right on Market Street through the heart of the Historic District to **Mount Olivet Cemetery,** where two of the city's most famous citizens, Francis Scott Key and Barbara Fritchie, are buried.

TIMING   It will take about three hours to cover these sights.

Sights to See

Mount Olivet Cemetery. Some of Frederick's most famous sons and daughters rest here, including Francis Scott Key and Barbara Fritchie. The cemetery also shelters the graves of more than 800 Confederate and Union soldiers killed during the battles of Antietam and Monocacy. ⊠ *515 S. Market St.* ☎ *301/662–1164* ⊙ *Daily.*

☾ **Rose Hill Manor Park/The Children's and Farm Museum.** Although this lovely Georgian manor is intended as a place for elementary-school children to study local and regional history, it's more than just this. Maryland's first governor, Thomas Johnson, lived here from 1798 to 1819. Guided tours of the gracious home focus on the early 19th century, covering the manor's owners and their lifestyles. During the tour, children can card wool, weave on a table loom, play with reproductions of old toys, and dress in period costumes. Also open are several outbuildings, including a log cabin, ice house, smokehouse, blacksmith shop, and large shed housing a carriage collection. You can also wander through herb, vegetable, and rose gardens. ⊠ *1611 N. Market St.* ☎ *301/694–1646* ⊕ *www. rosehillmuseum.com* 🖃 *$5* ⊙ *Apr.–Oct., Mon.–Sat. 10–4, Sun. 1–4; Nov., Sat. 10–4, Sun. 1–4.*

Schifferstadt Architectural Museum. Believed to be the oldest house in Frederick, this unusual stone structure was built in 1756 by German immigrants. Spared from the wrecking ball two decades ago by preservation-minded citizens, the house is considered one of the finest examples of German architecture in Colonial America. Because the rooms are barren, it's easy to observe structural details such as the sandstone walls, which are 2½-feet thick. ✉ *1110 Rosemont Ave.* ☎ *301/663–3885* ☞ *$3* ✆ *Call for hours.*

Community Bridge Mural. Confusing birds since it was built in 2000, this life-size optical illusion transforms an ordinary bridge into a public work of art. Detailed stonework, an archangel that seems to jump out at you, and ivy so real you can almost smell it are just a few delights of the mural, which is also a popular gathering place for summer festivals. ✉ *Carroll Street Bridge, between E. Patrick and E. All Saints Sts.* ⊕ *http://bridge.skyline.net.*

Where to Stay & Eat

$$–$$$$ ✕ **Bentz Street Raw Bar.** Fresh seafood and live music nightly are the hallmarks of this funky neighborhood hangout, which is Frederick's most eclectic restaurant. You can enjoy fresh Maryland crabs and oysters, steamers, soups, salads, sandwiches, and main dishes of seafood, beef, ribs, and barbecue. ✉ *6 S. Bentz St.* ☎ *301/694–9134* ⊕ *www.rawbar.com* 🖃 *AE, MC, V.*

$$–$$$$ ✕ **The Red Horse.** A local institution and landmark—note the red horse on the roof—the Red Horse is primarily a steak house. The rustic dining room has a stone fireplace, rafters, and large wagon-wheel chandelier. The service is first-rate; you can watch your steak being grilled from behind a window. A lower-level cigar parlor serves cognac, ports, sherries, and bourbons. ✉ *996 W. Patrick St.* ☎ *301/663–3030* 🖃 *AE, D, DC, MC, V.*

$–$$$ ✕ **Cafe Kyoko.** This sushi and Thai restaurant sets itself apart from the standard eateries in downtown. The sparsely decorated dining room is still inviting, with wooden booths along the window front, exposed rafters, and ceiling fans. In addition to the fresh and inventive sushi choices, pad thai is excellent and one of the more popular dishes. There's also chicken teriyaki, steak, and seafood entrées, and a vegetarian menu. The wine and beer selection is limited. ✉ *10 E. Patrick St.* ☎ *301/695–9656* 🖃 *AE, D, MC, V.*

$–$$$ ✕ **Firestone's.** In a 1920s-era building that in earlier incarnations was a bank, a sporting goods store, and an Irish pub, Firestone's is a casual, slightly upscale place for good American fare. At first glance, it seems more like a local pub, with a wooden bar dominating the main floor. Look more closely, and you can see the white linens covering the tables. Steak and seafood are plentiful on the menu, which also offers a few surprises, including marinated and roasted portobello mushrooms stacked with onions, peppers, eggplant, and zucchini. Desserts are made in-house. ✉ *105 N. Market St.* ☎ *301/663–0330* 🖃 *AE, D, MC, V* ✆ *Closed Mon.*

$–$$$ ✕ **Hagan's Tavern.** Yes, George Washington ate here, and the tavern enjoys a bit of fame as the one-time headquarters for the Blue as well as the Gray during the Civil War: some say ghostly soldiers still pace throughout the tavern. Built in 1785, the fieldstone structure served as a stopping point between Baltimore and Cumberland. Staff wear period dress, and all desserts and breads are made on the premises. The regional food on the menu has an Early American influence: specialties include house-smoked salmon, duck, and quail; Maryland-style roast chicken with lump-crabmeat sauce; and twin grilled duck breasts in a pear–orange confit. ⊠ *5018 Old National Pike, Braddock Heights* ☎ *301/371– 9189* ⊟ *AE, D, DC, MC, V* ☯ *Closed Mon.*

$–$$$ ✕ **Tauraso's.** The mouthwatering smell of pizza baked in a wood oven greets diners approaching the reservations desk of this wood-panel, white-tablecloth trattoria. Other specialties include pasta dishes, poultry, steaks, and seafood. A favorite appetizer is Tauraso's own homemade seafood sausage. The restaurant has a bar, separate dining room, and a garden patio open seasonally. ⊠ *6 East St.* ☎ *301/663–6000* ⊟ *AE, D, DC, MC, V.*

¢–$$$ ✕ **Isabella's.** This Spanish eatery brings some flair to downtown Frederick's predominantly American restaurant scene. Most people head here for the tapas—appetizers that originated in the Andalusia region of Spain. Isabella's tapas may include lamb, beef, chicken, and seafood with various spices, herbs, and wonderful sauces. Try the littleneck clams steamed in beer, garlic, cilantro, pepper, and tomato or the grilled lamb chops, served with a black currant sauce. Three or four tapas makes a meal. ⊠ *44 N. Market St.* ☎ *301/698–8922* ⊟ *AE, D, DC, MC, V* ☯ *Closed Mon. except for happy hour 4–6:30.*

$–$$ ✕ **Brewer's Alley.** Frederick's first brewpub was once a town hall and market building. The eatery is clean and bright, with copper brewing pots gleam next to the bar and the wooden tables. Substantial main dishes, such as large Maryland crab cakes, double-thick pork chops, steaks, and ribs are available, as are starters, salads, specialty sandwiches, pasta, and pizza. Several kinds of beer are made on the premises. ⊠ *124 N. Market St.* ☎ *301/631–0089* ⊟ *AE, DC, MC, V.*

$–$$$ ✕🔲 **Inn at Buckeystown.** An inviting wraparound porch fronts this B&B, an 1897 mansion in a village with pre–Revolutionary War roots, near the Civil War battlefield. The small but cozy rooms are furnished with Victorian accents that include lace bedspreads; heavy, floral curtains; and reproduction pieces. One room has a fireplace. A fixed-price five-course dinner is available for an additional fee of $40; high tea is available most days. You don't have to stay here to eat in the restaurant, but you do need a reservation. ⊠ *3521 Buckeystown Pike, Buckeystown 21717* ☎ *301/874–5755 or 800/272–1190* 🖷 *301/831–1355* ⊕ *www. innatbuckeystown.com* ⇝ *9 rooms, 5 with private bath* ⌂ *Restaurant, some cable TV, bar* ⊟ *D, MC, V* |◎| *BP.*

$–$$ ✕🔲 **Catoctin Inn and Conference Center.** Antiques, books, family pictures, and heirlooms decorate this large house from 1790. Its well-worn original floors attest to the traffic that has come and gone in this cozy inn a few miles south of Frederick. Three rooms have working fireplaces and hot tubs. The inn's restaurant is open to the public for dinner on Friday and Saturday with a fixed-price menu of three courses ($26). Maryland crab soup, hickory-smoked duck, crusted rack of lamb, and bacon-wrapped pork are all specialties. The Catoctin is no-smoking with the exception of one suite. ⊠ *3619 Buckeystown Pike, Buckeystown 21717* ☎ *301/874–5555 or 800/730–5550* 🖷 *301/874–2026* ⊕ *www.catoctininn.com* 🍽 *4 rooms, 4 cottages, 9 suites ♿ Restaurant, refrigerators, cable TV, in-room VCRs, outdoor hot tub, business services, meeting rooms, airport shuttle; no smoking except in 1 suite* ☰ *AE, D, DC, MC, V* ◉ *BP.*

★ **$$–$$$$** ✕☷ **Antrim 1844.** Once part of a 2,500-acre plantation, this pre–Civil War mansion, less than 10 mi from Gettysburg, is an elegant retreat. The owners have re-created the genteel spirit of a 19th-century estate. The nine mansion guest rooms are furnished with period antiques, working fireplaces, canopy feather beds, and marble baths or whirlpools. Other guest rooms are in a restored 19th-century carriage house, and buildings that were once an ice house and a plantation office. Don't miss the prix-fixe, six-course dinner ($62), an evening-long event. The menu includes seafood, beef, and poultry, all served with exquisite sauces. ⊠ *30 Trevanion Rd., Taneytown 21787* ☎ *410/756–6812 or 800/858–1844* 🖷 *410/756–2744* ⊕ *www.antrim1844.com* 🍽 *22 rooms, 7 suites ♿ Restaurant, putting green, tennis court, pool, croquet, lawn bowling, bar; no room TVs, no kids under 12, no smoking* ☰ *AE, MC, V* ◉ *BP.*

$ ✕☷ **Hollerstown Hill B&B.** Sprinkled with chintz and a pale-pink color scheme, this B&B is full of Victorian touches right down to the marble claw-foot tubs and pull-chain toilets. You can have a drink on the wraparound porch or a lively game of billiards in the game room. The Hollerstown is right across the street from a park and within walking distance of most of Frederick's restaurants and attractions. ⊠ *4 Clarke Pl., Frederick 21701* ☎ *301/228–3630* ⊕ *www.hollerstownhill.com* 🍽 *4 rooms, ♿ Wi-Fi; no smoking, no pets, no kids under 15* ☰ *AE, MC, V* ◉ *BP.*

$$$ ☷ **Tyler Spite House.** The furnishings in this Federal-style mansion could tell some stories. A peace treaty was signed by General MacArthur on the check-in desk, and the 10-foot-high pier mirror, from the old Frederick train station, was used by President Lincoln. The Chippendale-style mahogany-and-ebony grand piano was made in Baltimore for Francis Scott Key. Three of the guest rooms have working fireplaces. The large rooms are beautifully decorated in Federal-style colors, fabrics, and wallpaper. Lodging price includes room tax, a walking tour of Courthouse Square, a generous breakfast, and an extensive afternoon tea. ⊠ *112 W. Church St., 21701* ☎ *301/831–4455* ⊕ *www.tylerspitehouse.com* 🍽 *4 rooms, 1 suite ♿ Pool; no kids under 15, no pets, no smoking* ☰ *AE, D, MC, V* ◉ *BP.*

Nightlife & the Arts

Drop by the **Frederick Coffee Company** (⊠ Shab Row–Everedy Sq., 100 East St. ☎ 301/698–0039 or 800/822–0806) for pastries, soup, sandwiches, quiche, dessert, and—of course—exotic and traditional coffees and other beverages. As you walk in the door of this former 1930s gas station, you can smell the heady fragrance of beans roasting in front of you. The Frederick Coffee Company is open 7–9 weekdays and 9–9 weekends; folk and jazz musicians perform Saturday night.

The **Weinberg Center for the Arts** (✉ 20 W. Patrick St. ☎ 301/228–2828) was a movie house in the 1920s. Now the theater offers plays, musicals, and concerts throughout the year.

Sports & the Outdoors

Hiking

The famed **Appalachian Trail** crosses the spine of South Mountain just west of Frederick, from the Potomac River to the Pennsylvania line. Several well-known viewpoints can be found along Maryland's 40-mi stretch, including Annapolis Rocks and Weverton Cliffs. The best access points that have parking available are Gathland State Park, Washington Monument State Park, and Greenbrier State Park. For more information, contact the **Appalachian Trail Conference** (✉ 799 Washington St., Harpers Ferry, WV 25425 ☎ 304/535–6331 ⊕ www.atconf.org).

Shopping

In downtown Frederick, **Everedy Square & Shab Row** was once a complex of buildings that manufactured kitchen utensils and wares; now it's a center for retail shops, restaurants, and boutiques. At the family-owned **Candy Kitchen** (✉ 52 N. Market St. ☎ 301/698–0442) you can get hand-dipped chocolates.

The area's best outdoor store, **The Trail House** (✉ 17 S. Market St. ☎ 301/694–8448) sells and rents quality hiking, backpacking, camping, and cross-country skiing equipment. The store also stocks a good selection of maps and books. The **Museum Shop** (✉ 20 N. Market St. ☎ 301/695–0424) sells museum-quality ceramics, sculpture, hand-crafted jewelry, Whistler etchings, and Japanese woodcuts.

Away from downtown, **Wonder Book & Video** (✉ 1306 W. Patrick St. ☎ 301/694–5955) stocks more than 600,000 new and used books, videos, and compact discs.

SIDE TRIPS FROM FREDERICK

Not only is Frederick within easy driving distance of Baltimore and Washington, D.C., but it's also surrounded by other areas of interest, including historic towns, scenic parks, and national battlefields.

Numbers in the margin correspond to points of interest on the Side Trips from Frederick map.

Monocacy National Battlefield

2 mi south of Frederick via Rte. 355.

Monocacy National Battlefield was the site of a little-known, hugely mismatched confrontation between 12,000 and 13,000 Confederates and 5,800 Union troops on July 9, 1864; many historians believe the Union victory thwarted a Confederate invasion of Washington, D.C. Although the Union troops were outnumbered, they delayed the Rebels by burning a bridge along the Monocacy. This tactic, along with some inten-

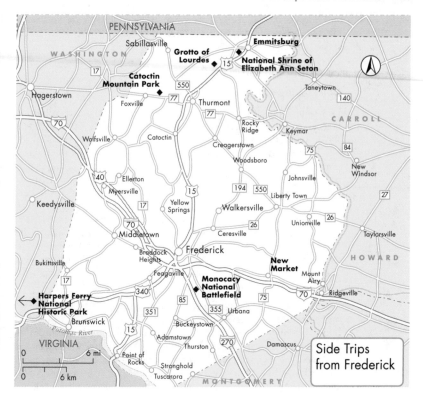

Side Trips
from Frederick

sive fighting in the river, delayed the Confederates' approach to Washington, allowing the federal government time to bolster its forts. The farmland surrounding the battlefield remains largely unchanged. An electronic map in the visitor center explains the battle. ⊠ *4801 Urbana Pike* ☎ *301/662–3515* ⊕ *www.nps.gov/mono* ⊠ *Free* ⊙ *Daily 8–4:30, until 5:30 Memorial Day–Labor Day.*

New Market

8 mi east of Frederick via Rte. 70.

The self-proclaimed antiques capital of Maryland, New Market is a 200-year-old village surrounded by farmland. Though some things have remained the same for the past two centuries, a new addition to town is the throngs of tourists walking Main Street in search of furnishings and knickknacks.

Where to Eat

$–$$$ ✕ **Mealey's.** Once a store and hotel on the National Pike, Mealey's today is a busy restaurant in the heart of New Market, appropriately decorated with antiques. A large stone fireplace dominates the spacious main dining room, which is often filled to capacity on weekend evenings and Sunday afternoons; smaller dining rooms offer more privacy. Beef and Chesapeake Bay seafood are the specialties. Desserts are worth saving room for—especially the bread pudding, served with a bourbon vanilla sauce. ⊠ *8 Main St.* ☎ *301/865–5488* ▭ *AE, D, DC, MC, V.*

Harpers Ferry National Historical Park

24 mi southwest of Frederick via Rte. 340.

Less than a mile from both Maryland's and Virginia's state lines is Harpers Ferry National Historic Park in West Virginia. Thomas Jefferson described the area that makes up the park best: "On your right comes up the Shenandoah, having ranged along the foot of the mountains a hundred miles to seek a vent. On your left approaches the Potomac, in quest of a passage also. In the moment of their junction they rush together against the mountain, rend it asunder, and pass off to the sea. . . . This scene is worth a voyage across the Atlantic." The spot where these rivers converge so dramatically is also where, on October 16, 1859, the radical abolitionist John Brown led his 21-man assault on the Harpers Ferry arsenal. Today, much of Harpers Ferry has been restored as it was during the time of John Brown's raid, and historic markers and exhibits tell the story of that infamous event and the town's tumultuous involvement in the Civil War.

The township of **Harpers Ferry** grew around a U.S. armory built in 1740, and many buildings have been preserved. Meriweather Lewis (of Lewis and Clark fame) stopped here in 1803 to outfit his expedition with rifles from the armory and arsenal. Lining the cobblestone streets are shops and museums in which park employees in period costume demonstrate Early American skills and interpret the evolution of American firearms. A portion of the Appalachian Trail winds along the Potomac River and climbs uphill through the town. On the second Saturday in October the park service stages Election Day 1860, when the presidential candidates on the slate in the region (Stephen Douglas, John Bell, and John Breckinridge—Abraham Lincoln was not on this ballot) again debate the hot topic of their day: states' rights versus a strong federal union. Parking is tricky and scarce in Harpers Ferry; most visitors park at the Cavalier Heights Visitor Center and take a free shuttle into the town. The visitor center has exhibits on John Brown and the Civil War as well as the wetlands in the area. ⊠ *Parking lot 1 mi past Shenandoah bridge on Rte. 340, Harpers Ferry, WV* ☎ *304/535–6298* ⊕ *www.nps.gov/hafe* ▭ *$6 per vehicle, $4 per person arriving by other means* ☉ *Memorial Day–Labor Day, daily 8–6; Labor Day–Memorial Day, daily 8–5.*

Above the park on High Street is the small, somewhat creepy **John Brown Wax Museum,** which depicts the abolitionist's raid on the town and the highlights of his life. ⊠ *High St.* ☎ *304/535–6342* ▭ *$4.50* ☉ *Daily 9–5* ☉ *Closed mid-Dec.–mid-Mar.*

Catoctin Mountain Park

15 mi north of Frederick via Rte. 15.

Hidden within this park is Camp David, the presidential retreat that was the site of the famous peace accords between Egypt and Israel. You won't find the camp, which has been used by presidents since Franklin D. Roosevelt, and even if you come close, you can run into security officers. What you will find are 6,000 acres of rocky outcrops and thick forests traversed by 20 mi of moderate to strenuous hiking trails, the most popular of which have scenic overlooks. A small visitor center has exhibits on the area's wildlife. Across Route 77 is **Cunningham Falls State Park,** the site of a cascading 78-foot waterfall and a man-made lake. Both parks have camping facilities. ⊠ *Rte. 77, west of Rte. 15, Thurmont* ☎ *301/663–9388* ⊕ *www.nps.gov/cato* ⊠ *Free* ⊙ *Visitor center Mon.–Thurs. 10–4:30, Fri. 10–5, weekends 8:30–5. Park daily dawn–dusk.*

Catoctin Wildlife Preserve & Zoo, 6 mi from the park, holds more than 350 animals on 30 acres. The zoo is easily navigable by children, and the tall trees and winding paths make for comfortable walking. Exotic animals here include tigers, macaws, monkeys, and boas. A petting zoo allows children to mingle with goats and other small animals. Throughout summer there are interactive shows, when children can touch snakes, talk to tigers, and learn about grizzlies. ⊠ *13019 Catoctin Furnace Rd., Thurmont* ☎ *301/271–3180* ⊕ *www.cwpzoo.com* ⊠ *Adults $3* ⊙ *Mar., weekends 10–4; Apr. and Oct., daily 10–5; early to late May and early to late Sept., daily 9–5; Memorial Day–Labor Day, daily 9–6.*

Where to Eat

¢–$ ✕ **Cozy Restaurant.** A local institution, the Cozy Restaurant became internationally famous during the 1979 Camp David Accords, when hordes of reporters stayed at the adjacent inn to cover the Israeli-Egyptian peace talks. Photographs, newspaper clippings, and memorabilia from that era are on display in the restaurant's entrance halls. The 750-seat restaurant is best known these days for its all-you-can-eat buffets ($6.19–$14), which include seafood, steaks, fried chicken, and a belt-loosening brunch. Like spice? Don't miss the "Wall of Fire," a collection of 200 mouth-burning hot sauces; some are so hot that diners sign waivers before trying them. ⊠ *103 Frederick Rd., Thurmont* ☎ *301/271–4301* ⊕ *www.cozyvillage.com* ▭ *AE, MC, V.*

en route Two of Frederick County's three covered bridges span creeks near Thurmont. The **Loy's Station Covered Bridge,** originally built in 1848 and reconstructed after a fire, is east of Thurmont off Route 77. **Roddy Road Covered Bridge,** built in 1856, is north of Thurmont, just off Route 15. Picnic areas are near both bridges.

Emmitsburg

24 mi north of Frederick via Rte. 15.

By the foothills of the Catoctin Mountains, Emmitsburg, founded in 1757, was the site of the first parochial school in the United States and the final home of the first American saint. Its Main Street remains a showcase of fine examples of Federal, Georgian, and Victorian architecture; many of the buildings are still in use as homes and businesses.

The **National Shrine Grotto of Lourdes** reproduces the famous grotto in France where a peasant girl saw visions of the Virgin Mary. The grotto, tucked into a mountain overlooking Mount Saint Mary's College, draws hundreds of thousands of people a year, and a sunrise Easter service attracts a crowd. Beautifully landscaped paths lead to the grotto and a small chapel. ⊠ *U.S. Rte. 15* ☎ *301/447–5318* ⊕ *www.msmary.edu/ grotto* ☜ *Free* ☉ *Daily dawn–dusk.*

The **National Shrine of St. Elizabeth Ann Seton** contains the home of the first American-born saint, who came to the Maryland mountains to establish the Sisters of Charity and the nation's first parochial school. Born to wealth in New York City, Elizabeth Ann Seton (1774–1821) was widowed with five children before her experiences in Italy led her to convert to Catholicism. A short film and exhibits tell her story, and a classroom contains authentic furnishings. She is buried in a small graveyard on the well-maintained and shaded grounds. She was canonized in Rome in 1975; Pope John Paul II designated the chapel of her shrine a minor basilica in 1991. ⊠ *333 S. Seton Ave.* ☎ *301/447–6606* ⊕ *www. setonshrine.org* ☜ *Donations requested* ☉ *Tues.–Sun 10–4:30.*

WESTERN MARYLAND

The South Mountains that divide Frederick and Washington counties once sheltered Confederates, who formed a defensive line against advancing Union soldiers just before the Battle of Antietam. Only a few monuments and road signs mark this lesser-known battle site today. Hikers and cyclists come to travel the South Mountains' section of the Appalachian Trail and marvel at panoramic views of the Potomac River and the valley that surrounds Hagerstown to the west.

Numbers in the margin correspond to points of interest on the Western Maryland map.

Hagerstown

❶ *25 mi west of Frederick via I–70, 75 mi west of Baltimore via I–70.*

Once a prosperous railroad hub and manufacturing center, Hagerstown is striving to redefine itself, spending millions refurbishing downtown buildings for offices and retail stores. Chic restaurants have opened along the Public Square, and plans call for the creation of an arts-and-entertainment district around the venerable Maryland Theatre. The region lost its bid to create a national Civil War museum, but did gain the headquarters of the nation's largest Civil War battlefield preservation group, the Association for the Preservation of Civil War Battlefields. The group has spent thousands of dollars to help preserve land at the nearby Antietam National Battlefield in Sharpsburg.

Hagerstown may have lesser ties to the Civil War than Frederick, but the city's past is being tapped as a tourism magnet—and there's some justification. The Battle of Antietam and the lesser-known Battle of South Mountain were both fought just outside Hagerstown, and Confederates occasionally came through town, most memorably in 1864, when they threatened to burn the city. The Rebels relented after city officials paid a $20,000 ransom.

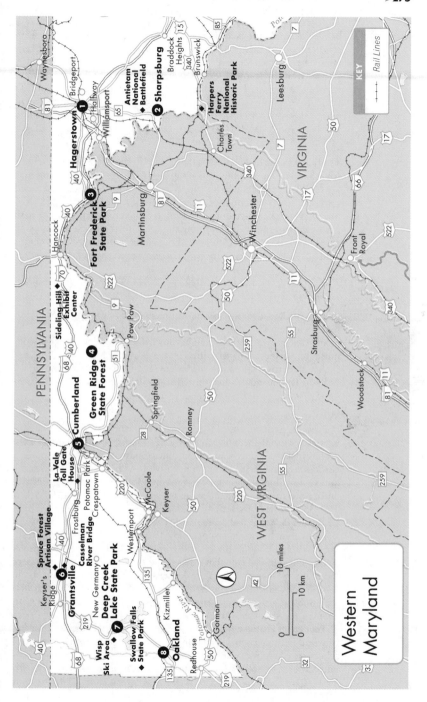

Western Maryland

KEY

Rail Lines

1 **Hagerstown**

2 **Sharpsburg**

Antietam National Battlefield

Harpers Ferry National Historic Park

3 **Fort Frederick State Park**

4 **Green Ridge State Forest**

Sideling Hill Exhibit Center

5 **Cumberland**

La Vale Toll Gate House

6 **Grantsville**

Spruce Forest Artisan Village

Casselman River Bridge

7 **Deep Creek Lake State Park**

Swallow Falls State Park

Wisp Ski Area

8 **Oakland**

PENNSYLVANIA

VIRGINIA

WEST VIRGINIA

Waynesboro

Bridgeport

Halfway

Williamsport

Braddock Heights

Brunswick

Leesburg

Charles Town

Martinsburg

Winchester

Front Royal

Hancock

Paw Paw

Strasburg

Woodstock

Springfield

Romney

McCoole

Keyser

Frostburg

Potomac Park

Crespatown

Westernport

New Germany

Keyser's Ridge

Kizmiller

Redhouse

Gorman

Potomac River

10 miles

10 km

★ The **Washington County Museum of Fine Arts** has an impressive collection of American paintings, drawings, prints, and sculpture from the 18th century to the present. The museum's holdings include the work of Benjamin West, James McNeill Whistler, and Norman Rockwell, as well as two portraits by Joshua Johnson, believed to be the first African-American portrait artist. The building is inside Hagerstown's beautiful **City Park,** a 27-acre wooded and landscaped haven with two small, man-made lakes—they're filled with ducks, geese, and swans in spring and fall. ⊠ *91 Key St.* ☎ *301/739–5727* ⊕ *www.washcomuseum.org* ⊠ *Free* ☉ *Tues.–Fri. 9–5, Sat. 9–4, Sun. 1–5.*

☺ The **Hager House and Museum** is the original home of the town's founder, Jonathan Hager, who built the home in 1739 over two springs to give his family a protected water supply and an indoor springhouse (used to refrigerate food). Built of uncut fieldstones, the house has 22-inch-thick walls and 18th-century furnishings. Colonial-style flower and herb gardens surround it. A small museum next to the house contains an extensive collection of 18th- and 19th-century coins, forks, and combs made of bone, pottery, buttons, and ironwork. The items were excavated during the house's 1953 restoration. ⊠ *110 Key St.* ☎ *301/ 739–8393* ⊕ *www.hagerhouse.org* ⊠ *$4* ☉ *Apr.–Dec., Tues.–Sat. 10–4, Sun. 2–5.*

☺ **Hagerstown Roundhouse Museum.** Although the city's 89-year-old roundhouse was demolished in 1999, photographs, artifacts, and memorabilia from Hagerstown's railroading heyday can be found in this two-story museum, inside a former office of the Western Maryland Railway. Lights, lanterns, bells, and whistles are among the artifacts, and model railroad layouts add to the fun. ⊠ *300 S. Burhans Blvd.* ☎ *301/739– 4665* ⊕ *www.roundhouse.org* ⊠ *Free* ☉ *Fri.–Sun. 1–5.*

Where to Stay & Eat

¢–$$ ✕ **Roccoco.** At downtown Hagerstown restaurant, the selections here go beyond the usual, including country garlic soup, crispy duck spring rolls, garlic chicken, and avocado pizza. Entrée standouts include a smoked chicken, mascarpone, and pine nut ravioli with a truffle cream sauce and veal scallopini with mushrooms and Madeira wine sauce. Pastries and desserts are made on the premises. ⊠ *20 W. Washington St.* ☎ *301/ 790–3331* ▭ *AE, D, MC, V* ☉ *Closed Sun.*

$$ ▥ **Wingrove Manor Bed & Breakfast.** The large, inviting front porch on this Victorian house on the north side of town has a brick stairway leading up to it, adding to the general grandeur. The four guest rooms are stately and dignified, and they also include TVs and VCRs (there's a large video library) for unwinding. Breakfast is served in the main dining room. ⊠ *635 Oak Hill Ave., Hagerstown 21740* ☎ *301/797–7769* 🖷 *301/ 797–8659* ⊕ *www.wingrovemanor.com* ⇗ *4 rooms* ⚹ *In-room VCRs, some in-room hot tubs* ▭ *AE, DC, MC, V* ⦿| *BP.*

¢–$ ▥ **Four Points Sheraton Hotel.** Blue-and-mauve color schemes and touches of wood in these rooms keep things looking warm for guests, many of whom stay here for business. Some business suites have Murphy beds and conference tables. ⊠ *1910 Dual Hwy., Hagerstown 21740* ☎ *301/ 790–3010* 🖷 *301/733–4559* ⊕ *www.sheraton.com* ⇗ *108 rooms*

☆ *Restaurant, room service, in-room data ports, pool, gym, sports bar, business services, meeting rooms* ☰ *AE, D, DC, MC, V.*

Shopping
Prime Outlets (✉ 495 Prime Outlets Blvd. ☎ 888/883–6288), open daily, is a cornucopia of more than 100 designer and specialty outlet stores like Polo Ralph Lauren, Coach, Banana Republic, Harry and David, Le Creuset, Nautica, and L. L. Bean.

Sharpsburg

❷ *10 mi south of Hagerstown via Rte. 65, 20 mi west of Frederick via Alt. Rte. 40 to Rte. 34.*

Fodor'sChoice Among the cornfields and woods that surround Sharpsburg is the
★ **Antietam National Battlefield,** where Union and Confederate troops clashed on September 17, 1862. It was the single bloodiest one-day battle of the war: more than 23,000 men were killed or wounded. Landmarks on the largely undisturbed battlefield include the Burnside Bridge, Dunkard Church, and Bloody Lane. The Union's victory at Sharpsburg gave President Abraham Lincoln the momentum to announce on September 22 that unless the Confederacy stopped fighting and rejoined the Union, an "Emancipation Proclamation" would be issued on January 1 that would free all slaves in Confederate states. At the visitor center are Civil War artifacts, a short film about Lincoln's visit, an hour-long documentary about the battle (shown at noon daily), and rental cassettes for narrated driving tours. An overlook provides a panoramic view of the battlefield and the countryside. ✉ *Rte. 65, Sharpsburg Pike* ☎ *301/432–5124* ⊕ *www.nps.gov/anti* ✑ *$3* ⊙ *Battlefield daily dawn–dusk; visitor center Labor Day–Memorial Day, daily 8:30–5; Memorial Day–Labor Day, daily 8:30–6.*

★ The modest house that holds the **Boonsborough Museum of History** is- jam-packed floor-to-ceiling with unique and just plain wacky artifacts that the owner, Doug Bast, has collected. Standout exhibits include Geronimo's walking stick, a Civil War cannonball lodged in a piece of wood, and a marble piece of the original White House. There's also a mummified hand, a re-created General Store with old-timey signage, and myriad Civil War scraps, from bullets to bibles, that were collected from the area's battlefields. The museum is a must-see if you want to see something out of the ordinary. ✉ *113 Main St., Boonsboro* ☎ *301/432–6969* ✑ *Donations accepted* ⊙ *May–Sept., Sun. 1–5 and by appointment.*

Where to Stay & Eat
$$–$$$ ✕ **Old South Mountain Inn.** Built in 1732, the South Mountain Inn was a trading post in its early days. Now a restaurant, the 18th-century stone structure is atop South Mountain along the National Pike (now Route 40). In addition to an indoor dining room, there's also an enclosed garden patio with white-wicker furniture and plants as well as a garden patio. Highlights on the continental menu include Rockfish Chesapeake, a fillet smothered in cream sauce dotted with lump crab and country ham, and Brace of Quail, quail stuffed with sausage (made in-house) and then braised in a wild mushroom and red wine sauce. ✉ *6132 Old*

National Pike, Boonsboro 21713 ☎ 301/432–6155 or 301/371–5400
🖷 301/432–2211 ⊕ www.oldsouthmountaininn.com ☰ AE, DC, MC,
V ☉ Closed Mon.

$–$$ 🏨 **Inn at Antietam.** Built in 1908, this Victorian home sits on 8 acres.
The site was once the campgrounds of Gen. George Pickett during the
Battle of Antietam, and now it's next door to the Antietam National
Cemetery. Common areas at the inn include a solarium, parlor, and
wraparound porch. The country lodgelike Gen. Burnside Smokehouse
Suite has a very low-ceilinged sleeping loft and an enormous Colonial
kitchen brick fireplace that takes up half the room. Breakfast, with a
menu that changes daily, often includes favorites like blueberry pancakes,
eggs Benedict, and Belgian waffles. ⊠ 220 E. Main St., Sharpsburg
21782 ☎ 301/432–6601 or 877/835–6011 🖷 301/432–5981 ⊕ www.
innatantietam.com ⇌ 4 suites, 1 penthouse ᗧ Library; no room phones,
no TV in some rooms, no kids under 6, no pets, no smoking ☰ AE,
MC, V ☉ Closed Jan.

$–$$ 🏨 **Jacob Rohrbach Inn.** The ornate Federal facade is so well preserved,
you half expect a Civil War soldier to step out from behind the unusual
pink-color front door. This inn served as a Civil War hospital, and some
guests have reported hearing footsteps when no one was there. But the
past is what draws people to the inn, which is near Antietam Battlefield,
and other historic sites like the C&O Canal and Harpers Ferry. Guests
can rent bikes ($6 per hour) and tour the battlefield at their leisure. ⊠ 138
W. Main St., Sharpsburg 21782 ☎ 301/432–5079 or 877/839–4242 ⇌ 4
rooms ᗧ Library, Internet; no room phones, no TVs in some rooms,
no children under 10, no pets, no smoking ☰ AE, D, MC, V.

Fort Frederick State Park

❸ 17 mi west of Hagerstown via I–70, 40 mi west of Frederick via I–70.

Along the Potomac River stands the only remaining stone fort from the
French and Indian War. Built in 1756, this was the first state park to be
established in Maryland. The barracks were reconstructed in the 1930s
by the Civilian Conservation Corps, to whom a small museum here is
dedicated. A visitor center displays artifacts from the French and Indian
War and the Colonial era. ⊠ 11100 Ft. Frederick Rd., Big Pool ☎ 301/
842–2155 ⊠ $3 ☉ Apr.–Oct., daily 8 AM–dusk; Nov.–Mar., weekdays
8 AM–dusk, weekends 10 AM–dusk.

en route Interstate 68 cuts through Sideling Hill—the mountain that separates
Washington and Allegany counties—thus exposing nearly 850
vertical feet of sedimentary rock formed 350 million years ago. At the
top of the mountain is the **Sideling Hill Exhibit Center,** which seeks
to explain one of the best rock exposures in the eastern United States.
The four-story visitor center also has interpretive exhibits of animals
native to western Maryland. Forty-minute tours that cover the center
and the mountain's geology are given at 11, 1, and 3 daily. Picnic
areas overlook the stunning valleys. ⊠ I–68, 5 mi west of Hancock
☎ 301/678–5442 ⊠ Free ☉ Daily 9–5.

Green Ridge State Forest

❹ *23 mi west of Ft. Frederick State Park via I–70 to I–68, 62 mi west of Frederick via I–70 to I–68.*

At nearly 40,000 acres, Maryland's second-largest forest stretches across most of eastern Allegany County. Its vast stands of oak, maple, hickory, and pine attract those from Baltimore, who come here to hunt, bike, and camp in fall and spring. Beneath the forest growth, decaying tombstones and crumbling stone foundations are remnants of the lives of the immigrants who worked on the C&O Canal and the railroad. Within the forest is a Potomac River overlook, where Union soldiers once stood on the lookout for Confederate saboteurs. A *Baltimore Sun* columnist called one of the park's overlooks, just off the interstate, "the best deck in Maryland" because of its phenomenal view of heavily wooded mountains. ⊠ *28700 Headquarters Dr. NE, Flintstone* ☎ *301/478–3124* 🖃 *Free* ☉ *Park office daily 8–4.*

Cumberland

❺ *17 mi west of Green Ridge State Park via I–68; 89 mi west of Frederick via I–70 to I–68, 142 mi west of Baltimore via I–70 to I–68.*

Cradled in the Allegheny Mountains, Cumberland was once America's gateway to the west. Pioneers, and later, trains and motorists, took advantage of a 1-mi-long natural pass in the mountains—the Narrows—to make their way west. The National Pike, the first federally funded highway, appropriated by Congress in 1806; the Chesapeake and Ohio Canal; and the Baltimore and Ohio Railroad all converged here in the mid-19th century. When the B&O Railroad beat the canal to Cumberland, it doomed the waterway as the future transportation route.

Today, Cumberland is revisiting its transportation heritage to help its economy and attract tourists. A two-lane highway and an excursion train now cross through the 900-foot-deep Narrows, whose exposed red shale and sandstone cliffs above make for a scenic ride. In addition, millions of dollars are being spent to restore a stretch of the canal and offer mule-drawn barge rides to visitors. The city's historic train station has been restored, and by 2007, the entire complex, known as Canal Place, will be finished to include recreational areas, pedestrian bridges, and other amenities.

In the mid- to late 19th century, Cumberland's leading politicians, doctors, lawyers, and businessmen lived in the **Washington Street Historic District,** which stretches along Washington Street from Wills Creek to Allegany Street and from Greene Street to Fayette Street. The six-block district, on the National Register of Historic Places, still reflects the architecture of the period, with prominent Federal, Greek Revival, Italianate, Queen Anne, and Georgian revival homes. Of particular interest is the **Emmanuel Episcopal Church and Parish Hall** (⊠ 16 Washington St.). It was built in 1849–50 on the site of the former Fort Cumberland, a frontier outpost during the French and Indian War. The

Gothic revival church, built of native sandstone and contains three large Tiffany windows.

The only surviving structure from Fort Cumberland, **George Washington's Headquarters** (⊠ Washington and Greene Sts. ☎ 301/777–5132 🎦 Free ⊘ By appointment) was used by the future president and military hero when he was an aide to General Braddock. The one-room cabin, built in 1754–55, stands at Prospect Square in Riverside Park, downhill from where Fort Cumberland once stood.

The Second Empire–style **Gordon-Roberts House** was built in 1867 by Josiah Gordon, president of the C&O Canal, on fashionable Washington Street. Today it's the home of the Allegany County Historical Society, and a repository for hundreds of items of local and national significance, including furniture, clothing, hats, accessories, and toys. ⊠ *218 Washington St.* ☎ *301/777–8678* ⊕ *www.historyhouse.allconet.org* 🎦 *$5* ⊘ *Tues.–Sat. 10–5.*

★ ☾ The **Western Maryland Scenic Railroad** allows riders to relive the glory days of trains in Cumberland. A 1916 Baldwin locomotive, once used in Michigan's Upper Peninsula, carries you uphill through the Narrows and up scenic mountains on a 32-mi round-trip to Frostburg. A 90-minute layover in Frostburg allows time for lunch at one of the many restaurants on the city's main street, just up the hill. A diesel engine typically runs on weekdays, with the more popular steam engine saved for weekends. Some rides have themes, such as murder mysteries or a train transformed into the North Pole Express. Also in Frostburg, the **Thrasher Carriage Collection Museum** (⊠ 19 Depot St. ☎301/689–3380 ⊕www. thrashercarriagemuseum.com 🎦 $4 ⊘ Mar.–Dec., Wed.–Sun. 10–3; Jan. and Feb. by appointment) contains almost every style of horse-drawn vehicle, including carriages, milk wagons, sleighs, and funeral wagons. These vehicles from another era were collected by James R. Thrasher, a local blacksmith's son who became a successful businessman. Museum admission is included in the train fare. ⊠ *13 Canal St.* ☎ *301/759–4400 or 800/872–4650* ⊕ *www.wmsr.com* 🎦 *$20* ⊘ *Departures at 11:30 AM: May–Sept., Wed.–Sun; Oct., daily; Nov.–mid-Dec., weekends.*

The **Cumberland Visitors Center—C&O Canal National Historical Park** explains Cumberland's role as the western terminus of the C&O Canal. Interactive exhibits relate to boatbuilding at the Cumberland boatyards and the regional coal industry, which used the canal to transport coal to D.C. You can walk through a re-created Paw Paw Tunnel, one of the landmarks along the nearly 185-mi canal. ⊠ *Western Maryland Railway Station, 13 Canal St.* ☎ *301/722–8226* ⊕ *www.canalplace.org* 🎦 *Free* ⊘ *Daily 9–5.*

Where to Stay & Eat

$$–$$$ ✕ **J. B.'s Steak Cellar.** A blazing fireplace, dark paneling, and cushioned chairs keep this basement-level restaurant cozy in winter, when skiers returning home from the Wisp Ski Area in neighboring Garrett County stop by. Cuts of beef and fresh seafood are displayed in a glass case in one of the two small dining rooms, and steaks are grilled in front of diners. The menu, predominantly beef, chicken, and seafood, also includes

pasta dishes such as seafood Alfredo and portobello mushroom linguine. Prime rib remains a favorite. ⊠ *12801 Ali Ghan Rd. NE, Exit 46, I–68, 1 mi east of Cumberland, Cumberland* ☎ *301/722–6155* ⊟ *AE, D, DC, MC, V.*

$–$$$ ✕**Au Petit Paris.** Murals of Paris street scenes welcome diners to this restaurant, where the three intimate dining rooms are decorated with pictures of the City of Light. Duckling, lamb, veal, and seafood are the specialties here. Signature dishes include ostrich medallions served in a wine sauce with mushroom caps, and baked shrimp stuffed with crab. The chateaubriand steak serves two and must be ordered 24 hours in advance. Desserts include bananas Foster and cherries jubilee. ⊠ *86 E. Main St., Frostburg* ☎ *301/689–8946* ⚍ *Reservations essential* ⊟ *AE, D, DC, MC, V* ⊗ *Closed Sun. and Mon.*

$–$$ ✕**City Lights.** This casual restaurant, inside a two-story building, has wooden booths and tables covered in white linens. Seafood, hand-cut steaks, and pasta dishes are the dinner staples here. The lasagna Florentine, an eye-popping 32-layer spinach lasagna, attracts attention most evenings. Housemade New York–style cheesecakes are among the desserts. ⊠ *59 Baltimore St.* ☎ *301/722–9800* ⊟ *AE, D, DC, MC, V* ⊗ *Closed Sun.*

¢–$$ ✕**When Pigs Fly.** It's a virtual pig explosion inside this local favorite. All creatures pink and pudgy grace the walls and the ceiling. Known for their sweet ribs (of course), there's also a comprehensive selection of all meats served BBQ-style. ⊠ *18 Valley St., Cumberland* ☎ *301/722–7447* ⊟ *AE, MC, V.*

★ $$–$$$ ✕▥ **Savage River Lodge.** Halfway between Grantsville and Frostburg, the Lodge is hidden in Maryland's largest state forest. This rustic retreat on a plot of 45 acres has 18 cozy, two-level cabins, a first-rate restaurant, and a lovable dog mascot. The handsome three-story lodge, with a towering stone fireplace that splits the room, is a short walk from the cabins. The cabins contain oversize furniture, queen-size beds in a loft, and gas log fireplaces and ceiling fans. Muffins and orange juice are delivered to your room every morning. The restaurant, open Thursday through Sunday, uses only the freshest local meats, dairy products and seasonal vegetables. The cornish hen with sausage and cornbread stuffing and the seared duck breast are particular favorites. Reservations are required. ⊠ *1600 Mount Aetna Rd., 5.2 mi off I–68, Exit 29, Frostburg 21532* ☎ *301/689–3200* ⌨ *301/689–2746* ⊕ *www. savageriverlodge.com* ⇆ *18 cabins* ⚘ *Restaurant, fishing, mountain bikes, hiking, cross-country skiing, bar, library, business services, meeting rooms, some pets allowed (fee); no room TVs* ⊟ *AE, D, MC, V.*

$$ ▥ **Rocky Gap Lodge and Golf Resort.** With Evitts Mountain and Lake Habeeb as a backdrop, this resort is in one of the state's most idyllic locales. The lobby, dining room, and lounge overlook a 243-acre man-made lake. In keeping with the nature outside, greens and browns are used throughout the six-story hotel. Rooms, larger than most, are appointed with Shaker-style furniture; most have views of a breathtaking ridge of mountains. Suites include a gas fireplace and sitting area. Try a spa treatment, 18 holes on the golf course, a hike along the park's trails, or boating, fishing, and swimming. ⊠ *Rocky Gap State Park, 16701 Lakeview Rd., Box 1199, Flintstone 21530* ☎ *301/784–8400 or 800/*

724–0828 📠301/784–8408 ⊕www.rockygapresort.com 🛏203 rooms, 15 suites ➴ 2 restaurants, 18-hole golf course, 3 tennis courts, spa, indoor-outdoor pool, lake, gym, beach, boating, fishing, hiking, bar, business services, meeting rooms 🖃 AE, D, DC, MC, V.

¢–$ 🏨 **Holiday Inn-Downtown.** Cumberland's only downtown hotel is within walking distance of the downtown mall, historic sites, and the C&O Canal. The hotel caters to many business travelers and includes the usual Holiday Inn amenities: in-room coffeemaker, hair dryer, iron, and ironing board. Rooms on the west side of the six-story hotel come with a panoramic view of the mountains. Passing night trains can sometimes bother those sleeping on the opposite side. ⊠ 100 S. George St., 21502 ☎ 301/724–4001 📠 301/724–4001 ⊕ www.cumberland-dtn.holiday-inn.com 🛏 130 rooms ➴ Restaurant, room service, pool, gym, bar, business services, meeting rooms, airport shuttle, some pets allowed 🖃 AE, MC, V.

$–$$ 🏨 **Inn at Walnut Bottom.** Within two 19th-century row houses connected by a modern addition, this charming country inn is within walking distance of Cumberland's historic district. Antiques and reproductions of 19th-century country furniture are standard in each of the guest rooms. Lemonade, apple cider, and homemade sweets are served every afternoon in an upstairs sitting room that's filled with games, puzzles, books, and magazines. You can rent bicycles for a ride along the flat towpath of the C&O Canal, and then unwind with a Danish massage treatment called Afspaending, which means "unbuckling." ⊠ 120 E. Greene St., 21502 ☎ 301/777–0003 or 800/286–9718 📠 301/777–8288 ⊕ www.iwbinfo.com 🛏 12 rooms ➴ Bicycles, massage; no smoking 🖃 AE, D, MC, V ⦿| BP.

Sports & the Outdoors

Allegany Expeditions Inc. (⊠ 10310 Columbus Ave. NE, Cumberland ☎ 301/722–5170 ⊕ www.alleganyexpeditions.com) offers guided backpacking, caving, canoeing, fishing, and kayaking tours. The company also rents out camping equipment.

en route Along the Old National Road out of Cumberland stands the only remaining tollhouse in Maryland. Built in 1836, the **LaVale Toll Gate House** is a four-room building that housed the gatekeepers who collected tolls until the early 1900s. ⊠ Historic National Rd., Rte. 40, LaVale ☎ 301/729–3047 ⊙ May–mid-Oct., weekends 1:30–4:30.

Grantsville

❻ 21 mi west of Cumberland via I–68.

Two miles south of the Mason-Dixon Line, Grantsville is a village amid some of the most productive farmland in the region. It is also in the heart of the county's Amish and Mennonite communities. To the west and south is Maryland's largest forest, the 53,000-acre Savage River State Forest. Mostly undeveloped, it's used by hikers, campers, anglers, and, in winter, cross-country skiers. Also nearby is New Germany State Park, which has hiking trails, campsites, and cabins.

By the time you see the **Casselman River Bridge** (✉ Rte. 40), you're almost in Grantsville. This single-span stone arch bridge ½ mi east of town was built in 1813; at the time it was the largest of its kind. Though the bridge is no longer in use, it serves as the backdrop for a small state park and picnic area.

The history and craftsmanship of Upper Appalachia are exhibited at the rustic **Spruce Forest Artisan Village and Penn Alps,** a museum village where spinners, weavers, potters, stained-glass workers, wood sculptors, and bird carvers demonstrate their skills. The Winterberg House, a log stagecoach stop, is the last remaining log tavern along the Old National Pike. It's now used as a crafts store and restaurant. ✉ *177 Casselman Rte., at Rte. 40* ☎ *301/895–3332* ⊕ *www.spruceforest.org* 🎫 *Free* ☉ *Mon.–Sat. 10–5.*

In the northern end of Savage River State Forest, the much smaller **New Germany State Park** (400 acres) contains stands of hemlocks and pines planted in the late 1950s. In winter this popular hiking spot's 8 mi of trails are groomed for cross-country skiing. A 13-acre man-made lake is available for swimming, fishing, and boating. The park also has picnic shelters, 39 campsites, and 11 rental cabins, fully equipped for year-round use. ✉ *349 Headquarters La., 25 mi southwest of Cumberland via I–68 and Lower New Germany Rd., Exit 24* ☎ *301/895–5453* ⊕ *www.dnr.state.md.us* 🎫 *$2, Memorial Day–Labor Day; $3 during ski season* ☉ *Daily dawn–dusk.*

Shopping

Yoder Country Market (✉ Rte. 669 ☎ 301/895–5148), open Monday through Saturday, began as a butcher shop on a Mennonite family farm in 1947. Today, the market sells breads, cookies, pies, and pastries baked on the premises. There's also a nice selection of bulk groceries, local food products, meats, and homemade jams and jellies. A Mennonite kitchen serves a limited menu.

Deep Creek Lake

21 mi southwest of Grantsville via I–68 and Rte. 219.

Garrett County's greatest asset, the 3,900-acre Deep Creek Lake was created in the 1920s as a water source for a hydroelectric plant on the Youghiogheny (pronounced "Yok-a-gainy") River—a favorite among kayakers and white-water rafters. Though much of Deep Creek Lake's 65-mi shoreline is inaccessible to the public, it's visible from Route 219 and from numerous restaurants and motels, many of which have private docks.

★ ❼ For best public access, visit **Deep Creek Lake State Park** (✉ 898 State Park Rd. ☎ 301/387–4111 ⊕ www.dnr.state.md.us). The 1,818-acre park hugs the eastern shore of the lake and has a public boat launch, small beach, and picnic and camping sites. At the park's Discovery Center are hands-on educational activities for children, a freshwater aquarium, native animals on display, and a small gift shop. The center is also a staging area for organized outdoor activities, including lake boat tours.

Near Deep Creek Lake is Maryland's only alpine ski resort, the **Wisp Ski & Golf Resort,** atop 3,080-foot Marsh Mountain. Called "the Wisp" by locals, the mountain has a humble history: its eastern face was once a cow pasture. Today it's one of the area's most popular destinations.

Where to Stay & Eat

The area's most popular lodging choice is the ski resort. You can also rent a private house through **Railey Mtn. Lake Vacations** (☎ 800/846–7368 or 301/387–2124 ⊕ http://rentals.deepcreek.com). Year-round options include lakefront chalets as well as log cabins inside the woods. Many of the rentals include amenities like outdoor hot tubs, double balconies, game rooms, stone fireplaces, whirlpool tubs, and private piers.

$–$$$ ✕ **Deep Creek Brewing Co.** You know it's not your typical brew pub when the menu includes Wild Stew—venison, elk, and ostrich cooked in beer. (There are also more traditional entrées like fish-and-chips, paninis, and a unique crab Caesar salad.) Just off Route 219 above Deep Creek Lake, the pub pours four handcrafted beers—golden and pale ales and stouts— as well as seasonal selections. No alcohol is served Sunday. ⊠ *75 Visitor Center Dr., McHenry* ☎ *301/387–2182* ⊕ *www.deepcreekbrewing. com* ⊟ *AE, D, MC, V.*

¢–$$ ✕ **Bumble Q's.** The Texas flavor of the barbecue here may seem out of place in Appalachia, but owner and Garrett County native Vivian Padgett spent some time cooking on a Texas ranch. Taste her pulled pork sandwich or BBQ ribs and you'll know why the unassuming joint is a local favorite. Her chili contains three types of beans and chopped roast beef. The homemade desserts are great. ⊠ *145 Bumble Bee Rd., just off Rte. 219* ☎ *301/387–7667* ⊟ *No credit cards* ☽ *No dinner Sun.–Tues.*

$ ✕ **Canoe on the Run.** This casual coffee bar and café near Deep Creek Lake serves a health-conscious menu. The food is freshly prepared and includes a selection of green salads as well as turkey, cheese, mushroom, and seafood sandwiches. Appetizers include red chili and a smoked gouda and chicken quesadilla; there are jumbo cookies, muffins, scones, and mini–bundt cakes for dessert. A short walk uphill from the lake, the café opens at 8 AM. ⊠ *2622 Deep Creek Dr., McHenry* ☎ *301/387–5933* ⊟ *AE, D, DC, MC, V.*

$$$ ▥ **Lake Pointe Inn.** This restored 1890 stone farmhouse sits on a cove 13 feet from Deep Creek Lake. A wraparound porch has rocking chairs in which you can pass the afternoon gazing out at the water. A stone fireplace dominates the inn's great room, where guests can relax by a blazing fire, or opt for a rejuvenating massage from the small spa menu. The floor and paneling on the first floor are original chestnut. All rooms have lake or ski slope views, and seven have fireplaces and spa tubs. Hors d'oeuvres are served in the great room in the evenings. ⊠ *174 Lake Pointe Dr., McHenry 21541* ☎ *301/387–0111 or 800/523–5253* 🖷 *301/387– 0190* ⊕ *www.deepcreekinns.com* ⊷ *9 rooms, 1 suite* ♻ *In-room VCRs, tennis court, lake, outdoor hot tub, dock, boating, bicycles; no smoking* ⊟ *D, MC, V* ⵊ *BP.*

★ $$–$$$ ▥ **Carmel Cove Inn.** This former monastery retreat sits on a ridge above a Deep Creek Lake cove. The chapel has been converted into an English-style great room, where you can play billiards or board games, watch movies, listen to music, or browse through magazines. Guests have free use of on-site sporting equipment, and a communal refrigerator is stocked with wine and beer. Breakfast can be taken in the small, bright dining room, in your room, or on the deck, weather permitting. Some rooms have private decks and fireplaces. ⊠ *290 Marsh Hill Rd., Oakland 21550* ☎ *301/387–0067* ⊟ *301/387–4127* ⊕ *www.carmelcoveinn.com* ◔ *10 rooms* ⚘ *Room service, in-room DVD players, tennis court, lake, outdoor hot tub, dock, boating, fishing, bicycles, billiards, cross-country skiing; no kids under 12, no smoking* ⊟ *D, MC, V* ¶◯¶ *BP.*

$$–$$$ ⊡ **Savage River Inn.** Way off the beaten path within the Savage River State Forest, this inn began as a farmhouse in 1934. Additions since have created a modern, four-story structure. The great room has a large stone fireplace and splendid views of mountain scenery. Outside, enjoy a landscaped garden, pool, and hot tub. Rooms are decorated with country furnishings, and two have sitting areas and fireplaces. ⊠ *Rte. 495 S to Dry Run Rd., Box 147, McHenry 21541* ☎ *301/245–4440* ⊕ *www.savageriverbandb.com* ◔ *4 rooms* ⚘ *Pool, hot tub, bicycles, hiking; no in-room TVs* ⊟ *MC, V* ¶◯¶ *BP.*

$–$$ ⊡ **Wisp Mountain Resort Hotel and Conference Center.** Rooms here include modern appliances, fluffy comforters, and comfortable lodge furniture to sink into after a long day on the slopes. ⊠ *290 Marsh Hill Rd., McHenry 21541* ☎ *800/462–9477 or 301/387–5581* ⊟ *301/387–8634* ⊕ *www.wispresort.com* ◔ *104 suites, 64 rooms* ⚘ *2 restaurants, food court, some kitchenettes, refrigerators, spa, skiing, bar, shop, some pets allowed (fee)* ⊟ *AE, D, DC, MC, V.*

Sports & the Outdoors

BICYCLING **High Mountain Sports** (⊠ *21327 Garrett Hwy., McHenry* ☎ 301/387–4199 ⊕ www.highmountainsports.com) rents mountain bikes, snow and water skis, kayaks, and snowboards and sells outdoor gear and equipment. Kayak, mountain bike, and other outdoor tours are available as well.

BOATING At the docks at Deep Creek Lake State Park, **Nature Lake Tours** (⊠ 898 State Park Rd. ☎ 301/746–8782) runs sunrise, nature, dinner, and family-oriented tours of the lake daily from April through October.

SKIING **Wisp Mountain Resort Hotel and Conference Center** has 94 acres of trails ranging from beginner to difficult; most are open for night skiing. The resort's Bear Claw Tubing Park has seven tubing lanes, each of which 15 foot wide and 800 foot long. ⊠ *290 Marsh Hill Rd., McHenry* ☎ *800/462–9477, 301/387–4911* ⊕ *www.wispresort.com* ◔ *104 suites, 64 efficiencies,* ⊟ *AE, D, MC, V* ⊙ *Closed Apr.–mid-Dec.*

Oakland

❽ *11 mi southwest of Deep Creek Lake State Park via Rte. 219.*

Though it's the Garrett County seat, the town of Oakland keeps a low profile. Tucked away in Maryland's extreme southwestern corner, the town sits atop a mountain plateau, 2,650 feet above sea level. Oakland prospered during the last half of the 19th century, when the famous Baltimore and Ohio Railroad reached town, bringing summer vacationers.

Trains no longer bring tourists, but Oakland survives as the government and commercial center of the county.

At **Swallow Falls State Park,** paths wind along the Youghiogheny River, past shaded rocky gorges and rippling rapids, to a 63-foot waterfall. The park is also known for its stand of 300-year-old hemlocks and for its excellent camping, hiking, and fishing facilities. ⊠ *222 Herrington La., off Rte. 219, Oakland* ☎ *301/334–9180* ⊕ *www.dnr.state.md.us* 🗒 *Memorial Day–Labor Day, $2; Labor Day–Memorial Day, $1* ☉ *Daily dawn–dusk.*

Where to Eat

$$–$$$ ✕ **Deer Park Inn.** French-born chef and owner Pascal Fontaine uses locally grown produce in many of his dishes at this French country restaurant. His favorite dish is confit of duck, which he marinates in its own juices after curing it overnight. Beef, seafood, chicken, and lamb round out the entrée choices. Dessert highlights include crêpes and a strawberry and rhubarb tart with crème fraîche. The restored Victorian mansion lies between Deep Creek Lake and Oakland. During the area's off-season months, the restaurant may be closed Monday–Wednesday, so call ahead. And if the name reminds you of that bottled water you're drinking, it's because this area contains one of the springs used to bottle the drink. ⊠ *65 Hotel Rd., Deer Park* ☎ *301/334–2308* ⊕ *www. deerparkinn.com* ⊟ *AE, D, MC, V* ☉ *Closed Sun. No lunch.*

$–$$$ ✕ **Cornish Manor.** Built in 1868, this ornate Victorian house was once the home of a Washington, D.C., judge. Today, the 7-acre grounds and expansive home have been turned into one of the area's best-known restaurants. Seafood dishes reflect U.S. states, including Floridian grilled tuna and Alaskan wild salmon. Perhaps the most decadent entrée is the chicken breast imperial, stuffed with jumbo lump crab and topped with a sweet béchamel sauce. The thick, butcher-block steaks and lobster raviolis aren't too shabby, either. Don't forget to pick up airy croissants, stacked muffins and dense fruit tarts at the on-site bakery. ⊠ *Memorial Dr.* ☎ *301/334–6499* 🍴 *Reservations essential* ⊟ *AE, D, MC, V* ☉ *Closed Sun. and Mon.*

Sports & the Outdoors

Ten minutes from Deep Creek Lake, **Precision Rafting** (⊠ Main St., Friendsville ☎ 301/746–5290) and **Upper Yough Whitewater Expeditions** (⊠ Macadam Rd., Friendsville ☎ 301/746–5808 or 800/248–1893) provide kayaking instruction and guided white-water rafting trips on the Upper Youghiogheny, Savage, Gauley and Cheat rivers.

WESTERN MARYLAND A TO Z

To research prices, get advice from other travelers, and book travel arrangements, visit www.fodors.com.

BUS TRAVEL

Greyhound Lines provides daily transportation to Frederick, Hagerstown, Cumberland, and Keysers Ridge in Garrett County, from Baltimore; Washington, D.C.; and Pittsburgh, Pennsylvania.

Greyhound Lines has daily runs to Hagerstown, Cumberland, Frostburg, and Keysers Ridge. Frederick, Hagerstown, and Cumberland all operate municipal bus lines. Fares vary.

Frederick Transit provides bus service within Frederick and to outlying towns, including Thurmont, Emmitsburg, Jefferson, and Walkersville. Shuttle buses transport commuters to the Washington Metro at Shady Grove and Maryland's commuter train at Point of Rocks. The shuttle fare is $1.10; children under 3 feet tall ride free.

🚍 Bus Depots **Frederick Train Station** ✉ 100 S. East St., Frederick ☎ 301/663-3311.
🚍 Bus Lines **Frederick TransIT** ☎ 301/694-2065. **Greyhound Lines** ☎ 800/229-9424 ⊕ www.greyhound.com.

CAR TRAVEL

The best way to see western Maryland is by car. Interstate 70 links Frederick to Hagerstown and intersects with Route 15 and I–270, the main highway to Washington, D.C. West of Hagerstown, I–68—the main road through western Maryland—passes through some of the most scenic stretches of the state. Follow Route 219 off I–68 to reach Deep Creek Lake and the more remote areas of Garrett County.

EMERGENCIES

🚨 Emergency Services **Ambulance, fire, police** ☎ 911.
🏥 Hospitals **Frederick Memorial Hospital** ✉ 400 W. 7th St., Frederick ☎ 240/556-3300. **Garrett County Memorial Hospital** ✉ 251 N. 4th St., Oakland ☎ 301/533-4000. **Memorial Hospital** ✉ 600 Memorial Ave., Cumberland ☎ 301/723-4000. **Sacred Heart Hospital** ✉ 900 Seton Dr., Cumberland ☎ 301/723-4200.

TOURS

Heritage Koaches provides horse-drawn trolley, carriage, and stage-coach tours of Cumberland. Mountain Getaway Tours offers guided bus tours of the mountains and historic sites in Allegany and Garrett counties and West Virginia and Pennsylvania. Westmar Tours conducts group bus tours of the Allegheny Mountain region and the Shenandoah Valley, led by guides in Colonial and 19th-century garb.

In Frederick, guides lead walking tours ($7) that focus on the town's 250 years of history by day. By night, visitors see the haunted side on the Candlelight Ghost Tour ($8), weaving a spooky trail through the city's most notorious and gruesome sites. Tours start at the visitor center, which also has brochures that outline a self-guided tour.

🚌 Bus Tours **Heritage Koaches** ✉ 13 Canal St., Cumberland ☎ 301/777-0293. **Mountain Getaway Tours** ☎ 800/459-0510. **Westmar Tours** ✉ 13 Canal St., Cumberland ☎ 301/777-0293.

TRAIN TRAVEL

The Maryland Area Rail Commuter line runs from Frederick southwest to Point of Rocks on the Potomac River and then onto Washington, D.C. Amtrak service is available from Washington, D.C., to Cumberland.

🚆 Train Lines **Maryland Area Rail Commuter** (MARC) ☎ 866/743-3682. **Amtrak** ☎ 800/872-7245.

Train Stations **Cumberland Station** ⊠ E. Harrison St. and Queen City Dr., Cumberland. **Frederick Train Station** ⊠ 141 B&O Ave., off East St., Frederick 🕾 301/539-5000. **Point of Rocks Station** ⊠ Clay St.

VISITOR INFORMATION

Tourist Information **Allegany County Tourism Department** ⊠ Western Maryland Station, 13 Canal St., Cumberland 21502 🕾 301/777-5132 or 800/425-2067 ⊕ www. mdmountainside.com. **Garrett County Chamber of Commerce** ⊠ 15 Visitors Center Dr., McHenry 21541 🕾 301/387-4386 ⊕ www.garrettchamber.com. The **Tourism Council of Frederick County** Visitor center ⊠ 19 E. Church St., Frederick 21701 🕾 301/228-2888 or 800/999-3613 ⊕ www.fredericktourism.org. **Hagerstown/Washington County Convention & Visitor's Bureau** ⊠ Elizabeth Hager Center, 16 Public Sq., Hagerstown 21740 🕾 301/791-3246 ⊕ www.marylandmemories.org.

ANNAPOLIS & SOUTHERN MARYLAND

8

Updated by
Laureen Miles

THE PAST IS NEVER FAR AWAY from the present among the coves, rivers, and creeks of the Chesapeake Bay's lesser known *western* shore. In the lively port of Annapolis, Colonial Maryland continues to assert itself. Today, "Crabtown," as the state capital is sometimes called, has one of the highest concentrations of 18th-century buildings in the nation, including more than 50 that predate the Revolutionary War.

The region south of Annapolis and D.C. is a peninsula broken in two by the Patuxent River, a 110-mi-long tributary to the Bay. The counties of Anne Arundel, Calvert, Charles, and St. Mary's, which make up the area, have all been supported since their founding in the 1600s through tobacco fields and fishing fleets. More recently, the northern parts of the counties have emerged as prime residential satellites for the Annapolis-Baltimore-D.C., metro triangle—but despite the subdivisions and concomitant shopping centers, southern Maryland retains much of its rural character. With the exception of the fair-weather getaway enclave, Solomons Island, and the archaeological site-in-progress, Historic St. Mary's City, the region remains largely undiscovered. All the better for travelers who do come to enjoy stunning water vistas, miles of scenic roads, dozens of historic sites, and a plethora of inns and bed-and-breakfasts on the water, in tiny towns, and in the fields and woodlands of its unspoiled countryside.

About the Restaurants & Hotels

In the beginning, there was crab: crab cakes, crab soup, whole crabs to crack. These days, most likely because of overfishing and habitat changes, crabs from the Bay are pretty scarce. Maryland's favorite crustacean is still found in abundance on menus, but most arrive from out of state. In addition, Annapolis has broadened its horizons to include eateries—many in the Historic District—that offer many sorts of cuisines. Ask for a restaurant guide at the visitor center.

Dinner reservations in Annapolis are recommended throughout the summer and at times of Naval Academy events.

There are many places to stay near the heart of Annapolis, as well as at area B&Bs and chain motels a few miles outside town (some of which offer free transportation to the downtown historic area). A unique "Crabtown" option is Boat & Breakfasts, in which you sleep, eat, and cruise on a yacht or schooner; book ahead. Contact the visitor center for information.

Hotel reservations are necessary, even a year in advance, during the sailboat and powerboat shows in the spring and fall and Naval Academy commencement in May.

Two reservation services operate in Annapolis. **Annapolis Accommodations** (✉ 41 Maryland Ave. ☎ 410/280–0900 or 800/715–1000 ⊕ www.stayannapolis.com) specializes in long-term rentals. The office is open 9–5 weekdays. **Annapolis Bed & Breakfast Association** (☎ 410/295–5200 ⊕ www.annapolisbandb.com) books lodging in the old section of town, which has many restaurants and shops as well as the Maryland State

House and the City Dock. The U.S. Naval Academy and St. John's College serve as the northern and western boundaries of the territory.

	$$$$	$$$	$$	$	¢
WHAT IT COSTS					
RESTAURANTS	over $30	$22–$30	$14–$22	$7–$14	under $7
HOTELS	over $250	$175–$250	$130–$175	$80–$130	under $80

Restaurant prices are per person for a main course at dinner. Hotel prices are for a standard double room, excluding state tax.

Exploring Annapolis & Southern Maryland

Annapolis and southern Maryland encompass the western shore of the Chesapeake Bay, an area within easy driving distance of Baltimore and Washington, D.C. Annapolis, on a peninsula bounded by the Severn and South rivers and the Chesapeake Bay, is a mid-Atlantic sailing capital and the gateway to southern Maryland. Calvert County, just south of Annapolis, promises compelling Bayside scenery that includes the imposing Calvert Cliffs and several miles of bay beaches. Beyond the Patuxent River, across the 1⅓-mi Thomas Johnson Bridge, lies St. Mary's County, a peninsula that protrudes farther into the Chesapeake, with the Patuxent and the Potomac rivers on either side of it.

ANNAPOLIS

In 1649 a group of Puritan settlers moved from Virginia to a spot at the mouth of the Severn River, where they established a community called Providence. Lord Baltimore, who held the royal charter to settle Maryland, named the area around this town Anne Arundel County, after his wife; in 1684 Anne Arundel Town was established across from Providence on the Severn's south side. Ten years later, Anne Arundel Town became the capital of Maryland and was renamed Annapolis after Princess Anne, who later became queen. It received its city charter in 1708 and became a major port, particularly for the export of tobacco. In 1774 patriots here matched their Boston counterparts (who had thrown their famous tea party the previous year) by burning the *Peggy Stewart,* a ship loaded with taxed tea. Annapolis later served as the nation's first peacetime capital (1783–84).

The city's considerable Colonial and early republican heritage is largely intact and, because it's all within walking distance, highly accessible.

Although it has long since been overtaken by Baltimore as the major Maryland port, Annapolis is still a popular pleasure-boating destination. On warm sunny days, the waters off City Dock become center stage for an amateur show of powerboaters maneuvering through the heavy traffic. Annapolis's enduring nautical reputation derives largely from the presence of the United States Naval Academy, whose strikingly uniformed midshipmen throng the city streets in crisp white uniforms during the summer and navy blue in winter.

Numbers in the text correspond to numbers in the margin and on the Annapolis map.

a good tour

You can see Annapolis in a single well-planned day. To get maps, schedules, and information about guided tours, begin your walking tour at the **Annapolis & Anne Arundel County Conference & Visitors Bureau** ❶ ▶. Exit the visitor center then turn left at West Street and walk to **St. Anne's Church** ❷, straight ahead a half block. The edifice incorporates walls from a former church that burned in 1858; a congregation has worshipped here continuously since 1692. Off Church Circle, take Franklin Street one block to the **Banneker-Douglass Museum** ❸, which portrays African-American life in Maryland. Return to the circle after a visit. Continue clockwise around the circle to the Maryland Inn and walk to the end of Main Street. On your way you can pass many boutiques and small restaurants as well as the **Historic Annapolis Foundation Museum Store** ❹, where you can rent audiotapes for self-guided walking tours. Along the water's edge, the **Kunta Kinte–Alex Haley Memorial** ❺ commemorates the 1767 arrival of the slave portrayed in Alex Haley's *Roots.* On the other side of City Dock in front of the Harbor Master's office, there's an **information booth** ❻, where you can get maps and information from April to October.

Return to Market Square and take a right onto Randall Street. Walk two blocks to the Naval Academy wall and turn right, entering the gate to the **United States Naval Academy** ❼ and its Armel-Leftwich Visitor Center. Here you can join a tour or continue solo through the academy grounds, where future U.S. Navy and Marine Corps officers are trained. Walk toward the Naval Academy Chapel dome and turn right on Buchanan Road and again at the Tecumseh statue, figurehead of the USS *Delaware,* to visit the academy's dormitory, Bancroft Hall. Return to Tecumseh and take the curvy walkway to the left to the chapel. From the chapel entrance the Naval Academy Museum is a half block to the left in Preble Hall.

From the museum, leave through Gate 3 to your right and walk down Maryland Avenue to the **Hammond-Harwood House** ❽ and the **Chase-Lloyd House** ❾, both designed by colonial America's foremost architect, William Buckland. The two homes are across the street from each other. Continue east on Maryland Avenue a block to Prince George Street; turn left and walk a block to the **William Paca House and Garden** ❿, home of another signer of the Declaration of Independence. Retrace your route and continue a block past Maryland Avenue to the campus of **St. John's College** ⓫, directly ahead at the College Avenue end of Prince George Street. After touring the campus, follow College Avenue away from the Naval Academy wall to North Street and go one block to the **Maryland State House** ⓬ in the middle of State Circle. After touring the capitol, stop and visit the **Thurgood Marshall Memorial** ⓭ in State House Square, close to Bladen Street and College Avenue. Then turn back toward State Circle and turn right, exiting State Circle via School Street. Keep an eye

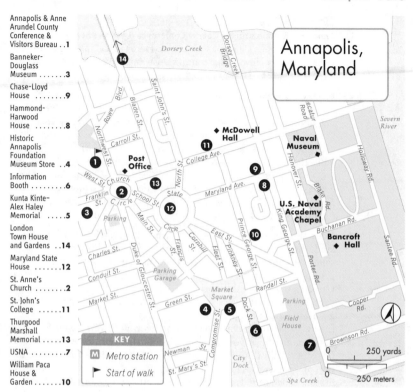

Annapolis, Maryland

Dorsey Creek

Dorsey Creek Bridge

Decatur Road

Severn River

McDowell Hall

Naval Museum

Post Office

College Ave.

Maryland Ave.

Hanover St.

Blake Rd.

King George St.

U.S. Naval Academy Chapel

Buchanan Rd.

Bancroft Hall

Holloway Rd.

Santee Rd.

Rowe Blvd.

Bladen St.

Saint John's St.

Northwest St.

Carroll St.

West St. Church

Franklin St.

School St.

State

Church Circle

Parking

Main St.

Charles St.

Duke of Gloucester St.

Conduit St.

Market St.

Circle

Cornhill St.

Francis St.

Fleet St.

East St.

Pinkney St.

Prince George St.

Porter Rd.

Cooper Rd.

Brownson Rd.

Field House

Parking

Randall St.

Market Square

Dock St.

Green St.

Compromise St.

Newman St.

St. Mary's St.

City Dock

Spa Creek

Parking Garage

KEY

Ⓜ *Metro station*

▶ *Start of walk*

0   250 yards

0   250 meters

out for the beautiful wrought iron fencing that surrounds Government House, a Georgian mansion with sculpture gardens that's the home of Maryland's governor. Walk down School Street, which leads back to Church Circle and West Street, where the tour began. From here you can drive to **London Town House and Gardens** ⑭, Maryland's largest archaeological excavation. The digging here continues to uncover parts of the abandoned town of London. The public can participate on scheduled dig days, and docents lead tours of a three-story brick home built there in 1760. To get here take Rowe Boulevard to Route 50 to Exit 22 onto Highway 665 and turn right onto Highway 2 south; cross the South River Bridge and turn left at Mayo Road; in less than a mile, turn left onto Londontown Road and follow it 1 mi to the site.

TIMING   Walking this route will take about an hour. Budget another half hour each for tours of the smaller historic homes and an hour each for the Paca and Hammond-Harwood houses. The Naval Academy deserves about two hours, plus another half hour if you visit the museum. The capitol takes a quarter hour to see. The drive to the London Town is about 15 minutes. Plan on 1½ hours for taking the tour and wandering the grounds. Note that traffic and parking in downtown Annapolis can be difficult, especially on weekends and during good weather.

Sights to See

❶ Annapolis & Anne Arundel County Conference & Visitors Bureau. Start your visit at Annapolis's main visitor center. Here you can pick up maps and brochures or begin a guided tour. ⊠ *26 West St., West Side* ☎ *410/280–0445* ☽ *Daily 9–5.*

☝ **❸ Banneker-Douglass Museum.** Named for abolitionist Frederick Douglass and scientist Benjamin Banneker, this former church and its next-door neighbor make up a museum that tells the stories of African-Americans in Maryland through programming, art, and interactive historic exhibits. The church hosts performances, lectures and educational programs, while the addition houses both permanent and changing exhibits. Audio and visual presentations and hands-on exhibits make the museum engaging for kids, while also bringing home the hardships of slave life. ⊠ *84 Franklin St., Historic Area* ☎ *410/216–6180* ⊕ *www.mdhousing.org/bdm/index.asp* ☞ *Free* ☽ *Tues.–Fri. 10–3, Sat. noon–4.*

❾ Chase-Lloyd House. Built by the prominent colonial architect William Buckland, the Chase-Lloyd House was begun in 1769 by Samuel Chase, a signer of the Declaration of Independence and future Supreme Court justice. Five years later the tobacco planter and revolutionary Edward Lloyd IV completed the work. The first floor is open to the public and contains some impressive sections of Buckland's handiwork, including a parlor mantelpiece with tobacco leaves carved into the marble. (Buckland was famous for his interior woodwork; you can see more of it in the Hammond-Harwood House across the street and in George Mason's Gunston Hall in Lorton, Virginia.) The house, furnished with a mixture of 18th-, 19th-, and 20th-century pieces, has a staircase that parts dramatically around an arched triple window. For more than 100 years the house has served as a home for older women, who live upstairs. ⊠ *22 Maryland Ave.,* ☎ *410/263–2723* ☞ *$2* ☽ *Mar.–Dec., Mon., Tues., Thurs., Fri. 2–4.*

❽ Hammond-Harwood House. Ninety percent of this 1774 home is original. A fine example of colonial five-part Georgian architecture (a single block with two connecting rooms and wings on each side), the Hammond-Harwood House is the only verifiable full-scale example of William Buckland's work. It was also his final project, as he died the year the house was completed. Exquisite moldings, cornices, and other carvings appear throughout (note especially the garlands of roses above the front doorway). The house was meant to be a wedding present from Matthias Hammond, a planter and revolutionary, to his fiancée, but she jilted him before the house was finished. Hammond died a bachelor in 1784. The Harwoods took over the house toward the turn of the 19th century. Today it's furnished with 18th-century pieces, and the garden's plants are also reflective of the period. Tours leave on the hour; the last begins at 4. ⊠ *19 Maryland Ave., Historic Area* ☎ *410/263–4683* ⊕ *www.hammondharwoodhouse.org* ☞ *$6* ☽ *Mid-Apr.–Oct., Wed.–Sun. noon–5; Jan. and Feb., weekends noon–4; Nov.–Dec. and Mar.–mid-Apr., Wed.–Sun. noon–4.*

❹ Historic Annapolis Foundation Museum Store. In a redbrick building at the base of Main Street, the store occupies the site of a warehouse that held supplies for the Continental Army during the Revolutionary War. Today it's filled with maps, Maryland history books, ceramics, and nautical knickknacks. You can rent taped narrations here for 90-minute walking tours. ⊠ *77 Main St., City Dock* ☎ *410/268–5576* ⊕ *www. hafmuseumstore.com* ⊠ *Free* ☉ *Sun.–Thurs. 10–8, Fri. and Sat. 10–10. Variable extended hours in summer.*

❻ Information Booth. From April to October the information booth on City Dock, adjacent to the harbormaster's office, is open and stocked with maps and brochures. ⊠ *Dock St. parking lot, City Dock* ☎ *410/ 280–0445.*

❺ Kunta Kinte–Alex Haley Memorial. A series of plaques along the waterfront recounting the story of African-Americans in Maryland lead to a sculpture group depicting the famed author reading to a group of children. On the other side of the street, a three-sided obelisk and plaque commemorates the 1767 arrival of the African slave immortalized in Alex Haley's *Roots.* ⊠ *Market Sq.* ⊕ *www.kintehaley.org.*

★ ⓮ London Town House and Gardens. This National Historic Landmark is on the South River, a short car ride from Annapolis. The three-story waterfront brick house, built by William Brown in 1760, has 8 acres of woodland gardens. The 17th-century tobacco port of London, made up of 40 dwellings, shops, and taverns, disappeared in the 18th century, its buildings abandoned and left to decay. The excavation of the town is still going on. Docents conduct 30- to 45-minute house tours; allow more time to wander the grounds. From March 15 to December, house tours leave on the hour (the last is at 3). ⊠ *839 Londontown Rd., Edgewater 21037* ☎ *410/222–1919* ⊠ *$7* ☉ *Mid-Mar.–Dec., Mon.–Sat. 10–4, Sun. noon–4; Jan.–mid-Mar.* ☉ *Closed weekends.*

⓬ Maryland State House. Completed in 1780, the State House is the oldest state capitol in continuous legislative use; it's also the only one in which the U.S. Congress has sat (1783–84). It was here that General George Washington resigned as commander in chief of the Continental Army and where the Treaty of Paris was ratified, ending the Revolutionary War. Both events took place in the Old Senate Chamber, which is filled with intricate woodwork (attributed to colonial architect William Buckland) featuring the ubiquitous tobacco motif. Also decorating this room is Charles Willson Peale's painting *Washington at the Battle of Yorktown*, a masterpiece of the Revolutionary War period's finest portrait artist. The Maryland Senate and House now hold their sessions in two other chambers in the building. Also on the grounds is the oldest public building in Maryland, the tiny redbrick Treasury, built in 1735. Note that you must have a photo ID to enter the State House. ⊠ *State Circle, Historic Area* ☎ *410/974–3400* ⊠ *Free* ☉ *Welcome center open weekdays 8:30–5, weekends 10–4; ½-hr tour daily at 11 and 3.*

need a break? **Chick and Ruth's Delly** (⊠ 165 Main St. ☎ 410/269–6737), is a longtime counter-and-table institution where the waitstaff is friendly and the sandwiches are named for state politicos.

❷ **St. Anne's Church.** Residing in the center of one of the historic area's busy circles, this brick building is one of the city's most prominent places of worship. King William III donated the Communion silver when the parish was founded in 1692, but the first St. Anne's Church wasn't completed until 1704. The second church burned in 1858, but parts of its walls survived and were incorporated into the present structure, built the following year. The churchyard contains the grave of the last colonial governor, Sir Robert Eden. ⊠ *Church Circle, Historic Area* ☎ *410/267– 9333* 🔲 *Free* ☉ *Weekdays 6–6, Sat. 6–2; services on Sun.*

⓫ **St. John's College.** As home to the Great Books curriculum, St. John's students all follow the same four-year, liberal arts curriculum, which includes philosophy, mathematics, music, science, Greek and French. Students are immersed the classics, through small classes conducted as discussions rather than lectures. Start a visit here by climbing the gradual slope of the long, brick-paved path to the cupola of **McDowell Hall.** The Annapolis campus of St. John's, the third-oldest college in the country (after Harvard and William and Mary), once held the last Liberty Tree, under which the Sons of Liberty convened to hear patriots plan the Revolution. Damaged in a 1999 hurricane, the 400-year-old tree was removed; its progeny stands to the left of McDowell Hall. The **Elizabeth Myers Mitchell Art Gallery** (☎ 410/626–2556), on the east side of Mellon Hall, presents exhibits and special programs that relate to the fine arts. Down King George Street toward the water is the **Carroll-Barrister House,** now the college admissions office. Once home to Charles Carroll (not the signer of the Declaration but his cousin), the house was built in 1722 at Main and Conduit streets and moved onto campus in 1955. ⊠ *60 College Ave., at St. John's St., Historic Area* ☎ *410/ 263–2371* ⊕ *www.sjca.edu.*

⓭ **Thurgood Marshall Memorial.** Born in Baltimore, Thurgood Marshall (1908–93) was the first African-American Supreme Court Justice and was one of the 20th century's foremost leaders in the struggle for equal rights under the law. Marshall won the decision in 1954's *Brown v. Board of Education,* in which the Supreme Court overturned the doctrine of "separate but equal." Marshall was appointed as United States Solicitor General in 1965 and to the Supreme Court in 1967 by President Lyndon B. Johnson. The 8-foot statue depicts Marshall as a young lawyer. ⊠ *State House Sq., bordered by Bladen St., School St., and College Ave., Historic Area.*

❼ **United States Naval Academy.** Probably the most interesting and important site in Annapolis, the Naval Academy runs along the Severn River and abuts downtown Annapolis. Men and women enter from every part of the United States and foreign countries to undergo rigorous study in subjects that include literature, navigation, and nuclear engineering. The academy, established in 1845 on the site of a U.S. Army fort, occupies 329 waterfront acres. The centerpiece of the campus is the bright copper-clad dome of the interdenominational **U.S. Naval Academy Chapel.** Beneath it lies the crypt of the Revolutionary War naval officer John Paul Jones, who, in a historic naval battle with a British ship, uttered the inspirational words, "I have not yet begun to fight!"

FodorśChoice
★

Near the chapel in Preble Hall is the **U.S. Naval Academy Museum & Gallery of Ships** (⊠ 118 Maryland Ave., Historic Area ☎ 410/293–2108), which tells the story of the U.S. Navy through displays of model ships and memorabilia from naval heroes and fighting vessels. The U.S. Naval Institute and Bookstore is also in this building. Admission for the museum, institute, and bookstore is free; hours are Monday through Saturday from 9 to 5 and Sunday from 11 to 5.

On the grounds, midshipmen (the term used for women as well as men) go to classes, conduct military drills, and practice or compete in intercollegiate and intramural sports. **Bancroft Hall,** closed to the public, is one of the largest dormitories in the world—it houses the entire 4,200-member Brigade of Midshipmen. The **Statue of Tecumseh,** in front of Bancroft Hall, is a bronze replica of the USS *Delaware*'s wooden figurehead, "Tamanend." It's decorated by midshipmen for athletics events, and for good luck during exams, students pitch pennies into his quiver of arrows. If you're there at noon weekdays in fair weather, you can see midshipmen form up outside Bancroft Hall and parade to lunch accompanied by the Drum and Bugle Corps.

Adjoining Halsey Field House is the **USNA Armel-Leftwich Visitor Center** (⊠ 52 King George St., Historic Area ☎ 410/263–6933), which has exhibits of midshipmen life, including a mockup of a midshipman's room, and the Freedom 7 space capsule flown by astronaut Alan Shepard, an Academy graduate. Walking tours of the Naval Academy led by licensed guides leave from here. You must have a photo ID to be admitted through the Academy's gates, and only cars used for official Department of Defense business may enter the grounds. ⊕ *www.navyonline. com* ⚓ *Grounds tour $7.50* ⊙ *USNA Armel-Leftwich Visitor Center: Mar.–Dec., daily 9–5; Jan. and Feb., daily 9–4. Guided walking tours generally leave Mon.–Sat. 10–3 on the hour and Sun. 12:30–3 on the ½ hour; call ahead to confirm and for Jan. and Feb. tour times.*

★ ❿ **William Paca House and Garden.** A signer of the Declaration of Independence, Paca (pronounced "PAY-cuh") was a Maryland governor from 1782 to 1785. His house was built in 1765, and its original garden was finished in 1772. Inside, the main floor (furnished with 18th-century antiques) retains its original Prussian blue and soft gray color scheme. The second floor contains a mixture of 18th- and 19th-century pieces. The adjacent 2-acre garden provides a longer perspective on the back of the house, plus worthwhile sights of its own: upper terraces, a Chinese Chippendale bridge, a pond, a wilderness area, and formal arrangements. An inn, Carvel Hall, once stood on the gardens. After the inn was demolished in 1965, it took eight years to rebuild the gardens, which are planted with 18th-century perennials. You can take a self-guided tour of the garden, but to see the house you must go on the docent-led tour, which leaves every hour at half past. The last tour leaves 1½ hours before closing. ⊠ *186 Prince George St., Historic Area* ☎ *410/263–5553* ⊕ *www.annapolis.org* ⚓ *House and garden $8, house only $5, garden only $5* ⊙ *House and garden mid-Mar.–Dec., Mon.–Sat. 10–5, Sun. noon–5; Jan.–mid-Mar., Fri. and Sat. 10–4, Sun. noon–4.*

Where to Eat

$$$–$$$$ ✕ **aqua terra.** This funky restaurant gives history-minded Annapolis an alternative to the Colonial flavor found at most other downtown eateries. Inside are blond-wood furniture, an open kitchen, and a handsome granite counter under a row of blue teardrop-shape lamps. The menu changes with each season, but each employs seafood, beef, and pasta as regular features. A summer menu includes Cajun New York strip: a handsome cut of beef topped with pink curls of shrimp, butter, and chopped garlic. The summer's linguine is tossed with lumps of crab, fresh tomatoes, and shallots. ☒ *164 Main St., Historic Area* ☎ *410/263–1985* ⊟ *AE, MC, V* ☺ *Closed Mon. No lunch.*

$$$–$$$$ ✕ **Treaty of Paris Restaurant.** An age-blackened brick fireplace along with period reproduction furniture and fabrics bring back a bit of the 18th century to this handsome dining room. Continental dishes like roasted pheasant or rack of lamb complement seafood selections like the Atlantic strudel, a puffed pastry stuffed with snapper, lobster, crab, and prawns. ☒ *Maryland Inn, 16 Church Circle, Historic Area* ☎ *410/ 216–6340* ⊟ *AE, D, DC, MC, V.*

$$–$$$ ✕ **Carrol's Creek.** You can walk, catch a water taxi from City Dock, or drive over the Spa Creek drawbridge to this local favorite in Eastport. Whether you dine indoors or out, the view of historic Annapolis and its harbor is spectacular. The all-you-can-eat Sunday brunch ($20) is worth checking out, as are the seafood specialties. Any of the entrées, including the herb-encrusted rockfish or Muscovy duck breast, can be turned into a four-course meal, with the addition of soup, salad, and dessert for $12 more. ☒ *410 Severn Ave., Eastport* ☎ *410/263–8102* ⊕ *www.carrolscreek.com* ⊟ *AE, D, DC, MC, V.*

★ **$$–$$$** ✕ **Harry Browne's.** In the shadow of the State House, this understated establishment has a reputation for quality food and attentive service that ensures bustle year-round, especially during the busy days of the legislative session (early January into early April) and special weekend events at the Naval Academy. The menu clearly reflects the city's maritime culture, but also has other seasonal specialties, such as rack of lamb and wild mushroom ravioli. Live Irish music is performed in the lounge every Monday night. The sidewalk café is open, weather permitting, April through October. ☒ *66 State Circle, Historic Area* ☎ *410/263–4332* ⊟ *AE, D, DC, MC, V.*

$$–$$$ ✕ **Breeze.** The icy blue color scheme and wide open spaces of this stylish eatery suggest a maritime dining experience without using all the typical nautical clichés. Daily specials, capitalizing on the area's bounty of fresh, local ingredients, augment the menu, which includes seared halibut and New York strip steak. A lunch buffet, which might feature pasta one week and Chinese cuisine the next, is just $12. ☒ *Loews Annapolis Hotel, 126 West St., West Side* ☎ *410/263–1299* ⊟ *AE, D, DC, MC, V.*

$$–$$$ ✕ **Café Normandie.** Ladder-back chairs, wood beams, skylights, and a four-sided fireplace make this French restaurant homey. Out of the open kitchen comes an astonishingly good French onion soup, made daily from scratch. Bouillabaisse, puffy omelets, crepes, and seafood dishes are other specialties. The restaurant's breakfast, served only on weekends, includes poached eggs in ratatouille, eggs Benedict, seafood omelets, and crepes, waffles, and croissants. ✉ *185 Main St., Historic Area* ☎ *410/263–3382* ☰ *AE, D, DC, MC, V.*

$$–$$$ ✕ **Middleton Tavern.** Horatio Middleton began operating this "inn for seafaring men" in 1750; Washington, Jefferson, and Franklin were among his guests. Today, two fireplaces, wood floors, paneled walls, and a nautical theme make it cozy. Seafood tops the menu; the Maryland crab soup and pan-seared rockfish are standouts. Try the tavern's own Middleton Pale Ale, perhaps during happy hour or during a weekend blues session in the upstairs piano bar. Brunch is served on weekends, and you can dine outdoors in good weather. ✉ *City Dock at Randall St., City Dock* ☎ *410/263–3323* ⊕ *www.middletontavern.com* ☰ *AE, D, DC, MC, V.*

$–$$$ ✕ **Cantler's Riverside Inn.** Opened in 1974, this local institution was founded by Jimmy Cantler, a native Marylander who worked as a waterman on the Chesapeake Bay. The no-nonsense interior has wooden blinds and floors and nautical items laminated beneath tabletops. Food is served on disposable dinnerware; if you order steamed crabs, they'll come served atop a "tablecloth" of brown paper. Waterview outdoor dining is available seasonally. Boat owners can tie up at the dock; free parking spaces are rare during the busy summer season. Specialties include steamed mussels, clams, and shrimp as well as Maryland vegetable crab soup, seafood sandwiches, oysters, crab cakes, and numerous finfish. This place is easiest to find by boat, so if you're coming by car, call for directions. ✉ *458 Forest Beach Rd.* ☎ *410/757–1311* ⊕ *www.cantlers.com* ☰ *AE, D, DC, MC, V* ⊙ *Sun.–Thurs. 11–11; Fri. and Sat. 11 AM–midnight.*

★ $$ ✕ **Rams Head Tavern.** A traditional English-style pub also houses the Fordham Brewing Company, which you can tour. The Rams Head serves better-than-usual tavern fare, including spicy shrimp salad, crab cakes, beer-battered shrimp, and daily specials, as well as more than 170 beers—26 on tap—from around the world. Brunch is served on Sunday. The nightclublike Rams Head Tavern On Stage brings in nationally known folk, rock, jazz, country, and bluegrass artists. Dinner-show specials are available; the menu has light fare. ✉ *33 West St., West Side* ☎ *410/268–4545* ⊕ *www.ramsheadtavern.com* ☰ *AE, D, DC, MC, V.*

$–$$ ✕ **El Toro Bravo.** A local favorite, this authentic Mexican restaurant is family-owned. The wooden colonial exterior conceals colorful, South-of-the-Border scenes hand painted on the interior walls, hanging plants, and padded aqua booths. There's often a line, but takeout is available. Lunch and dinner specials include a variety of enchiladas, fish tacos, grilled shrimp, and steak. The guacamole is made on the premises. ✉ *50 West St., 1 block from visitor center, West Side* ☎ *410/267–5949* ☰ *AE, D, DC, MC, V.*

$–$$ ✕ **49 West Coffeehouse and Gallery.** In what was once a hardware store, this eclectic, casual eatery has one interior wall of exposed brick and another of exposed plaster; both are used to hang art for sale by local artists. Daily specials are chalked on a blackboard. Menu staples include a large cheese and pâté plate, deli sandwiches, and soups and salads. There's free Wi-Fi and live music every night but Sunday. ✉ *49 West St., West Side* ☎ *410/626–9796* ☰ *AE, D, DC, MC, V.*

¢–$$ ✕ **McGarvey's Saloon and Oyster Bar.** An Annapolis institution since 1975, this dockside eatery and watering hole is full of good cheer, great drink, and grand food. A heritage of seasonal shell- and finfish dishes, the finest burgers and steaks, as well as unstinting appetizers, make Mc-Garvey's menu one of the most popular in the area. The full menu is available daily until 11 PM. ⊠ *8 Market Space, City Dock* ☎ *410/263–5700* ▭ *AE, DC, MC, V.*

¢–$ ✕ **Chick and Ruth's Delly.** Deli sandwiches (named for local politicos), burgers, subs, and milk shakes and other ice-cream concoctions are the bill of fare at this counter-and-table institution. Built in 1901, the edifice was a sandwich shop when Baltimoreans Chick and Ruth Levitt purchased it in 1965. They ran a little boardinghouse with 12 rooms and only two bathrooms above the deli. ⊠ *165 Main St.* ☎ *410/269–6737* ⊕ *www.chickandruths.com* ▭ *No credit cards.*

Where to Stay

$$$$ ▦ **Annapolis Marriott Waterfront.** You can practically fish from your room at the city's only waterfront hotel. Rooms have either balconies over the water or large windows with views of the harbor or the historic district. The outdoor bar by the harbor's edge is popular in nice weather. ⊠ *80 Compromise St., Historic Area, 21401* ☎ *410/268–7555 or 800/336–0072* 🖷 *410/269–5864* ⊕ *www.annapolismarriott.com* 🛏 *150 rooms* ↺ *Restaurant, in-room data ports, gym, boating, 2 bars, shop, laundry service, concierge, business services, meeting rooms, parking (fee), no-smoking rooms* ▭ *AE, D, DC, MC, V.*

$$$$ ▦ **The Annapolis Inn.** An extraordinarily elegant B&B, this circa 1770 house has richly colored rooms decorated in the formal style of the home's original era. The master suite has a sitting room and two fireplaces. Each suite has a king-size bed with luxury linens and a bathroom with hand showers, bidets, and heated towel holders and marble floors. From the third-floor suite's sundeck there's a close-up view of the domes of the Naval Academy Chapel and the state capitol and the harbor. Breakfast is a sumptuous three-course event served in the stately dining room. TVs are placed in the rooms on request. ⊠ *144 Prince George St., Historic Area, 21401* ☎ *410/295–5200* 🖷 *410/295–5201* ⊕ *www.annapolisinn.com* 🛏 *3 suites* ↺ *Dining room, in-room data ports, free parking; no kids, no smoking* ▭ *AE, MC, V* ⑩ *BP.*

$$$–$$$$ ▦ **Loews Annapolis Hotel.** Although its redbrick exterior blends with the city's 1700s architecture, the interior is airy, spacious, and modern. Guest rooms, decorated in a sailing theme, include coffeemakers and terry robes. A free hotel shuttle bus takes you anywhere you want to go in Annapolis, and a complimentary breakfast is served in the Breeze restaurant for concierge-level guests. ⊠ *126 West St., West Side, 21401* ☎ *410/263–7777 or 800/235–6397* 🖷 *410/263–0084* ⊕ *www.loewsannapolis.com* 🛏 *210 rooms, 7 suites* ↺ *2 restaurants, room service, in-room data ports, minibars, gym, hair salon, bar, laundry service, concierge, concierge floor, business services, meeting rooms, airport shuttle, parking (fee), no-smoking floors* ▭ *AE, D, DC, MC, V.*

$$$–$$$$ ▦ **O'Callaghan Hotel.** When this Irish-owned and -operated hotel opened in 2002, it was the city's first new downtown hotel in more than two

decades. Floor-length drapes and the lush, blue carpets flecked in gold colors were custom-made in Ireland (much of the attentive staff is from the Emerald Isle as well). Meeting rooms are named after counties in Ireland, and maps and pictures of the Old Country adorn the elegant guest rooms. The first-floor restaurant and bar overlooks West Street and carries a limited but fine selection of entrées. ☒ *174 West St., West Side, 21401* ☎ *410/263–7700* 🖷 *410/990–1400* ⊕ *www.ocallaghanhotels-us. com* ⇨ *120 rooms, 2 suites △ Restaurant, cable TV with movies and video games, Internet, health club, bar, laundry service, concierge, business services, meeting rooms, parking (fee)* ▭ *AE, D, DC, MC, V.*

$–$$$$ ▦ **Sheraton of Annapolis.** Next to Westfield Shoppingtown, and near numerous chain restaurants, this large Sheraton has a free hourly shuttle bus to and from downtown Annapolis. (Traffic and parking there can be difficult.) The lobby is outfitted with marble floors, fresh flowers and ferns, and two sitting areas among marble columns. The café is adjacent to the lobby. Rooms are furnished with blond woods, geometric carpeting, and burgundy-print bedspreads. ☒ *173 Jennifer Rd., I–97/Rte. 50 Area, 21401* ☎ *410/266–3131 or 888/627–8980* 🖷 *410/ 266–6247* ⊕ *www.sheraton.com/annapolis* ⇨ *196 rooms △ Café, room service, in-room data ports, indoor pool, gym, lobby lounge, business services, meeting rooms, free parking, no-smoking rooms* ▭ *AE, D, DC, MC, V.*

★ $$$ ▦ **Historic Inns of Annapolis.** Three 18th-century properties in the historic district are now grouped as one inn with registration for all three at the **Governor Calvert House.** Built in 1727, Calvert House is steps from the capitol building. Also on State Circle, **Robert Johnson House** was built for the Annapolis barber in 1772. The **Maryland Inn** on nearby Church Circle has some rooms that date back to the Revolutionary era. The Treaty of Paris Restaurant and two pubs serve all three inns. Guest rooms are individually decorated with antiques and reproductions; all have coffeemakers and hair dryers, and some have kitchenettes, sitting suites, or whirlpools. ☒ *58 State Circle, Historic Area, 21401* ☎ *410/263–2641 or 800/847–8882* 🖷 *410/268–3613* ⊕ *www. annapolisinns.com* ⇨ *110 rooms, 10 suites △ Restaurant, in-room data ports, some kitchenettes, health club, bar, 2 pubs, laundry service, concierge, business services, meeting rooms, parking (fee), no-smoking rooms* ▭ *AE, D, DC, MC, V.*

$$$ ▦ **William Page Inn.** Built in 1908, this dark-brown, cedar-shingle, wood-frame structure was the local Democratic party clubhouse for 50 years. Today its wraparound porch is furnished with Adirondack chairs. The third-floor suite, with dormer windows and a sloped ceiling, includes an Italian-marble bathroom with whirlpool. Breakfast is served in the common room. There's a two-night minimum for weekend stays. ☒ *8 Martin St., Historic Area, 21401* ☎ *410/626–1506 or 800/364–4160* ⊕ *www.williampageinn.com* ⇨ *4 rooms, 2 with shared bath, 1 suite △ Free parking, no-smoking rooms; no TV in some rooms* ▭ *MC, V* ⦿ *BP.*

$$–$$$ ▦ **Gibson's Lodgings.** Three detached houses from three decades—1780, 1890, and 1980—are operated together as a single inn. One of the houses' hallways is strikingly lined with mirrors. Guest rooms are furnished with pre-1900 antiques. One first-floor room, which has a private bath and porch, is designed for disabled access. Free parking in the courtyards is a big advantage in the heart of this small Colonial-era city (the houses are opposite the U.S. Naval Academy). Continental breakfast is served in the formal dining room of the 18th-century Patterson House. Some rooms have free Wi-Fi. ⊠ *110–114 Prince George St., Historic Area, 21401* ☎ *410/268–5555 or 877/330–0057* 🖶 *410/268– 2775* ⊕ *www.avmcyber.com/gibson* 🛏 *21 rooms, 4 with shared bath* ⚲ *Meeting rooms, free parking* ☐ *AE, MC, V* ℺ *CP.*

$–$$ ⌑ **Country Inn & Suites.** True to its name, a cozy, country mood, as well as the gentle aroma of potpourri, permeates this suburban hotel. Rooms all have standard chain-hotel decor, but a large fireplace, wooden floors, and overstuffed sofas make the lobby an inviting place to linger. Exterior windows, trimmed with shutters and latticework, look out at a wooded area or a shopping plaza. Within walking distance of Annapolis's largest mall, the hotel also has free shuttle that can take you to the historic district and to business parks. Four rooms have whirlpool tubs and two have fireplaces. ⊠ *2600 Housely Rd., I–97/Rte. 50 Area, 21401* ☎ *410/571–6700 or 800/456–4000* 🖶 *410/571–6777* ⊕ *www.countryinns.com* 🛏 *100 rooms* ⚲ *Microwaves, refrigerators, indoor pool, gym, laundry facilities, meeting rooms* ☐ *AE, D, DC, MC, V* ℺ *CP.*

$–$$ ⌑ **Hampton Inn and Suites.** A two-sided fireplace separates the check-in area from the lobby's bright and airy breakfast space. Just off I–97, this hotel is minutes from historic Annapolis. Guest rooms are traditional, but the spacious apartment-style suites have fully equipped kitchens. ⊠ *124 Womack Dr., I–97/Rte. 50 Area, 21401* ☎ *410/571–0200 or 800/426–7866* 🖶 *410/571–0333* ⊕ *www.hamptoninn.com* 🛏 *86 rooms, 31 suites* ⚲ *In-room data ports, pool, exercise equipment, billiards, shop, laundry facilities, laundry service, business services, meeting rooms* ☐ *AE, D, DC, MC, V* ℺ *BP.*

$–$$ ⌑ **Scotlaur Inn.** On the two floors above Chick and Ruth's Delly, rooms in this family-owned B&B are papered in pastel colonial prints. The high beds are topped with fluffy comforters and lots of pillows. Chandeliers in each room and marble floors in the private bathrooms bring this place a long way from its first days as a boardinghouse with only two bathrooms. Check-in as well as breakfast are done in the famous deli downstairs. ⊠ *165 Main St., Historic Area, 21401* ☎ *410/268–5665* 🖶 *410/ 269–6738* ⊕ *www.scotlaurinn.com* 🛏 *10 rooms with bath* ⚲ *Restaurant, cable TV, in-room VCRs, Internet* ☐ *MC, V* ℺ *CP.*

Nightlife & the Arts

Bars & Clubs

The lounge at **Harry Browne's** (⊠ 66 State Circle ☎ 410/263–4332) gives people something fun to do on Monday night: listen to live Irish music.

Middleton Tavern (⊠ City Dock ☎ 410/263–3323) presents local and regional acoustic musicians nightly at its Oyster Bar lounge. The Oyster Shooter—raw oysters served in a shot glass with vodka and cocktail sauce and washed down with beer—supposedly originated here. The upstairs piano bar is open on Friday and Saturday nights.

The **Rams Head Tavern on the Stage** (✉ 33 West St., Historic District ☎ 410/268–4545 ⊕ www.ramsheadtavern.com) hosts nationally known folk, rock, jazz, country, and bluegrass groups. Past performers include Lyle Lovett, Ralph Stanley, and Linda Thompson. Dinner combinations are available; the area is nonsmoking.

Music & Theater

Annapolis Summer Garden Theater (✉ 143 Compromise St., at Main St. ☎ 410/268–9212 ⊕ www.summergarden.com) stages a mix of musicals and plays outdoors (May–September), including occasional works by local playwrights. The **Colonial Players** (✉ 108 East St. ☎ 410/268–7373 ⊕ www.cplayers.com/pol.html) active since the 1940s, is the city's principal theater troupe.

Entertainment at the **Naval Academy** (☎ 410/293–2439 for schedules, 800/874–6289 for tickets) includes the Distinguished Artists Series, The Masqueraders (the Academy's theatrical club), chamber music recitals, and Glee Club concerts. **Naval Academy Band** (☎ 410/293–0263) concerts, many held outside during fair weather, are free.

Sports & the Outdoors

Sandy Point State Park (✉ 1100 E. College Pkwy., Rte. 50, 12 mi east of Annapolis ☎ 410/974–2149 ⊕ www.dnr.state.md.us) has beaches for fishing and swimming, 22 launching ramps for boats, rock jetties extending into the bay, and a fishing pier. Admission is about $5 per person or $3 a vehicle (depending on the season and day of the week) from April to October; from November to March admission is $3 per vehicle.

Participant Sports

BIKING The **Baltimore and Annapolis (B&A) Trail** (✉ Boulters Way, Arnold ☎ 410/222–6244 ⊕ www.dnr.state.md.us/greenways/statewidetrails.html) runs through 13 mi of farmland and forests as well as urban and suburban neighborhoods, from Annapolis to Glen Burnie. It follows the old Baltimore and Annapolis Railroad and is linked directly to the 12½ mi trail encircling Baltimore-Washington International Airport. The trail is open sunrise to sunset to hikers, bikers, runners, and rollerbladers. Access to the northern end of the trail is via Dorsey Road off I–97 Exit 15 near Friendship Park. Parking there is free but limited.

Pedal Pushers Bike Shop (✉ 546 Baltimore and Annapolis Blvd., Rte. 648, Severna Park ☎ 410/544–2323) rents bikes for the B&A Trail.

FISHING **Anglers** (✉ 1456 Whitehall Rd. ☎ 410/757–3442) sells equipment for archery and hunting as well as for fresh- and saltwater fishing. Anglers is also a full-service Orvis fly-fishing dealer.

SAILING **Annapolis Sailing School** (✉ 601 6th St. ☎ 800/638–9192 or 410/267–7205 ⊕ www.annapolissailing.com) bills itself as America's oldest and largest sailing school. The inexperienced can take a two-hour basic lesson. In addition, live-aboard, cruising, and advanced-sailing programs are available, as are boat rentals.

Womanship (✉ 137 Conduit St. ☎ 410/267–6661 or 800/342–9295 ⊕ www.womanship.com) is a sailing school with programs for girls (ages 12–17), for mother/daughter partners, for couples, and for family groups. Classes can be custom designed for special needs or desires. Men are welcome to take classes as half of a couple or as part of a group.

Spectator Sports

The teams of the **United States Naval Academy Athletic Association (NAAA)** (☎ 800/874–6289 ticket office ⊕ www.navysports.com) compete in about 20 varsity sports, most notably football. The team plays home games in the fall at the Navy–Marine Corps Stadium on Rowe Boulevard in Annapolis.

BOAT RACES **Annapolis Yacht Club** (☎ 410/263–9279 ⊕ www.annapolisyc.com) sponsors sailboat races at 6 PM each Wednesday from mid-May through early September in Annapolis Harbor, starting at the Eastport bridge.

JOUSTING For more than 40 years the **Amateur Jousting Club of Maryland** (⊕ ajc. psyberia.com) has been providing details on the state sport's tournaments and events, which take place from April through November in rural areas like southern Maryland.

Shopping

Along Maryland Avenue as well as on Main Street in downtown Annapolis you'll find antiques and fine art, fashions, arts and crafts, home furnishing, and gifts and souvenirs as well as nautical clothing and other necessities for seasoned salts and would-be sailors alike.

A destination in itself, the **Arundel Mills** (✉ 7000 Arundel Mills Circle, Hanover ☎ 410/540–5100) shopping mall holds more than 200 well-known retailers and eateries, including Ann Taylor Loft, Kenneth Cole, Bass Pro Shops, and T. J. Maxx. Many of the shops are outlets with great bargains, making the 40-minute trip from Annapolis well worth it for some.

Art & Antiques

Dealers in fine antiques and art abound along Annapolis's "other main street," Maryland Avenue. At **The Annapolis Pottery** (✉ 40 State Circle ☎ 410/268–6153) you can actually watch the potters at work as you browse the store filled with their wares. Other shops are in West Annapolis. **Annapolis Antique Gallery** (✉ 2009 West St. ☎ 410/266–0635) is a consortium of 35–40 dealers with an inventory that includes Victorian and art deco pieces. **Ron Snyder Antiques** (✉ 2011 West St. ☎ 410/ 266–5452) specializes in 18th- and 19th-century American furniture displayed in seven tastefully decorated rooms.

Clothing

Inside the Annapolis Marriott Waterfront, **Pussers Company Store** (✉ 80 Compromise St. ☎ 410/268–7555) is part of a small chain originating in another big sailing destination, the British Virgin Islands. The store peddles Pussers Rum merchandise as well as seasonal chutneys, nautical knickknacks, purses, and sundries, but the main product here is nautical clothing—raffia hats, khaki shorts, and pin-stripe shirts with collars—that will have you looking the part of a sailor.

CALVERT COUNTY

The long, narrow peninsula between the Patuxent River and the Chesapeake Bay is Calvert County, an area that has not yet been completely overrun by tourism. Two principal routes—Route 2 from Annapolis and Route 4 from Washington, D.C.—merge near Sunderland and continue on together to the county's southern tip. Exploring the Bayside and riverside communities to either side of the highway, as well as the inland sites and attractions, will immerse you quickly in the tangible history and heritage of agriculture and fishing.

North Beach

31 mi south of Annapolis, via Rte. 2, Rte. 260, and Rte. 261.

In some ways a quieter, more residential extension of Chesapeake Beach, North Beach has a fishing pier and a quiet boardwalk. When it was founded in 1900, it was a resort for family summer vacations. Amusement centers, bingo halls, theaters, and bathhouses defined the town until the Great Depression. Then, in 1933, a hurricane ravaged the beach and destroyed many of its buildings. Post-WWII programs sponsored by the Veterans Administration facilitated a building boom, turning North Beach into a year-round community.

Where to Eat

$–$$ ✕ **Neptune's.** Modest Neptune's claims of preparing "the world's best mussels" rings true with many, making the trip to this tiny town just north of Chesapeake Beach worthwhile. Attached to the small bar, a glass-enclosed dining room with a brick floor is a friendly, informal spot to dig in to its signature dish. Also on the menu are also seafood pastas, burgers, and cuts of Angus beef. ⊠ *8800 Chesapeake Ave., at 1st St.* ☎ *410/257–7899* ▤ *AE, D, MC, V.*

Chesapeake Beach

⑮ *1 mi south of North Beach, via Rte. 261, 32 mi south of Annapolis, via Rte. 2, Rte. 260, and Rte. 261.*

This charming little town beside the Bay was founded at the close of the 19th century as a resort to rival those along the French Riviera. It was served by steamboats from Baltimore and by a railroad from Washington, D.C. Steamboat service diminished over time and the railroad failed in 1935, but the town survived as private automobiles became more readily available. It boomed again in 1948 with the legalization of slot machines, although they lasted only 20 years. Today Chesapeake Beach is once again staging a tourism comeback with the addition of a water park and a new waterfront hotel.

The **Chesapeake Bay Railway Museum,** housed in the railroad's 1898 trackside terminus, provides memorable glimpses of the onetime resort's turn-of-the-20th-century glory days. Among its exhibits are a glass-en-

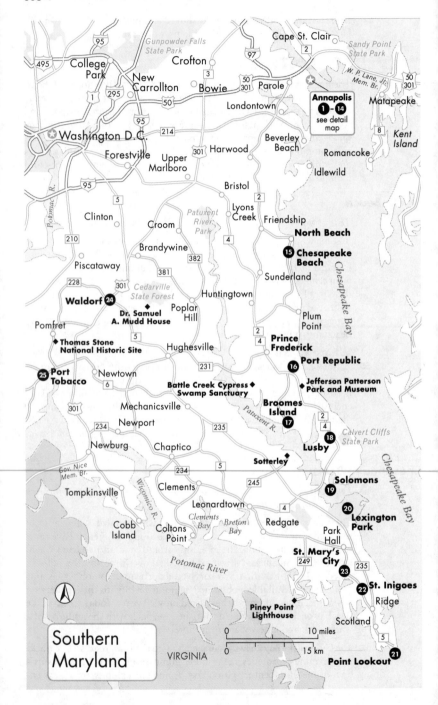

95
495
College
Park
New
Carrollton
295
1
Washington D.C.
95
Forestville
Gunpowder Falls
State Park
Crofton
97
3
50
301
Bowie
Parole
Londontown
214
301
Harwood
Upper
Marlboro
Bristol
Cape St. Clair
2
Sandy Point
State Park
W. P. Lane, Jr.
Mem. Br.
50
301
Annapolis
1 - **14**
see detail
map
Matapeake
8
Kent
Island
Beverley
Beach
Romancoke
Idlewild

5
Clinton
Croom
Patuxent
River
Park
Lyons
Creek
Friendship
210
Piscataway
Brandywine
382
381
Cedarville
State Forest
Huntingtown
Poplar
Hill
North Beach
15 Chesapeake
Beach
Sunderland
Plum
Point
Chesapeake Bay

228
301
Waldorf **24**
Dr. Samuel
A. Mudd House
5
Pomfret
◆Thomas Stone
National Historic Site
Hughesville
231
2
4
**Prince
Frederick**
Port Republic
16
◆ Jefferson Patterson
Park and Museum

25 Port
Tobacco
Newtown
6
301
Mechanicsville
234
Newport
Newburg
Chaptico
235
Battle Creek Cypress ◆
Swamp Sanctuary
Patuxent R.
**Broomes
Island**
17
2
4
Lusby
18
Calvert Cliffs
State Park
Chesapeake Bay

Gov. Nice
Mem. Br.
Tompkinsville
Wicomico R.
234
Clements
5
Leonardtown
245
Redgate
4
Sotterley
Solomons
19
20
Lexington
Park

Cobb
Island
Clements
Bay
Coltons
Point
Breton
Bay
Park
Hall
**St. Mary's
City**
249
23
235
22 St. Inigoes
Ridge

Potomac River

Piney Point
Lighthouse
Scotland
5

Southern
Maryland

VIRGINIA

0   10 miles
0   15 km

Point Lookout
21

closed model of the town of Chesapeake Beach, a gleaming, black Ford Model T that once carried guests from the station to their hotels, a hand-carved horse from the magnificent carousel, and a slot machine as well as photos of early vacationers. One of the railroad's passenger cars rests nearby. ⊠ *4155 Mears Ave., Rte. 261* ☎ *410/257–3892* 💲 *Free* ☉ *May–Sept., daily 1–4; Apr. and Oct., weekends 1–4 and by appt.*

Families make a day of it at **Chesapeake Beach Water Park** (⊠ Gordon Stinnett Ave., at Rte. 261 ☎410/257–1404), which has a children's pool, beach, and many slides. The park is open from Memorial Day until the first day of school. Admission is $15–$17.

Where to Stay & Eat

$$–$$$ ✕ **Rod 'n' Reel.** This family-owned restaurant opened optimistically in 1936, the year after the demise of the railroad from Washington. Since then it has remained synonymous with superb seafood. Now connected to the Chesapeake Beach Hotel by a large canopy, its bayside location still provides stunning views. The extensive menu includes succulent southern Maryland specialties such as rockfish stuffed with crab imperial, fried oysters, and the region's ubiquitous crab cakes. ⊠ *Rte. 261 and Mears Ave.* ☎ *410/257–2735 or 877/763–6733* ⊕ *www.rodnreelinc.com* 🗃 *AE, D, MC, V.*

★ **$–$$$** ✕🏨 **The Chesapeake Beach Hotel.** Opened in 2004, this luxury hotel and spa is a key part of the revitalization of the town's tourism business. The public spaces pay homage to the beachfront community's history. A mural in the lobby depicts the old roller coaster that once thrilled vacationers, and framed photographs line the corridors, tracing the town's changes from its Victorian heyday to the present. The whitewashed oak furniture and sand-colored walls give the rooms a elegant yet beachy style. The hotel was built right on the water's edge, and its suites and deluxe rooms have balconies that seem to hang over the Bay. There's also a fishing charter company on the premises. ⊠ *4165 Mears Ave.* ☎ *410/257–5596 or 301/855–0096* ⊕ *www.chesapeakebeachhotelspa. com* 🛏 *72 rooms, 6 suites* ⟡ *3 restaurants, café, in-room data ports, indoor pool, gym, sauna, spa, boating, fishing, shop, video game room, Internet, business services, meeting room, free parking* ☉❘ *BP* 🗃 *AE, D, DC, MC, V.*

Port Republic

⑯ *17 mi south of Chesapeake Beach.*

Christ Episcopal Church traces its origins to 1672, when a log-cabin church stood at the site. Its 1772 brick replacement, coated with plaster, is notable for its biblical garden, planted with species mentioned in the scriptures. Port Republic School No. 7 is on the church's property. Since immediately after the Civil War the grounds have been a venue for jousting (Maryland's state sport) on the last Saturday in August. ⊠ *3090 Broomes Island Rd., Rte. 264* ☎ *410/586–0565* 💲 *Free* ☉ *Daily dawn–dusk.*

Port Republic School No. 7, a classic one-room schoolhouse built in the 1880s, looks for all the world as if today's lesson could begin any minute. Here, you can find a restored classroom with archetypal desks, inkwells, and a school bell. Until 1932 a single teacher taught children in seven grades here. ⊠ *3100 Broomes Island Rd., Rte. 264* ☎ *410/ 586–0482* 🖃 *Free* ☉ *Memorial Day–Labor Day, Sun. 2–4 and by appt.*

With the northernmost naturally occurring stand of bald cypress trees in the United States, the 100-acre **Battle Creek Cypress Swamp Sanctuary** provides close-up looks at the forest primeval. A ¼-mi elevated board-walk at the bottom of a steep but sturdy column of steps gives you a good vantage point to see the swamp, thick with 100-foot trees that are more than 1,000 years old. Guides at the nature center can alert you to the seasonal permutations of the vegetation and the doings of squirrels, owls, and other wildlife. Indoor exhibits focus on the area's natural and cultural history. The swamp is about 5 mi west of Port Republic. ⊠ *Sixes Rd., Rte. 506, Prince Frederick* ☎ *410/535–5327* ⊕ *www.calvertparks. org* 🖃 *Free* ☉ *Tues.–Sat. 10–4:30, Sun. 1–4:30.*

en route | Behind 2½ mi of scenic Patuxent riverfront stretch 544 acres of woods and farmland. The 70-odd archaeological sites have yielded evidence of 9,000 years of human habitation—from prehistory on through to Colonial times. At the **Jefferson Patterson Park and Museum,** you can follow an archaeology trail to inspect artifacts of the successive hunter-gatherer, early agricultural, and plantation societies that once roamed and settled this land. Displays include primitive knives and axes, fragments of Native American pottery, and Colonial glassware. Stroll along the nature trails to take a look at wildlife, antique agricultural equipment, and fields of crops. The park is 2 mi south of Port Republic. ⊠ *10115 Mackall Rd., Rte. 265, St. Leonard* ☎ *410/586–8500* ⊕ *www.jefpat.org* 🖃 *Free* ☉ *Mid-Apr.–mid-Oct., Wed.–Sun. 10–5.*

Broomes Island

⑰ *7 mi south of Port Republic, via Rte. 264.*

An area without specific boundaries, Broomes is not even an island per se, except during a very high tide or in a strong storm. It's made up of little more than a few houses and stores, a post office, and a church. This little area at the mouth of Island Creek is a portrait of a water-de-pendent community amid change: weather-beaten structures of its past now mingle with new, expensive waterfront homes.

Where to Eat

★ **$–$$** ✕ **Stoney's Seafood House.** Popular with boaters who tie right up to the dock, this restaurant overlooking Island Creek has one dining room that actually juts out over the water and another on higher ground with great views from its floor-to-ceiling windows. There's also ample seating—and a tiki bar—outside. Stoney's hefty crab cakes are made with plenty of back fin meat and little filler. Oyster sandwiches and Stoney's Steamer—handpicked selections of fresh seafood—are also good choices. The intense, house-made desserts, such as the strawberry shortcake and the Snickers pie, are not for the faint of heart. ⊠ *Oyster House Rd.* ☎ *410/586–1888* 🖃 *AE, D, MC, V* ⊘ *Closed Nov.–early Mar.*

Lusby

🔞 *12 mi southeach of Broomes Island.*

Ⓒ Like its better known neighbor Calvert Cliffs State Park, **Flag Ponds Nature Park** has spectacular views of the cliffs, but with just a short stroll to the beach, this county park is the more accessible of the two. Until the 1950s the area was a busy fishery, and some of the buildings from that era still stand. Today, it beckons with bathhouses, a fishing pier, 3 mi of gently graded hiking trails, observation decks at two ponds, a boardwalk through wetlands, and indoor wildlife exhibits. Soaring cliffs, flat marshland, and wildflowers (including the Blue Flag Iris, for which the park is named) provide stunning contrasts. A shark's tooth dating back 10–20 million years ago is the big prize in a fossil hunt on the beach, one of the park's most popular activities. ⊠ *Rte. 2/4* ☎ *410/586–1477* ⊕ *www.calvertparks.org* 🖃 *$6 per vehicle Apr.–Oct.; $3 per vehicle Nov.–Mar.* ⊘ *Memorial Day–Labor Day, weekdays 9–6, weekends 9–8; Labor Day–Memorial Day, weekends 9–5.*

Nightlife & the Arts

For a taste of the tropics *and* the South Pacific along St. Leonard's Creek, wet your lips with an umbrella-topped cocktail at **Vera's White Sands** (⊠ Rte. 4, Lusby ☎ 410/586–1182), a celebration of owner Vera Freeman's world travels and exotic tastes. For years, clad in her trademark long gowns and feather boas, she's taken her place at the piano and entertained diners and bar patrons in her tiki bar. Open May through October, Vera's maintains a swimming pool that is, as Vera says, "for all the fun times" and a deepwater (15-feet) marina with 84 slips.

Solomons

🔞 *8 mi south of Lusby.*

On the tip of the peninsula, Solomons is where the Patuxent empties into the Chesapeake. The town has become a popular getaway for sailors, boaters, and affluent professionals. But it's still a laid-back waterfront town—at least when compared with, say, Annapolis or St. Michaels. Several excellent boatyards and marinas cater to powerboaters and sailors, with nautical services from the simplest to the most sophisticated. There are several antiques, book, gift, and specialty shops and galleries side by side, parallel to the boardwalk. Wherever you go, stunning views surround you at nearly every turn.

Ⓒ The **Calvert Marine Museum** is concerned with the history of both the river
FodorśChoice and the Bay. The bright, spacious exhibition hall contains models and
★ life-size examples of historically significant types of working and pleasure boats. A grouping of 17 tanks holds examples of marine life; the river otters here are often at play. The jaws of a white shark open above an exhibit on fossils, and children can sift through sharks' teeth and other specimens and examine them under microscopes. Outside, small craft of different periods are on display in a waterside shed, and on many sum-

mer afternoons you can take a cruise aboard a converted 1899 bugeye sailboat, the *William B. Tennison*. There's also a restored hexagonal lighthouse from 1883 that's perched like an insect on six slender legs. The **J. C. Lore & Sons Oyster House** (☉ June–Aug., daily 1–4:30, May and Sept., weekends 1–4:30), operated by the museum, is a processing plant built in 1934 that's now a museum of the local seafood industries. This National Historic Landmark displays the tools used by oystermen, crabbers, and fishermen. ✉ *Rte. 2 at Solomons Island Rd.* ☎ *410/326–2042, 410/326–8217 weekends* ⊕ *www.calvertmarinemuseum.com* ✇ *$7* ☉ *Daily 10–5.*

A world-class sculpture and botanical venue, **Annmarie Garden on St. John** is a 30-acre property on the St. John Creek. The sculptural art is by artists both local and from around the world. One of the more intriguing installations is a series of 13 "Talking Benches." Each tells an ecological story by depicting a plant that grows in southern Maryland, including dogwood, loblolly pines, papaw trees, and tobacco. Smooth, user-friendly pathways curve through the grounds. Little here is off-limits, and picnickers are welcome to settle in virtually anywhere. Be sure to visit the mosaic-filled rest rooms. ✉ *Dowell Rd.* ☎ *410/326–4640* ⊕ *www.annmariegarden.org* ✇ *Free* ☉ *Daily 9–5.*

Where to Stay & Eat

$$–$$$ 🍽 **DiGiovanni's Dock of the Bay.** It's rare to be able to enjoy elegant waterside dining and professional service at budget prices. The chef creates succulent Italian dishes using fresh herbs and spices. The *cacciucco* (seafood soup) alone is worth a special trip, as is the homemade crab-stuffed ravioli. A folk singer entertains on Wednesdays. ✉ *14556 Solomons Island Rd.* ☎ *410/394–6400* ▤ *AE, D, MC, V* ☉ *Closed Sunday. in Jan.–May. No lunch.*

$$–$$$ 🍽 **Back Creek Inn.** The bar is a reproduction of an oyster boat, and fishing nets and pictures of old Solomons set the mood. Gas lanterns illuminate the polished wood tables and the exposed ceiling beams. Diners on the first floor have a view of Solomons Harbor on Back Creek; on the second floor, patrons look onto the creek toward the Patuxent River. The catch of the day is frequently sautéed, and the chef's crab cakes' recipe is closely guarded. On weekends in the warmer months you can order lighter fare on the partially covered "quarterdeck." ✉ *14636 Solomons Island Rd.* ☎ *410/326–2444* ⊕ *www.lighthouse-inn.com* ▤ *AE, D, DC, MC, V* ☉ *No lunch.*

★ $–$$$ 🏨 **Back Creek Inn.** Built for a waterman in 1880, this blue wood-frame house sits in a residential neighborhood on well-tended grounds at the edge of Back Creek. You can soak in the open-air hot tub or lounge on the deck next to a beautiful perennial garden. Three rooms have water views, and one opens onto the garden. Breakfast is served in the dining room or by the lily pond. ✉ *Calvert and Alexander Sts., 20688* ☎ *410/326–2022* 🖷 *410/326–2946* ⊕ *www.bbonline.com/md/backcreek* ⇱ *4 rooms, 2 suites, 1 cottage* ⚷ *Dining room, cable TV, Internet, outdoor hot tub, bicycles, no-smoking rooms; no kids under 12* ▤ *MC, V* ☉ *Closed mid-Dec.–early Jan.* ⑩ *BP.*

$–$$$ 🏨 **Holiday Inn Select Conference Center and Marina.** In this five-story waterfront hotel, every guest room has a water view (if you count the swimming pool); rooms look onto the cove, the open creek, or the courtyard. Whirlpools are available in some suites. Designed to accommodate conventions and meetings business, the hotel is often heavily booked, so try to reserve early. ✉ *155 Holiday Dr., Box 1099, 20688* ☎ *410/326–6311 or 800/356–2009* 🖷 *410/326–1069* ⊕ *www.solomonsmd.hiselect.com* 🖙 *276 rooms, 50 suites* ♿ *Restaurant, room service, in-room data ports, some kitchenettes, 2 tennis courts, pool, gym, sauna, volleyball, 2 bars, shop, laundry facilities, Internet, business services, meeting rooms, no-smoking rooms* 🖃 *AE, D, DC, MC, V.*

ST. MARY'S COUNTY

"Just at the mouth of the river, we observed the natives in arms. That night, fires blazed through the whole country and since they had never seen such a large ship, messengers were sent in all directions, who reported that a 'canoe' like an island had come with as many as there were trees in the woods."—Father Andrew White, recounting the arrival of the *Ark* and the *Dove* in 1634.

Father White arrived in the New World in 1634 as a member of Lord Baltimore's contingent of 140 colonists. The two "canoes" the Native Americans spotted were the tiny sailing vessels that had just crossed the Atlantic to reach the southernmost tip of Maryland's western shore, where the Potomac River meets the Chesapeake Bay. The peninsula between the Potomac and the Patuxent rivers is today St. Mary's County, easily one of the state's most beautiful regions, and gradually attracting development because of its easy access to Washington, D.C., to the north.

Like so much of Maryland south of Annapolis and Washington, many scenic drives throughout St. Mary's County bring together charming inland and waterside towns and historic sites. Hearty food and homey places to stay are easy to find.

Lexington Park

20 *9 mi southeast of Solomons, 68 mi south of Annapolis, via Rte. 2/4 to Rte. 235.*

The **Patuxent Naval Air Museum** houses items from the research, development, test, and evaluation of naval aircraft. Nineteen vintage aircraft are displayed outside. Inside, you can climb into a cockpit trainer and view some of the more improbable creations that failed to passed muster, such as the Goodyear "Inflatoplane." ✉ *Patuxent River Naval Air Station, Rte. 235, Three Notch Rd.* ☎ *301/863–7418* ⊕ *www.paxmuseum.com* 🖃 *Free* ☼ *Tues.–Sun. 10–5.*

The St. Mary's River, which once powered **Historic Cecil's Old Mill,** is just a trickle in this area now, so the water wheel now runs on electricity. Today, the building, which dates to 1900, contains an artist co-op as well as a small display of artifacts and photographs of the mill. In keeping with the setting, most of the arts and crafts on sale are quaint and rustic: rural scenes painted on circular saw blades or lighthouses on driftwood, crocheted placemats, and colorful quilts. ✉ *Indian Bridge Rd.*

off Rte. 5, Great Mills ☎ *301/994–1510* ⊙ *Mar.–Oct., Thurs.–Sat. 10–5, Sun. 11–5; Nov.–Dec., Mon.–Sat. 10–5, Sun. 11–5.*

<table>
<tr><td>

off the
beaten
path

</td><td>

SOTTERLEY – The distinguished house on the grounds of this 18th-century plantation is the earliest known (1717) post-in-ground structure in the United States: in place of a foundation, cedar timbers driven straight into the ground support it. The house is a sampler of architectural styles and interior design from the last two centuries. On the grounds of this National Historic Landmark are other buildings from the 18th through early 20th centuries, including a Colonial customs warehouse, a smokehouse, a "necessary" (an outhouse), and a restored slave cabin. ⊠ *Rte. 245 near Hollywood, 12 mi north of Lexington Park via Rte. 235 and Rte. 245* ☎ *301/ 373–2280* ⊕ *www.sotterley.com* 💲 *$7* ⊙ *May–Oct., Tues.–Sat. 10–4, Sun. noon–4. Grounds open year-round.*

</td></tr>
</table>

Where to Eat

$$–$$$$ ✕ **The Roost.** Like the place itself, food at the Roost is homey but still elegant. A large fireplace dominates the spacious dining room, which is accented by green floral wallpaper, Depression-era chandeliers, and ladder-back chairs. The adjacent bar holds a collection of Navy memorabilia. Oyster stew (in season), grilled lamb chops, and broiled rainbow trout are on the regular menu, but around the holidays look for the region's signature dish, stuffed ham. Steaming apple dumplings topped with a dollop of ice cream are a treat year-round. ⊠ *198 Great Mills Rd.* ☎ *301/863–5051* 🗐 *AE, MC, V.*

Point Lookout

㉑ *20 mi south of Lexington Park, 88 mi south of Annapolis, via Rte. 2/ 4 and Rte. 235 to Rte. 5.*

When Father Andrew White came to Point Lookout and saw the Potomac at its side, he mused that the Thames was a mere rivulet in comparison. Instead of being overwhelmed by the wildness of the New World, he observed that "fine groves of trees appear . . . growing in intervals as if planted by the hand of man."

On the approach to **Point Lookout State Park,** two memorial obelisks remind travelers of the dark history of this starkly alluring point of land. Beginning in 1863, a Union prison stood at the farthest tip of the peninsula, just across the Potomac from Confederate Virginia. During those last two years of the conflict, nearly 4,000 of the 50,000 Confederate soldiers here died because of disease and poor conditions. All that remains of the prison are some earthen fortifications, partially rebuilt and known as Fort Lincoln, with markers noting the sites of hospitals and other buildings. A small museum supplies some of the details. The 500-acre state park has boating facilities, nature trails, and a beach for swimming. The RV campground, with hook-ups, is open year-round; tent camping facilities close from early November through late March. ⊠ *Rte. 5* ☎ *301/872–5688* ⊕ *www.dnr.state.md.us* 💲 *Weekends and holidays May–Sept. $5 per person, all other times $3 per vehicle* ⊙ *Year-round, daily 6 AM–sunset.*

Where to Stay & Eat

$–$$$ ✕ **Spinnakers Restaurant at Point Lookout Marina.** This restaurant has brought the best of southern Maryland to the shores of Smith Creek. Specialties include grilled rockfish, Kansas City steaks, and excellent crab cakes. Subdued lighting, fresh flowers, and linen-covered tables make it an elegant, casual space. The enthusiastic staff makes dining here a comfortable experience. Sunday brunch is a local tradition. ⊠ *Point Lookout Marina, 32 Millers Wharf Rd., Ridge* ☎ *301/872–4340* ▭ *AE, D, DC, MC, V* ⊗ *Closed Jan.–mid-Feb.*

¢–$ ▦ **St. Michael's Manor & Vineyard.** Joe and Nancy Dick have run their B&B on Long Neck Creek since the early 1980s—and they've harvested grapes from their 3 acres of vines nearly as long as that. Rooms, which overlook the water, are decorated with antiques and family heirlooms, the beds covered with hand-sewn quilts. There's a working fireplace at each end of the public space in the Federal-style main building. Nancy's eggs Benedict are always popular, and her airy Austrian puff pancakes over fresh apples or peaches are delicious. Upon arrival guests are invited to sample wine from the vineyards. ⊠ *50200 St. Michael's Manor Way, Scotland 20687* ☎ *301/872–4025* ⊕ *www.stmichaels-manor.com* ⊸ *4 rooms, 3 with shared bath* ⚲ *Pool, bicycles, no smoking* ▭ *No credit cards* ⊗ *Closed Nov.–mid Feb.* ◉ *BP.*

Sports & the Outdoors

Scheibel's (⊠ Wynne Rd., Ridge ☎ 301/872–5185) will arrange fishing charters.

St. Inigoes

㉒ *9 mi northwest of Point Lookout, via Rte. 5, 77 mi south of Annapolis.*

St. Ignatius Church, built in 1758, is all that survives of the pre-Revolutionary plantation of St. Inigoes. A church dating from the 1630s had stood where this church, named for the founder of the Jesuits, stands now; the graveyard is one of the oldest in the United States. Several veterans of the Revolution are buried here, alongside Jesuit priests who served here. To see inside the church, ask for the key at the sentry box of the naval installation next door. ⊠ *Villa Rd. off Rte. 5, St. Inigoes* ☎ *301/872–5590* ▱ *Free.*

St. Mary's City

㉓ *73 mi south of Annapolis, via Rte. 2/4 to Rte. 235 to Rte. 5 North.*

An intrepid group of 140 English settlers sailed the *Ark* and the *Dove* up the Potomac and into one of its tributaries, the St. Mary's River. About halfway up, on an east bank, they founded St. Mary's City, the fourth permanent settlement in British North America and eventually the first (albeit short-lived) capital of Maryland.

Long before a Constitution or a Bill of Rights, the first law of religious tolerance in the New World was enacted in St. Mary's City, guaranteeing the freedom to practice whatever religion one chose. Here, too, almost three centuries before American women achieved suffrage, Mistress Margaret Brent challenged the status quo and requested the right to vote (she didn't get it). The settlement served as Maryland's capital city until 1695, when the legislature moved to Annapolis and the county seat moved to Leonardtown. St. Mary's City virtually vanished, its existence acknowledged only in historical novels and textbooks. Today, the city is home to a living history park and a small liberal arts college that share its name. St. Mary's College of Maryland, which dates to 1840, functions as the cultural center for the surrounding community.

In 1934, a first step in the rebirth of St. Mary's was taken. In commemoration of the 300th anniversary of Maryland, the Colony's imposing State House, originally built in 1676, was reconstructed. In the early 1970s, a vast archaeological-reconstruction program began in earnest, a project that has revealed nearly 200 individual sites. The entire 800-plus acres have become a living-history museum and archaeological park called **Historic St. Mary's City.**

★ ☾

The historic complex includes several notable reconstructions and reproductions of buildings. The **State House of 1676,** like its larger and grander counterpart in Williamsburg, has an upper and a lower chamber for the corresponding houses of Parliament. This 1934 reproduction is based on court documents from the period; the original was dismantled in 1829, with many of the bricks used for Trinity Church nearby. The small square-rigged ship, *Maryland Dove,* docked behind the State House, is an accurate replica of one of the two vessels that conveyed the original settlers from England. The nearby **Farthing's Ordinary** is a reconstructed inn.

Godiah Spray Tobacco Plantation depicts life on a 17th-century tobacco farm in the Maryland wilderness. Interpreters portray the Spray family—the real family lived about 20 mi away—and its indentured servants, enlisting passive onlookers in such household chores as cooking and gardening or in working the tobacco field. The buildings, including the main dwelling house and outbuildings, were built with period tools and techniques.

Throughout Historic St. Mary's City, you're encouraged to explore other sites and exhibits-in-progress, including the town center, the location of the first Catholic church in the English Colonies, a "victualing" and lodging house, and the woodland Native American hamlet. Historic interpreters in costume—and in character—add realism to the experience. ⊠ *Rte. 5* ☎ *240/895–4990 or 800/762–1634* ⊕ *www. stmaryscity.org* 🎫 *$7.50* ☾ *Call for exhibit hours.*

off the
beaten
path

PINEY POINT LIGHTHOUSE – The first permanent lighthouse constructed on the Potomac River is now the center of a small, 6-acre park. The park's museum is closed due to damage from Hurricane Isabel, but the lighthouse is open on weekends as is the museum store. The grounds, which are free, have a boardwalk, pier, and picnic tables. ⊠ *Lighthouse Rd., Piney Point* ☎ *301/769–2222* ⊕ *www.co.saint-marys.md.us/recreate/museums* 🎫 *$3* ☾ *Weekends noon–5.*

Where to Stay & Eat

★ $–$$$ ✕⊡ **Brome-Howard Inn.** Set on 30 acres of farmland, this 19th-century farmhouse provides a trip through time to life on a tobacco plantation. Rooms are decorated with original family furnishings. Relax on one of the big outdoor porches or patios and watch the lazy St. Mary's River nearby. In the evening, there are two candlelit dining rooms—the foyer or the formal parlor. Five miles of hiking trails lead to St. Mary's City, and the inn has bikes for the use of guests. The restaurant ($$–$$$) specializes in seafood and occasionally serves such exotic items as bison, ostrich, or shark. ⊠ *18281 Rosecroft Rd., 20686* ☎ *301/866–0656* 📠 *301/866–9660* ⊕ *www.bromehowardinn.com* ⤴ *3 rooms, 1 suite* ♿ *Restaurant, bicycles, hiking, library* ⊟ *AE, MC, V* ⊚| *BP.*

CHARLES COUNTY

To the north of St. Mary's County and about 35 mi southwest of Annapolis, relatively rural Charles County is flanked on its west by the Potomac River's big bend as it flows south from Washington, D.C. In what used to be tobacco country, less-traveled county and state roads crisscross the pristine countryside dotted with depot towns, riverfront ports-of-call, wildlife preservation centers, and unsung historical sites.

Waldorf

㉔ *40 mi south of Annapolis on Rte. 301.*

The **American Indian Cultural Center and Piscataway Indian Museum** strives to be a source for information on the art and culture of the Piscataway Native Americans; the museum emphasizes the life of Maryland's indigenous people prior to the 17th century. Artifacts, tools, and weapons are on display, and there's a full-scale reproduction of a traditional longhouse. ⊠ *16816 Country La.* ☎ *301/372–1932* ⊕ *www.piscatawayindians.org* 🎟 *$3* ⊙ *Sun. 11–4; other times by appt. only.*

The **Dr. Samuel A. Mudd House** is where John Wilkes Booth ended up at 4 AM on Good Friday, 1865, his leg broken after having leaped from the presidential box at Ford's Theater. Most likely, the 32-year-old Dr. Mudd had no idea his patient was wanted for the assassination of Abraham Lincoln. Nonetheless, Mudd was convicted of aiding a fugitive and sentenced to life in prison. (President Andrew Jackson pardoned him in 1869.) Today the two-story house, set on 10 rolling acres, looks as if the doctor is still in. The dark purple couch where Mudd examined Booth remains in the downstairs parlor, 18th-century family pieces fill the rooms, and the doctor's crude instruments are displayed. There's a 30-minute guided tour of the house, an exhibit building, and Mudd's original tombstone. ⊠ *14940 Hoffman Rd.* ☎ *301/645–6870* ⊕ *www.somd. lib.md.us/MUSEUMS/Mudd.htm* 🎟 *$4* ⊙ *Late Mar.–late Nov., Wed. and weekends 11–4.*

Port Tobacco

㉕ *11 mi southwest via Rte. 301 and Rte. 6 from Waldorf.*

One of the oldest communities in the East, Port Tobacco first existed as the Native American settlement of "Potopaco." (The similarity between this Native American name—meaning "the jutting of water inland"—and the name for the plant that was to become a cornerstone of the region's economy—is purely coincidental.) Potopaco was colonized by the English in 1634, and later in the century emerged as the major seaport of Port Tobacco. The Historic District includes the reconstructed early-19th-century courthouse; Catslide House, one of the area's four surviving 18th-century homes; and a restored one-room schoolhouse, dating to 1876 and used as such until 1953.

★ **Thomas Stone National Historic Site,** built in the 1770s, was the Charles County home of Thomas Stone, one of four Maryland signers of the Declaration of Independence. It has been painstakingly rebuilt after a devastating fire left it a shell in the late 1970s. The restoration re-created the distinctive five-part Georgian house inside and out. The two-story main plantation house is linked to the two wings and adjoining hallways in an arc rather than a straight line. All the rooms have exquisite details, such as built-in cabinets, elaborate moldings, a table set in fine china, gilded mirrors, and a harpsichord. The house and family grave site are just a short stroll from the parking lot and visitors center, where you can examine a model of the house or watch a video about Stone. ⊠ *6655 Rose Hill Rd., between Rtes. 6 and 225, 4 mi west of La Plata* ☎ *301/392–1776* ⊕ *www.nps.gov/thst* ☜ *Free* ☾ *Mid-June–Aug. daily 9–5; Sept.–mid-June, Wed.–Sun. 9–5.*

SOUTHERN MARYLAND A TO Z

To research prices, get advice from other travelers, and book travel arrangements, visit www.fodors.com.

ADDRESSES

The Colonial streets of downtown Annapolis fan out not from the waterfront but from Church Circle and the larger State Circle. Anne's Church and the Maryland state capitol, which once dominated the Annapolis skyline, remain city landmarks.

There's not much other rhyme or reason to the layout of the city's streets, but it's good to know that Main Street, Duke of Gloucester Street, Maryland Avenue, and East Street are main thoroughfares. Main Street leads to the City Dock and the busy waterfront. Once Main Street is northwest of Church Circle, it becomes West Street.

AIRPORTS

Baltimore-Washington International Airport is convenient to Annapolis and attractions in southern Maryland.

🛅 Airport Information **Baltimore-Washington International Airport** (BWI) ⊠ Exit 2 off Baltimore-Washington Pkwy. ☎ 410/859-7100 ⊕ www.bwiairport.com.

TRANSFERS The most convenient way to get to Annapolis is by car or taxi (the fare is roughly $50). From BWI, follow airport exit signs and then take I–97 south to Route 50 east. Take Exit 24 onto Rowe Boulevard and follow signs to the Annapolis visitor center.

You can also reach Annapolis by bus or shuttle. The Sky Blue Bus Route runs from the International Terminal Bus Stop to Annapolis. You can transfer from the Spa Road stop to other routes, several of which stop near the visitor center.

BWI Ground Transportation has information on Super Shuttle and Airport Vans.

🚩 **BWI Ground Transportation** ☎ 800/435-9294. **Sky Blue Bus Route (Dept. of Public Transportation)** ☎ 410/263-7964.

BIKE TRAVEL

Take a Step, an Annapolis brochure that has biking maps and more information, is available at the visitor center or by contacting the Department of Public Transportation.

🚩 **Department of Public Transportation** ☎ 410/263-7964 ⊕ www.annapolis.gov/government/depts/transport/go.asp. **Washington Area Bicyclist Association** ⊕ www.waba.org.

BOAT & FERRY TRAVEL

To get around the Annapolis waterfront, call the Jiffy Water Taxi, which runs from May to October.

🚩 **Boat & Ferry Lines Jiffy Water Taxi** ☎ 410/263-0033 ⊕ www.watermarkcruises.com/taxi.shtml.

BUS TRAVEL

Maryland's Mass Transit Administration offers regularly scheduled bus service from Baltimore to Annapolis (it's about one hour and 20 minutes one-way from downtown Annapolis). The fare is $1.60.

Bus service between Washington, D.C., and Annapolis is geared to commuters rather than vacationers. Weekday mornings and afternoons, buses arrive at and depart from the Navy–Marine Corps Stadium parking lot, from College Avenue by the state buildings, and also from St. John's College. The one-way fare is $4.25. On weekends Greyhound makes one trip daily, arriving at and departing from the stadium.

🚩 **Bus Lines Dillons Bus Service** ☎ 800/827-3490 or 410/647-2321 ⊕ www.dillonbus.com. **Greyhound** ☎ 800/231-2222 ⊕ www.greyhound.com. **Mass Transit Administration (MTA)** ☎ 410/539-5000 ⊕ www.mtamaryland.com.

CAR TRAVEL

Annapolis is normally 35–45 minutes by car from Washington, D.C., on U.S. 50 (Rowe Boulevard exit). During rush hour (weekdays 3:30–6:30 PM), however, it takes about twice as long.

From Baltimore, following Routes 3 and 97 to U.S. 50, travel time is about the same. To tour southern Maryland, follow Route 2 south from Annapolis, and Route 4, which continues through Calvert County.

PARKING   Parking spots on Annapolis's historic downtown streets are scarce, but you can pay $5 to park at the Navy–Marine Corps Stadium (to the right of Rowe Boulevard as you enter town from Route 50), and ride a free shuttle bus downtown. Parking garages on Main Street and Gott's Court (adjacent to the visitor center) are free for the first hour and $1 an hour thereafter with an $8 maximum but are often full on weekdays. On weekends these garages cost $4 a day. Street parking in the Historic Area is metered (in effect 10–7:30 daily) or limited to two hours for those without a residential parking permit.

EMERGENCIES

⑦ **Ambulance, Fire, Police** ☎ 911.

⑦ Hospitals **Anne Arundel Medical Center** ✉ 2001 Medical Pkwy., off Jennifer Rd., Annapolis ☎ 443/481-1000. **Calvert Memorial Hospital** ✉ 100 Hospital Rd., Prince Frederick ☎ 410/535-8344. **St. Mary's Hospital** ✉ 25500 Point Lookout Rd., Rte. 5, Leonardtown ☎ 301/475-8981.

TOURS

The *Schooner Woodwind* and the *Schooner Woodwind II* are twin 74-foot boats that have two to four sails Tuesday through Sunday between April and October, with some overnight trips. Two-hour sails are $27 to $32.

When the weather's good, Watermark Cruises runs boat tours that last from 40 minutes to 7½ hours and go as far as St. Michaels on the Eastern Shore, where there's a maritime museum, yachts, dining, and boutiques. Prices range from $8 to $55.

Discover Annapolis Tours leads one-hour narrated minibus tours ($14) that introduce you to the history and architecture of Annapolis. Tours leave from the visitor center daily April through November and most weekends December through March.

Walking tours are a great way to see Annapolis's Historic District. The Historic Annapolis Museum Store rents two self-guided (with audiotapes and maps) walking tours: "Historic Annapolis Walk with Walter Cronkite" and "Historic Annapolis African-American Heritage Audio Walking Tour." The cost for each is $5.

Guides from Three Centuries Tours wear Colonial-style dress and take you to the state house, St. John's College, and the Naval Academy. The cost is $11. Tours depart daily April through October at 10:30 from the visitor center and at 1:30 from the information booth, City Dock. From November through March one tour a week leaves on Saturday at 1:30 from the information booth.

Legacy Promotions offers historic walking tours of streets not often visited by most tourists. The tour focuses on the town's African-American heritage.

⑦ *Schooner Woodwind* and **Schooner Woodwind II** ✉ Annapolis Marriott Hotel dock, Annapolis ☎ 410/263-7837 ⊕ www.schooner-woodwind.com. **Watermark Cruises** ✉ City Dock, Historic District ✑ Box 3350, 21403 ☎ 410/268-7600 or 410/268-7601 ⊕ www.watermarkcruises.com.

🚌 Bus Tours **Discover Annapolis Tours** ✉ 31 Decatur Ave., Historic District ☎ 410/626-6000 ⊕ www.discover-annapolis.com.

🚶 Walking Tours **Historic Annapolis Foundation Walking Tours** ✉ 77 Main St., Historic District ☎ 410/268-5576 ⊕ www.annapolis.org. **Legacy Promotions** ✉ 7632 McNamara Dr., Glen Burnie ☎ 410/280-9745. **Three Centuries Tours** ✉ 48 Maryland Ave., Historic District ☎ 410/263-5401 🖶 410/263-1901 ⊕ www.annapolis-tours.com.

VISITOR INFORMATION

Crain Memorial Welcome Center is a good place to pick up information if you're traveling north from Virginia.

ℹ Tourist Information **Annapolis–Anne Arundel County Conference and Visitors Bureau** ✉ 26 West St., Annapolis 21401 ☎ 410/280-0445 ⊕ www.visit-annapolis.org. **Calvert County Dept. of Economic Development & Tourism** ✉ County Courthouse, Prince Frederick 20678 ☎ 410/535-4583 or 800/331-9771. **Charles County Office of Tourism** ✉ 8190 Port Tobacco Rd., Port Tobacco 20677 ☎ 800/766-3386. **Crain Memorial Welcome Center** ✉ U.S. Rte. 301, 12480 Crain Hwy., near Newburg, 1 mi north of Governor Nice bridge over the Potomac River ☎ 301/259-2500. **St. Mary's County Tourism** ✉ 23115 Leonard Hall Dr., Leonardtown 20650 ☎ 301/475-4411.

THE EASTERN
SHORE

9

STAY AND DINE IN LUXURY
where the food rivals the rooms:
the Kent Manor Inn ⇨*p.323*

FIND THE CRAB CAKES OF YOUR DREAMS
at Harris Crab House, near the dock ⇨*p.327*

MAKE $5 GO A LONG LONG WAY
at Dixon's Furniture Auction ⇨*p.330*

FIND THOSE FAMOUS PONIES
in the shadow of Chincoteague ⇨*p.359*

VISIT WATERMEN AND THEIR PAST
with a cruise to Tangier Island ⇨*p.363*

Updated by
Loretta
Chilcoat

SAILING THE CHESAPEAKE BAY nearly four centuries ago in search of new territory for his English king, Captain John Smith wrote that "heaven and earth never agreed better to frame a place for man's habitation." Today the counties of Maryland and Virginia on the eastern side of the Bay retain an enchanting culture and landscape of calm despite their proximity to Baltimore and Washington, D.C.

The Eastern Shore's first permanent English settlement—indeed, the first in Maryland and one of the earliest along the Atlantic—took root on Kent Island, now Queen Anne's County, in 1631. The region's long heritage is not only recorded in architecture and on paper and canvas, but continues to reveal itself through recent archaeological research, such as that being done at East New Market. Many Eastern Shore families have been here for many generations; residents of Smith Island still retain a peculiar Elizabethan lilt in their dialogue.

A thorough visit to the Shore might consist of exploring hospitable communities and historic sites, strolling through wildlife parks and refuges, pausing at a few of the myriad shops, dining at third-generation-owned waterfront restaurants, and overnighting at inns and bed-and-breakfasts. One of the region's most popular summertime destinations is Ocean City, which clings to a narrow barrier island off the southeastern edge of Maryland's Eastern Shore. Its ocean-side culture differs dramatically from that of the Chesapeake, lacking as it does the early-American aura that pervades the rest of the peninsula.

To understand the Eastern Shore, look to the Bay. The Chesapeake is 195 mi long and the nation's largest estuary (a semi-enclosed body of water with free connection to the open sea). Freshwater tributaries large and small flow south and west into the Bay, ensuring the agricultural wealth of the peninsula as well as the bounty of the Bay ("Chesapeake" is an Algonquian word meaning "great shellfish"). At day's end look west across Chesapeake Bay and you can see the sun set over water—a rare sight for any East Coast resident.

Exploring the Eastern Shore

The Eastern Shore takes up most of the Delmarva (for Delaware-Maryland-Virginia) Peninsula, which reaches down from Pennsylvania and stretches some 200 mi to its tip just above Norfolk and Virginia Beach, Virginia. Only two bridges connect the Eastern Shore to the western and southern mainland. To the north, the William Preston Lane Jr. Bridge, or "the Bay Bridge," crosses just above Annapolis, its dual spans stretching 4½ mi across. To the south, the impressive, 17½-mi Chesapeake Bay Bridge-Tunnel connects Norfolk, Virginia Beach, and other Tidewater-area towns with the peninsula.

Whether you choose road, air, or water, it's easy to get around on the Eastern Shore. The rural roads make for pleasant driving and easy cycling, the airports allow for regional air service, and the dozens of marinas have many years' experience with almost every vessel type.

For glimpses into the past, stop by towns with deep roots, including Chestertown, Easton, Oxford, and St. Michaels. The life of the waterman—as Bay fishermen are traditionally known—still reigns in Crisfield, on Smith Island, and on Tilghman Island. A visit to Virginia's Eastern Shore, the slim peninsula running from the Maryland line to the Chesapeake Bay Bridge-Tunnel, calls for getting off U.S. 13 to take in the 300-year-old port town of Onancock, secluded Tangier Island, popular Chincoteague Island, and the Chincoteague National Wildlife Refuge.

About the Restaurants & Hotels

Outside of Cambridge and Ocean City, the great majority of accommodations throughout Maryland's and Virginia's Eastern Shore are B&Bs, inns, and budget chain hotels. Many, if not most, of the B&Bs and small inns throughout both Maryland's and Virginia's Eastern Shore require two-night minimum stays on weekends during the summertime as well as in the late spring and early fall. This policy often applies during special events such as fairs and festivals. Long-term rentals are available year-round in Ocean City, and many B&Bs welcome long-term stays.

Like larger hotels and motels, many smaller inns have teamed up with other businesses to create packages that include boat tours, golf, tennis, galleries, and museums. Some offer incentives for longer stays.

WHAT IT COSTS				
	$$$$	**$$$**	**$$**	**$**	**¢**
RESTAURANTS	over $30	$22–$30	$14–$22	$7–$14	under $7
HOTELS	over $250	$175–$250	$130–$175	$80–$130	under $80

Restaurant prices are per person for a main course at dinner. Hotel prices are for a standard double room, excluding state tax.

QUEEN ANNE'S COUNTY

The eastern landfall of the Bay Bridge, which carries U.S. 50/301, is Kent Island, near the hamlets of Stevensville and Chester. This island gateway is 5 mi wide where U.S. 50/301 crosses it, and 14 mi long. William Claiborne established Maryland's first permanent settlement here in 1631 as part of Virginia. Today, the small towns in this onetime trading post all have their share of churches and homes that recall the region's past.

Numbers in the margin correspond to points of interest on the Maryland's Eastern Shore map.

Stevensville

❶ *10 mi east of Annapolis via U.S. 50/301.*

Tiny Stevensville, just north of the Bay Bridge's eastern landfall, is emerging as an enclave of artisans and craftspeople. Its galleries and studios sell original pottery, stained glass, and painted furniture as well as antiques and fine art. Its historic center has been on the National Register since 1986.

The **Old Stevensville Post Office,** now owned by the Kent Island Heritage Society, is a small building from the late 1800s. On a narrow lot, the structure stands with its side facing the street. ⊠ *408 Love Point Rd.* ☎ *410/643–5969* 💲 *Donations accepted* ⊙ *May–Oct., 1st Sat. of month and by appt.*

Completed in 1809, the **Cray House** is a glimpse into middle-class life of the early 19th century. The two-story cottage, furnished with period pieces, sits in a little yard surrounded by a picket fence. Also on the site, the restored **Stevensville Train Depot,** from the early 1900s, was the western terminus of the old Queen Anne's Railroad Company system. ⊠ *Cockey's La.* ☎ *410/643–5969* 💲 *Donations accepted* ⊙ *May–Oct., 1st Sat. of month and by appt.*

The **Old Christ Church** served as the sanctuary for Maryland's Anglican church and, at the time, represented the only Anglican settlement in the colony. The current congregation moved to another site in 1995, but the church is still used for religious purposes. The curious Gothic church, built in 1880, is mostly wood, but bricks from a church that stood on nearby Broad Creek in 1652 form the chimney, and its peaks and eaves make it seem medieval. ⊠ *Rte. 8, 117 E. Main St.* ☎ *410/758–0835* ⊙ *May–Oct., 1st Sat. of month and by appt.*

Where to Stay & Eat

$–$$$$ ✕ **Hemingway's.** A broad veranda and an upper-level section indoors both have great views west across the Bay, at its narrowest here, and of Annapolis beyond. The sunsets can rival those off Key West, home of the restaurant's namesake. This long-popular restaurant serves tapas, soups, and salads; entrées include Atlantic salmon and coconut sesame shrimp. In summer a very informal bar and grill opens on the lower level, with tables on the lawn adjacent to its private dock. Live music on weekends enhances its simple soup and sandwich menu. ⊠ *Pier One Rd. off Rte. 8* ☎ *410/643–2722* 🟰 *AE, D, MC, V.*

$$–$$$ ✕ **Tavern on the Bay.** Soothing blues and whites set a relaxing mood at the Tavern, and every table has a prime view of the fiery orange sunsets across the Bay. The menu at the Tavern include succulent steaks and well-made crab cakes, but don't overlook the daily "freshline" fish specials. In warmer months, you can have a cocktail on the beach while kicking back in a roomy Adirondack chair. ⊠ *Chesapeake Bay Beach Club, 500 Marina Club Rd., off Rte. 8 near Rte. 50/301* ☎ *410/604–1033* ⊕ *www.chesapeakebaybeachclub.com* 🟰 *AE, MC, V.*

$–$$ ✕ **Love Point Cafe.** Don't let the unassuming exterior fool you into thinking you're in a traditional café—it's more than that. Silky cream-of-crab soup with smoky hints of sherry, meltaway eggs Benedict Chesapeake-style, and a belt-loosening stuffed rockfish are all standouts on the menu. ⊠ *401 Love Point Rd.* ☎ *410/604–0910* 🟰 *AE, D, MC, V* ⊙ *Closed weekdays Jan.–Mar.*

$$–$$$ ✕🛏 **Kent Manor Inn & Restaurant.** A summer hotel since 1898, this imposing antebellum manor house is on 226 acres of farmland along Thompson Creek, near the Chesapeake Bay. Many guest rooms have cozy window seats, others Italian marble fireplaces. All rooms on the upper floors open onto semiprivate verandas. The restaurant ($–$$$$)

Fodor'sChoice ★

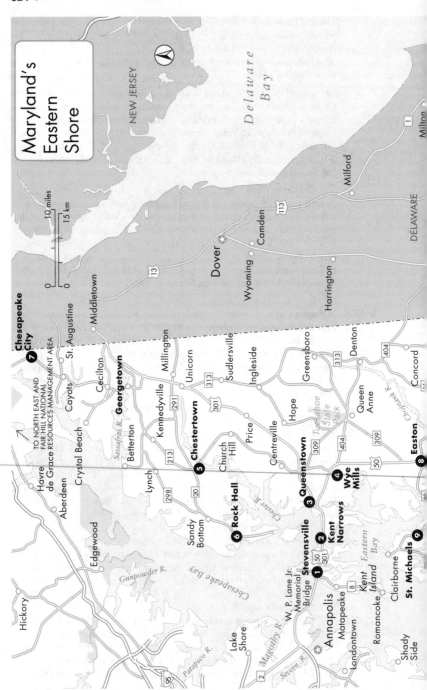

Maryland's
Eastern
Shore

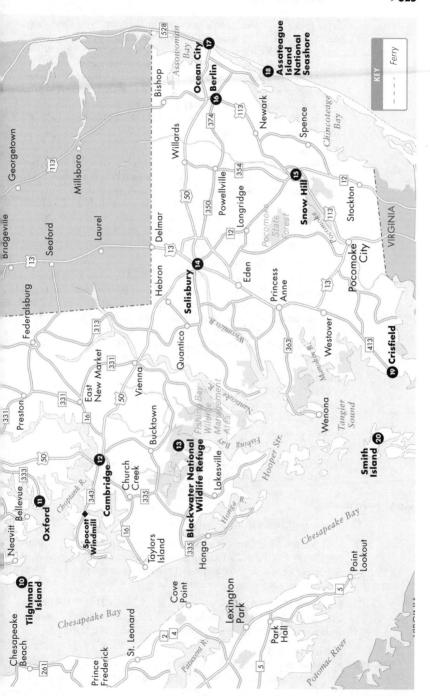

serves meals in two elegant Victorian dining rooms or in an enclosed porch. You can follow a tangy Crab Cosmo starter served in a martini glass with Chef Kent's Trio, which includes beef tenderloin medallions, plump New England sea scallops, and a fat jumbo lump crab cake. ⊠ *500 Kent Manor Dr., 21666* 🕾 *410/643–7716 or 800/820–4511* ⊕ *www. kentmanor.com* 🚗 *20 rooms, 4 suites* 🛆 *Restaurant, cable TV, pool, dock, paddleboats, tennis, croquet, volleyball, bar, meeting rooms; no smoking* ▭ *AE, D, MC, V* ☉ *Restaurant closed Mon. and Tues., except for guest breakfast* ⚭ *BP.*

Nightlife

The **Chesapeake Bay Beach Club** (⊠ 500 Marina Club Rd., off Rte. 8, near Rte. 50/301 🕾 410/604–1933 ⊕ www.chesapeakebaybeachclub.com) is a happening place open year-round, but summer brings the liveliest times here. It includes two pubs, the Sunset Bar, and a shrimp shack. Live music on weekends spans the generations, and when the weather cooperates, the buff and the not-so gather for sports in, nearby, and on the water, including beach volleyball. The beach is free and open to the public.

Sports & the Outdoors

You can stroll or roll along the **Cross Island Trail** between Kent Narrows on the western edge of Kent Island—5½ mi wide here—and Bay beachfront on its eastern side. Here the smoothly paved or hard-packed trail joins the **Terrapin Nature Area**, 279 flat, lush acres that hug the Chesapeake Bay. The area, made up of five identifiable habitats, including wetlands, woodlands, and wildflower meadows, as well as tidal ponds and sandy beaches, has ample parking at both of its ends.

Shopping

Ye Olde Church House (⊠ 426 Love Point Rd. 🕾 410/643–6227) in old Stevensville is just that, but now it's a shop filled with crafts and handspun yarn, hand-dipped candles, old-fashioned soap and candy, and the occasional antique. With sheep grazing in the pasture next door, it's hard to miss and worth seeking out.

Old Stevensville's popular art gallery, the **Kent Island Federation of Art** (⊠ 405 Main St. 🕾 410/643–7424), showcases local artists.

Kent Narrows

❷ *5 mi east of Stevensville, 15 mi east of Annapolis via U.S. 50/301.*

Kent Narrows is a slim, but vital, channel between Kent Island and the mainland of Maryland's Eastern Shore, near the town of Grasonville. A number of eclectic bars and restaurants have congregated at this intersection of road- and waterway traffic.

Exploration Hall (⊠ 425 Piney Narrows Rd., Chester 21619 🕾 410/604–2100 or 888/400–7787 ⊕ www.qac.org), the county's visitor center, has an interactive exhibit on Chesapeake Bay ecology and history.

Where to Eat

$$$-$$$$ ✕ **The Narrows.** Overlooking the namesake waterway separating Kent Island from the Eastern Shore, this restaurant has views that include the

home port of one of the region's largest commercial fishing fleets. The atrium of the contemporary dining room, with a skylight and large windows, is airy. Specialties include a Caesar salad with fried oysters and grilled peppered tuna, served over sautéed spinach. ⊠ *3023 Kent Narrows Way S, Grasonville* ☎ *410/827–8113* ▭ *AE, D, DC, MC, V.*

★ **$$–$$$$** ✕ **Harris Crab House.** On the mainland side of Kent Narrows, this family-friendly institution provides ample docking space for diners arriving by boat. Some of the seafood comes directly from local watermen. Cream-of-crab soup and back-fin crab cakes are among the best around—the cakes are spicy enough to promote plenty of beer drinking. A nautical theme prevails in the large dining room; oyster cans and other relics from an adjacent abandoned oyster house are all on display. You can get expansive water views from a table on the deck. ⊠ *433 Kent Narrows Hwy., Grasonville* ☎ *410/827–9500* ⊕ *www.harriscrabhouse. com* ▭ *MC, V.*

Sports & the Outdoors

BOATING Queen Anne's County has 18 public landings for boats of all sizes. Of these, nine have trailer launching ramps, but the others are "unimproved" and can be used only for canoes, kayaks, and other small boats that can be carried to the water. A seasonal or daily permit is required to launch a boat from public landing ramps and for parking at these sites. For locations where permits may be purchased, contact **Parks and Recreation** (☎ 410/758–0835).

C & C Charters (⊠ Mears Point Marina, 506 Kent Narrows Way N ☎410/827–7888 or 800/733–7245 🖷410/827–5341 ⊕www.cccharters. com) has an extensive fleet of power- and sailboats over 30 feet. It's one of the northern Bay's most experienced and hospitable boat firms. **Island Boat Rentals** (⊠ 201 Wells Cove Rd., Exit 42 off Rte. 50 ☎ 410/ 827–4777) provides small skiffs or pontoon boats for use on the Chester River and the eastern Bay. All necessary equipment is provided for short- or long-term rentals. **Tuna the Tide Charter Service** (⊠ 404 Greenwood Creek La. ☎ 410/827–5635 or 410/827–6188 🖷 410/827–9331 ⊕ www.exploredelmarva.com) has two boats for light tackle and fly-fishing expeditions as well as for crabbing or sightseeing.

Join Captain Michael Hayden as part of the crew of *Nellie L. Byrde* (☎410/ 886–2906) part of the Bay's historic skipjack fleet.

Nightlife

Like other aspects of Kent Island, its nightlife revolves around the water. Most of the bars here are attached to restaurants. One exception is **Gravity Lounge** (⊠ 51 Piney Narrows Rd. ☎410/604–6955). This steadfast waterman's community is an odd location for a groovy martini and sushi bar, but it works. Dress like you didn't just step off a fishing boat and order the whopping "Best of the Bite" sushi platter to share with friends. The full sushi menu here comes with stellar waterfront views of Piney Cree.

In addition to having live music and a seafood menu, the **Crab Deck at the Fisherman's Inn** (⊠ 3116 Main St., Grasonville ☎ 410/827–6666) also has a duck pond to amuse the kids. The deck is closed in winter.

With its blinding hot green and yellow colors **The Jetty** (⊠ 201 Wells Cove Rd., Grasonville ☎ 410/827–4959) helps re-create a slice of the tropics among its very laid-back crowd, especially when it's Karaoke night or when there's live music on weekends.

The raucous, open-air **Red Eye's Dock Bar** (⊠ 428 Kent Narrows Way North, Grasonville ☎ 410/827–3937)is a hopping, good place to grab a brew—as long as you don't have a problem with the wildly popular bikini contests here.

Shopping

Eastern Bay Trading is a barn of a building packed with a near-random gathering of castoffs and antiques. It's a great place for rummaging. ⊠ 4917 Main St., Rte. 18, Grasonville ☎ 410/827–9286 ☉ Thurs.–Mon. 11–5.

Queenstown

❸ 11 mi east of Stevensville, 21 mi east of Annapolis via U.S. 50/301.

The cove of Queenstown's harbor is protected by a bend of the mouth of the Chester River. Established in 1707 as "Queen Anne's Town," it became an important enough port to be attacked by the British during the War of 1812. A pleasantly sleepy little community, it's worth a short visit.

Where to Stay

$$$ ▦ **Lands End Manor on the Bay.** On 17 secluded acres on Eastern and Prospect bays, a 10-minute drive east of Queenstown, this stunningly decorated former hunting lodge has see-forever views from its three spacious rooms, which all have king-size beds. The cozy common areas include a great room, gun room, and solarium. When evening arrives, homemade cookies and sherry are set out. Deep-draft docking is available for guests. ⊠ 232 Prospect Bay Dr., Grasonville 21638 ☎ 410/827–6284 ⊕ www.bbonline.com/md/landsend ⇌ 3 rooms ₺ Refrigerators, pool, dock, boating, bicycles; no smoking ☰ MC, V ◯ BP.

Sports & the Outdoors

Queenstown is home to a pair of the finest golf courses in the region, both of which are part of **Queenstown Harbor Golf Links** (⊠ 32 Links La., off Rte. 301 ☎ 410/827–6611 or 800/827–5257 ⊕ www.mdgolf.com). The River Course and the adjacent Lakes Course, par 71 and par 72 respectively, have 36 holes beside the place where the Chester River flows into the Bay. Fees range from $36 for 9 holes on weekdays to $89 for 18 holes on weekends.

Operated by the Wildfowl Trust of North America, the 500 acres of the **Horsehead Wetlands Center** will open your eyes, ears, and mind to the wildfowl and waterscapes that characterize Maryland's Eastern Shore. The aviary and waterfowl ponds are full of ducks, geese, swans, and birds of prey. Pause a moment in a secluded blind and explore native woodlands, marshes, and meadows along 4 mi of trails. A visitor center and picnic facilities are both on the grounds. ⊠ 600 Discovery La., Grasonville ☎ 410/827–6694 ⊕ www.wildfowltrust.org ⊠ $5 ☉ Daily 9–5.

Shopping

A major layover between the western shore and the beaches, **Prime Outlets at Queenstown** (✉ U.S. 50/301 ☎ 410/827–8699), 10 mi east of the Bay Bridge, includes more than 60 factory outlet stores, including Brooks Brothers, Polo Ralph Lauren, Liz Claiborne, Jones New York, Nike, and L. L. Bean. If you reach the mall around lunch, grab an overstuffed sandwich and a slice of homemade cheesecake at **Chesapeake Gourmet** (☎ 410/827–8686).

The popular **Christmas Goose** (✉ 4628 Ocean Gateway, at U.S. 50 ☎ 410/827–5252 ⊕ www.xmasgoose.com) stocks Yuletide decorations and gifts the whole year through.

Wye Mills

❹ *5 mi south of Queenstown, 14 mi southeast of Stevensville.*

The **gristmill** for which this village is named was built—and rebuilt—in the late 1600s. It supplied flour to George Washington's troops during the War of Independence. The first and third Saturday of each month, from mid-April to early November, you can still buy fresh cornmeal as well as whole-wheat and buckwheat flour. ✉ *Rte. 662* ☎ *410/827–6909 or 410/685–2886* 🎟 *$2 donation requested* ☉ *Mid-Apr.–mid-Nov., Mon.–Thurs. 10–1, Fri. and Sat. 10–4.*

Where to Stay

$$$$ 🏨 **Irishtown B&B.** Operated by the Pintail Point resort, this renovated but still rustic early 1900s farmhouse can sleep 6 to 10 people. Rates are $500 per night for up to 6, then $50 per person up to a maximum of 10. ✉ *511 Pintail Point La., near Rte. 50* ☎ *410/827–7029* 🖷 *410/827–7052* ⊕ *www.pintailpoint.com* 🛏 *1 house* 🕭 *Pool, bicycles, kennel; no room phones, no room TVs, no smoking* ▭ *D, MC, V* ◎l *CP.*

$$$–$$$$ 🏨 **Manor House.** One of two B&Bs on the Pintail Point property (the other is Irishtown), this imposing 1930s English Tudor–style structure is perched on the end of an idyllic peninsula in the Wye River. The English club touches include overstuffed seating and Oriental rugs. A broad, fully furnished veranda stretches the width of the house. Guest room furnishings are conservatively contemporary with nautical accents. Vistas, most over the water, are stunning from any window. A full breakfast is served on weekends. ✉ *511 Pintail Point La., near Rte. 50* ☎ *410/827–7029* 🖷 *410/827–7052* ⊕ *www.pintailpoint.com* 🛏 *2 rooms, 1 suite, 1 cottage* 🕭 *Cable TV, pool, outdoor hot tub, bicycles, billiards, library, kennel; no room phones, no smoking* ▭ *D, MC, V* ◎l *CP.*

Sports & the Outdoors

The **Pintail Point** (✉ 511 Pintail Point La., near Rte. 50 ☎ 410/827–7029 ⊕ www.pintailpoint.com) complex on the Wye River defies easy definition. It's a semiprivate resort with two bed and breakfasts open year-round. There's shooting and fly-fishing instruction, clay shooting and lessons, upland game and waterfowl hunting, freshwater pond fishing, and a four-boat charter boat fleet for Chesapeake Bay fishing as well as for catered meals and receptions. Biking and hiking trails as well as canoeing creeks abound. An 18-hole golf course, Hunters Oak, is adjacent.

Shopping

★ Looking for that pink flamingo piñata? You're almost guaranteed to find one at **Dixon's Furniture Auction** (⊠ 2017 Dudley Corner Rd., at intersection of Rtes. 290 and 544, Crumpton ☎ 410/928–3006 ⊕ www.crumptonauction.com), which is much more than furniture. At this a rite-of-passage for antique (and flea market) bargain hunters, you browse among acres of objects, from genuine antiques to everyday "other people's treasures," then bid against amateurs and pros alike. Want to bid low? Start at the $5 field—the loot is divided into sections, and minimum bids increase by $5 increments. Some of the food and beverage concessions here are run by members of the local Amish community. The auction takes place every Wednesday from 9 PM and ends when the last pink flamingo piñata is sold.

KENT COUNTY

The communities on the upper reaches of Maryland's Eastern Shore are steeped in history and determined to preserve it. Those in Kent County, whose idyllic location between the Chester and Sassafras Rivers is enhanced by a long, ragged Chesapeake Bay shoreline, are among the most fiercely protective. Hidden hamlets untouched by time savor their quiet anonymity; others struggle to balance acceptance of their recent renown with a heritage of 300 years.

Chestertown

❺ *47 mi northeast of Annapolis via U.S. 50/301 to Rte. 213, 24 mi north of Wye Mills via U.S. 50 to Rte. 213.*

Second only to Annapolis in its concentration of 18th-century houses, Chestertown was a major international port in Colonial days: a tall, brick customhouse continues to dominate the High Street waterfront. Still the home of families whose local roots go back many generations, the town has its share of newer residents, many of them retirees. Today, inns and good restaurants, fine art galleries and antiques shops line the brick pavements of High Street, Chestertown's broad, tree-lined main street. To walk along its narrow streets, some of them cobbled, is to commune quietly with some of the country's oldest history. At the northern edge of Chestertown is **Washington College,** one of the nation's oldest liberal-arts institutions. George Washington helped found the college in 1782 through a gift of 50 guineas.

Geddes-Piper House, home of the Historical Society of Kent County, is a splendid Federal-style home containing 18th-century furniture and an impressive teapot collection, a historical library, and shop. It's a good place to begin a visit to Chestertown. ⊠ *Church Alley* ☎ *410/778–3499* ⊕ *www.hskcmd.com* 💲 *$3* ⏱ *Wed.–Fri. 10–4.*

The *Sultana,* a reproduction of a 1768 Colonial schooner by the same name, was launched in 2001. With a length of only 97 feet, the original *Sultana* was the smallest schooner ever registered on the Royal Navy Lists. The mission of this "Schoolship of the Chesapeake" is to provide unique, hands-on educational experiences in Colonial history and environmental science. Several two-hour public sails ($25) are available each month from April through November. Daylong and multiday public sails are also scheduled regularly. The *Sultana* can be seen close-up when she is anchored in the Chester River, at the end of Cannon Street. ✉ *105 S. Cross St.* ☎ *410/778–5954* ⊕ *www.schoonersultana.com.*

Where to Stay & Eat

$$–$$$ ✕ **Blue Heron Café.** This relaxed, contemporary dining room has high, sloped ceilings and skylights. Among the café's most sought-after entrées is baked rockfish, but don't overlook the oyster fritters, a signature dish. The service here is genuine and attentive. ✉ *236 Cannon St.* ☎ *410/778–0188* ⊟ *AE, MC, V* ⊗ *Closed Sun.*

$$–$$$ ✕ **Kennedyville Inn.** In a little town 8 mi north of Chestertown, the Kennedyville is known for its legendary pit barbecue and microbrews as well as daily seafood specials and light fare. The polished service and personal attention are as fine as the food, and the wine and spirits selection has been carefully chosen. It's not open long hours: seating is Wednesday and Thursday 5–8, Friday and Saturday 5–9, and Sunday 3–6:30. ✉ *Rte. 213, east side, Kennedyville* ☎ *410/348–2400* ⊕ *www.kennedyvilleinn.com* ⊟ *D, MC, V* ⊗ *Closed Mon. and Tues.*

¢–$ ✕ **Feast of Reason.** Head to this lunch spot for extraordinary sandwiches with uncommon ingredients, including roast beef with pesto mayonnaise on French bread, or tomatoes, spinach, zucchini, and sprouts in a garlic herb wrap. For dessert, have a cookie, brownie, granola bar, or "fuslbous." "Fuslbous"? Ask the proprietor for the story of how this delicious item got its name. ✉ *203 High St.* ☎ *410/778–3828* ⊟ *No credit cards* ⊗ *Closed Sun. No dinner.*

¢ ✕ **Play It Again, Sam.** This is one of those card shop/bookshop/coffee shop/snack shop/general store enterprises that give some insight into a community's character. Washington College students and others mingle happily at sidewalk tables when weather permits and in the "reading room" when it doesn't. ✉ *108 S. Cross St.* ☎ *410/778–2688* ⊟ *No credit cards.*

$–$$$$ ✕▦ **Imperial Hotel and Restaurant.** This three-story brick structure at the intersection of Chestertown's two main downtown streets was built in 1903. Guest rooms and suites are decorated with original artwork, authentic period furnishings, and custom-designed and handcrafted pieces, some of which hide TVs and telephones. The hotel's two dining rooms ($$$) are bright and airy, both serving regional dishes such as rack of lamb with toasted pecans and peanuts as well as Asian-Mediterranean cuisine. Don't overlook the creations of the restaurant's own pastry chef. ✉ *208 High St., 21620* ☎ *410/778–5000* 🖷 *410/778–9662* ⊕ *www.imperialchestertown.com* ↵ *11 rooms, 2 suites* ♿ *Restaurant, cable TV, meeting room; no smoking* ⊟ *AE, D, MC, V* ⊗ *Restaurant closed Mon. and Tues. No lunch, except Sun.*

★ $–$$$ ▦ **White Swan Tavern.** Step back in time at this inn, restored to its appearance circa 1790. Built as a home in 1733, it was a tavern, then a general store; it may be the town's oldest building. Brick fireplaces and deep window seats, an old writing desk, and pewter candleholders are all in keeping with its Colonial past. The original kitchen, shaded by a giant elm, is the inn's most requested guest room. Its rough ceiling beams, brick floor, and large fireplace attest to its antiquity. Afternoon tea is served in the dining room, on the rear stone patio, or in guest rooms. ⊠ *231 High St., 21620* ☎ *410/778–2300* 🖶 *410/778–4543* ⊕ *www. chestertown.com/whiteswan* 🛏 *4 rooms, 2 suites* ⚬ *Meeting room; no room phones, no room TVs, no smoking* ☰ *MC, V* ⎮◯⎮ *CP.*

$–$$ 🖵 **The Inn at Mitchell House.** The long history of this 1743 manor house includes the tale of a War of 1812 British commander who died of his wounds here in 1814: his body left for England preserved in a barrel of rum. The inn sits on 10 serene acres surrounded by woods about 10 mi from downtown Chestertown. Nature enthusiasts are as much at home here as the songbirds, migrating geese, white-tailed deer, and eagles. With access to Tolchester Marina and its private beach, it's convenient to boating, fishing, crabbing, and swimming, as well as to biking, hiking, hunting, sporting clays, golf, and tennis. Four guest rooms have working fireplaces. ⊠ *8796 Maryland Pkwy., 21620* ☎ *410/ 778–6500* ⊕ *www.innatmitchellhouse.com* 🛏 *6 rooms* ⚬ *Lounge, meeting room; no room phones, no room TVs, no smoking* ☰ *MC, V* ⎮◯⎮ *BP.*

★ $ 🖵 **Hill's Inn.** Before they began the restoration of this Victorian inn, the proprietors already had the set of 1870s stained-glass windows that are now installed here. On the ground floor are painted faux fireplaces and hand-painted plaster ceilings; "Jenny Doors" (tall, wide windows that open upward to create doorways) lead to a gracious veranda. All rooms are furnished with period antiques and have queen- or king-size beds. An English tea, complete with clotted cream and scones made from scratch, is part of the experience, as is a glass of sherry in the evening beside the fireplace. Therapeutic massages are available on request. ⊠ *114 Washington Ave., 21620* ☎ *410/778–1926* 🖶 *410/778–3606* 🛏 *4 rooms* ⚬ *No room phones, no room TVs, no kids under 12, no smoking* ☰ *MC, V* ⎮◯⎮ *BP.*

Nightlife & the Arts

Younger and older "C'town" residents alike head to **Andy's** (⊠ 337½ High St. ☎ 410/778–6779) when they're looking for an unpretentious nightspot. Its simple menu ($) includes burgers, pizza, and "blue plate specials." Bluegrass, country, folk, jazz, rock, and pop bands play on Friday and Saturday. Andy's is closed on Sunday and serves no lunch.

Sports & the Outdoors

At the mouth of the Sassafras River, about 12 mi north of Chestertown, **Betterton Beach,** the bay's only jellyfish-free beach, has a bathhouse, boardwalk, picnic pavilion, and boat ramp. To fully enjoy this tiny community, bike, boat, and kayak rentals are available in and around Chestertown.

Shopping

Robert Ortiz Studio (⊠ 207 S. Cross St. ☎ 410/810–1400 ⊕ www. ortizstudios.com) is a place to find uncommonly handsome handcrafted furniture.

Rock Hall

6 *13 mi southwest of Chestertown via Rte. 291 to Rte. 20.*

No longer just a side trip, Rock Hall, its hardy maritime character intact, has emerged as a viable destination in its own right, to be reached either by road or by boat. It reveres its heritage, despite the pleasure boats anchored in its waters and moored at its docks that far outnumber actual working fishing boats.

The **Waterman's Museum** profiles the hard life on the Bay in absorbing detail, celebrating a Chesapeake way of life that in many ways is dying out. On display are exhibits on oystering and crabbing that include historical photos and local carvings, as well as preserved examples of his all-important boats and a reproduction of a waterborne shanty. ⊠ *20880 Rock Hall Ave.* ☎ *410/778–6697* 🖅 *Free* ☉ *May–Sept., daily 8–5; Oct.–Apr., weekdays 8–5, Sat. 9–5, Sun. 10–4.*

The tiny **Tolchester Beach Revisited Museum** recalls the nearby holiday resort and Bay ferry destination. The beach, which had a grand hotel and a dizzying Ferris wheel, closed in 1962. The eclectic collection of memorabilia amounts to a charming survey of late-19th- and early-20th-century Chesapeake-area culture. ⊠ *Oyster Court Cluster, Sharp and Main Sts., Rock Hall* ☎ *410/778–5347* ☉ *Weekends 11–3 and by appt.*

At the tip of the Eastern Neck peninsula, at the mouth of the Chester River, is the superb **Eastern Neck National Wildlife Refuge.** This 2,285-acre park, 8 mi south of Rock Hall, is a prime place to spot migratory waterfowl, wild turkey, Delmarva fox squirrels, and southern bald eagles, undeterred by the experimental power-generating solar panels and wind turbines installed nearby. Nearly 6 mi of roads and trails and an observation tower provide excellent vantage points. ⊠ *1730 Eastern Neck Rd.* ☎ *410/639–7056* ⊕ *easternneck.fws.gov* ☉ *Daily dawn–dusk.*

Where to Stay & Eat

$–$$$ ✕ **Waterman's Crabhouse.** This casual dockside restaurant looking out toward the Chesapeake Bay Bridge has lots of local color. The menu includes ribs, steaks, and fried oysters, but its crab dishes are legendary: so are its homemade cheesecake and key lime pie. Warm summer weekends mean live entertainment and seating on the 40-foot deck. There's a deep-draft dock for diners arriving by boat. ⊠ *21055 Sharp St.* ☎ *410/639–2261* ▤ *AE, D, MC, V* ☉ *Closed Jan. and Feb.*

$$–$$$ ✕🏠 **The Inn at Osprey Point.** On 30 lush acres along Swan Creek, this stately Colonial-style building has brick fireplaces and exposed beams. It's worth staying here for the views alone. Rooms have four-poster, canopied beds; the spacious two-room Escapade suite has French doors and a marble bath with a whirlpool hot tub. At the inn's restaurant ($$–$$$; closed Tuesday and Wednesday), regional fare is served. The cream-of-crab soup with sherry is a favorite among regulars, as are entrées such as Maryland jumbo lump crab cakes and pan-seared duck breast. ⊠ *20786 Rock Hall Ave., 21661* ☎ *410/639–2194* ⊕ *www. ospreypoint.com* 🔁 *6 rooms, 1 suite* ⌂ *Restaurant, picnic area, cable*

TV, pool, marina, meeting rooms; no room phones, no kids, no smoking. ⊟ *D, MC, V* ⍾⍜⍾ *CP.*

Sports & the Outdoors

Canoeing and kayaking on quiet creeks and rivers throughout the Eastern Shore's ragged western shorelines are popular pastimes here. Two firms in Kent County provide rentals, tours, and lessons for the area: they're also good sources for waterside camping advice. One is **Kayak-Canoe,** (⊠ Swan Creek Rd., 4 mi north of Rock Hall ☎ 410/639–9000 ⊕ www.kayakcanoe.com). The other is **Chester River Kayak Adventures** (⊠ 5758 Main St., Rock Hall ☎ 410/639–2001 ⊕ www. crkayakadventures.com). These entrepreneurs also operate two B&Bs. Canoes and kayaks are also available to guests of some B&Bs and in some nature parks.

CECIL COUNTY

Cecil County includes the northern extremities of Chesapeake Bay. Its western boundary with Harford County, the Susquehanna River, is the Bay's principal northern tributary. Its southern boundary with Kent County is another tributary, the Sassafras River. The all-important Chesapeake and Delaware (C&D) Canal is cut between Cecil's third major river, the Elk, and the Delaware River, a major shipping route that connects Chesapeake Bay with Delaware Bay and the Atlantic Ocean. Some 12,000 acres of public parks and forests in addition to a wildlife management area help preserve connections with nature and the outdoors.

Chesapeake City

❼ *31 mi north of Chestertown via Rte. 213.*

A town split dramatically in two by the C&D Canal, Chesapeake City homes and businesses face each other across the busy waterway. Those sitting at the restaurants and taverns next to the canal often marvel at the giant oceangoing vessels that slide by—seemingly within arm's reach. Chesapeake City's own well-protected harbor cove welcomes visiting pleasure craft virtually year-round.

Where to Stay & Eat

★ **$$–$$$** ✕ **The Bayard House.** One of the few restaurants in Chesapeake City, the Bayard House's cuisine and service would stand out almost anywhere. Patrons in the know travel to this canal-shop eatery for dishes such as grilled breast of duck; tournedos Baltimore, twin fillets of beef topped with crab and lobster; and the de rigueur Maryland crab cakes. The Maryland crab soup is even more widely renowned. ⊠ *11 Bohemia Ave.* ☎ *410/ 885–5040* ⊟ *AE, D, MC, V.*

$$–$$$ 🏠 **Ship Watch Inn.** Three levels of broad decks mean that every room has a place from which to relax and watch international watercraft sail in and out of the C&D Canal just yards away. (A canal-side hot tub offers an even closer view.) Built as a residence in 1920, the elegant, eclectic furnishings of this waterfront B&B blend well with the modern amenities. The decades-old black-and-white photos hanging in the public areas reveal much about the roles the owner-innkeepers' families played in the history of Chesapeake City. ⊠ *401 1st St., 21915* ☎ *410/885–5300* ⊕ *www.shipwatchinn.com* ⊋ *8 rooms* ⚘ *Cable TV, meeting rooms; no smoking* ⊟ *AE, MC, V* |⊙| *BP.*

North East

12 mi northwest of Chesapeake City via Rte. 213 and Rte. 40.

Uncommon neighborliness along a main street of antiques and collectibles shops and homey eateries gives Cecil's riverside county seat its welcoming charm.

You could spend a weekend in the **5&10 Antique Market.** Originally the Hotel Cecil, it became Cramer's 5&10, an old-fashioned variety store with hard-to-find items, penny candy jars, and a pair of proprietors who themselves became historic treasures. The building's enterprising current owner created an antiques mart but fully restored the building's exterior and retained its well-worn wood flooring, candy jars, and display counters. ⊠ *111 S. Main St.* ☎ *410/287–8318.*

The **Day Basket Factory** has been crafting oak baskets by hand since 1876. Skilled craftspeople and weavers use techniques passed down through the generations; you can often watch them as they work. ⊠ *714 S. Main St.* ☎ *410/287–6100* ⊕ *www.daybasketfactory.com* ⊙ *Daily Wed.–Fri. 10:30–5, Sat. 10–5, Sun. 1–5; until 6 PM on Sat. in summer.*

The two spacious buildings of the **Upper Bay Museum** at the head of the North East River preserves the rich heritage of both the commercial and recreational hunter. This unusual museum houses an extensive collection of boating, fishing, and hunting artifacts native to the Upper Chesapeake Bay: sleek sculling oars, rare working decoys, and the outlawed "punt" gun and "gunning" rigs. ⊠ *Walnut St. at Rte. 272* ☎ *410/287–2675* ⊙ *Sat. 10–3, Sun. 10–4.*

About 6 mi south of the town of North East, **Elk Neck State Park** juts into the headwaters of the Chesapeake Bay to its west, with the Elk River flowing along its eastern flank. You can drive almost the length of the peninsula and then walk about a mile through pleasant woodlands to the cliffs on its tip. There you can find the sparkling-white Turkey Point Lighthouse. No longer in use, it's maintained by volunteers. The 270-plus-degree view from Turkey Point is stunning. Camp sites are available here, as are some charming 1950s-era wooden cabins that are admirably well maintained. Elk Neck is a prime location for picnicking as well as for fishing and swimming off sandy beaches. ⊠ *Rte. 272 south of North East* ☎ *410/287–5333 or 888/432–2267* ⊕ *www.dnr.state. md.us/publiclands/central/elkneck.html.*

Where to Stay & Eat

$–$$ ✕ **Woody's Crab House.** You can get the crabs here, of course, and have them served any number of imaginative ways. But slurp one of the thick homemade soups, or down the famous Carolina shrimp burger, to understand why this funky little eatery is so popular. The kids' menu is a thoughtful extra. But go easy on the real food: Woody's ice-cream parlor, next door, includes seasonal favorite flavors such as apple, pumpkin, and Fourth of July (a celebration of red, white, and blue ice creams). ⊠ *29 S. Main St.* ☎ *410/287–3541* ♻ *Reservations not accepted* ▭ *D, MC, V.*

★ **$$–$$$** ▦ **Elk Forge B&B Inn and Retreat.** An easy hour's drive from either Baltimore or Philadelphia, Elk Forge is an appealing destination unto itself. On 5 acres of woods and gardens, the inn is along the Big Elk Creek. Each of the 12 guest rooms is uniquely decorated and well appointed. A daily afternoon tea includes the innkeepers' own herbal blends; services at the Spa in the Garden include Swedish massage and aromatherapy facials. ⊠ *807 Elk Mills Rd., Rte. 316, Elk Mills 21920* ☎ *410/392–9007 or 877/355–3674* ⊕ *www.elkforge.com* ➩ *12 rooms* ♿ *In-room data ports, cable TV, in-room VCRs, outdoor hot tub, massage, spa, badminton, croquet, meeting rooms; no smoking* ▭ *AE, MC, V* ⦿ *BP.*

Fair Hill National Resources Management Area

10 mi northeast of North East.

Cecil County has long been known for its horse farms, and its many pastures, surrounded by white fences, are a testament to that equestrian heritage. The 5,613 acres that make up the Fair Hill National Resources Management Area were once the private preserve of the DuPont family. It now includes the Fair Hill Training Center for racehorses, where you can watch Triple Crown hopefuls run. In addition, both steeplechase and flat races are held regularly on a "turf course." Other events, including dog shows and Civil War reenactments, are held here from time to time. Fair Hill's extensive trail system is open for hiking, mountain biking, and horseback riding, and Fair Hill Stables provides group rides and lessons, as well as rides in restored antique carriages. Big Elk Creek, which runs through Fair Hill, is a great place for angling. A covered bridge, built in the 1800s, is nearby. ⊠ *Three entrances off state Hwy. 273, 2 mi south of state line; follow signs to "Office" at 300 Tawes Dr.* ☎ *410/ 398–1246 Dept. of Natural Resources* ⊕ *www.dnr.state.md.us/ publiclands.*

Where to Stay & Eat

$ ▦ **Tailwinds Farm B&B.** Your hosts—the dynamic managers of nearby Fair Hill Stables—welcome you to their restored Victorian-era farmhouse and invite you to help gather eggs from the henhouse, visit with Jeepers the goat, or simply watch horses graze from your guest room window. After a hearty farm breakfast you can take a riding lesson or a carriage ride. If you're traveling with your own horses, you may board them overnight in Tailwinds's 17-stall barn for a small extra charge. ⊠ *41 Tailwinds La., North East 21901* ☎ *410/658–8187* 🖷 *410/658–9677* ⊕ *www.fairwindsstables.com* ➩ *2 rooms* ♿ *Pond, horseback riding, horseshoes; no room phones, no smoking* ▭ *No credit cards* ⦿ *BP.*

TALBOT COUNTY

Water defines the landscape of Talbot County, which has some of the region's most vibrant little towns, including Easton, Oxford, and St. Michaels. The Chesapeake Bay forms its western border, and the meandering Choptank River slices through the Delmarva Peninsula to form its southern and eastern borders. Waterfront hamlets that started as fishing villages now include comfortable inns and downtown B&Bs. Fine waterside restaurants and folksy main street taverns are also part of this comfortably refined region.

Easton

★ ❽ *79 mi south of North East and 36 mi south of Chestertown via Rte. 213 and U.S. 50, 36 mi southeast of Annapolis via U.S. 50/301 to U.S. 50.*

Well-preserved buildings dating from Colonial through Victorian times still grace the downtown of this affluent, genteel town. Fine art galleries, high-quality antiques shops, and gift boutiques sit side by side along North Harrison Street and others make up the small midtown mall called Talbottown.

Rebellious citizens gathered at the **Talbot County Courthouse** to protest the Stamp Act in 1765 and to adopt the Talbot Resolves, a forerunner of the Declaration of Independence. Today, the courthouse, built in 1712 and expanded in 1794, along with two wings added in the late 1950s, is still in use. The two-tier cupola is topped by a weather vane. ⊠ *11 N. Washington St.* ☎ *410/770–8001* ☉ *Weekdays 8–5.*

The white, wood-frame **Third Haven Friends Meeting House**, built in 1684, reflects the simplicity its Quaker builders revered. Quakers still have meetings here, 10 AM Sunday and 5:30 PM Wednesday. ⊠ *405 S. Washington St.* ☎ *410/822–0293* ☉ *Daily 9–5.*

★ In its 1820s-era schoolhouse, the **Academy Art Museum** houses a permanent collection of fine art by such American artists as James McNeil Whistler, Grant Wood, Lichtenstein, and Rauschenberg, as well as Chagall and Dürer. Special exhibitions often cover Eastern Shore artists, and the juried art show the museum holds in early October is one of the finest in the region. ⊠ *106 South St.* ☎ *410/822–2787 or 410/822–0455* 🖷 *410/822–5997* ⊕ *www.art-academy.org* 🎫 *$2* ☉ *Mon. and Sat. 10–4, Tues.–Thurs. 10–9.*

A three-story Federal brick house, restored by a Quaker cabinetmaker in 1810, houses the **Historical Society of Talbot County,** which maintains a small museum of local history and manages Tharpe Antiques. The society also operates Three Centuries Tours, a one-hour overview of authentically furnished homes of the 17th through 19th centuries. ⊠ *25 S. Washington St.* ☎ *410/822–0773* 🎫 *$5* ☉ *Mon.–Sat. 10–4. Guided house tours Tues.–Sat. 11:30 and 1:30.*

Where to Stay & Eat

$$-$$$ ╳ **General Tanuki's.** What's available here is an unusual blend of sushi and California-surf cuisine. You can choose from a traditional à la carte sushi menu or (for the more adventurous) try the "morphing quesadillas." They're not as scary as they sound. Tanuki's opens at 3 on Saturday and 5 every other day of the week. ⊠ *25 Goldsborough St.* ☎ *410/819–0707* ▭ *MC, V* ☉ *No lunch.*

★ $$–$$$ ✕ **Mason's.** A family-run landmark for more than 30 years, Mason's uses fresh ingredients from its own garden when making its dishes. Pink snapper, ahi tuna, and Pacific striped marlin from Hawaii are appreciated by seafood lovers, and the restaurant's tenderloin is second to none. Next door is a coffee bar and a food store that sells hard-to-find cheeses and meats, wonderful hand-crafted chocolates, and all manner of esoteric edibles. ⊠ *42 E. Dover St.* ☎ *410/822–3204* ▤ *AE, D, MC, V* ⊗ *Closed Sun.*

$$–$$$ ✕ **Out of the Fire.** A spare, modern interior sets this neighborhood bistro apart from its Colonial neighbors. Of note is the owner's insistence that all equipment and furnishings—including a trompe l'oeil mural, faux-finish walls, and pottery—be obtained locally. One of the more interesting entrées is Caribbean spiced pork with ginger mango chutney. Breads are baked in a stone-hearth oven; desserts are produced on-site. Enjoy one of more than 100 labels at the wine bar or in the overstuffed seating off to one side of the open kitchen. ⊠ *22 Goldsborough St.* ☎ *410/770–4777* ▤ *AE, D, MC, V* ⊗ *Closed Sun.*

★ $$$ ✕▥ **Inn at Easton.** This B&B operates one of the finest restaurants ($$$–$$$$) in the country. Delightfully imaginative creations include green Thai bouillabaisse, but the signature dish is roasted lamb sirloin with a Dijon herb crust. With a colorful interior that's full of antiques and gracious touches, this circa 1790 Federal mansion is a bit like a boutique hotel. Original paintings by the Russian impressionist Nikolai Timkov are hung in the common areas. Upstairs, the seven rooms and suites skillfully combine old-time charm with modern amenities. ⊠ *25 S. Harrison St.* ☎ *410/822–4910 or 888/800–8091* ▤ *410/820–6961* ⊕ *www.theinnateaston.com* ☝ *3 rooms, 4 suites* ⚐ *Restaurant; no room TVs, no kids under 9, no smoking* ▤ *AE, D, MC, V* ⊗ *No lunch* ▮◯▮ *BP.*

$$–$$$ ▥ **The Tidewater Inn & Conference Center.** This stately four-story brick hotel was built in 1949. Beyond its first-story archways, a Colonial theme pervades its spacious common areas, where there are hurricane lamps, huge fireplaces, and paintings of old Easton. Mahogany reproduction furniture fills the charming rooms, done in greens and golds. In the hotel's full-service dining room, a "hunting breakfast" is available early every morning in season. ⊠ *101 E. Dover St., 21601* ☎ *410/822–1300 or 800/237–8775* ⊕ *www.tidewaterinn.com* ☝ *114 rooms, 7 suites* ⚐ *Restaurant, cable TV, pool, bar, business services, meeting rooms, kennel, no-smoking floors* ▤ *AE, D, MC, V.*

$–$$ ▥ **The Bishop's House.** Elaborate, elegant hats surround those entering the grand foyer of the home. Built for a former state governor around 1880 and later owned by the Episcopal diocese, this red-trim Victorian house now awes guests with its wraparound porch, huge bay windows, and fireplaces with tiled mantels. Second-floor guest rooms have 12-foot ceilings and 19th-century oak, walnut, and mahogany furnishings. Three guest rooms have working fireplaces. The third-floor sitting room has a VCR and mini kitchen appliances. ⊠ *214 Goldsborough St., Box 2217, 21601* ☎ *410/820–7290 or 800/223–7290* ▤ *410/820–7290* ⊕ *www.bishopshouse.com* ☝ *5 rooms* ⚐ *Some in-room hot tubs, cable TV, bicycles, meeting rooms; no room phones, no kids under 12, no smoking* ▤ *AE, D, DC, MC, V* ▮◯▮ *BP.*

Nightlife & the Arts

Avalon Theatre (⊠ 40 E. Dover St. ☎ 410/822–0345 ⊕ www. avalontheatre.com), a former vaudeville house built in 1921, has been restored as a venue for the Talbot Chamber Orchestra and the Eastern Shore Chamber Music Festival, as well as films and other performances.

With a name like **Chez Lafitte** (⊠ 13 S. Washington St. ☎ 410/770–8868), you might think that this bar is going to ooze pretentiousness. But no. The owners, a New York actress and her husband, named this intimate yet welcoming piano jazz bar after their Great Dane. The rich furnishings, including giant gilded mirrors and crushed velvet drapes, evoke Parisian bistros.

The **Washington Street Pub** (⊠ 20 N. Washington St. ☎ 410/822–9011) has a raw bar, 19 beers on tap, hardwood floors, a brick wall behind a bar that stretches on and on, and serves the town's legendary "pub chips."

Shopping

Attic Artifacts (⊠ 305 E. Dover St. ☎ 410/770–8828) is a mishmash of funky paintings, elaborate lamps, and vintage clothing. Owner Lorrie Walpole also runs a cat rescue, and they earn their keep as honorary shopkeepers.

St. Michaels

❾ *9 mi west of Easton via Rte. 33, 49 mi southeast of Annapolis.*

St. Michaels, once a shipbuilding center, is today one of the region's major leisure-time destinations. Its ever-growing popularity has brought more and more shops, cafés, waterfront restaurants, and inns. In warmer months, tourists and boaters crowd its narrow streets and snug harbor.

"The town that fooled the British" in the War of 1812 diverted fire from targets by strategically placing lanterns under the fog cover. The shelling hit just one structure, the **Cannonball House**, built in 1805. It's not open to the public, but you can see it on Mulberry Street at the northwest edge of St. Mary's Square. This square, dedicated to public use, is the core of a neighborhood whose architecture has remained largely unchanged since the 1800s.

In a 17th-century half-timber cabin, the **St. Mary's Square Museum** preserves local artifacts. The most prominent item in the collection was a shipyard bell that still rings at the start of the workday, at lunch, and at quitting time. The museum also occupies the adjoining Teetotum Building, a yellow clapboard house of the Civil War era named for a children's toy it was thought to resemble. ⊠ *St. Mary's Sq.* ☎ *410/745–9561* 🎫 *Donation suggested* ⊗ *May–Oct., weekends 10–4.*

★ ☺ The **Chesapeake Bay Maritime Museum**, one of the region's finest, chronicles the Bay's rich history of boatbuilding, commercial fishing, navigating, and hunting in compelling detail. Exhibits among nine buildings on the 18-acre waterfront site include two of the Bay's unique skipjacks among its more than 80 historic regional boats. There's also the restored 1879 Hooper Strait Lighthouse, a working boatyard, and a "waterman's wharf" with shanties and tools of oystering and crabbing. In the Bay

Building, you can see a dugout canoe hewn by Native Americans and a crabbing skiff. The Waterfowl Building contains carved decoys and stuffed birds, including wood ducks, mallards, and swans. ⊠ *Mill St. at Navy Point* ☎ *410/745–2916* ⊕ *www.cbmm.org* ✒ *$7.50* ۞ *June–Sept., daily 9–6; Oct., Nov., and Mar.–May, daily 9–5; Dec.–Feb., daily 9–4.*

Where to Stay & Eat

★ **$$$** ✕ **208 Talbot.** Unobtrusively situated on St. Michaels' busy main street, 208 Talbot has several intimate dining rooms with exposed brick walls and brick floors. Seafood specialties include such starters as baked oysters with prosciutto, pistachio nuts, and champagne, and baked salmon in a tomato, mushroom, and tarragon sauce. Entrées, all served with tossed salad, include roasted halibut with lobster and mashed potatoes. On Saturday, there's a prix-fixe menu ($50). ⊠ *208 N. Talbot St.* ☎ *410/745–3838* ⊕ *www.208talbot.com* ▭ *D, MC, V* ۞ *Closed Mon. and Tues.*

$$–$$$ ✕ **Town Dock Restaurant.** Every seat in this vast restaurant overlooks the water, and every window frames its own scene; the deck is also open. Fresh seafood dishes such as local red snapper and rockfish and Atlantic salmon are favorites. For a finale, sample some strawberries hand-dipped in chocolate. ⊠ *125 Mulberry St.* ☎ *410/745–5577* ⊕ *www. town-dock.com* ▭ *AE, D, DC, MC, V* ۞ *Closed Tues. and Wed. Nov.–Mar.*

$–$$ ✕ **Crab Claw Restaurant.** Owned and operated by the same family since 1965, this St. Michaels landmark started as a clam- and oyster-shucking house for watermen long before that. Diners at both indoor and outdoor tables have panoramic views over the harbor to the river beyond, but eat dockside if you can. As the name suggests, this is *the* down-home place for fresh steamed and seasoned blue crabs. But the extensive menu also includes sandwiches and other light fare as well as other seafood and meat dishes. Children's platters are available, too. ⊠ *End of Mill St., at the Harbor* ☎ *410/745–2900 or 410/745–9366* ▭ *No credit cards* ۞ *Closed late Dec.–early Mar.*

★ **$$$–$$$$** ✕🛏 **Inn at Perry Cabin.** Set on 25 acres beside the Miles River, this luxury inn employs a nautical theme throughout to elegant effect. Each guest room has unique charm and elegant appointments; standard amenities include heated towel racks, fresh flowers in all rooms, and afternoon tea. Above all, staying here means finding impeccable service. Dining at the inn's restaurant with its flawless cuisine and stellar wine selection is an event. The signature crab spring roll with pink grapefruit, avocado, and toasted almonds, and the lamb shank glazed with honey and tarragon are both exquisite. ⊠ *308 Watkins La., 21663* ☎ *410/745–2200 or 800/722–2949* 🖷 *410/745–3348* ⊕ *www.perrycabin.com* 🛏 *54 rooms, 27 suites* ᕱ *Restaurant, in-room data ports, pool, pond, exercise equipment, massage, sauna, steam room, dock, bar, library, concierge, meeting rooms, helipad; no smoking* ▭ *AE, DC, MC, V.*

★ **$$$–$$$$** 🛏 **Five Gables Inn & Spa.** Three circa 1860 houses have been turned into an elegant and comfortable getaway. All rooms have a private porch or balcony, and all are decorated with antique furnishings, fine linens and towels, and down comforters. The hot stone massage and invigorating rosemary mint body wrap are treatments in the spa. Refreshments are served daily at 3. ⊠ *209 N. Talbot St., 21663* ☎ *410/745–0100 or 877/ 466–0100* 🖷*410/745–2903* ⊕*www.fivegables.com* ⋑*11 rooms, 3 suites* ᛘ *Dining room, cable TV, in-room hot tubs, in-room VCRs, pool, sauna, spa, steam room, bicycles, shops, some pets allowed (fee); no phones in some rooms, no smoking* ▭ *AE, MC, V* ⊺⊖⊺ *CP.*

$$–$$$ 🏠 **Victoriana Inn.** Adirondack chairs line a sloping expanse of lawn leading to the formal gardens of what was once a Civil War army officer's home. Set on the town's harbor and across a footbridge from the Maritime Museum, this inn is a relaxing haven. All rooms include queen-size beds; two have fireplaces and three overlook the water. The suite has a private water-view deck and a fireplace as well as a TV. There's a nightly happy hour that includes wine, beer, and light hors d'oeuvres. ⊠*205 Cherry St., 21663* ☎ *410/745–3368* ⊕ *www.victorianainn.com* ⋑*6 rooms, 1 suite* ᛘ *Bicycles, some fireplaces; no room phones, no TV in some rooms, no kids under 13 on weekends, no smoking, no pets* ▭ *MC, V* ⊺⊖⊺ *BP.*

★ **$$–$$$** 🏠 **Wades Point Inn on the Bay.** Combining the serenity of the country and the splendor of the Chesapeake Bay, this complex of three brick and Colonial wood-frame Victorian buildings is on 120 acres of fields and woodland. The two sun-bright corner rooms in one wing are closest to the water, but each carefully decorated period room has a private porch or balcony. Cows and goats grazing along a 1 mi trail through the property welcome hikers, joggers, and bird-watchers. All are welcome with an unusual stipulation—fishermen, hunters, and children under 14 need to stay on the first floor of one of the buildings. ⊠ *Wades Point Rd. (Rte. 33, Box 7), 21663* ☎ *410/745–2500 or 888/923–3466* ⊕ *www. wadespoint.com* ⋑*23 rooms, 1 farmhouse* ᛘ *Some kitchenettes, pond, dock, hiking, meeting rooms; no a/c in some rooms, no room phones, no room TVs, no kids under 1, no smoking* ▭ *MC, V* ⊺⊖⊺ *CP.*

Sports & the Outdoors

Town Dock Marina (⊠ 305 Mulberry St. ☎ 410/745–2400 or 800/678–8980) rents bicycles as well as surrey-top electric boats and small power-boats. *The Patriot* (⊠ docked near Crab Claw Restaurant and Chesapeake Bay Maritime Museum, St. Michaels ☎ 410/745–3100 ⊕ patriotcruises. com), a 65-foot steel-hull yacht, departs four times daily, from April through October, for one-hour cruises on the Miles River. The tour covers the ecology and history of the area as it passes along the tranquil riverfront landscape.

Shopping

Talbot Street, the main street in St. Michaels, is lined with restaurants, galleries, and all manner of shops, including a hardware store that doubles as a retro gift shop. Stroll between Mill Street, the lane to the Chesapeake Bay Maritime Museum, and Willow Street, or head just beyond to Canton Alley.

Tilghman Island

❿ *13 mi southwest of St. Michaels via Rte. 33.*

A visit to Tilghman Island provides intriguing insight into the Eastern Shore's remarkable character. Leave your car and explore by bike or kayak.

THE VENERABLE SKIPJACKS OF THE CHESAPEAKE BAY

S ETTLEMENT ALONG THE FERTILE SHORES of the Chesapeake Bay was an obvious choice for 17th-century English immigrants, who soon farmed the cash crop of tobacco and plucked plentiful blue crabs and plump oysters from its bottom. Among the reminders of the Bay's fishing culture, which endures, are its dwindling fleet of native skipjacks: broad, flat-bottom wooden sailing vessels for dredging oysters. Economical to build, skipjacks had the shallowest draft—the distance from the waterline to the lowest point of the keel—of any boat in the Chesapeake Bay. This made them essential for cruising above the grassy shoals favored by oysters.

At first, oyster harvesters would stand in small boats and use simple, long-handle tongs, like a pair of scissored rakes, to grasp clumps of oysters from the bottom and bring them aboard. It was tiresome, difficult work. But in the early 1800s, sturdy Yankee schooners, having left the depleted waters of New England, entered the Chesapeake Bay with dredges, ungainly iron contraptions that dragged up oysters along the bottom. With their first large harvest, Chesapeake's fishing industry changed forever.

Dredging was banned initially as exploitive and intrusive, first by Virginia and later by Maryland, but after the Civil War drained the region's economy, Maryland changed its mind and legalized the practice, allowing it under certain conditions for boats powered only by sails. By 1875, more than 690 dredging licenses were issued to owners of pungies, schooners, and sloops. Soon, more sophisticated dredgers emerged, such as "bugeyes" and "brogans." All were loosely called bateaux, French for "boats."

The oyster bounty was not to last. After peaking in 1884 with 15 million bushels, less than a third of that amount was caught in 1891. Despite the growing use of steam and gasoline power on land and water, "only under sail" laws prevailed in the Bay. As the 19th century drew to a close, boatbuilders were forced to experiment with boat designs that were cheap to build and yet had sails that would provide enough power for dredging and transporting the harvests. In 1901, one of these new bateaux appeared in Baltimore's harbor. She caught the eye of a Baltimore Sun newspaper reporter, who wrote that their "quickness to go about may have earned for them the name of skipjack . . .applied by fishermen on the New England coast to the bonita, a flymember of the fish family." The name stuck.

Oysters—and the Chesapeake's renowned blue crab—are still harvested by a dwindling number of watermen, their fleets concentrated in locales such as Crisfield and Kent Narrows, and Smith Island.

Only a dozen sail-powered skipjacks are still working. Taking a ride on one of them (generally from early April through October, when they're not dredging) is an exhilarating way to fully experience the culture and history of the Chesapeake. The region's second-largest working skipjack, the Nellie L. Byrde, is docked in front of Explorer Hall beside Kent Narrows. The Nathan of Dorchester is berthed in Cambridge. The Herman M. Krentz, built in 1955, and the 80-foot Rebecca T. Ruark, originally built in 1886, both sail from Tilghman Island or nearby St. Michaels.

A handful of B&Bs and small inns provide excellent accommodations here. A small fleet of working fishing boats, including a few of the region's remaining skipjacks, call Dogwood Harbor "home port."

Where to Stay & Eat

$$$–$$$$ ✕⌂ **Tilghman Island Inn.** Warm, welcoming conviviality and casual elegance define this compact, modern resort overlooking the Chesapeake Bay (there are also views of a neighboring waterfowl marsh). Five deluxe waterside rooms have hot tubs, fireplaces, and spacious decks. Dishes served at the Gallery Restaurant ($$–$$$) include the unusual black-eyed pea cake and Oysters Choptank. The 5-acre complex includes a 20-slip transient marina and a small fleet of tandem and single kayaks available for rent. ⊠ *Coopertown Rd., Box B, 21671* ☎ *410/886–2141 or 800/866–2141* ⊕ *www.tilghmanislandinn.com* ⌇⟿ *15 rooms, 5 suites* ♌ *Restaurant, in-room data ports, cable TV, tennis court, pool, dock, marina, croquet, 2 bars, meeting rooms, some pets allowed; no smoking* ⊟ *AE, D, DC, MC, V* ⫶○⫶ *CP.*

$$–$$$$ ⌂ **Lazyjack Inn on Dogwood Harbor.** Although this beautiful island inn was severely damaged during a 2003 hurricane, it has since resurfaced with aplomb, now sitting 6 feet higher than its original 1855 foundation. The impeccable rooms are equipped with down comforters and candles in the windows. Guests are welcomed with fresh flowers and a tray of sherry on the bureau. Both suites include a fireplace and an oversize hot tub. You can reserve a sail on the innkeepers' restored 1935 45-foot boat, the *Lady Patty.* ⊠ *5907 Tilghman Island Rd., 21671* ☎ *410/886–2215 or 800/690–5080* ⊕ *www.lazyjackinn.com* ⌇⟿ *2 rooms, 2 suites* ♌ *Boating; no room phones, no room TVs, no kids under 12, no smoking* ⊟ *AE, MC, V* ⫶○⫶ *BP.*

★ $ ⌂ **Sinclair House.** Built in the 1920s as a fishermen's inn, Sinclair House eventually became Tilghman's first B&B. Today, the innkeepers' former lives in international relations are tastefully reflected here. Each guest room is decorated with crafts and artwork from a different culture: baskets and tapestries from southern Africa; rattan furniture and puppets from Indonesia; hand-painted headboards and antique mirrors from Morocco; textiles and *retablos* (small devotional paintings) from Peru. American, European, or Latin specialties are served at breakfast. The common room has satellite TV, along with a VCR and a group of classic films. ⊠ *5718 Black Walnut Point Rd., 21671* ☎ *410/886–2147 or 888/859–2147* ⊕ *www.sinclairhouse.biz* ⌇⟿ *4 rooms* ♌ *Library* ⊟ *AE, D, MC, V.*

Sports & the Outdoors

Tilghman Island's tiny Dogwood Harbor is the home port of two of the region's revered skipjacks. They are available for tours between early April and late October. The ***H. M. Krentz*** (⊠ Dogwood Harbor, Tilghman Island ☎ 410/745–6080 ⊕ www.oystercatcher.com) is U.S. Coast Guard–certified for 32 passengers. A two-hour tour costs $30.

The ***Rebecca T. Ruark*** (⊠ Dogwood Harbor, Tilghman Island ☎ 410/886–2176 or 410/829–3976 ⊕ www.skipjack.org ⫟ 2-hr hands-on learning cruise $30) is U.S. Coast Guard–certified for 49 passengers.

en route	The **Oxford-Bellevue Ferry,** begun in 1683, may be the oldest privately owned ferry in continuous operation in the United States. It crosses the Tred Avon River between Bellevue, 7 mi south of St. Michaels via Routes 33 and 329, and Oxford. ⊠ *N. Morris St. at the Strand, Oxford* ☎ *410/745–9023* ⊕ *www.oxfordbellevueferry.com* 🖃 *Ferry: $7 car and driver one-way, $2 pedestrian, $3 bicycle, $4 motorcycle* ☉ *Mar.–Memorial Day and Labor Day–Nov., weekdays 7 AM–sunset, weekends 9 AM–sunset; Memorial Day to Labor Day, weekdays 7 AM–9 PM, weekends 9–9.*

Oxford

⑪ *7 mi southeast of St. Michaels via Rte. 33 and Rte. 333.*

Tracing its roots to 1683, Oxford remains secluded and untrammeled. Robert Morris, a merchant from Liverpool, lived here with his son, Robert Morris Jr., a signer of the Declaration of Independence. The younger Morris helped finance the Revolution but ended up in debtor's prison after losing at land speculation.

On the riverbank stands a replica of the tiny, one-room **Customs House,** where Jeremiah Banning, the first federal collector of customs, kept track of the traffic at this crucial 18th-century port. The replica of the original 1777 structure is simply but comfortably furnished with antiques of the period. A docent tells the story of the port. ⊠ *N. Morris St.* ☎ *410/226–5122* 🖃 *Free* ☉ *Apr.–Oct., Fri.–Sun. 2–5.*

The **Oxford Museum** displays models and pictures of sailboats. Some boats were built in Oxford, site of one of the first Chesapeake regattas (1860). Check out the full-scale racing boat by the door. Other artifacts include the lamp from a lighthouse on nearby Benoni Point, a sail-maker's bench, and an oyster-shucking stall. Docents elaborate on the exhibits, which set the context for a walking tour of nearby blocks. ⊠ *Morris and Market Sts.* ☎ *410/226–5122* 🖃 *Free* ☉ *Apr.–Oct., Fri.–Sun. 2–5.*

Where to Stay & Eat

$$$–$$$$ ✕ **Latitude 38.** A whimsical red, white, and green color scheme; painted vines climbing the walls; and polished wooden floors distinguish this bistro. Weather permitting, you can eat outdoors at wrought-iron tables in a brick courtyard. The creative and diverse menu changes twice a month and includes such dishes as veal scallopini topped with crab and hollandaise sauce, and crab ravioli in an herbed cream sauce. ⊠ *26342 Oxford Rd.* ☎ *410/226–5303* ⊟ *AE, D, MC, V.*

$–$$$$ ✕ **Robert Morris Inn.** In the early 1700s, this building on the banks of the Tred Avon River was crafted as a home by ships' carpenters using ship nails, hand-hewn beams, and pegged paneling. In 1738 it was bought by an English trading company as a house for its Oxford representative, Robert Morris. Four guest rooms have handmade wall paneling and fireplaces built of English bricks used as boat ballast. Other buildings in the complex include a newer manor house on a private beach. Circa 18th-century murals of river scenes adorn the walls of the main room in the inn's restaurant ($$–$$$), known for its meticulous preparation of the Chesapeake Bay's bounty. ⊠ *314 N. Morris St., 21654*

☎ *410/226–5111* 🖷 *410/226–5744* ⊕ *www.robertmorrisinn.com* 🖙 *35 rooms* ⚭ *Restaurant, taproom, Internet, meeting rooms; no room phones, no TV in some rooms, no smoking* ⊟ *AE, MC, V.*

★ **$$$$** 🏢 **Combsberry.** This 1730 brick house, together with a carriage house and cottage and a formal garden, is set amid magnolias and willows on the banks of Island Creek. Inside are five arched fireplaces, floral chintz fabrics, and polished wood floors. All the rooms and suites of this luxurious B&B have water views and are furnished with English manor–style antiques, including four-poster and canopy beds. Some also have hot tubs and working fireplaces; the two-bedroom Carriage House has a kitchen. ⊠ *4837 Evergreen Rd., 21654* ☎ *410/226–5353* ⊕ *www. combsberry.com* 🖙 *2 rooms, 2 suites, 1-bedroom cottage, 2-bedroom carriage house* ⚭ *Dining room, library, some pets allowed; no room phones, no room TVs, no kids under 12* ⊟ *AE, MC, V* 🍽 *BP.*

DORCHESTER COUNTY

One of the larger, yet sparsely populated counties on Maryland's Eastern Shore, Dorchester retains bits of early America in its picture-postcard towns and waterfront fishing villages. Gunslinger Annie Oakley and Underground Railroad activist Harriet Tubman are among the county's most famous residents. The expansive Choptank River, its northern boundary, and the rambling 28,000-acre Blackwater National Wildlife Refuge are idyllic locales for biking and boating, hiking and camping, and hunting and fishing (including crabbing).

Cambridge

⓬ *15 mi southeast of Oxford via U.S. 50, 55 mi southeast of Annapolis via U.S. 50/301 to U.S. 50.*

In this county seat, Annie Oakley used to aim at waterfowl from the ledge of her waterfront home. Graceful Georgian, Queen Anne, and Colonial Revival buildings abound: with an art gallery here and a museum there, a night or two in Cambridge can be very refreshing.

The three-story, 18th-century Georgian **Meredith House** is headquarters of the Dorchester County Historical Society. Chippendale, Hepplewhite, and Sheraton period antiques fill the first floor. The Children's Room holds an impressive doll collection, cradles, miniature china, and baby carriages. Portraits and effects of seven former Maryland governors from Dorchester County adorn the Governor's Room. There's also a restored smokehouse, blacksmith's shop, and medicinal herb garden. ⊠ *902 La Grange Ave.* ☎ *410/228–7953* 🎟 *Free* ☉ *Year-round, weekdays 10–1, Sat. 10–4 Apr.–Oct., and by appt.*

The **James B. Richardson Maritime Museum** in downtown Cambridge celebrates and chronicles Chesapeake boatbuilding with impressive, scaled-down versions of boats peculiar to the Chesapeake Bay, such as bugeyes, pungies, skipjacks, and log canoes—and the tools used to build them. Photos, a film, and a model boatbuilding workroom complement the models. ⊠ *401 High St.* ☎ *410/221–1871* 🎟 *Free* ☉ *Wed. and weekends 1–4 and by appt.*

The small **Harriet Tubman Museum** dedicated to the former slave who helped lead more than 300 other slaves to freedom along the Underground Railroad. Tubman was born and raised in and around Cambridge. At the museum, artifacts and documents about her life are on display. ⊠ *424 Race St.* ☎ *410/228–0401* 🖃 *Donations accepted* ☉ *Weekdays 9–5.*

off the
beaten
path

SPOCOTT WINDMILL – Maryland's only English post windmill—which, unlike stationary Dutch windmills, can rotate 360-degrees—stands 6 mi west of Cambridge on Route 343. It's a replica of one destroyed in an 1888 blizzard. Also open to the public are the miller's tenant house, a one-room schoolhouse dating to 1868, and a country store from the 1930s. The windmill operates only sporadically for celebrations, but a good gust of wind will give you a great snapshot to take home. ⊠ *Rte. 343* ☎ *410/228–7090* 🖃 *Free; donations accepted* ☉ *Mon.–Sat. 10–5.*

Where to Stay & Eat

$–$$$ ✕ **Snappers Waterfront Cafe.** Join regulars at this casual waterside restaurant and bar on the edge of town. Choose from an extensive menu of dishes with a Southwestern flavor, healthy portions of steak, and such entrées as baked stuffed shrimp. ⊠ *112 Commerce St.* ☎ *410/228–0112* 🚍 *AE, D, MC, V.*

$$$$ 🏨 **Hyatt Regency Chesapeake Bay Golf Resort, Spa and Marina.** This 370-acre complex is the Eastern Shore's first full-service, year-round resort, and one that takes full advantage of the soothing natural light and spectacular views of the Choptank River. The resort includes an 18-acre Blue Heron rookery, an 18,000-square-foot spa, and a golf course designed by Keith Foster. All rooms and suites have a private balcony; those on the upper level have raised ceilings. The resort's restaurants include the self-service Bay Country Market and the Blue Point Provision Company for seafood. Two outdoor sandstone fireplaces make perfect s'more hubs, and a 30-foot-high wall of windows welcome you to Michener's Library. ⊠ *100 Heron Blvd., 21613* ☎ *410/901–1234* 🖶 *410/901–6301* ⊕ *chesapeakebay.hyatt.com* ⇆ *384 rooms, 16 suites* ♿ *5 restaurants, snack bar, room service, in-room data ports, in-room safes, refrigerators, cable TV, 18-hole golf course, 4 tennis courts, indoor-outdoor pool, health club, spa, beach, marina, bar, lounge, shops, concierge, Internet, business services, convention center, meeting rooms* 🚍 *AE, D, MC, V.*

$$ 🏨 **The Cambridge House.** Set on a brick, tree-lined row of stately sea captains' homes in the old part of town, the Cambridge House has been refurbished from its former use as an apartment building. The interior is pure Victorian, with a stunning guest parlor with crimson walls, fringed lamps and curtains, and a cherub border on the ceiling. A back deck leads to gravel paths and ponds. ⊠ *112 High St., 21613* ☎ *410/ 221–7700 or 877/221–7799* 🖶 *410/221–7736* ⇆ *6 rooms* ♿ *In-room data ports, cable TV, in-room VCRs, pond; no kids under 8, no smoking* 🚍 *AE, D, MC, V* 🍴 *BP.*

$$ 🏨 **Glasgow Inn.** A long driveway crossing a broad landscaped lawn leads to this stately white plantation house that evokes its genteel 18th-

century beginnings. All rooms are filled with period prints and furniture, including four-poster beds. Front rooms look out over the lawn to the Choptank River. ⊠ *1500 Hambrooks Blvd., 21613* ☎ *410/228–0575* ⊕ *410/221–0297* ✍ *10 rooms, 5 with bath* ⚭ *Dining room, croquet, meeting rooms; no room phones, no TV in some rooms, no smoking* ⊟ *No credit cards* ⦵ *BP.*

Sports & the Outdoors

All of the land of the **Fishing Bay Wildlife Management Area,** bordering Blackwater National Wildlife Refuge, is along **Fishing Bay** at the southern end of Dorchester County. Here you can take a pair of "water trails" through some scenic rivers and streams—it's reminiscent of Florida's Everglades. A short canoeing or kayaking trek down one of these water trails—recommended only for paddlers with some experience—is an exceptional way to experience a salt marsh and the wildlife that lives in one. Contact the Dorchester County Department of Tourism (410/228–1000) for more information, as well as a waterproof map.

The ***Nathan of Dorchester,*** a skipjack replica, cruises the Choptank River from Long Wharf at the foot of High Street in Cambridge. In summer the 28-passenger *Nathan* sets sail on most Saturday evenings and Sunday afternoons. Two-hour cruises cost $20. ⊠ *Long Wharf, 526 Poplar St.* ☎ *410/228–7141* ⊕ *www.skipjack-nathan.org.*

The paddle wheelers *Dorothy & Megan* and **Choptank River Queen** run a full schedule of sightseeing, lunch, and dinner cruises between April and December from their berth at the unluckily named Suicide Bridge Restaurant. A 90-minute sightseeing tour costs $14. ⊠ *6304 Suicide Bridge Rd., Hurlock* ☎ *410/943–4689* ⊕ *www.suicidebridge.com* ⊟ *MC, V.*

Blackwater National Wildlife Refuge

⑬ *8 mi south of Cambridge via Rte. 16 to Rte. 335, 63 mi southeast of Annapolis.*

The largest nesting bald eagle population north of Florida makes Blackwater its home. You can often see the birds perching on the lifeless tree trunks that poke from the wetlands here, part of nearly 28,000 acres of woods, open water, marsh, and farmland. In fall and spring, some 35,000 Canada and snow geese pass through in their familiar V formations to and from their winter home, joining more than 15,000 ducks. The rest of the year, residents include endangered species such as peregrine falcons and silver-hair Delmarva fox squirrels. Great blue heron stand like sentinels while ospreys dive for meals, birds sing, and tundra swans preen endlessly. By car or bike, you can follow a 5-mi road through several habitats or follow a network of trails on foot. Exhibits and films in the visitor center provide background and insight. ⊠ *Rte. 335 at Key Wallace Dr.* ☎ *410/228–2677* ⊕ *www.friendsofblackwater.org* ✑ *$3 car, $1 pedestrian or cyclist* ☉ *Wildlife drive daily, dawn–dusk. Visitor center weekdays 8–4, weekends 9–5.*

THE LOWER EASTERN SHORE

The three counties of Maryland's lower Eastern Shore—Wicomico, Worcester, and Somerset—contain the contrasting cultures of the Chesapeake Bay and the Atlantic coast but still share a common history.

From the north, the Nanticoke River flows out of southern Delaware across fertile farmland into the Chesapeake Bay near the Blackwater National Wildlife Refuge. To the east, the Atlantic alternately caresses and pounds sturdy shorelines and fragile barrier islands stretching from the Delaware Bay to easternmost Virginia. In the Eastern Shore's southwestern corner, a few towns cling to the shoreline of Tangier Sound among vast Wildlife Management Areas.

The small towns throughout the region sometimes seem a century away from the oceanfront's summertime bustle. Main Street shops, Early-American inns, and unsung restaurants are a far cry from the boutiques and galleries, the high-rise hotels and condos, and eateries of nearby Ocean City, which clings to a narrow, sandy strip.

Salisbury

⓮ *32 mi southeast of Cambridge via U.S. 50, 87 mi southeast of Annapolis via U.S. 50/301 to U.S. 50.*

Barges still ply the slow-moving Wicomico River between the Bay and Salisbury, the Eastern Shore's second-largest port after Baltimore. The tree-shaded waterfront is a popular draw for hiking, biking, boating, fishing, and shopping. Antiques shops and galleries, along with some exemplary Victorian architecture, fill the six blocks that make up downtown.

The Federal-style **Poplar Hill Mansion** provides a glimpse of gentility in the early 1800s. The mansion, among the few old buildings to survive devastating fires in 1860 and 1866, displays meticulous attention to details large and small—the fluted pilasters framing the door, the two-story Palladian window that floods the arched 12-foot hallway with light, the hand-carved moldings in ornate rooms. ⊠ *117 Elizabeth St.* ☎ *410/749–1776* ⊴ *$2* ☉ *By appt. only.*

★ Operated in partnership with Salisbury University, the **Ward Museum of Wildfowl Art** presents realistic marshland and wildfowl displays. Two brothers from Crisfield, Lem and Steve Ward, helped transform decoy making from just a utilitarian pursuit to an art form; their re-created studio is a must-see exhibit. Besides the premier collection of wildfowl art, the 30,000-square-foot museum has some 2,000 other artifacts as well as a gift shop and library. ⊠ *3416 Schumaker Pond, at Beaglin Park Dr.* ☎ *410/742–4988* ⊕ *www.wardmuseum.org* ⊴ *$7* ☉ *Mon.–Sat. 10–5, Sun. noon–5.*

Ocelots, otters, and bears are a few of the wild animals at the **Salisbury Zoo.** What started out as a foster home for some stray deer and a bear in 1954 has grown into a delightful glimpse of the wild. ⊠ *755 S. Park Dr.* ☎ *410/548–3188* ⊟ *410/860–0919* ⊕ *www.salisburyzoo.org*

🎟 *Free* ⏲ *Labor Day–Memorial Day, daily 8–4:30; Memorial Day–Labor Day, daily 8–7:30.*

Arthur W. Perdue Stadium, home of the Class A Delmarva Shorebirds, an affiliate of the Baltimore Orioles, combines modern niceties with a nod to old-time ballparks. A tent-covered picnic deck sits behind first base, and children flock to a carousel and playground. You can enjoy a game from the Hardball Café, behind home plate, or in the Birdsview Restaurant, on the first-base side. Home games are played from April through August. ✉ *Hobbs Rd. and U.S. 50* 🕿 *410/219–3112 or 888/ 247–3796* ⊕ *www.theshorebirds.com* 🎟 *Games $6.*

Where to Stay & Eat

$–$$$ ✕ **The Red Roost.** Inside a former chicken barn, inverted bushel baskets now serve as light fixtures at this down-home crab house, where hammering mallets rival the beat of piano and banjo sing-alongs. The Red Roost gets rave reviews for its seafood specialties and ribs, as well as its meaty steamed crabs. ✉ *Rte. 352 and Rte. 362, Whitehaven* 🕿 *410/ 546–5443 or 800/953–5443* ⊟ *AE, MC, V* ⏲ *Closed Nov.–Mar. and Mon. and Tues., Labor Day–Memorial Day. No lunch.*

$–$$ ☷ **Whitehaven Bed & Breakfast.** In a secluded waterside village where George Washington's mother once lived, this mid-19th-century inn, a handsome, white Victorian main house and a cottage, puts a premium on tranquillity. Surrounded by bike-friendly country roads with little traffic, only the three-car, cable-driven ferry that crosses the river to Princess Anne disturbs the peace. All rooms have a coffeemaker. Rates include wine in the early evening, cookies and fruit cordials at bedtime, and an elegant breakfast served on fine china. The B&B also operates boat tours on a Chesapeake workboat. ✉ *23844–48 River Rd., 18 mi southwest of Salisbury, Whitehaven 21856* 🕿 *410/873–3294 or 888/205–5921* 🖷 *410/873–2162* ⊕ *www.whitehaven.com* ⤴ *5 rooms, 3 with private bath* ⚓ *Boating, bicycles, library, some pets allowed; no room phones, no room TVs, no smoking* ⊟ *AE, D, MC, V* ⋈ *BP.*

Shopping

At **Salisbury Pewter** (✉ U.S. 13, between Salisbury and the Delaware border 🕿 410/546–1188), shoppers can watch pewter being turned by hand and buy quality seconds, factory overruns, and discontinued pieces in many styles. It's closed on Sunday.

Snow Hill

⓯ *19 mi southeast of Salisbury via Rte. 12, 106 mi southeast of Annapolis.*

The streets of Snow Hill, the Worcester County seat, are lined with huge sycamores and stately homes the reflect its days as a shipping center in the 18th and 19th centuries.

The **Julia A. Purnell Museum** tells the town's story with spinning wheels, mousetraps, and other miscellany illustrating the 100-year life of its subject, an ordinary citizen who died in 1943. ✉ *208 W. Market St.* 🕿 *410/632–0515* ⊕ *www.purnellmuseum.com* 🎟 *$2* ⏲ *Tues.–Sat. 10–4, Sun. 1–4.*

The redbrick **All Hallows Episcopal Church,** (✉ 109 W. Market ☎ 410/632–2327) completed in 1756, occupies the site of an earlier sanctuary. Inside is a Bible that belonged to Queen Anne. The church is one of the Snow Hill historic structures that appear in a walking-tour brochure available at the Julia A. Purnell Museum or, on weekdays, at Town Hall, at the corner of Green and Bank.

Where to Stay

$$ 🏨 **Chanceford Hall.** This mansion's Georgian front section was begun in 1759 and later three times. Chimneys seem to soar from every corner. Ten working fireplaces and the contrast of cool Williamsburg greens and blues welcome you throughout the guest rooms and public areas. A huge fireplace mantel moved from the ballroom overlooks a 12-place dining table and a breakfront bookcase crafted of yew wood. ✉ *209 W. Federal St., 21863* ☎ *410/632–2900 or 888/494–8817* ⊕ *www.chancefordhall.com* ⇨ *4 rooms* ⚴ *Pool, bicycles, croquet, volleyball, meeting rooms; no room phones, no room TVs, no smoking* ☰ *MC, V* 🍽 *BP.*

Sports & the Outdoors

CANOEING **Pocomoke River Canoe Company** (✉ 312 N. Washington St., Snow Hill ☎ 410/632–3971 🖷 410/632–2866 ⊕ www.atbeach.com/amuse/md/canoe) rents canoes, offers lessons, and leads tours along the Pocomoke River, a habitat for bald eagles, blue herons, and egrets.

The Bald Cypress tidal river winds gently through miles of pristine woodland. You can paddle a canoe through this environment on an **inn-to-inn tour** (☎ 410/632–2722 ⊕ www.inntours.com) arranged by the River House B&B. After a full breakfast at a participating inn, you spend the day drifting past waterside homes, hidden landings, and abundant wildlife. Have a picnic lunch on a quiet bank or in a riverside park. Dinner awaits at your next overnight inn; then continue on for a second day (luggage transfers are included). A standard two-day, two-night, all-inclusive self-paddling trip is $700 for two, and is one of several tours available spring, summer, and fall. Shorter itineraries are available and trips may be customized.

Berlin

⑯ *15 mi northeast of Snow Hill via Rte. 113, 22 mi east of Salisbury via U.S. 50; 7 mi west of Ocean City via U.S. 50.*

Berlin is a short drive from Ocean City but is far less strident and loud in temperament. Magnolias, sycamores, and ginkgo trees line streets filled with predominantly Federal- and Victorian-style buildings (47 are on the National Register of Historic Places). By the way, the name comes not from the German city but from Burleigh Inn, a Colonial way station.

Where to Stay & Eat

★ ¢–$$$ ✕🏨 **Atlantic Hotel.** This fully restored 1895 inn blends the taste of grand living with modern conveniences. Guest rooms are spacious and have four-poster beds on hardwood floors. Beneath chandeliers, the hotel's formal dining room ($$–$$$) serves scrumptious entrées that may include a pistachio duck dish or rockfish topped with oysters, ham, and crabmeat. In the tavern, a very talented waiter periodically joins the pianist and sings. The second-floor parlor, done in bold red-and-green hues with ornate furnishings, is a perfect place to relax. ⊠ *2 N. Main St., 21811* ☎ *410/641–3589 or 800/814–7672* ☎ *410/641–4928* ⊕ *www. atlantichotel.com* ↪ *17 rooms* ⚐ *Restaurant, café, cable TV, in-room phones, library, meeting rooms; no smoking* ⊟ *AE, MC, V.*

Ocean City

⓱ *7 mi east of Berlin and 29 mi east of Salisbury via U.S. 50.*

Stretching some 10 mi along a narrow barrier island off Maryland's Atlantic coast, Worcester County's Ocean City draws millions annually to its broad beaches and the innumerable activities and amenities that cling to them, as well as to the quiet bayside.

On the older, southern end of the island, where the 3-mi Boardwalk begins, is a restored 19th-century carousel as well as traditional stomach-churning amusement park rides and a fishing pier. The north–south roads, as well as the Boardwalk itself, are crowded with shops selling the prerequisites of resort destinations everywhere, from artwork to T-shirts to snack food to beer. Beyond the northern end of the Boardwalk (27th Street), high-rise condos prevail, and the beaches are less congested.

Lodging options include modern high-rises, sleepy motels, two B&Bs, and older hotels with oceanfront porches filled with wooden chaises longues and rocking chairs. Cuisine here includes Thrasher's renowned "Boardwalk" fries, available from three outlets throughout Ocean City, to fine restaurant fare accompanied by impressive wine lists. Fresh seafood abounds.

A year-round destination, Ocean City is particularly appealing in the fall and early winter, then again in late winter and early spring, when the weather is mild. Most hotels and better restaurants remain open year-round, although the latter may operate on fewer days and/or shorter schedules. Furthermore, many festivals and other special events are scheduled for the off-season.

★ On the southernmost tip of the island, the **Ocean City Life Saving Station Museum** traces the resort to its days as a tiny fishing village in the late 1800s. Housed in an 1891 building that once held the U.S. Lifesaving Service and the Coast Guard, the museum's exhibits include models of the grand old hotels, artifacts from shipwrecks, boat models, five saltwater aquariums, an exhibit of sands from around the world, and even itchy wool swimsuits and an old mechanical laughing lady from the Boardwalk. Press the button, and you can be laughing with her. ⊠ *Boardwalk at the Inlet* ☎ *410/289–4991* ⊕ *www.ocmuseum.org* ☒ *$3* ⊗ *June–Sept., daily 11–10; May and Oct., daily 11–4; Nov.–Apr., weekends 10–4.*

☾ **Trimper's Amusement Park,** at the south end of the Boardwalk, has a "boomerang" roller coaster; the rickety and terrifying "Zipper"; and the Hirschell Spellman Carousel, from 1902. The park has been owned by the Trimper family since it opened in 1890. ⊠ *Boardwalk and S. 1st St.*

☎ 410/289–8617 ◻ *Pay per ride or attraction* ◷ *Memorial Day–Labor Day, weekdays 1* PM*–midnight; weekends noon–midnight. Labor Day–Memorial Day indoor portion only, weekends noon–midnight.*

Wheels of Yesterday. This museum of antique or otherwise collectible cars has famed comedian Jack Benny's Overland and other cars and trucks from throughout the 20th century. All but a handful of the vehicles make up a private collection—and all are roadworthy. ⊠ *12708 Ocean Gateway, Rte. 50* ☎ *410/213–7329* ◻ *$4.*

Where to Eat

★ **$$–$$$$** ✕ **Fager's Island.** This bayside restaurant gives you white-linen treatment and views of soothing wetlands and the bay, and stunning sunsets through its large windows. White stucco walls and white columns contrast with red tile floors and brass chandeliers. Entrées include prime rib, fresh mahimahi, and salmon. There's an outside deck for more informal dining and a raw bar with lighter fare. On a whimsical note: Tchaikovsky's *1812* Overture is played every evening, with the tumultuous finale timed to coincide with the setting of the sun. ⊠ *60th St. at the Bay* ☎ *410/524–5500* ⊕ *www.fagers.com* ⌂ *Reservations essential* ☰ *AE, D, DC, MC, V.*

$$–$$$ ✕ **Harrison's Harbor Watch Restaurant and Raw Bar.** Overlooking the Ocean City Inlet at the island's southernmost tip, this sprawling, two-story seafood restaurant includes only freshly prepared sauces, soups, breads, and dressings on its menu, with fish and meat cut and prepared daily. A raw bar is also available. Comfortable booths have tile tabletops and clear ocean views. There's seashell-pattern carpeting, ocean scenes on the walls, and huge fish-market signs and lobster artwork hanging from a sloped wood-beam ceiling. ⊠ *Boardwalk at the Inlet* ☎ *410/289–5121* ☰ *AE, D, DC, MC, V.*

$$–$$$ ✕ **The Hobbit.** Dedicated to Bilbo Baggins and other literary creations of J. R. R. Tolkien, this elegant bayside dining room has murals depicting scenes from the classic novel, and wood table lamps are carved in the shapes of individual Hobbits. The deck is popular with summer diners. Veal with pistachios is sautéed in a sauce of Madeira, veal stock, prosciutto, mushrooms, shallots, and heavy cream. Hobbit Catch is the fish of the day (typically salmon, swordfish, or tuna). Light fare is served in the adjoining bar as well as in the café. A gift shop sells Hobbit-related T-shirts and gifts. ⊠ *101 81st St.* ☎ *410/524–8100* ⊕ *www.hobbitgifts. com* ☰ *AE, D, MC, V.*

$$–$$$ ✕ **Phillips Crab House & Seafood Buffet.** Feast on crab cakes, crab imperial, or stuffed and fried shrimp at the original 1956 home of a restaurant that has since become a chain. The dark-panel dining room has decorative stone floors, hanging Tiffany-style lamps, stained-glass windows, and funky wall art. Its wildly popular buffet is served in an upstairs dining room. ⊠ *21st St. and Philadelphia Ave.* ☎ *410/289–6821 or 800/549–2722* ⊕ *www.phillipsoc.com* ☰ *AE, D, MC, V.*

Where to Stay

During the high-season months of summer, Ocean City has about 10,000 hotel rooms to choose from. A narrow island means that no lodging is far from either the ocean or the bay. Rates vary dramatically through the year, with the lowest typically between mid-November and mid-March, and the highest during the months of July and August. A room with an ocean view will almost always come with a premium rate.

★ $$$$ ▦ **The Edge.** Opened in 2002, the Edge's accommodations exude quality and style. In this boutique hotel, each of the rooms is uniquely furnished to evoke such locales as Bali or the Caribbean, the French Riviera or southern Italy, and even the *Orient Express*. From queen- and king-size feather beds to gas-fed fireplaces, no amenity is amiss. Windows that take up the entire west-facing room walls allow for panoramic views at sunset. ⊠ *56th St. at the Bay, 21842* ☎ *410/524–5400 or 888/371–5400* ⊟ *410/524–3928* ⊕ *www.fagers.com* ⟿ *10 rooms, 2 suites, 1 penthouse* ⟁ *In-room hot tubs, minibars, refrigerators, pool* ⊟ *AE, D, DC, MC, V.*

$$–$$$$ ▦ **Dunes Manor Hotel.** The Victorian theme of the lobby, with immense crystal chandeliers and a carved ceiling, sets the tone for this hotel, built in 1987 to replicate a 19th-century seashore resort. Step beyond the lobby and settle into a green rocking chair overlooking the ocean. All rooms are oceanfront and have two double beds, pickled-pine furniture, and private balconies; suites include a full kitchen. Formal, white-glove High Tea, open to nonguests, is served on silver each afternoon. The hotel is a block beyond the north end of the Boardwalk. ⊠ *2800 Baltimore Ave., at the Boardwalk, 21842* ☎ *410/289–1100 or 800/523–2888* ⊟ *410/289–4905* ⊕ *www.dunesmanor.com* ⟿ *160 rooms, 10 suites* ⟁ *Restaurant, microwaves, refrigerators, indoor-outdoor pool, gym, hot tub, bar, free parking* ⊟ *AE, D, DC, MC, V.*

★ $–$$$$ ▦ **Lighthouse Club Hotel.** This elegant all-suite hotel is a Chesapeake Bay "screwpile" lighthouse look-alike of uncommonly quiet luxury, just blocks from the busy Coastal Highway. Its airy, contemporary suites have high ceilings and views of sand dunes that slope to the Assawoman Bay. Rooms have white-cushion rattan furniture and marble bathrooms with two-person hot tubs and the convenience of coffeemakers and plush terry robes. Sliding glass doors lead to private decks with steamer chairs. ⊠ *60th St. at the Bay, 21842* ☎ *410/524–5400 or 888/371–5400* ⊕ *www.fagers.com* ⟿ *23 suites* ⟁ *Minibars, refrigerators, hot tubs* ⊟ *AE, D, DC, MC, V.*

$–$$ ▦ **Atlantic Hotel.** Family owned and operated, the three-story, H-shape frame hotel—Ocean City's oldest—is a replacement of the original Victorian hotel that burned in 1922. Rooms are plainly furnished and decorated just as they were originally, but now with modern comforts, such as air-conditioning. This is oceanside vacationing as it was in a calmer era. ⊠ *Boardwalk and Wicomico St., 21843* ☎ *800/328–5268 or 410/289–9111* ⊟ *410/289–2221* ⊕ *www.atlantichotelocmd.com* ⟿ *90 rooms* ⟁ *Cable TV* ⊟ *MC, V* ⊗ *Closed Oct.–Apr.*

¢–$$ ▦ **The Lankford Hotel & Apartments.** Opened in 1924, the Lankford is still owned by the family of the original owners. Many combinations of rooms in the hotel and the adjacent lodge are available for small groups of friends and families. Bicycle storage and Ocean City Golf Course privileges are included in the rate. Lazing in a rickety rocking chair on the front porch off the small (unair-conditioned) lobby, cooled by overhead fans, is a true throwback to quieter times. (All guest rooms are air-conditioned.) ⊠ *8th St. at the Boardwalk, 21842* ☎ *410/289–4041 or 800/282–9709 late May–Sept., 410/289–4667 Oct.–late May* 🖶 *410/ 289–4809* ⊕ *www.ocean-city.com* ↩ *23 rooms, 28 suites and apartments* ⬡ *Laundry facilities, free parking* ▭ *No credit cards* ⊘ *Closed Columbus Day weekend through Apr.*

Nightlife & the Arts

In summer Ocean City provides enough entertainment for everyone, ranging from refined to rowdy. Some bars and clubs close in midwinter, but most of those with live music remain open.

BARS   Open since 1976, the large sports saloon known as the **Greene Turtle** (⊠ Coastal Hwy. at 116th St. ☎ 410/723–2120) has been hugely popular.

The waterside **Seacrets Bar and Grill** (⊠ 49th St. at the Bay ☎ 410/524–4900) often presents four live bands at four different entertainment venues. The crowds run in age from those in their early 20s on through baby boomers, proving that you're never too old to sip a piña colada on an inner tube.

DANCE CLUBS   One of the most versatile complexes for older teens and those in their twenties, **Big Kahuna** (⊠ Coastal Hwy. at 17th St. ☎ 410/289–6331) is a DJ-driven "party place"; others include the **Paddock,** pumping out heart-thumping recorded and live music with a bit more volume and flash; and **Rush,** a Miami-style dance club for a well-dressed clientele.

The huge **Bonfire Restaurant & Nightclub** (⊠71st St. and Ocean Hwy. ☎410/ 524–7171) serves an all-you-can-eat buffet and an à la carte menu. It caters to thirties-and-over diners enjoying the live Top 40 music played by local groups. It's closed Monday–Thursday, mid-October–mid-March.

Sports & the Outdoors

Although Ocean City is mainly a summertime resort, there are also lots of outdoor things to do once you feel like getting up off your beach towel. The Atlantic Ocean and Assawoman Bay is the biggest playground. But besides fishing of many kinds, power boating and sailing, you can also kiteboard, parasail, and jet ski. For the less adventurous, kayaks and canoes glide through the gentle Bay wetlands. Back on land there's biking, tennis, volleyball, and (especially) golf.

BICYCLING   A portion of Coastal Highway has been designated for bus and bicycle traffic. Bicycle riding is allowed on the Ocean City Boardwalk from 5 AM to 10 AM in summer and 5 AM to 4 PM the rest of the year. The bike route from Ocean City to Assateague Island (U.S. 50 to Rte. 611) is a 9-mi trek, and Assateague itself is crisscrossed by a number of clearly marked, paved trails.

Bike rentals are available throughout Ocean City, "every three blocks" according to some. One of the oldest bike rental, sales, and service enterprises is the highly respected **Mike's Bikes** (⊠ N. Division St. and Baltimore Ave. ☎ 410/289–5404 ⊕ www.mikesbikesoc.com ⊠ N. 1st St. at the Boardwalk ☎ 410/289–4637). Rates are $5 for the first hour, $3 for every hour thereafter for regular adult bikes up to $20 an hour for a six-passenger-and-two-toddler surrey.

BOATING   Assawoman Bay, between the Ocean City barrier island and the mainland, is where you can go deep-sea fishing, sailing, jet skiing, and paragliding. **Sailing, Etc.** (⊠ 5305 Coastal Hwy. ☎ 410/723–1144) rents sailboats, catamarans, kayaks, and Windsurfers and teaches sailing and windsurfing.

FISHING   No fishing licenses are required in Ocean City. Public fishing piers on the Assawoman Bay and Isle of Wight Bay are at (south to north) 3rd, 9th, 40th, and 125th streets and at the inlet in Ocean City. Other fishing and crabbing areas include the U.S. 50 bridge, Oceanic Pier, Ocean City Pier at Wicomico Street and the Boardwalk. Crabbing is especially good at Northside Park.

Bahia Marina (⊠ 21st St. and the Bay ☎ 410/289–7438 or 888/575–3625) is a great venue for sportfishing enthusiasts. It has spotless charterboats, live bait and tackle, and opportunities for bottom fishing.

Ocean City Fishing Center (⊠ U.S. 50 and Shantytown Rd., West Ocean City ☎ 410/213–1121 ⊕ www.ocfishing.com) is Ocean City's largest deep-sea charter boat marina with some 30 vessels and Coast Guard–licensed professional captains. In addition to catering to preformed groups, the Fishing Center will form fishing groups of individuals who are on their own.

GOLF   Now rivaling premier golfing destinations around the United States, Ocean City is within easy driving distance of more than 21 golf courses. For a complete listing of courses and details, contact the Worcester County Tourism office or Ocean City Visitor Center. The Web site **Ocean City Golf Getaway** (⊕ www.oceancitygolf.com) is full of good information about courses.

VOLLEYBALL   The **Eastern Volleyball Association** (☎ 410/250–2577) coordinates a series of professional and pro–am tournaments at several beach locations on summer weekends.

Shopping

Ocean City's 3-mi-long boardwalk is lined with retail outlets for food, gifts, and souvenirs, as well as several specialty stores. Side streets are rife with still more. Shopping malls are along the length of the island on Coastal Highway. Factory outlets are just across the U.S. 50 bridge.

The Kite Loft (⊠ 5th St. at the Boardwalk ☎ 410/289–6852 ⊠ 45th St. Village ☎ 410/524–0800 ⊠ Coastal Hwy. at 131st St. ☎ 410/250–4970) has a dazzling line of kites as well as banners, flags, and wind socks, hammocks and sky chairs, whirligigs and wind chimes.

The Lankford Shops (⊠ 8th St. at the Boardwalk ☎ 410/289–8232), operated by the Lankford Hotel, sell bikinis, handicrafts, hobby supplies— such as miniature furniture for dollhouses—and ocean-side souvenirs.

Ocean City Factory Outlets (⊠ U.S. 50 and Golf Course Rd. ☎ 800/625–6696 ⊕ www.ocfactoryoutlets.com), which has more than 80 stores, is made up of mostly big-name retailers like Gap, Ann Taylor, Tommy Hilfiger, Carter's for Kids and Harry & David.

Assateague Island National Seashore

18 *11 mi south of Ocean City.*

FodorsChoice
★

The Assateague Island National Seashore occupies the northern two-thirds of the 37-mi-long barrier island: a small portion of the seashore is operated as Assateague State Park. ("Assateague" means "a marshy place across.") The southern third of the island is the Chincoteague National Wildlife Refuge, in Virginia. Although most famous for the small, shaggy, sturdy wild horses (adamantly called "ponies" by the public) that roam freely along the beaches and roads, the National Seashore is also worth getting to know for its wildland, wildlife (including the beautiful Sika deer), and opportunities for having fun outdoors. In summer the seashore's mild surf is where you can find shorebirds tracing the lapping waves back down the beach. Behind the dunes, the island's forests and bayside marshes are well worth exploring, and there are three self-guided nature trail walks that let you do just that.

Swimming, biking, hiking, surf fishing, picnicking, and camping are all available on the island. The visitor center at the entrance to the park has aquariums and hands-on exhibits about the seashore's birds and ocean creatures as well as the famous ponies. ⊠ *7206 National Seashore La., Rte. 611* ☎ *410/641–1441* ⊕ *www.assateagueisland. com* ☒ *7-day pass Maryland/Virginia section $3/$10 per vehicle; $2 per person for bicycles and pedestrians* ☉ *Visitor center daily 9–5, park daily 24 hrs.*

Crisfield

19 *33 mi southwest of Salisbury via U.S. 13 to Rte. 413.*

In William W. Warner's study of the Chesapeake Bay, *Beautiful Swimmers,* Crisfield was described as a "town built upon oyster shells, millions of tons of it. A town created by and for the blue crab, Cradle of the Chesapeake seafood industries, where everything was tried first." The number of seafood processing plants here—where workers still pick crabs and shuck oysters as they have for more than a century, by hand—has dwindled to just three from more than 150, but you can still marvel at the craft and listen to workers singing hymns as they work.

Where to Stay

¢–$ ⊞ **Bea's B&B.** Sunshine streaming through the stained-glass windows in this 1909 home personifies Bea's cheerful hospitality. There's a screened porch for summer and fireplaces that are soothing in summer. A steam room adds a touch of modernity. ⊠ *10 S. Somerset Ave., 21817* ☎ *410/ 968–0423* ⊕ *www.beasbandb.com* ☜ *3 rooms* ♿ *Cable TV; no room phones, no kids under 10, no smoking* ⊟ *No credit cards* ⏐⊚⏐ *BP.*

Sports & the Outdoors

Eco-Tours on the *Learn-It* (⊠ Crisfield City Dock, 1021 W. Main St. ☎ 410/968–9870) depart daily at 10 and 1:30 from the Captain's Galley restaurant. Learn about the wildfowl and water creatures of the Chesapeake Bay, find out why bay grasses are important, explore the effects of shoreline erosion, and visit an experienced waterman—as Bay fishermen are known—at work, all while aboard the comfortable 40-foot bay workboat, which has been certified by the U.S. Coast Guard.

Janes Island State Park nearly surrounded by the waters of the Chesapeake Bay and its inlets, has two distinct areas: a developed mainland section with cabins and camping areas (April through October) a minute's drive from Crisfield and a portion accessible only by boat. Miles of isolated shorelines and marsh areas beckon those who enjoy the peaceful of nature. The original island inhabitants were Native Americans of the Annemessex Nation. ⊠ *26280 Alfred Lawson Dr., Crisfield* ☎ *410/968–1565* ⊕ *www.dnr.state.md.us/publiclands.*

Shopping

Don't leave Crisfield without tasting the two local delicacies—crab cakes and Smith Island Cake. You can sample both at the locally famous **Captain's Galley** (⊠ 1021 W. Main St. ☎ 410/968–3313). The crab cakes are packed with juicy lumps of backfin and virtually no filler. The "Captain's Combo" is also a good introduction to the area's seafood harvest. For dessert, order a towering slice of Smith Island Cake, made up of seven paper-thin layers of yellow cake with chocolate ganache drizzled in between and all over. **Watermen's Inn** (⊠ 901 W. Main St. ☎ 410/968–2119) is also a good spot for a snack.

If you want a whole Smith Cake to take home, head to **Delmarvalous Cakes** (⊠ 605 W. Main St. ☎ 410/968–2566), which is closed on Sunday. You can choose from more than 30 flavors; cakes start at $20.

The Ice Cream Gallery (⊠ 5 Goodsell Alley ☎ 410/968–0809) is a sweets emporium that doubles as a crafts outlet for local artisans. From here there's a spectacular view out over the Bay. **Tropical Chesapeake** (⊠ 712 Broadway ☎ 410/968–3622) prepares oven-baked deli sandwiches and sells gifts and clothing.

Smith Island

 12 mi west of Crisfield by boat.

For more than three centuries, Smith Islanders have made their living coaxing creatures from the Chesapeake Bay. Today, the tiny island's three villages (Tylerton, Ewell, and Rhodes Point) made up of simple homes, churches, and a few stores, remain reachable only by boat, fiercely independent, and fairly remote (cable TV didn't arrive here until 1994). Listen for the residents' distinct accents, which echo that of their 17th-century English ancestors. A midday visit by passenger ferry allows ample time for a stroll around the island and a leisurely meal overlooking watermen's shanties and workboats. Stop by **Ruke's,** a venerable general store that serves excellent fresh seafood.

Air-conditioned **Smith Island Cruises** leave Crisfield's Somers Cove Marina for the 60-minute trip to Smith Island at 12:30 PM daily from Memorial Day to mid-October. ⊠ *Somers Cove Marina, Crisfield* ☎ *410/425–2771* ⊕ *www.smithislandcruises.com* ⊒ *$22.*

Another way to get to Smith Island is via the mail boat, *Island Belle* (☎410/968–1118). There are two departures daily (12:30 and 5 PM) and the cost is $20 round-trip.

Two freight boats, *Captain Jason I* and *Captain Jason II* (☎ 410/425–4471), also take passengers to Smith Island for $20 round-trip. All three boats depart daily at 12:30 PM and return to Crisfield at 5:15 PM, year-round, weather permitting. You can ride back to Smith Island later in the evening; both captains live on the island.

The **Smith Island Center** traces the island's history through such exhibits as an equipped workboat, photos, a time line, and a 20-minute video narrated by islanders. ⊠ *Just off town dock, Ewell* ☎ *410/425–3351 or 800/521–9189* ⚏ *$2* ⊘ *Apr.–Oct., daily noon–4 and by appt.*

The first privately owned facility of its kind on the island, tiny **Smith Island Marina** hugs the water's edge adjacent to the Ewell Tide Inn and B&B. ☎ *410/425–2141 or 888/699–2141.*

Started in 1996 by 12 gutsy Smith Island women, **Smith Island Crabmeat Co-op** produces the finest, shell-less quality crabmeat, with all proceeds going straight back to the women and their families. Visitors can drop by and see the lightning-fast pickers at work. Don't forget to pick up a pound before you leave, and ask Janice (the founder and president) about her secret crab cake ingredient. ⊠ *3019 Union Church Rd., Tylerton* ☎ *410/968–9000* ⊕ *crabs.maryland.com.*

Where to Stay

An overnight on Smith Island gives new meaning to the term "getaway." Your neighbors include more egrets, heron, osprey, and pelicans than people.

$ ▦ **Ewell Tide Inn and B&B.** On the northern tip of Smith Island, downhome hospitality is heartily extended by a licensed ferry- and charterboat captain and his wife. Dinner is available, but must be ordered in advance. Open year-round, the inn welcomes children, as well as pets, on weekdays, and complimentary drinks and snacks are served throughout the day. This couple also operates Ewell's Driftwood General Store as well as the adjacent marina, a separate operation. ⊠ *Ewell 21824* ☎ *410/425–2141 or 888/699–2141* ⊕ *www.smithisland.net* ⤸ *4 rooms, 2 without bath* ⚭ *Dining room, in-room data ports, cable TV, dock, bicycles, pub, meeting rooms, some pets allowed; no room phones, no smoking* ⊟ *MC, V* ⦿ *BP.*

$ ▦ **Inn of Silent Music.** Part of a town that's separated by water from the other two villages on Smith Island, this remote English cottage–style inn takes its soothing name from a phrase in a poem by the mystic St. John of the Cross, a Carmelite monk. Tylerton has no restaurants, but the eclectic innkeepers will cook a fresh seafood dinner for guests for an extra charge. ⊠ *Tylerton 21866* ☎ *410/425–3541* ⊕ *www.innofsilentmusic.com* ⤸ *3 rooms* ⚭ *Dining room, dock, bicycles; no room phones, no room TVs, no kids under 12, no smoking* ⊟ *No credit cards* ⊘ *Closed mid-Nov.–early Mar.* ⦿ *BP.*

VIRGINIA'S EASTERN SHORE

A narrow 70-mi-long peninsula between the Chesapeake Bay and the Atlantic Ocean, Virginia's Eastern Shore has one main artery bisecting its full length. U.S. 13's occasional gentle curves interrupt an otherwise straight, flat route through unremarkable landscape. It's the wild ponies, a small slice of NASA, gloriously uncrowded beaches, and waterfront views in every direction draw thousands of snowbirds here every summer. Tiny hamlets remain scattered among farms and protected wildlife habitats, and along the shore watermen still struggle for their living.

At its southernmost tip, the extraordinary Chesapeake Bay Bridge-Tunnel sweeps 17½ mi across the Chesapeake Bay to connect with the Virginia Tidewater towns of Hampton Roads, Norfolk, and Virginia Beach.

Numbers in the margin correspond to points of interest on the Virginia's Eastern Shore map.

Chincoteague Island

㉑ *27 mi southeast of Snow Hill, MD via U.S. 13 to Rte. 175, 43 mi southeast of Salisbury, MD via U.S. 13 to Rte. 175.*

Just south of the Maryland-Virginia line, the Virginia Eastern Shore's only island resort town (Chincoteague, meaning "large stream or inlet," is pronounced "**shin**-coh-teeg") exudes a pleasant aura of seclusion, despite the renown it has gained since the publication of the 1947 children's book *Misty of Chincoteague,* the story of one of the wild ponies that are auctioned off every summer. Chincoteague Island's inns, restaurants, and shops are eminently reachable by walking; relatively uncrowded beaches stretch out nearby.

Islanders and visitors alike savor one of the shore's specialties during October's **Chincoteague Oyster Festival** (⊠ 6733 Maddox Blvd. ☎ 757/336–6161 ⊕ www.chincoteaguechamber.com), which can sell out months in advance. The Chincoteague Chamber of Commerce sells tickets.

The **Oyster and Maritime Museum** chronicles the local oyster trade with displays of mostly homemade tools; elaborate, hand-carved decoys; marine specimens; a diorama; and audio recordings based on museum records. ⊠ 7125 Maddox Blvd. ☎ 757/336–6117 ⊠ $3 ⊙ June–Sept., daily 10–5; Mar.–May, Sat. 10–5, Sun. noon–4.

Most of Virginia's **Chincoteague National Wildlife Refuge** occupies the southern third of Assateague Island, directly off Chincoteague Island. (The northern two-thirds, part of Maryland, is taken up by the Assateague Island National Seashore.) Created in 1943 as a resting and breeding area for the imperiled greater snow goose as well as other birds, this refuge's location makes it a prime "flyover" habitat. It also protects native and migratory nonavian wildlife, including the small Sika deer that inhabit its interior pine forests. A 3.2-mi self-guided wildlife loop is a great introduction to the refuge. Bike or walk it; it's open to vehicles only between 3 PM and dusk. The Chincoteague ponies

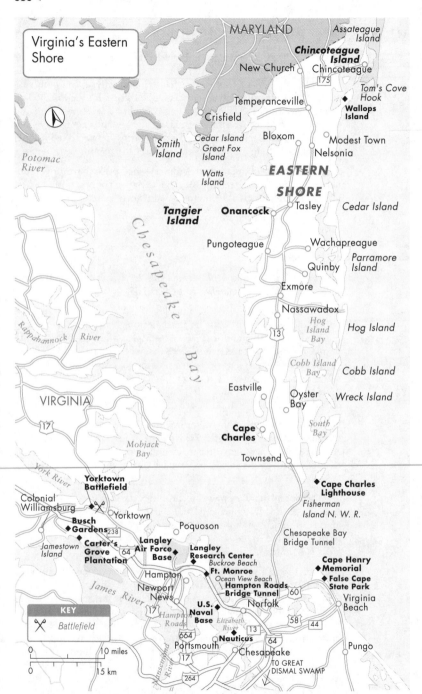

Virginia's Eastern
Shore

MARYLAND

Assateague
Island

*Chincoteague
Island*

New Church   Chincoteague

175

Temperanceville   Tom's Cove
Hook

Crisfield   **Wallops
Island**

*Smith
Island*   *Cedar Island*
*Great Fox
Island*   Bloxom   Modest Town

Nelsonia

Watts
Island   *EASTERN*

SHORE

Tasley   *Cedar Island*

*Tangier
Island*   **Onancock**

*Potomac
River*

Che

Pungoteague   Wachapreague

sapeake

Quinby   *Parramore
Island*

Exmore

Rappahannock   River   *Bay*

Nassawadox

13

*Hog
Island
Bay*   *Hog Island*

*Cobb Island
Bay*   *Cobb Island*

VIRGINIA

17

Eastville   Oyster
Bay   *Wreck Island*

*Mobjack
Bay*   **Cape
Charles**   *South
Bay*

Townsend

York River   **Yorktown
Battlefield**   ◆ **Cape Charles
Lighthouse**

Colonial
Williamsburg   Yorktown   *Fisherman
Island N. W. R.*

238   Poquoson

**Busch
◆Gardens**   Chesapeake Bay
Bridge Tunnel

**Carter's
Grove
Plantation**   **Langley
Air Force
Base**   **Langley
Research Center**

*Jamestown
Island*   64   *Buckroe Beach*

◆Ft. Monroe   **Cape Henry
◆Memorial**

Hampton   *Ocean View Beach*   **◆False Cape
State Park**

Newport
News   **Hampton Roads
Bridge Tunnel**   60   *Virginia
Beach*

James River   Norfolk

17   *Hampton
Roads*   **U.S.
◆Naval
Base**   *Elizabeth
River*   13   58   44

KEY	
✂	*Battlefield*

664   **◆Nauticus**   Pungo

Portsmouth   Chesapeake   64

0   10 miles

0   15 km   17   *TO GREAT
DISMAL SWAMP*

264

occupy a section of the refuge isolated from the public, but they may still be viewed readily from a number of spots. ✉ *Herbert H. Bateman Educational and Administrative Center and entrance: 8231 Beach Rd.* ☎ *757/336–6122* ⊕ *www.nps.gov/asis* 🖃 *$10 per car, valid for 7 days* ⊙ *Refuge hrs: May–Sept., daily 5 AM–10 PM; Oct. and Apr., daily 6 AM–8 PM; Nov.–Mar., daily 6–6. Visitor center hrs vary seasonally; call for information.*

Where to Stay & Eat

$–$$$ ✕ **AJ's on the Creek.** The warm scent of fresh herbs wafts in from the garden as you dine on the screened porch and take in live music and breezes off Eel Creek. Start with one of the scrumptious oyster appetizers and proceed to one of the many creative seafood entrées. ✉ *6585 Maddox Blvd.* ☎ *757/336–5888* ⊟ *AE, D, DC, MC, V.*

★ ¢–$$ ✕ **Shucking House Cafe.** This relaxed eatery is just the place to unwind after a day on the water. Featuring oyster, crab, and fish sandwiches along with fish-and-chips, this café is a pleasant change from fancy restaurants or fast-food franchises. Be sure to try the rich New England or Manhattan clam chowders, both prepared with local mollusks. A sister property, **Landmark Crabhouse** (☎ 757/336–3745), is a bit more upscale, with the same fresh, locally harvested seafood dishes and peaceful waterfront views. ✉ *6162 Landmark Pl.* ☎ *757/336–5145* ⊟ *MC, V.*

$$–$$$ 🏠 **Cedar Gables Seaside Inn.** Tucked away in the northeast of town, this stunning, modern waterfront B&B is a refreshing alternative to those that are more traditional. Each of the four professionally designed and decorated rooms have their own unique character. The Captain's Quarters, with a brass king-size bed, occupies the third floor by itself. ✉ *6095 Hopkins La., 23336* ☎ *757/336–1096 or 888/491–2944* ⊕ *www.cedargable.com* 🛏 *4 rooms* ♺ *Fans, in-room data ports, refrigerators, cable TV, in-room VCRs, pool, outdoor hot tub; no kids under 14, no smoking.*

★ $–$$$ 🏠 **Channel Bass Inn.** This three-story, beige clapboard house just off Chincoteague Bay was built in the 1870s, then expanded and converted to an inn 50 years later. Its luxurious rooms all have comfortable sitting areas. In addition to its full breakfast, the inn serves afternoon tea daily in the public tearoom. Delicacies such as *apfel kuchen* (German apple cake), firm scones, and an extraordinary multilayer trifle, all homemade, are served on Wedgwood china. ✉ *6228 Church St., 23336* ☎ *757/336–6148 or 800/249–0818* ⊕ *www.channelbass-inn.com* 🛏 *8 rooms, 1 suite* ♺ *Shop, some pets allowed; no room phones, no room TVs, no kids under 6, no smoking* ⊟ *AE, D, MC, V* ⊣⊙⊢ *BP.*

$–$$$ 🏠 **Miss Molly's.** Operated by the same innkeepers as the Channel Bass Inn, this unassuming 1886 Victorian inn claims fame as the temporary home of author Marguerite Henry, who wrote *Misty of Chincoteague.* Here, in 1946, she spent two of her six weeks in Chincoteague preparing the background for her renowned children's novel. Miss Molly, the daughter of the home's builder, spent most of her life here. Genuine high tea is served every afternoon at the Channel Bass. ✉ *4141 Main St., 23336* ☎ *757/336–6686 or 800/221–5620* 📠 *757/336–0600* ⊕ *www.missmollys-inn.com* 🛏 *7 rooms* ♺ *No room phones, no room TVs, no kids under 6, no smoking* ⊟ *AE, D, MC, V* ⊙ *Closed Jan. and Feb.*

$–$$ 🏨 **Island Motor Inn Resort.** There are views of the ocean and bay from the private balcony off every room in this three-story motel beside the Intercoastal Waterway. Stroll the inn's private 600-foot boardwalk or relax in the quiet garden area beside the koi pond. One of the two gyms is set aside for weights, with a personal trainer on call. In addition to the pools, there's a hot tub on the third floor. For when you must be inside, every room has a 27-inch cable TV. ✉ *4391 Main St., 23336* ☎ *757/336–3141* 🖷 *757/336–1483* ⊕ *www.islandmotorinn.com* 🛏 *60 rooms* ♿ *Café, room service, in-room data ports, refrigerators, cable TV, 2 pools (1 indoor), 2 gyms, hot tub, laundry facilities, meeting rooms* 🚭 *AE, D, DC, MC, V.*

★ **$–$$** 🏨 **The 1848 Island Manor House.** The unusual design of the Island Manor House was a result of splitting the home in two, providing adequate privacy for the original owners, who were brothers, and their wives, who were sisters. Most rooms have water views of the channel and an intimate brick patio with a multitier fountain, makes a nice summer gathering place. ✉ *4160 Main St., 23336* ☎ *757/336–5436 or 800/852–1505* 🖷 *757/336–1333* ⊕ *www.islandmanor.com* 🛏 *8 rooms, 2 with shared bath* ♿ *No room phones, no TVs, no kids under 10, no smoking, no pets* 🚭 *MC, V* ⦿| *BP* ☉ *Closed Jan.*

Sports & the Outdoors

Nearby beaches open to the public, managed by the National Park Service, are at the eastern end of Beach Road (☎ 757/336–6577).

You can rent boats for fishing or for a spin around the bay from **Captain Bob's** (✉ 2477 S. Main St. ☎ 757/336–6654) or **R&R Boats** (✉ 4183 Main St. ☎ 757/336–5465).

Shopping

Chincoteague Country Corner (✉ 4044 Main St. ☎ 757/336–5771) carries gifts, crafts, and model boats, both assembled and in kits.

Listen for the sounds of fine jazz and inhale the aroma of good coffee that wafts from the windows of the **mainStreet shop & coffeehouse** (✉ 4288 Main St. ☎ 757/336–6782 ⊕ www.mainstreet-shop.com). This corner venue is a lively mix of color and art and people. The enclosed front porch of this little house has tiny tables for java and munchies. Inside are clothes, shoes, graphics, mirrors, lighting, and more.

The wildlife sculpture by renowned artisan Donald White and the jewelry by Joan's Jems are reason enough to visit **White's Copperworks** (✉ 6373 Maddox Blvd. ☎ 757/336–1588 ⊕ www.whitescopperworks. com). Also available are hand-carved wood flowers, wind chimes, matted photos, prints, and puzzles.

off the
beaten
path

WALLOPS ISLAND – NASA's Wallops Flight Facility Visitors Center fires the imagination with full-scale rockets, films on space and aeronautics, and displays on NASA projects. Although this was the site of early rocket launchings and NASA occasionally sends up satellites here, the facility now focuses primarily on atmospheric research. ✉ *Rte. 175, 20 mi southwest of Chincoteague* ☎ *757/824–2298 or*

757/824–1344 ⊕ *www.wff.nasa.gov* ☒ *Free* ☉ *July and Aug., daily 10–4; Sept.–June, Thurs.–Mon. 10–4, closed Dec. and Jan.*

Onancock

㉒ *30 mi southwest of Chincoteague via Rte. 175 to U.S. 13.*

Four miles from the Chesapeake Bay at the mouth of Onancock Creek, Onancock, pronounced Oh-NAN-cock and which means "foggy place," was once the home of a handful of Algonquin families. It was established as a port in 1690 and later emerged as an important ferry link with the burgeoning waterside cities of Maryland and Virginia. Today, this quiet community of 1,600, the second-largest town on Virginia's Eastern Shore, is worth a short visit for a flavor of its past as a transfer point between water and land.

Where to Stay & Eat

$–$$$ ✕ **Trawler Restaurant and Lounge.** This inland restaurant 17 mi from Onancock maintains a nautical attitude in its appearance and menu. "Rick and Steve" is a delicious combination of scallops, shrimp, and crabmeat sautéed in butter with fresh garlic and mushrooms. The menu also includes she-crab soup and crab cakes. Meals are accompanied by sweet-potato biscuits, which have achieved a widespread reputation (and whose recipe is a guarded secret), and a salad bar. Wildlife drawings and hand-carved duck decoys, mostly by local artists, decorate the three dining areas. There's live entertainment and karaoke several days a week. ☒ *U.S. 13, Exmore* ☎ *757/442–2092* ☐ *D, MC, V.*

$–$$ ✕ **Hopkins & Bros. General Store & Eastern Shore Steamboat Co. Restaurant.** Beside the wharf, inside a general store (circa 1842) on the National Register of Historic Places, you can imagine yourself waiting for a steamer to Baltimore. At the charming eatery adjacent to the store, there's fresh baked grouper with locally picked crabmeat stuffing as well as prime meats that are hand cut to order. ☒ *2 Market St.* ☎ *757/787–3100* ⊕ *www.onancock.net* ☐ *MC, V* ☉ *Closed Sun. No lunch.*

$$ ✕☐ **Inn and Garden Cafe.** This 1880s house is now an intimate inn and creative restaurant ($–$$) with stunning waterfront views. A wall of windows encloses the dining room. The inn has four guest suites. ☒ *145 Market St., 23417* ☎ *757/787–8850* ⊕ *www.theinnandgardencafe. com* ⬠ *4 suites* ☐ *MC, V* ☉ *Restaurant closed Sun.–Tues. No lunch.*

$ ☐ **1840's 76 Market Street.** Within walking distance to the Tangier Island ferry, this circa-1840s Victorian house is pleasantly simple, with three warmly welcoming rooms: Blue, Rose, and Yellow, which all have queen-size beds. There's cable TV with a VCR in the common room. Guests regularly rave about the innkeeper's breakfasts. ☒ *76 Market St., 23417* ☎ *757/787–7600 or 888/751–7600* ☐ *757/787–2744* ⊕ *www.76marketst.com* ⬠ *3 rooms* ⚅ *Croquet, volleyball; no room phones, no room TVs, no kids under 6, no smoking* ☐ *AE, MC, V* ◯| *BP.*

Tangier Island

Crab traps stacked 10 feet high, watermen's shanties on the water, and a landscape virtually devoid of excessive commercialization await those who come to this Virginia fishing community in the Chesapeake Bay. You can't bring a car, but you can join a guided tour near the boat dock, rent a golf cart to roam the few narrow roads, or simply soak in the timelessness on foot. Stop by the Waterfront Sandwich Shop or head to the Islander Seafood Restaurant. As on Maryland's Smith Island, you can hear the distinct accents that reveal the English origins of the residents' 17th-century ancestors. Note that Tangier Island is "dry"; you may bring your own alcohol for personal use, but you must use discretion.

Narrated trips from Onancock to the island are available on **Tangier-Onancock Cruises** (☎ 757/891–2240) at 10 AM daily Memorial Day–October 15. The return trip leaves Tangier at 2 PM, allowing ample time to explore.

Where to Stay

$ 🏠 **Shirley's Bay View Inn.** You may stay in one of two guest rooms in one of the oldest houses on the island and have breakfast on 100-year-old china, hosted by members of the home's original family, or you may stay in one of the adjacent cottages. Either way, an overnight on Tangier Island is an uncommon experience. A visit to Shirley's should include a visit to her ice-cream parlor, where music from the 1950s plays. ⊠ *16408 West Ridge Rd., 23440* ☎ *757/891–2396* ⊕ *www.tangierisland. net* ⬦ *2 rooms, 7 cottages* ⚬ *Refrigerators, cable TV, beach; no room phones, no smoking* ⊟ *No credit cards.*

Cape Charles

㉓ *30 mi south of Onancock via U.S. 13.*

Cape Charles, established in the early 1880s as a railroad-ferry junction, quieted down considerably after its heyday, but in the past few years its very isolation has begun to attract people from farther and farther away. The town holds one of the largest concentrations of late-Victorian and turn-of-the-20th-century buildings in the region. Clean, uncrowded public beaches beckon, as do a marina, renowned golf course, and the Eastern Shore of Virginia National Wildlife Refuge.

Where to Stay

$–$$ 🏠 **Chesapeake Charm.** Two blocks from the beach, this B&B feels like a summer beach house. It's also one of the few family-friendly B&Bs in Virginia. Golfing packages for play at the Arnold Palmer Signature Course at Bay Creek are also available. ⊠ *202 Madison Ave., 23310* ☎ *757/331–2676* ⊕ *www.chesapeakecharmbnb.com* ⬦ *4 rooms* ⚬ *Golf privileges, boating, fishing, bicycles; no room TV in one room, no kids under 12, no smoking* ⊟ *D, MC, V.*

$$ 🏠 **Pickett's Harbor.** Clinging to the southernmost tip of the peninsula, this land parcel is part of a 17th-century grant to the owner's family. The current clapboard B&B was built in 1976 according to a Colonial-era design, with floors, doors, and cupboards from several 200-year-old James River farms reinstalled here. All guest rooms overlook small sand dunes and the Chesapeake; the backyard is actually 27 acres of private beach. Runners and bikers are likely to find the area's long country lanes and untrafficked paved roads a delight. ⊠ *28288 Nottingham*

Ridge La., Cape Charles 23310 ☎*757/331–2212* ⊕*www.pickettsharbor. com* 🛏 *6 rooms, 4 with bath* ⚏ *Beach, bicycles, some pets allowed (fee); no room phones, no room TVs, no smoking* ☰ *No credit cards* ⦿ *BP.*

National Wildlife Refuges

13 mi south of Cape Charles.

At the southernmost tip of the Delmarva Peninsula, the unique Eastern Shore of Virginia and the Fisherman Island National Wildlife Refuges, including nearby Skidmore Island—were established in 1984. Their maritime forest, myrtle and bayberry thickets, grasslands, and croplands, as well as ponds are used by such species as bald eagles and peregrine falcons. Each fall, between late August and early November, migrating birds "stage," or gather in large groups, on refuge lands until favorable winds and weather conditions allow for easy crossing of the Chesapeake Bay. ⊠ *Southern extremity of Rte. 13* ☎ *757/331–2760* ⊕ *easternshore.fws.gov* 🗺 *Free.*

THE EASTERN SHORE A TO Z

To research prices, get advice from other travelers, and book travel arrangements, visit www.fodors.com.

BIKE TRAVEL

Flat and friendly, the Eastern Shore is a great region to go biking. The most popular places are in Kent Island along the Cross Island Trail, St. Michaels, Oxford, Chestertown, Wicomico County's 100-mi Viewtrail 100 loop, and Ocean City's Boardwalk in the mornings. Call Maryland's Department of Transportation for a state bicycle map and for more information.

Bicycles are available for rent at Stevensville's Happy Trails Bike Repair, which is open from 10 to 6 Monday through Saturday. Happy Trails will pick up and drop off bikes for boaters in local marinas and guests at local hotels and B&Bs. On Sunday at 9 AM, Happy Trails also hosts escorted group rides of 15 to 30 mi, when the weather allows.

Chestertown's Bikework Bicycle Shop rents bikes for adults and children; helmets are included in the rate. A group, open to those just visiting, rides up to 60 mi every Sunday at 8 AM, weather permitting. The shop is open Tuesday through Friday 9–5, Saturday 9–3, and Sunday and Monday by appointment.

You can also bike inn to inn with InnTours, which maps out a relatively flat route between Berlin in Maryland and New Church, Virginia near Chincoteague. Prices start at $350 per couple per day and includes inn accommodation, luggage transportation, and all meals.

Viewtrail 100, a marked 100-mi biking circuit, runs along less-traveled secondary roads between Berlin and Pocomoke City. For a brochure and map, contact the Worcester County Tourism Office.

🚲 **Bikework Bicycle Shop** ⊠ 208 S. Cross St., Chestertown ☎ 410/778-6940 ⊕ www. bikeworkbicycleshop.com. **Happy Trails Bicycle Repair** ⊠ 111 Cockey La. ☎ 410/643-

0670. **InnTours** ☎ 410/632-2722 ⊕ www.inntours.com. **Maryland Dept. of Transportation** ☎ 800/252-8776. **Oxford Mews Emporium** ✉ 105 Morris St., Oxford ☎ 410/820-8222.

BUS TRAVEL

Carolina Trailways makes several round-trip runs daily between Baltimore or Washington and Easton, Cambridge, Salisbury, and Ocean City.

Greyhound Lines leaves regularly from Norfolk and Virginia Beach for destinations on the Eastern Shore.

When you're in Ocean City, you can avoid the aggravation of driving in slow-moving traffic by taking **The Bus,** which travels 10-mi-long Coastal Highway 24 hours a day, in its own lane, with service about every 10 minutes. Bus-stop signs are posted every other block, and there are shelters at most locations. A $2 ticket is good for 24 hours.

A park and ride facility on the mainland—on Route 50 just west of Ocean City—has free parking for some 700 vehicles. It's on the Bus's route.
🚍 **Bus Depots Cambridge** ✉ 2903 Ocean Gateway Dr., at Rte. 50 ☎ 410/228-5825. **Easton** ✉ FastStop Convenience Store, U.S. 50, 2 mi north of town, opposite airport ☎ 410/822-3333. **Ocean City** ✉ 2nd St. and Philadelphia Ave., at U.S. 50 bridge ☎ 410/289-9307. **Salisbury** ✉ 350 Cypress St. ☎ 410/749-4121.
🚍 **Bus Lines The Bus** ☎ 410/723-1607. **Carolina Trailways** ☎ 800/231-2222. **Greyhound Lines** ☎ 800/231-2222.

CAR TRAVEL

A car is indispensable for touring the region. To reach the Eastern Shore from Baltimore or Washington, D.C., travel east on U.S. 50/301 and cross the 4½-mi Chesapeake Bay Bridge (toll collected eastbound only, $2.50) northeast of Annapolis.

The extraordinary 17½-mi Chesapeake Bay Bridge-Tunnel, officially the Lucias J. Kellam Jr. Bridge-Tunnel, is the only connection between Virginia's Eastern Shore and Norfolk, Virginia Beach, and other Tidewater-area towns. There's a toll of $12 in either direction.

The bridge and tunnel complex comprises 12 mi of trestled roadway, two mile-long tunnels, two bridges, almost 2 mi of causeway, and four man-made islands, on one of which there's a restaurant and on another a fishing pier. U.S. 13 is the main route up the spine of the peninsula into Maryland.

TRAFFIC   In summer, Friday afternoon eastbound (beach-bound) traffic can be very heavy; conversely, Sunday and sometimes Saturday afternoon westbound traffic (from the beaches toward Baltimore and Washington, D.C.) can be equally congested.
🚗 **Chesapeake Bay Bridge-Tunnel** ☎ 757/331-2960 in Maryland, 410/974-0341 in Virginia ⊕ www.cbbt.com.

DISABILITIES & ACCESSIBILITY

The B&Bs and small inns that represent the majority of the accommodations throughout Maryland's and Virginia's Eastern Shore may not always be handicapped accessible. Contact DisabilityGuide for a comprehensive list of accessible accommodations and attractions in Maryland and Virginia.

Furthermore, because some of the region's towns are 200–300 years old, sidewalks are often brick, stone stairs are well worn, and roads are sometimes still cobbled.
🔲 **DisabilityGuide** ⊕ www.disabilityguide.org.

TOURS

Besides any number of tours by boat from several of the waterside towns on Maryland's and Virginia's Eastern Shore, there are day-trip tours into the region from Annapolis and Baltimore. Larger towns, including Annapolis as well as St. Michaels, are home port for diesel- or gasoline-powered tour boats and yachts. As part of its Day on the Bay Cruise series, the Annapolis-based Watermark Cruises operates between there and St. Michaels on Saturday, May through September, and also on Monday in summer, a thoroughly enjoyable way to visit one town while staying in the other. It costs $55 per adult. Chesapeake Bay Lighthouse Tours offer a rare chance to see the Bay's lighthouses up close. Passengers on the all-day Great Circle Route visit 12 lighthouses, and those on the Passage, a half-day tour, visit five. There's also a "two light" sunset cruise. Bring your camera. A full day costs $120 for an adult, a half day $60, and two hours costs $35. Board the *Cambridge Lady* to explore the Choptank River and its tributaries. In addition to Cambridge, some departures are available from Denton and Oxford. The *Lady* sails from May through October; tours are $20.

Rock Hall Trolleys, with 35 stops, is the way to explore this burgeoning Bayside community (adults, $2; children, $1)—and to travel between here and Chestertown ($5 per person, round-trip). It runs Friday–Sunday.

A self-guided walking tour of downtown Salisbury is available from the chamber of commerce. A walking map of Ocean City's historic sites—available from its Visitor Information Center, provides insight into its growth and evolution as a vacation resort. Historic Chestertown and Kent County Tours schedules guided, narrated walking tours from 1½ to 2 hours that focus on history and architecture, particularly that of the 18th century. Tours are by appointment only. Guided tours of Crisfield are run by the J. Millard Tawes Historical Museum. From May through October, the tours include a visit to a crab processing plant.

Chesapeake Horse Country Tours allow you to roll through Cecil's stunning acres of emerald grassland. The tours head to horse farms that have produced such notable racing legends as Northern Dancer and Kelso.
🔲 Boat Tours **Cambridge Lady** ☎ 410/221-0776 ⊕ www.cambridgelady.com. **Chesapeake Bay Lighthouse Tours** ☎ 410/886-2215 or 800/690-5080 ⊕ www.chesapeakelights.com. **Watermark Cruises** ☎ 410/268-7601 Ext. 104 ⊕ www.watermarkcruises.com.
🔲 Trolley Tours **Rock Hall Trolleys** ☎ 410/639-7996 or 866/748-7658 ⊕ www.rockhalltrolleys.com.
🔲 Walking Tours **Chesapeake Horse Country Tours** ☎ 410/287-2290 or 800/874-4556 ⊕ www.uniglobehill.com. **Historic Chestertown and Kent County Tours** ☎ 410/778-

2829. **The Port of Crisfield Tour and Crisfield Heritage Tour** ✉]. Millard Tawes Historical Museum at Somers Cove Marina ☎ 410/968-2501 💲 $2.50 ☉ May–Oct., daily 9–4:30; Nov.–Apr., weekdays 9–4:30.

VISITOR INFORMATION

▮ Tourist Information in Maryland **Bay Country Welcome Center** ✉ 1000 Welcome Center Dr., Centreville ☎ 410/758-6803. **Cecil County Tourism** ✉ 1 Seahawk Dr., Suite 114, North East 21901 ☎ 410/996-6290 or 800/232-4595 🖶 410/996-6279 ⊕ www. seececil.org. **Chesapeake House Welcome Center** ✉ Chesapeake House Service Area, I-95, between exits 93 and 100, near Perryville ☎ 410/287-2313. **Dorchester County Tourism Department** ✉ 2 Rose Hill Pl., Cambridge 21613 ☎ 410/228-1000 or 800/522-8687 🖶 410/221-6545 ⊕ www.tourdorchester.org. **Kent County Tourism Development Office** ✉ 400 High St., Chestertown 21620 ☎ 410/778-0416 🖶 410/778-2746 ⊕ www.kentcounty.com. **Ocean City Department of Tourism** ✉ 4001 Coastal Hwy., at 41st St., Ocean City 21842 ☎ 410/289-2800 or 800/626-2326 🖶 410/289-0058 ⊕ www. ococean.com. **Queen Anne's County Office of Tourism** ✉ 425 Piney Narrows Rd., Chester 21619 ☎ 410/604-2100 or 888/400-7787 🖶 410/604-2101 ⊕ www.qac.org. **Salisbury Chamber of Commerce** ✉ 114 E. Main St. ☎ 410/749-0144. **Somerset County Tourism Office and Visitors Center** ✉ 11440 Ocean Hwy., Princess Anne 21853 ☎ 410/651-2968 or 800/521-9189 🖶 410/651-3917 ⊕ www.visitsomerset.com. **Talbot County Office of Tourism** ✉ 11 S. Harrison St., Easton 21601 ☎ 410/770-8000 🖶 410/770-8057 ⊕ www. tourtalbot.org. **U.S. 13 Welcome Center** ✉ 144 Ocean Hwy., Rte. 13, 15 mi south of Snow Hill, Pocomoke City ☎ 410/957-2484. **Wicomico County Convention & Visitors Bureau** ✉ 8480 Ocean Hwy., Delmar 21875 ☎ 410/548-4914 or 800/332-8687 🖶 410/341-4996 ⊕ www.wicomicotourism.org. **Worcester County Tourism Office** ✉ 104 W. Market St., Snow Hill 21863 ☎ 410/632-3110 or 800/852-0335 🖶 410/632-3158 ⊕ www. visitworcester.org.

▮ Tourist Information in Virginia **Chincoteague Chamber of Commerce** ✉ 6733 Maddox Blvd., Box 258, Chincoteague 23336 ☎ 757/336-6161 ⊕ www.chincoteaguechamber. com. **Eastern Shore of Virginia Tourism** ✉ Rte. 13, Box 460, Melfa 23410 ☎ 757/787-2460 ⊕ www.esvachamber.org.

INDEX